caring for ... series

caring for
preschool children
third edition

Derry G. Koralek

Diane Trister Dodge

Peter J. Pizzolongo

Teaching Strategies inc.
Washington, DC

Updates to modules 2 and 9 © 2006
Updates to module 13 © 2008

Editors: Toni S. Bickart, Laurie Taub
Cover, book design, and computer illustrations: Carla Uriona

Teaching Strategies, Inc.
P.O. Box 42243
Washington, DC 20015
www.TeachingStrategies.com
ISBN: 978-1-879537-75-0

Library of Congress Cataloging-in-Publication Data

Koralek, Derry Gosselin.
  Caring for preschool children / Derry G. Koralek, Diane Trister Dodge, Peter J. Pizzolongo.-- 3rd ed.
    p. cm.
  Previous ed. has Diane Trister Dodge as first author.
  Includes bibliographical references.
  ISBN 1-879537-75-3
  1. Child care--Study and teaching. 2. Early childhood education. I. Dodge, Diane Trister. II. Pizzolongo, Peter J. III. Title.
  HQ778.5.D64 2004
  362.71'2'071--dc22
                        2004003368

Printed and bound in the United States of America
2010
10 9 8 7 6

Acknowledgments

Caring for Preschool Children has a long history. We are pleased to bring you this completely updated and redesigned third edition. Carolee Callen, former head of the Navy Child Development Services Branch and M.-A. Lucas, Director, Child and Youth Services, Headquarters Department of the U.S. Army, were both instrumental in the development of the original work, which was then adopted by all branches of the military. We thank M.-A. Lucas for inspiring us to update these materials for a new generation of child care providers.

Our deepest appreciation goes to Toni Bickart, Vice President, and Laurie Taub, Developmental Editor, for their editing. We thank Carla Uriona, Design and Production Manager, for her engaging design and Carla and Terri Rue-Woods, Production Assistant, for working so hard at layout and for their efforts to keep us on deadline.

It is our hope that this third edition of *Caring for Preschool Children* will have a positive impact on the quality of early childhood programs by giving staff developers and teachers a practical and comprehensive tool to support their important work.

Table of Contents

Orientation

Welcome to *Caring for Preschool Children*, a personalized training program designed for teachers who work with preschool children. The training program consists of two books: *Caring for Preschool Children* and a *Skill Building Journal*. This book, *Caring for Preschool Children*, contains all the readings for the 13 modules in the training program. It also includes a glossary of terms used throughout the training, a list of references, and a bibliography of additional resources. The *Skill-Building Journal* is a personal record of your learning. It includes the instructions and forms for the activities you will do to apply what you have read about each topic and to reflect on your practice.

Whether you are new to the profession or have years of experience, this training program offers practical information on topics central to teaching preschool children. We use the term *teacher* to mean any adult who works with young children in a classroom setting, including mentor teachers, lead teachers, teacher aides, teacher assistants, caregivers, and volunteers. We use the term *trainer* to refer to the individual who is guiding your participation in this training program.

Several features of *Caring for Preschool Children* make it unique:

- The materials are appropriate for both **new and experienced teachers**.

- You take **responsibility** for your progress through the training program, with **guidance and feedback** provided by a trainer.

- The training program is **individualized**; you work independently, according to your own schedule, and at your own pace.

- The information presented in the modules is **practical** and of **immediate use** in your daily work with children.

- Many of the learning activities ask you to **observe** children to learn about their skills and interests. Observation is a key way to get to know children and to plan a program that responds to each child's individual skills, needs, interests, and other characteristics.

- Your completed learning activities become a **professional resource** and record of your growth and competence.

How the Training Program Can Help You

Caring for Preschool Children is designed to help you gain the knowledge and skills to provide a high-quality program for preschool children. The modules describe the typical developmental stages of children ages 3–5 and include many examples of how you can apply this knowledge every day in your work. Once you begin this training program, you will discover that you already have many skills addressed in the modules. Completing the modules will let you extend and expand on the skills and knowledge you already have. The training will help you to meet the profession's standards and to become a more competent teacher.

Completing *Caring for Preschool Children* can help you meet the requirements for achieving a nationally recognized credential that acknowledges your skills as a teacher of preschool children. The training program is based on the Child Development Associate (CDA) Competency Standards defined by the Council for Professional Recognition (the Council) in Washington, DC. The 13 CDA functional areas define the skills and knowledge base of competent teachers.

Functional Areas of the Child Development Associate (CDA) Competency Standards

Safe
Provide a safe environment to prevent and reduce injuries.

Healthy
Promote good health and nutrition and provide an environment that contributes to the prevention of illness.

Learning Environment
Use space, relationships, materials, and routines as resources for constructing an interesting, secure, and enjoyable environment that encourages play, exploration, and learning.

Physical
Provide a variety of equipment, activities, and opportunities to promote the physical development of children.

Cognitive
Provide activities and opportunities that encourage curiosity, exploration, and problem-solving appropriate to the developmental levels and learning styles of children.

Communication
Communicate with children and provide opportunities and support for children to understand, acquire, and use verbal and nonverbal means of communicating thoughts and feelings.

Creative
Provide opportunities that stimulate children to play with sound, rhythm, language, materials, space, and ideas in individual ways to express their creative abilities.

Self
Provide physical and emotional security for each child and help each child to know, accept, and take pride in himself or herself and to develop a sense of independence.

Social
Help each child to feel accepted in the group, help children learn to communicate and get along with others, and encourage feelings of empathy and mutual respect among children and adults.

Guidance
Provide a supportive environment in which children can begin to learn and practice appropriate and acceptable behaviors as individuals and as a group.

Families
Maintain an open, friendly, and cooperative relationship with each child's family, encourage their involvement in the program, and support the child's relationship with his or her family.

Program Management
Use all available resources to ensure an effective operation.

Professionalism
Make decisions based on knowledge of early childhood theories and practices, promote quality in child care services, and take advantage of opportunities to improve competence both for personal and professional growth and for the benefit of children and families.

Each of the modules in *Caring for Preschool Children* addresses one of the functional areas. Teachers may apply for a CDA credential from the Council when they have completed 120 clock hours of training and can demonstrate that they have acquired the skills and knowledge outlined in the CDA Competency Standards. Contact the Council at www.cdacouncil.org or 1-800-424-4310 for more information about the requirements for a CDA credential.

Working With Your Trainer

An important part of the training process is the feedback and support you receive from a trainer. The trainer might be a colleague, mentor teacher, supervisor, education coordinator, college instructor, or other individual who can observe you working with children and provide meaningful feedback to support your professional development. Although the modules are meant to be self-instructional, you will benefit most if an experienced trainer reviews and discusses your responses to learning activities, answers questions, and comments on your interactions with children and families. A trainer can provide feedback on-site at the program, during a phone conference, via electronic mail (e-mail), or in a group meeting.

Beginning the Program

After reading this *Orientation*, your next step is to complete the *Self-Assessment* in your *Skill-Building Journal* (section 0-1). *The Self-Assessment* lists the three major areas of competence related to the topic of each module. You read each item and check the box that describes your current level of implementation. You will want to respond as objectively as possible, so you can identify your strengths and interests as well as areas that need strengthening. Afterward, you discuss your responses with your trainer and choose three modules to work on first.

You and your trainer will also develop a tentative schedule for completing the entire training program. You can expect to spend 4–6 weeks on each module. It generally takes 12–18 months to complete the entire training program.

You might begin with a module of particular interest precisely because you think you have already acquired many of the relevant skills. Alternatively, you might begin with a module that addresses a training need identified through the *Self-Assessment* or your trainer's observations. If this training program is part of a course or seminar, your trainer might ask you to begin with a particular module so you can participate in group meetings with others working on the same module. Your program director might ask you to begin with a module that addresses a program need, such as improving partnerships with families.

Completing Each Module

Each of the 13 modules follows a consistent format using both books. The chart that follows shows how the sections of the books are related.

Section	Caring for Preschool Children	Skill-Building Journal
Overview	An introduction to the topic addressed in the module, identification of three major areas of competence, related strategies, and three brief examples of how teachers apply their knowledge and skills to support children's development and learning.	Questions about each of the examples and sample answers.
Your Own Experiences	A short discussion of how the topic applies to adults.	A series of questions about personal experiences related to the topic.
Pre-Training Assessment (presented only in the *Skill-Building Journal*)		A checklist of how often teachers use key strategies and a question about skills to improve or topics to learn more about.
Learning Activities (4–5 per module)	Objectives for each *Learning Activity* and several pages of information about the topic.	Instructions for applying the reading to classroom practices. This may involve answering questions; observing children and using the information to address individual needs and interests; completing a checklist; trying new teaching strategies; or planning, implementing, and evaluating a new activity. When appropriate, *Answer Sheets* are provided.
Reflecting on Your Learning (presented only in the *Skill-Building Journal*)		An opportunity to consider how the topic relates to curriculum implementation and building partnerships with families. Questions help teachers summarize what they learned.

As you can see from the chart, the two books are coordinated. Each section of a *Caring for Preschool Children* module includes an instruction that directs you to the corresponding section of the *Skill-Building Journal*. Look for the *what's next?* box at the bottom of the page. Similarly, each section of the *Skill-Building Journal* explains whether to continue with the next section of the Journal or to return to your reading of *Caring for Preschool Children*.

When you are directed to a section of the *Skill-Building Journal,* you can identify the correct forms by finding the corresponding section numbers in the upper right-hand corner of the pages. The first part of the section number (to the left of the hyphen) indicates the number of the module. The second part of the number (to the right of the hyphen) indicates the step of the module that you are working on. If the step has more than one form, a lowercase letter has been added.

Although the content and activities in the modules vary, you will follow the same process for completing each module. That process is described in the following paragraphs and illustrated in the diagram on page xi. As you complete each step, be sure to record your feedback sources in section 1 of each *Skill-Building Journal* module.

Overview

You will read a short introduction to the topic addressed in the module. For each related area of competence, you also review strategies that teachers use and three stories about how they apply their knowledge and skills. Then you answer questions about each story and compare your answers to those on the *Answer Sheet* at the end of the module in the *Skill-Building Journal.*

Your Own Experiences

Next, you will read about how the topic relates to adults and answer questions about how it relates to your own experiences, both on and off the job. You examine how personal experiences affect your approach to your work with children and families and your choice of teaching strategies.

Pre-Training Assessment

The next step is to complete the *Pre-Training Assessment*—a list of the strategies that competent teachers use—by indicating whether you do these things regularly, sometimes, or not enough. Then you will review your responses and identify 3–5 skills you want to improve or topics you want to know learn more about. You may refer to the *Glossary* at the end of *Caring for Preschool Children* for definitions of the terms used.

Next, you will want to schedule a meeting with your trainer to discuss your responses to the *Overview* questions and *Pre-Training Assessment.* After your discussion, you will be ready to begin the learning activities for the module.

Learning Activities

Each module includes four or five learning activities. After reading several pages of information about the topic, you will apply your knowledge while working with children and families. For example, you might answer questions related to the reading and to your own teaching practices; complete a checklist; try out suggestions from the reading and report the results; plan, implement, and evaluate an activity; or observe and record children's behavior and interactions and then use your observation notes to individualize the program. Examples of completed forms, summaries, and charts are provided, when needed, to demonstrate the activity.

Your trainer will be an important source of support as you complete the learning activities. Your trainer might observe the way you implement an activity, conduct a co-observation of a child, review your plans and help you collect materials, or discuss and answer your questions about the content.

After you have completed a learning activity, schedule a time to meet with your trainer, individually or with a group of teachers who completed the same activity. This will be an opportunity to discuss the content of the module, report what you did and learned, and voice your concerns. For some activities, you will also meet with colleagues or a child's family, or review an *Answer Sheet* at the end of the module. It is always best to discuss your work on a learning activity while it is fresh in your mind, so it is important to let your trainer know when you are ready for a feedback conference. A full understanding of each activity is particularly important when an activity builds on the knowledge and skills addressed in the previous one.

Reflecting on Your Learning

After completing all of the learning activities, take time to summarize your progress. Review your responses to the *Pre-Training Assessment* and describe your increased knowledge and skills. For some modules, you will also review and add examples to a chart created in one of the learning activities.

After summarizing your progress, you will meet with your trainer to review your learning and to discuss whether you are ready for the knowledge and competency assessments. When you are ready, schedule a time to complete the *Knowledge Assessment* and set another time for your trainer to conduct the *Competency Assessment* observation. If you need more time to learn about the knowledge and skills addressed in the module, your trainer can suggest supplemental strategies and resources. *Caring for Preschool Children* also includes a bibliography of resources for early childhood professionals.

Assessing Knowledge and Competence

There is a *Knowledge Assessment* for each module and a *Competency Assessment* for modules 1–12. The *Knowledge Assessment* is a short written test about information presented in the modules. For the *Competency Assessment,* your trainer will conduct a focused observation of how you apply your knowledge and use key skills in your work with children. You will need to achieve a score of 80% or higher on each assessment before starting another module. Your trainer will discuss the assessment process in greater detail.

Documenting Progress

As you successfully complete each section and assessment for a module, you can record your progress on the Individual Tracking Form that your trainer will provide and sign.

what's next?

Read "The Training Process" chart.
Go to **Skill-Building Journal,** section **0-1** *(Self-Assessment).*

The Training Process

Complete the Orientation

Read about the training program
Complete the Self-Assessment
Develop a module-completion plan

Feedback
and
Discussion

Complete a Module

Overview

Read about the topic and three related areas of competence
Review examples of what teachers do
Answer questions

Your Own Experiences

Relate topic to own experiences
Answer questions

Pre-Training Assessment

Assess own use of strategies
List skills to improve or topics to learn about

Learning Activities

Read about topic
Apply knowledge
Answer questions

Reflecting on Your Learning

Review responses to Pre-Training Assessment
Summarize skills and knowledge gained
Discuss readiness for assessments

Feedback
and
Discussion

Not ready for assessment
Review or repeat activities

Ready for assessment
Schedule times

Assessments
Knowledge Assessment
Competency Assessment

Feedback
and
Discussion

Did not demonstrate competence
Review or repeat activities

Demonstrated competence
Document progress
Begin next module

Overview

Maintaining Practices and Environments That Prevent or Reduce Injuries

Planning for and Responding to Injuries and Emergencies

Helping Children Learn to Take Precautions

Your Own Need for Safety

Learning Activities

A. Creating and Maintaining Safe Environments

B. Keeping Children Safe on Trips Away From the Program

C. Handling Injuries and Emergencies

D. Helping Children Learn to Take Precautions

1. Safe

Children feel safe when they trust adults to keep them from harm.

Adults feel safe when they are in control of situations, know how to prevent injuries, and know what to do if injuries occur. To feel safe, children must trust adults to keep them from harm and to know what to do when injuries occur. As children become more independent, they learn how to control some parts of their environments and become better able to explore safely.

Some risk-taking is common to preschool children. As they try new challenges and explore their independence, they may act without direct adult supervision. Because taking risks may lead to injuries, children must learn to consider the possible consequences of their actions and to understand how to take precautions. Most accidents that cause injuries to children are preventable.

Teachers are responsible for protecting children.

As stated in the National Association for the Education of Young Children's Code of Ethical Conduct, child safety is your professional responsibility.

> *P-1.1—Above all, we shall not harm children. We shall not participate in practices that are emotionally damaging, physically harmful, disrespectful, degrading, dangerous, exploitative, or intimidating to children.* This principle has precedence over all others in this Code.[1]

Teachers help children develop safety habits.

Teachers use three key safety strategies. First, arrange classroom and outdoor areas to provide structure and clear limits, and keep all areas free from hazards. Second, model and talk with children about safety and, when necessary, intervene in children's play to prevent injuries. Third, know and follow your program's established procedures to ensure children's safety every day and during emergencies. When you follow these procedures calmly during drills and emergencies, you help children learn how to keep themselves safe. Each of these strategies helps children develop safety habits as you guide them to be self-disciplined individuals who think ahead and solve problems.

You can keep children safe by

- maintaining practices and environments that prevent or reduce injuries

- planning for and responding to injuries and emergencies

- helping children learn to take precautions

Maintaining Practices and Environments That Prevent or Reduce Injuries

1. **Check indoor and outdoor areas daily and remove or place out of reach any hazardous materials.** Remove plastic bags; balloons; latex/vinyl gloves; small objects that may cause choking; and other materials that can harm children, such as toxic substances.

2. **Check the room daily to see that all electrical outlets are covered and electrical cords are placed away from water, traffic paths, and children's reach.** Cover unused outlets with spring-loaded plates. Use screw-in plug covers for outlets in use.

3. **Check materials and equipment daily for broken parts, loose bolts, or jagged edges; make sure that imperfect materials and equipment are repaired or replaced.** Cushion furniture edges with masking tape, secured bubble wrap, or commercial corner guards. Hardware fasteners and connecting devices should be tight and not removable without tools.

4. **Arrange the room with clear exit paths and no long or open spaces that tempt children to run.** Use bookcases, furniture, and other equipment to create interest areas and to prevent running.

5. **Check safety equipment monthly to ensure that it is in good condition and easy to reach.** Notify the appropriate person if there are problems.

6. **Convey to children, in actions and words, that the program is a safe place and that they will be protected.** "Benjamin, would you like me to stand next to the slide while you go down?"

7. **Work with colleagues to supervise all children at all times.** Plan the day so at least two teachers supervise children's play at all times. When an activity, such as woodworking or cooking, requires a teacher to be present for the entire time, other teachers should supervise other areas and intervene when necessary.

Ms. Kim Prevents an Injury

Ms. Kim notices 3-year-old Sara across the room, climbing on a large cardboard box that had been placed in the Library Area as a getaway space. It was moved to the Block Area and is sagging with Sara's weight. Ms. Kim alerts the teacher on that side of the room. Ms. Richards moves to Sara's side. "Sara," she says calmly, "I'm going to help you climb down. The box isn't safe for climbing, because it isn't strong enough to hold you, but this box will make a nice place for reading. What can we use to make it cozy, so that everyone knows it's our new getaway space?" They move the box back to the Library Area and put a blanket and pillow inside. "Thank you for helping make a cozy reading nook," says Ms. Kim. "You can climb on the climber when we go outside."

Planning for and Responding to Injuries and Emergencies

8. **Develop and post injury and emergency procedures.** Keep them in a prominent place near the telephone.

9. **Make sure the telephone is easy to reach and working properly.** Know where to find families' emergency telephone numbers.

10. **Respond quickly and calmly to children in distress.** "I'm sorry that you pinched your finger. Let me see if you need a bandage."

11. **Check the first-aid kit regularly to make sure it has the required supplies.** Take the first-aid kit on neighborhood walks and other trips away from the center.

12. **Maintain current emergency information for all children.**

13. **Know how to recognize and respond to a medical emergency.** Have ready an emergency plan and supplies. Be prepared to meet the special emergency needs of individual children.

14. **Know and follow established procedures for leading children to safety during fire and other hazard drills and in real emergencies, and post evacuation routes in each room.** "Remember, when we leave the building during a fire drill, we walk quietly down the hall toward the doors."

example

Mr. Lopez Responds to Leo's Injury

Mr. Lopez and his group of 4-year-olds walk into the building. Leo trips and falls. "You scraped your knee a little," explains Mr. Lopez as he helps Leo to his feet. When they get back to the room, Mr. Lopez gets the first-aid kit from the shelf. He opens the kit and reviews the chart taped to the inside lid that describes how to treat minor injuries. Mr. Lopez puts on latex gloves, then washes Leo's knee with soap and water. Leo winces. "You're being brave," says Mr. Lopez. "I know this stings a bit, but your knee needs to be clean so it will heal." At Leo's request, he puts a bandage on the scrape. Leo helps stick it in place. Mr. Lopez assures him, "You're all set and ready to play again." He fills out an injury report form and writes a note on the daily chart so, at the end of the day, he will remember to tell Leo's parents to read and sign the injury report.

Helping Children Learn to Take Precautions

15. **Take safety precautions in a calm and reassuring manner without overprotecting children or making them fearful.** Tell the children what they should do as you guide them appropriately.

16. **Involve children in making safety rules for indoor and outdoor equipment, materials, and activities.** Help children phrase safety rules so they state what they may do, rather than what they may not, such as "Use the steps to climb into and out of the loft," rather than, "Do not use the bookshelf to climb into the loft."

17. **Remind children of safety rules and emergency procedures by using diagrams, pictures, and words.** "Hold your funnel over the table so the water doesn't spill. Someone might slip and fall if the floor gets wet."

18. **Demonstrate proper ways to use potentially dangerous materials and equipment.** "Jorge, see how I do this? I hold the wood steady with my left hand when I'm sawing, keeping my fingers away from the blade. "

19. **Teach children to follow safety rules when taking neighborhood walks and study trips.** "Let's make sure everyone has a partner and knows which group he is in for tomorrow's trip."

20. **Use positive guidance to respond immediately when children are involved in unsafe activities.** "It hurts Michelle when you drive into her ankles. If you want to pass, ask her please to move onto the grass."

21. **Point out potential hazards so children will learn how to prevent injuries.** "Amanda, please help me trim the loose strings on the edge of this rug so nobody trips."

example

Ms. Williams Helps Oanh Stay Safe

Five-year-old Oanh builds a structure as high as her head. "I want to build my house bigger than I am," she says to the other children in the block area. Ms. Williams overhears her. "None of the children has built a building that tall yet. Let's talk about how to do that safely," she says. "It's only a problem if someone knocks it down," says Oanh. "I know!" volunteers Amanda, "Take tape and make a circle around the building so no one gets too close." "You solved the problem!" exclaims Ms. Williams. "You'll have to let the other children know." They decide to make a "Safety in the Block Area" chart, with pictures and words, so everyone will know the guidelines.

what's next?

Skill-Building Journal, section **1-2** *(Overview),* section **1-10** *(Answer Sheets),* and section **1-1** *(Feedback).*

Your Own Need for Safety

Feeling safe is a basic human need.

Everyone needs to feel protected from harm in order to function well. Safe environments make us feel secure, relaxed, confident, and able to enjoy ourselves. When people do not feel protected, they are often fearful and anxious.

The increasing violence in many communities today, especially random, unpredictable violence, makes many of us feel unsafe. We see violence on television and might also experience it in our homes and neighborhoods. A sense of security is important for everyone.

When you are in charge of your environment, you can keep it free from hazards most of the time. You have probably done things that were potentially dangerous, but you took steps to make these activities safer. Do you remember when you

- climbed a ladder while someone held it to keep it stable

- parked your car at night in a well-lit area of the shopping mall

- carefully unplugged a lamp with a frayed cord and had the wiring replaced

Learning about safety begins in childhood.

Your life experiences have taught you how to stay safe. When you were a child, the important adults in your life may have covered the electrical outlets to keep your bedroom safe and helped you develop safety habits, such as wearing a helmet when you rode your bike. As you grew older, you learned what you could do to minimize danger in a variety of situations.

what's next?

Skill-Building Journal, section **1-3** *(Your Own Need for Safety)*, section **1-1** *(Feedback)*, and section **1-4** *(Pre-Training Assessment).*

Learning Activities

LEARNING ACTIVITY

A. Creating and Maintaining Safe Environments

In this activity you will learn to

- establish and maintain indoor and outdoor environments and practices that promote safety for preschool children

- use daily and monthly safety checklists to identify and correct potential hazards in indoor and outdoor areas

Teachers help children learn how to minimize risks as they explore.

Many activities have elements of risk, but almost every risk can be minimized by anticipating and eliminating potential hazards. Early childhood teachers have dual responsibilities to children. They must keep them safe while also providing challenges that encourage development of cognitive, social/emotional, and physical skills. When selecting materials, arranging the environment, guiding learning, and responding to injuries, preschool teachers must consider how to encourage children to take risks while showing them how to do so safely. To do so, teachers think about what preschool children are like, what they can do, and what skills they are still developing. (The first learning activities in modules 4–10 offer many examples of what preschool children can do.)

Teachers work together to keep children free from harm.

You can expect preschool children to run, climb, and jump whenever they have a chance. To prevent injuries, you and your colleagues need to work together to make sure that all areas are continually supervised. You make sure that, indoors and outdoors, at every moment of the day, each child can be seen by you or your colleagues. You use what you know about each child's abilities and personality to anticipate what he or she might try to do, and intervene when necessary. If a child is about to endanger himself or others, you step in to stop the action before it starts. You model and talk about safety with children: using equipment properly, eliminating potential hazards, and following other safety practices and routines. You explain cause and effect—what might cause an injury and how someone could be hurt—through simple language and demonstration.

Daily and monthly safety checks will help you maintain an uncluttered environment, free from potentially dangerous items and with plenty of room for children to move their bodies safely. In addition, children are less likely to run inside, jump off tables, or climb on shelves when the daily schedule offers time for active play, both indoors and out. Because injuries tend to happen when children are tired, you also alternate vigorous activities with more quiet ones that help children rest.

Creating a safe environment can prevent injuries.

Preschool children show a lot of initiative; they are curious learners who try to make sense of their world. As children try to find out how things work, they sometimes use materials in ways that adults don't intend. Offer toys and materials that are well constructed and durable enough to withstand children's play and novel uses.

The way you arrange your space can prevent injuries. Constant supervision of indoor and outdoor environments—and intervening when necessary—also ensures safety. Because children don't always think ahead to predict the consequences of their actions, you have to do it for them.

Know the guidelines for keeping children safe.

The first step in arranging a safe environment is to provide sufficient space for children's activities. *Caring for Our Children: National Health and Safety Performance Standards: Guidelines for Out-of-Home Child Care Programs*[2] (http://nrc.uchsc.edu) explains safety requirements that will help you to keep children safe from harm. Section 1-5 of the *Skill-Building Journal* also lists safety conditions that reflect these performance standards. Ask your supervisor for information on the program's guidelines for environmental safety and applicable licensing requirements. Many of these requirements are designed to prevent injuries.

Consider these tips for making indoor interest areas and activities safe:

- Set up interest areas using low dividers or shelves, so it is easy to see all children at all times.

- Display and store materials on low, open shelves, not in chests with heavy lids that can fall on children.

- Place heavy toys on bottom shelves so children won't pull them down on themselves.

- Make sure each area has enough room for the activities that children engage in there.

- Create clear traffic paths so children don't get in each other's way.

- Provide a sufficient quantity of developmentally appropriate materials so children do not have to wait for a long time to use desired items.

Each interest area requires specific safety practices.

Try these suggestions for maintaining safe interest areas:

Blocks: Set up in a large space where the wall(s) and shelves create three sides and where the floor is level. Cover the floor with low-pile or indoor-outdoor–type carpeting, if possible. Place tape on the floor to define where children may build. Store blocks on low, open, labeled shelves with the largest on the bottom. Involve children in setting and posting guidelines for the height of structures.

Dramatic Play: Set up so the wall(s), shelves, and furniture create three sides. Remove drawstrings that could strangle a child. Shorten sleeves and hems of adult dress-up clothes so children won't trip while walking. Check furniture regularly to make sure it is free of rough edges, splinters, and loose hardware. Props should meet the standards set by the U.S. Consumer Product Safety Commission (www.cpsc.gov): no sharp points or edges, no pieces small enough to be swallowed, and no pieces that can be used as projectiles.

Toys and Games: Make sure all play materials meet the standards discussed above for dramatic play props. Use labeled storage containers so children can easily find and put away items. Teach children to check the floor regularly so they don't trip over small items.

Art: Locate art activities near a source of water and a washable floor. Provide sponges and towels for wiping up spills. Adjust open easels to children's height and fasten them securely. Store scissors with the points facing down. Use nontoxic materials, certified as safe by an organization such as the Art and Craft Materials Institute (http://www.acminet.org). Allow woodworking activities only when a teacher can closely supervise no more than four children at a time. Provide sturdy, real tools that children can use successfully. Require both children and adults to wear safety goggles.

Library: Place tape recorders and other electronic equipment near outlets. Help children use book-making and book-repair tools, such as hole punches, staplers, and scissors, without hurting themselves.

Discovery: Display indoor plants that you know are nontoxic and only animals that are not wild or dangerous. (Dangerous animals include turtles, birds of the parrot family, and ferrets.[3]) Teach children safe practices with animals, and be sure that children and adults always wash their hands after handling and feeding animals. If you use a take-apart table with mechanical objects or small appliances (for children to investigate springs, levers, gears, and other moving parts), use appliances other than computers or televisions, which contain toxic materials. Cut off cords, and remove batteries and glass.

Sand and Water: Locate these materials away from electrical outlets and cords. Use newspapers, drop cloths, or towels to control spills; have a mop, towels, and sponges nearby. Limit the number of children using the area at one time.

Music and Movement: Place CD players and other electronic equipment near outlets. Check rhythm instruments regularly to make sure they don't develop sharp corners or loose parts from being struck and shaken. Use tumbling mats for gymnastics and under indoor climbing equipment.

Cooking: Set up near a source of water and a fire extinguisher. Use a work surface that is at children's level. Regularly check the cords and functioning of electric appliances and place them near outlets. Teach children how to use small sharp knives without cutting themselves. Provide supplies to clean up spills and to handle hot food and equipment. Closely supervise all food preparation and cooking activities.

Computers: Place computers, printers, and other electronic equipment near outlets. Screw a power strip/surge protector into the bottom of the computer table, and plug all equipment into the power strip. Secure wires away from children's feet. Children should sit no closer than 18 inches from the screen, with the monitor angled so they do not have to look up.

Outdoors: Whether you use an outdoor play area at your program or a neighborhood park, it must have the safety features that are referenced in module 1 of the *Skill-Building Journal*. Make sure that your outdoor area is safe and under adult supervision whenever children are playing there.

Use safety checklists regularly.

Regular maintenance is necessary to keep the environment free from hazards. Because children use materials and equipment continuously, wear and tear can make a safe item or area dangerous. Teachers need to stay one step ahead of the children. They must continually check toys and equipment for sturdiness, make sure that exit paths stay clear, and repair or replace unsafe items.

what's next?

Skill-Building Journal, section **1-5** *(Learning Activity A)* and section **1-1** *(Feedback).*

Learning Activities

B. Keeping Children Safe on Trips Away From the Program[4]

In this activity you will learn to

- keep children safe while walking near traffic

- plan and implement safe study trips with children

During the preschool years, children expand their understanding of the world around them. One way you can support children's growing interest in their community is by planning neighborhood walks and study trips to interesting places. Remember, however, that taking children away from the program involves risks. You and the children might have to cross busy streets, travel in cars or vans, or take public transportation to new and unfamiliar locations. You can minimize risks by teaching children how to cross streets and walk near traffic, and by following the program's procedures for safe trips.

Walking Safely Near Traffic

Trips away from the program require safety planning.

Neighborhood walks are opportunities for children to learn about their community and to develop new concepts and skills. You might take a listening walk or visit a local store to purchase something the group needs. Preschool children are capable of learning and following rules about walking near traffic safely. Guidelines for taking walks with children follow.

Before taking a walk with children, review and discuss the following safety guidelines:

- Obey the crosswalk signals, *Walk* and *Don't Walk*.

- Cross at the corner and stay within the crosswalk.

- Never walk out from between parked cars.

- Always walk on the sidewalk.

- Look left, right, and left again before crossing, even when the signals indicate that it is safe to walk.

During the walk, review and discuss the following safety guidelines:

- Talk to children about safety: "We will cross the street at the corner."

- Point out traffic signs and talk about how they help keep people safe.

- Use a knotted clothesline or rope to keep the group together; have each child hold onto a knot.

- Make the walk fun by singing a song, looking for objects or shapes, or playing "Follow the Leader."

- Know which children may need close attention and be sure an adult is assigned to be with them.

- Return to the program if children seem tired or frustrated, or if they are behaving in unsafe ways.

Study trips can introduce children to interesting but unfamiliar places. Appropriate trips for preschool children are to nearby sites and last no more than a few hours. For example, most preschool children are ready for a morning trip to a children's museum to see a specific room or exhibition. An all-day trip would be too tiring and overwhelming for this age group.

Plan ahead so that you and the children can enjoy the trip.

The children are likely to be both excited and apprehensive about an upcoming trip. Some children may be fearful about leaving the program, changing the normal routine, and going to a strange place. They may worry that their parents won't know where to find them. You, too, may be nervous about supervising the children in an unfamiliar location. If you are driving, you might be anxious about getting to and from the place or about parking. If you are taking public transportation, you might worry about children who get separated from the group. For these reasons, it is important to plan ahead, anticipate potential problems, and take precautions to ensure children's safety on study trips. Guidelines for trips follow.

Study Trips: Planning and Logistics

Pre-trip planning:

Recruit volunteers to help supervise the children. They might be family members, senior citizens, or high school or college early childhood students. Always pair volunteers with someone from the program who knows the policies and procedures for trips.

Obtain signed permission slips for each trip so families know when their children will be leaving the program, where they will be going, and when they will return.

Review the route to be sure you have correct directions and have allocated adequate time for travel and the visit.

Inspect the first-aid kit and replace missing or outdated items. Provide a first-aid kit for each vehicle and/or group of children, as well as coins for pay phones.

Create a trip folder with a planning checklist, a list of emergency phone numbers, signed parent emergency forms (be sure information is current), signed permission slips, and information about the site.

Plan for car travel by checking that you have a size- and age-appropriate seat restraint for each child and adult.

Learn the current fares and obtain correct fare payment if using public transportation. Plan how to get the children on and off the vehicle safely.

Visit the site in advance, if possible, by traveling there using the same route you will follow on the trip. Look for potential problems, such as detours, one-way streets, or parking restrictions. Adjust the trip schedule if necessary.

Locate essential or emergency facilities at the site, such as telephones, restrooms, shelters for poor weather, and where to go for emergency assistance.

Make individual tags or badges stating the name and telephone number of your program and the child's first name. Last names are not necessary and could make it easier for an abductor to encourage a child to go with him or her.

Prepare children for the trip by discussing what you will see and do. Involve children in setting safety rules. Give clear instructions about what children should do if they get separated from the group.

Plan for children with special needs such as allergies, asthma, diabetes, or seizures. The supervising adult needs to know how to recognize and respond to a medical emergency and have on hand an emergency plan, supplies, and needed medications.

Immediately before leaving:

Review the trip folder to make sure it is complete.

Distribute first-aid kits to each group or vehicle.

Study Trips: Planning and Logistics (continued)

Traveling by car or van:

Secure each child. Place only one child in each safety restraint.

Remove dangerous objects (e.g., sharp, heavy) from the vehicle, in case of a sudden stop.

Review safety rules for traveling (e.g., keeping seat belts buckled and bodies completely inside the vehicle).

Traveling by bus or subway:

Review safety rules for traveling, including procedures for getting on and off the vehicle.

Make sure you have correct change for each passenger's fare.

Traveling to and from the site:

Engage children. Talk about passing scenery and discuss what to expect upon arrival. Remind children of the safety rules.

Stop the vehicle in case of unruly behavior. If children misbehave or undo their seat belts, pull off the road and stop. Do not try to discipline children while driving.

Supervise children at all times while inside the vehicle.

At the site:

Follow prearranged procedures on arrival.

Closely supervise all children, all of the time. Pay attention to children's behavior. If children seem tired or frustrated, cut the visit short and return to the program.

Leaving the site:

Account for everyone. Count children and adults at least twice.

Secure each passenger in a safety restraint.

Review safety rules for traveling.

what's next?

Skill-Building Journal, section **1-6** *(Learning Activity B)* and section **1-1** *(Feedback).*

Learning Activities

C. Handling Injuries and Emergencies

In this activity you will learn to

- prepare for responding to injuries and other emergencies

- follow your program's procedures for dealing with injuries and emergencies

Most child care programs require staff members to take first-aid training. Cardiopulmonary resuscitation (CPR) training might also be required (particularly for programs that include swimming and wading activities). The information in this activity is a reminder of the most important content from such training. It is not meant to be a substitute for CPR and first-aid training led by qualified medical personnel.

Even the most safety-conscious and well-prepared teacher will have to deal with injuries and emergencies from time to time. Because injuries and emergencies can occur at any time, it is wise to be ready for them. Part of keeping children safe is knowing and following the program's policies and procedures for responding to injuries and emergencies. The more familiar you are with these procedures, the more quickly and effectively you can respond.

Responding to Children's Injuries and Emergencies

Most injuries are minor—bumped heads or sore knees—requiring only soothing words and perhaps a bandage. For minor injuries such as cuts and bruises, your program probably has an injury form that you must complete. Be sure to inform parents of the incidents when they pick up their children at the end of the day, and ask them to read and sign the forms. In addition, let your supervisor know about the injuries.

Stay calm and follow proper procedures.

Sometimes, children's injuries are serious enough to require first aid on site. Rarely, a trip to the hospital may be necessary.

Your program should have a plan for emergency transportation to the closest hospital or health care facility. If you accompany the child in the ambulance, bring the child's signed medical history and emergency authorization forms. The director or a colleague should contact the child's family and ask them to meet you at the hospital as soon as possible.

Know and follow your program's policies and procedures for determining when and how to get immediate medical help. The following summary may be helpful.

Getting Immediate Medical Help[5]

Ask the family to come right away or meet you at the hospital if you observe that a child

- is at risk for **permanent injury**

- is **acting strangely**, is much less alert, or is much more withdrawn than usual

- has **difficulty breathing** or is unable to speak

- has **discolored skin or lips** that look blue, purple, or gray

- has a **seizure** (rhythmic jerking of arms and legs and a loss of consciousness)

- is **unconscious**

- is less and **less responsive**

- after a head injury, has a **decreased level of alertness**, confusion, headache, vomiting, irritability, or difficulty waking

- has increasing or **severe pain** anywhere

- has a **cut or burn that is large**, deep, or won't stop bleeding

- is **vomiting blood**

- has a **severe stiff neck, headache, and fever**

- is significantly **dehydrated**: sunken eyes, lethargic, not making tears, not urinating

---

Other situations require immediate family notification and warrant medical attention within one hour, although not necessarily ambulance transport. These include a feverish child who looks more than mildly ill, a quickly spreading purple or red rash, and blood in the stools.

First-Aid Procedures

Maintain well-stocked first-aid kits.

First aid is the immediate care you provide to a child who is injured or ill. It is a way to manage the situation until further medical care can be given. In cases of drowning, electric shock, and smoke inhalation, CPR is used to clear the patient's throat, help him or her to breathe, and restart the heart if necessary. Make sure that your knowledge and skills in first-aid and CPR are up-to-date.

Maintain at least two well-stocked first-aid kits: one for program use and another for travel (e.g., neighborhood walks, study trips). Keep supplies in a closed container accessible to staff but out of children's reach. Outdoors, staff should carry a mini-kit (including latex gloves, gauze, bandages, and tissues) for immediate use and protection from body fluids. Restock kits after each use and check them monthly. Also stock extra blankets, pillows, and ice packs.

If you must administer more than simple first aid, remain calm. Reassure the child. To clear the area, ask others to move away. Ask someone else to call 911 for assistance. If more than one person is hurt, begin by administering first aid to the person in the greatest danger. All staff members need to be trained in using gloves for contact with body fluids and in waste disposal, to protect against the spread of pathogens such as HIV/AIDS and hepatitis B.

When giving first aid, remember these important rules:

- Do no harm. Harm might occur if you fail to treat the injury, as well as if you make the injury worse.

- Do not move a child with serious head, neck, or back injury except to save a life. Moving the child might cause further injury.

Steps for Evaluating Emergency Situations and Giving First Aid[5]

Follow your program's policies and procedures, which are likely to recommend these steps:

1. **Evaluate the situation:** who is hurt, what is wrong, how the injury occurred, and if there is still danger.

2. **Check for life-threatening problems.** If the child is not conscious, determine if he or she is breathing.

3. **If the child is not breathing, follow correct procedures for mouth-to-mouth resuscitation. Begin CPR if necessary.** Make sure that you have current training for both procedures..

4. **If the child is conscious, ask questions** such as, "What's your name?" to help determine the child's condition. Keep checking breathing and pulse.

5. **Check for injuries**, starting at the head. Medical personnel will ask you for this information.

6. **Decide whether to call an ambulance.** If in any doubt, call an ambulance. Then call the child's parents.

7. **Check the condition of any other injured children.** Calmly explain to everyone present that you are taking care of the injured children.

8. **Wash any minor wounds** to reduce chances of infection.

9. **Complete an injury report form.** Follow procedures for reporting the injury and give a copy of the form to the parents.

Make sure poisons are out of children's reach.

A poison emergency occurs when a toxic substance touches someone in a harmful way. This can happen when someone swallows a toxic substance, gets chemicals in the eyes or on the skin, or breathes toxic fumes. The following common substances might be poisonous: cleaners and laundry products, hair care products, prescription and over-the-counter drugs, art supplies, plant food and lawn care chemicals, cigarettes, alcoholic beverages, paint and paint removal products, lighter fluids, berries and leaves of certain plants, pesticides, room deodorizers, and workroom supplies. None of these should be stored within children's reach.

If you know or suspect that a child has been poisoned, call the poison control center or a medical clinic immediately. Tell the person answering the phone what product or chemical the child was exposed to, and have the container with you when you make the call. Tell the person how much the child took or was exposed to and when.

Responding to Fires

Every month, you and your co-workers should hold an emergency drill so all the children and adults will know what to do if they must quickly leave the building during a fire or other emergency. The program's emergency procedures and evacuation routes should be posted in every classroom. If you designate specific staff responsibilities in advance, all adults can work as a team to lead the children to safety. Emergency responsibilities might include administering first-aid if needed, overseeing building evacuation, accounting for all children and adults, and calling 911.

Know when it is appropriate to use a fire extinguisher.

It is important to know when and when not to use a fire extinguisher. Do not try to fight fires that spread beyond the spot where they started. For example, you can probably put out a grease fire in a frying pan, but, if it gets out of control or threatens to block an exit, you and the children should get out of the building immediately. Use an extinguisher only if the following conditions exist:

- All children are safely out of the area and in the care of a responsible person.

- You can get out fast if your efforts fail.

- You are nearby when the fire starts, or you discover the fire soon after it has started.

- The fire is small and confined to a space such as a trash can, cushion, or small appliance.

- You can fight the fire with your back to an exit.

- The extinguisher is in working order and you can stand back about 8 feet; aim at the base of the fire, not the flames or smoke; and squeeze or press the lever while sweeping from the sides of the fire to the middle.

When in doubt, get out!

If you have the slightest doubt about whether to fight the fire or get out, leave the building and call the fire department. Your safety is more important than the property you might save.

If the building is filled with smoke, have the children crawl under the smoke to safety. If a child's clothes catch fire, tell him or her to drop and roll. You can practice this procedure during one of your emergency drills.

what's next?

Skill-Building Journal, section **1-7** (*Learning Activity C*), section **1-10** (*Answer Sheets*), and section **1-1** (*Feedback*).

Learning Activities

D. Helping Children Learn to Take Precautions

In this activity you will learn to

- teach children how to stay safe throughout the day

- develop safety rules with children

The first step in teaching children safety is to show them—by your actions—how you take precautions and prevent injuries. Children need to see adults acting in safe ways, such as

- walking, not running, in the room

- sitting, not standing, on chairs

- using a step stool to reach high cupboards

- using sharp tools properly for woodworking and cooking

Model and explain safe practices.

When you and your colleagues use potentially dangerous items or take other risks, talk to the children about what's happening and why.

> Mr. Chanute is changing the light bulb over the water table. He's moving the water table out of the way. Now he can set up the stepladder right under the light. Now, he's opening up the ladder and fastening the safety latches. The latches help to keep the ladder steady so he won't fall. Mr. Lopez will stand nearby to pass Mr. Chanute the new bulb and to be ready to help.

Preschool children can sometimes make plans and think before acting, but they frequently forget to do so. They may not consider what might happen if they ride a tricycle too fast, climb up the slide, or splash water on the floor under the sink. There are numerous opportunities throughout the day to explain and demonstrate the safe way to use materials, play games, and carry out routines. In addition to the safety practices discussed in the *Overview* of this module, here are some suggestions for teaching children to do things safely:

Stand near the equipment children are using and comment on their use of precautions. "Aimee, you remembered to make sure nobody was in the way, and you said, 'I'm going to jump.'"

Supervise and interact with the children. Hold conversations with other teachers during break and planning times.

Step in quickly to ensure safe practices. "Use the step stool, not the table."

Be consistent in applying rules and acknowledge children who follow them. "Tyrone, I see you remembered to wear a safety helmet while riding your trike."

Remove the child from the situation if he or she continues to break a safety rule, and explain why he or she is being removed. "Janelle, put the scissors down. I have told you to stop waving the scissors in the air because someone could get hurt. Choose another area to work in now."

Involve children in clean-up routines so they will learn that potentially hazardous equipment should be stored safely. "That's right. You put the knives in the basket. I'll put them on top of the cabinet until I can wash them and put them away."

Help children predict and avoid unsafe situations.

Preschool children are beginning to understand cause and effect, which helps them recognize how injuries happen and what can be done to prevent them. They can make predictions and talk about past, present, and future events. Using simple language, you can talk with children about dangerous situations and remind them of previous situations in which children did or did not stay safe. "Do you remember what happened last week when Leo and Tony ran around the room? They bumped into each other and banged their heads." You can also demonstrate, using concrete objects and experiences, the correct ways to use materials and equipment.

Most preschool children can understand and follow safety rules, although they are likely to need frequent reminders. The children in your group are more likely to understand and remember to follow safety rules that they have helped set. To develop safety rules with children, you might start a discussion by saying

- "What can you tell me about . . .?"

- "What could happen when . . . ?"

- "What might happen if . . . ?"

For example, assume you are planning a cooking activity that involves use of an electric skillet. Before the activity, you can meet with the children to set some rules for safe use of the skillet. You might say, "What can you tell me about cooking with skillets?" The children will offer several different comments: "It's fun," and "It gets really hot." Then ask, "What might happen if you put your hand on a hot skillet?" "You would get burned," a child answers. Now you can lead the group in developing the following rules for using the skillet:

- Only one child may use the skillet at a time.

- Keep your hands off the skillet.

- Use a pot holder to hold the handle.

- Use long-handled utensils to move the food.

By participating in safety discussions, children learn that they can take steps to keep themselves safe. As teachers offer safety reminders while supervising activities, children begin to develop the skills and sound judgment needed to keep themselves safe.

what's next?

Skill-Building Journal, section **1-8** (*Learning Activity D*), section **1-1** (*Feedback*), and section **1-9** (*Reflecting on Your Learning*).

Overview

Maintaining Indoor and Outdoor Environments That Promote Wellness

Helping Children Develop Habits That Promote Good Hygiene and Nutrition

Recognizing and Reporting Child Abuse and Neglect

Your Own Health and Nutrition

Learning Activities

A. Creating and Maintaining a Hygienic Environment

B. Responding When Children Are Sick

C. Encouraging Good Nutrition

D. Helping Children Learn Healthy Habits

E. Recognizing and Reporting Child Abuse and Neglect

2. Healthy

Healthy people feel good about themselves.

Good health is a state of physical, mental, and social well-being, not simply the absence of disease. Healthy people generally are well-rested and energetic, eat the right foods, feel competent, and get along well with others.

Teachers help children develop good health practices.

Teachers play a key role in keeping children healthy. Although preschool children can do many things for themselves, teachers need to maintain environments that promote wellness.

Children learn about good health practices by following adults' examples. You model handwashing, and you alternate periods of exercise and rest. You offer nutritious snacks and encourage children to help you keep the room clean. You eat family style with the children and help them to learn the importance of starting each day with a balanced meal.

Preschool children can use self-help skills to stay healthy. They put on their jackets before going out on a cold day, brush their teeth after meals, and wash their hands after using the toilet. Children can also learn to select, prepare, and eat nutritious foods. Cooking activities and family-style meals allow preschoolers to learn about good nutrition. When good health and nutrition habits are developed at an early age, they are likely to continue throughout a person's life.

Sometimes teachers are the only witnesses to the signs of abuse and neglect.

This module also addresses an important but disturbing aspect of keeping children healthy: recognizing the signs of abuse and neglect and reporting them to appropriate authorities. Other than the children's families, teachers may be the only persons who have daily contact with young children. Because you know the children well, you are likely to notice unusual changes in their behavior and/or unexplained injuries. All teachers have the ethical and legal responsibility to report suspected child abuse and neglect.

You can promote children's health by

- maintaining indoor and outdoor environments that promote wellness

- helping children develop habits that promote good hygiene and nutrition

- recognizing and reporting child abuse and neglect

Maintaining Indoor and Outdoor Environments That Promote Wellness

1. **Check the room daily for adequate ventilation and lighting, comfortable temperature, and sanitary conditions.** While teachers typically do not have direct responsibility for controlling the classroom temperature and air circulation and for replacing light bulbs, you need to be aware of environmental conditions and report problems to your supervisor.

2. **Provide tissues; paper towels; soap; and plastic-lined, covered waste containers within children's reach.** When children use these supplies, they help you maintain a healthy environment.

3. **Complete daily health checks and stay alert to symptoms of illness throughout the day.** "Oanh, your eyes look watery today. Are you feeling okay?"

4. **Recognize symptoms of common childhood illnesses, such as strep throat and chicken pox.** Stay in regular contact with families. Follow your program's policy for contacting families when you suspect that a child might be ill.

5. **Use the handwashing methods recommended by the Centers for Disease Control and Prevention (CDC) to prevent the spread of germs.** Children and adults should wash their hands properly throughout the day.

6. **Clean and disinfect table surfaces before and after preparing and serving food.** Use a bleach solution to disinfect tables after you or the children wash them.

7. **Follow a flexible daily schedule that offers a balance of relaxing and vigorous indoor and outdoor activities.** Allow all children sufficient time to rest. Nap/rest time is typically scheduled after lunch, and some children may require additional rest.

Mark Blows His Nose

When Ms. Williams conducts the morning room check, she notices that the children's soap dispenser is full but the paper towel roll is empty. As she installs a new roll, the children begin to arrive. She greets each child warmly, checking to see if anyone has signs of the cold that several children in the program have had. "You have the sniffles today, Mark. Please blow your nose with a tissue from the box next to the sink," she says. Mark is having difficulty, so Ms. Williams asks if she can help. "It's hard," he says. "It goes through the tissue!" She doubles the tissue and helps him blow his nose. After putting the used tissue into the can, she says, "Now let's both wash our hands to make sure all the germs are gone."

Helping Children Develop Habits That Promote Good Hygiene and Nutrition

8. **Encourage children to use self-help skills for toileting, handwashing, toothbrushing, and at snack and mealtimes.** Use different strategies to help children learn self-help skills so that each child is successful in keeping himself healthy.

9. **Model healthy habits, such as handwashing, using tissues, eating nutritious foods, and sanitizing materials and surfaces.** "Uh-oh, here comes a big sneeze! I'd better get a tissue."

10. **Introduce health and hygiene concepts through daily routines, conversations, books, cooking activities, and visiting health professionals.** "Chef Chavez, Jorge's dad, is going to help us make some healthy treats. Before we handle any food, we all need to wash our hands."

11. **Plan and serve nutritious meals and snacks.** Select nutritious recipes for cooking activities and encourage the program to plan meals and snacks that are high in nutrients.

12. **Sit with children, family-style, during snacks and meals to encourage conversation and to model healthy eating habits.** "I've never had tofu before, but I'm going to try some. In Asian countries, people eat it all the time. Aimee, would you like to try some?"

13. **Help children recognize when their bodies need rest, food or water, or movement.** "Leo, you've been painting all afternoon. How about playing catch with us?"

14. **Tell families how you and your colleagues promote wellness.** Provide copies of snack and meal menus; share an article about preventing colds through frequent handwashing; and post a chart on the symptoms of common childhood diseases.

Crunchy Apples and Shiny Teeth

"What a delicious lunch," says Mr. Lopez. "These crunchy juicy apples are good for us," he explains as he passes a bowl of slices to Benjamin. As the children finish lunch, they clear their dishes and wipe their place mats. Then they go to the sink to wash their hands and brush their teeth. Each child uses one squirt of soap and vigorously washes wrists and hands. After drying their hands and tossing the used paper towels in the waste container, the children take their toothbrushes from a Styrofoam egg-carton holder. The brushes are labeled with the children's names and stored in the same slot each day. Mr. Lopez joins the children at the sink. "Remember to brush up and down," he says. Janelle watches Mr. Lopez brush his teeth. "I'm brushing my teeth," she says proudly, with toothpaste in the corners of her broad smile. "So am I," says Mr. Lopez. "Do my teeth look clean?"

Recognizing and Reporting Child Abuse and Neglect

15. **Respond to children in caring ways while avoiding situations that might be questioned by others.** Work with your supervisor to make sure that all staff and family members are aware of appropriate ways for teachers to nurture children, so that the program supports staff in doing their jobs.

16. **Know the definitions of physical abuse, sexual abuse, emotional abuse or neglect, and physical neglect.** If you are unclear about the definitions of abuse and neglect, talk with your supervisor.

17. **Recognize and be alert to the physical and behavioral signs that a child might be a victim of abuse or neglect.** The signs of abuse and neglect include, but are not limited to, bruises and marks, often covered by clothing; dizziness; and talking about being beaten or sexual acts.

18. **Report suspected child abuse and neglect to authorities according to applicable laws and program policies.** Your program should provide information about teachers' responsibilities as persons who are required to report suspected problems.

19. **Support families by helping them get the services they need.** Talk with your supervisor and other colleagues about agencies and organizations your program uses for referrals.

example

Noticing Some Unexplained Bruises

When Betty spills juice down the front of her shirt, Ms. Kim quickly moves to help her find a clean shirt. As Betty takes off the wet shirt, Ms. Kim sees that the child's back is criss-crossed with loop-shaped bruises. Some look fresh; others seem older. When Ms. Kim asks what happened, Betty replies, "I was bad, so I got whipped." Ms. Kim tells Ms. Lee, the director, what she has seen and heard. They discuss the signs of possible child abuse. Ms. Kim decides she must report the incident to Child Protective Services (CPS), the local agency that responds to child abuse and neglect. She writes down her observations and concerns, so this information will be available when she calls CPS. Ms. Lee says, "We both need to keep this situation confidential. I will be here if you need someone to talk to." Ms. Kim calls CPS and files a report. She then arranges to meet privately with Betty's parents at pick-up time to let them know she has filed a report and to offer her support.

what's next?

Skill-Building Journal, section **2-2** (*Overview*), section **2-11** (*Answer Sheets*), and section **2-1** (*Feedback*).

Your Own Health and Nutrition

Staying healthy improves your life.

We all know that good health and proper nutrition are important. The national focus on staying fit has provided much useful information about how staying healthy improves the quality of life and can actually prolong life.

To maintain wellness, perhaps you have

- begun walking or jogging more often

- joined a gym or taken an exercise class

- quit smoking or vowed never to start

- added more vegetables, fruits, and whole-grain foods to your diet

- maintained an appropriate weight using a sensible eating plan

- begun eating more fibrous foods and less sugar, fat, and salt

- used healthy strategies to manage stress

- experienced the positive effects of relaxation techniques

Change your health and nutrition habits one step at a time.

You may have discovered, though, that changing too much too quickly can lead to discouragement and failure. Have you found yourself saying these things?

- "I tried to quit smoking, but I felt like I was going crazy, and I couldn't stop eating!"

- "I don't have time to run and still work, take care of my family, and do the gardening."

- "I'd like to serve healthier meals, but they take too long to plan and prepare."

It can be hard to change health and nutrition habits. We may know what to do but not actually do it. It can help to think of change in terms of more and less. Try to develop more good habits, such as

- exercising

- eating foods low in fat, salt, and sugar

- getting enough sleep

- spending time with family and friends

Try to stop or lessen unhealthy habits, such as

- smoking

- eating foods high in fat, salt, or sugar

- drinking alcohol

- letting stress build up

The *Dietary Guidelines for Americans*, developed by the U.S. Department of Agriculture (USDA) and the U.S. Department of Health and Human Services (DHHS), provide recommendations for maintaining good health and nutrition habits. The Guidelines also include special advice for children about such matters as exercise, milk consumption, and the amount and sources of fats.

The USDA and DHHS jointly update and publish these guidelines every five years. You can obtain the Dietary Guidelines online (www.health.gov/dietaryguidelines/dga2005/document). A booklet that explains the guidelines may also be viewed and downloaded from the Internet (www.healthierus/gov/dietaryguidelines) or ordered by calling 888-878-3256. Here are some tips from the guidelines.

Dietary Guidelines for Americans*

Eat a variety of foods and maintain a healthy weight.

- Eat a variety of nutritious foods in amounts that meet your daily energy needs (calories).

- Include selections of fruits, vegetables, whole grains, fat-free or low-fat milk and milk products, lean meats, poultry, fish, eggs, dried beans and peas, and nuts.

- Increase your physical activity.

- Drink plenty of water.

Choose a diet low in saturated and trans fatty acids.

- Choose lean meat, fish, poultry, beans, peas, nuts, and seeds as protein sources.

- Use skim or low-fat milk and milk products.

- Limit your intake of fats and oils, especially saturated fat and oil (butter, cream, lard, palm oil, coconut oil) and heavily hydrogenated fats and oils (some margarines and shortenings).

- Broil, bake, or boil rather than fry.

- Read labels carefully to determine both the amount and type of fat in foods.

*United States Department of Agriculture and United States Department of Health and Human Services. (2005). *Dietary guidelines for Americans: Key recommendations for the general population*. Retrieved May 11, 2005, from http://www.health.gov/dietaryguidelines/dga2005/recommendations.htm

Dietary Guidelines for Americans, continued

Choose plenty of vegetables, fruits, and whole grains.

- Choose a variety of foods that are good sources of fiber, such as whole-grain breads and cereals, fruits, vegetables, beans, and peas.

Use sugar in moderation.

- Choose food and beverages with few added sugars or caloric sweeteners. Avoid soft drinks, candy, cake, and cookies.

- Avoid eating sweets between meals and practice good oral hygiene.

- Read food labels for information about sugar content. Sucrose, glucose, maltose, dextrose, lactose, and fructose are various kinds of sugars.

Use salt in moderation.

- Learn to enjoy the flavors of unsalted foods.

- Cook without salt or add only small amounts of salt, and do not add more salt at the table.

- Try flavoring foods with herbs, spices, and lemon juice.

- Limit your intake of salty foods such as chips, pretzels, salted nuts and popcorn, condiments, pickled foods, cured meats, and some canned vegetables and soups.

- Read labels carefully to determine the amounts of sodium (salt) they contain. At the same time, choose potassium-rich foods, such as fruits and vegetables.

what's next?

Skill-Building Journal, section **2-3** (*Your Own Health and Nutrition*) and section **2-4** (*Pre-Training Assessment*).

Learning Activities

A. Creating and Maintaining a Hygienic Environment[6]

In this activity you will learn to

- maintain indoor and outdoor spaces that minimize germs and promote wellness

- follow procedures recommended by health professionals for handwashing, sanitation, and toileting

Caregiving environments for preschool children can be germ-filled places where illnesses are passed among children and adults. When you think about typical scenes in a preschool room, it is easy to understand why germs might be spread easily.

> Jamie wet his pants, which is not uncommon for 3-year-old children who are mastering toileting. His pants, underwear, and shirt front are soaked. Ms. Kim asks him to go to the restroom to change. She puts on disposable gloves and helps Jamie remove his wet clothes, wash himself with a disposable cloth, dry off, and put on clean clothes. She puts Jamie's soiled clothes in a plastic bag, seals the bag with a twist-tie, and writes his name on the bag.

> While playing outdoors, Michelle sneezes into her hand, then picks up a ball and tosses it to Mark. Mark grabs the ball after it hits the ground and rolls it to Oanh. As Mark pushes the ball on the ground, he scrapes his fingers. He puts them in his mouth as he cries and runs toward Ms. Frilles.

It's a major part of your job to work with your colleagues to make sure your comfortable, activity-oriented setting also promotes wellness and minimizes illness and disease. You can eliminate disease-producing germs and preserve everyone's good health through daily practices. These include checking your classroom to make sure it is clean and uncluttered and reporting any problems to your supervisor; cleaning spills as they occur; disinfecting tables before and after eating and after the classroom pet has run across them; and throwing garbage away promptly. You can invite children to assist with these chores and keep tissues, sponges, and paper towels within their reach.

Germs can be passed from one person to another.

Most childhood illnesses are contagious. Sick children can leave germs on tables, materials, and equipment, and germs grow on perishable foods. Germs can be spread from one child to another through saliva, mucus, urine, vomit, and stool. Each time a child sneezes or coughs, shares food, or forgets to wash his or her hands after using the toilet, disease-causing germs can be transmitted. You can't always tell who has a contagious illness by whether he looks sick. Sometimes diseases can be contagious even when the child appears healthy. Most illnesses (such as flu or chicken pox) are contagious for several days before symptoms appear. Some can be carried for a long time without any symptoms (such as giardia, hepatitis B, and HIV). That's why it is essential to follow universal precautions—handwashing, cleaning and disinfecting, and using gloves for contact with body fluids—to prevent the spread of diseases among children and adults.

Handwashing Procedures

Health professionals agree that frequent, thorough handwashing can reduce the spread of disease in child care programs by 50 percent and protect adults and children from various illnesses. Handwashing is for everyone. Teachers wash their own hands and help as children wash their hands

- upon arrival and before going home

- before and after preparing, eating, and serving snacks and meals

- before and after giving medication

- after handling your or a child's body fluids (mucus, blood, vomit, urine, and so on) or soiled clothes

- after using the toilet or helping a child use the toilet

- after caring for a child who may have a contagious illness

- after cleaning the room, bathroom surfaces, or toys

- after emptying, cleaning, or changing the plastic bag in a trash can

- after handling pets, cages, or pet supplies

- before and after playing in water that was used by more than one person or that has been standing for more than a few hours

- after playing in sandboxes

- after playing outdoors

How to Wash Your Hands

- Make sure a clean paper towel is available.

- Remove rings. (Rings can hide germs.[7])

- Turn on warm water; moisten hands with liquid soap.

- Rub your hands together vigorously until lather appears; continue rubbing for at least 10 seconds.

- Wash all surfaces: backs of hands, wrists, palms, fingers, between fingers, under fingernails.

- Rinse your hands well. Leave the water running.

- Dry your hands with a paper towel.

- Turn off the water using a paper towel instead of bare hands. Throw away the towel.

Help children wash their hands by following the steps described in the box above. Make a poster that shows these steps with a series of pictures and words, sequenced from left to right and hung above the sinks. If you do not have a child-size sink, have each child stand on a safety step at a height at which her hands can hang freely under the running water. Wash your own hands when the children's hands are clean and dry.

Washing and Disinfecting Surfaces, Toys, and Equipment

Use a bleach solution to disinfect surfaces and materials.

Children who have been exposed to germs that cause infectious diseases can leave bacteria, parasites, and viruses on tables, materials, toys, equipment, and clothing. The best line of defense is to thoroughly wash surfaces, toys, and equipment with soap and water, then disinfect them to kill germs. Some programs disinfect washable toys in the hot cycle of a dishwasher, separately from dishes, or in a washing machine. Otherwise, use the following safe bleach solutions to disinfect surfaces and other items effectively.

Surface Bleach Solution	Cleans
1/4 cup of liquid chlorine bleach to 1 gallon of water or 1 tablespoon of liquid chlorine bleach to 1 quart of water	All surfaces except play materials, including tabletops and counters; bathroom fixtures; walls; door frames and doorknobs; floors; brooms, dustpans, and mops used to wipe up body fluids

Follow these steps to clean and disinfect surfaces:

- Wash the surface with detergent and water. Rinse with clear water.

- Coat the surface with bleach solution (dispensed from a spray bottle).

- Let the surface air dry. If you want to dry the surface with a paper towel, wait for 2 minutes before drying.

Mild Bleach Solution	Cleans
1 tablespoon of liquid chlorine bleach to 1 gallon of water or 1 teaspoon of liquid chlorine bleach to 1 quart of water	All play materials and objects children have put in their mouths

Follow these steps to clean and disinfect toys and other washable objects handled by children:

- Clean toys and other items with detergent and water. Scrub with a brush to reach all parts.

- Rinse in clear water.

- Coat the surface with bleach solution (dispensed from a spray bottle) and place in a rack or on a clean towel to air dry.

If you use a soaking method to sanitize toys, use a more concentrated solution (because each object can introduce germs into the solution): 3/4 cup of bleach to 1 gallon of water. Put toys in a net bag, soak them for 5 minutes, rinse with clean water, and hang the bag to air dry.

Dishwashing Bleach Solution	Cleans
1 1/2 teaspoons of liquid chlorine bleach to 1 gallon of water	Dishes and utensils, during the third step of dishwashing when those items are not washed and dried in a dishwasher

Make fresh bleach solutions every day.

One of your daily tasks is to mix new batches of bleach solutions. Pour *surface* bleach solution into labeled spray bottles and place them in the food preparation and toileting areas. Pour the *mild* bleach solution and the *dishwashing* bleach solution into separate labeled containers. Store all solutions away from direct sunlight and out of children's reach. Discard unused bleach solutions at the end of the day because they weaken and lose effectiveness very quickly.

Hygienic Food Practices

Everyone can help keep food safe to eat.

In programs that serve meals and snacks, the food service staff usually prepares the food. Your classroom might have a food preparation area where you position a cart before delivering food to the tables where the children and teachers eat, or where you prepare food brought from the children's homes. The food preparation area should be located near a sink and used only for preparing food. The following strategies will help everyone keep food fresh and safe to eat.

Serving snacks and meals

- Make sure food from home is in containers labeled with the child's name, the date, and a description of the contents. Examine the food when it arrives to make sure it is not spoiled or dirty. Refrigerate food at 40° F or cooler, or keep warm food at 140° F or hotter.

- Use only cooking equipment, dishes, and utensils that can be washed and disinfected or discarded.

- Make sure each serving bowl has a spoon or other serving utensil.

- Make sure children use their own plates, cups, and utensils, and do not share food they have touched or started to eat.

Cleaning up

Children can help with these activities, to the extent their abilities allow.

- Throw leftover food away or return it to the kitchen. Do not discard whole raw fruit and cut or raw vegetables that can be thoroughly washed, and packaged foods that have not been unwrapped and do not spoil.

- Allow children to help wash counters and table tops with soap and water before the teacher disinfects the surfaces with surface bleach solution.

- Scrape food off dishes and utensils into a trash container and place the dishes and utensils in a basin to be returned to the kitchen.

Promoting Wellness While Children Sleep at the Center

Sanitize cots and bedding regularly.

Even while children are sleeping, germs can pass from one person to another. When a sick child sleeps next to another child, both may end up with the same illness. Sharing cots and linens can also spread disease. Hygienic practices can minimize the spread of germs while children are sleeping.

- Set up cots at least 3 feet apart.

- Assign each child to a specific cot (or mat), labeled with the child's name and stored so sleeping surfaces do not touch each other.

- Make sure children sleep in assigned beds. If a child accidentally sleeps in another child's bed, disinfect it and change the linens before the assigned child uses it again.

- Label each child's sheets, pillows, pillowcases, and blankets; store them separately so they aren't touching another child's bedding.

- Clean and disinfect cots at least weekly and whenever soiled or wet.

Maintaining the Bathroom as a Hygienic Environment

Keep bathrooms well-stocked with soap and paper towels.

The bathroom environment is a source of germs. Check bathrooms daily to make sure they are clean and supplied with soap and paper. It is easier and more sanitary for children to use liquid soap in a dispenser than to use bar soap, which is slippery and can harbor germs. Place dispensers for paper towels, tissues, and toilet paper within children's reach. Refill the soap dispensers, paper towels, tissues, and toilet paper as needed. Discard paper products in washable trash containers lined with plastic bags. Trash containers with lids operated by foot pedals are ideal, because no one has to touch any surfaces.

The sinks that children use for daily hygiene should be kept clean.

Typically, children use classroom sinks for brushing teeth and washing hands. Store toothbrushes in sanitary containers that allow air drying. You can make a suitable container by cutting slots in a Styrofoam egg carton turned upside down or in a plastic milk container. Paper egg cartons are not appropriate because they cannot be washed. Use a different sink to clean toxic materials or items that have been contaminated by body fluids such as urine, blood, or vomit.

To support children's independent use of the bathroom, your program should have child-size toilets or seats that attach to adult-size toilets (with a washable step stool nearby). If you do not have a sink that is low enough for children to reach easily, provide a step stool. Paper towels should be hung where children can reach them. Provide a plastic-lined trash container with a pedal-operated lid. When children have accidents, help them clean themselves and change into clean clothes. Wear disposable latex or vinyl gloves whenever contact with body fluids is likely. Wash your hands and make sure children wash theirs.

what's next?

Skill-Building Journal, section **2-5** (*Learning Activity A*) and section **2-1** (*Feedback*).

Learning Activities

B. Responding When Children Are Sick[8]

In this activity you will learn to

- recognize symptoms of common childhood illnesses

- follow your program's policies regarding sick children

Few illnesses necessitate sending a child home.

Few illnesses require that a child be excluded from a program. Some common childhood illnesses are not contagious, and many contagious illnesses, such as the common cold, begin to spread before symptoms appear. By the time you know a child is sick, others in the group may have already been exposed to the germs. If the child is coughing, feverish, or unable to participate in daily activities, he should be sent home to rest.

Most children with mild illnesses can safely attend your program, although the program may have policies regarding specific symptoms (such as a fever over a specified temperature). Because you know the children well, you can determine whether a mildly ill child can participate in activities and whether you and your colleagues can adequately care for the child without affecting the care of other children. When sick children remain at the center, they need extra attention. For example, depending on the illness, a child might need

- additional time to rest or sleep

- appropriate food and drinks, especially to prevent dehydration

- medication (dispensed according to program policy, written physician's instructions, and written permission from the parents or guardians)

- close supervision and comfort

The family may ask the program to administer medication. You must have the parents' or guardians' written permission, and the medication must be in the original dated container with a child-protective cap. Medications must include instructions for use and disposal and be labeled with the child's name and that of the health care provider. Refrigerate medications when appropriate, storing them away from food and out of children's reach.

When administering medication, follow your program's policies and procedures. Be sure to read the instructions carefully so you are clear about the required dosage. Never administer one child's medication to another. Keep accurate records noting the child's name, the date and time, and the name and amount of medicine administered. Be alert to possible side-effects of the medicine.

Conduct daily health checks to look for signs of illness.

There are times, however, when an ill child should not be cared for at the center. You and your colleagues should conduct daily health checks to look for specific signs of more serious illnesses. A daily health check upon arrival will help you identify children who might be ill.

As you greet children and parents, be alert for the following signs of illness:

- difficulty breathing

- yellowish skin or eyes

- unusual spots or rashes

- feverish appearance

- severe coughing (red or blue in the face, high-pitched croup or whooping sound)

- pinkeye (tears, redness of eyelid lining, irritation, swelling, discharge of pus)

- infected skin patches or crusty, bright-yellow, dry, or gummy skin areas

- unusual behavior (child is cranky, less active or more irritable than usual; child feels general discomfort or just seems unwell)

Children may become sick while at the program.

During the day, be alert for signs that a child might be ill:

- frequent trips to the bathroom

- diarrhea not associated with a diet change or medication

- difficulty urinating or defecating

- sore throat or trouble swallowing

- headache or stiff neck

- nausea and vomiting

- loss of appetite

- frequent scratching of the body or scalp (may be a sign of lice or scabies)

Your state licensing agency has specific policies concerning diseases that require a child to go home and remain out of the program until no longer contagious. The chart that follows summarizes information about the symptoms of contagious illnesses transmitted through direct contact, the intestinal tract, and the respiratory system, and guidance as to when it is safe for a child to return to the program. This information is provided as a general guide. For information about when a child may return to the program after being ill, refer to the most recent edition of *Caring for Our Children: National Health and Safety Performance Standards: Guidelines for Out-of-Home Child Care Programs* (available online: http://nrc.uchsc.edu/CFOC/XMLVersion/NewTOCwoSubs.xml). Also check with your supervisor.

Common Childhood Diseases

Diseases spread through the intestinal tract	Symptoms	When child may return to the program
Diarrheal diseases	Increased liquid and number of stools in an 8-hour period	Diarrhea has stopped (if caused by *Salmonella typhi* or other infection, may require that a stool culture be taken by a physician)
Some illnesses that cause vomiting	Abdominal pain, digested/undigested stomach contents, refusal to eat, headache, fever	When vomiting has stopped or until a health care provider determines that the cause of the vomiting is not contagious
Hepatitis A	Fever, loss of appetite, nausea, yellowish skin and whites of the eyes, dark brown urine, light-colored stool	One week after illness begins, if fever is gone, or as directed by the health department

Diseases spread through the respiratory system	Symptoms	When child may return to the program
Bacterial meningitis	**For younger children:** fever, vomiting, unusual irritability, excessive crying with inability to be comforted, high-pitched crying, poor feeding, and activity levels below normal **For older children:** fever, headache, neck pain or stiffness, vomiting (often without abdominal complaints), decrease in activity, and complaints of not feeling well	After fever has gone and a closely supervised program of antibiotics has been completed Health department may recommend preventive medicine for exposed children and staff
Colds and flu	**Colds:** stuffy or runny nose, sore throat, sneezing, coughing, watery eyes, and perhaps a fever **Flu:** sore throat, fever, muscular aches, and chills	When coughing has subsided, fever is gone, and child can participate in daily activities
Strep throat	Red and painful throat, often accompanied by fever	Generally when fever has subsided and child has been on antibiotics for at least 24 hours

Diseases spread by direct contact (touching)	Symptoms	When child may return to the program
Chickenpox	Fever, runny nose, cough, rash (pink/red blisters)	When sores are crusted and dry (usually 6 days after onset of blisters)
Head lice	Whitish-gray nits (eggs) attached to hair shafts or presence of adult lice	After treatment and removal of nits, and child's clothes and bedding have been washed in hot water (140° F) to destroy lice and eggs
Herpes (mouth or cold sore)	Sores on lips or inside mouth	No need for exclusion if sores are covered
Impetigo	Red oozing sore capped with a golden yellow crust that appears stuck on	Twenty-four hours after treatment has begun
Measles	Fever, runny nose, cough, and red-brown blotchy rash on the face and body	Four days after the rash appears
Mumps	Swelling of the glands at the jaw angle accompanied by cold-like symptoms	Nine days after swelling begins
Pertussis (whooping cough)	Cold-like symptoms that develop into severe respiratory disease with repeated attacks of violent coughing	Five days after antibiotic treatment has been completed
Pinkeye (purulent conjunctivitis)	Eyes are pink/red, watery, itchy, lid swollen, sometimes painful, and pus is present	Twenty-four hours after treatment has begun (not all pinkeye is contagious)
Ringworm	**Skin:** reddish scaling, circular patches with raised edges and central clearing or light and dark patches on face and upper trunk or cracking peeling of skin between toes **Scalp:** redness, scaling of scalp with broken hairs or patches of hair loss	No need to exclude child; advise parents about need for treatment
Scabies	Crusty wavy ridges and tunnels in the webs of fingers, hand, wrist, and trunk	After treatment has been completed
Shingles	Blisters in a band or patch	No need for exclusion if sores are covered

When you see any symptoms of an illness that requires the sick child to be away from the program, isolate the child in a quiet, comfortable, supervised area until a family member arrives. Inform your supervisor so you can discuss how to notify other parents of the contagious illness.

Share the information in this chart with families. Encourage them to tell you when their child has been exposed to one of these illnesses so you can take necessary precautions to keep the illness from spreading.

Facts About HIV

HIV (human immunodeficiency virus) is the cause of AIDS (acquired immune deficiency syndrome). HIV attacks the immune system that normally protects the body from viruses and bacteria. This makes it hard for the body to fight infection. HIV is not transmitted through casual contact or from being around someone who is infected. It cannot be transmitted by mosquitoes or pets. The virus does not live by itself in the air. You cannot get it by

- being in the same room with someone who has the virus

- sharing drinks or food

- being near someone who coughs or sneezes

- hugging, shaking hands, or kissing as friends do

- sharing a swimming pool, bath, or toilet

HIV is transmitted through blood, semen, and vaginal secretions.

A person **can** be infected with HIV

- **from mother to child (perinatal) during pregnancy or delivery.** If the mother has HIV infection, her blood can transmit the virus to the baby during pregnancy or delivery. Most children under age 13 with HIV are infected in this way.

- **through sexual intercourse** with a man or woman who has HIV disease. Sexually abused children are at risk for HIV infection.

- **by sharing or getting stuck with intravenous needles** that contain infected blood from a previous user.

- **from blood and blood product transfusions prior to 1985,** before blood was tested for HIV. Many people were infected this way as children, including those with hemophilia.

Children with HIV can remain healthy for long periods of time. They develop AIDS when the virus has severely damaged the immune system. Because they are more susceptible to illnesses, good hygiene is very important.

Always take universal precautions when handling blood.

Because you and your colleagues might not know whether a child has HIV disease and because HIV is carried in the blood, **always** take universal blood precautions. Wear disposable, heavy-duty gloves to create a barrier between yourself and any person's blood when giving first-aid or cleaning up spills. In addition, if you have been exposed[9] to blood or other body fluids, Federal regulations require the following measures:

- Wash the exposed body part.

- Clean and disinfect spills.

- Report to the supervisor.

- Document the exposure.

- Have a medical exam within 24 hours.

- Receive follow-up and treatment as necessary.

Children with HIV infection may have special nutritional and therapeutic needs. Encourage parents to share pertinent medical information so you can provide the best care for their child. If a child has HIV disease or any other medical condition, programs should have a special care plan outlining medications, emergency procedures, and measures to prevent and recognize illness. If you care for a child with HIV infection, get specific training so you will know how to meet the child's needs.

Lice Happen!

Even when you and your colleagues practice good hygiene, you may have an outbreak of head lice, tiny brown bugs that make themselves at home on people's hair. Adult lice lay sesame-seed-size eggs (nits) on human hair strands, about 3/4" from the scalp. Seven to ten days later the eggs hatch, and lice emerge and begin to bite the scalp. These bites make a person's head itch. If you see a child scratching his or her head repeatedly (or if your own head itches), lice may be the cause. You may see the tiny white nits attached to strands of hair, or the adult lice moving around. Unlike dandruff, nits do not move when the hair is moved.

A joint home and program response is needed to get rid of lice.

Head lice are quite common, do not carry diseases, and are not caused by unsanitary conditions. They are, however, extremely hardy and are easily transferred from one person to another, either from head to head or from pillows, rugs, seatbacks, combs, bedding, hats, and so on. You need to respond immediately to rid the lice from children and the environment. When lice and nits are off the body (on clothes or stuffed animals), they die within seven days.

Your first step in lice removal is to send a letter to families. Use a light-hearted tone for the letter. Let them know that lice are harmless and, although they are annoying, there is nothing to be ashamed of. Include the following information in the letter:

A description of the life-cycle of lice: Lice are very resilient. You must use a thorough and vigorous approach to ridding your child and home of lice.

How to identify lice: Check the whole family immediately and continue checking over the next few weeks. Someone who is free of lice one day can have them after the eggs hatch. Let us know if your child does have lice so we can keep track of the seriousness of the outbreak.

What to do about lice on human heads: Call your pediatrician for information on appropriate anti-lice shampoos for children and adults. Follow the shampoo directions carefully; then use a fine-toothed comb to remove the dead adults and nits.

How to rid the home of lice: Lice travel to bedding, clothing, stuffed animals, combs and brushes, carpets, and furniture. These items can be dry cleaned or washed in water that is at least 140° F. Items that are difficult to clean, such as stuffed animals, can be placed in sealed plastic bags for 10–14 days. Wash combs and brushes in anti-lice shampoo. Vacuum carpets, mattresses, and furniture thoroughly and tie the vacuum bag in a plastic bag. Then place the bag in an outside trash can.

Use the lice outbreak as a teachable moment.

An equally thorough response is needed at the program. Begin by checking all staff so they can use anti-lice shampoo if they need to and take steps to rid their homes of lice. Let the children know about the lice. Describe your lice removal plans. Explain that head lice are harmless and not caused by dirt or carelessness. Remind children not to share combs, brushes, or hats.

Next, use the methods described above to clean all the items at the program to which lice may have attached. In addition to items listed already, you must clean dress-up clothes (especially hats), carpet squares, pillows, and mattresses. Send home children's bedding and special blankets and stuffed animals, to be cleaned by parents.

Once you have survived your first outbreak of lice, you will be better prepared to tackle the next, and there will be one. As long as children are cared for in groups, lice are likely to follow.

what's next?

Skill-Building Journal, section **2-6** (*Learning Activity B*) and section **2-1** (*Feedback*).

LEARNING
ACTIVITY

Learning Activities

C. Encouraging Good Nutrition

In this activity you will learn to

- teach children that healthy bodies need a variety of foods every day

- help children select and enjoy nutritious foods for snacks and meals

Preschool children can learn about nutrition.

Teaching children good nutrition habits is a wise investment in their future. The foods children eat affect their well-being, physical growth, ability to learn, and overall behavior. Attitudes about foods and eating develop early in life and are difficult to change. Eating moderately, eating a variety foods, and eating in a relaxed atmosphere are healthy habits for young children to form. Teachers can help children enjoy a variety of foods from their own and other cultures, and to learn what their bodies need to be strong, flexible, and healthy.

Some adults make the mistake of using food to reward or punish children. This inappropriate practice may promote poor eating habits that continue into adulthood. When an adult tells a child, "You can't have dessert because you didn't eat your peas," the child learns that desserts are more desirable than peas. Children should be learning that it is best to eat a variety of nutritious foods.

Your program should support healthy nutrition for young children.

Much of the nutrition education in an early childhood program is indirect. It occurs when you serve a variety of healthy foods for snacks and meals; share relaxed, family-style meals; taste all the foods served and encourage children to do the same; take "water breaks" throughout the day; and offer cooking as an interest area or activity. Children can also learn about healthy foods by talking with a visiting nutritionist, planting a vegetable garden, and looking at books.

To ensure that children receive nutritious snacks and meals, the U.S Department of Agriculture's *MyPyramid for Kids* (http://teamnutrition.usda. gov/resources/mpk_poster2.pdf) can be a helpful guide. Serving muffins rather than cakes, fresh vegetables rather than potato chips, and milk or juice rather than artificially flavored drinks will help children learn to make healthy choices. Your program also might provide workshops for families on topics such as nutrition, menu planning, family-style meals, sanitation, and using a variety of recipes.

Nutritious foods are good for bodies and teeth.

An important topic related to nutrition is dental health. Almost everyone (98 percent of the population) gets cavities. Many young children know sweet, sticky foods can cause cavities. However, children may not realize that, to prevent tooth decay, they must cut down on the number of times a day they eat sugary foods. It is always a good idea to have children brush their teeth after eating foods such as

- peanut butter

- bananas, dried fruit, and fruit packed in syrup

- bread (except 100% whole wheat) and crackers

Although some of these foods are nutritious, they all stick to the teeth!

Serving and Eating Family-Style Meals

One way to make meal times relaxed and pleasant is to serve and eat meals family-style. This means that a teacher sits with a group of children at each table. Everyone eats the same foods, serves himself or herself, and enjoys pleasant conversation. During family-style dining, children are more likely to try new foods because they serve themselves. They can decide for themselves whether to put one pea or a spoonful on their plates. The following tips can help you begin or enhance family-style dining.

Serve and eat meals family-style.

Before the meal:

- Arrange the furniture so tables are far enough apart to walk between but close enough for quiet conversation and so that five or six children and one adult can be seated at each table.

- Ask children who are assisting to set the tables.

- Serve the food in serving bowls or on platters, and supply drinks in small pitchers, so children can serve themselves. Use utensils as needed and according to children's abilities: forks, knives with serrated blades, and/or spoons.

- Do not provide additional salt and sugar.

- Suggest that, before eating, everyone take a deep breath, relax. You might ask the children to talk about being thankful for the food, to think about how the food will make them strong and healthy, and so on.

- Be aware of and respect cultural traditions. For example, in some cultures, a respectful silence is appropriate before the meal begins and talking during meals is considered inappropriate. Some children may wish to thank the cook or say a prayer.

During the meal:

- Invite children and teachers to begin serving as soon as everyone is seated. Keep a calm and relaxed manner, and maintain a leisurely pace so children don't feel hurried.

- Allow children to refuse food, but encourage them to taste a little of everything.

- Encourage children to take only as much as they can to eat. If they can't finish what's on their plate, don't force them.

- Model good hygiene, safety practices, and manners; ask children to clean up their own spills.

Try these suggestions after the meal.

- Encourage conversation about the foods served, the day's events, or other topics of interest to the children.

- Allow children to leave the table when finished. They may clean their dishes, wash their hands, brush their teeth, and then choose an activity.

- Ask the children who are assisting to help clean up and wash the tables.

Cooking With Children[10]

Cooking is one of the best ways to teach children about nutrition. Although the children may not know about vitamins or saturated fats, spreading a vegetable cottage cheese dip on whole wheat crackers and mashing bananas for muffins give much healthier messages than opening a package of chocolate cookies or a bag of corn chips.

Cooking provides many opportunities for learning.

Through cooking activities children develop self-help skills, improve fine motor coordination, increase cognitive skills, socialize with friends, and share in the responsibilities of daily living. They are proud to help snap the ends off beans, crack eggs, and stir raisins and cinnamon into yogurt to make a dip. Your job is to encourage each child to participate according to his or her interest and skill level.

It is not necessary to plan special menus or use simplified versions of recipes to include children in cooking. The snacks and meals children cook can be part of the regular menu for the program. Here are some simple cooking activities preschool children might enjoy.

Children enjoy making simple foods.

Mashed potatoes. Children can peel potatoes, cut them into pieces, drop them into the cooking pot, and mash them after they cool.

Fresh vegetables and fruit, cooked or served raw with dips. Children can grate carrots, slice apples, shell peas, wash grapes, break cauliflower or broccoli flowerets, and snap the ends off beans.

Fruit smoothies. Children can use a blender to mix milk and/or yogurt with fresh fruits.

Lemonade. Have children roll fresh lemons on the table top, then twist them on the juicer. Add some sugar and water to taste. Slice a lemon to put in the pitcher.

Pizzas. Spoon tomato sauce and sprinkle grated cheese and spices on English muffins, French bread, pita bread, bagels, tortillas, or freshly made dough.

Children can follow simple recipe cards.

You might make recipe picture cards. On 5" x 8" pieces of cardboard, describe and illustrate each step in the recipe. Number each card so they are easy to keep in order. Cover the cards with clear Contact paper to protect them from spills. Children can lay out the picture cards, left to right on the table, so they can follow the recipe. This will make them more independent and help them understand a purpose for reading.

You can also ask the children's parents to suggest cooking projects. By cooking their favorite foods, you show respect for children and their families. This also allows you to introduce family traditions into your program.

Here are some suggestions to help make cooking a success:

- Plan food preparation activities for small groups to select during choice time. Each participating child should have a task to complete without waiting long.

- Use a work table that is no higher than the children's waists and located near a sink or other water supply.

- Use an electric frying pan or wok as a substitute for a stove.

- Place electric appliances within reach of an electrical outlet so an extension cord is not needed. An adult should plug and unplug appliances. Hang the cords behind the table so children don't trip.

- Provide duplicates of favorite utensils so children won't be frustrated or lose interest while waiting for a turn.

- Provide plastic knives with serrated blades or blunt-ended scissors if they will do the job. When metal knives are essential, supervise their use carefully.

- Make and display signs and posters on cooking safety. Remind children of safety guidelines before you start and during the activity. Comment when you see children following a safety rule.

- Provide aprons or smocks for all children. Messes are inevitable.

- Keep cleaning supplies, such as mops, sponges, and paper towels, within children's reach. Lock up cleansers.

what's next?

Skill-Building Journal, section **2-7** (*Learning Activity C*) and section **2-1** (*Feedback*).

Learning Activities

LEARNING ACTIVITY

D. Helping Children Learn Healthy Habits

In this activity you will learn to

● model and talk about healthy habits during daily routines and activities

● help children learn how to keep themselves healthy

Earlier in this module you read about ways to keep the children in your care healthy, and then you applied your knowledge on the job. It's also important to help young children gradually learn how to take care of their own health and nutrition needs. It will be many years before they can be completely responsible for their physical, mental, social, and emotional well-being, but the learning begins now!

Children learn good health habits through routines.

The first step in teaching children good health habits is to practice them daily in your classroom. Through routines such as regular toothbrushing, frequent handwashing, using and discarding tissues, and careful food handling, children can learn good health habits. Encourage children to do as much as possible for themselves: pumping soap on their hands, squeezing toothpaste on a toothbrush, setting the table, serving themselves, dressing for outdoor play. In addition, invite children to help you maintain a healthy environment. Although you may not expose children to toxic cleaning substances, they may wash the table before you spray it with a bleach solution. They can shake out a new plastic bag for the waste can or help you empty and clean the tray at the bottom of the hamster's cage. After completing routines such as these, be sure that the children and adults wash their hands.

During the day you can also help children learn good health habits as they play and participate in activities. Here are some suggestions.

Dramatic play. Provide props such as a cot, stethoscope, bandages and a white jacket so children can set up a hospital or dentist's office. This is particularly appropriate if one of the children or a friend or family member is ill or will be going to the hospital in the near future. Children might also rehearse upcoming visits to the doctor or dentist for check-ups and immunizations. Ask the children open-ended questions to help them recall what they know from their own experiences. In addition, stock the house corner with empty boxes or cans of healthy foods and pretend fruits and vegetables. Comment on the healthy meals children are preparing. "Your vegetable soup looks very tasty. I know it will help me stay strong and healthy."

Water play. Encourage children to bathe dolls and wash clothes. Talk about different parts of the body and how taking baths and showers helps remove germs.

Puppet shows. Suggest that puppets represent nurses, doctors, dentists, and other caregivers. Invite children to make up stories about caring for someone who is sick or retell what happened when they visited the doctor or dentist.

Special events. Visit a farm to pick berries and learn about where food comes from. Take a behind-the-scenes tour of the supermarket. Invite a health professional to talk to the children about taking good care of themselves. Ask a parent and a new baby to visit the program and discuss what babies need to grow and develop.

Books. Read and plan follow-up activities for books such as *Pete's a Pizza,* by William Steig; *Dumpling Soup,* by Jam Kim Rattigan; and *This Is the Way We Eat Our Lunch: A Book About Children Around the World,* by Edith Baer. You and the children can make books about topics such as dressing for the weather or preparing a special meal.

Toys and games. Make lotto or bingo games featuring pictures of food and healthy routines. Provide puzzles featuring body parts, health providers, farms, and supermarkets.

Art activities. Trace children's bodies on large pieces of newsprint and invite them to draw the features—such as hair, nails, and eyes—and clothing. Make collages about topics related to health, such as exercise, healthy foods and junk foods, and ways to relax.

Going outdoors. Let the children use self-help skills to put on and take off outdoor clothing. Discuss how hats, gloves, and coats help us stay warm on cool days. Point out that boots keep our feet dry and cozy on wet days. Encourage children to drink water and play in the shade as much as possible on hot days.

Involving families is also important for helping children learn healthy habits. Tell parents what you do to keep children healthy. Focus on practices they can do at home, such as handwashing, toothbrushing, and serving nutritious finger foods. Share information with parents about their child's growing self-help skills so they can encourage the child to use them at home.

what's next?

Skill-Building Journal, section **2-8** (*Learning Activity D*) and section **2-1** (*Feedback*).

LEARNING ACTIVITY

Learning Activities

E. Recognizing and Reporting Child Abuse and Neglect

In this activity you will learn to

- recognize the signs of possible child abuse and neglect

- report suspected cases of child abuse and neglect in accordance with state and local laws.

Child abuse and neglect include any behavior of an adult that causes physical or emotional harm to a child or youth under age 18 for whose care and well-being the adult is responsible. Abuse and neglect can result from an act (doing something to cause harm) or an omission (not taking action to protect a child). Abuse and neglect can involve a single incident, such as burning a child's hand, or a pattern of behavior that continues over time, such as failing to give a child sufficient food or love and attention.

It is very likely that, at some time in your career, you will care for a child who has been abused or neglected. Teachers play two key roles in preventing and stopping child abuse and neglect. First, because they care for children daily, they may identify the signs of possible abuse or neglect that otherwise would go unnoticed. Second, all states require teachers to report their suspicions of abuse and neglect in accordance with state and local laws.

There is no typical profile of adults who mistreat children. Children may be mistreated by relatives or nonrelatives, by people they know or by strangers, by males or females. Adults who abuse children come from every income level, race, and ethnic group. They can be of any age.

There are physical and behavioral signs of child abuse and neglect.

Children may exhibit physical and/or behavioral signs of their abuse and neglect. Physical signs, whether mild or severe, are those you can actually see, such as bruises or broken bones. Behavioral clues, ranging from subtle changes to extreme withdrawal or fear, may be present with or without physical signs. Clues may be found in the way a child looks and acts, what a parent or other responsible adult says, or how he or she relates to the child. They might be seen in the way an adult and child behave when they are together. No single sign or clue proves abuse or neglect, but repeated signs or several signs together indicate the **possibility** of abuse or neglect.

In federal, state, and local laws, most definitions of child abuse and neglect include four types of maltreatment. Descriptions and signs of each type follow.

Physical Abuse

Physical abuse includes nonaccidental physical injuries caused by an adult in single or repeated episodes. Sometimes physical abuse is intentional, such as when an adult burns, bites, pokes, cuts, twists, shakes, or otherwise harms a child. Such injuries can be the result of overdiscipline or inappropriate physical punishment, such as when an angry or frustrated adult lashes out at a child. Physical abuse can cause minor injuries such as cuts and bruises, or major injuries such as brain damage and broken limbs. It can hinder a child's healthy social/emotional development and leave emotional problems that last into adulthood.

Notice where the injury is located on the child's body.

Active preschool children sometimes fall down and bump into things. These accidents may cause injuries to their elbows, chins, noses, foreheads, and other bony areas. Bruises and marks on the soft tissue of the face, back, neck, buttocks, upper arms, thighs, ankles, backs of legs, or genitals, however, are more likely to be the result of physical abuse. Another sign to look for is bruises that are at various stages of healing, as if they resulted from more than one incident. When helping a child take off a shirt, you might see bruises or burns that were covered by clothing. An adult might try to cover the signs of abuse by dressing the child in long sleeves or long pants, even when the weather calls for cooler clothes.

Injuries to a young child's abdomen or head, particularly vulnerable spots, are often undetected until symptoms appear. Abdominal injuries can cause swelling, tenderness, and vomiting. Head injuries may cause swelling, dizziness, blackouts, retinal detachment, and even death.

In addition to physical signs, a child **might** also exhibit behavioral signs of physical abuse. Children's remarks often provide clues. Therefore, it's important to listen carefully to what children say, as well as to notice what they do.

> When a teacher notices another big bruise on his leg, Troy tells her, "I fell down the stairs again."

> On most days, Daniel's mother picks him up. He finishes what he's doing, then gathers his belongings. Yesterday, Daniel saw his father at the door and said, "Uh-oh, I'm not ready. My dad doesn't like to wait." Today, when a teacher asked about his painting, Daniel said, "This is a bad boy. He got a whipping because he acted like a baby."

Signs of Sexual Abuse

Sexual abuse includes a wide range of contacts or interactions in which a child is used for the sexual stimulation of an adult or older child. It includes fondling a child's genitals, intercourse, rape, sodomy, exhibitionism, incest, and commercial exploitation through pornographic pictures or films.

The physical signs of sexual abuse include some that a teacher would notice while caring for young children. For example, while helping a child use the bathroom you might see torn, stained, or bloody underclothing, or bruised or bleeding genitals or anal areas. If a child says it hurts to walk or sit, or she complains of pain or itching in the genital area, take note and watch to see if this is a recurring condition.

Children who have been sexually abused may also exhibit behavioral signs. They might act out their abuse using dolls or talk with other children about sexual acts. Their premature sexual knowledge is a sign that they have been exposed to sexual activity. They might show excessive curiosity about sexual activities or touch adults on the breast or genitals. Some children who have been sexually abused are very afraid of specific places, such as the bathroom or a bed. Older children who have been sexually abused may be very uncomfortable in situations where they have to undress. For example, an abused child might refuse to put on a swimsuit to run through the sprinkler.

Some examples of signs that **might** indicate a child is being sexually maltreated include the following:

> The children and teachers are outside on the playground. Simone needs to go inside to the bathroom. Ms. Fox says, "I'll take her." The other teacher, Ms. Young, says, "But it's my turn." Ms. Fox insists that she will take the child. Simone says, "I don't have to go any more." Ten minutes later Simone comes up to Ms. Young and says, "I want you to take me. You don't hurt me."

> The children are sitting at the table eating breakfast. Nancy is wiggling around in her seat a lot. A teacher asks her if she needs to go to the bathroom. Nancy says, "No, it's not that. My bottom hurts where Gary poked me." Gary is her 12-year-old brother.

Physical Neglect

Physical neglect is failing to provide a child with adequate or proper food, appropriate shelter, clothing, health care, supervision, or education, when the responsible person has adequate financial resources to meet these needs. Neglect tends to be chronic, an ongoing pattern of behavior. Some neglected children suffer from malnourishment, frequent illnesses, and high levels of stress. Neglectful families often appear to have many problems they cannot handle. Signs of neglect include poor hygiene, inadequate or inappropriate clothing for weather conditions, and inattention to health needs. In addition, developmental disorders, such as being extremely small for his or her age, might indicate that a child is neglected.

When considering the possibility of neglect, it is important to look for patterns. Do the signs of neglect occur rarely or frequently? Are they chronic (present almost every day), periodic (appearing after weekends, vacations, or absences), or episodic (for example, seen twice during a period when the child's mother was in the hospital)?

Some examples of signs that **might** indicate a child is being neglected include the following:

> Joanie falls down outside and badly scrapes her knee. A teacher cleans the knee with soap, puts on a bandage, and prepares an accident report for Joanie's parents. Four days later, Joanie complains her knee hurts. The teacher looks at her knee and notices the bandage has not been changed and the wound is infected.

> Andrea tells a teacher she is tired today because her baby brother Max woke her up in the night. She says, "My mommy wasn't home yet, so I made Max a bottle and gave it to him. Then he finally went back to sleep."

Emotional Abuse or Neglect

Emotional abuse or neglect includes actively, intentionally blaming, belittling, ridiculing, and disparaging a child so as to cause low self-esteem, undue fear or anxiety, or other damage to the child's psychological well-being. It also includes passive-aggressive inattention to emotional needs, nurturing, or psychological well-being. It is the most difficult form of maltreatment to identify because the signs are rarely physical and the effects may not show up for years. Also, the signs of emotional abuse are similar to those for emotional disturbance. Emotional abuse is almost always present along with other types of maltreatment. The effects can last a lifetime.

The following are examples of signs that a child might be a victim of emotional abuse or neglect:

> Each time he picks up Nathan, Mr. Wheeler makes fun of his son's efforts. Typical comments include: "Can't you button that coat right? You never get the buttons lined up with the holes. You look like an idiot." "What's that a picture of? It looks like a five-legged horse." "Can't you climb to the top of the climber yet? All the other kids climbed to the top. What's the matter with you, are your legs too short?" Mr. Wheeler told a teacher, "I like to give Nathan a hard time. I don't want him to think he's better than anyone else. He needs to remember that he's got a lot to learn."

The Jackson family has two children enrolled in the program. Five-year-old Neesie is an outgoing leader who excels at everything. Three-year-old Tiffany is a quiet child who plays alone or with one or two friends. Most days, when Mrs. Jackson picks up the girls she ignores Tiffany and lavishes praise and attention on Neesie. Today she says, "Neesie, let me see what you made today. Where's Tiffany? Sitting in the corner again?" Mrs. Jackson tells a teacher, "I know Neesie will do well in life; she's so smart. But Tiffany—I don't know what will happen to her!"

Picking Up Clues From Observations and Conversations

Programs for preschool children should be family oriented, encouraging much formal and informal communication between teachers and parents. You may gather important information from routine conversations with children and parents. Young children enjoy talking about their families, so they, too, may share information about life at home. During daily drop-off and pick-up times and at scheduled conferences, parents describe family life, discuss discipline methods, or ask for help with problems. Conversations with family members can provide clues to how the adult feels about the child. Be alert to the possible signs of child abuse and neglect if the family member constantly

- blames or belittles the child ("I told you not to drop that. Why weren't you paying attention?")

- sees the child as very different from his or her siblings ("His older sister Terry never caused me these problems. She always did exactly what she was told to do.")

- sees the child as "bad," "evil," or a "monster" ("He really seems to be out to get me. He's just like his father, and he was really an evil man.")

- finds nothing good or attractive about the child ("Oh well, some kids are just a pain in the neck. You can see this one doesn't have much going for her.")

- seems unconcerned about the child ("She was probably just having a bad day. I don't have time to talk about it.")

- fails to keep appointments or refuses to discuss problems the child is having in the program ("That's what I pay you for—it's your job to make her behave.")

- misuses alcohol or other drugs.

Isolation and extreme stress can lead to child abuse or neglect.

When you know a family well, you are in a better position to evaluate the seriousness of a problem. You can gauge whether it is a chronic condition or a temporary situation, a typical childhood problem that the program and family can handle, or one that requires intervention. Family circumstances may also provide clues. The risk of abuse or neglect increases when families are isolated from friends, neighbors, and other family members, or if there is no apparent lifeline to which a family can turn in a crisis. Marital, economic, emotional, or social crises are among the causes of family stress that can lead to child abuse or neglect.

Abuse and Neglect in a Program

Abuse or neglect can occur in an early childhood program.

You may find it hard to imagine that child abuse and neglect could take place at an early childhood program, but it does happen. Thinking about this possibility may make you feel as though you are suspicious of your colleagues or that your supervisors will be spying on teachers. You are responsible for keeping children safe and healthy. One important way to do this is to be alert to the possibility of child abuse and neglect taking place right at the program site.

Many of the physical and behavioral signs described above apply to abuse and neglect in early childhood programs. In addition, the signs listed below also warn of possible abuse or neglect in a child care setting.

A child

- refuses to participate in activities supervised by a particular teacher

- shows extreme fear of a particular staff member

- states that he or she has been hurt by a staff member

A teacher

- spends long periods of time out of sight with one child

- takes unscheduled breaks without telling his or her colleagues

- says a child is "bad," "spoiled," or "needs to be taught a lesson"

- shows favoritism to one child and gives that child special attention and treats

- holds a child often, although the child seems tense and tries to get away

If you see any of these signs, or others that cause you to suspect the possibility of child abuse or neglect, discuss your observations with your supervisor.

Understand the difference between nurturing children and possible child abuse.

There are situations in which teachers fear that hugging a child or letting a child sit on his or her lap could be viewed as child sexual abuse. Children's safety in the program is certainly the most important concern. However, program supervisors must support staff members' ability to perform their jobs, and that includes comforting and nurturing children in appropriate ways. All staff and family members should be aware of program policies regarding child nurturance. Talk with your supervisor if you have questions about how you may respond to children in caring ways.

Reporting Child Abuse and Neglect

In every state and the District of Columbia, teachers are mandated reporters, which means that you have a legal obligation to report suspected child abuse and neglect. In addition, you have an ethical and professional responsibility to know, understand, and follow the reporting requirements and procedures of your state, community, and program.

Each state law specifies one (or more) agencies to receive reports of suspected child abuse and neglect. Often reports are made to the Department of Social Services; the Department of Human Resources; the Division of Family and Children's Services; or Child Protective Services of the city, county, or state government. In some states the police department also receives reports. Some states require either a written or an oral report. Others require an immediate oral report, followed by a written report within 24–48 hours. It is important to know who receives reports of suspected child abuse and neglect in your jurisdiction. State reporting statutes include this information. Check your state law for the specific requirements. The National Clearinghouse on Child Abuse and Neglect Information (http://nccanch.acf.hhs.gov/) maintains current online reports on state statutes.

Most states require reporters to provide the following information:

- child's name, age, and address

- child's present location (for example, at the program)

- parent's or guardian's name and address

- nature and extent of the injury or condition observed

- reporter's name and location (sometimes not required but very useful for the agency conducting the investigation)

Most programs have established policies defining the duties and responsibilities of the staff in reporting child abuse and neglect. If you don't have a copy of your program's child abuse and neglect reporting procedures, ask your director for one.

Overcoming Barriers to Reporting

You do not have to prove your suspicions.

When you suspect a child is being abused or neglected, you may be very reluctant to file a report. Some teachers find their personal feelings are a barrier to reporting child abuse or neglect. They prefer not to get involved or convince themselves there is a perfectly good explanation for the child's injuries or behavior. They may fear that parents, their supervisors, and their colleagues will think them incompetent or an alarmist.

Another potential barrier to reporting is the special relationship between parents and a teacher or between two colleagues. When teachers observe signs of abuse or neglect, they may give parents or colleagues the benefit of the doubt. Even when they do suspect child abuse or neglect, they may expect the parent or colleague to be hostile, indignant, or distressed, or retaliate by filing a lawsuit. People who are required by law to report their suspicions are not responsible for damages if they made the report with good intentions, even if investigators decide that abuse and neglect are not involved. If you are sued, the case will be dismissed when the court learns you are required by law to file a report.

Your primary responsibility is to protect children.

Regardless of why you might feel uneasy about reporting, you have legal and professional responsibilities to protect children and to support their families. By reporting your suspicions to the appropriate authorities, you are protecting children and beginning the helping process. In addition, you are helping families (or your colleagues) get the assistance they need to change their behavior. Focus on your responsibility to report your suspicions. Remember, your report is not an accusation, and you are not required to have proof or to conduct an investigation.

Getting Ready to Report

When you suspect a child is being abused or neglected, file your report as soon as possible. Obviously, this is not a pleasant task. You will probably feel at risk, confused, and generally uncomfortable. It helps to organize your thoughts and secure the support you will need once the report is filed. Here are steps to follow as you prepare to report.

Reporting Child Abuse and Neglect

Document your suspicions:

1. Review your observation notes and anecdotal records.

2. Identify what caused you to suspect abuse or neglect. List the physical and behavioral signs you have observed.

3. Describe adult-child interactions you observed when the parent (or a colleague) spoke badly of the child. Include examples of the parent's lack of interest in the child.

4. Discuss with your colleagues the physical and behavioral signs you have documented. If they suspect abuse or neglect, discuss their reasons.

Secure support:

5. Ask your supervisor what support he or she will provide once you file the report and what the program will do if the parent tries to remove the child.

6. Set up a support system so you can talk with others about your feelings and concerns without breaching confidentiality.

File the report:

7. Review the program's reporting policy.

8. Collect the information needed to file the initial report.

9. Look up the phone number and address of the agency to which you will report (or ask your director for the phone number).

10. Obtain forms or use a piece of paper, if a written report is required.

11. Make your oral and/or written report.

12. Notify your supervisor that you have filed the report.

13. Notify the child's parents that you have filed a report.

14. Use your support system.

In some cases, you will not be able to complete all of these steps because the seriousness of the case requires you to report your suspicions immediately.

Offer support to the child and family.

Notifying the child's parents is usually a difficult conversation. Maintain a professional tone while describing what you reported ("repeated incidences of cigarette burns on Carl's arm"), when ("this morning"), and to whom ("Child Protective Services"). Explain that you have carried out your legal, professional, and ethical responsibilities to report your suspicions and are not involved in investigating or proving the case. In addition, offer the family support as they deal with this difficult situation. They may not accept your gesture immediately. However, it is important to let them know that you are not judging anyone. Instead, you have reported signs of possible abuse so their child and the family can get the help they need.

Your report may receive no response.

In some states and local jurisdictions, the agency receiving reports of abuse and neglect is so overwhelmed they cannot respond to every case. Internal agency policies may require staff to respond first to cases that are life-threatening or extremely clear-cut. You may not see action after you file a report. If this happens, continue supporting the child and family and advocating for them to receive needed services. Stay alert to physical and behavioral signs of abuse or neglect. If necessary, file a second or even third report. Some states have a child abuse and neglect hotline. Find out if there is one in your state, and use it if necessary.

what's next?

Skill-Building Journal, section **2-9** (*Learning Activity E*), section **2-11** (*Answer Sheets*), section **2-1** (*Feedback*), and section **2-10** (*Reflecting on Your Learning*).

3
Learning Environment

Overview

Organizing Indoor and Outdoor Areas That Encourage Play and Exploration

Selecting and Displaying Materials and Equipment That Interest and Challenge Children

Planning and Implementing a Schedule and Routines That Support Children's Development and Learning

Your Own Responses to the Environment

Learning Activities

A. Using Your Knowledge of Child Development to Create a Learning Environment

B. Setting Up and Maintaining Classroom Interest Areas

C. Organizing the Outdoor Environment

D. Planning the Daily Schedule and Routines

3. Learning Environment

The physical environment affects how children and adults feel.

You and the children spend many hours of the day together. If the physical environment is attractive and well-designed, children are encouraged to engage purposefully in activities. As a result, you may discover that your work with children is more enjoyable. The quality of the learning environment affects how both children and adults feel and act.

Many features influence the quality of the indoor environment, such as the size of the room, the colors of the walls, the type of flooring, the amount of light, and the number and size of windows. While there are some things you can't change, you can decide how to arrange furniture, organize materials, and display children's work.

Indoor and outdoor spaces should be well defined and offer a variety of choices.

A well-organized classroom allows you more time to observe and interact with children in positive ways. When you arrange the furniture to define a variety of interest areas, children can play and learn cooperatively in small groups and on their own. The selection of materials and how you display them convey powerful messages to children. Well-organized interest areas invite children to choose activities and to take care of materials.

The outdoors offers children a whole new range of experiences and textures. A good outdoor environment has soft and hard surfaces, shady and sunny areas, and safe places for children to play. In a well-designed outdoor space children can run, jump, skip, throw and catch a ball, and use loud voices. These experiences allow children to stretch their muscles, breathe fresh air, take in the sunshine, and enjoy the freedom possible outdoors.

The daily schedule, routines, and transitions are part of the learning environment.

Your program's schedule, routines, and transitions also help create a comfortable atmosphere. When children know what to expect each day, it helps them feel secure. Each day will go more smoothly if the schedule, routines, and transitions meet children's needs.

The following pages give examples and stories of how teachers create effective indoor and outdoor learning environments for preschool children.

You can establish and maintain a learning environment by

- organizing indoor and outdoor areas that encourage play and exploration

- selecting and displaying materials and equipment that interest and challenge children

- planning and implementing a schedule and routines that support children's development and learning

---

Organizing Indoor and Outdoor Areas That Encourage Play and Exploration

1. **Offer a variety of well-defined and equipped indoor and outdoor interest areas.** Each area reflects the current skills and interests of individual children and of the group.

2. **Create soft, cozy areas where children can get away from the large group.** There are places for children to play alone, look at books, listen to music, or talk with a friend.

3. **Organize separate spaces indoors and outdoors for active and quiet play.** Decide what activities will work well near one another and which will not.

4. **Make changes to the environment, if necessary, to include children with disabilities.** Children in wheelchairs can get from one area to another and reach the furniture and materials; support props such as bolsters are available.

5. **Provide enough storage for children's personal belongings.** Individual cubbies and bins have labels with the children's names and pictures.

6. **Arrange the outdoor area to support a variety of activities.** There are places and equipment for climbing, swinging, building, running, riding, digging, and playing ball.

example

Mr. Lopez Organizes the Outdoor Area

Mr. Lopez looks around the play yard. He sees that several children seem to be frustrated. Sarah is in the shed, pulling on a tire that is under a tangle of boards, riding toys, and rakes. Benjamin struggles to pull a tricycle out of the shed. Andy drops the watering can when a child chasing a ball races by the tomato plants he is watering. "This place needs some organizing," Mr. Lopez decides. Over the next week, he makes changes to encourage children's play and exploration. First, he arranges the tires and boards so that children can get them easily. He hangs the gardening tools within easy reach on the door of the storage shed. He moves the trikes to the path and the balls to the grass away from the garden. He tells the children about the different areas and reminds them where to ride their trikes and throw balls.

Selecting and Displaying Materials and Equipment That Interest and Challenge Children

7. **Provide a variety of materials to encourage different kinds of play**: dramatic play, blocks, toys and games, art, music and movement, reading and writing, sand and water, and discovery (science).

8. **Display learning materials related to children's current interests.** After a trip to the firehouse, Ms. Williams adds firefighter hats, fire engines, and books on firefighters to interest areas.

9. **Display materials so children can find and return them independently.** Store materials on low, open shelves and label with print and pictures.

10. **Include materials that honor diversity.** Include dolls, picture books, photographs, and toys showing different ethnic groups, people with disabilities, and women and men doing all kinds of jobs.

11. **Store materials and supplies that are used together in the same place.** Put pegs in a box near the pegboards; place markers and crayons near plain drawing paper.

12. **Display materials in an attractive way.** Materials are neat and clean and organized in ways to attract children's attention and show they are valued.

Ms. Williams Plans Changes to the Environment

Ms. Williams is using rest time to make a list of the materials and activities she wants to offer children tomorrow. Today the children made get-well cards to send to a child in the hospital. Several children showed great interest in doctors and hospitals, so Ms. Williams brought out two books about going to the hospital. On her list she writes, "hospital prop box" which she will add to the dramatic play area. She will put two white lab coats, a stethoscope, ace bandages, and a pad and pencil in the box. She remembers that several children have seemed anxious during the past few days. She decides to open the water table because she knows water play is a calming activity. She makes a note to add blue coloring to the water and to set out plastic squeeze bottles, eye droppers, measuring cups, and plastic tubes for children to use.

Planning and Implementing a Schedule and Routines That Support Children's Development and Learning

13. **Plan a schedule with large blocks of choice time.** Choice time lasts at least one hour each morning and afternoon when children are free to select the interest area(s) where they want to play.

14. **Offer a balance of activity choices.** The schedule includes active and quiet activities; indoor and outdoor times; and individual, small-group, and large-group activities.

15. **Plan time each day for children to play outdoors.** Children go outdoors twice a day for 45– 60 minutes each time.

16. **Allow time for children to use their self-help skills in daily routines.** Procedures are in place for children to wash hands, brush teeth, set the tables for meals, and clean up.

17. **Plan for transitions between activities so children won't be bored and restless.** "If your shoes have more than one color, you can get up now, walk to your cubby, and get on your coat."

Ms. Richards and Ms. Kim Keep the Children Involved During Clean-Up Time

It is clean-up time in the 3-year-old room. Ms. Richards is helping a small group in the block area to put the blocks away. "We have a big job in the block area today," she says. Holding up a triangular block, she says, "Let's start by finding all the triangles." When all the triangular blocks are on the shelf, Ms. Richards says, "Jamie, what shape should we clean up next?" Jamie holds up a cylinder. "OK," says Ms. Richards, "Let's find all the cylinders next." Ms. Kim realizes that the other children are going to be ready before the block builders. She visits each interest area and tells the children to go to the meeting area when they are finished cleaning up and select a book to look at. "I'll be there to read our story in just a few minutes," she says. When the block builders are finished, Ms. Kim is ready to read the story.

what's next?

Skill-Building Journal, section **3-2** (Overview), section **3-10** (Answer Sheets), and section **3-1** *(Feedback).*

Your Own Responses to the Environment

We are not always aware of how an environment makes us feel.

People react to their environments. Our surroundings affect our feelings, comfort level, behavior, and ability to accomplish tasks. Consider how you react in the following situations:

You are standing in a hot, crowded bus or subway, sandwiched between strangers. Perhaps you pull your shoulders in, try to avoid any contact with others, and count the minutes until you get off.

You are eating in a special restaurant with a favorite friend. The lights and noise level are low. The smells are delicious. You are probably relaxed, enjoying the conversation and your food.

You are preparing a meal in an unfamiliar kitchen. You may be very frustrated because you can't figure out how the kitchen is organized. You spend lots of time looking for the things you need. You may not cook as well as usual.

It's easy to see in these examples how the environment can affect actions and feelings, but the influence of our surroundings is not always so clear. Your work environment should support and help you do your job. Your job becomes easier and more enjoyable if the environment is well-organized and appropriate for the children you teach. If it is a pleasing place to be, you and the children will enjoy being there. Often when people describe their favorite places, they identify

- a quiet place to be alone

- a soft and comfortable place to stretch out

- a place where music is playing or where only the sounds of nature can be heard

- a bright and sunny place with clean air

- a colorful and attractive place

Try to find ways to incorporate the features you like best inside and outdoors. A comfortable environment for young children makes them want to be there and engages them in learning.

what's next?

Skill-Building Journal, section **3-3** (*Your Own Responses to the Environment*), section **3-1** (*Feedback*), and section **3-4** (*Pre-Training Assessment*).

Learning Activities

LEARNING ACTIVITY

A. Using Your Knowledge of Child Development to Create a Learning Environment

In this activity you will learn to

- recognize some typical behaviors of preschool children

- use what you know about child development to create a good environment for learning

Children ages 3–5 are at a stage of development where they are eager to try new things. This is what Erik Erikson called the stage of initiative. Preschool children are full of ideas about what to do and how to do it. They like having a variety of materials and activities that help them explore their varied interests and that develop skills. The more preschool children are encouraged to come up with ideas and try them, the more confident they become in their own abilities.

- Sara (age 3) takes great pride in knowing exactly where each of the pots and pans goes on the shelf.

- Janelle (age 4) gets the box of gears and some tools and sets up shop in the dramatic play area

- Tyrone (age 5) goes to the writing table to get paper and pencils so he can write a letter to his grandmother.

Preschool children are active learners.

A good learning environment for preschool children invites them to explore. It lets them work cooperatively with others, get messy, and take responsibility for cleaning up. Preschool children enjoy challenges and eagerly explore the new, interesting materials you put out for their use.

Preschool children can express their ideas and feelings in many ways. Using crayons, markers, and paints, they draw simple pictures to show their ideas with symbols. Playing with blocks or in the dramatic play area, they remember scenes from books and from their own experiences. In the process they begin to understand the world around them.

Preschool children enjoy being with others.

Preschool children are very social. They are learning how to take turns and beginning to value working together. They learn these skills by having many opportunities to play with other children. A good learning environment is divided into many interest areas where small groups of children can work together without getting in each other's way.

Preschool children have lots of energy. They are building their large- and small-muscle skills, and they want to practice these skills, over and over again. A good learning environment offers children many opportunities to use their large muscles by, for example, climbing, running, and jumping, and their small muscles with playdough, pegs and pegboards, and with drawing and writing tools. When they have opportunities to use these muscles, they can practice their new skills.

Planning an effective learning environment for preschool children means creating a setting and providing appropriate materials that correspond to what you know about the developmental characteristics of young children.

Developmental Characteristics of Preschool Children

Preschool children typically

- enjoy large-muscle activities such as running, jumping, climbing, kicking balls, and riding tricycles

- are building the small muscles in their hands used for tasks such as stringing beads, drawing and writing, and pouring

- are learning to take turns

- can play cooperatively with other children and often have "best friends"

- sometimes need to get away from the group and be by themselves

- have a lot of energy but can tire easily

- like being helpful and can help keep the classroom neat

- engage in dramatic play, re-enacting family roles, community events, and super-heroes

- have lots of interests

- draw pictures and make constructions that represent real things

---

what's next?

Skill-Building Journal, section **3-5** *(Learning Activity A)*, section **3-10** *(Answer Sheets)*, and section **3-1** *(Feedback)*.

Learning Activities

LEARNING ACTIVITY

B. Setting Up and Maintaining Classroom Interest Areas

In this activity you will learn to

• organize the classroom into separate interest areas

• select and display materials in each interest area that reflect children's families, cultures, abilities, and interests

Well-defined interest areas offer clear choices and help children play well with others.

A preschool classroom includes a variety of separate interest areas, for two reasons. First, young children work best in small groups. By dividing your space into smaller areas, you can limit the number of children in any one area. In smaller spaces, children focus and their play becomes complex.

A second reason for creating interest areas is to offer children clear choices. Areas set aside for books, art activities, or toys and games allow several choices for quiet activities. Areas set aside for dramatic play, block building, woodworking, or large-muscle activities offer children more active choices.

Creating Interest Areas

Several factors make interest areas work well.

Most preschool classrooms have interest areas for dramatic play, blocks, toys and games, art, books and writing (library), sand and water, and a discovery table. Many have areas for cooking and a place to listen to music or play instruments. Computers may be in several areas.

In setting up your indoor environment, keep in mind the following guidelines:

• Separate quiet areas (e.g., books, art, toys and games) from noisier areas (e.g., blocks, dramatic play, and woodworking) as much as possible.

• Separate areas by using shelves, furniture, and rugs.

• Locate the areas for art and sand and water play near a source of water and on a washable floor.

• Keep in mind which areas need to be near electrical outlets (e.g., computers, cooking, music and movement).

• Create an area large enough to fit the whole group for meetings and music and movement.

Arranging Interest Areas to Engage Children

Interest Area	Arrangement	What Children Do
Blocks	Away from traffic and protected by shelves Near the dramatic play area Low, open, labeled shelves Smooth, flat carpeting Wooden unit blocks stored on shelves by size and shape Props (people, animals, vehicles), small blocks, and construction materials in open containers	Learn about sizes and shapes. Solve problems. Cooperate to build group projects. Engage in pretend play. Learn about numbers, patterns, and measurement. Write signs for their buildings.
Art	Near the sink Washable floor Two-sided easels Table and chairs Low shelves to hold art materials	Express ideas and feelings. Develop fine motor skills as they use paint brushes, crayons, scissors, and other tools. Explore materials and make discoveries.
Dramatic Play	Shelves and furniture Child-sized furniture and equipment (stove, table and chairs, sink, refrigerator) Dress-up clothes hung on low hooks Pots, pans, and other kitchen equipment on shelves or hung on peg board	Recreate familiar situations—family roles, community events. Conquer fears—getting a shot from the nurse or fighting monsters. Develop social skills—taking turns, negotiating, compromising. Develop abstract thinking skills—create mental images, relate one event to another.
Sand and Water	Near a source of water Washable floor Smocks and a variety of props within children's reach	Release tension. Learn about shape, size, and volume. Test ideas. Make discoveries. Cooperate with others. Use small muscles to pour and dig.
Library	A quiet corner Carpeted floor Good light Comfortable places to sit Books reflecting children's families, cultures, and ethnicities, on a stand with covers facing out Small table and chairs A variety of materials for reading, writing, and listening Story retelling materials (puppets, flannel board)	Look at books. Learn about books and reading behaviors. Listen to story tapes. Read books with an adult. Spend time alone. Use small-muscle skills. Practice writing. Re-enact a familiar story.

Interest Area	Arrangement	What Children Do
Toys and Games	Away from noisy areas such as blocks and dramatic play Low shelves Table and chairs Toys (e.g., beads and laces, bottle caps to sort, pegs and pegboards, small blocks) in open containers on shelves Puzzles on racks	Notice the characteristics of things. Group items that are the same. Make patterns and constructions. Use small muscles to manipulate pieces. Follow the rules in playing games. Count objects. Explore and investigate.
Discovery	Near natural light Table to hold displays and collections Shelf to store materials Trays Tools	Use tools to examine materials. Observe and notice things. Share discoveries with others. Develop small-muscle skills.
Computers	Away from water, food, and paint Next to another quiet area such as the library One or more computers and a printer set up against a wall or divider Two chairs at each computer Electrical cords out of children's reach Developmentally appropriate software	Follow directions. Learn by experimenting. Cooperate with other children. Share knowledge with another child. Explore math and science concepts. Develop literacy skills.
Music and Movement	Open area with carpeting, if possible Storage for musical instruments: a shelf, pegboard, or box Storage for tapes, CDs Tumbling mats Musical instruments: drums, tambourines, kazoo, rhythm sticks, bells, triangles, xylophones, shakers	Make and listen to music. Cooperate with others. Explore creative movement. Follow directions. Develop large-muscle skills.
Cooking	Near a water source and electrical outlet; away from computers Table and chairs Shelf or pegboard to store materials and equipment Cooking supplies and equipment Recipe cards Place mats, dishes, flatware	Read and follow directions. Explore numbers and counting. Observe and notice how things change. Learn by experimenting. Develop small-muscle skills. Use tools.

Selecting and Displaying Materials

Well stocked interest areas invite children to explore.

The materials you select and the way you display them influence what and how children learn from their environment. Think about the children's many different interests; how their skills vary, and what kinds of life experiences they have had. Consider what you want children to learn and how you want them to take care of materials. Then plan to offer a variety of challenging materials, keep interest areas attractive and well organized, and regularly rotate and add new materials to attract children's attention and inspire them to explore.

In selecting each material, ask yourself these questions:

Will it interest the children? Daily observations will help you identify the interests of individual children and the group.

Do the children have the skills to handle it? For example, are some children ready for 10-piece puzzles while others need puzzles with only five pieces?

Will it challenge children to think and explore? Assorted buttons or bottle caps will be just as interesting as colored shapes for sorting.

Does it reflect the families, cultural backgrounds, and special needs of the children? Pictures in children's books, wooden figures for the block area, and dolls in the dramatic play area should reflect the diversity of society and help children accept and respect these differences.

Does it promote equal use by boys and girls? Be sure, for example, to include male dress-up clothes in the dramatic play area, and pictures that show men and women in many roles.

Is it durable and in good condition? This means no broken parts and no missing pieces. Materials should be clean and free of splinters or any jagged edges.

Is it an open-ended material that encourages children's creativity? For example, blocks, art materials, and many construction toys can be used in a variety of ways.

Does it help achieve the program's goals for children? For example, will it help children develop creativity? Learn to think? Develop language skills? Strengthen small and large muscles?

In modules 4–10 you will find many ideas for selecting materials that will promote children's physical, cognitive, social, and language development.

Take time to organize materials logically and display them attractively.

The organization and display of materials in the classroom are as important as your choice of materials.

- Identify a specific place for each material.

- Group materials that are used together (e.g., crayons and markers with paper, utensils with playdough, small cars and figures with blocks).

- Label the shelves with pictures and words so children can find and return the materials they use. Laminate or cover the labels with clear Contact paper to make them last longer.

- Store toys with small parts or pieces in open, labeled containers, such as boxes or dish pans, on low, open shelves.

You may need to make changes to the environment to include children with disabilities.

If you have children with physical disabilities in your program you will need to make the space safe and accessible. You may take steps such as the following:

- Make sure that traffic patterns between interest areas are wide enough for a child using a wheelchair or a walker.

- Adjust tables so wheelchairs will fit underneath or equip the chairs with trays. Provide tall stools so other children can sit comfortably at a raised table.

- Provide bolsters or other equipment so children who need extra physical support can participate in floor activities.

- Use puzzles with knobs for children with fine motor delays.

An expert consultant can help you to evaluate your classroom and outdoor areas to determine what changes, if any, are needed to give all children the best possible opportunities to participate in all program activities.

what's next?

Skill-Building Journal, section **3-6** *(Learning Activity B),* section **3-10** *(Answer Sheets),* and section **3-1** *(Feedback).*

Learning Activities

LEARNING
ACTIVITY

C. Organizing the Outdoor Environment

In this activity you will learn to

- organize the outdoor environment to offer children a variety of choices

- determine what materials and equipment are needed to improve your outdoor space

Whether your program operates in a rural, suburban, or city environment, the outdoors can offer children a variety of new experiences. Some programs have only blacktop and a fence surrounding their outdoor spaces; others have natural surroundings that readily invite exploration. Even in the most limited outdoor environments, you can do much to offer children a range of experiences.

The outdoor environment offers children a wide range of experiences.

The outdoor space is as important as the classroom, and teachers need to plan outdoor activities as carefully as they plan indoor ones. Of course, the outdoor area must be safe for children. See module 1, *Safe*, for information on maintaining a safe outdoor area at all times.

The outdoor environment ideally should include

- easy access to and from the indoor space

- a drinking fountain and water spigot for attaching a hose

- nearby bathrooms

- a storage shed outdoors or indoors near the door to the outdoor area

- soft materials that absorb falls, such as sawdust, sand, or bark, under swings, slides, and climbers (Check local and state regulations that apply to your program.)

- a hard-surfaced area for riding, chalk drawings, and games

- a covered area for use in wet weather

- sunny and shady areas

- places to be alone or with one or two friends (boxes, tents, logs, bushes)

- open, grassy spaces for tumbling, running, and sitting

- open space for active or group play

Children and staff need to dress for the weather.

Children should have time outdoors twice a day, unless the weather is severe. You and the children will enjoy the outdoors more if you are dressed appropriately for the weather. On cold days, dress in layers (long sleeve shirt, sweater, and coat or jacket) and wearing a hat and gloves or mittens. On warm days, dress in loose clothing made from light fabrics and perhaps wear a hat with a visor. Keep a box of extra clothes: loose T-shirts, shorts, and baseball caps in the summer, and scarves, hats, gloves, and sweaters in the winter.

- What do you like or dislike about outdoor time?

- How can you extend or overcome these feelings?

- How can you make the most of outdoor time to promote children's development and learning?

You may need to make changes to the outdoor environment for children with disabilities.

Children with disabilities benefit from outdoor time, as all children do. However, depending on the type and severity of the disability, the outdoors can be overwhelming or frightening to a child who is unsure of how to get around an open space safely.

Evaluate the space from the child's point of view. For example, a child with a visual disability will need help to move around. You will have to orient the child to the location of different play structures. Allow the child to touch the equipment as you describe its features and guide the child's first attempts. Stay close by to supervise and teach other children to assist those with visual impairments. For children with hearing problems, point out possible hazards, such as swings, where they might not hear a verbal warning.

Special equipment or other changes may be necessary for children with other physical disabilities. Here are some suggestions:

- Provide bucket seats or straps on swings.

- Build ramps over uneven surfaces or on inclines for children in wheelchairs or who have poor balance.

- Place handholds and rails on climbing equipment and structures.

- Offer activities, such as sand and water play and table art, so children in wheelchairs can participate with others.

- Place straps on pedals of wheeled toys.

The outdoor environment should offer a range of choices. In addition to traditional outdoor activities. Many indoor activities can be brought outdoors.

Organize the outdoor environment to offer children choices.

The outdoor space should be organized by types of activities. Locate active play areas near each other and separate them from the quieter ones. Mark clear pathways for wheeled toys, to help prevent injuries. Store equipment and materials used outdoors in a storage shed or bring them outdoors from the classroom.

The following chart lists the types of activities you can offer children outdoors. Notice the materials and equipment needed, and what children are likely to do.

Materials and Equipment for Outdoor Activities

Activity	Materials and Equipment	What Children Do
Sand Play	Large sand box with cover Pails, scoops, muffin tins, shovels, molds, funnels Plastic people, animals, vehicles Pine cones, stones, twigs, leaves Access to water	"Bake" pies and cakes. Learn about shape, size, and volume. Make roads, castles, and tunnels. Dig, pour, sift, mold. Investigate and solve problems.
Water Play	Water table, tub, or wading pool Plastic buckets, cups, spray bottles Large brushes and painters' hats Hose and sprinkler Liquid soap and bubble-blowing props	Release tension. Learn about shape, size, volume. Use small muscles to pour, spray, scrub. Paint with water. Blow bubbles. Run through a sprinkler.
Wheeled Toys	Tricycles Wagons Wheelbarrows Scooters Large set of traffic signs Set of cones Hats and caps	Ride bikes. Pull wagons. Push wheelbarrows. Pretend to drive cars, trucks or ambulances. Follow rules and boundaries. Learn to share and take turns. Read traffic signs.
Games	Rubber balls (different sizes) Large bats (plastic, hollow) Bean bags Parachute Balance beam Hula hoops Ropes Tunnels	Throw, kick, catch, bounce, jump, and balance. Explore new ways to move their bodies. Crawl forward and backward. Play with others. Learn to take turns. Follow rules and directions.

Activity	Materials and Equipment	What Children Do
Construction	Boards and saw horses Wooden boxes Large hollow blocks Tires Cartons and crates	Lift and carry. Build structures. Pretend. Cooperate with others. Exercise large muscles. Measure and develop spatial sense.
Woodworking	Workbench or large tree stump Safety goggles Hammers, saws, hand drill C-clamps and vises Wood scraps (soft) Nails with large heads Sandpaper Rulers and measuring tapes	Hammer, saw, drill. Pull out nails. Sand and file wood. Use large and small muscles. Create constructions. Measure and compare. Learn about size and shape. Solve problems.
Quiet Activities	Games and puzzles Books Writing materials CD/tape player with CDs or tapes Table blocks and toys Collections Art supplies	Spend time alone or with one or two others. Look at books. Be creative. Sort and categorize. Listen to music.
Science and Nature	Pets Pet food, cages, water bottles Magnifying glasses Containers for collections Trowels Thermometers Rain and snow gauge Writing materials	Care for and play with pets. Dig in the dirt. Collect and examine natural items. Observe and categorize. Learn new words. Graph rain and snowfall. Record their observations.

what's next?

Skill-Building Journal, section **3-7** *(Learning Activity C)* and section **3-1** *(Feedback).*

Learning Activities

LEARNING ACTIVITY

D. Planning the Daily Schedule and Routines

In this activity you will learn to

- develop a daily schedule and routines that meet children's developmental needs and support learning

- plan ahead so all parts of the day go smoothly

Every day has a structure, the daily schedule that shows what happens each day and when. This schedule includes activities, routines, and transitions, when children move from one activity or routine to another. With careful planning, each aspect of the day will proceed smoothly for you and for the children.

When the schedule is the same each day, children can learn to predict what will happen. This sameness helps children feel competent and secure. An appropriate schedule for preschool children should offer

- **a balance** between active and quiet times; large-group, small-group, and individual activities; child-initiated and adult-led activities; and indoor and outdoor play periods

- **at least 60 minutes a day for each choice time** so children can become deeply involved in their play

- **outdoor play** every day, for 45–60 minutes each time (two outdoor periods in full-day programs)

- **large-group activities** that are planned and limited to 15 minutes so children remain interested and involved

- **opportunities for small-group activities** when teachers work with a few children to introduce new concepts or materials, lead a game, or teach a skill

- **well-planned routines and transitions** so children know what is expected and, can move from task to task independently.

- **book reading** for the whole group, small groups, and to individual children several times a day

The sample schedule that follows shows what a typical day might look like in a preschool program.

The daily schedule should offer a balance of activities and be predictable.

DAILY SCHEDULE

30 minutes (8:00–8:30 a.m., or earlier in child care programs)	**Planning/preparation time:** Review the plans for the day. Conduct health and safety check (e.g., refill bathroom supplies, remove any broken or torn materials, check outside for trash). Prepare interest areas (e.g., mix paint, place puzzles on a table, display new books). Set out name cards in sign-in area. Think about individual children, any special needs, current projects. Set out self-serve breakfast.
30 minutes (8:30–9:00 a.m., or longer in child care)	**Arrival:** Greet families and children individually. Help children store belongings, select a quiet activity, or serve themselves breakfast
10–15 minutes (9:00–9:15 a.m.)	**Group meeting:** Give signal to gather the group and lead children in singing songs and fingerplays and sharing news. Read a poem, talk about the day's activities, and talk about the choices for the morning. Consider the needs of children who are not ready for large-group activities (e.g., hold two smaller groups, have one teacher sit close to children who need extra attention).
60–75 minutes (9:15–10:15 or 10:30 a.m., depending on how snack will be served)	**Choice time and small groups:** Guide children in selecting interest areas. Observe and interact with individual children to extend play and learning. Lead a short, small-group activity that builds on children's skills and interests. Work with children engaged in special projects. **Cleanup:** Help children put away materials in each interest area.
15 minutes (10:15–10:30 a.m.)	**Snack time:** Sit with children and enjoy a snack together or supervise the "snack bar." *Note:* Self-serve snacks can be incorporated into indoor or, in warm weather, outdoor choice time.
10 minutes (10:30–10:40 a.m.)	**Group time:** Invite children to share what they did, lead music and movement activity, read aloud (e.g., story, poem), record ideas, or write experience story.
60 minutes (10:40–11:40 a.m.)	**Outdoor choice time:** Supervise playground activities. Observe and interact with children as they jump rope, play ball games, blow bubbles, make nature discoveries, and so on. Extend special project work outdoors, if appropriate. Help children to put away or carry in toys and materials, hang up jackets, toilet, and wash up.

Caring for Preschool Children

DAILY SCHEDULE

10 minutes (11:40–11:50 a.m.)	**Story time:** Read and discuss a storybook. Use props to help children retell stories.
55 minutes (11:50 a.m.–12:45 p.m.)	**Lunch:** Help children to prepare the tables for lunch. Encourage conversations about the day's events, the meal itself, and topics of interest to children. Guide children in cleaning up after lunch, brushing teeth, setting out cots/mats, and preparing for rest.
60–90 minutes (12:45–2:15 p.m.)	**Rest time:** Help children relax so they can fall asleep. Supervise rest area, rotating responsibility so each teacher gets a break. Provide quiet activities for children who don't sleep. Adjust length of rest time to suit age of group and needs of individual children.
30 minutes (2:15–2:45 p.m.)	**Snack/quiet activities:** Set up snack so children can serve themselves and participate in quiet activities.
15 minutes (2:45–3:00 p.m.)	**Group activity:** Lead group meeting/activity. Help children reflect on the day and prepare for home. Read aloud.
60 minutes (3:00–4:00 p.m.)	**Outdoor choice time:** Supervise and interact with children. Plan some special activities.
60 minutes (4:00–5:00 p.m.)	**Choice time and small groups:** Set out a limited number of choices for children, such as computers, library, toys and games. Lead a small-group activity.
60 minutes (5:00–6:00 p.m.)	**Closing and departures:** Lead group discussion about the day and plans for the next day. Involve children in quiet activities, hanging up their artwork and preparing for the next day. Greet parents and share something about the child's day.
As time allows during the day	**Planning and reflection:** Discuss how the day went and the progress of individual children (skills, needs, interests); work on portfolios and observation notes related to the *Developmental Continuum*. Review and make plans for the next day.

Sample Daily Schedule

Displaying the schedule with pictures and words offers a literacy experience that helps children learn the order of the day's events.

A schedule with pictures and words helps children predict and recall the order of daily events. You can make one using drawings or photographs. For example, a series of photographs could show children arriving in the morning, working in the interest areas, getting ready to go outdoors, playing outside, and so on. This can be particularly helpful for children who have very little consistency in their lives and who do not have a sense of control over what takes place.

- Do the children in your classroom understand the daily schedule? How do you know?

- What could you do to make sure all the children know what happens next?

When they first arrive in the morning, children might need reminders of what happens during the day. For example, "During choice time we usually stay indoors. We'll go outside after snack." Children feel powerful when they can say what comes next: "First I eat lunch. Then I brush my teeth."

Routine activities can offer opportunities for learning.

Routines are the events that take place every day: arriving and leaving, eating, sleeping or resting, toileting, dressing and undressing, and cleaning up. Think of routines as opportunities for teaching and helping children develop self-confidence. For example, you can explain the importance of good health practices as children go through routines. Children will feel more in control when they know that each day, after eating lunch, they go to the sink to brush their teeth and wash their hands, get their blankets from their cubbies, and go to their cots.

When children participate in routines they develop

- small-muscle skills as they brush teeth, pour juice, serve themselves, and zip or button clothing

- large-muscle skills as they set up cots or arrange chairs

- social and language skills as they talk with each other and adults during relaxed, family-style meals

- self-help skills as they wash their hands

- cognitive skills, such as one-to-one correspondence (an important math concept), as they set places at the table

- social skills as they work together to prepare for a meal

In full-day programs, the daily schedule includes a block of time when children nap or rest while doing quiet activities. Some children find it easy to fall asleep immediately; others need extra attention to help them relax enough to fall asleep. Many teachers find it helps to rub children's backs, play music at low volume, read stories, and sing songs softly to help children fall asleep. Those who can't sleep or who get up early can enjoy a restful time looking at books, drawing, or playing with quiet toys such as beads and laces or puzzles.

- Do children know what to do during routines?
- How do you adapt routines for individual children?
- Do you use routines to promote learning?

Transitions can be difficult if children don't know what to do.

Transitions—the periods between one activity and the next—can be learning opportunities or problem times. If children have nothing to do while waiting, they may become restless. Because they are bored, they sometimes act out, wrestling with one another or running around the room.

During a transition, there are often some children who are still busy completing an activity and some just waiting for the next one. If one teacher is helping the children who are finishing an activity and the other teacher plans something for the rest of the group, transitions are usually easy. Here are some tips:

Give children a warning. "In five minutes it will be time to clean up."

Involve children in transition activities. Children can help set the tables for meals, collect the trash, wash the paint brushes, or help a friend zip a coat.

Provide clear directions. State them clearly and simply. "Please find your mat and sit in the listening area. I'll be right there to teach you a new fingerplay."

Be flexible whenever possible. Allow children extra time to complete special projects or activities when they seem very interested and involved. "We're going to let Jan and Eric finish weighing the rocks they collected while the rest of us start to clean up. Then we can all hear which rock was the heaviest."

Allow children to share their work. Children are often more willing to clean up if they have an opportunity to share and talk about their work. Gather the children in the meeting area before cleanup. Invite them to talk about what they did and show their work. Then ask for volunteers to clean up each of the areas.

Keep children occupied. If children have something specific to do, they are less likely to cause problems. For example, those who are finished eating or cleaning up could work on a group puzzle while they wait for the others, or get their coats on and go outside with one teacher.

Establish a signal for quiet. When the noise level gets too high, use a signal, such as a bell, raising a hand, or blinking the lights, to get children's attention.

Transition times can be used to teach new concepts, to practice skills, and to encourage creativity. Here are some ideas:

Transitions can be learning times.

- Play a game of follow the leader. You can lead the children in picking up, going outdoors, making funny gestures, and so forth.

- Use categories to move children from one activity to another. ("Everyone wearing shoes with laces may go quietly to the juice table.")

- Ask children to try unusual ways of moving. ("Let's go to our meeting place like big, slow, heavy elephants.")

- Play a clapping game—such as 2 loud claps and 3 soft claps—and encourage children to follow your pattern. Use the pattern as a signal when you want children to be quiet.

- Teach the children fingerplays and special songs.

- Ask children to help each other. ("Kim, will you please help Sara find her mittens?")

- What transitions in the day are easy for the children?

- What do you do to make these times go smoothly?

what's next?

Skill-Building Journal, section **3-8** *(Learning Activity D),* section **3-1** *(Feedback),* and section **3-9** *(Reflecting on Your Learning).*

4
Physical

Overview

Providing Materials, Equipment, and Opportunities for
Gross Motor Development

Providing Materials and Opportunities for Fine Motor Development

Reinforcing and Encouraging Children's Physical Development

Taking Care of Your Body

Learning Activities

A. Using Your Knowledge of Child Development to Promote
Physical Development

B. Creating an Environment That Supports Physical Development

C. Observing and Responding to Children's Growing Physical Skills

D. Promoting Children's Gross Motor Skills

4.

Physical

Overview

Physical development involves the use and coordination of fine and gross motor skills.

A tremendous amount of physical development takes place during the first five years of life. During this time, young children learn to control their muscles and practice the physical skills they will use for the rest of their lives. They use their large muscles to walk, run, jump, and hop, as well as throw, catch, and kick. They use small muscles to hold, pinch, and flex fingers as they cut with scissors. They learn coordination; to balance; to start and stop their large muscles; and to direct their foot and hand movements accurately. By using their senses and coordinating their movements, children make discoveries about their world and the effects of their actions. Children must have many opportunities to move their bodies and use their physical skills if they are to develop properly.

Physical activity should be regular.

The experiences preschool children have using their physical skills set the stage for a lifetime of physical fitness. When children have positive experiences engaging in physical activities, they are more likely to become adults with healthy lifestyles. For most healthy adults, physical fitness involves moderate amounts of physical activity on a regular basis, not necessarily performing like Olympic athletes!

Physical fitness is related to a child's positive sense of self. Many children develop views of themselves and attitudes about attempting new tasks on the basis of how they feel about their bodies and what they think they can or cannot do physically. Young children who have had many successful experiences using their fine and gross motor skills tend to feel competent. This sense of competence carries over into other activities. They are more likely to explore materials and attempt new challenges without worrying about failure.

Teachers support children's physical development by making sure that they have opportunities to use their large and small muscles every day, throughout the day, indoors and outdoors. Teachers thus help children develop physical fitness habits. They set up challenging experiences that help children to feel good about the things they are learning to do.

You can promote physical development by

- providing materials, equipment, and opportunities for gross motor development

- providing materials and opportunities for fine motor development

- reinforcing and encouraging children's physical development

---

Providing Materials, Equipment, and Opportunities for Gross Motor Development

1. **Encourage children to use their large muscles throughout the day.** Routines, such as setting the table and cleaning up; group time activities; work in interest areas; and outdoor times provide many opportunities for children to learn and practice gross motor skills.

2. **Schedule time for active outdoor play every day.** The daily schedule should include a 45- to 60-minute outdoor time for half-day programs and two 45- to 60-minute outdoor times for full-day programs.

3. **Provide opportunities for active indoor play during bad weather.** "During choice time today we'll use the hallway for riding trikes, bowling, and tumbling."

4. **Encourage the development of self-help skills that involve the use of large muscles.** "Oanh, that was a good idea. You used the hollow block as a step stool to reach the sink."

5. **Offer indoor and outdoor activities that challenge children to improve their gross motor skills.** "Now that the children have mastered the obstacle course, they're losing interest. Let's invite them to rearrange the equipment to offer new challenges!"

6. **Provide a variety of materials and equipment to encourage all children to use their large muscles.** Balance beams, ramps, slides, climbers, rope ladders, balls, bats, hoops, ropes, and other materials allow children to practice many skills.

Ms. Williams and Ms. Frilles Lead a Rainy Day Activity

It's a rainy day, and choice time is very noisy as the children crash blocks and bang pots and pans. "I think we need to move our bodies," Ms. Williams tells the children. "But we can't go outside," Mark moans. "It's raining hard!" "You're right. It's too wet to go out. Let's clean up, then we can try some new ways to move our bodies," she suggests. When the last blocks are put away, Ms. Williams and several children push the shelves against the wall. "We'll need this space for moving," she says. Ms. Frilles uses several long ropes to make large circles on the floor. "Now, Tyrone, Amanda, and Michelle, show us how many different ways you can move inside the circle without bumping into each other." Ms. Frilles announces, "Tyrone is jumping! Amanda is galloping! Michelle looks like she's floating!" Meanwhile, Ms. Williams invites children to go to the other circles. The children walk, hop, leap, skip, slide, and crawl.

Providing Materials and Opportunities for Fine Motor Development

7. **Encourage children to use their small muscles throughout the day.** As with large muscle development, routines, group time activities, work in interest areas, and outdoor times provide many opportunities for children to learn and practice fine motor skills.

8. **Encourage the development of self-help skills that involve the use of small muscles.** "Avida, you zipped your jacket all by yourself today! You've been working on that for a while!"

9. **Provide a variety of materials that fit together so children can practice their fine motor skills.** "Leo, you made a house with the table blocks yesterday. Would you like to use them again or build with Lincoln Logs?"

10. **Provide materials and activities that accommodate different skill levels.** Some children put 7-piece puzzles together, while others are ready for puzzles with more pieces.

11. **Encourage children to participate in daily routines.** "Jorge, you're doing a very careful job of setting the table. You're making sure that each place has one plate, one napkin, and one fork."

Ms. Kim Encourages the Use of Small Muscles at Mealtime

example

"Here's the pitcher," says Ms. Kim to Marcus. "Hold your cup with one hand so it stays in place." Marcus holds his cup and pours the milk very quickly; it overflows. "Oops, that milk came out too fast, didn't it?" smiles Ms. Kim. "There's a sponge near the sink you can use to clean it up." Marcus gets the sponge and wipes up the spill. "Would you like to practice pouring slowly so the milk doesn't overflow?" asks Ms. Kim. "You can pour a glass of milk for me!" Marcus picks up the pitcher. "I can make it go slow. Watch me." Marcus holds the pitcher and pours the milk very slowly, stopping before it gets to the top of her cup. "You got the milk into the cup without spilling, Marcus," observes Ms. Kim. "Your hand and arm muscles were working well." "My peas keep falling off my fork," explains Sara. "You could use your spoon," says Marcus. "That would help, wouldn't it?" says Ms. Kim. "What else could you do?" Sara looks up and says, "I could stick my peas on the fork like this," and spears four peas on her fork. Several other children at the table begin spearing their peas. "Well, we certainly solved that problem," says Ms. Kim.

Reinforcing and Encouraging Children's Physical Development

12. **Offer a variety of materials and activities for different skill levels.** For example, have balls of different sizes so each child can pick the one that feels comfortable for kicking, throwing, and catching.

13. **Encourage children to coordinate use of their large and small muscles.** Describing children's actions, offering suggestions, and providing cues can help children have successful experiences as they roll playdough, pour milk, stack hollow blocks, and toss bean bags into a hoop on the ground.

14. **Help children develop an awareness of rhythm so they can coordinate their body movements.** "Avida and Tony are hopping to the music. Benjamin and Aimee are swaying. How else can we move to the music?"

15. **Introduce cooperative games and activities that build children's physical skills.** Games in which children play *with* each other, and that do not lead to identifying winners and losers, are appropriate for preschool children.

16. **Help older children begin learning skills they can use to play sports and games.** "Tyrone, put the wiffle ball on the tee. Pick up the bat with both hands near the bottom. Then stand back and swing!"

example

Ms. Thomas Encourages Appropriate Physical Activities

When Ms. Díaz comes to pick up her daughter, Avida, she sees children steering tricycles, pulling wagons, and crawling through boxes. She sees Avida kicking a ball with Janelle. Turning to Ms. Thomas, Ms. Díaz says, "Now that Avida's almost 5, we'd like her to play soccer with the neighborhood league." "Has Avida said she wants to play soccer?" asks Ms. Thomas. "No, not really," says Ms. Díaz, "but I want her to exercise." "That's important," says Ms. Thomas. "We provide opportunities for children to move their bodies every day, and we encourage families to exercise, too. Most 5-year-olds, however, aren't ready for competitive sports such as soccer. Are you familiar with the community center's family fitness programs? I think you and Avida would enjoy the cooperative games they play." "Oh," says Ms. Díaz. "We could have fun and stay fit together."

what's next?

Skill-Building Journal, section **4-2** *(Overview),* section **4-10** *(Answer Sheets),* and section **4-1** *(Feedback).*

Taking Care of Your Body[11]

Teachers of young children engage in a lot of physical activity every day.

As a teacher, you are concerned about children's physical development. However, you must take care of yourself, too. Think about how often you

- bend from the waist to pick up a child or an item on the floor

- lean over a step stool in front of a sink to wash your hands

- sit on the floor and bend forward to play with a child

- sit on a child-size chair

These actions are typical for teachers, producing sore backs and limbs. Back problems are the most common cause of occupational injuries for child care staff.

Try these suggestions to prevent back injuries:

- Keep your lower back as straight as possible and avoid slouching when sitting or standing.

- Shift your weight from side to side and change positions when standing for a long time.

- Bend your knees, not your back, when you lean forward.

Back injuries are common among adults who care for young children.

- Wear low-heeled, comfortable shoes with good shock absorption. Use shoe inserts to increase absorption.

- Bend your knees, tuck in your buttocks, and pull in your abdominal muscles when lifting a child or a heavy object.

- Avoid twisting when lifting or lowering a child or a heavy object. Hold the child or object close to you.

- When you sit on the floor (such as during circle time), sit against a wall or use a large pillow to support your back.

- Talk with your supervisor and colleagues about staff coverage for short breaks. Do some stretching exercises and relax.

Teaching is a physically demanding job. Remember to take care of yourself!

what's next?

Skill-Building Journal, section **4-3** *(Taking Care of Your Body),* section **4-1** *(Feedback),* and section **4-4** *(Pre-Training Assessment).*

Learning Activities

LEARNING ACTIVITY

A. Using Your Knowledge of Child Development to Promote Physical Development

In this activity you will learn to

- recognize typical gross and fine motor skills of preschool children

- use what you know about children to promote their motor skills

Each child learns and uses motor skills according to an individual timetable.

As with other areas of development, each child follows an individual schedule for mastering physical skills. In any group of preschool children there is likely to be a wide range of physical abilities. For example, one 4-year-old can skip with both feet, while another can skip with only one foot. Although the age when children accomplish a skill varies from child to child, the pattern rarely does. For example, children control their head movements first; then their torsos and arms, and finally their legs. Gross motor skills, such as rolling over, usually appear before those involving small muscles, such as picking up small objects. Development normally begins with muscles close to the body center and moves outward as the child matures. Teachers need to observe individuals and understand the typical sequence of development to be able to promote preschool children's motor skills.

The following descriptions illustrate the sequence of gross and fine motor development during the preschool years. You will probably notice that the children in your group are developing several motor skills at the same time. As you observe children indoors and outdoors, you can learn which skills they have mastered and which ones they are developing.

Three-Year-Olds

- Jamie likes to dance to music.

- Marcus can serve himself from the big bowl at lunch.

- Linda moves the tricycle by stepping on the ground; she is just beginning to use the pedals.

Three-year-olds move in a variety of ways.

Three-year-olds are becoming sure and nimble on their feet. They can walk, run, and turn sharp corners with ease. They might hold their arms out to their sides for balance or swing them for sureness. They can climb stairs using alternate feet and perhaps jump from the bottom stair and land on both feet. Three-year-olds like to run, gallop, and dance to music. They can hop several times in a row, balance on one foot for a few seconds, and walk along a line made with tape or a rope. They enjoy pushing and pedaling tricycles; using swings, and throwing, catching, and kicking large balls.

Three-year-olds develop fine motor skills through routines and activities.

Three-year-olds are gaining greater control of their fingers, hands, and wrists. They can spoon food from serving dishes, pass platters, and use eating utensils. Most have learned to pull their pants up and down, put on shoes, and use large buttons and zippers. They can wash their own hands by turning the faucet on and off, pumping soap from a dispenser, and tearing paper towels off a roll.

Three-year-olds enjoy using a variety of materials. They can string beads, build towers and bridges with blocks, begin to use scissors to cut paper, and turn the pages of a book one page at a time. With practice, they progress from holding crayons with their fists to using their first two fingers and thumb.

Four-Year-Olds

- Aimee likes to spend most of her time outdoors climbing the ladder and sliding.

- Leo can write the letters of his first name; he sometimes reverses the *L*.

- Avida can throw and catch a bounced ball.

Four-year-olds can control their large muscles.

Four-year-olds have greater control over their large muscles. They can typically hop in a sequence of two or three hops, as they move toward skipping on one foot, then taking a walking step forward with the other. Balancing on a board, broad jumping, and throwing balls overhand are other favorite activities. Many fours can climb ladders and playground equipment with assurance and fearlessness. They skillfully pedal, steer, and turn corners on tricycles.

Four-year-olds have greater control over finger, hand, and wrist movements.

Four-year-olds have more refined small muscle movements and eye-hand coordination than 3-year-olds. They can cut more skillfully with scissors and begin to draw pictures that represent real things. They can zip and snap most clothing, pour from small pitchers without spilling, serve and eat with a fork and spoon, and use knives for spreading and some cutting. Finger, hand, and wrist control allows them to build detailed structures with construction materials. They can use tools to form shapes and objects with playdough and clay. As their coordination increases, they are able to use smaller versions of the materials they used when younger, such as Legos, beads and strings, and pegs and pegboards.

Five-Year-Olds

- Michelle skips in the outdoor area almost every day.

- Tyrone likes to use the sharp knife when we have a cooking activity.

- Mark can catch a ball thrown underhanded.

Five-year-olds can use their ball-handling skills to play games.

By age 5, most children can run fast, ride tricycles with great speed and skill, and climb high structures freely. They can hop on one foot for a long distance and usually master skipping with alternating feet. They can also walk the full length of a balance beam without stepping off. Because 5-year-olds can usually succeed in getting a ball where they want it to go, they enjoy ball games. Some 5-year-olds are learning to jump rope, do somersaults, and use an overhead ladder on a climber.

Five-year-olds are refining their fine motor skills.

Most 5-year-olds have well-developed fine motor skills. Their drawings and paintings include much detail, and they can cut shapes with scissors. They can use utensils properly to serve and eat food. Five-year-olds can handle most buttons, snaps, zippers, and buckles, and are learning to tie shoes. Most can reproduce some letters and numerals and write words, especially their own names.

Development: It's All Connected

Preschool children use their fine and gross motor skills every day, all day. Their physical development is closely connected to all other aspects of their development. Here are a few examples:

Cognitive
Children use eye-hand coordination as they stack and balance unit blocks to make a bridge, noticing that they need an equal number of blocks on each side for the bridge to stay up.

Emotional

When children use their large-muscle skills and coordination to move in different ways, such as like a galloping horse, a waddling penguin, and a lumbering elephant, they feel competent that they can control how their bodies move.

Social

Children interact with friends while running, jumping, and climbing.

Language

Children develop their small muscles (needed for writing) when they work playdough, string beads, and place pegs in a pegboard.

Physical Development Alerts[12]

If you notice over time that a child cannot do several of these activities and no reason is known, suggest that the parents discuss their child's physical development with a health professional.

By age 4	By age 5
• cannot throw a ball overhand	• cannot build a tower of 6–8 blocks
• cannot ride a tricycle	• seems uncomfortable holding a crayon
• cannot stack four blocks	• has trouble taking off clothing
• has difficulty scribbling	• cannot brush her teeth efficiently
• cannot grasp a crayon between thumb and fingers	• cannot wash and dry his hands

---

A pediatrician or other health specialist can determine the child's skills and needs and suggest specific strategies for the program and home.

what's next?

Skill-Building Journal, section **4-5** (*Learning Activity A*), section **4-10** (*Answer Sheets*), and section **4-1** (*Feedback*).

Learning Activities

LEARNING
ACTIVITY

B. Creating an Environment That Supports Physical Development

In this activity you will learn to

- select materials and equipment that help children develop gross motor skills

- select materials and equipment that help children develop fine motor skills

When teachers know the range of physical skills that children can learn at a given age and stage of development, they can set up an environment that encourages further development of these skills.

An early childhood environment should be a safe place in which children feel confident and assured as they climb, balance, draw, hop, dance, build, serve themselves, and clean up. A safe environment encourages children to practice skills they have mastered and try new ones.

The environment should support children's development of physical skills.

The types of materials and equipment you provide should reflect the range of skills, strengths, needs, and interests of the children in your group. Many open-ended materials, such as blocks and art supplies, are ideal for meeting diverse needs, because they can be used in different ways by children at different skill levels. Older preschool children who have had many opportunities to use their large and small muscles can usually have success with more challenging learning materials and equipment than can 3-year-olds and children with limited experiences. It is crucial to provide a wide variety of items that offer children challenges without causing frustration.

THINK

- What open-ended materials do you have in your classroom for building fine motor skills?

- How does each interest area support fine and gross motor skills?

Children can use their large and small muscles indoors in every interest area as well as outdoors. The following chart lists examples of materials that preschool children use that promote fine and gross motor skills.

Caring for Preschool Children

Children's Use of Fine and Gross Motor Skills

Area	How Children Use Fine and Gross Motor Skills
Dramatic Play	Lift dolls, utensils, and pots and pans. Push and pull carriages and wagons. Set the table and pass serving bowls. Use zippers, buttons, buckles, and snaps on dress-up clothes. Write an order in a restaurant; write messages. Hold cups and pretend to drink.
Toys and Games	Take out and put in puzzle pieces. Snap together Bristle Blocks and Legos. String beads. Pick up and drop sorting items (buttons, bottle caps) into trays. Pick up and place dominoes on a tabletop or floor.
Blocks	Lift unit blocks and hollow blocks. Place one block on top of another. Move wooden people, cars, and trucks. Write signs to label or protect structures.
Art	Finger paint. Paint large strokes at the easel. Draw with crayons and markers. Paste and glue paper, fabric, feathers, and other materials to make collages and assemblages. Mold and stretch playdough and clay. Use scissors.
Library	Turn the pages of books. Place headsets on ears. Move felt pieces on a flannel board. Press buttons on a tape recorder. Write and bind books.
Computers	Press keys on a keyboard. Use a mouse. Insert a disk into the drive. Fill the printer with paper.

Area	How Children Use Fine and Gross Motor Skills
Music, Movement, and Large Muscle (indoors)	Climb the rungs of an indoor climber. Balance in a rocking boat. Crawl through a cardboard box. Walk on a balance beam. Toss bean bags in a basket. Move to music. Use rhythm instruments.
Sand and Water	Pour from a pitcher. Squeeze sponges and basters. Direct the stream from a squeeze bottle. Feel the textures of wet and dry sand. Rotate wrist or forearm to use eggbeaters and screw jar lids.
Discovery	Sprinkle food into a fish bowl. Pick up rocks, shells, and other collections. Look at objects through a magnifying glass. Carry a pitcher to water plants. Adjust a microscope. Take apart broken mechanical objects.
Woodworking	Hold a nail in one hand and use a hammer with the other. Turn the rod on a vise. Place tools on pegboard hooks. Make back-and-forth motions with a saw or sandpaper. Pick up screws and nails.
Cooking	Pour liquid into a measuring cup from a pitcher. Knead dough. Roll dough with a rolling pin. Stir ingredients in a bowl. Grate carrots onto a cutting board. Slice celery with a knife.
Outdoors	Throw, catch, and kick balls. Run, hop, skip, and jump. Swing from rungs on a climber. Crawl through tunnels. Pull a wagon. Dig in the sandbox or a garden. Create games, such as rolling a ball back and forth.

As you set up and change your environment to match children's developing skills, think about safety first. Consider how children typically play in each interest area and outdoors with the materials you have provided, and plan accordingly. (More information on safety is provided in module 1, *Safe.*)

- What safety precautions should you keep in mind when planning physical activities?

- Which activities require an adult to be present throughout the activity?

- How can the children be involved in developing safety rules for each interest area?

Remember: Children need adequate amounts of time to practice their gross and fine motor skills. Choice time should allow children opportunities to use their large and small muscles in several interest areas: Blocks, Art, Sand and Water, and so on. Active outdoor play should be scheduled for each day: 45–60 minutes in half-day programs and two 45- to 60-minute outdoor times for full-day programs. During severe weather, rearrange the classroom furniture and equipment and use the hallways to create space for your group to have indoor active play, such as climbing an indoor climber, crawling through a tunnel, and moving to music.

what's next?

Skill-Building Journal, section **4-6** *(Learning Activity B)* and section **4-1** *(Feedback).*

Learning Activities

LEARNING ACTIVITY

C. Observing and Responding to Children's Growing Physical Skills

In this activity you will learn to

- observe how children use their fine and gross motor skills

- help children develop and refine their physical skills

To help children develop and refine their physical skills, teachers need to understand the sequence of fine and gross motor skills that most 3- to 5-year-old children use. Because each child acquires and uses these skills according to his or her own pattern of development, observing what each child can do is important. With this information, you can respond to their actions and plan experiences based on what children can do now and what you expect them to be able to do next.

It is helpful to use a continuum of fine and gross motor skills for preschool children as you plan for your group, interact with children, and conduct activities. Knowing the sequence of development helps you to have appropriate expectations and helps you track each child's physical development.

Continuum of Fine and Gross Motor Development[13]

A continuum of fine motor development for 3- to 5-year-old children includes the following:

General skill	Most children can do this, before...	They can do this, before...	They can do this
Controls small muscles of hands	Manipulates objects with hands (*Example: places large pegs in pegboard*)	Manipulates smaller objects with increasing control (*Example: squeezes a clothespin to hang a painting*)	Manipulates a variety of objects requiring increased coordination (*Example: cuts with scissors along lines*)
Coordinates eye-hand movements	Performs simple manipulations (*Example: rolls and pounds playdough*)	Performs simple manipulations with increasing control (*Example: pours water into a funnel*)	Manipulates materials in a purposeful way, planning and attending to detail (*Example: creates a tall, balanced structure from table blocks*)
Uses tools for writing and drawing	Holds a marker or crayon with thumb and two fingers; makes simple strokes	Makes several basic strokes or figures; draws some recognizable objects	Copies and draws simple shapes, letters, and words

A continuum of gross motor development for 3- to 5-year-old children includes the following:

General skill	Most children can do this, before...	They can do this, before...	They can do this
Demonstrates basic locomotor skills (running, jumping, hopping, galloping)	Moves with direction and beginning coordination *(Example: hops in place once or twice)*	Moves with direction and increasing coordination *(Example: does a running jump with both feet)*	Moves with direction and refined coordination *(Example: gallops smoothly)*
Shows balance while moving	Attempts to walk along a line, stepping off occasionally	Walks along a wide beam	Walks forward easily, and backward with effort, along a wide beam
Climbs up and down	Climbs a short, wide ladder	Climbs up and down stairs and ladders, and around obstacles	Climbs and plays easily on ramps, stairs, ladders, or sliding boards
Pedals and steers a tricycle or other wheeled vehicle	Pedals in a forward direction, steering around wide corners	Pedals and steers around obstacles and sharp corners	Rides with speed and control
Demonstrates throwing, kicking, and catching skills	Throws, catches, and kicks objects with somewhat awkward movements	Throws, catches, and kicks with increasing control	Throws and kicks at a target and catches with increasing accuracy

From your daily observations, you will be able to identify the child's level on the continuum of physical development. This information will help you to decide how to respond. Of course, knowing about each child's temperament and interests, as well as his or her physical abilities, also helps you determine your responses. Children's views of themselves and their attitudes about attempting new tasks are connected to what they think they can or cannot do physically. Your responses to children's physical activities should promote their feelings of competence and encourage them to keep trying to master physical skills.

Responding to a Child's Use of Fine and Gross Motor Skills

Encourage a child who is eager to accomplish a goal, pointing out what she does successfully.

Reassure a child who is reluctant or frightened.

Intervene when a child is doing something that is not safe, such as climbing up the slide rather than the ladder.

Review or explain how to do an activity correctly before children try it.

Suggest a new activity that challenges the child to go to the next step on the continuum when he has mastered a skill.

Share a child's pleasure in gaining a new skill by describing the accomplishment.

Respect a child's progress, without making comparisons to other children.

Suggest how to overcome an obstacle or prevent a problem.

Keep track of every child's developing skills.

When you know what each child is capable of doing, you can provide opportunities for children to practice and refine their skills. Children feel good about themselves when they see how competent they are in using their bodies. This feeling of competence will encourage them to try new physical skills, and this feeling will carry over to other areas of development as well.

what's next?

Skill-Building Journal, section **4-7** *(Learning Activity C)* and section **4-1** *(Feedback).*

LEARNING ACTIVITY

Learning Activities

D. Promoting Children's Gross Motor Skills

In this activity you will learn to

- give children cues to use and expand their physical skills

- use skill challenges to encourage children to practice their skills

Maturation plays a primary role in the physical development of very young children. Most infants crawl and eventually stand and walk. Most toddlers walk with increasing ease. During the preschool years, children can learn to use many gross motor skills at a beginning level on their own, if you simply provide enough space for them to move around. For mastery, however, children need some instruction and opportunities to practice new skills.

Offering Cues to Help Children Refine Their Skills[14]

Encourage children as they discover how to make their bodies move.

Most children explore and discover the many ways they can make their bodies move, as they begin to throw, catch, hop, climb, hit an object with a stick, and so on. Encourage children's attempts, allow them to practice their skills, and share their pleasure as skills develop, without interrupting or trying to change their approaches. Of course, you keep safety in mind as children are discovering ways to move. Set clear limits and offer reminders so that they stay safe.

Offering cues helps children practice physical skills successfully.

As children have opportunities to use the skills they are developing, they learn more efficient ways to perform. A way to provide instruction is to offer a cue, that is, a word, phrase, or demonstration that helps children perform a task better than the way they are performing it on their own. Cues provide information that will help children to be successful. For example, Janelle wants to jump far and land without falling. She must learn to bend her knees, swing her arms, and land with both feet at the same time. You provide cues by demonstrating the technique and explaining what you are doing.

Cues help children to be aware of their actions. You can offer cues as demonstrations, as direct statements, or as open-ended questions. By offering cues, you focus children's attention on their actions and make them aware of the component parts. You also help children avoid frustration as they try to refine their skills, and you encourage their independent problem solving.

Teacher Cues to Promote Physical Skills

Running: "Swing your arms and bend your elbows." "Keep your head up."

Skipping: "Lift your knees." "Hop and land on one foot; then hop and land on the other foot."

Galloping: "Keep the same foot forward."

Hopping: "What would happen if you kept your arms out and your knee up?"

Jumping and landing: "Bend your knees and swing your arms." "Land with both feet at the same time." "Keep your balance when you land."

Balancing: "Stand very still." "Tighten your muscles and extend your arms."

Throwing: "Hold your arm way back and step with your opposite foot." "Remember to follow through." "Keep that arm moving."

Catching: "Watch the ball." "Reach for it, grab it, and pull it in."

Kicking: "What would happen if you kicked the ball with your instep, rather than the front of your shoe?"

Dribbling: "Use the pads of your fingers." "Keep your knees bent." "Put your hands on top of the ball."

Offer cues to a child when you think that child is developmentally ready to refine a skill. For example, when you see Jorge jumping and falling with each landing, you might demonstrate an upright landing and explain, "Try it this way and see what happens: Bend your knees and land with both feet at the same time." After observing Jorge's jump, you might add, "If you swing your arms, I'll bet you'll go farther!"

Using Skill Challenges

Children refine their skills through practice. A way to help children increase practice time is to present challenges, such as trying a skill in a different way or suggesting a more difficult goal without changing the activity, itself. For example, if Tony is kicking a ball in a general direction, you might ask if he can kick it toward a target. When Amanda has demonstrated that she can gallop, you could set up an obstacle course for her and the other children to gallop through. If Leo has become a good ball bouncer, you might challenge him by asking, "How many times can you bounce the ball with your right hand?"

By using cues and skill challenges in the activities you plan and conduct regularly for your group, you help children to use their physical skills efficiently and successfully. Success with skills that are typical for 3- to 5-year-olds lays the groundwork for later physical development. Successful experiences encourage children to continue to engage in activities that promote physical fitness. For most healthy adults, physical fitness requires physical activity on a regular basis. You are setting the stage for children to become adults with healthy lifestyles!

what's next?

Skill-Building Journal, section **4-8** *(Learning Activity D)*, section **4-1** *(Feedback),* and section **4-9** *(Reflecting on Your Learning).*

5

Cognitive

Overview

Creating an Environment That Invites Children to Explore and Investigate

Interacting With Children in Ways That Stimulate Thinking and Problem Solving

Providing Opportunities for Children to Learn About Their World

Your Own Experiences With Learning

Learning Activities

A. Using Your Knowledge of Child Development to Promote Cognitive Development

B. Encouraging Children to Explore and Investigate

C. Helping Children Learn About Mathematics

D. Engaging Children in a Study

5.   Cognitive

Overview

Cognitive development refers to the acquisition and use of thinking skills.

Cognitive development is a child's increasing ability to think and reason. Children are active participants in learning processes. They have their own ideas and try to figure out how things work, what they can do, and what will happen if they act. When they learn something new, they are excited and eager to learn more.

Cognitive skills include learning how to learn. Children are curious about what they observe. They ask questions, make predictions about what might happen, and test their ideas. They recall past experiences and apply what they know to new situations in order to understand them. Scientists use the same skills.

Cognitive skills also include mathematical thinking.

Children are also developing mathematical skills. For example, they match one-to-one when they set a table. They sort objects and explain how they classified them: "These are all red, and the other pile has all the blue ones." They compare and use mathematical language: "I have more leaves than you do." "My brother is two, but I'm four, so I'm bigger." Preschool children are interested in measuring: "Which one is heavier?" They can arrange objects in a sequence, e.g., large to small. They can also recognize and repeat patterns, such as stringing beads using red/yellow/blue, red/yellow/blue.

Teachers build on children's interests to promote cognitive development.

Teachers who understand cognitive development take note of children's interests and build on their natural curiosity. They ask open-ended questions and encourage children to think of different ways to do things and solve problems. They plan activities and provide resources so children can find answers to their questions, express what they have learned, and construct deeper understandings about their experiences. When preschool children pretend in their dramatic play and when they build a farm or apartment house with blocks, they are using cognitive skills to recall experiences and represent their ideas with symbols (blocks or other objects).

You can promote children's cognitive development by

- creating an environment that invites children to explore and investigate

- interacting with children in ways that stimulate thinking and problem solving

- providing opportunities for children to learn about their world

---

Creating an Environment That Invites Children to Explore and Investigate

1. **Organize and display toys and materials logically by categories and attributes.** Organize unit blocks by size and shape on a low shelf with labels to show where each one goes; put props in labeled containers.

2. **Provide objects for children to take apart and examine.** Place appliances, like clocks and tape recorders, in the Discovery Area, along with screwdrivers, tweezers, hammers, pliers, and safety goggles.

3. **Offer materials that invite children to sort, classify, and order.** Set out interesting collections of colored bottle caps, beans, buttons, and shells on trays.

4. **Include living things for children to care for and observe.** Choose a class pet, such as a rabbit, gerbil, fish, or guinea pig, and place plants in the classroom and/or an outdoor garden.

5. **Provide tools children can use to explore and investigate.** Supply tools such as magnifying glasses, magnets, shovels, containers, funnels, plastic tubing, binoculars, and flashlights.

6. **Offer materials that encourage children to explore cause and effect and make predictions.** "What will happen when you add water to the sand?"

Ms. Thomas Introduces a Balance Scale

Janelle and Leo have been exploring a new collection of shells in the Discovery Area. They are each holding a large shell. Janelle says, "I bet mine is heavier than yours." Leo shakes his head and says, "Uh, uh. Give it to me so I can see." Taking one shell in each hand, he holds them up, balancing them, and declares, "No, mine is heavier. And it's bigger too. Can't you see?" Ms. Thomas, who has been observing the children, goes to the closet and brings out a balance scale. She says, "I see you noticed the new shells and you are wondering how heavy they are. Leo, you made your hands into a balance scale. That's what this is. Would you like to try weighing the shells on this scale?" Leo puts his shell on one side and Janelle's shell on the other. They all watch the scale swing up and down until the two pans are just about even. Ms. Thomas says, "Wow! Look at that. What happened?" Janelle and Leo exclaim, "They're the same!" "Let's try weighing some other shells," suggests Leo.

Interacting With Children in Ways That Stimulate Thinking and Problem Solving

7. **Show children that you respect their work and ideas.** "I never noticed that before! Our caterpillar only likes certain leaves. You were really looking carefully to make that discovery."

8. **Comment on children's work in ways that introduce new words and encourage them to extend their ideas.** "I see you are fixing your car. Car fixers are called *auto mechanics*. You're an auto mechanic!"

9. **Ask questions to help children understand how past experiences relate to what is happening now.** "Remember the last time we made playdough that was too sticky? How did we solve that problem?"

10. **Point out children's use of logical thinking skills.** "You made a pattern with the beads. You put red/green/yellow, red/green/yellow, all around the necklace."

11. **Encourage children to think of several possible answers or solutions.** "I'm afraid someone might get hurt on that crowded climber. What could we do to make it safer?"

12. **Ask questions that help children think about cause and effect and make predictions.** "Why do you think our plants look so droopy on Monday mornings?"

Ms. Williams Helps the Children Solve a Problem

Ms. Williams is watching three children build a tall tower in the block area. She knows that the building is likely to fall if they add any more blocks, but she can see that no one will get hurt if it does fall. When the building comes crashing down, Ms. Williams quietly goes into the Block Area and kneels down near the children. "I see your building fell down," she says calmly. "Why did that happen?" Terry says, "We made it too tall." Ms. Williams asks, "Do all tall buildings fall down?" "No," says Heather, "this one was too skinny." Ms. Williams then asks, "How could you build a tall building so it won't fall down?" After thinking a minute, Sam responds, "We could make it fatter so it would be stronger." Ms. Williams encourages, "Try that and see what happens!"

Providing Opportunities for Children to Learn About Their World

13. **Set up activities and provide materials that allow children to test their ideas.** Metal, wooden, and plastic objects are displayed on a tray, along with large magnets and an illustrated sign that reads, "What does the magnet pick up?"

14. **Build on children's interests and extend their ideas.** "Look at all the worms you found under that old log! Would you like to keep some in our terrarium so we can learn more about them?"

15. **Help children apply what they have learned to new situations.** "Last week you made purple by mixing red and blue paint together. What color would you add to blue to make green?"

16. **Provide books and other resources so children can search for answers to their questions.** Two books on caterpillars are displayed on a table holding a terrarium with the caterpillars the children have found on their playground.

17. **Plan studies on topics that interest children, are worth investigating, and engage them in research.** Last year, with a building site across from the school, the children studied construction. This year, a study on firefighters interested the children.

18. **Take trips and walks to extend children's understandings about the world.** "Let's see how many different kinds of leaves and seeds we can find on our walk today."

Ms. Kim Helps the Children Answer Their Own Questions

example

Marcus and Maria are examining the worms they collected on the playground. Marcus says, "I'll get the magnifying glass so we can see better." Ms. Kim comes over. "What do you see?" she asks. "They move funny," Marcus responds. "First they scrunch together and make themselves small. Then they get long and move. Then they scrunch small again." Ms. Kim watches the worms and says, "Look at that. You discovered something very interesting about how worms move." Maria exclaims, "I can't see their eyes! How do they know where they're going?" Ms. Kim responds, "That's a good question, Maria." Marcus looks more closely with his magnifying glass and says, "I don't see any eyes either." Ms. Kim brings out a library book about worms. "I wonder if we can find out more about worms in this book," she says. "If not, we can look on the Internet."

---

what's next?

Skill-Building Journal, section **5-2** *(Overview)*, section **5-10** *(Answer Sheets)*, and section **5-1** *(Feedback)*.

Your Own Experiences With Learning

People are capable of learning throughout their lives.

Confident learners generally have some of these characteristics:

- They enjoy a challenge and speak up about what they think.

- When they confront a problem, they don't give up if they can't solve it right away. They try to figure out what to do.

- They are curious and interested in learning new things.

- They are creative thinkers; they can see several possibilities.

People learn in different ways.

People have different styles or ways of learning that are best for them. Some people need to read directions and think about them for a while. Others prefer to watch someone demonstrate a task or need to hear directions several times.

Many factors affect a person's ability to learn something new. If you know you will use the information, you are more likely to make the effort to learn it. You are probably most interested when the new information is related to something you already know or to something you've wanted to know for some time. Other factors affect a person's ability to learn: how the information is presented, how it is organized, and whether it is at an appropriate level. If you are tired, distracted, or unsure of what is expected, learning is more difficult.

This training program is designed for different kinds of learners.

This training program is designed to help you increase your skills:

- Learning activities are short and focused.

- All the learning activities relate to your work.

- Examples in each module help you understand the content.

- You complete many activities while caring for children.

- You can get feedback along the way.

- Your *Skill-Building Journal* is an ongoing reference tool.

As you enhance your skills and understanding, you will become a more confident teacher. In each of the 13 modules, you will try many ideas and discover for yourself what approaches work best for you and for the children in your care.

what's next?

Skill-Building Journal, section **5-3** *(Your Own Experiences With Learning)*, section **5-1** *(Feedback)*, and section **5-4** *(Pre-Training Assessment)*.

Learning Activities

LEARNING ACTIVITY

A. Using Your Knowledge of Child Development to Promote Cognitive Development

In this activity you will learn to

- recognize some typical behaviors of preschool children that are related to cognitive development

- use what you know about child development to promote children's thinking and problem-solving skills

Have you ever wondered why preschool children ask so many questions? It's because they are curious about the world and eager to make sense of what they experience. They believe there is a purpose and explanation for everything, and they come up with their own ideas to explain what they observe.

- Carlos (age 3) points to the goosebumps on his arm on a cold day and asks Ms. Richards, "What are these bumps?"

- Aimee (age 4) notices her plant is drooping and asks Mr. Lopez, "Why isn't it standing up like the other ones?"

- Oanh (age 5) looks intently at the fish swimming in the tank. She asks Ms. Williams, "Do the fish ever sleep?"

Preschool children are scientists and mathematicians.

Preschool children not only ask questions, but they want to find answers to their questions. They are scientists and mathematicians as well as storytellers and artists. They use scientific skills when they ask questions, explore and take things apart, try ideas to see what happens, and guess what will happen next. Like scientists, preschool children wonder about things and make predictions: "If I put one more block on top of my tower, I think it's going to fall down." Then they want to test their ideas to find out what happens. Preschool children are able to recall past experiences and apply what they know to new situations. For example, they may remember that, if the playdough is too sticky, they can add more flour to fix it.

Preschool children are interested in mathematical concepts. They make comparisons, trying to figure out who has more and who has less. They sort their toys into categories, as when putting all the cars in one basin and all the animals in another. When they have snacks to share, they are able to figure out how many each child should receive. They use numbers to count the milk cartons that were delivered.

Children make sense of information by focusing on one feature of an object at a time.

Young children do not necessarily judge things by what is logical to an adult. They may think that a tall, thin glass holds more water than a short, wide one, even when they see the identical amount of water poured from one glass to the other. At this stage of thinking, children tend to focus on one feature of an object at a time: in this case, the height of the glass and not its width. You may have noticed that the children in your class like to break up their crackers at snack time. Lots of small pieces, they reason, are more than one large piece.

As they gain experience handling objects and experimenting with materials, children come to understand that the amount of water in both glasses is the same no matter how it looks. This understanding comes when children are capable of thinking more abstractly and when they have had many direct experiences exploring water and other liquids. Young children grow cognitively as they play with real objects and materials and when adults talk with them about their experiences.

One of the joys of teaching young children is the funny things they sometimes say. When you understand how preschool children think and how hard they work to understand the world around them, you will gain new respect for their ideas, even if what they say is not logical.

Preschool children are literal thinkers.

Typically, young children don't realize that a word can have different meanings depending on how it is used. Because preschool children are still learning multiple meanings, they can get confused.

- A 3-year-old told her mother, "We went on a walk at school today. We were looking for signs of winter, but all I saw was one *stop* sign."

- A teacher put on a tape and told the children to "move to the music," meaning "move your bodies as the music makes you feel." The children got up and moved over to the tape player.

These children took the words they heard literally. They had a different understanding of what the words meant from the meaning that the adult intended. While adults find such mistakes amusing, it is important to respond in ways that respect children's efforts to learn.

- "The word *sign* has several meanings. I think your teacher was saying, 'What can we see that tells us spring is coming, like buds on the trees?' We call these *signs of spring*."

- "You did just what I asked you to do. Now try listening to the music and see how it makes you want to move your arms and legs and bodies."

Preschool children make connections to explain things, and they are not always right.

Preschool children are interested in cause and effect. They make a connection between what they observe and what they have experienced in the past. Sometimes they put ideas together that are not related.

- "Today we are having fish for lunch because the teacher is late. Whenever the teacher is late, we have fish."

- A 4-year-old noticed that a friend didn't want ice cream for dessert. Later that night, the friend got sick. The next day, when offered ice cream, the child said, "Yes, because, if I don't have ice cream, I'll get sick too."

- "Thunder makes it rain."

Even though these children were not correct in their conclusions, they were recalling past experiences and making connections to try to understand and predict events in their lives.

Preschool children can be egocentric.

Young children also tend to be egocentric. They believe that your thoughts are just like theirs. This doesn't mean they are selfish or focused only on themselves. It means that they have trouble understanding that each person is unique and has different thoughts and feelings.

- A 3-year-old with a toothache was asked if his tooth hurt. "Yes," he replied, "Can't you feel it?"

- "Don't you know that?" children will ask in surprise, as if everyone should know what they know!

Listening to what children say is an excellent way to learn how they think and attempt to make sense of their world. Children teach us a lot about what they understand and what they are ready to learn.

Promoting children's cognitive development means planning appropriate experiences and responding to what children do and say based on what you know about developmental characteristics.

Developmental Characteristics of Preschool Children

Preschool children typically

- use all their senses—smell, taste, touch, sight, and hearing—to explore and investigate

- are curious and want to explore what is around them

- like to gather information about the world

- are interested in cause and effect (what makes things happen)

- can talk about what they are doing and explain their ideas

- gain deeper understandings by representing what they've learned through drawing, constructing, and dramatic play

- believe there is a purpose for everything and ask many questions: What? Why? How?

- construct understandings by making connections between new experiences and ideas and what they already know

- develop an understanding of mathematical concepts by playing with and talking about real objects

- can match, sort, classify, and compare objects

Development: It's All Connected

Children's cognitive development is related to their physical, social, emotional, and language development. Examples follow.

Physical

As preschool children develop increasing control over their small muscles, they can manipulate objects more purposefully to sort, group, and organize them. They can use tools, such as tweezers, magnifying glasses, and magnets, to investigate and make discoveries. They can also paint and draw pictures and build structures to show what they have learned and to reach deeper understanding of their experiences.

Emotional

Preschool children often call attention to what they have done or created. They seek approval from adults. As they gain confidence in their abilities, they are more likely to express their ideas, to explore, and to make discoveries on their own.

Social

Preschool children are increasingly able to cooperate with others to complete a task, whether it's agreeing on a scene for dramatic play, sorting objects, or solving a problem. They understand the concept of taking turns, although they are not always able to do so. They can also participate in group activities, sharing ideas and listening to what others have to say.

Language

During the preschool years, children expand their vocabularies and can engage in extended conversations with others. Their verbal abilities enable them to talk about people and objects that are not present, and both past and future events. They can use words to solve problems, ask and answer questions, and describe their discoveries.

what's next?

Skill-Building Journal, section **5-5** *(Learning Activity A),* section **5-10** *(Answer Sheets),* and section **5-1** *(Feedback).*

Learning Activities

LEARNING ACTIVITY

B. Encouraging Children to Explore and Investigate

In this activity you will learn to

- encourage children's natural interest in exploring and investigating

- ask questions that encourage children to observe carefully, solve problems, and think for themselves

Young children are active explorers and investigators.

From birth, young children are interested in what they see, hear, smell, taste, and touch in the world around them. They explore and investigate to learn about everything that crosses their paths. By the time they are preschool-aged, they have become much more purposeful about what they do and what they want to find out. They wonder and ask questions.

- "Where did the puddle go?"

- "How do the roots know to grow down?"

- "Do the fish sleep drink the water?"

- "How can I make my truck go faster down the ramp?"

- "What is that thing that's flying around?"

- "How does the water get hard into ice cubes?"

Children and teachers ask questions.

Different types of questions need different types of answers. Sometimes a simple answer is all that is required: "That's a worm." Other times you can use questions to encourage children to find their own answers: "How could we find out what worms like to eat?" Children might suggest trying different kinds of food to see what worms like best, getting a book about worms, or even looking at a Web site on the Internet. If they don't have these ideas, you might suggest one and help children do their own research.

Children are not the only ones who ask questions. Teachers do as well, but for different purposes. Teachers ask questions to find out what children know and to encourage children to think and talk about their ideas. It's important to understand what kind of questions to ask children to promote cognitive development.

Teachers ask open-ended questions to help children learn.

Open-ended questions can be answered in many different ways. Closed questions have one right answer. For example, if you ask the children the open-ended question, "What did you discover the magnet will pick up?," you will get a variety of responses. If you ask the closed question, "Will the magnet pick up these paper clips?," the children will answer either *yes* or *no*. They will not have to stretch their thinking to recall much about the topic in order to respond.

Because there are many possible responses, open-ended questions help children to think and build on what they already know. Answering open-ended questions requires thinking and imagination, so you learn much more about children's understanding from their answers. With practice, you can become very good at asking children open-ended questions that encourage them to think.

To answer open-ended questions children have to

- recall a past event: "What happened last time when ...?" "Do you remember when . . .?"

- explore cause and effect: "Why do you think that happened?"

- express their ideas: "Can you tell me more about that?" "Why did you decide to do it that way?"

- make a prediction: "What do you think will happen if you...?" "What do you think will happen next?"

- think of several possibilities: "What other ways can you ...?" "How many different ways could you. . .?"

- interpret what someone did: "Why did he do that?"

Teachers can encourage children to answer their own questions.

In their investigations, preschool children try to figure out why things happen.

Five-year-old Mark noticed that the water level in the fish tank had gone down. He said to Ms. Frilles, "We have to put more water in the fish tank because the fish are drinking the water!" Ms. Frilles could have explained to Mark about evaporation. Instead, she asked open-ended questions and suggested a way for him to find out for himself what really caused the water to go down.

- "What makes you think the fish are drinking the water?"

- "You mean, if we put out a bowl of water without any fish, the water wouldn't get lower? Let's try it and see what happens."

Next, Mark observed that the water level also dropped in the bowl without fish. Noting that other children became interested in Mark's scientific experiment, Ms. Frilles planned some activities so the children could learn more about the concept of evaporation. They painted with water on a chalkboard and watched the water disappear. They took a walk after a rain shower, made circles around the puddles with chalk, and noted that the puddles disappeared soon after the sun came out.

The more you encourage children to notice what happens, the more they will want to explore and investigate. They start making predictions: "What might happen if . . .?" or "What might happen next . . . ?" They can apply what they have learned about cause and effect to new situations.

Children construct an understanding of information as they explore and investigate.

When children discover something that interests them, like a caterpillar crawling along a leaf, it's not enough for them just to look it. They want to touch it, pick it up, examine it closely, and even smell it. By using all of their senses, young children develop new understandings about caterpillars. When you say the word *caterpillar*, children learn a label for something they have explored firsthand. Another day, when they see a worm, the same children may say, "Look at that caterpillar!" This is because they have noticed that a worm and a caterpillar have many characteristics in common. Although they are not actually correct, they are applying their new understanding to a similar situation and striving to make sense of it.

As their knowledge increases, children test their ideas and make discoveries. In so doing, they re-examine their previous ideas. Sometimes their experiences reinforce what they already know, and sometimes they change their ideas, like the child who thought the fish were drinking the water. In the process, children are building a clearer and (usually) more accurate understanding of their world and how things work.

Children learn from each other as well as from adults.

Children also learn from each other. Listen to two or more children playing with water, building with blocks, finger painting, or engaging in dramatic play. They talk about what they are doing, share information, give each other advice, and correct one another. All learning doesn't come from the teacher.

Four-year-old Leo watches Janelle at the sand table scooping up sand and pouring it to make a sand wheel spin. Later that day, while playing at the sand table, Leo gets the same scoop and dumps the sand into the top of the sand wheel, but nothing happens. He tries more sand, but it just piles up in the opening and the wheel doesn't move. Then he notices that the sand he scooped up is wet and sticks together. He dumps the wet sand out, scoops up some dry sand, and grins as the wheel begins to spin.

Leo observed how another child was able to make the sand wheel turn. He remembered what he had seen and applied what he thought. When it didn't work, he had to figure out what was wrong and try another approach. His first idea—adding more sand—didn't work. His next idea—trying dry sand—did work. Thus, Leo constructed his own understanding of how to make the sand wheel work. Because he figured it out himself, he will be more likely to remember what he learned. Even more important, he is gaining confidence in himself as a learner.

Preschool children can learn an endless number of concepts. As important as what they learn, however, is whether they are learning how to learn. Children who are encouraged to explore and make discoveries on their own become self-confident learners who want to learn more.

what's next?

Skill-Building Journal, section **5-6** *(Learning Activity B)* and section **5-1** *(Feedback).*

Learning Activities

C. Helping Children Learn About Mathematics

In this activity you will learn to

- identify the important math content areas and skills preschool children can learn

- provide opportunities for children to use mathematical thinking skills every day

Mathematics is a way of thinking about and organizing information. It involves finding order, quantifying, comparing objects, recognizing patterns, seeing relationships, making predictions, and solving problems. It uses a special language: *more, less, equal, the same,* and so on. You often hear children using math concepts and language.

- "He has more cars than I do."

- "I can run faster than you."

- "We have the same."

- "I'm four."

Standards developed by the National Council of Teachers of Mathematics, identify five content areas of mathematics in which preschool children should learn.[15] They recommend that children have opportunities to explore number concepts, patterns and relationships, geometry, measurement, and collecting and organizing information. As they explore this math content, preschool children should be solving problems, reasoning, communicating, making connections, and representing what they are thinking. This may seem like a lot for preschool teachers to address, but you'll soon see how to provide these experiences every day in your classroom.

Understanding number concepts involves being able to count and know what each number means.

Understanding numbers involves learning about symbols and number names. When children use real objects, they learn that, for example, a group of three items can be represented by the symbol 3. They learn that ✳ ✳ and Δ Δ can be labeled 2. Have children compare groups of objects and use terms like *more than, bigger than, less than,* and *the same as.* Use numbers daily to help children gain understanding: "I need two helpers for this job: Leo is one, and Janelle is two." Through these experiences, children eventually learn the value of each number: a group of three objects has one more than a group of two and one less than a group of four.

In addition to learning number names, children learn the counting order of numbers. You may have heard a child count proudly, "1, 2, 7, 5, 8, 9, 10." This is a first step. Many songs and finger plays—such as "1-2-3-4-5, I caught a fish alive; 6-7-8-9-10, I threw him back again"—teach children the names and correct order of numbers.

When children count real things, they learn that each number can be matched with something.

Another concept children need in order to understand numbers is *one-to-one correspondence*. The child might count much faster than she can point to objects, or say more than one number as she touches an object. When children set the table, placing a napkin and plate at each chair, they are practicing one-to-one correspondence. When you show a child how you touch each item as you say a number, you are teaching how counting and number operations work.

Finding patterns and relationships is part of all mathematical thinking.

Patterns are regular arrangements that are repeated. There are many different kinds of patterns:

- colors: red/yellow/blue, red/yellow/blue

- shapes: circle/square, circle/square

- sounds: clapping a beat such as loud/loud/quiet, loud/loud/quiet

- size: big/little/little, big/little/little

- seasons: fall/winter/spring/summer, fall/winter/spring/summer

Call children's attention to different kinds of patterns.

Preschool children need many opportunities to notice and talk about the characteristics of different objects; to recognize, create, and copy patterns; and to use language to describe and compare relationships. Every classroom should have materials such as shape blocks of different colors and sizes, pegboards and pegs, colored cubes, colored beads, and nesting cups.

As children play with these materials, you guide their learning. You can challenge children by asking questions to further their thinking and learning. Here are some examples:

- "Can you find another square that is bigger than this one?"

- "How are these two buttons the same? How are they different?"

- "You made a pattern with your beads: red/yellow, red/yellow. What color comes next?"

Geometric shapes are everywhere in a preschool classroom and outdoors.

Children explore geometry and spatial sense when they play with different shapes. They learn shape names and how to describe their characteristics. Unit blocks are available in squares, rectangles, triangles, and cylinders. When you organize them on the shelf according to size and shape, children become aware of their characteristics by selecting, using, and returning each block to its appropriate place. If you use shape names as children play with blocks, children will learn what each shape is called. You might say, "Let's put away all the square blocks first," or "It looks like you need a long rectangular block to finish your road."

The toys and games area should include small wooden shapes of different sizes that children can use to build and sort and make patterns. You can help children learn the similarities and differences between shapes. For example, show them a square and another kind of rectangle and ask, "How are these shapes the same? How are they different?"

Help children explore the characteristics of shapes and their many uses.

Outside, you might point out how tree branches form triangles. You can ask children to compare the shapes of STOP signs and YIELD signs. You can also tell children that windows are usually rectangles and ask them to find other rectangles as you take a walk.

Of course, naming shapes is not enough. Children need opportunities to handle and manipulate three-dimensional shapes. They develop spatial sense when they have many experiences noticing and talking about where things are located in relation to others. As they use materials and explore spaces with their bodies, you can use words to describe their positions in space: *on, off, under, over, on top of, behind, below, near, far, next to, up, down, around.*

Measurement includes ideas about height, age, weight, amount, and speed.

Children often use the language of measurement: *taller, older, bigger, longer, heavier,* and *faster.* They learn about measurement by using non-standard measures before ever using standard ones like rulers, tape measures, scales, and thermometers. They might, for example, measure the length of the table using a shoe. They can use a piece of string to measure the size of a pumpkin. You should also introduce standard measuring tools for children to explore and use in their play and investigations. Have a variety of measuring tools for children to use

- to measure length: rulers, yardsticks, tape measures

- to measure volume: measuring cups and spoons

- to measure weight: balance scale, digital scale

- to measure time: sand timer, clock, timer

As always, your interest in what children are doing and your involvement in their explorations and play will encourage them to stretch their thinking and learn.

- "What a long snake you made with the playdough. How could you make one that is longer than this one? How could you make one that is shorter?"

- "I wonder how many yardsticks it would take if we lined them up across our floor. How could we find out?"

Children love to collect and organize things when they have a reason to keep records.

Collecting information and organizing it logically is part of mathematical thinking. When children sort, classify, make graphs, and compare, they are developing very important cognitive skills. Collections of objects—keys, buttons, seeds and pits, shells, leaves, and plastic bottle caps—are ideal materials. As children explore them, you can challenge their thinking by posing questions:

- "What do you notice about this collection of keys?"

- "What different groups could we make with these bottle caps?"

- "You sorted the buttons by color. What other groups can you make?"

- "How are all the shapes in this group alike?"

- "How are these two shells the same? How are they different?"

After sorting and classifying a collection of objects, the next step is for children to compare what they have. You might ask, "What do you notice about the different groups you made? Which one has more? How could we find out?" A concrete way for children to answer this question is to line the objects up in a three-dimensional graph. You can start with empty egg cartons so children can put one object in each hole and then compare which row of objects is longer. Making a grid with masking tape is another way to give children a structure for comparing groups.

You can provide children with opportunities every day to use mathematical thinking to solve problems and complete tasks.

what's next?

Skill-Building Journal, section *5-7 (Learning Activity C)* and section *5-1 (Feedback).*

Learning Activities

D. Engaging Children in a Study

In this activity you will learn to

- identify appropriate topics for children to study over a period of time

- involve children in investigating a topic and finding answers to their questions

A study is an in-depth investigation of a topic that interests children enough to want to learn more. It is much richer than a theme or a unit. It is a project that can be conducted over many weeks or even months. Katz and Helm describe the term *project approach* as

> *...an in-depth investigation of a topic worth learning more about... The key feature of a project is that it is a research effort deliberately focused on finding answers to questions about a topic posed by the children, the teachers, or the teacher working with the children.*[16]

Planning a Study

The first step in planning a study is to identify a good topic. The most successful topics grow out of the children's interests and what is occurring in their own community. For example, children living in a fishing village in Alaska might learn about different kinds of fish; children in a city might investigate different stores in the neighborhood, and children in a rural area might explore the operation of a farm. Some topics interest children everywhere, like a study about different kinds of balls or a study about water.

Select a topic that will interest your children.

An appropriate topic matches the developmental abilities and interests of the children. Three-year-olds are primarily interested in themselves and their families. Four-year-olds want to know about other children and their neighborhoods. Five-year-olds typically ask questions about how things are made, who does what jobs, and how things work.

In selecting a good topic, ask yourself the following questions:

- Does the topic reflect children's interests?

- Is the topic relevant to children's experiences and appropriate for preschool children?

- Will children have questions about the topic?

- Can children explore the topic firsthand to find answers to their questions?

- Are resources available, such as people to talk with, places to visit, objects or living things to observe and explore, and books to read?

- Can the topic be explored in a variety of ways over an extended period?

- Does the topic connect to your curriculum goals and objectives?

- Will it address content standards?

- Is the topic worth investigating?

Sometimes a topic emerges quite unexpectedly.

Ms. Kim reads aloud the story, *Something Good*, by Robert Munsch, which takes place in a grocery store. The children love the story and ask to hear it again and again. She notices that the children are playing grocery store in the dramatic play area. Ms. Richards adds some empty food containers, and their play becomes more complex. At their next planning meeting, the teachers consider that a study of a grocery store might interest the children and offer many opportunities for learning. To identify all the possible important ideas this study could help children learn about, they make a web.

Make a web to identify what children can learn.

Webbing a topic is best accomplished as a brainstorming activity that involves several colleagues and, later, the children. Start with a large sheet of paper. Write the name of the topic in the middle. Then try to think of all the possible "big ideas" that could be explored. On the topic of a grocery store, your web might look like the image that follows.

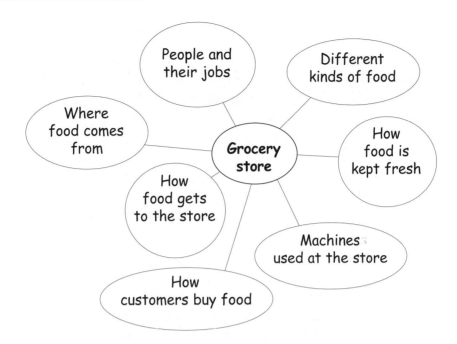

To help you come up with ideas, look at children's books on the topic. A children's librarian can help you find relevant books. Gather pictures, books, and other items related to the topic so children can begin to investigate. Parents can be excellent resources and may, in fact, be experts on the topic. Involving family members in a study is a wonderful way to enrich children's experiences.

Find out what children know about the topic.

At group time, talk with the children to find out what they know about the topic and their level of interest. On the topic of a grocery store, children might raise questions such as the following:

- From where does the food come?

- Why don't the fruits and vegetables rot in the grocery store?

- Who puts the food on the shelves?

- What are the striped lines (bar codes) on the boxes?

- Why does the door open when you walk in front of it?

- How much does food cost?

Make a web with the children, recording their questions and ideas. This web should remain in a meeting area where you and the children can refer to it and add their new ideas as they investigate the topic.

Finally, confirm for yourself that the topic will enable you to address content in a meaningful way.

A Study of the Grocery Store

Content Area	How a Study of the Grocery Store Addresses Content
Literacy	Read books about food and the grocery store. Add empty containers of familiar products to Dramatic Play. Add supermarket ads and coupons to Dramatic Play. Make up, write down, and read an advertising jingle. Add paper and writing tools for creating signs and shopping lists. Learn new vocabulary words about the grocery store (names of foods, workers, equipment).
Math	Use scales to weigh fruits and vegetables. Count foods to be purchased. Use numbers on signs and products. Use measurement terms (pound, ounce). Use play money to purchase groceries. Sort and classify groceries.
Science	Take apart an old scale to see how it works. Grow real vegetables for the class store. Find out where food comes from. Sort healthy foods from junk food. Find out what happens if food is not refrigerated.
Social Studies	Taste various ethnic foods. Learn about the different jobs in the store. Draw a map of a grocery store. Find out the "rules" in a grocery store (standing in line, express lane). Find out how people with little money buy food.
The Arts	Use clay to create fruits and vegetables for the store. Create a display of products. Use newsprint to create advertising. Draw posters to hang in the store. Play soft music in the background. Sing songs about healthy foods.
Technology	Learn how the grocery store uses technology to make work easier (conveyer belts, fork lifts, scanner, bar codes, microphones). Use the computer to create signs for the grocery store. Take digital photos of food products for signs, coupons, advertising.

Exploring the Topic With Children

Knowing children learn best when they can actively question, explore, and research the answers to their questions, you want to offer a variety of ways for children to investigate the topic. Investigative experiences can take many forms. Children investigate when they

- pose questions
- visit a relevant site
- look at pictures
- have discussions
- explore materials

- create experiments
- examine and use objects
- observe objects and events
- listen to and ask questions of experts

The experiences you plan will vary according to the topic. A grocery store study might involve several trips to a neighborhood store, taking photographs to bring back to the classroom, interviews with the people who work there, looking through books, and creating a store in the classroom. For a study about caterpillars and butterflies, investigation might involve collecting caterpillars, finding out what kind of environment they need and what they eat, making an appropriate caterpillar or butterfly home in the classroom, observing them closely over time, taking a trip to a nature center to see an exhibition, talking to experts, and taking photos of how the insects change.

Children's cognitive skills grow when they make representations and talk about the topic of study.

Children need a variety of opportunities to increase their understanding of new information. When they learn something new and then describe it in their own words, draw a picture of it, build a model, or act it out, they make sense of their experiences. As they represent their ideas in drawings, block structures, or other models, they reach higher levels of thinking and show their current levels of understanding of the material.

Some materials children can use to document and represent what they are learning about a topic include

- unit and hollow blocks
- markers, crayons, pencils, and paper
- tempera paint and water colors
- clay and playdough

- collage materials
- journals
- cartons and boxes

In dramatic play, children take on different roles, create imaginary settings and situations, use relevant props, dress up, interact with others, and recall sequences of events. For example, children could set up a grocery store in the classroom after visiting one and interviewing the people who work there. This would involve creating or obtaining the appropriate props, deciding who will take different roles, and arranging for "customers" to come and purchase food.

When you plan a study that engages children's interest, they come up with new ideas and questions about the topic. This often leads to new investigations and the desire to represent what they have discovered. You have to be a good observer and be willing to change plans, add new props and materials, and follow children in new directions. Children and teachers become co-constructors of understanding.

Concluding a Study

Some studies last for more than a month; others might last just a few weeks. The length of a study depends on how involved children become and the variety and depth of experiences and materials you can offer children as they explore the topic.

When considerable time is spent on a study, it is important to identify how children can document what they are learning and ways they can share their understanding with others. Depending on the study, there might be graphs to make, murals to paint, or a group book to produce.

It's also important to think about how this documentation might be used as part of closing activities for a study. Closing activities might be making a class book of drawings and photographs on the topic, displaying the children's projects and artwork, or presenting a play to family members. Closing activities give children a chance to share what they have learned and feel pride in their accomplishments.

what's next?

Skill-Building Journal, section **5-8** *(Learning Activity D)*, section **5-1** *(Feedback)*, and section **5-9** *(Reflecting on Your Learning)*.

6

Communication

Overview

Reading Aloud and Talking With Children About Books, Ideas, and Experiences

Helping Children Focus on the Sounds and Structure of Language

Making Connections Between Speech and Print

Your Own Experiences With Communication

Learning Activities

A. Using Your Knowledge of Child Development to Support Language Development

B. Creating a Literacy-Rich Environment

C. Encouraging Children to Listen and Speak

D. Reading Aloud and Talking About Books

6. Communication

The first five years are prime times for language development.

Communication is the sharing of ideas and feelings with others. People communicate in many ways, through gestures, facial expressions, touch, pictures, speech, and writing. They communicate to think, plan, solve problems, figure out what others think and feel, and build relationships with others. Effective verbal communication involves listening, speaking, reading, and writing.

Preschool children can learn a lot about reading.

Language skills are most easily acquired during the first five years of life. Children understand and respond to language before they can speak. By interacting with adults who listen to and talk with them, they learn to understand and say thousands of words and make sense of the rules for using words. By preschool age, children converse, talk about the past and future, and tell stories.

Adults can nurture children's use and enjoyment of language. From shared experiences with oral and written language, children learn that speech and writing are related but different. They learn the letters of the alphabet, recognize rhymes, understand how stories are told, and discover how books work.

Reading and writing go together.

Young children scribble on paper and tell another person what they wrote, showing that they have understandings about reading and writing. Soon their scribbling begins to look like letters and words. When writing tools and paper are readily available, and children's names and the alphabet are prominently displayed, children are inspired to write for many purposes. They make signs for their buildings, sign their artwork, and write notes to friends. This happens when teachers purposefully create a literacy-rich environment and plan experiences and activities to encourage these important skills.

You can promote children's communication skills by

- reading aloud and talking with children about books and a wide range of ideas and experiences

- helping children focus on the sounds and structure of language

- offering an environment that encourages children to make connections and understand the differences between speech and print

Reading Aloud and Talking With Children About Books, Ideas, and Experiences

1. **Read aloud daily at story time and in response to children's requests.** Introduce children to many kinds of texts and purposes for reading and writing, including stories, poems, lists, letters, and informational books.

2. **Invite children to participate during read-aloud sessions.** Pause so children can join in with repeated phrases and rhymes. Ask questions that help children recall the plot of a familiar story or predict what might happen next: "Do you remember what happened after the rainbow fish learned to share?"

3. **Provide opportunities for children to deepen their understanding of stories and topics.** Offer props, dress-up items, and puppets so children can retell a story, make up a new ending, or incorporate characters in their play. Relate books to children's own experiences: "Your doll's quilt looks like one of the quilts in *Tar Beach*."

4. **Offer materials for making books about concepts, topics, and events that are important to children.** Encourage children to share the books they make. "Let's listen to Bonnie read her book about the day we made pretzels."

5. **Encourage family reading and writing times.** Set up a lending library so every family has access to books. Secure materials and services from libraries and book distribution programs, share tips for reading aloud and talking about books, and distribute paper and writing tools.

Ms. Williams Invites the Children to Participate

A small group of children sits facing Ms. Williams, eagerly awaiting a story. She shows the cover of the book and asks, "Who's that?" "Minerva Louise!" shout the children.[17] "It sure is," agrees Ms. Williams. "She's holding a pencil in her beak. I wonder what she's going to do in this story." These 3-year-olds have heard several stories about this fluffy white chicken. Sara says, "She will be silly." Several children nod their heads in agreement. Ms. Williams reads the first page, then pauses so the children can examine the picture. After reading the second and third pages, she points to a red building in the picture and asks, "Where do you think she is going?" Several children predict at once, "It's a school. She's going to school." Ms. Williams continues the story, stopping often to invite the children to comment on Minerva Louise's many mistakes. "Those aren't nesting boxes;" observes Janelle, "They're cubbies. We have cubbies." When Ms. Williams finishes the story, she closes the book. Several children say, "Read it again, please." "Okay," Ms. Williams agrees, "and this time you can read with me."

Helping Children Focus on the Sounds and Structure of Language

6. **Learn a few words, songs, chants, and rhymes in the children's home languages.** Support children's language and literacy skills in their home language as you help them learn English. "¡Buen (What a good idea!), Selena! Your pipe-cleaner people are just the right size to sit in the car."

7. **Read aloud books with rhymes, repetition, and silly words.** Pause often so children can say the next sentence or make up their own rhymes.

8. **Teach children short poems, chants, rhymes, and finger plays.** Invite children to join in during transitions and activities. Add a personal touch by including a child's name: "This is the way Jack cleans the brushes, cleans the brushes, cleans the brushes!"

9. **Accept every child's way of speaking, while modeling conversational skills and standard language.** If a child says "I throwed the ball," the teacher would say, "Yes, you threw the ball a long way."

10. **Plan activities that focus on the sounds of letters and words.** "Yesterday we thought of sounds and words that rhyme with cat. Today, let's think of words that start with *ch*, like *chicken* and *Charlie*."

Ms. Kim and the Children Make Up a New Song

When Ms. Kim asks, "What would you like to sing today?" several children make suggestions. "The teapot song." "B-I-N-G-O." "Roll Over." "What good ideas!" she exclaims. "Let's start with Bingo." After singing the song twice, Ms. Kim invites the children to make up a new song. "Suppose the farmer were a teacher and she had a different kind of pet." "There was a teacher had a . . . " She pauses to see what the children suggest. "Kitten," says Luis. "We have a kitten." "There was a teacher had a kitten . . . ," sings Ms. Kim along with a few children. Now who can think of a name that rhymes with Bingo?" "I know, I know," says Deanne, "Ringo. My friend's cat is called Ringo. She has stripes round her tail." Ms. Kim leads the children in song, "There was a teacher had a kitten, and Ringo was her name-o. R-I-N-G-O, R-I-N-G-O, R-I-N-G-O, and Ringo was her name-o."

Making Connections Between Speech and Print

11. **Provide a print-rich environment that shows how written language is used to communicate.** Post labels and signs; create a word wall with children's names and familiar words and sounds; provide alphabet books and charts; put books, paper, and writing tools in each interest area.

12. **Create comfortable, well-stocked library and writing areas.** "Carlos, if you want to read another *Clifford* book, look for his picture on the cover and the letter *C*, as in the beginning of your name."

13. **Post charts and lists with words and pictures that ask children to provide and organize information.** Children can write their names on sign-in lists, on a chart of snack choices, and on the classroom job chart.

14. **Encourage children to communicate ideas and requests through pictures and writing.** Provide writing tools, paper, envelopes, and mailboxes; write children's dictated stories; invite them to read their writing aloud.

15. **Show children how adults use reading and writing.** Read aloud a note to or from home; invite children to help write a shopping list for snack supplies; talk about what you are doing: "Let's see what it says in the instruction book that came with our new computer program. 'Step One: Click on the menu bar.'"

16. **Select and display a variety of books.** Include some in children's home languages and books that reflect children's abilities, interests, cultures, and families. Consult observation notes, families, and librarians when choosing books. Keep favorites on hand and update the collection regularly.

example

Mr. Lopez and Ms. Nolan Encourage Story Writing

"Welcome back!" says Mr. Lopez as Kara, Avida, and Ms. Nolan, an intern from the community college, return from a walk. "What did you see?" "We saw a big bird!" Grace tells him. "And a nest," Kara adds. "The bird was flying around and then it sat on its nest," Avida explains. Mr. Lopez suggests they write about what they saw. Kara and Avida get paper and markers from the shelf and begin to draw and write. Ms. Nolan asks, "What do you want to say?" "That's the bird," Kara says while pointing to a picture and two letters, B and R. "It says bird." "Tell me more about the bird you saw," says Ms. Nolan, "and I'll write down what you say." "The bird had big wings," Kara dictates. "It sat on its nest in a tree," Avida adds. Ms. Nolan writes their words and then invites the girls to read them with her.

what's next?

Skill-Building Journal, section **6-2** *(Overview)*, section **6-10** *(Answer Sheets)*, and section **6-1** *(Feedback)*.

Your Own Experiences With Communication

We use language skills all day, every day.

Communication requires listening, talking, reading, and writing well enough to send and receive messages. As lifelong learners, we use communication skills to increase our knowledge and understanding of the world, do our jobs, and explore special interests. We send and receive messages orally (using words and tone of voice), nonverbally (facial expressions and gestures), and in writing. You use language skills all day, every day, on and off the job. On a typical morning, you might

- *listen* to the voice of a radio announcer giving today's weather report

- *talk* with family members about what is happening that day

- *read* the instructions on a box of oatmeal to learn how to cook it in the microwave

- *write* a note to your trainer saying you are ready to discuss a learning activity

It is important to send clear messages.

To send clear verbal messages, it is important to say what you mean. If you want someone to help you choose books, you might say, "I'd like to order some new informational books. Will you help choose the titles?" An unclear message could be misinterpreted. For example, asking, "Do you think we have enough informational books for our group?" might not encourage anyone to help choose titles because you did not directly request help. You also need to pay attention to your nonverbal communications. Make sure your body language matches your message.

Communication also involves receiving and interpreting messages from other people. Listen carefully to the sender's words and note nonverbal cues. To make sure you understand a message correctly, you sometimes have to ask for more information. To confirm your understanding, you might use questions and statements like the following:

- Are you saying that . . . ?

- Do you mean . . . ?

- Do I understand correctly that . . . ?

- It sounds like you want . . .

Teachers regularly communicate through written messages such as notes, daily logs, and e-mails. Be sure to write clearly so colleagues and families receive accurate information that will not be misunderstood. Use a dictionary or style guide if you have questions about spelling, punctuation, or grammar.

Read for your own pleasure.

In addition to reading so you can learn more about caring for preschool children, we hope you read for pleasure. Reading is a life-long activity that introduces people, places, events, and experiences you might never encounter firsthand. Choose whatever you enjoy. It could be a newspaper or magazine, fiction or non-fiction, a short story or full-length novel.

what's next?

Skill-Building Journal, section **6-3** *(Your Own Experiences With Communication),* section **6-1** *(Feedback),* and section **6-4** *(Pre-Training Assessment).*

Learning Activities

LEARNING ACTIVITY

A. Using Your Knowledge of Child Development to Support Language Development

In this activity you will learn to

● recognize some typical language and literacy behaviors of preschool children

● use what you know about preschool children to support language and literacy development

Language and literacy skills begin developing in infancy.

The strong drive to communicate is apparent even during the first few months of life. Infants are active communicators. They cry, coo, and wave their arms and legs. As families and other caregivers respond to their coos and smiles, sing lullabies, and play peek-a-boo, babies learn that it's fun and rewarding to talk with another person, and they learn to communicate intentionally. They make sounds while pointing at objects they want or while raising their arms to be picked up.

Learning to read and to write is also rooted in warm and meaningful family experiences. When a father reads to his 3-month-old daughter, she does not know what books are or understand what he is reading. She does enjoy being with him and listening to the sound of his voice. Throughout life she will retain these warm, comforting feelings and continue to think of reading as a pleasant activity if her attempts to find meaning in print are encouraged.

Most toddlers understand and begin to use language to communicate. They like listening to stories and, because they are active learners, eagerly explore books on their own. They hold crayons and make marks on paper: the first step on the road to writing. Some 2- and 3-year-old children can identify the familiar signs, labels, and logos they see at home and in the community.

Preschool children use language to learn.

By the time they are preschool-aged, children use language to learn. They can take part in conversations, talk about past and future activities, and tell stories about real and imaginary characters and events. Many children learn to understand and say thousands of words and they come to understand the rules for using words, by interacting with adults who listen to them, talk with them, and introduce them to reading and writing.

As with other areas of development, the language skills of preschool children vary greatly. Some children talk constantly, while others speak mainly when spoken to. Some speak in long, complex sentences, while others make brief statements and need to be encouraged to expand upon their ideas. Some children pronounce sounds and words with great precision, while others are still learning to master vowels and consonant sounds.

Preschool children learn about literacy by observing, exploring, and acting.

Preschool children learn a lot about reading and writing by observing adults and older children and by exploring books and writing materials on their own. Activities such as singing songs, listening to stories, and paying attention to print in the environment also teach children about literacy. Through these and similar experiences, most children come to understand that

- drawing and writing are different

- print corresponds to speech but is different from spoken language

- reading books is enjoyable and satisfying

- alphabet letters have names

- books have a beginning and end, and they are read from front to back

- the words on each page are read in a particular order (in English and many other languages, from left to right and top to bottom)

Songs, rhymes, chants, and fingerplays help children pay attention to the sounds of letters and words.

In order to become readers and writers, children need to develop *phonological awareness*, the ability to attend to the sounds, rhythms, rhymes, and other patterns of speech. Children acquire this skill if teachers call their attention to sounds and rhymes when they sing rhyming songs, do finger plays, and teach simple poems. Teachers omit the last word that rhymes in a familiar story refrain so children can predict it. They have everyone clap out the syllables in each child's name and compare the number of claps they need, e.g., one for *Mark*, two claps for *Carlos*, and three for *Benjamin*. They also point out initial sounds: "Marcus, can you think of someone here whose name starts like your name? Right, Maria! Both of your names begin with the same sound: *m*." There are many enjoyable ways to teach phonological awareness.

Preschool children can learn a lot about print, reading, and writing.

Young children make step-by-step progress as they learn about print and reading. Here are some of the early literacy understandings that preschool children construct:

"**I can read books, too.**" At first, children might turn the pages and make up a story to go with the pictures. They may ask to have a favorite book read again and again, because they like the story and because they feel competent when they know a story so well they can retell it on their own. Predictable stories and those with repeated refrains are particularly useful in helping children discover the structure of stories. Repeated readings also help children figure out print conventions, both how to handle books and how to decode print.

"**Stories have a beginning, middle, and end.**" The more experience children have with books and retelling stories, the more they can recall details and the order of story events.

"**Print has meaning.**" Before children gain this insight, they may ask you to read a page without print or hold their hands over the print on a page while asking you to read. More experienced children might observe, "Now you can start reading again," when you turn to a page with print. They realize that printed words serve a different purpose from pictures and that both stand for people, objects, and ideas.

"**Written words and spoken words are related.**" It is a major accomplishment for children to realize that print records speech and thought and that the words we say are the same as those we read and write. As you read to children who are developing concepts about words, they may run their fingers along the text, although their pointing might not necessarily correspond to the words you are reading.

"**I know what that word says.**" Children may ask questions about print. They may ask, "What does this say?" or "Where does it say that?" You may notice them starting to decode printed words in the classroom and on neighborhood walks. They are developing a sight vocabulary as they learn to recognize words on signs, their own names, and sometimes the names of other children in the class.

Young children imitate adult writing before they write recognizable letters.

Children learn about the purposes of written language when they see adults reading (books, charts, bulletin board messages, etc.) and writing (shopping lists, notes, recording a child's description of a painting, etc.) and when they have opportunities to write, themselves. They practice writing long before they can make conventional letters. Using pencils, pens, crayons, and other writing tools, they strive to imitate adult writing. If you make a shopping list, a 3-year-old may want to help. If you write a letter, a 4-year-old may decide to write one, too. Here are some of the understandings about writing that are part of early literacy development:

"**I can make my own marks.**" Young children imitate adult writing by making marks on the page. At first these marks appear completely random to adults. Later, they look more like letters of the alphabet.

"I wrote a letter." As children gain more experience, they begin to point out letters in their writing. Soon they are writing many letters.

"I can write lots of letters." Children begin to realize that they can decide to write particular letters, often letters found in their names. They write the letters again and again, although the letters may not be in standard order when they write their names.

"Print must be written and read in a specific order, to be meaningful." With lots of practice with print and developmental writing, children learn that there is a standard order for writing letters and words. They come to realize that, in reading and writing English, print goes from left to right, and spaces are left between words.

"Letters stand for sounds." As children begin to recognize individual letters, they also learn that letters represent sounds. They begin writing words and making up their own spelling by paying attention to the sounds of letters and words, for example, *kt* for *cat*. Children's developmental spelling is a sign of progress and gives you information about what the child knows. Ask the child to read what he or she has written.

Developmental Characteristics of Preschool Children

Preschool children typically

- use language for many purposes: to plan, gain information, understand concepts, express feelings, share ideas, make requests, and solve problems

- tell stories about real and imaginary experiences that took place in the past as well as those in the present and future

- participate and take turns in conversations with peers and adults

- retell familiar stories, gradually mastering the correct sequencing of events

- learn most rules of grammar without direct instruction but may make mistakes because there are exceptions to rules

- learn that printed words are symbols for spoken words and convey messages

- make marks and write letters and words that, over time resemble conventional letters and words

- enjoy a wide variety of books and may have particular favorites

- memorize songs, poems, rhymes, and books with repetitive language patterns

- learn print concepts, such as, in English, that text is written and read from left to right

Development: It's All Connected

Language and literacy development evolves with cognitive, social, emotional, and physical growth. Examples follow.

Cognitive

Preschool children's expanding vocabularies help them understand and describe experiences and concepts, think and solve problems, make predictions, ask questions, create stories, and talk about the past and future. Older preschool children might use the pictures in information and reference books to explore an interest or answer a question.

Social

Preschool children have fun talking and playing with others. Children who can express their ideas and feelings are more likely to enjoy the company of others. During dramatic play they talk about what they want to do, who will play what role, and what will happen. They may write signs and create props to use during play. As their skills grow, they learn how to give and get information and what kinds of speech are appropriate in a variety of situations.

Emotional

Preschool children feel competent when they realize they can send oral and written messages to other people. They see themselves as successful communicators when they make their ideas comprehensible to others, name their feelings, take part in conversations, join in during read-aloud experiences, retell stories, and begin to recognize and write letters of the alphabet and a few important words.

Physical

Preschool children continue to develop the small muscles of their hands and fingers that are used to hold and manipulate books and writing tools. They strengthen these muscles while enjoying materials and activities, such as rolling playdough, stirring raisins into muffin batter, buttoning and zipping, building with small blocks, and using a computer keyboard.

Some preschool children have extremely limited language skills and show few signs of progress. If there is no other explanation for a child's limited language skills, he or she may have a language delay (such as a physical abnormality with the teeth, palate, tongue, or vocal cords; a respiratory problem; a hearing problem; or a speech disorder such as lisping. The following developmental warning signs could indicate possible concerns in hearing, speech, or areas that affect language development.

Language and Communication Development Alerts[18]

If you notice over time that a child shows several of these characteristics, suggest that the parents discuss their child's language development with a health professional.

By age 3

- frequently speaks in sentences with fewer than three words

- uses speech that is mostly unintelligible to familiar listeners

- understands only a few opposites (go-stop; big-little; up-down)

- seldom talks about activities

or if, by age 4,

- speaks in an unclear voice

- uses simple sentences with few details

- uses speech that is mostly unintelligible to strangers

- has trouble sticking to the topic when telling stories

- repeats syllables or words

- makes many, many grammatical errors

- has difficulty pronouncing the sounds of many letters and parts of words

- has difficulty communicating with other children and adults

If several of the above signs are present over an extended period of time, it is a good idea to refer the parents to a speech pathologist, a specialist who can conduct a comprehensive language assessment and determine the child's skills and needs. The speech pathologist can suggest specific strategies to use at the program and at home.

what's next?

Skill-Building Journal, section **6-5** *(Learning Activity A),* section **6-10** *(Answer Sheets),* and section **6-1** *(Feedback).*

Learning Activities

LEARNING
ACTIVITY

B. Creating a Literacy-Rich Environment

In this activity you will learn to

- set up well-stocked, inviting library and writing areas

- support reading and writing indoors and outdoors

Teachers demonstrate how they use literacy skills.

A literacy-rich environment for preschool children is filled with books, writing materials, and meaningful print displayed at the children's eye-level. Teachers—a very important part of a literacy-rich environment—support early literacy as they model talking, listening, reading, and writing for many different purposes. For example, while looking up the number for the nature center in the phone book, a teacher might say, "The names in the phone book are listed in the same order as the alphabet. *Nature* starts with an *n*, so I'm going to look for it after *m* and before *o*." When reading big books, teachers point to the text to help children learn print concepts, such as, in English, that we read from the front of the book to the back, and from left to right on each page.

Children can engage in literacy activities in well-stocked library and writing areas and throughout the classroom and outdoors. When children have many opportunities to see a variety of uses for print, to explore reading and writing materials, and to talk with peers and adults, their skills and understandings grow.

Setting Up a Library Area

The library area invites literacy learning.

Every preschool room needs an inviting place where children can sit comfortably while exploring many different kinds of texts. The best location for the library area is a quiet corner, away from noisy activities such as blocks and woodworking.

Make it soft and comfortable. Put a rug on the floor, as well as some large pillows. Include places to sit, such as an overstuffed bean-bag chair, a rocking chair, or a mattress covered with attractive and cheerful fabric. A tent can provide a cozy space, or a reading nook can be made from a large box. Offer a few stuffed animals or dolls children can read to or use to enact stories.

Include a table and two or three chairs. Some children like to sit and look at books at a table. Cover it with a colorful cloth and decorate it with a small plant or an interesting object.

Display books attractively. Use a shelf that allows books to be displayed with covers in view. Be sure to feature books you recently read aloud. Keep books in good repair, not torn or marked. Laminate the attractive covers on new books or cover them with clear Contact paper.

Organize the books, using categories that identify different kinds of text. Have separate baskets or areas for poetry, story books, books about animals, other information books and so on.

Decorate the area. Hang book covers and posters. Display photographs of children and adults reading books. Create a display related to a favorite book.

Provide good lighting. Locate the area near a window so natural light is available. Add a standing lamp or ceiling fixture if additional light is needed.

Include materials related to books read aloud. Puppets, hats, dress-up clothes, and other props children to retell stories or make up new tales about the same characters.

Choosing Books for Preschool Children

A preschool classroom should include books in children's home languages and English. Choose books that match children's skills and interests and depict their cultures, heritage, families, and abilities in positive ways. Provide five to eight books for each child in your class.

Include many types of books.

It is important to vary the selection of books throughout the year. Always offer some familiar favorites, while adding new books that correspond to children's growing skills and changing interests. Be sure to add to all interest areas books that are tied to current areas of study and activities.

Choosing Different Types of Books

Picture books about

- everyday life (for example, making pancakes or getting ready for bed)

- feelings, fears, and challenges (for example, adjusting to a new baby)

- self-awareness (what makes each of us unique)

- fairy tales, folk tales, fables, fantasy stories, and nonsense stories

Pattern books with

- repeated words and phrases children can master

- predictable plots

- rhyme and rhythm (poetry, songs, fingerplays)

Big books (enlarged versions of popular books that let children build print and book concepts during group read-aloud time and then reread on their own)

Informational books about non-fictional topics (for example, plants, dinosaurs, fish) that

- relate to the children's current interests

- introduce new ideas and topics

- include facts, charts, maps, captioned illustrations or photographs

Reference books (simple dictionary, software manuals, cookbooks)

Concept books (opposites, colors, shapes)

Alphabet books

Counting books

Wordless books

References (simple dictionary, nature guides, software manuals, cookbooks)

"Easy readers" with controlled vocabulary, rhyme, and repetition, for children who are ready to read

Look for award-winning children's books.

Children's librarians are experts on choosing appropriate books. If you describe the children's current skills and interests, a librarian can direct you to books that are just right for your group. While at the library, look for books that were nominated for or won awards, such as the Caldecott medal for picture books, the Coretta Scott King Award for exemplary children's books by African American authors and illustrators, and the Pura Belpré Award presented to Latino writers and illustrators for work that celebrates the Latino cultural experience in literature for children. Review book lists from the American Library Association and the International Reading Association. The library may carry journals, such as *The Horn Book,* that review new children's books.

Teachers can help children learn to love and care for books.

As with other materials in your classroom, well-loved books can wear out. This is often a sign that children love books and reading. Replace these favorites with new copies. If you pay too much attention to keeping books in new condition, some of the more active children in your class may be discouraged from reading. Nevertheless, preschool children can learn to take care of books. You and the children can set a few simple rules, such as "Write on paper, not in books," and post them in the library area. At first children may need gentle reminders to help them learn to care for books. Point out your own actions. "I'd love to read to you. First, I'll wash my hands so I don't get paint on the book."

Repair damaged books. There is little you can do if pages are missing, but you can erase pencil marks and tape torn pages or covers. Create a book repair kit in a shoe box or basket that is stocked with transparent and cloth tape, erasers, correction fluid to cover marks, and scissors. Older preschool children will soon learn to fix books on their own. Younger children will be more likely to report damaged books and ask for your help.

Set Up a Writing Area

Preschool children will make good use of a writing area filled with materials for making books and writing signs, lists, stories, letters, cards, and messages. If space allows, locate the writing area in or near the library area to reinforce the connections between reading and writing. Furnish the writing area with a desk or a table and several chairs. Include a shelf, a bulletin board, and mailboxes. The writing area is a good place for a computer set on a table with two chairs and a printer.

A Well-Stocked Writing Area

Tools for writing:

- pencils (thick lead; regular and colored)
- erasers
- markers (washable, non-toxic)
- chalk (white and colored)
- crayons
- alphabet charts

Surfaces to write on:

- chalkboards (with white and colored chalk and erasers)
- "magic" slates with pencils
- cardboard
- index cards
- paper (lined and unlined, white and colored, different sizes, weights)
- message center (large piece of paper hung on wall with pencils or markers attached or nearby)

Book-making materials:

- ready-made blank books (stapled sheets of paper)
- paper
- index cards
- cardboard, heavy paper, or wallpaper for covers
- laces, yarn, string
- twist ties for binding pages

Office equipment and supplies:

- desk and chair
- typewriter
- file folders, envelopes
- erasers
- stapler, hole punch
- blunt-ended scissors
- clipboards
- paste, glue, tape, stickers
- mailbox

Play props:

- junk mail
- catalogs, magazines
- coupons, stamps
- receipt books, order forms
- small pads of paper
- tickets

Computer station:

- furniture (computer table, chairs, printer stand)
- computer
- software
- printer
- paper

Samples of children's writing:

- child-made books
- message board
- mailboxes (so children can send messages to each other)
- bulletin board

Adults rely on books and printed materials for different reasons: for entertainment, to look up a recipe, answer a question, or explore a special interest. When planning a project or study of a special topic, include literacy materials and opportunities to read and write. Outfit each interest area with appropriate books and reading matter, along with writing tools and drawing paper, so children can make reading and writing part of their work every day.

Literacy Materials in Interest Areas	Literacy Learning
Blocks books about transportation, buildings, bridges, and tunnels a basket filled with index cards, markers, and masking tape props with writing on them, such as wooden traffic signs	Children can get ideas for their buildings, make signs for constructions, and write or dictate messages such as "Please don't touch our road."
Dramatic Play storybooks, cookbooks, magazines, catalogs, telephone books, grocery advertisements, junk mail clipboards, pads of paper, and pencils reading and writing props related to real activities, such as coupons, empty food containers, and menus	Children can use the materials in their play. In a pretend doctor's office, children might use office supplies, write prescriptions, give eye exams, create a clinical record, and look at pamphlets in the waiting room.
Art books about famous artists and their work art posters (e.g., modern and classical, paintings and sculpture, different artists) a variety of writing and drawing supplies children's work hung at their eye level; their dictated, descriptive sentence strips posted under the work	Children can use the art books and posters as reference tools. A variety of supplies lets them try different techniques in their own work and build small muscle skills.
Music and Movement song books rhythm instruments large charts of the words to songs	Children can use the rhythm instruments to mark the syllables in words. They can follow along the words to familiar songs.
Cooking cookbooks and recipe cards tools such as an egg beater and large spoons	Reading recipes shows children that print carries meaning. Using cooking tools and utensils helps children develop small muscle skills used for writing.
Computers software manuals books made by children on the computer age-appropriate software for reading and writing	Children observe adults learning to use software from manuals. Making and displaying books supports developing reading and writing skills.
Outdoors basket of books—stories and informational books on plants and animals, weather, gardening, and games clipboards, paper, writing and drawing tools	Children can read for pleasure and find information about outdoor interests.

Use Meaningful Print in the Classroom and Outdoors

Including print in the classroom and outdoors helps children make connections between spoken and written language. When children hear spoken words and then see them in writing, they come to understand how and why language is recorded in print. The print you provide should be meaningful; it should serve a purpose. For example, shelf labels tell where materials are stored, and name and picture labels tell whose belongings are stored in which cubby. Here are some additional ways to provide meaningful print.

Call attention to print throughout the classroom.

Communicate important information to the children, sometimes using English and sometimes home languages. For labels in many bilingual classrooms, teachers use different colors for each language to help children distinguish which words are written in which language. When a color-coding system is used, it should be introduced and explained to the children.

Invite children to help you. Together you can make print and picture labels for shelves and containers, to show were materials belong.

Use pictures and writing to post the daily schedule. Children like to show they know the order of the day's activities by reading the schedule. This is a great way to present information in print for children with a range of literacy skills.

Make signs for each interest area. In addition to the name of the area, signs can tell how many children may use it at a time and list a few simple reminders about how to use the area.

Point out environmental print. On a walk, show children traffic signs and explain what they mean. Read aloud the signs posted in store windows and on the sides of buses and other vehicles. Show children the print on various products, such as the tissue box, snack containers, and the toothpaste tube.

Make experience charts. After a trip or shared experience, ask children to describe what happened and write their statements on a large piece of paper. As you and the children read their story aloud, point to the words and move your finger along each line. Older preschool children may take turns pointing to the words and helping you read. Post the finished story in the room.

Write where children can see you and tell them what you are writing: "I'm writing this note to your dad to let him know that your sniffles are much better today." Ask children to help you make a list of things you need for a trip or an activity. They can draw what you need, while you write the words next to the pictures.

Write a recipe or the steps in a simple activity on a large piece of paper, while children are watching. Talk about what you are writing: "This is the recipe for English muffin pizzas. First, we pull the muffins apart to make two pieces." Post the paper in the appropriate interest area.

Provide many opportunities for children to write.

Another way to help young children realize that spoken and written languages correspond is to encourage children to write often. For example, young children can indicate their favorite fruit on a chart, providing information the group can discuss. Writing gives children chances to share their ideas and feel competent. Here are some more ideas to try out with the group:

Make attendance and helper charts. Attach a pencil or marker on a string so children can write a mark, a few letters, or their whole names to indicate that they have arrived or chosen a weekly job.

Introduce a few important words. Make and post index cards with each child's name so children can address messages to each other. Create a word wall with key words related to children's experiences.

Include alphabet references and materials. Children can play lotto, matching, and number games with words and numbers as well as with pictures. Provide published and homemade alphabet books and puzzles; letter stamps, sponges, and tiles for making words; and alphabet references such as charts hung at the children's eye level, strips taped to a table, and laminated, portable cards.

Introduce formats for displaying data. Children can show the results of their investigations by making simple graphs and charts.

Create a system for taking turns with popular materials. Post a piece of paper and a marker attached with a string. Children may write their names and cross them off after their turns.

Invite children to write their own books. Offer as much help as children need to carry out their plans. Children may use teacher-made blank books (just staple several pieces of paper together) or bind the pages using a hole punch and yarn or another method. (Office supply stores are a good source of inexpensive but strong bindings.) Children can illustrate their books with photographs or drawings. Put the finished books in the library area for others to read.

Help Families Provide Literacy-Rich Homes

Most children have their first literacy experiences at home. Preschool children's literacy development is enhanced when families continue to present reading and writing as fun and functional activities. Even the busiest families need to set aside time to read aloud regularly. You can help families be literacy models and promoters by making sure they have books and writing materials at home. Try these suggestions:

- Share a flyer about the local library: hours of service, special programs, and lists of good books for preschoolers.

- Establish a book library so families may borrow books to read at home.

- Sponsor book giveaways from groups such as First Book or Reading Is Fundamental.

- Encourage families to look for books at garage sales and secondhand shops. Ask family members to give books as gifts and to trade books with friends.

- Encourage family members to read to children in the language they read the best. If you learn that family members are illiterate, provide information about literacy programs.

In addition, when your program receives donations of paper, pencils, crayons, or markers, share them with families. Your director might be able to include money in the budget to purchase materials for children to use at home.

what's next?

Skill-Building Journal, section **6-6** *(Learning Activity B)* and section **6-1** *(Feedback).*

Learning Activities

C. Encouraging Children to Listen and Speak

In this activity you will learn to

- use the environment to encourage oral communication

- help children learn how to participate in conversations

The more opportunities children have to listen and speak, the more their communication skills will grow. A room in which children are encouraged to talk is not a quiet room. Teachers must be willing to accept a moderate level of chatter and noise to encourage language development.

Some children lack the oral language skills that support literacy development.

For almost 2 1/2 years, researchers Betty Hart and Todd R. Risley[19] observed and documented the language development of a group of very young children. They found that, by age 3, the children whose parents spent the most time talking with them had much larger vocabularies than children who were talked with less. This advantage held true when the children were tested again at age nine. Hart and Risley estimated that the children who were exposed to the least language would require 41 hours per week of language-rich interventions to catch up with their more verbal peers.

Many of the strategies for creating a learning environment discussed in module 3 encourage preschool children to practice and expand their language skills.

The environment can be set up so children have reasons to talk and listen.

Here are some specific ideas:

Set up interest areas where children can work and play in small groups. Join in children's play to introduce new vocabulary and concepts that expand their thinking and talking.

Offer interesting materials—like an old radio to take apart or funnels and plastic tubing for the water table—that encourage children to explore, ask questions, talk about their ideas, learn new words, and interact with each other.

Provide dramatic play props that encourage children to listen and speak. Two or more telephones can lead to many lively conversations. Children can set up a restaurant with "servers" and "customers" if you provide the menus and tablecloths.

Plan some group projects, such as painting a mural or making bread. Help the children plan projects together and carry out their ideas.

Take trips and walks in the neighborhood to expand children's experiences and give teachers and the group new things to talk about.

Offer materials that promote language use, such as puppets and flannel boards.

Eat family-style meals at small tables where five or six children and a teacher can take part in interesting conversations.

Ask families to make audiotapes of the children's favorite books. Place books and tapes in plastic bags and display them in the library area near the tape player and headphones.

Children who are comfortable and relaxed feel free to express themselves.

Most children will express their ideas and feelings more freely if they are comfortable and relaxed. First they may need to get to know you and the other children, learn to follow your predictable schedule, explore new and unfamiliar materials, remember what to do during routines, and master their feelings about separating from their families.

You've probably noticed that the more verbal children tend to make friends easily. It's especially important to be aware of shy children who may require your help to feel accepted by their peers and to learn how to express themselves. Similarly, children are more likely to respond to your questions and share their thoughts after they learn that you will honor their ideas and feelings.

Accepting children's efforts to communicate means

- encouraging both verbal and nonverbal attempts to communicate

- never belittling what a child says

- waiting patiently until a child is ready to speak

- positioning yourself at the child's level and listening carefully and patiently

Every culture has conversational guidelines.

To be effective communicators, children need to learn how to take part in conversations. Every culture has guidelines that people follow when talking with one another that govern wait time before responding. For example, when someone wants to start or join a conversation, he or she says something and then waits for a response. Good conversationalists know not to interrupt and to stay on the topic. If they don't understand what is said, they ask questions to help the speaker clarify his or her message.

You probably know both children and some adults who find it hard to participate in conversations. It can be very difficult to give someone else a turn to talk, to resist the urge to interrupt, or to explain one's ideas. Children learn to be partners in conversations, gradually, over time, and with much practice.

Teachers can engage children in one-on-one conversations during transitions, while doing chores such as washing paint brushes, or at the beginning or end of the day when it's easier to provide undivided attention. By talking with children, teachers can model how to engage in conversation.

Starting Conversations With Children

Join in the children's play so you can encourage conversation. "I like green peppers on my pizza. What do you like on yours?"

Offer an interesting observation that invites a response. "The prism in the window is making rainbows on our floor."

Ask an open-ended question that narrows the topic. When open-ended questions are too broad, children have no idea how to respond. For example, you might ask, "What did the clowns do?" instead of, "What did you see at the circus?"

To keep a conversation going ask for more information. "Did your dog get sick after he ate your whole ice cream cone?"

Repeat or comment on what the child says; then ask a related question. "That's right. Your plant is much taller than last week. What did you do to make it grow so fast?"

Ask for clarification of an unclear message. You might say, "Will you explain that again, please?" "Try to use different words to tell me what you did."

Redirect a child back to the topic. "Will you finish telling me about what happened at the dentist?"

While helping children learn the rules of conversation, you can introduce new words and model standard uses and patterns of language. This helps children expand their vocabularies and learn about the world. Later, they will use this knowledge when learning to make sense of words they read. Here are some suggestions:

Talk about how things look, feel, smell, taste, and sound. Because children use all of their senses to learn, they tend to be aware of the sensory characteristics of objects. Encourage them to describe what they experience. "Yes, this rock feels smooth. Is it as smooth as ice?"

Ask open-ended questions that encourage thinking. "What could we use this for?" "What might happen if?" "What would you do if...?"

Introduce new vocabulary. New words can describe something a child is wearing or doing. "You are wearing corduroy pants today." "I see you're making a pattern: red, red, yellow; red, red, yellow." "What a winding road you made with the blocks!"

Speak in complete and detailed sentences. When a child asks where something is located, don't simply point and answer, "Over there." Take time to explain, "The markers are on the art shelf next to the drawing paper."

Use a soft tone of voice. A harsh voice makes children tense. A loud voice makes them talk louder and raises the noise level of the room.

Introduce categories. "That <u>color</u> is blue." "We're having apples today for snack. What <u>fruits</u> do you like?" "Here are some <u>farm animals</u>: a horse, a cow, and a pig."

Describe the specific characteristics of objects or actions. Say, "Roll the rubber ball to me" rather than, "Roll it." "Put the paint brushes in the sink," rather than, "Put the brushes here." "Look at how fast Kris is riding the tricycle!" rather than, "Look at Kris." "See how high the bird is flying—up to the top of the tree," rather than, "See the bird."

Talk about and name feelings. Help a child who is upset to use words to express his or her feelings. Sometimes you have to model the words. "I think you might be feeling frustrated because you have to wait for your turn. Would you like some help finding something to do while you wait?"

Supporting English Language Learners

Your group may include children who are building communication skills in more than one language, their home language and English. As children listen to stories, sing, look at books, and engage in other activities in their home language, they acquire language and literacy skills and concepts about the world. They then use what they already know about words and print to learn the second language—English.

It is important for children to continue language development in their home language.

The home language gives a child lifelong connections to family and culture. Listening to adult discussions and taking part in family conversations conducted in their home languages support children's language and cognitive growth. If children lose their home language skills they may also lose opportunities to stretch their thinking skills as they try to make sense of complex and abstract ideas expressed by older siblings and adult family members.

Teachers need to keep language simple when talking with English language learners.

When you talk with English language learners, it is important to consider individual skill levels. If spoken language is too far above a child's level of comprehension, he or she will not be able to determine meaning. Keep messages simple and clear and talk about things and events in the present. Show your respect and reassure a child by learning the correct pronunciation for both the child's first and last names. Learning a few words in the home language also goes a long way toward helping a child feel comfortable in the classroom.

Strategies for Supporting English Language Learners[20]

Speak slowly and clearly; pause at natural breaks for a longer time than you would for children whose home language is English.

Use words that are heard frequently; limit your use of slang and non-standard language.

Talk and use cues such as gestures, pictures, and objects.

Repeat words that are important to the meaning of what you are saying.

Emphasize the most important words by saying them more loudly, exaggerating intonation, or through body language.

Accept the child's attempts at using language without pointing out mistakes. Instead, respond by rephrasing or expanding on what the child said.

English language learners need to be accepted by others in the class so they will have opportunities to play and learn. However, to be socially accepted by others, children have to be able to understand and speak the language used most often in the class. Teachers play an important role in helping children gain social acceptance, thereby setting the stage for second-language learning.

what's next?

Skill-Building Journal, section **6-7** *(Learning Activity C)* and section **6-1** *(Feedback).*

Learning Activities

LEARNING ACTIVITY

D. Reading Aloud and Talking About Books

In this activity you will learn to

- read aloud with individual children and small groups of children

- talk about books with preschool children

Children are more likely to develop a love for reading when they are read to regularly and introduced to the power and pleasure of print. In addition, reading aloud and talking about books support development of early literacy skills. Reading aloud lets preschool children[21]

- pay attention to the language of books and begin to notice how written language differs from speech

- listen to the sounds of language and notice similarities, differences, and patterns

- build their vocabularies with words they understand and can use

- gain background knowledge about a variety of topics

- talk about story characters, settings, and plot and relate them to their own lives

- learn more about print concepts, such as that letters and words are written in a certain order and that written words are separated by spaces

Selecting Appropriate Books to Read Aloud

What makes a book good for reading aloud?

Books written for preschool children can help them learn more about themselves and the world around them. When books depict familiar experiences—a new baby at home, making friends, starting a new school—children can better understand and deal with their feelings. When children discover that the situations and feelings of characters in books are similar to their own, they seek out books to help them make sense of their experiences.

Three- and 4-year-old children tend to focus on themselves, their families, their homes, and their friends. They like stories about animal and human characters with whom they can identify. Books that are appropriate for young preschool children have

- a simple plot about familiar experiences

- predictable language and plot

- colorful, bold, realistic illustrations that children can understand

- lots of repetition in the telling of the story

- happy endings that encourage a sense of security

- rhymes, nonsense words, and interesting language

Most older preschool children (4- and 5-year-olds) enjoy books with more complex plots. They can pay attention for a longer period of time and appreciate humorous and imaginative characters and events. Books that are appropriate for 4- to 5-year-olds have

- imaginative plots they can follow

- humorous characters and events, and perhaps a surprise ending

- information that extends their understanding of the world

- colorful, detailed illustrations

THINK

- What are some of your favorite books to read aloud with children?

- What do these books have in common with each other?

- Why do the children like them?

Reading With Children

Reading aloud with a group brings children together for a meaningful social experience. Children react to the story and comment on the pictures and what is happening. Sometimes they correct the reader for missing a word or leaving out an important detail in a familiar story. The ability to remember the words and events in a story is an important step in learning to read, because it supports the development of children's understanding of story structure and their efforts to learn the written code.

Read aloud to children every day.

When reading aloud is a regular part of the schedule every day, you may see children looking at familiar books and telling the story to themselves. These children may not know the meaning of all the words on the page, but they demonstrate their understanding of print concepts as they point to words, stop to examine pictures, and look at and turn the pages of the book from the front to the back.

Read-alouds can take place during a scheduled story time as well as in response to children's requests throughout the day. You might read to two children in the library area, a small group seated under a shady tree, one child curled up with you in the easy chair, or a group of ten gathered around your chair. Young preschool children can generally listen to a story for five to ten minutes. Older children can listen a little longer, between 10 and 15 minutes.

- Where in your indoor and outdoor environments do you read aloud to one or two children?

- What makes these read-aloud times special for the children and for you?

Get to know a book before reading it aloud.

Begin by carefully selecting the books you will read aloud. Use the criteria suggested in this module and be sure to consider the interests and abilities of your group.

Characteristics of a Good Book to Read Aloud

- The adult reader likes it.

- The topic is already or likely to be of interest to the children.

- It is a good match for the children's developmental stages (e.g., for young preschool children, the book has lots of rhymes and repetition; for older preschool children, the story has suspense, plot twists, dialogue, and engaging characters).

- It relates to the children's unique experiences and interests.

- A familiar—and favorite—author wrote it.

- The story and illustrations are relevant to children's families and culture.

- The story and illustrations introduce new family and cultural experiences.

- It is a well-loved favorite that children like hearing again and again.

- New information and ideas are presented through text and pictures.

When you plan to introduce a new book, read it several times, yourself, so you can become very familiar with the words, characters, and plot. Write questions and reminders on Post-it® notes; then stick them on the appropriate pages so you will know how and when to prompt the children's thinking. As you consider the appropriateness of a book, consider the following questions:

- How long will it take to read? Can the children pay attention for that length of time?

- Will any concepts or ideas be unfamiliar to the children? How can I explain them?

- Do the illustrations have tiny details or hidden surprises to point out to the children?

- How can I make sound effects (e.g., animal noises or sirens) part of the story?

- How can I vary my voice for the different characters?

- What props (e.g., hats or musical instruments) would enhance the story?

- How can I invite the children to participate? Can they say rhymes, join in with the last word of repetitive phrases, predict what might happen next, or answer questions?

Start the reading by giving children a reason to listen to the book.

The first step in reading aloud is to gain the children's attention and help them focus on the book. You might read the title, author, and illustrator, look at the cover and discuss what the book might be about, and suggest things the children can look and listen for. Here are some more suggestions for introducing a book:

- Explain how the story is related to familiar feelings or a recent experience. "We all have angry feelings sometimes. If someone took the last place on the swings, we may feel angry. This book is about feeling angry. It's called, *I Was So Mad!*"

- Share an object that is an important part of the story. "Here's a nice round stone I found outside. Do you think we could make soup from this stone? Let's see what happens in this book called *Stone Soup*."

- Relate a new book to a familiar one. "Do you remember *The Very Hungry Caterpillar?* This book has the same author. It's called *The Very Lonely Firefly*."

- Explain how the book is tied to what the children are studying. "The title of this book is *How a House is Built*. I think it will give us some new ideas for our building."

While reading, use strategies that are fun and that provide information about books and print.

Make sure the children are seated comfortably and can see the pictures. Start to read as soon as you have the children's attention. Here are some tips to use when reading aloud:

- Hold the book to one side so the children can see the pictures.

- Use your voice and facial expressions to make the characters and experiences come alive.

- Change or define words to help children understand the story.

- Stop to talk about the pictures, answer questions, discuss what might happen next, and think about what the characters might be feeling.

- Answer questions related directly to the book; save other questions for later.

- Run your finger under the text.

- Pause at the end of sentences.

- Invite children to join in with repeated and predictable words, phrases, and rhymes.

- Discuss interesting words and expressions and ask what the children think they mean.

- Repeat words that rhyme or have sounds like those found in other words the children know.

Extend children's interest in a read-aloud book.

When you have finished the book, talk about the plot and characters. For non-fiction books, review the interesting things you learned, discuss what you might still want to know, and talk about how to find out. Offer materials and activities that enhance children's enjoyment and understanding of the book. Here are some examples:

- Discuss what the characters did and ask the children to share their own experiences.

    "Have you ever felt the way Andrew did? How would you feel if you had something important to say and people did not listen to you?"

    "It was really hard for Frances when it was her sister's birthday. Have you ever felt the way Frances did? What did you do?"

- Provide dress-up clothes and props so children can act out the story.

- Make flannel board cutouts so children can retell favorite stories themselves.

- Display the books you have read prominently so children can enjoy them again and again.

- Refer to a non-fiction book when you need information to answer a question.

Create opportunities for all children to be read to every day.

Some children find it difficult to sit with a group. There is little point in forcing a child to sit still when he or she is not yet ready to do so. It is best to allow such children to leave the group if they lose interest in the book. Another teacher can help the child find something else to do. Later you can read to the child, one-on-one. Reading to one or two children at a time allows you to adjust the reading to their special needs and interests and share a special time of closeness. As children grow older they will remember these times and continue to associate reading with feelings of warmth and security.

what's next?

Skill-Building Journal, section **6-8** *(Learning Activity D),* section **6-1** *(Feedback),* and section **6-9** *(Reflecting on Your Learning).*

7A

Creative

Overview

Arranging the Environment to Encourage Exploration and Experimentation

Offering a Variety of Materials and Activities That Promote Self-Expression

Encouraging and Respecting Children's Ideas

Your Own Creativity

Learning Activities

A. Using Your Knowledge of Child Development to Encourage Creativity

B. Supporting Creativity Throughout the Day

C. Encouraging Self-Expression Through Music and Movement

D. Offering Art Experiences That Invite Exploration and Experimentation

7. Creative

All aspects of the curriculum offer opportunities for creativity.

Creative people are willing to try new ways of doing things. They combine ideas and materials in different ways for new purposes. They are curious about how things work and why things happen. They are willing to take risks. When their strategies are unsuccessful, they learn from their mistakes and try other approaches.

Children invent characters and act out roles and stories. They move their bodies in different ways while responding to music. Block builders try different ways to build towers. Young artists experiment with techniques and materials while painting and making collages. Children analyze problems and suggest solutions, such as how to take turns with popular toys or how to figure out which jar holds the most marbles.

Arrange the environment to support children's creativity.

Young children are imaginative, inventive learners who use all of their senses to explore the world. In environments that support creativity, children may make messes, store their work so they can return to it another time, and move their bodies freely. Teachers arrange the indoor and outdoor environments so children have the freedom and safety to explore and experiment. They also encourage creativity by planning a daily schedule that allows children plenty of time to explore and work at their own pace.

Open-ended materials encourage creative self-expression.

As preschool children develop greater physical, language, and thinking skills, their play and work become more inventive. Teachers support creative expression by providing a rich variety of open-ended art materials and tools, music for listening and moving, instruments for making music, and props for imaginative play.

Teachers support creativity by encouraging and respecting children's ideas.

Teachers support creativity by encouraging children to think, explore, solve problems, reflect, evaluate, and revise. Children's ideas and answers may not always make sense to adults, but children gain confidence and want to continue experimenting when they know their ideas are valued by other people. Encouraging and respectful relationships between children and adults are the foundation for nurturing creativity.

You can promote children's creativity by

- arranging the environment to encourage exploration and experimentation

- offering a variety of materials and activities that promote self-expression

- encouraging and respecting children's original ideas

Arranging the Environment to Encourage Exploration and Experimentation

1. **Display and store materials within children's reach on open shelves that are no taller than 3 feet.** "Jamie, the cars are in a basket on the shelf. You can get them yourself."

2. **Offer spaces where children can explore, make noise, move their bodies, and be messy.** Create open spaces by rearranging moveable furniture and provide mats for tumbling.

3. **Provide protected spaces where children may save both finished and unfinished creations.** "You may put your clay pot in this plastic container so it stays soft. Then you can work on it again tomorrow."

4. **Help children display their work attractively.** "Linda, which of your paintings do you want to hang on the wall?"

5. **Display interesting pictures and objects within reach and invite children to explore them.** "The dancing feather fans Sara's grandma brought us are hanging on the hooks in the music area. You may get them when you want to use them."

6. **Adapt the schedule, when appropriate, so children have enough time to act on their ideas.** "Marcus is still making the cover for his book. Let's start cleaning up without him. He'll join us when he's done."

example

Ms. Kim Helps the Children Save Their Block Creation

When it's almost time to clean up, Ms. Kim walks over to the Block Area where Carlos, Sara, and Marcus have been working. "That is the biggest block house I ever saw!" she exclaims. "You must have worked hard building that." All three children ask, "Please, please, can we leave it up?" Ms. Kim smiles and says, "Yes, you may, but your building needs some protection. How can you let everyone else know that you want to save your building?" Carlos replies, "We can make a sign." "Does everyone want to try Carlos' idea?" asks Ms. Kim. The children nod in agreement. "There are markers, paper, and tape on the shelf," Ms. Kim reminds them. After helping the children make the sign, Ms. Kim continues, "Do you have any ideas about how we could remember this house for a long time?" "Take a picture!" says Marcus. Ms. Kim laughs, "You children have lots of good ideas. Would you like to be in the picture, too? I'll get the camera."

Offering a Variety of Materials and Activities That Promote Self-Expression

7. **Assess the children's current interests and provide a variety of appropriate materials, props, and objects.** Include books, CDs or tapes, rhythm instruments, and art materials.

8. **Offer materials, props, and objects that reflect the cultures and ethnicities of all children in the class.** "Aimee's mom brought us some beautiful fabric and one of her saris from India. Maybe she will show us how to put on a sari."

9. **Plan activities and ask questions that encourage children to use their imaginations.** "The dragon ate three tons of mashed potatoes, two boxes of hot dogs, and a carrot. What do you think he ate next?"

10. **Provide a variety of materials for children to use in different ways depending on their interests, ideas, and plans.** Include open-ended materials, such as blocks, musical instruments, art supplies, dress-up clothes, and woodworking tools and scraps, to encourage children's self-expression.

11. **Offer messy open-ended activities such as finger painting; bubble blowing; and water, sand, and mud play.** "Leo, using the spray bottle to dampen the sand worked well. Now your tunnel for the cars doesn't collapse."

---

example

Ms. Thomas Invites the Children to Create Their Own Baker's Hats

Benjamin, Tony, and Avida decide to open a bakery in the Dramatic Play Area after a class trip to the bakery near the program. As they gather the props and supplies they are going to use, Avida exclaims, "Hats! We need to wear hats and aprons like the bakers we talked to." "We have aprons but no hats," Tony responds. Ms Thomas asks the children how they could get hats like the bakers wore. "We can make them. I'll get paper and glue," replies Tony. "We can each make it the way we want," adds Benjamin.

Encouraging and Respecting Children's Ideas

12. **Invite children to express their ideas and feelings.** "How do the soap suds feel on your hands?" "What do you think about when you listen to this music?"

13. **Extend and expand children's dramatic play by assuming pretend roles or offering a new prop.** "My hair is too long. Do I need an appointment or is this a walk-in barber shop?"

14. **Show respect for the creative process as well as the creative product.** "Mark, you experimented by painting with your hands and then with your elbows."

15. **Ask open-ended questions that encourage children to solve problems and think in new ways.** "Tyrone, you're right, our tomato plants are falling over. How can we fix them?"

16. **Accept and value each child's unique ideas and expressions.** "After our field trip to the pet store, Jeremy and Jorge made some snakes out of clay, and Oanh painted a colorful picture of tropical fish."

Ms. Williams Focuses on the Creative Process

Ms. Williams watches Jorge use both hands to make large circles with finger paint on a tray. He gets some paint on the elbow of one sleeve, which has started to slip down. She pushes up his sleeve gently and says, "Jorge, tell me about those enormous circles you are making." Jorge smiles and explains, "First, I made some big circles. Now I'm going to make small ones." Ms. Williams continues watching for a while. When Jorge appears to be finished, she asks, "Would you like some paper to make a print of your circles?" "No, thanks," says Jorge, as he erases the circles with his hand. "That's enough circles. It's time to make some wavy lines." Ms. Williams gets up to see what the other children are doing. "They sure are wavy! I wonder what kinds of lines you are going to make next."

what's next?

Skill-Building Journal, section **7-2** *(Overview)*, section **7-10** *(Answer Sheets)*, and section **7-1** *(Feedback)*.

Your Own Creativity

Creative people are innovative and resourceful. They adapt ideas, plans, and materials to solve problems or make something new. You don't have to be able to paint a picture, play an instrument, or write a book to be creative. Artists and musicians are creative people, and so are cooks, plumbers, and teachers.

Teachers of preschool children have many opportunities to be creative.

Early childhood teachers are living examples of the saying, "Necessity is the mother of invention." They are creative in the ways they recycle materials, respond to challenging behavior, and invite family involvement. Adjusting plans in response to children's changing interests and needs is an important part of a teacher's job. Thinking of new ways to help children make friends, making up a special song to sing at the end of the day, and rearranging the room to provide an area for dancing are all ways teachers are creative.

Creative teachers are lifelong learners about themselves and the world. They understand how they

- approach problems and address challenges

- make decisions

- share ideas and listen to other people

- respond to stimuli

Creative teachers use this self-awareness as they establish environments that support children's creativity and as they interact with children to encourage self-expression.

Creativity can be very satisfying.

Creative expression can be very satisfying. Think about how you feel when you use leftovers to create a delicious meal; turn an old pair of boots into petunia planters; or come up with new ways to involve fathers, as well as mothers, in the program. Those emotions are similar to the pride children feel when they figure something out for themselves and their pure joy when moving in response to music. Creative teachers recognize these feelings in themselves and strive to promote them in young children.

what's next?

Skill-Building Journal, section **7-3** *(Your Own Creativity)*, section **7-1** *(Feedback)*, and section **7-4** *(Pre-Training Assessment)*.

Learning Activities

A. Using Your Knowledge of Child Development to Encourage Creativity

In this activity you will learn to

- recognize some typical behaviors of preschool children that are related to creativity

- use what you understand about children to encourage their creativity

Preschool children are very creative.

Preschool children are very creative. They have vivid imaginations, are extremely curious, and are very good at solving problems that arise during their explorations.

- Jamie (3 years old) hears a truck outside. Before Ms. Kim can step in, he drags a chair to the window so he can climb up and look outside.

- Avida (4 years old) wants to join the group playing pet store. She picks up a stuffed dog and says, "Look! I found the lost puppy!"

- Mark (5 years old) is making a mobile, adding things to balance it.

Three key characteristics of preschool children are linked to creativity.[22] They are sensitive to internal and external stimuli. They are increasingly aware of their own emotions, even if they cannot name them, and pay attention to what is going on around them. Most young children lack inhibition. They don't have an inner voice that says, "Stop," or, "No, you can't do that." They are willing to experiment and test their ideas. They also become completely absorbed in an engaging activity and stay involved as long as their interest lasts.

Maria, 3 years old, demonstrates these three characteristics when she encounters finger paint for the first time.

> Placing her hands in the thick paint, Maria responds to the texture of this new substance, "It's wet and slimy." She lets it ooze through her fingers, then uses the palm of her hand to spread it across the tray. She turns her hand over and says, "My hand is all red." Next, Maria uses one finger to make wavy lines. She sees Carlos add a blob of yellow paint to his tray and keeps watching him for several minutes. Maria then adds her own yellow blob. With both hands she mixes the two colors together. Maria scratches her nose, leaving an orange smudge. She barely notices when Ms. Richards pushes up the sleeve of her shirt to get it out of the way. For a long time, Maria stays focused on the finger paint—fully engaged in exploring how it looks and feels and how it responds to her actions.

Children can manipulate tools and materials as their small-muscle skills develop.

Physical development during the preschool years affects children's ability to express themselves. Because their rate of growth slows down, preschool children do not tire as quickly as toddlers. They stay involved in an activity for long periods of time, if they are interested and engaged. Preschool children also have much greater control over the large muscles used to run, jump, climb, throw, and carry. Their small-muscle skills and hand–eye coordination are increasing. Increased control over small muscles allows children to use a variety of materials and equipment, such as brushes, markers, crayons, and other drawing tools; scissors; rhythm instruments; sand, water, and dramatic play props; a computer keyboard and mouse; beads and strings; and so on.

Children gather and use information as their cognitive development progresses.

Preschool children's rapid cognitive development also supports creativity. As they move, dig, build, lift, climb, handle, taste, fill, empty, and manipulate, children gather and use information about objects and events in their environment: "These things are different." "These look and taste the same." "When you put this color next to that color, it looks different." Preschool children are natural scientists. Their curiosity leads them to ask, "Why?" again and again. When teachers encourage children to make their own discoveries, children construct their own understanding of math and science concepts. Language growth is also rapid; children learn new words and use them to describe what they see and experience. They make up stories; describe their paintings; talk with teachers and each other; and ask many, many questions.

Children's creativity is important to their development of social skills. Children invent new ways to share and take turns with favorite toys. Some children use creative problem-solving skills to negotiate with others: "If you let me play, too, we can use more puppets and put on a bigger show."

Dramatic play is very important. As preschool children make sense of their experiences, they invent roles and scenarios and think of new ways to use props and wear dress-up clothes. Dramatic play themes frequently carry over from one day to the next. Teachers can respond by providing new materials and by offering indirect suggestions that extend the play: "Those muffins look really tasty. Tell me how you made them."

Children think creatively to solve social problems.

Preschool children can be creative in every activity, routine, and interest area. While art and music activities are typically thought of as creative, alert, observant teachers have many opportunities throughout the day to encourage children to express themselves, solve problems, and carry out plans and ideas.

what's next?

Skill-Building Journal, section **7-5** *(Learning Activity A)* and section **7-1** *(Feedback).*

Learning Activities

B. Supporting Creativity Throughout the Day

In this activity you will learn to

- provide a variety of materials for children to actively explore and use in different ways

- listen to and talk with children in ways that encourage their efforts

Children experience the challenge and joy of discovery when the environment is arranged to support active exploration and when materials are interesting and varied. Positive interactions with teachers encourage children to test their ideas.

Open-ended materials invite children to be creative.

One of the easiest ways to promote children's creativity is to provide open-ended materials that children can use in a variety of ways. Because they have multiple uses, open-ended materials interest children of different ages and stages of development. For example, given a box of recycled materials (e.g., fabric squares, catalogs, greeting cards, wire hangers, cardboard tubes), children might sort and classify the items, make mobiles, or decorate masks. They might investigate weight and use the materials as dramatic play props.

Look around your room.

- What open-ended materials have you provided?

- How are children using them? What items could you add?

Because children are creative in many different ways, include open-ended materials that invite discovery in all interest areas. Here are examples of how teachers encourage children's creativity in different areas.

Tyrone and Mark are **Outdoors,** using a piece of string to measure the height of marigold seedlings. Some plants are much taller than the others. Ms. Frilles asks, "Why do some plants grow faster than others?"

Leo is in the **Library Area,** writing and illustrating a story. He tells Ms. Thomas that he would like to make a book. She suggests using cardboard for a cover and demonstrates using a hole punch and a shoelace to bind the pages together.

Aimee and Janelle are setting up a bakery in the **Dramatic Play Area.** They display their playdough cakes and cookies on shelves made from shoe boxes. Mr. Lopez stops by to purchase a birthday cake.

Amanda and Michelle are in the **Toys and Games Area,** making designs with a set of small colored cubes. Ms. Williams comments on their choice of materials, "Amanda, you are using red and blue blocks for your design. Michelle, your design includes all the colors."

Tony is using a drawing program on the **Computer.** He is learning how to draw circles, squares, and triangles to use in his design. Ms. Thomas asks, "How do you put a triangle inside a circle?"

Sara and Linda are in the **Cooking Area.** They are discussing which ingredients to put in the trail mix. Ms. Kim asks, "How can you both make the kind of trail mix you like best?"

Teachers' enthusiastic support encourages children to use their imaginations.

Your daily interactions with children can help them gain confidence in their abilities. What you say, how you ask and answer questions, and the ways in which you encourage discovery all nurture children's creativity. Careful listening to what children say and recognizing each child as a unique individual are crucial. Your enthusiasm for children's efforts and successes greatly support their explorations and imagination. These practices also help children develop positive attitudes about persevering and learning from mistakes. When these attitudes are encouraged during the preschool years, they are likely to have lasting effects on the child's entire development.

THINK

- Do you take time to listen to each child every day?

- What do you learn about children when you listen carefully?

Open-ended questions can be answered correctly in a number of different ways.

Open-ended questions encourage preschool children to think creatively. These questions can be answered correctly in a number of different ways. In the following example, Mr. Lopez asks open-ended questions to help Leo and Janelle play with the same doll.

Mr. Lopez:	*"How could you both play with the doll? Janelle, tell us your idea."*
Janelle:	*"I should get it first because I'm older. Then he can have a turn."*
Mr. Lopez:	*"Now, Leo, tell us your idea."*
Leo:	*"I could have the doll, and Janelle could have the carriage."*
Mr. Lopez:	*"What things could you do with the doll together?"*
Leo:	*"We could give her a bath."*

Mr. Lopez's open-ended questions and prompts help the children solve the problem. His approach allows the children to use creative thinking to arrive at an agreeable solution. As a result, the children feel competent; learn a problem-solving strategy they can use in the future; and practice compromising, an important social skill. (See module 5, *Cognitive*, to learn more about asking open-ended questions.)

Questions That Encourage Creative Thinking

- What do you think about...?
- Why did that happen?
- What would happen if...?
- How does this work?
- What else can we use this for?
- How did you...?
- What else is like this?

- How could you...?
- Is there another way to do this?
- What's similar about these?
- What if we added this?
- In what ways are these different?
- What if we take this away?

---

what's next?

Skill-Building Journal, section **7-6** *(Learning Activity B)* and section **7-1** *(Feedback).*

Learning Activities

LEARNING ACTIVITY

C. Encouraging Self-Expression Through Music and Movement

In this activity you will learn to

- recognize how music and movement foster children's creativity

- encourage children to express themselves through music and movement

Most young children enjoy music. They sing their favorite songs over and over and aren't concerned with the quality of their voices or their teacher's ability to carry a tune. They experience the pure joy of playing with sounds and moving their bodies. Because children easily connect movement with music, listening to music invites them to explore what their bodies can do and to become aware of how their bodies move in space.

Children easily connect music with body movements.

From a very early age, children respond to music. Infants smile when adults sing to them. They begin to move their bodies when they hear music, and they respond to toys that make sounds. Soon children hum, sing, and make up chants. As their coordination increases, children begin moving deliberately to music. They sway, dance, bounce up and down, clap their hands, and stamp their feet.

Preschool children are becoming aware of rhythm and can use simple rhythm instruments. They like to sway, walk, or jump when someone claps rhythmically or plays an instrument. They discover new ways to move their bodies and use props such as scarves, streamers, and hula hoops.

Listening to Sounds and Music

Teachers can provide opportunities throughout the day for children to listen to different sounds and types of music. Children develop listening skills when you call their attention to sounds, play background music, and offer special listening activities.

Encourage children to listen to the sounds that are all around us.

Preschool children enjoy guessing games in which they close their eyes and try to identify familiar sounds: a ringing telephone, rain banging on a window, leaves rustling in the wind. Point out sounds during walks: "Do you hear the birds singing?" "The wind sounds like a howling dog." "Our shoes sound different on the sidewalk from the way they sound on grass."

Introduce different kinds of music.

In addition to songs and music written for children, preschool children enjoy different musical styles, including classical, jazz, marches, musical plays, and traditional music from a variety of cultures. Different types of music have different effects on children's moods. Some classical music and quiet instrumentals can be relaxing at naptime, while a march or lively jazz can prompt dancing or parading around the room. Many public libraries have selections of children's CDs and tapes, as well as other types of music. Ask families what kinds of songs and music their children like to listen to at home and try to include these preferences when playing music in your room.

Use various strategies to focus children's attention.

To help older preschool children strengthen their listening skills, encourage them to listen to music and other sounds with you. Younger children might not be able to sit still and listen for very long, but they can enjoy listening to music while they do something else. For example, play music in the Art Area. Ask the children to think about the music as they paint or draw.

"What does the music make you think of?"

"What different colors do you think of as you listen?"

"Does this music make you feel like painting quickly or slowly?"

Play music selectively, however. When music is playing all the time, it becomes background noise rather than sound to attend and enjoy.

Singing With Children

Singing is a part of every preschool program because it is fun; builds a sense of community; and supports development of phonemic awareness, hearing the sounds that make up letters and words. Young children like simple, lively, repetitive songs because they are easy to learn. Even a child who can't remember all of the words can join the chorus. Preschool children also enjoy songs with finger or larger movements, such as "I'm a Little Teapot." To encourage creativity, invite children to change the words to favorite songs or add new movements.

Suggestions for Singing With Preschool Children

Ask families to share their favorite songs. This is a wonderful way to bring children's cultures and languages into the program.

List simple songs the children know. Post the list in the room as a reminder of songs everyone knows. As the children learn new songs, add them to the list.

Sing during transitions. For example, sing while getting ready for lunch or during clean-up. When children have to wait for a short time, sing to use the time well.

Make specific songs a part of familiar routines. Tie special songs to daily routines, such as starting the day or cleaning up. Some children gain a sense of security from knowing that certain events always occur in the same way. They quickly point out the omission if you forget to include specific songs at their regular times.

Play singing games. Encourage everyone to sing while playing games such as "London Bridge" and "The Farmer in the Dell."

Act out story songs. Make props for several songs, such as "The Old Woman Who Swallowed a Fly," so children can sing and act at the same time.

Make audiotapes of children singing alone or in a group. Most children enjoy hearing their own voices on tape. You can share the tapes with family members.

Sing the same song in different ways. Sing the same song with and without instruments, loudly, softly, in a whisper, quickly, slowly, sitting, standing, marching, or hopping.

Use a familiar tune to turn a rhymed, repetitive story into a song. This is a great way to have fun with music and language.

Make up new songs with the children. Use familiar tunes and make up words to go along with what children are doing. "This is the way we make ice cream, make ice cream, make ice cream…"

Introduce new songs. Choose songs with simple words and melodies and with repetition. Sing each song several times, encouraging children to join you. Shorten the phrases if they are too long for preschool children to remember.

Playing Rhythm Instruments

Most children love to make their own music. They even use their bodies as their first rhythm instruments. Start clapping and invite children to join you: "How softly can you clap? How loudly can you clap? Can you clap slowly like this? Can you clap really fast?"

Preschool children can use harmonicas, xylophones, hand bells, kazoos, electronic keyboards, and pianos. They enjoy making music with simple rhythm instruments, purchased or homemade, that produce interesting and varied sounds. A set of rhythm instruments includes

- drums/cymbals
- xylophones
- triangles
- rhythm sticks
- hand bells
- tambourines
- clackers
- sandpaper blocks
- maracas/shakers

Making Rhythm Instruments

Drums: Glue lids to oatmeal or ice cream containers. Use dowels of different lengths and diameters for drumsticks.

Cymbals: Flatten aluminum pie plates, make holes, and use string to attach noisemakers such as thread spools or large buttons.

Shakers: Fill small boxes or plastic containers with pebbles or beans. Tape the lids securely so the contents won't fall out.

Kazoos: Use a rubber band to attach a piece of waxed paper around the end of a short cardboard tube. (For health reasons, use paper towel rolls cut in thirds.)

Sand blocks: Use thumbtacks to fasten coarse sandpaper to small blocks of soft wood, and attach cabinet knobs to make a handle on each block.

Hand and wrist bells: Sew bells on a piece of wide elastic, and sew the ends of the elastic together.

Give children plenty of time to explore the properties of rhythm instruments.

The first time you introduce rhythm instruments, give each child the same kind. When the children are ready for a greater variety of instruments, provide duplicates of the popular ones to minimize conflicts over taking turns. Name each instrument and allow plenty of time for children to explore its properties. Have children take turns demonstrating the variety of sounds they can make with their instruments. Ask questions, such as, "How can you make different sounds with the maracas? How can you make them sound louder or softer?"

Parade the children's marching band.

Play recorded marching music and encourage the children to move around the room playing their instruments. Their marching band can have a parade if children make flags or banners to carry as they proceed around the playground or through the halls. Marches and parades are opportunities to talk about how people of different cultures celebrate special days such as Thanksgiving, Cinco de Mayo, Mardi Gras, Juneteenth, the Fourth of July, and so on.

Encouraging Creative Movement

Music and movement tend to go together. Children enjoy experimenting with different movements, and some children are kinesthetic learners who learn best when they move. It's important to have plenty of space for movement activities. Children need to be free to move without bumping into things or each other.

You can encourage their creativity by asking questions:

> "What can your feet do?"

> "How can you move your arms?"

> "How would a family of ducks (or cows) walk across the street?"

> "Can you move only your hands?"

Invite children to:

> "Bend from your waist."

> "Wiggle your fingers."

> "Stamp your feet as loudly as you can."

> "Tiptoe in place."

Open-ended props invite creative movement.

To increase children's enjoyment and stimulate their imaginations, add open-ended props to use while moving to music. Children can wave streamers, scarves, and feathers; swirl pieces of light fabric; chase balloons; toss foam balls; jingle wrist bells; and wear capes while moving and dancing to music. Think of different ways to use hula hoops in movement activities. There is no right or wrong way to use these props, so children are free to discover their own ways.

Families can promote children's creativity by sharing traditional music and dances that are important to them. A parent might visit the classroom to teach a dance. Once children learn the basic steps, you can encourage them to try variations.

what's next?

Skill-Building Journal, section **7-7** *(Learning Activity C)* and section **7-1** *(Feedback).*

Learning Activities

D. Offering Art Experiences That Invite Exploration and Experimentation

In this activity you will learn to

- provide a variety of open-ended materials and activities that encourage children to express themselves through art

- offer materials and experiences that correspond to children's individual skills and interests

Art activities are an important part of any preschool program. Children relax and use all of their senses as they paint, draw, glue things together, and roll lumps of playdough. Art activities encourage children to use their imaginations and create something of their own. They make choices and try out their own ideas without thinking that there has to be a right or wrong result. The daily schedule should include long periods of time during which children may decide what to do, gather the materials they need, and carry out their plans.

Recognize that younger preschool children enjoy the creative process.

Younger preschool children tend to be more interested in art processes than in products. They want to discover what will happen if they use the side of a crayon or if they paint with their fists or elbows. Young preschool children enjoy the physical experience of scribbling with crayons and pounding playdough. As their small-muscle skills and coordination grow, they are pleased to be able to control their marks and determine the width of a playdough "snake." As they learn to use a variety of media, they experiment with colors, brush strokes, textures, and combinations of shapes. Older preschool children begin to care about art products, and they examine and think about their work. Invite children who draw to tell you about their creations. Listen carefully to what they tell you; their pictures and words are both forms of communication.

Many teachers wonder if it is a good idea to offer coloring books, photo copies, patterns for particular products, models, or craft kits to preschool children. The answer is simple: **No, it is not a good idea.** First, asking children to use the same materials in the same way does not allow them to express their ideas in original ways. Coloring books and projects that require children to match a model or follow specific instructions do not promote creativity. They do not encourage children to experiment, use their imaginations, and express their own ideas as they can with open-ended materials.

Appropriate art experiences offer children choices.

Plan open-ended art experiences that offer choices such as whether to participate, what colors to use, and how to use a technique or materials. Some activities require supervision or guidance, at least the first time they are offered. Children might need help learning how to use tools or materials safely, or they may need a simple step-by-step explanation of a technique or process. When activities are very messy, have children wear smocks and remove anything from the area that might get damaged. Explain that everyone will help clean up and put things away when the activity is over.

Examples of open-ended art activities include

- weaving with paper, cloth strips, yarn, and natural items such as feathers and leaves

- making puppets

- painting murals, pictures, and structures

- making sculptures using wood scraps, recycled items, and school glue or nails

- making prints using paint and objects such as Styrofoam packing trays, lengths of string, and pieces of sponge cut in a variety of shapes

Typically, the activities discussed in the following sections should be offered every day. When the children are enjoying and learning from an activity, offer it for several days. Add new materials to expand their explorations.

Drawing and Painting

Drawing and painting allow children to explore the properties of different materials; discover what they can do with various tools; explore concepts such as size, color, and shape; and develop fine motor skills and coordination. Of course, they also support children's self-expression.

Children's drawing and writing skills progress through predictable stages.

Young children go through similar stages as they explore drawing and painting. When teachers understand and recognize the stages of children's artistic development, they can respond with appropriate materials and activities and encourage children to continue experimenting and learning. Think about how you can promote children's self-expression with new materials and ideas, and ask children to talk about their creations.

The following chart summarizes children's stages as they develop drawing and painting skills.

Developmental Stages of Children's Art[23]

Literacy Materials in Interest Areas	Literacy Learning
Early scribbles Make random marks in many directions. Enjoy physical motions.	
Later scribbles Make circles, lines, or zigzags. May cover whole paper. Control use of a drawing tool.	
Basic shapes Recognize and repeat shapes, such as circles, rectangles, and crosses.	
Mandalas Combine designs, for example crosses with circles or rectangles.	
Suns Draw circles or ovals with lines at the edges or marks in the middle. Adults think they look like suns or human faces.	
Humans Combine shapes and lines to make a figure that represents a person.	
Animals and trees Combine the same shapes and lines to draw animals and trees. Animals have ears on top of circle. Later animals are no longer upright. Trees begin as rectangles with a circle on top.	
Making pictorial drawings Combine shapes and figures. Size and color may not be realistic. Objects on the same page may be unrelated and free-floating.	

Children move through the same stages in painting as they do in drawing. At first, children focus on how it feels to paint. They love the way the brush slides across the paper and usually are not very interested in the color or design that results. This is why many first paintings look the same: every inch of available space is covered with a brownish-purplish color that results when the child brushes layer upon layer of color onto the paper.

When needed, demonstrate basic painting techniques.

First-time painters may need help learning basic techniques, such as how to hold the brush and how to wipe the brush against the side of the container to remove excess paint. It's best to put small amounts of paint in each container, because it is easier for children to control paint when there is not too much of it. Also, brushes tend to last longer when the paint level is below the bristles. Teachers should assist children who request help, while at the same time allowing all children to experiment and learn through trial and error. Most 4- and 5-year-olds use a wide range of colors if it is offered. They mix colors together and add white paint to create pastels. They like using colors such as purple and black, as well as the primary colors. Gradually, children become more purposeful in their painting. They request specific colors and want to place things on the paper in particular ways. They may be concerned when drips disrupt what they are trying to do. Eventually, they reach the stage where they plan their paintings.

Change the paper, paint, and tools to offer a variety of painting experiences.

Painting experiences can be varied by simply changing the tools, the paint, or the paper. Here a few examples:

- blow painting—dip one end of a straw in paint; blow through the other end to splatter the paint across the paper

- squirt bottle painting—make thick paint by mixing 1 part salt, 1 part flour, and 1 part water with 2 parts dry tempera paint; pour into squirt bottles; provide thick paper or cardboard

- spatter painting—place leaves, feathers, and shells on paper; position a screen on top; use a toothbrush to force the paint through the screen; remove the items when dry

- crayon-resist painting—make crayon designs on paper and then paint over them with diluted paint

- folded painting—put paint on a piece of paper, fold it, then unfold it

Collages and Structures

Collages are made by gluing a variety of thin materials on a flat surface. Structures are three-dimensional creations made by fastening a variety of objects together. Both of these art activities offer wonderful opportunities for creative expression and exploring concepts.

To make collages, children need a variety of materials: fabric scraps, ribbon, wood scraps, Styrofoam, feathers, magazine pictures, and buttons. Children glue selected items on a sturdy surface, such as cardboard, heavy corrugated paper, construction paper, or poster board. Paper can be used as the underlying support for collages made with paper scraps.

As children gain experience in making collages, they can use scissors to cut pieces of paper or thin materials (such as wallpaper samples or ribbon) to the size and shape they want.

To make three-dimensional structures, children need a framework, items to attach to it, and fasteners to secure the items to the framework. Materials include

- for the framework: blocks of wood, shoe boxes, plastic containers, berry boxes

- for attachments: tile pieces, Styrofoam, cork, fabric, paper, sponges, wooden clothespins, dowels, items such as those used for collages

- for fasteners: toothpicks, wire, wooden dowels, straws, paper fasteners, yarn, nails, pipe cleaners, school glue, and tape

Creating three-dimensional structures invites experimentation and reinforces children's natural curiosity. Arranging objects requires children to plan and organize. Learning that a big piece of cork is too heavy to be secured by one toothpick is a scientific discovery. Trying different ways to make a structure stand upright is practice in solving problems. Looking at other people's work is part of learning to appreciate unique approaches to self-expression and problem solving.

Exploring Playdough and Clay

Given playdough for the first time, most children smell, taste, poke, and pinch it; squeeze it between their fingers; push it around; and pound it with their hands. Children need plenty of time to explore this material, experience its texture, and discover what they can do with it.

Children can use playdough directly on a table top. As they become familiar with this material, offer props such as wooden spoons, wooden mallets, rolling pins, and cookie cutters. Make sure you have duplicates of the most popular items. Children have as much fun making playdough as they do using it, especially when they vary the texture and color. The chart on the following pages includes two popular playdough recipes. Store the playdough in a refrigerator, in sealed plastic bags or containers; put it out each day for children's use.

Children enjoy using modeling clay and clay that hardens.

Two types of clay match the developmental skills of preschool children: soft modeling clay, which does not dry and harden, and clay that can be baked or left to air dry. If possible, provide both types of clay in your Art Area. Children enjoy manipulating soft clay and using it to make balls, snakes, or different shapes. Rolling pins, cookie cutters, and tongue depressors are useful tools that encourage further exploration with soft clay. Clay that hardens is a good choice for children who want to save their work. Once the clay hardens, children can paint their creations.

Display individual containers of clay and playdough and an assortment of props to use with them on low, open shelves where children can reach them. Children may choose the material and tools they want to use.

Art Materials for Preschoolers

Items	Tips for Teachers
Paper and cardboard	A variety of papers (tissue, construction, wrapping, sandpaper) and shapes (circles, squares, triangles) lets children experiment with texture, color, shape, and absorbency. Ask a local newspaper or printer to donate end rolls of newsprint; ask for outdated wallpaper and fabric sample books at other local stores. Businesses may save scrap paper for your class. When ordering paper, get large sizes (at least 12" x 18") so children can make bold movements.
Brushes and other painting tools	Brushes 1" in width and 5" or 6" in length, with thick handles, are easiest for preschool children to use. Offer brushes in other sizes and shapes, along with sponges (whole or cut in shapes), cotton balls, paper towels, marbles, ink stamps, feathers, leaves, tongue depressors, straws, strings, eye droppers, rollers, plastic squeeze bottles, whisk brooms, and so on, so children can explore tools and techniques.
Easels	Purchase or build simple easels, or hang a piece of plastic on the wall (indoors or outdoors) and tape or clip paper on the plastic.
Paint	Liquid tempera paint, although expensive, is long-lasting and produces vibrant colors. Powdered tempera is much cheaper but must be mixed. Add a few drops of alcohol or wintergreen while mixing, to prevent tempera from souring. Add soap flakes to improve consistency and make it easier to wash paint from clothes. Offer sawdust, sand, and salt to sprinkle on paper or to add to the paint, to encourage experiments with texture.
Finger paint	**Recipe:** Combine 1 C liquid starch with 6 C water, 1/2 C soap flakes, and a few drops of food coloring. **Alternative Recipe:** Mix 3 T sugar with 1/2 C cornstarch in a pan; then add 2 C cold water. Cover and cook the mixture over low heat until thickened. Cool; then add food coloring. Paint on a washable table, on a table covered with oilcloth or a shower curtain, on cookie sheets or plastic trays, or on glossy paper. Make sure children have ample room to experiment with paint and fingers.
Scrap building materials	Supply various sizes of linoleum, tiles, wallboard, wire, wire mesh, wood, and wooden dowels.

Items	Tips for Teachers
Crayons and other drawing materials	Large, good crayons produce even, vibrant, colors. (Less expensive crayons have less color.) For variety, offer white and colored chalk, pens, pencils, and washable markers. **Recipes:** Soap crayons (for water play): Mix 1/8 C water with 1 C soap flakes; add food coloring. Pour mixture into plastic ice cube trays or popsicle molds. Remove when hardened. Crayon cookies (to reuse old, broken crayons): Peel crayons. Place 5–7 crayons in each section of a non-stick muffin tin. Melt at 250°. Turn oven off, leaving tin inside. Remove tin when oven is cold. Push bottom of each section to remove.
Playdough	**Recipe:** Combine and knead 2 C flour, 1 C salt, 2 T oil, 1 C water, and a few drops of food coloring. For smoother playdough, add 1T cream of tartar to above ingredients and heat in a pan, stirring constantly, until dough pulls away from sides of the pan and forms a lump. Then knead the dough. Store in plastic bags or containers in the refrigerator. Commercial playdough can be harmful if swallowed and is difficult to remove from carpets.
Clay	**Recipe:** Soft clay: Mix and knead 2 C corn starch, 1 C baking soda, 1 C water, and food coloring. Modeling clay: 1 C salt, 1 1/2 C flour, 1/2 C warm water, 2T oil, and food coloring. This dough will harden. Store in plastic containers.
Tools for playdough and clay	Provide short, thick dowels; rolling pins; cookie cutters; and tools that make impressions, such as a meat tenderizer.
Paste or glue	Inexpensive white paste and school glue work well for most projects and activities. Paper-mâché and woodworking may require specific kinds of glue.
Scissors	Supply good scissors with blunt ends. Provide left-handed scissors as needed.
Natural items	Collect acorns, feathers, flowers, pinecones, seashells, seeds, stones, pebbles, and so on for collages and decorating.
Sewing supplies	Provide beads, braids, buttons, cotton balls, ribbons, shoelaces, snaps, hooks and eyes, yarn, and felt. Offer fabric scraps of different colors, sizes, and textures, such as burlap, canvas, denim, felt, fake fur, lace, leather, oilcloth, and terry cloth. (Ask families or fabric stores to contribute to the supply.) Purchase large plastic sewing needles, thick yarn, and plastic canvas at craft stores.

Items	Tips for Teachers
Household items	Ask families to help keep the classroom stocked with items such as aluminum foil, bottle tops, plastic wrap, parchment, corks, egg cartons, clean bleach bottles, empty containers, boxes, packing supplies, cans with smooth rims, doilies, spray bottles, string, and toothpicks.
Other art supplies	Provide glitter, confetti, appliance parts, pipe cleaners, beads, stamp pads and stamps, marbles, shredded paper, old business cards, hangers, and wire. Your community might also have a reusable resource center where you can purchase interesting materials for a nominal charge.
Clean-up items	Provide plenty of mops, sponges, brooms, and towels so all the children can help clean up. Store toxic cleaning products in locked cabinets.

what's next?

Skill-Building Journal, section **7-8** *(Learning Activity D),* section **7-1** *(Feedback),* and section **7-9** *(Reflecting on Your Learning).*

8

Self

Overview

Helping Children Learn About Themselves and Others

Respecting Each Child as an Individual

Providing a Program That Enables Children to Be Successful

Your Own Sense of Self

Learning Activities

A. Using Your Knowledge of Child Development to Help Children Build a Sense of Self

B. Appreciating Each Child as an Individual

C. Offering a Program That Promotes Success

D. Using Language That Conveys Respect for Children and Their Feelings

8.   Self

Overview

A sense of self is rooted in the family.

From birth, children begin to learn about themselves. They learn who they are, how they are like other people, and how they are different. When a baby reaches out to touch her reflection in a mirror, she collects information about herself. A sense of self includes recognizing physical traits and much more. When her parents and teachers smile and laugh with her, marvel at her growing skills, and celebrate her very being, she learns that she is a person of value.

Preschool children need opportunities to work hard and meet challenges.

Children's sense of self is rooted in home and community experiences. Preschool children are interested in learning about families, cultures, and communities and in understanding their place in the world. They are not afraid to take on challenging tasks, and they will work hard to accomplish goals they set for themselves. A preschool child can write a letter to a friend (often asking for help in writing what he wants to say), set the table for lunch, or figure out which paint colors to mix to get purple. With acknowledgment of both efforts and accomplishments, children begin to build self-esteem. This confidence enables them to tackle problems, attempt new challenges, help others, recover from setbacks, and learn from mistakes.

Families and teachers are the greatest influence on children's sense of self.

Preschool children learn about themselves when the program offers an interesting environment, challenging activities, and meaningful routines. However, along with family members, you are the greatest influence on children's sense of self. When you listen to children you let them know that you understand and appreciate their feelings. When you comment on their efforts and accomplishments you help them feel good about who they are and what they can do.

As a teacher, your supportive interactions help children learn about and value themselves and others. When you offer help in solving a problem or comment on a new painting technique, you are fostering the child's sense of self. By demonstrating respect for each child you show that each person is valued. Young children need opportunities to succeed and to experience the satisfaction that comes from mastering a skill and helping another person. By offering appropriate materials, activities, and experiences, you encourage children to try new things, function as a member of a group, and experience success in a variety of situations.

You can promote children's sense of self by

- helping children learn about themselves and others

- respecting each child as an individual

- providing a program that enables children to be successful

Helping Children Learn About Themselves and Others

1. **Offer a bias-free program that respects differences such as gender, ability, culture, ethnicity, and family background.** "Aimee, tell Leo that of course girls can build with blocks. Look at those pictures of construction workers. There are men and women."

2. **Provide opportunities for children to learn about and appreciate people of different cultures and ethnic groups.** Invite families to share recipes, books, music, games, dances, and their time, by completing tasks at home or volunteering in the classroom.

3. **Encourage children to share and build on their interests.** "Tyrone, here's a magnifying glass. You can use it to get a closer look at the roly-poly bugs you found under the rock."

4. **Show appreciation for children's positive behavior.** "Marcus, I saw you showing Sara how to make a print of her finger painting. You like to help others."

5. **Learn and use a few words in the home languages of children whose first language is not English.** "Jorge, ¿puedes ayudarme buscar estos libros por favor?" ("Jorge, can you help me look for those books?")

6. **Encourage children to talk about their feelings and take their concerns seriously.** "I think you are worried about moving to a new house. Do you want to talk about it? It might help you feel better."

example

Ms. Kim Helps Carlos Learn About His Painting Style

Ms. Kim approaches the easels where Carlos is painting. Carlos smiles as he looks at his picture. Ms. Kim stops to talk. "Carlos, would you like some help hanging your picture?" Carlos nods. They each hold one side of the picture, hang it on the line, then step back to look at it. Ms. Kim points to Carlos's brushstrokes and says, "It looks like you used the side of the brush to make those marks. I see you used a lot of blue paint, as you did last week. Blue seems to be one of your favorite colors." Carlos says, "Yeah, I like blue." Ms. Kim points to a print by the artist Picasso that is hanging above the sink in the art area. She explains, "Picasso painted many blue paintings at one time in his life." Carlos says, "That's what I am. I'm a blue painter." He returns to the easel and starts another blue painting. Ms. Kim writes a brief note on the index card in her pocket, "Introduce Carlos to shades of blue."

Respecting Each Child as an Individual

7. **Observe each child regularly to learn about individual needs, skills, abilities, interests, culture, and family experiences.** "Marcus seems to be getting used to having a baby sister. I saw him holding a doll and heard him say, 'Don't cry. I'll get you a bottle.'"

8. **Know what each child can do and show that you value individual interests and abilities.** "I see you are interested in learning more about gerbils. This new library book might have answers to your questions."

9. **Offer verbal and gentle nonverbal contact to show you care about the child's well-being.** Give a child a hug, a touch, or a smile to communicate your positive feelings.

10. **Spend individual time with each child every day.** "I'm coming right now to hear all about your experiment. You can tell me what you found out about melting ice."

11. **Help children learn how to handle their strong feelings.** "It's hard to say goodbye to Grandma. Would you like to write a letter to give her when she comes back at the end of the day?"

12. **Show by what you say and do that you respect each child.** "Amanda, I put a new book about whales in the library because you told me how much you like them."

Mr. Lopez Helps Benjamin Express His Feelings

example

Benjamin places another button on the scale. "Look," he calls to Mr. Lopez. "Now it balances." "It took you a long time, but you did it," comments Mr. Lopez, bending down for a closer look. Benjamin smiles proudly. Just then, Janelle walks by, swinging her arms. Crash! The scale tips over and there are buttons all over the table and the floor. "No!" shouts Benjamin. "I wanted to count the buttons." He lifts his arm to hit Janelle. "Benjamin," Mr. Lopez says, reaching up to stop Benjamin's swing. "Janelle hit the scale by accident, but I can't let you hit her. Tell Janelle how you feel." Benjamin turns to Janelle and says, "I'm angry. You messed up my hard work. Be careful." Janelle says, "I'm sorry Benjamin. Can I help you pick up?" "Okay," says Benjamin. "You can help."

Providing a Program That Enables Children to Be Successful

13. **Provide a range of activities and materials that can be enjoyed by children with varied interests, abilities, and skills.** Offer puzzles that range in complexity, playdough utensils, books, table blocks, beads and string, and other open-ended materials that can be used by children in different ways.

14. **Acknowledge children's efforts as well as their accomplishments.** "Tony, every day you go a little further along the monkey bars. That takes hard work, doesn't it?"

15. **Allow children to do as much as possible for themselves, even if they take a long time.** Follow a flexible schedule and coordinate with colleagues so children who need extra time may have it.

16. **Repeat activities so children can practice, master skills, and experience success.** "It's time for lunch, now, so we have to put the bean bags and baskets away. Tomorrow you may play this game again."

17. **Accept mistakes as a natural part of learning.** "Whoops! You poured too much juice in the cup, and it spilled. Get a sponge from the sink so you can clean it up. Then you may try again. "

18. **Consider children's individual characteristics when setting up the environment, choosing materials, and planning activities.** "Before we rearrange the room, we need to measure the traffic paths to make sure there will be room for Frankie's wheelchair."

Ms. Williams Helps Mark Succeed

example

Ms. Williams observes Mark getting out one of the new animal puzzles that has 16 pieces. Ten minutes later, she notices that Mark is no longer at the puzzle table, but the polar bear puzzle pieces are all over the table. She finds him in the library area and says, "Mark, it looks like you had trouble finishing that new puzzle. If you come back to the table, we can work on it together. Puzzles with lots of pieces are hard to do at first. You'll be able to do it alone after you try it a couple of times." Mark and Ms. Williams return to the puzzle. They talk about the pieces—where the legs belong, the bear's head, his back—until the entire puzzle is put together. "Sometimes it takes hard work to finish something," says Ms. Williams. "You didn't think you could do a puzzle with so many pieces, but you did!"

what's next?

Skill-Building Journal, section **8-2** *(Overview)*, section **8-10** *(Answer Sheets)*, and section **8-1** *(Feedback)*.

Your Own Sense of Self

People with positive self-esteem value their abilities and accomplishments.

How an individual feels about his or her personal characteristics is one part of a sense of self, which is also called self-esteem. People with a positive sense of self are comfortable with who they are, what they can do, and what they have accomplished. They have achieved meaningful goals and set new ones. Overall, they have a realistic appreciation of their abilities and contributions and feel valued by others.

Teachers' sense of self, or self-esteem, affects their understanding of children.

Do you describe yourself by your physical appearance or other personal attributes? Perhaps you say, "I am lots of fun, a hard worker, a helpful neighbor, a loving parent, a thoughtful colleague." Your sense of self reflects your experiences. Your culture, home life, school experiences, successes, and failures contribute to your sense of self. They also affect your understanding of child development and of individual children. Do you sometimes make assumptions about children whose characteristics and experiences differ from yours? Do those assumptions turn out to be true or false?

Think about your likes, dislikes, learning style, opinions, and feelings. What are your individual characteristics and abilities? How are you the same as and different from other people in your family, at work, in the community, in the country, in the world? The more you know about yourself, the more you can help children understand and appreciate themselves and their peers.

Our experiences shape our views and interactions.

As you think about your childhood experiences and what was important in your home and community, consider how your values have changed over time. Your experiences (or lack of experiences) with people of diverse backgrounds may have helped to shape your views and interactions with people today. With self-awareness, you can make a conscious decision to keep the beliefs and behaviors that match your current experiences and change those that don't.

With greater personal awareness, you will be able to help children accept and appreciate their individual characteristics. You can help them identify with and feel positive about their own families, culture, ethnicity, and home language. With your support they will learn that there is a place for everyone in the group and that people are alike and different in many ways. How you interact and respond to children conveys your respect and acceptance of them. Respect and acceptance are what most children and adults ultimately want from others.

what's next?

Skill-Building Journal, section **8-3** *(Your Own Sense of Self)*, section **8-1** *(Feedback)*, and section **8-4** *(Pre-Training Assessment).*

Learning Activities

LEARNING ACTIVITY

A. Using Your Knowledge of Child Development to Help Children Build a Sense of Self

In this activity you will learn to

- recognize some typical characteristics of preschool children

- use what you know about children to promote a sense of self

Like other kinds of development and learning, building a sense of self begins early in life. When adults respond to babies with coos and smiles, infants learn that they are important people. Later adults talk with babies about what they look like and what they can do." "Your eyes are brown." "You have strong legs." "You are patting your bottle." Such comments help a child understand who she is and that other people value her.

Young children's self-awareness becomes obvious in the toddler years. Their growing language skills—"My shoe," Mine!" and "Me do it."—provide the evidence. Two-year-olds begin to pay attention to characteristics such as eye and hair color. They learn how to name some of their feelings, but they often have difficulty coping with anger and frustration.

Preschool children learn about themselves through interactions with peers and adults.

Preschool children tend to be social and develop strong friendships. They learn about themselves while playing with other children and through relationships with adults. Some young children can understand and name their feelings; others are still working on this skill. Most preschool children need adults to teach them how to handle strong feelings and express them in acceptable ways that do not harm people or things.

- Sara (age 3) pulls on Ms. Kim's sleeve and says, "You said I could pick the story to read today. Did you forget?"

- Janelle (age 4) crawls through the tunnel as fast as she can. She tells Mr. Lopez, "I don't want the monsters to get me."

- Jorge (age 5) writes his name over and over again. he says, "J-O-R-G-E. That spells me, Jorge."

Preschool children can learn about themselves when they have opportunities to use real skills to do meaningful work. Most preschool children are not ready to learn to read and write, do arithmetic, and memorize facts as they will in elementary school. Nevertheless, teachers can help children to acquire knowledge and develop concepts. They can provide developmentally appropriate materials and activities that introduce children to literacy, mathematics, science, social studies, the arts, and technology.

Preschool children thrive on a mix of self-directed play and teacher-led activities.

Some teachers and families worry that children will not be prepared for school. They expect preschool children to learn too much, too soon. This approach may work in the short term. However, when children are pushed too hard in formal learning tasks, without enough time for exploration, they may lose interest in learning. A more effective way to support learning is to offer a balanced mix of self-directed play and exploration and teacher-led activities for individuals and small groups.

On the other hand, sometimes adults don't understand how capable preschool children are. They may continue to provide help, even when children can do things for themselves. They may also think that preschool children are too young to learn. Children want to learn new things and be independent. When preschool children are aware of their abilities, they feel confident, competent, and ready to try new things.

Social/emotional development occurs throughout life.

Social/emotional development is closely linked with gaining a sense of self. At every stage of life, children (and adults) must deal with age-specific challenges before they move on to the next stage. If these challenges are handled successfully, children's social/emotional development is enhanced. Psychologist Erik Erikson outlined eight stages of social/emotional development from infancy to old age.[24] Erikson's last five stages cover the school-age years, adolescence, young adulthood, marriage, work, and parenting, and maturity. They focus on industry, identity, intimacy, the ability to reach out to others, and reflect on one's life. Erikson's message is that social/emotional development continues throughout our lives.

In Erikson's first stage of development, infants resolve the conflict between **trust** and mistrust. When responsive adults meet babies' basic needs quickly and consistently, infants learn to feel safe and secure in their world. A sense of trust supports infants as they explore the environment, try new activities, develop new skills, and interact with others. Feelings of trust continue to grow and support development and learning throughout childhood and into the adult years. A sense of trust supports the development of autonomy, which usually begins during the toddler years.

Toddlers resolve the conflict between **autonomy** and shame and doubt. Autonomy concerns being independent, doing things for oneself, making decisions, and exploring the world. As toddlers and young 3-year-olds assert their growing independence, they are likely to say "no" and insist on doing everything themselves. Autonomy is essential to the development of initiative, which generally takes place during the preschool years.

Preschool children resolve the conflict between **initiative** and guilt. Preschool children tend to be active, talkative, creative, and eager to learn and have new experiences. They seem to have endless energy. They can build, draw, mold, paint, climb, and swing with increasing skill. If you encourage them to explore, solve problems, and do things for themselves, they will show initiative. Their sense of self and self-confidence grow as their knowledge and skills increase.

Developmental Characteristics of Preschool Children

Preschool children typically

- want to please adults and may seek approval and attention

- may be afraid of such things as monsters, the dark, animals, or some people

- can eat, dress, wash hands, go to the bathroom, and do many other things for themselves

- are learning to recognize, name, and express feelings in acceptable ways

- like to try new things and may take risks without thinking about the consequences

- identify with their gender, family, culture, ethnic group, and community

- are eager to learn and develop new skills in all areas of development

- have lots of physical energy and want to gain physical skills

Development: It's All Connected

In addition to social and emotional skills, building a sense of self relies on physical, cognitive, and communication skills. For example:

Physical

Preschool children are very aware of their physical skills. When a child learns to throw a ball, jump a distance, or cut with a pair of scissors, the sense of accomplishment is enormous. Mastering physical skills helps children feel good about their abilities. This sense of confidence and competence leads to emotional security and a willingness to risk learning other social and cognitive tasks, as well as physical. Encouraging children's physical development promotes their growth in all areas and contexts.

Cognitive

Preschool children are eager, hard-working learners. When asked why he enjoyed an activity, one child responded, "It was really hard." They use their growing classification skills to group both objects and people. They learn to identify themselves by gender, ethnicity, and culture, and are curious about how they are the same as and different from other people. Preschool children are sensitive to adult attitudes about individual characteristics and form views about their own characteristics and those of others.

Language

Preschool children tend to talk a lot. They have rapidly growing vocabularies and can share their ideas, interests, and feelings verbally. They like to talk about themselves and to engage in conversations with others.

what's next?

Skill-Building Journal, section **8-5** *(Learning Activity A),* section **8-10** *(Answer Sheets),* and section **8-1** *(Feedback).*

Learning Activities

LEARNING
ACTIVITY

B. Appreciating Each Child as an Individual

In this activity you will learn to

- identify each child's individual characteristics

- show respect and appreciation for individual children

Every child follows an individual pace and timeline for development.

Child development theories and principles describe a general pattern and path for development. However, each child develops according to an individual pace and time line. The stages of child development are guidelines, but within any age group there can be great variation. A child might be faster or slower than the age group average or might be more advanced than age-mates in one area. For example, Michelle can read a few words, but she is still learning how to play successfully with other children.

The program should accommodate children's varied skills, abilities, and interests.

Preschool children tend to have a wide range of interests and abilities, so teachers need to consider both developmental and individual characteristics. For example, a teacher can set up the art area for children new to painting and children with more complex skills. One easel can have only one or two colors of paint and wide brushes, while another has five colors and brushes in several widths. The library area can include some books that are mostly pictures along with those with several sentences on each page. Another way to respond to and challenge all children is to plan activities to accommodate varied skills, abilities, and interests.

Children also vary according to traits such as temperament and personality. Here are some examples:

Adaptability. One child loves to try new foods; another prefers to eat familiar items. Janelle adjusts easily when a sudden thunderstorm delays a planned nature walk, but Aimee keeps asking when the rain will stop.

Activity levels. Amanda is constantly moving. She runs more often than she walks, and she throws her whole body into every activity. Mark is usually content to play quietly while watching what's going on around him.

Body rhythms. Some children do best when routines—eating meals and snacks, resting, using the bathroom—occur at the same time each day. Children with less predictable body rhythms need a schedule that allows them to eat when hungry and rest when tired.

Intensity. Some children express their emotions quietly, others with great gusto. Aimee raises her voice and wiggles when excited or happy, while Tony smiles and speaks in a quiet voice.

Attentiveness. Maria focuses on what she's doing without being distracted by a slamming door or other children's conversations and activities. She falls asleep easily no matter what else is going on in the room. Marcus frequently leaves buildings, pictures, and puzzles unfinished and finds it hard to fall asleep unless his cot is in a protected corner of the room.

Persistence. Leo spends long periods of time making patterns or practicing something new, such as using an egg beater. Avida needs encouragement to take on a new challenge or to stay with a difficult task.

Resilience. Some children can easily cope with daily disappointments and difficulties. They bounce back and move on when a favorite toy is in use or all of the spaces at the water table are filled. Other children need a teacher's help to recover from frustrating experiences. They need to be reminded that their turn will come soon or told that you understand their feelings.

Think about your personal style and how it affects your relationships with children. Where do you fit in the following continuums?

- I like . . . versus . . . avoid physical contact?

- I prefer quiet. . . versus . . . exciting times?

- I am slow . . . versus . . . quick to get angry?

- I am "thick skinned" . . . versus . . . likely to have my feelings hurt easily?

The differences described above are neither good nor bad traits. They simply describe the different ways children (and adults) respond to people and experiences in their lives. As you get to know each child, keep these characteristics in mind. You can use the information you collect as you plan and implement a program that responds to children as individuals.

Learning about individual interests, needs, skills, temperament, culture, language, and family experiences, demonstrates your respect and appreciation for every child. Planning a program that responds to individuals, as well as to the group, helps children learn about and value themselves. Children who know and like themselves are more likely to like and get along with others.

Here are several suggestions to help you understand and appreciate each child:

Communicate frequently with children's families. Children's sense of self is rooted in their relationships with parents and other family members. Share information with parents frequently. Ask them to keep you up-to-date about their child's experiences and activities at home and in the community. Effective early childhood programs involve families as meaningful partners. (See module 11, *Families,* for more information on communicating with families.)

Accept and respect individual differences without trying to change the child. Children need to know that other people appreciate them in order to learn to value themselves. Plan a program that fits the children rather than expecting children to adapt to materials and activities that are not appropriate for the individual or the group.

Plan activities and offer materials with individual children in mind. Learn about children's special interests, abilities, and preferred learning styles through your observation and those of families and colleagues. When you respond to a child's interests or adapt an activity to accommodate the child's learning style, you are saying, "You are important to me. I know you will like this."

Observe children frequently. Record a child's behavior for five minutes, several times a day for a week. Review your observation notes and ask yourself what the child might be feeling and thinking. Look for patterns that give you insight into the child's behavior. Use your insights to plan the program and tailor your interactions with the child.

Ask a colleague, your supervisor, or your trainer to observe a child whose behavior you do not understand or with whom you find it hard to work. Compare and discuss the observation notes. A fresh perspective can lead to greater awareness of the reasons for a child's behavior and ideas for responding in supportive ways.

Listen as children express their feelings. Sharing feelings makes them more manageable. Though you may not like to hear complaining or crying, when you listen, you show respect. You help children learn that you are available to listen to their concerns.

Talk with children about their families during the day. Look at family pictures. Encourage children to make pretend calls to their parents. Comments such as, "Did your grandma put that bow in your hair?" or "Tell me about helping your dad cook dinner," can help children feel connected to their families. Such comments tell children that you think their families are important too.

- What do you remember about your own childhood? How did you and your siblings feel and behave in different situations?

- Is there a child in your class whom you find it difficult to get to know? What can you do to get to know that child so you can support him or her?

what's next?

Skill-Building Journal, section **8-6** *(Learning Activity B)* and section **8-1** *(Feedback).*

Learning Activities

LEARNING ACTIVITY

C. Offering a Program That Promotes Success

In this activity you will learn to

- plan an environment and activities that match children's interests and abilities

- offer new challenges to encourage growth and learning

Preschool children are developing the physical, cognitive, social, and emotional skills they will use throughout their lives. Every day they acquire information, develop new interests, and gain a greater understanding of themselves and their world. As children master new skills, they come to see themselves as capable and competent people.

Plan the program so children can do many things for themselves.

Many of the practices described in module 3, *Learning Environment,* help children to feel competent as they become more independent and cooperative. For example, teachers display materials on low shelves, labeled with pictures and words, so children have access to what they need and can return things at clean-up time. They plan a schedule with long blocks of time during which children may choose what they want to do and with whom. Teachers also encourage children to make and carry out their plans and become fully involved in activities.

You and your colleagues probably spend much of your day doing things for children that they cannot do for themselves. It is important, however, to recognize when children are ready to help themselves and to provide opportunities for them to be successful and feel competent. For example, you might help 3-year-old Sara climb up the slide while holding her hand, show 4-year-old Tony a puzzle he's never done before, or put some sturdy plastic knives next to the peanut butter and crackers so all the children can make their own snacks. Children feel good about themselves when they can practice skills they already have and learn new skills in a safe and accepting atmosphere.

Here are some suggestions for offering a program that promotes success through experiences that build independence and cooperation:

Respond to children's current interests and skills and challenge them to extend their learning. For example, if children are studying butterflies, provide pads of paper and markers so their drawings can document the changes they see.

Provide materials that offer challenges and lead to success. When items are too simple, children can get bored. When items are too difficult, children are likely to fail. After several failures a child may feel incompetent.

Reflect children's homes, family structures, cultural backgrounds, and home languages in songs, books, pictures, dolls, music, games, and so on. When children's backgrounds are evident in the program, they tend to feel secure, accepted, and eager to get involved.

Offer open-ended materials and activities. There is no right or wrong way to make a collage out of recycled items, sort a collection of shells, or weigh and measure found objects. As children gain new skills and interests, they will find new ways to explore open-ended materials and activities.

Plan activities that help children understand and handle fears. Provide dress-up clothes and props children can use to overcome fears and make sense of things they don't understand. Give children lots of time for art and other creative outlets and read and discuss books about typical preschool worries and fears. Encourage children to do as much as possible for themselves. Children gain self-confidence as they pour juice, tie shoelaces, and help a friend put her cot on the top of the stack.

Invite children to help do meaningful jobs for the classroom community, such as washing paintbrushes or restocking the paper towel supply. Preschool children like meaningful work and feel proud of their contributions to making the classroom run smoothly.

The children in your program will change a great deal during the year. To promote children's sense of competence, observe them frequently and change the program to reflect their new abilities and interests.

Be specific when you pay attention to a child's work.

When children work hard and apply new skills, avoid offering vague statements such as, "Good job." This kind of praise does not tell a child that you paid attention and noticed what he did. Praise can have a negative effect. When children receive too much praise, they may do things just because it will please their teachers and families. This can prevent them from becoming self-motivated individuals who love learning and trying new experiences. Educator Alfie Kohn believes that praise motivates children to get more praise. Instead of promoting children's sense of self and self-esteem, praise gets in the way of independence, pleasure, interest, and achievement.[25]

Instead of praise, teachers can make thoughtful comments to help children recognize their own efforts and accomplishments and how they helped others. Such an approach acknowledges children and helps them see the value of their work. For example, you might describe what you see or hear a child do, "You put the farm animals in one basket and the zoo animals in the other one." Then add a statement that shows appreciation for what the child did. "Now the other children can find what they are looking for."

Providing the Right Level of Support

One of the hardest things for a teacher to know is when to offer help to a child trying something new and when to gradually withdraw this support so the child can manage independently. Teachers must use their knowledge of individual capabilities and limitations to provide the right kind of support and teaching as children approach new tasks. For example, some children can learn to move the computer mouse or recognize the letters in their name with little support from adults. Other children need encouragement and support for their efforts. Still others might need to be taught indirectly ("I'll hold the paper for you while you clip it to the easel.") or through direct instruction ("Benjamin's ready to throw the ball to you. Follow the ball with your eyes, and keep your arms stretched out."). It is important to remember that sometimes the most supportive thing you can do is to give a child an uninterrupted opportunity to practice a new skill. Rather than stepping in to help, stand back so the child can experience the pleasure of doing something independently.

Intervene only when necessary so children can build a sense of competence.

Observe children closely so you will know who needs support throughout the learning process, who needs words of encouragement, and who simply needs you to nod or smile at them as they try a new activity. If you intervene only when necessary, you help children acquire new skills in a way that builds their sense of competence.

In the following example, the teacher uses knowledge of each child to tailor her approach to providing support.

> Ms. Thomas has ordered a new indoor climber for her room. She knows that the children's reactions to the new equipment will be as varied as their abilities to climb and jump. Before the climber arrives, she plans how she will support the children.

> Leo is very curious, but may be timid about trying the climber. To support Leo and children with similar needs, Ms. Thomas will display pictures of the climber and talk about how children can use it.

Tony and Janelle and are both risk takers. They will be excited about the climber and may act without thinking. To meet their needs, Ms. Thomas will use group time to discuss safety limits. Later she and Mr. Lopez will provide ongoing guidance to encourage safe play.

Avida and Benjamin may take a long time to adjust to the new climber. The group time discussion might make them more fearful. Ms. Thomas plans to talk to these children so she can reassure them that they are capable of climbing safely. She will stay with them at the climber as long as they need her support.

Building relationships with children is part of being a professional. You may enjoy being with some children more than with others and find some children harder to get to know and like. Make it a point to spend individual time regularly with every child in the group. Challenge yourself to find something special about each child that may not have been obvious at first.

what's next?

Skill-Building Journal, section **8-7** *(Learning Activity C)* and section **8-1** *(Feedback).*

Learning Activities

LEARNING ACTIVITY

D. Using Language That Conveys Respect for Children and Their Feelings

In this activity you will learn to:

- listen carefully to children and try to identify what they might be thinking and feeling

- talk with children in ways that convey understanding and respect

Caring language helps children feel valued and respected.

Young children learn a lot about themselves through their interactions with the important adults in their lives. Teachers and family members are like mirrors, reflecting back to children images of their individual characteristics, abilities, and importance. Our nonverbal communications—smiles, hugs, and nods in a child's direction—convey the message, "I am taking the time to notice you and what you are doing." Our words are even more powerful and may stay with children long after they are uttered. When these words are caring, they help a child feel valued and respected.

Listening and Responding to Children

Talking with children respectfully requires the skills of listening and responding. Listening includes hearing what is said, along with paying attention to tone of voice, facial expressions, and nonverbal gestures. Place yourself at the child's level—kneel, crouch, or sit—so you can look at the child and focus your full attention on the meaning of his or her words. Try to relate the words and gestures to your own experiences. Perhaps you will be able to understand what the child is trying to say and what feelings might be behind the words.

Respond to children's words and feelings.

In responding to childrens' words and feelings, use the same courteous voice you would use when speaking with friends and family. It is important to first acknowledge what was said, perhaps by repeating the child's words. Sometimes, however, a child's words don't convey what the child is really feeling. That's why it's so important to try to understand what a child is trying to communicate.

In this example, Ms. Frilles demonstrates respect for Tony's feelings without judging them.

> Since 4-year-old Tony joined the class, he has never painted. One day Ms. Frilles sees him looking at the paintings hanging in the art area. He says to her, "These pictures are ugly." Ms. Frilles bends down and puts her arm around Tony. She responds, "You think these pictures are ugly. That's okay. In our classroom, everyone may paint a different way. That's what makes it interesting. You can have fun experimenting and trying out different ideas. When you want to paint, I'll help you find a smock and an empty easel. I think you will enjoy it."

Ms. Frilles listened to what Tony said and tried to figure out what he might be feeling. She thought that perhaps Tony was worried about his own ability to paint and that's why he called the paintings ugly. Her response showed Tony that she understood his worried feelings and respected his concerns. She encouraged him to try painting and assured him that his effort will be valued.

Personalizing Your Morning Greetings

Morning drop-off times can set the tone for the day. Some preschool children find it hard to say good-bye to their families at drop-off times. Others are ready to start the new day. When children arrive each morning, take time to welcome each child and family with a personal greeting. Here are some examples of individual greetings to children and their family members and what messages they convey.

> "Tyrone, you're the first to arrive today. Would you like to play lotto?" (This says, "I enjoy our one-on-one times together.")

> "Jamie, I see you smiling this morning. Are you looking forward to playing in the loft again today?" (This suggests, "I remember you and the important things you do here.")

> "Avida, is this your Grandpa Fred whom I heard so much about? I know you're glad he came to visit." (The message is, "I listen to the things you tell me. I know you are excited about your grandfather's visit.")

> "Leo, your Grandma went to her job at the airport. She thinks about you even when she is at work. She will be back to pick you up, just as she does every day." (This says, "It's okay to miss your family during the day. I will help you cope.")

Giving Children Attention

Most preschool children are eager to please adults. They want you to watch what they can do, listen to what they have to say, respond to their ideas, encourage their efforts, and meet their needs. Children share things that happen at home: "Last night we hung my new painting on the refrigerator." They want you to notice the results of their hard work: "Watch me. I can skip." Sometimes they need your help to solve a problem: "We want to play this game, but the spinner won't spin. Can you help us?"

Respond to children's requests for attention.

When children seek your attention, it is important to respond in ways that communicate respect and understanding. "Tell me what your Mom and Dad said about your painting." "As soon as I am finished here I'll come watch you skip." "Let's take a look at the spinner. It must be stuck."

Children also ask for attention through their behavior. For example, when Oanh wiggles at group time, her teacher might say, "I can see you are having trouble sitting still today. Would you like to do something else?" This tells Oanh, "I have noticed you. I understand that you are feeling restless today. It's okay to feel restless sometimes. We have other things you can do." Such words pay attention to Oanh's needs and help foster her positive sense of self.

When teachers ignore children or respond with angry or thoughtless words, children may begin to question their own worth. They may think the teacher's words carry more meaning than was intended. Upon hearing an angry or thoughtless statement: "Can't you sit still and listen?" a child could translate the words into a negative self-image: "I am a bad person because I can't sit still." When children hear such words over and over again, they may lose self-confidence, stop trying new challenges, or perhaps begin to use challenging behavior. It's as if they are saying, "If you think I am a bad person, then I must be one."

Practice until caring language is a natural part of every day.

Using caring language takes some practice. When you take the time to get to know and appreciate each child, it becomes very natural to show your respect when you talk with children. You will be rewarded when the children you care for let you know how much better they feel because of your understanding and care.

what's next?

Skill-Building Journal, section **8-8** *(Learning Activity D),* section **8-1** *(Feedback),* and section **8-9** *(Reflecting on Your Learning).*

9
Social

Overview

Offering a Program That Helps Children Develop Social Skills

Teaching Children the Skills to Play and Learn With Others

Building a Positive Relationship With Each Child

Your Own Social Development

Learning Activities

A. Using Your Knowledge of Child Development to Promote Social Development

B. Offering a Program That Supports Social Development

C. Supporting Children's Dramatic Play

D. Helping Children Learn Caring Behavior

E. Helping Children to Make Friends

9. Social

Overview	

Most preschool children enjoy playing and learning with others.

Social development is learning to relate to other children and adults. Social skills are evident as infants respond to the familiar voice or touch of a parent or caregiver, toddlers learn to play alongside others, and preschool children engage in pretend play and play cooperatively with friends. As children develop socially, they learn to take turns, cooperate, negotiate, and eventually to share with others. Although they sometimes argue and disagree, most children enjoy playing and learning with others. They learn to compromise so that play and other activities can continue.

Social skills are critical to success in school and life.

When asked to identify the characteristics of children who are ready for school, teachers list social skills such as taking turns, following directions, sharing, and getting along with others. Children who have positive relationships with other people, and who know how to make and keep friends, tend to be confident and eager to learn. Children who lack social skills are more likely to behave in ways that interfere with their learning. In fact, children who do not achieve minimal social competence by age 6 are likely to be at risk throughout life.[26]

To develop social skills, children need many opportunities to play and learn together. In a balanced, well-planned program, teachers help children learn to respect the rights of others, so that everyone can enjoy the benefits of being part of a group. In addition, teachers help children understand their own feelings and teach them acceptable ways to express themselves. (Because children's feelings about themselves affect their social development, you may want to review module 8, *Self*, while working on this module.)

A sense of security supports children's development of social skills.

Children's social development is strengthened through secure relationships with families and teachers. Through these relationships, children learn acceptable social behavior. As a teacher, you let children know that they are loved and accepted; you meet their needs as consistently and promptly as possible. This helps children feel secure, which in turn allows them to appreciate, respect, and get along with other children and adults.

You can promote children's social development by

- offering a program that helps children develop social skills

- teaching children the skills to play and learn with others

- building a positive relationship with each child

Offering a Program That Helps Children Develop Social Skills

1. **Include large blocks of time in the daily schedule when children may choose their play activities and partners.** Provide a variety of options by setting up well-stocked interest areas that will engage children in learning as they interact with others.

2. **Hold daily class meetings.** Allow time for children to share ideas, discuss feelings, and solve problems affecting individuals and the group. This will help them build the skills they need to function as members of a community.

3. **Plan classroom jobs and routines so two or more children can work together.** "The plants in our garden look very dry. They need a lot of water. Leo and Tony, will you please take care of them?"

4. **Involve children in setting a few simple rules about respecting themselves, each other, and the toys and materials.** "Let's think about how to talk to each other when we want a person to do something. For example, if someone is in your way, say, 'Please move so I can get by.' After she moves, say, 'Thank you.'"

5. **Provide materials and activities that encourage two or more children to play together.** "Maria, Sara likes to play lotto. You can ask her to play with you."

6. **Introduce children to the community beyond the classroom and program.** Plan activities, projects, trips, and visits from community representatives that let children learn about their world and relate to people beyond their immediate environment.

example

Ms. Richards and Three Children Help Each Other Get Ready

The children are getting ready to go outside. "Where's your other shoe?" Ms. Richards asks Linda. "It disappeared," she says. "I took it off when we were playing house. Now I can't find it anywhere." Jamie and Carlos, who are ready to go out, are standing by the door. "We have to find Linda's shoe before we go outside," Ms. Richards explains. "Jamie and Carlos, will you help Linda find her shoe? Then we can all get outside faster." They begin searching. "Here it is," they call. "It was under the pillows." Jamie holds up the shoe proudly and hands it to Linda so she can put it on. "Thanks," says Linda. Ms. Richards says, "This bag of balls is very heavy. Who can help me carry it?" The children and teacher each hold a part of the bag. "Thanks everyone. With your help we are all ready to go outside to play."

Teaching Children the Skills to Play and Learn With Others

7. **Model caring behavior.** "Ms. Kim, I have an extra pair of gloves you may wear when we go on our walk."

8. **Provide time and encouragement for children to solve their problems and conflicts.** "You both want to use the dump truck. How could you take turns?"

9. **Join in children's play by following their lead.** Watch and listen to the children's play for a few minutes; then think of a way to join them to extend the interaction between children.

10. **Read and discuss stories about coping with feelings and difficult situations.** "Can you think of a time when you had a 'terrible, horrible, no-good, very bad day'?" (after reading *Alexander and the Terrible, Horrible, No-Good, Very Bad Day*, by Judith Viorst)

11. **Point out and endorse children's positive solutions to their problems.** "Mark and Jorge both wanted to drive the car. They decided that Jorge should go first because Mark was the driver yesterday."

12. **Share your own feelings when appropriate.** "I'm frustrated because I can't find our song book. Will anyone help me find it?"

Ms. Frilles Helps Two Friends Play Together

example

Ms. Frilles looks around the room to see what the children are doing. Amanda and Michelle, two good friends, are playing in the dramatic play area. Michelle is waving her arms and looks very angry. Amanda, with one hand on her hip, is shaking her head. Ms. Frilles gets closer so she can hear their conversation. The girls are playing restaurant, and both want to be the waitress. Ms. Frilles says to them, "I ate in a restaurant last week. There were so many customers, they needed two servers." Then she steps back. The girls look at each other, and then Amanda says, "Let's sit the dolls in the chairs. Then we can both be waitresses." Ms. Frilles said, "That's good thinking. You found a way for both of you to be waitresses." As Ms. Frilles walks away she sees two dolls sitting at a table in the "restaurant."

Building a Positive Relationship With Each Child

13. **Describe in words what you think a child is feeling.** "I wonder if you are having a bad day because you miss your mom a lot when she goes on a trip."

14. **Introduce and repeat the words used to express feelings.** "When Tony teases you, it makes you feel unhappy, so you cry. Tell Tony, 'I want you to stop teasing me.'"

15. **Assist a child who has difficulty joining a group at play.** Observe the group at play with the child, point out what they are doing, and suggest a way to join.

16. **Respond to individual needs and requests consistently and as quickly as possible.** "I heard you ask for more French toast. It's all gone. If you are hungry, you may have a banana or a bowl of cereal."

17. **Help a child understand the potential and actual consequences of certain behavior.** "Brianna, Jorge doesn't want to play with you because you knocked down his building. He worked on the tower for a long time, so he felt angry when you kicked it."

Mr. Lopez Helps Two Children Handle Their Feelings

example

Mr. Lopez observes the children outdoors. He sees Leo begin to climb the ladder to the slide, then stop. Benjamin, who is next in line, tells him to hurry. He puts his hand on Leo's back and pushes. Leo pushes him back. Mr. Lopez quickly walks over and says, "Stop. It's not safe to push someone on the ladder. What's happening here?" Benjamin replies, "He's taking too much time." Mr. Lopez responds, "Leo, I think you are worried about going down the slide too fast. You're climbing slowly because it helps you feel calm and ready to slide." Leo nods. "Benjamin, you like going fast and don't like to wait." "Yeah," admits Benjamin. "How can you solve this problem together?" asks Mr. Lopez. Benjamin suggests. "Leo, let me go first, then you can take your time." Leo climbs down, and Benjamin has his turn. Leo takes a little more time to get ready, then climbs up again. As Mr. Lopez walks away, he hears Benjamin encouraging Leo, "The slide is fun, Leo. It doesn't hurt!"

what's next?

Skill-Building Journal, section **9-2** *(Overview)*, section **9-11** *(Answer Sheets)*, and section **9-1** *(Feedback).*

Your Own Social Development

Adults use social skills every day.

When you yield to another car in traffic, share your lunch with a colleague who forgot hers, or wait for your turn to speak at a staff meeting, you are using social skills. Adults who cooperate, compromise, share, take turns, negotiate, empathize, and so on tend to get along well with others in their families, workplaces, and communities.

Social skills help us get used to new people and situations.

Sometimes adults need to adapt to a new group of people. Perhaps you just joined a reading group or started attending an exercise class. In such situations you use social skills to get to know the other members and to adjust to the group's accepted ways of doing things. "We always start our meeting by catching up with each other's lives. Then we move on to discuss the book."

Some adults find it very hard to adjust to new situations. This difficulty may be due to characteristics of their temperament or personality. It's possible, though, that during childhood they didn't have many opportunities to get to know new people.

When teachers model positive social behavior, everyone benefits.

Young children learn how society expects them to behave by watching adults interact with each other as well as with children. When children see the important adults in their lives working cooperatively, sharing feelings and ideas, having friendly conversations, and enjoying each other's company, they learn important lessons. Sometimes teachers are so busy that they forget to say "please" or "thank you" and don't take time to enjoy the company of their colleagues. However, when teachers feel positive about their jobs and the people they work with, children can gain a more complete picture of what it's like to be an adult. They see adults working out problems, sharing happy experiences, and cooperating with each other.

what's next?

Skill-Building Journal, section **9-3** *(Your Own Social Development),* section **9-1** *(Feedback),* and section **9-4** *(Pre-Training Assessment).*

Learning Activities

LEARNING ACTIVITY

A. Using Your Knowledge of Child Development to Promote Social Development

In this activity you will learn to

- recognize some typical social behaviors of preschool children

- use what you know about preschool children to support social development

A child's social development begins at birth. Newborn babies are entirely dependent on their families and caregivers. Through their interactions with the adults who comfort, diaper, feed, and talk to them, infants learn to trust people. This trust is the foundation for social development.

Toddlers work hard to define themselves as separate and independent beings with minds of their own. When they run; climb; jump; test limits; and shout, "No! Me do!" they are saying, "This is who I am!" The experiences of being loved, cared for, and working together, help toddlers feel good about themselves and let them know what positive social interaction feels like.

Preschool children understand what social behavior is acceptable.

By the preschool years, most children understand which behaviors are acceptable and which are not. Preschool children are eager to be liked. They spend more time playing with their peers and, although they value adult approval, they are growing more and more independent. They learn from adults and other children and frequently copy what they see other people do.

- Sara (age 3) sets the table in the dramatic play area with three placemats, forks, plates, and cups for herself and her two friends.

- Janelle (age 4) remembers to follow the classroom rules and eagerly reminds her classmates when they don't follow them.

- Tyrone (age 5) slings his backpack over one shoulder in the same the way his Daddy carries his pack and says to his friend, "Time to go to work."

Preschool children sometimes reject each other from play.

The preschool years are also characterized by exclusion. Researchers have found that up to one half of children's requests to join others in play situations are rejected.[27] Although this is typical behavior, exclusion can hurt feelings and prevent the development of important social skills. Vivian Paley, a noted teacher and author, noticed that in her class a few children controlled who was allowed to play and who was not. She established a simple but firm rule, "You can't say that you can't play." By enforcing this rule, the classroom became a more caring community and children gained a sense of belonging.[28]

Play helps children grow in all areas, and it is one of the most important ways in which children develop social skills. Through play, children have fun, try ideas, make friends, and learn about the world. They learn to take turns, share favorite things, understand friendship, and express their feelings in acceptable ways. In addition, play helps children try out adult roles and overcome their fears.

Most infants are fascinated by other people. They will put their fingers in your mouth, touch your hair, and pull on your earrings or glasses. This and other play helps them understand that they are separate persons, learn to enjoy being with other people, and develop trust, which is the foundation for further social development. Mobile infants explore eagerly, crawling and then walking where they want to go. They enjoy watching other children and often imitate what they see others do.

Through their play, toddlers work hard to learn about themselves and others. They observe carefully to figure out relationships, and their ability to do things with each other grows rapidly. Toddlers can be very sensitive to each other, but they may need your help to begin playing, to continue, and to handle disagreements.

Preschool children enjoy the challenges and rewards of sociodramatic play.

Preschool children begin to spend most of their time playing in groups (for example, playing together in the dramatic play area). They organize their own activities, assign roles, make up rules, give out specific tasks, and usually work toward a common goal. For example, a group of children may decide to build a town in the block area. Through discussion and negotiation, they decide who will build the roads, houses, and stores. They resolve conflicts through compromise. The results, both the completed town and the process of working together, are more rewarding than building alone. Children at this level of play enjoy working and playing together. Enjoying the company of other people is an important part of their social development, just as it is for infants and toddlers.

Developmental Characteristics of Preschool Children

Preschool children typically

- can help make and follow a few simple rules

- are learning to share and take turns

- like to imitate adult activities

- talk with other children, in pairs and in groups

- can learn to solve problems through negotiation and compromise

- often exclude other children from their play

- have strong emotions and are learning how to name and express them appropriately

- begin to recognize and understand the feelings of others

- develop friendships and may have a best friend

- gain some awareness of the larger community

- enjoy pretend play alone and with others

- seek and value adult approval

Development: It's All Connected

Children's social development is related to their physical, cognitive, language, and emotional development. Examples follow.

Physical
Children engage with others as they use motor skills to create dramatic play settings and handle props. They take turns, negotiate, and cooperate as they climb stairs, crawl into box houses, and roll out cookie dough.

Cognitive
Children think as they use social skills, such as compromising, negotiating, and problem solving, to make plans with other children that give everyone a role. They learn to use props, such as blocks, as substitutes for other objects, such as phones. This skill in using symbols is needed for higher-level thinking.

Language

Children use language to share ideas, make plans, relate their experiences, and converse with others. They use verbal and written communication in their dramatic play. As their language skills grow, children's play becomes more complex.

Emotional

Children need to understand their own feelings so they can figure out how to get along with others. Playing and learning in groups helps preschool children find out what they do well, develop a sense of competence, and build confidence.

There are a number of reasons why a child might seem to be delayed in gaining social skills. Both personality and temperament play a role in social development, as do family relationships. Acceptable social behaviors may vary in different cultures.

Social Development Alerts[29]

Share concerns with a family if their preschool child frequently

- has feelings and behavior that prevent participation in classroom activities

- loses control, hurts self and others, and shows no concern

- is aggressive and seems pleased to have hurt someone

- acts impulsively without considering consequences

- cries now and then throughout the day

- cries to get others to do what he or she wants

- fails to engage in play or activities with other children

If several of these signs are present over an extended period of time, refer the family to a mental health specialist who can conduct a comprehensive assessment, determine the child's skills and needs, and suggest specific strategies for the program and home.

---

what's next?

Skill-Building Journal, section **9-5** *(Learning Activity A),* section **9-11** *(Answer Sheets),* and section **9-1** *(Feedback).*

LEARNING
ACTIVITY

B. Offering a Program That Supports Social Development

In this activity you will learn to

- arrange the physical environment to encourage social development

- plan a program that allows children to develop and use social skills

A classroom that functions as a community supports social development.

To promote social development, teachers need to make sure children have many opportunities to cooperate, take turns, and help. In addition, it is important to minimize or eliminate the conditions that lead to disagreements and aggressive behavior. One of the most effective ways to help children feel comfortable in a group setting is to create a classroom that functions as a community, with a supportive program that responds to individual and group needs, skills, and interests. The elements of a supportive program include the physical environment (arrangement of furniture and equipment in the indoor and outdoor spaces used by children, interest areas, and the way materials are displayed). In addition, the program includes the daily schedule, routines, transitions, activities, and interactions.

Arranging the Physical Environment

A physical environment divided into interest areas enables small groups of children to work together and focus on what they are doing. Like adults, children respond to the characteristics of the physical environment. An attractive room with homelike features, such as walls painted in warm colors, window curtains, soft lighting, and pictures hung at children's eye-level with plenty of space between them, provides an uncluttered, calm setting for children's play. Consider the following guidelines when planning the preschool environment:

Less is more. Offer a variety of materials to stimulate children's interests, but not so many that children are overwhelmed by too many choices.

Provide a place for everything to be stored. Display toys on low, labeled shelves, store play materials with loose pieces (such as Legos) in separate open containers, and put materials together that are used together (such as paper and crayons). A well-organized environment lets children find what they need. Cleanup proceeds well because it's easy to see where things belong.

Place interest areas near needed resources. For example, locate the art area near the sink and the computer area near an electrical outlet. That way, children won't drip paint on the way to the sink or trip over extension cords.

Rearrange to meet current needs. Create a flexible room layout so teachers can move furniture and equipment when children need space to spread out or to store unfinished projects.

A concrete system for taking turns lets children monitor their own use of interest areas.

Conflicts are common in preschool rooms. Children get in each other's way, knock down buildings, and bump into each other. Some children interpret these incidents as intentional and may respond aggressively. Limiting the number of children in an interest area or on a piece of outdoor equipment minimizes crowding and prevents accidents, thus reducing disagreements. Children can monitor the area themselves if you set up a concrete system that lets them know when there's room for them to play, e.g., five hooks to hang name tags limits the area to five children.

Some disagreements occur when children can't get in or out of an area easily. They may feel trapped or frustrated because movement is limited. To avoid this problem, make sure there is more than one way to get in or out of each area. "Remember to use the steps to climb up to the loft. The rope ladder is for climbing down."

Locating the block area away from the line of traffic offers protection and allows children to work on their structures without worrying about being disturbed. If the block area is in an unprotected space, children passing by are likely to get in the way of the builders and may accidentally knock down their creations.

Every classroom needs a few places where children can be by themselves.

Although preschoolers spend most of their time playing in groups, even the most outgoing children sometimes want to be alone for a while. They may take time out from group living because they are tired and need to rest. Some children need to spend time alone because they are overwhelmed by strong feelings. Time away from the group prevents them from losing control and acting in inappropriate ways. Every classroom should have several places where children can be by themselves. These places could include a listening area with a CD player and earphones; small enclosed spaces like a platform, loft, or large cardboard box; a small defined area with pillows; a small beanbag chair; or a desk or small table with one chair.

When children want to play with just one or two others, they need spaces sized to accommodate a few friends. Indoors, you can use shelves as dividers to create small spaces, group a pile of pillows in a corner, or turn a large appliance carton into a cozy nook. Outdoors, a tire swing holds two children. Large hollow blocks and planks are ideal for children who wish to build their own spaces. A tractor tire sandbox is the perfect size for a small group.

Lookouts let children see and hear what is going on before joining in.

To help children who find it difficult to enter a group, you can create lookouts—places from which a child can observe others at play until he or she feels ready to join. A loft can be a lookout, or a quiet area can serve as a lookout for a noisier one. For example, while painting a picture in the art area, Tony watches several children who are playing house nearby. The art area serves as a lookout point so Tony can watch the noisier, more interactive play in the dramatic play area and learn what the children are doing. This information gives him confidence and a way to enter the play. For example, if he sees other children pretending to cook, he can express his interest in joining by saying, "I'm hungry. What's for dinner?"

Planning the Program

Your daily schedule, routines, transitions, activities, and group time can also support social development. These aspects of the program are less concrete than interest areas, materials, and equipment. However, your careful planning of these parts of the program can help children learn social skills as they function as members of a community by helping, cooperating, and enjoying the company of others.

Follow a daily schedule that has long blocks of time when children may make choices about what to do, what to use, whom to play with, and when to move to something new. Include opportunities for children to play alone, with one or two others, in a small group, and in a large group.

Use routines and other opportunities to encourage children to see themselves as members of a community with specific roles and responsibilities. Children can use self-help skills when washing hands or brushing teeth. Set up a system for rotating assigned chores, so children can work together to maintain the classroom. In addition, ask for children's help at other times, such as finding a lost puzzle piece, carrying something heavy, or teaching another child a skill.

Announce transitions in advance so children can finish what they are doing. Some children find it difficult to move from one activity to the next. They may need several reminders that the transition is coming, one-on-one attention from a teacher, or extra time to finish what they're doing.

Plan activities that correspond to the interests of a child who seldom engages in group play. This lets the child know he or she has been noticed and gives the child an opportunity to interact with others. You can also plan activities that encourage interactions and cooperation, such as painting a mural, making a collage, planting a garden, and building an obstacle course.

Use daily group times to play cooperative games, solve problems, and discuss topics such as feelings, friendship, and helping. Try using puppets to act out a conflict resolution strategy, reading a story in which the characters face and solve a disagreement, or involving children in setting rules for a new area or piece of equipment. This sends the message that members of a community work together.

Provide a balance between structured and unstructured activities. Ideally, provide enough structure for children to feel secure, but not so much that they can't make choices and interact with each other. In a balanced program, children can spend most of the day doing activities of their own choosing (some of which are planned by teachers in advance). At the same time, teachers observe and guide children's play and learning. Teachers stay alert to opportunities to reinforce social skills, address aggressive behavior, and involve children who are reluctant to participate.

what's next?

Skill-Building Journal, section **9-6** *(Learning Activity B)* and section **9-1** *(Feedback).*

Learning Activities

C. Supporting Children's Dramatic Play

In this activity you will learn to

- help children learn to take their play to a higher level

- interact with children in ways that help them become fully involved in play

Sara Smilansky, an early childhood researcher, has identified four kinds of play young children enjoy—functional play, constructive play, games with rules, and sociodramatic play.[30]

Through **functional play** children explore and examine the properties of objects and materials and find out how things work. When preschoolers take apart an old radio or make designs with colored blocks, they are enjoying functional play. During **constructive play**, children use materials—for example, blocks, Legos, or sand—to create a representation of something real or imagined. **Games with rules** include card and board games, many computer games, sports, or any type of play governed by a set of rules that the players understand and follow. Preschoolers enjoy simple games with rules—such as Candyland and lotto—and group games led by the teacher.

Through dramatic play children try new roles and make sense of the world.

Smilansky identifies the fourth type of play as **sociodramatic play**, often called dramatic play. Children pretend to be real or imaginary characters, try different roles, and invent stories and situations to act out. Children develop and use a number of social skills during dramatic play. They generate ideas, share what they know, listen to each other, compromise, and see somebody else's point of view. Through dramatic play, children can learn to control the ways they express their own feelings and emotions. They can role play being mean and nasty because it doesn't really count; it's only pretend. They can also confront real fears, such as going to the dentist or moving to a new place. The social skills children develop through dramatic play can help them cope with many other situations in everyday life.

Young preschool children may spend more time planning than actually playing.

Children's dramatic play differs according to their age and stage of development. Threes and young 4s typically spend much of their time running away from monsters or imitating what they have seen firsthand. At this age, children do a lot of collecting and gathering, packing suitcases, filling tote bags, planning trips. Often the planning is the extent of the play experience.

As they get older, children continue to be fascinated by superheroes and scary monsters. Their play expands to include creating safe places to hide so the monsters can't get them. They like dress-up clothes and other props, and develop a wide variety of roles to play. As they begin to understand the difference between fantasy and reality, you may hear them say, "Let's pretend that . . ."

Older preschool children engage in complex dramatic play.

The dramatic play of 4- and 5-year-olds involves complex sets of characters and situations. It may include real people or fantasy figures from books or television. For many children, dramatic play is a way to practice doing something they fear, such as getting a shot at the doctor's or going on an airplane trip. Children also may use dramatic play to work through anxieties about situations in their lives, such as a new baby at home or a parent's absence during a trip.

Creating Settings for Dramatic Play

Dramatic play can take place in almost any indoor or outdoor setting. It can occur spontaneously, as when two children at the water table begin pouring "coffee" into cups and serving each other. It can also be planned and organized. For example, after a parent visits the classroom to tell children about his job as a flight attendant, several children might pretend to take a plane trip. With some help from their teacher, they talk about who will be the pilot, navigator, passengers, and flight attendants; they decide where they will go and what will happen. They use social skills, such as negotiation and cooperation, to carry out their plans.

Relaxing materials and activities invite conversation.

The materials in some interest areas invite social interaction. Most preschool children like the feel of materials such as sand, water, playdough, and finger paint, and they feel relaxed when they use them. As they play, they begin to share and talk to each other. When additional props are offered, children begin to pretend and make up play episodes with each other. A basket filled with rolling pins, cookie cutters, plastic knives, and cups and saucers to use with playdough can lead to dramatic play about cooking, baking, and serving. Dramatic play also occurs in the block area. Young children need time to explore the properties of blocks before they can create a setting for dramatic play. Props such as wooden and rubber animals, people, and cars encourage children to use blocks to create settings for dramatic play.

There are many opportunities for dramatic play outdoors.

The outdoor play area also serves as a site for dramatic play. Children might hold picnics or cook meals in the sandbox, turn the climber into a space ship, or pretend to drive cars. A collection of open-ended materials, such as milk crates, pieces of garden hose, ropes, and clothespins, inspires children in many different ways. Children can drape a blanket or table cloth over a table or lay it on the ground to set the stage for playing house, store, or any other theme of interest. Outdoors, there are fewer restrictions to children's dramatic play. Outdoor play may be louder and take up more room than indoor play.

Indoors, an area is set aside for dramatic play.

The dramatic play area is usually set up initially as a housekeeping area. It should feature props that encourage play revolving around the family, such as cooking, cleaning, caring for babies, going to the grocery store. A child-size table and chairs can set the stage for a variety of dramatic play scenes, from family scenes to a restaurant or doctor's office.

Guiding and Extending Children's Play

Some preschool children can use their imaginations and creativity to get fully engaged in complex forms of dramatic play. Others do not understand how to turn a paper plate into a steering wheel or a shoe box into a baby bed. They know of only one way to play house and can't think of new scenarios to act out. There are a number of strategies teachers can use to help such children become experts at dramatic play, while also taking all of the players to higher levels.[31]

Provide open-ended props that can be used for a number of purposes. For example, a large empty cardboard box can be a desk, a car, a train, a tent, or a cave.

Offer materials for children to make their own props. For example, children can use different colors of playdough to make fruits or burgers for the house corner. With a pad of paper and markers, children can make tickets for a puppet show, write prescriptions, take orders in a restaurant, or make a sign for a store.

Expand children's knowledge of potential play scenarios. Read books, display pictures, and take field trips that introduce new places and roles. Focus on the activities of different people, the tools they use, and how they interact with each other. For example, on a visit to a veterinary clinic, the teacher can help children notice the customers, the receptionist, and the veterinary assistant, as well as the veterinary doctor.

Introduce a planning process to help children prepare for dramatic play. Discuss the theme of the play, roles different children can assume, and what will happen.

Offer new props to build on individual or group experiences or a long-term study. For example, provide a greater variety of baking and cooking tools when a field trip to a bakery evolves into a long-term study of bread. Props can also relate to something important in children's lives, like a child's trip to the emergency room or a neighborhood fire the children witnessed.

Prepare for and follow up on study trips in the community. For example, before taking a behind-the-scenes tour of a grocery store, offer a cash register, play money, empty food cans and boxes, and shopping bags. Help children think about what they might see and do at the store. Later, add more props that allow children to recall what they saw and did. This will allow them to use the props to prepare for the visit and to recreate and understand their experiences.

Change the props and the setting of the dramatic play area as children's interests and experiences change. While many of the home-related props and furniture can remain in the dramatic play area throughout the year, you can extend children's play by incorporating new settings. Set up a store, post office, restaurant, or doctor's office. The new settings can stay in place as long as they are capturing children's interests. Ask the children to help you think about what to include in these new settings.

Observe children's play. Note which children do and do not get along with one another, what roles they play in the group, and what problems or anxieties individual children are experiencing. Observation also lets you know what is going on in play situations and when your guidance might be useful. Your interventions should be gentle and indirect, such as providing a suitable prop to help a child get involved in the play. "Kia, here is some money to give the storekeeper. I think he has run out of change."

Create prop boxes. To create a prop box, think of a specific theme, such as a health clinic or a shoe store, that corresponds to children's interests or recent experience. Then identify items children can use for dramatic play around the theme. Collect the materials and put them in a sturdy container until you are ready to introduce them to the children.

Participate in children's dramatic play by following their lead and taking on a role. For example, sit in the dramatic play area for 20–30 minutes while a colleague oversees the rest of the room. Chat with the children as they come and go or pretend to talk on the telephone. From this vantage point you can observe and perhaps comment on what the children are doing. You might be able to offer information or give indirect suggestions about what the group might do next. You might also model behavior that the children can imitate.

Here are some examples:

Marcus is banging two pots together. Ms. Richards says: "I'd really like some soup. Will you please put the soup on the stove to get hot?"

This suggestion gives Marcus an idea, a way to pretend. He is reminded that stoves are used to heat food and soup is served hot. Marcus puts the pot on the stove and says, "The soup will be hot in a minute."

Janelle starts to leave the area. Ms. Thomas asks, "Where's Janelle going?"

This stops Janelle from wandering away and helps her feel included and important. Janelle says, "I'm going to the store."

In response, Ms. Thomas offers a few ideas: "Janelle, do you have enough money? Will you please buy some milk?"

Janelle feels free to leave but also has a good reason for coming back.

Jorge stands next to the stove, watching two other children wash dishes at the sink. Ms. Williams talks to Oanh on the phone: "Yes, we're pretty busy here. Jorge is cooking. Hey, Jorge, Oanh wants to know what you're cooking."

Jorge may not have had a purpose for being by the stove. Ms. Williams' description helps him focus on what he is doing. Jorge thinks for a minute. Then he gets a spoon from the rack and a pot from the cupboard. He says, "Tell Oanh I'm cooking beans."

what's next?

Skill-Building Journal, section **9-7** *(Learning Activity C)* and section **9-1** *(Feedback).*

Learning Activities

D. Helping Children Learn Caring Behavior

In this activity you will learn to

- recognize caring behavior used by individual children

- help children develop and use caring behavior

Caring or prosocial behavior is valued in group programs and school communities. Caring behavior includes taking turns, sharing, and helping, as well as higher level social skills such as feeling empathy and being generous. Preschool children are learning to take turns. This is the beginning of learning to share. Empathy is the ability to recognize and identify with another person's feelings. Children who are aware of their own emotions are more likely to be able to empathize with and respond to another person's happiness, sadness, or pain. Generosity is the ability to give to others and is related to sharing and taking turns. A child who is generous is able to give something to another person or willingly shares a toy or snack. Children who are generous may make paintings and other presents to give to family members or to a special friend.

- What kinds of caring behavior do the children in your group use?

- How do you acknowledge children who are kind, thoughtful, or generous?

It takes time to learn to care.

Children develop caring behavior over a long period of time. Infants begin to bond with parents and caregivers. They react to changes in adult voices, for example, by frowning if a voice is loud or angry, and they cry when they hear another infant crying. Between the ages of 1 and 2, children begin to show real concern for others. When this concern is recognized and reinforced by parents and caregivers, children continue to develop caring behavior. Between the ages of 2 and 6, children begin to develop skills in responding appropriately to the needs and feelings of others.

Adults serve as models for the use of caring behavior.

The most direct way in which children learn caring behavior is by watching the adults who care for them. During a typical day you might model caring behavior in a number of ways. When you pass a bowl of carrots to a child, congratulate a child who finishes a difficult puzzle, and listen to a child's concerns, your dependable and responsive interactions help all of the children feel secure. This security allows children to show concern for others and to be cooperative members of the group.

- What caring behavior was valued in your own family and community as you grew up?

- What caring behavior is valued by the cultures of the children in your group?

Here are some ways teachers can help preschool children learn to care:

Plan thoughtful group activities that emphasize a sense of community. For example, make get-well cards for a sick child, to let him know he is missed and that the class hopes he feels better soon.

Use each child's name often. Refer to children by their given names when you talk with them. Practice saying each name as pronounced by the child's family. Hang pictures of children and families on the wall at children's eye level and talk about each family. Label children's artwork and cubbies. Help children learn the names of everyone in the group by singing songs or saying chants that include children's names.

Suggest ways for small groups to cooperate as they work and play together. Cooperative activities could include moving a large box, folding a large blanket, or creating a collage.

Read and discuss books about being helpful and having friends. "What are some ways to be a good friend?" (after reading *Best Friends for Francis*, by Russell Hoban).

Take photographs to record special occasions, exciting events, and daily activities. Ask a parent to help by putting the pictures in small albums that children can handle easily. Children will enjoy remembering events and talking about what they did together. Families will enjoy seeing what their children do in your program. Include the photographs in communications with families. "Jorge, you baked a beautiful loaf of bread. May I take a picture of it for the family newsletter?"

When children's own needs are met, they can begin to think about the needs of others.

Caring behavior is not learned quickly; teachers must be patient as children slowly learn the skills of negotiation, sharing, and cooperation. It is very natural for young children to put their own needs first. When their needs are met, children gradually learn to think about the needs of others. Frequently, you may have to reassure children with little experience in group living that their own wants will be satisfied.

what's next?

Skill-Building Journal, section **9-8** *(Learning Activity D)* and section **9-1** *(Feedback).*

LEARNING ACTIVITY

Learning Activities

E. Helping Children to Make Friends

In this activity you will learn to

- use classroom strategies to support friendships

- recognize the signs that a child needs help to make friends

In a classroom community, children practice the skills they need to make friends.

Every young child needs to have at least one friend with whom to talk, play, care, disagree, and make up. Some children seem to know instinctively how to make friends and find their place in their group. Other children may take longer, but, once they feel comfortable, they are able to join a group and make friends. When you purposefully build a classroom community where everyone feels safe, helps one another, and sees himself as part of a group, children are more likely to be able to learn the skills needed to make and keep friends. A well-planned environment and activities create the setting for positive social interactions and social problem solving.

Teachers can use specific strategies to support children's efforts to make and keep friends.[32]

Have discussions about making friends. Teachers can read books, such as *Will I Have a Friend?* by Miriam Cohen and *The Rainbow Fish* by Marcus Pfister and T. Alison James, to introduce a discussion.

Coach children. Teachers can help children practice social skills by modeling them. They show children how to ask questions, make positive comments, join a group, and interact with children.

Pair children to work together on a task. Teachers can organize activities so that two children who are not usually together share a job or a project.

Interpret children's actions. Some children don't understand how their behavior sometimes causes problems. By describing their actions in words, you help them become more conscious of their behavior and better able to change it. "Did you notice that when you sat down in the middle of the floor you were in the way of the block builders? Next time try asking the others, 'Where can I play?' Let's see if that works better."

Point out the benefits of caring behavior. When you say, "Look at the smile on Crystal's face. You can tell she is happy that you shared the markers with her." A child who recognizes the positive consequences of a behavior is more likely to repeat it in the future because the skill pleased another child and enables her to become a successful member of the group.

Minimize rejection. Because young children often want to exclude others, create a classroom environment where this behavior is not tolerated. With a rule such as, "You can't say you can't play," you promote a sense of community where children are assertive about inclusion rather than exclusion.

There are some children, however, who have extreme difficulty making friends. They may be shy or withdrawn, overly aggressive, or rejected by their peers for other reasons. Because their peers do not accept them, the children have fewer chances to develop social skills. They cannot break the cycle of rejection. These children need to learn how to make friends so they can avoid serious problems in school and in later life. They need an adult who can observe, analyze the information, and offer specific help.

Helping Children Who Are Very Shy Learn to Make Friends

Almost every group of children includes one or two who appear to be shy. Before offering assistance, observe to see if a child is simply a bit more reserved than others or truly needs help. One child may need opportunities to play alone successfully before being ready to play and work with others. Another child might need to watch and listen to others at play to figure out how to become part of the group. A child might begin by playing with one or two children; then, after becoming more skilled, she can play with a larger group of children.

Use a subtle approach to help a shy or withdrawn child learn social skills.

Some children, however, are so shy or withdrawn that they need a teacher's assistance. A subtle approach is most successful. Public statements such as "Be nice to Bret" or "Will you let Pam play too?" tend to make the shy child feel self-conscious and embarrassed. The other children may go along with your requests for a time, but the child who is shy will not develop the social skills to cope when you aren't there to intervene.

Try the following suggestions to help shy children develop the social skills needed to make friends:

Observe the child. When the child is playing alone, does she concentrate on her own activity, or does she also watch what other children are doing? Review your observation notes and talk with colleagues to identify the child's skills and favorite activities. Consider how the child behaves in different settings and at different times of the day. Use this information to guide your decisions.

Build a supportive relationship with the child. Use your observations to have a conversation. "I see Tyrone and Mark are playing at the water table." If the child responds, ask a question to extend the conversation, "Do you think Mark's cup will hold more water than Tyrone's?" Offer a suggestion, "Perhaps you can play at the water table tomorrow and figure out the answer."

Comment on what the child is doing. "I see you are lining up the shells by size." Such comments help the child feel more secure and valued because she knows the teacher is paying attention.

Notice and respond to the child's special interests. For example, if you know a child really likes to cook, plan to bake a snack with several children working together. Invite the child to take part. Ask open-ended questions to get her involved and try to engage her in conversation with the other children.

Help a child find a good friend. Pair a shy child with a socially competent and sensitive child to help you do a task. "Drew, will you please help Leo and me carry the toys outside?" You might also tell the children about an activity you think is of interest to both. "Drew and Leo, Ms. Johnson is setting up the woodworking bench. I think there's room for two more carpenters."

Help the child understand and cope with feelings of shyness. "It's okay to want to play alone when you don't know the other children too well. When you feel more comfortable, I will help you play with the others."

Helping Aggressive Children Learn to Make Friends

Many preschool children push, shove, hit, or kick some of the time. When they are upset, they act on their feelings without considering the consequences. They are still learning to use words to express their feelings and may act in anger or frustration. They use aggression—an intentional behavior that harms a person or things—but do not necessarily understand that their aggressive actions are hurtful.

Children who demonstrate aggressive behavior may lack social skills.

In a group of preschool children, however, there may be one or two children who have extreme difficulty in regulating their negative emotions. Their aggression can be a way to express unhappiness, to get what they want, or to hurt someone they think has harmed them. Because many children who are aggressive do not know how to take turns, negotiate, or cooperate with others, they get stuck in a negative cycle. Because of their aggressive behavior, other children don't want to play with them. Without opportunities to play, they are not able to practice and build positive social skills.

Children who are aggressive may be unhappy or insecure.

Teachers also may have trouble relating to children who are aggressive. It's hard to like a child who hurts others or destroys classroom materials. It may help to remember that children who hit or bully others often are emotionally troubled or in pain. They may feel unhappy or insecure. Regardless of the reasons for their aggression, these children need a caring adult to help them feel safe and valued. Then they will be ready to learn the social skills needed to make friends and play with other children.

Try these suggestions for helping these children learn the social skills needed to make friends:

Talk with the child about the consequences of his or her actions. "I think you want to play too, but the girls get angry when you grab their babies. Grabbing doesn't make them want to play with you."

Suggest an appropriate way to gain control of angry feelings. "Shawn, I know you feel very angry, but I won't let you hurt other children, and I won't let anyone hurt you. You may sit in the comfy chair until you calm down, or you may read in the library area. When you are ready, let's talk about what happened."

Use a special signal to help the child recognize when he or she is about to lose control. Agree on what to use as a special signal. The signal might be a single word that serves as a reminder, such as *snowflakes*; a tap on the shoulder; or the chorus to a familiar song, such as "E-I-E–I-O."

Spend time alone with a child after an aggressive outburst. "David, let's sit in the big chair and read a story together. We have some new books I think you might like."

Join the child in watching a group at play. Interpret the players' actions to explain how social skills are used. "Maria and Sara are baking cakes in the sandbox. Here comes Carlos. I think he wants to play with them. Maria smiled at him. Sara handed him a pan. Now Carlos is making a cake. He offered it to Sara. I think he's pretending to be her neighbor."

Help the child develop ways to achieve goals without being aggressive. "I know you want to be the doctor, but Michelle is the doctor now. Ask the children if there are lots of doctors at this hospital."

Acknowledge children's expressions and behaviors even when they can't have or do what they want. "You want to go home right now. You don't want to wait for your grandpa to pick you up. He will come get you after your nap. Then you can go home together."

Use the child's interests and positive behaviors to foster acceptance by the group. "Nicole collected some beautiful leaves on our walk. Let's put them on the table where everyone can see them."

Helping Other Children Learn to Make Friends

There are children in every class who are neither aggressive nor shy yet still have difficulty making friends. These children, who may be loud, clumsy, or bossy, do not know how to get involved with their peers. They want to play with others, but, because they are not able to understand what the other children are doing, they don't know how to get involved. They seem to be unaware of the effects of their behavior. You may hear complaints about these children. "She's always butting in." "He talks too loud." "He keeps riding his trike into the back of mine."

Coach children who need help making friends.

Some of the previous ideas for assisting children who are shy or aggressive can also help children who lack friends for other reasons. In addition, you can coach the child privately about how to develop social skills and make friends.

Help the child follow the group's accepted social practices. "Felipe, when it's time to go outdoors, try to get your coat on more quickly. Then the other children won't have to wait and we can all go outside and have fun."

Suggest ways for the child to find out what the other children are doing. "Jack, try asking questions, such as 'What are you doing?' 'Who are you pretending to be?' 'What are you building?'"

Help the child give the other children reasons why he or she should be included. "You can say to the children, 'I'd like to play, too. There are only three people in the sandbox, and four children can play here.'"

Explain the other children's nonverbal cues and tones of voice. "See how Avida turned away from you? She wants to be alone for a little while. You may sit here, next to Leo."

what's next?

Skill-Building Journal, section **9-9** *(Learning Activity E),* section **9-1** *(Feedback),* and section **9-10** *(Reflecting on Your Learning).*

Overview

Minimizing Problem Behavior and Encouraging Self-Discipline

Using Positive Guidance to Help Each Child Learn

Helping Children Express Their Strong Feelings in Acceptable Ways

Your Own Self-Discipline

Learning Activities

A. Using Your Knowledge of Child Development to Guide Children's Behavior

B. Guiding Children Toward Self-Disciplined Behavior

C. Setting Rules and Limits

D. Teaching Children to Use Problem-Solving Skills

E. Responding to Challenging Behavior

10. Guidance

Children need adult guidance to learn self-control.

In early childhood, children need to learn how to behave in ways expected by their families, culture, and community. Children learn the difference between right and wrong when caring adults who have realistic expectations guide their behavior in positive and supportive ways. Children also learn what is expected by observing and copying the behavior of the people around them.

With adult guidance, children learn to identify their emotions, use words to express strong feelings, and think before acting. Children begin to develop self-discipline during the preschool years and become more able to control their own behavior. Self-disciplined people make independent choices, balance their own needs with those of others, accept responsibility for their actions, and delay gratification.

Children misbehave for many reasons.

Children sometimes misbehave because they do not understand or cannot meet adult expectations. Some children act out when forced into a schedule that conflicts with their natural rhythms. Others are confused because rules and expectations at home differ from those at the center. At certain developmental stages children typically test the limits of their own control. The first step in offering positive guidance is to consider the reasons for a child's behavior.

Positive guidance means minimizing inappropriate behavior and encouraging appropriate behavior.

Many effective strategies teach children to behave appropriately and help them develop self-control. Some actions, such as setting up safe places to run or building supportive relationships with individual children, minimize unwanted behavior and encourage positive behavior. Other actions, such as redirecting children to climb on the climber rather than the table, teach children which activities are appropriate and which are not. Both kinds of positive guidance help children learn to monitor their own behavior. With adult guidance in a well-planned, appropriate program, most children learn acceptable behavior.

In any group, there are likely to be a few children whose challenging behavior has to be addressed in a more focused way. Teachers and families can work together to identify and address the reasons behind a child's problem behavior, and develop strategies to help the child learn alternative behavior.

Guiding children's behavior involves

- organizing a program that minimizes problem behavior and encourages self-discipline

- using positive guidance to help each child learn acceptable behavior

- helping children express their strong feelings in acceptable ways

Minimizing Problem Behavior and Encouraging Self-Discipline

1. **Provide open-ended materials and activities that support varied interests and skills.** Offer a wide variety of art materials, blocks, dramatic play props, and equipment for physical play.

2. **Establish a comfortable setting that looks and feels like children's homes.** Include items that reflect children's families, culture, and languages.

3. **Create cozy spaces where a child can be alone for a while, yet still be visible to adults.** "When Amanda needs some quiet time, she sits in a beanbag chair in the reading nook."

4. **Follow a schedule that allows children to choose their own activities for most of the day.** "Good morning, Carlos. What would you like to do before the breakfast cart arrives from the kitchen?"

5. **Arrange the room so traffic paths, interest areas, and the large group area are clearly defined.** "Now that we moved that table, there's plenty of room for the children who want to turn somersaults."

6. **Provide materials and activities that allow children to explore and express their feelings.** Children can paint and draw, listen to and discuss stories about feelings, and act out situations with dramatic play props and puppets.

Ms. Kim and Ms. Richards Assess Their Program

"I'm glad it's Friday," sighs Ms. Kim. "It's been a frustrating week. The children complained every day about waiting around with their coats on. And getting them to help with cleanup was like pulling teeth." Ms. Richards nods in agreement. "I know what you mean," she says. "We may need to make some changes." Ms. Kim responds, "I've noticed that some of the children get their coats on faster than others. They get hot and uncomfortable while waiting for the rest of the group to be ready go outside. Let's divide the group. One of us can take the children who are ready while the other helps the children who need more time." Ms. Richards says, "That's a good idea. I also think the children might help with cleanup if we make labels with pictures and words and tape them to the shelves and containers. Then the children will know where things are stored. I think that making these changes will prevent some of the problem behavior we've been seeing."

Using Positive Guidance to Help Each Child Learn Acceptable Behavior

7. **Build trusting, supportive relationships with individual children.** Work with colleagues to make sure all of the children have ongoing, positive interactions with their teachers.

8. **Teach problem-solving skills and help children apply them to negotiate and resolve disagreements.** "Oanh and Michelle, use the talking chairs to discuss your problem and see if you can find a way to settle it."

9. **Involve the children in setting a few important rules.** Explain why the rules are needed and ask children to share their ideas for rules that will work.

10. **Redirect children to acceptable alternative activities.** "Leo's reading that book, Aimee. You can choose another book to look at."

11. **Use simple, positive reminders that tell children what to do, rather than what not to do.** "Please walk in the classroom, Tony. It's okay to run when we go outside."

12. **Assume a firm, authoritarian role only when necessary to keep children safe.** "Stay on the sidewalk, Sara! A car is coming."

13. **Model appropriate ways to identify and express feelings.** "Whew! I feel tired after our walk. I need to sit down and rest for a minute. Then I'll be ready to play with you."

Ms. Williams Redirects Benjamin So He Can Throw Safely

example

Ms. Williams and the children are outside in the play yard. Benjamin, a very active child, has collected some pine cones and is throwing them at other children. Ms. Williams walks over to him. She bends down, looks at him, and says, "Benjamin, you are learning to be a good thrower. But if you hit someone with a pine cone, they might be hurt or angry. Where can you practice your throwing safely?" "I like to hit things," replies Benjamin. "I see," responds Ms. Williams. "You like to have a target for the pine cones you throw. What could you use as a target where no one would get hurt? Benjamin looks around and answers, "How about that tree?" Ms. Williams nods and says, "Yes, that's a good idea. There aren't any children over there." Benjamin picks up his pine cones and walks near a large tree. Ms. Williams watches him throw for a few minutes and then goes to the sandbox to interact with other children.

Helping Children Express Their Strong Feelings in Acceptable Ways

14. **Look for the reasons why a child might behave inappropriately.** Work with the child's family to learn what happens before and after the behavior and to plan strategies to help the child learn alternative behavior.

15. **Acknowledge frustrating experiences and suggest ways to cope with them.** Tell children you accept their feelings, even though you do not accept their actions.

16. **Identify and discuss feelings and suggest appropriate ways to express them.** Read and discuss the feelings and actions of characters in books and relate them to those of the children in the group

17. **Help children understand the effects of their actions on people and things.** "You were angry with Avida because she had the crayon you wanted to use. Then you pulled her hair and she screamed. She doesn't want to play with you because you hurt her."

18. **Work with a family to help a child with challenging behavior learn acceptable ways to express strong feelings.** "Sheila had a great day today. She used the words we practiced to tell the other children what she wanted."

example

Mr. Lopez Helps Sara Talk About Her Feelings

"No!" screams Sara. With arm extended, Sara leans over ready to hit Marcus, who has just grabbed a piece of orange from her plate. "Sara," says Mr. Lopez, extending his hand between Sara's hand and Marcus' arm. Sara looks at Mr. Lopez. "That was good stopping," Mr. Lopez says. "I know you are hungry. You don't like it when someone takes your food. It's okay to feel that way. You can talk to people when you are angry, but I can't let you hit them. Tell Marcus not to take your orange." Sara looks at Marcus and screams, "Don't take my orange!" Marcus puts the piece of orange down and goes back to eating his own lunch. "That was good," says Mr. Lopez. "Next time you don't have to scream. He can hear you very well."

what's next?

Skill-Building Journal, section **10-2** *(Overview)*, section **10-11** *(Answer Sheets)*, and section **10-1** *(Feedback)*.

Your Own Self-Discipline

Self-discipline makes some behavior automatic.

Much adult behavior is automatic. When you put money in a parking meter, come to work on time, or thank a store clerk, you are probably acting without thinking about what you are doing. You have learned and accepted certain rules of behavior, and because you have self-discipline, you don't need to be reminded of them.

Self-discipline guides your behavior at work.

- You let the center director know when you're sick so a substitute can be called.

- You ask a colleague for her help rather than complaining about a problem.

- You volunteer to help plan a weekend field trip for families.

Self-discipline also guides your behavior at home.

- You water the plants because you know they'll die if you don't.

- You clean the coffee pot so it will be ready to use in the morning.

- You resist eating cake because you are watching your weight.

Few people use self-discipline all the time and in every situation. Sometimes we experience very strong feelings that make us feel out of control, and sometimes we lose control. Fortunately, most of us have learned ways to regain control. We use different strategies to calm ourselves. For example, if we are very angry, we might count to ten before responding, breathe deeply, or take a walk. Once we have calmed down, we are better able to make clear statements about our feelings instead of lashing out and accusing someone which only makes that person defensive.

Being in control of your own behavior frequently enhances self-esteem. Having positive feelings about your abilities will make you a more effective and skilled teacher. Your self-discipline is a good model for the children. They will learn a lot from being cared for by a responsible and competent person.

what's next?

Skill-Building Journal, section **10-3** *(Your Own Self-Discipline)*, section **10-1** *(Feedback)*, and section **10-4** *(Pre-Training Assessment)*.

Learning Activities

A. Using Your Knowledge of Child Development to Guide Children's Behavior

In this activity you will learn to

- organize a program that minimizes behavior problems and helps children develop self-discipline

- recognize some typical behavior of preschool children

In a well-planned program children feel respected and become engaged.

An appropriate program for preschool children can support the development of self-discipline. Well-defined interest areas enable children to work in small groups, make choices about where to work and what materials to use, and find and replace materials easily. When these materials interest children and allow them to explore and make discoveries, they stay focused and engage in complex learning across all areas of development. Teachers who have built caring relationships can observe children's work and consider ways to guide and extend learning. In such a program, children feel they and their work are valued and respected. They are more likely to demonstrate appropriate behavior.

Positive guidance is based on a knowledge of child development.

Helping children learn self-discipline begins with having reasonable expectations based on knowledge of each stage of development. Social and emotional development are most closely linked to the ability to learn positive behavior. You can then plan a program that reflects developmental and individual characteristics. Because such a program supports children, problem behavior is minimized. Information on child development appears in previous modules in the training program.

Here are some examples of typical preschool behavior and supportive teacher responses that minimize problems and encourage children's self-discipline.

Developmental Characteristics and Teacher Responses

Preschool children...	Supportive Responses
can sit still and pay attention but often get fidgety after 10–15 minutes	Read books and plan group time activities that don't go beyond this time limit.
use the toilet independently and might have occasional toileting accidents	Ask parents to provide extra clothes. Respond to accidents in a matter-of-fact way and allow the child to clean up with minimal adult assistance.
like to play with others and are still learning to share and take turns	Provide duplicates of popular toys. Set up a turn-taking system, such as timers, hooks for hanging up name tags, or a waiting list for interest areas. Order sufficient consumable materials (such as paints) for the size of the group. Offer activities more than once so all interested children can take part.
can follow simple instructions, but may need help with instructions with several steps	Keep directions simple and clear. Ask children to repeat instructions to make sure they understand what they were asked to do.
have strong feelings that they are learning to identify and name, and they might act out or lose control without considering the consequences of their actions	Step in immediately to stop the behavior and stay with the child until he or she is calm. Help all of the children learn the names for different feelings and use words to express their emotions and desires. Create private areas such as a large box, a pile of pillows in the corner, a small table and chair for one child, a sheet draped over three sides of a table, where children can go to relax or to regain control.
can move their bodies in different ways and sometimes don't think about safety	Arrange the furniture to create pathways between interest areas. Provide an open area for music and movement and equipment for indoor physical activities (climber, tumbling mats, hula hoops). Use halls or an empty classroom for active play. Go outdoors every day (even if it is cold or rainy).
have a wide range of abilities and interests and gain new skills and find new interests regularly	Provide materials that match the children's interests and skill levels and challenge them to grow and learn.
make independent decisions and choices and may take risks without thinking about consequences	Follow a schedule that lets children spend most of the day making choices about what to do. Observe children and plan activities that respond to their interests. Maintain safe indoor and outdoor environments. Talk with children about safety and what they can do to take risks safely.

Preschool children...	Supportive Responses
can take care of their own belongings and may lose things or take things belonging to other children	Provide individual, labeled cubbies within children's reach. Involve children in setting a rule about only going in their own cubbies.
are learning about cause and effect and do not always see how their actions affect other people and things or result in certain responses	Point out immediate and natural consequences of actions: "You put your carpet square too close to Leo so he moved to a new spot. He wants more space." Respond calmly to accidents and involve children in repairs and clean up.
are increasingly aware of self, family, and culture, and recognize how they are the same as and different from others in the group	Choose toys, books, materials, and displays that reflect children's families, ethnicity, and culture. Read and discuss books about different kinds of families and situations.

what's next?

Skill-Building Journal, section **10-5** *(Learning Activity A)* and section **10-1** *(Feedback).*

LEARNING ACTIVITY

Learning Activities

B. Guiding Children Toward Self-Disciplined Behavior

In this activity you will learn to

- use positive approaches to guide children's behavior

- tailor positive guidance to match individual skills and needs

Punishment does little to develop the skills used to make good choices.

Often the words punishment and discipline are used to mean the same thing, but they are actually very different. Punishment responds to intentional or mistaken behavior by imposing a physical or emotional penalty on the child. The actual penalty, or fear of the penalty, may make children behave because they are afraid of what might happen to them if they don't. Punishment may stop children's negative behavior temporarily, but it doesn't teach them what to do. Punishment frequently harms children's self-confidence and hampers their ability to make good decisions.

Self-discipline is a life skill we all need.

Discipline means guiding and directing children toward acceptable behavior. It teaches children what behaviors are acceptable and helps them learn how to solve problems and behave in positive ways in future situations. The most important goal of discipline is to help children learn how to control their own behavior.

Children learn self-discipline through daily interactions with other children and adults. It takes a long time to learn self-discipline, but it is time well spent. Children who are self-disciplined tend to be more successful in school and in life. They can set goals and take the steps needed to accomplish them. They find it easier to get along with their peers and with adults.

Children often communicate their feelings through their behavior.

Many preschool children are not aware of their feelings or how to express them. Even children with strong verbal skills may find it hard to put their feelings into words. When children destroy materials, don't follow the rules, or hurt others, it is important to think about what their behavior means. What is the child trying to express? What are the reasons behind the behavior?

Children's behavior may be telling you many different things.

> "I feel lonely because my friend is playing with someone else. That's why I can't find anything to do."

> "I am angry because this morning I spilled juice on my favorite shirt and I had to wear something else. That's why I lost my temper and hit my friend."

> "I am afraid. That's why I won't let go of your hand."

> "I want to be good at something. That's why I keep ripping up my pictures."

> "I need you to set some limits. That's why I'm running around."

> "I can't do what you asked me to do. That's why I threw my sneaker at the wall."

When children feel upset, help them get engaged in soothing activities.

It's important for teachers to recognize and accept children's negative feelings. Through observation, you learn to recognize that a child is upset. Then you can respond by suggesting ways to express feelings without hurting oneself, other people, or the toys and materials. For example, when you see children who seem frustrated, redirect them to soothing activities that might help them feel better. There are no right or wrong ways to pound playdough, play with sand in a basin, or listen to music. Children can enjoy activities such as these without worrying about being successful. When children feel angry, them time and space to calm down and then help them find the words to express their needs. Focus attention on what a child may need rather than on what the child is doing.

Your words and tone of voice can be powerful positive guidance tools.

Angry, insensitive words can make children feel sad, ashamed, or angry. Positive words, however, can promote children's self-discipline. Your caring words help children understand their own feelings and those of others. When adults use a loud disciplinary voice, children sometimes don't really attend to the meaning of the words. Instead, talk to children in a natural but firm voice. When children hear a quiet, firm tone, they are more likely to feel cared for and safe. When talking with a child, crouch or kneel at the child's level, look into the child's eyes, and gently touch an arm or shoulder. Give the child your full attention, and make sure you have the child's attention. (Note: In some families and cultures, children are taught that it is disrespectful to look an adult in the eye. Be sensitive to differences.)

Effective guidance considers children's individual and developmental characteristics.

Effective guidance techniques are based on these principles:

- Expectations for children's behavior are realistic because they reflect an understanding of child development.

- Each child's unique characteristics are considered as well as the situation and the child's skills and needs.

Positive Guidance Strategies

Positive Guidance Strategy	Examples
Tell children you noticed their positive behavior during private moments.	"Carlos, when you gave Marcus the helicopter to play with he felt so happy."
Help children learn how to solve their own problems.	"I think you want to kick the ball with Leo and Tony. What can you say so they will stop to let you in the game?"
Anticipate and plan ways to minimize or prevent problem behavior.	"Let's talk about tomorrow's trip to the firehouse. First, how will we get there?"
Describe a positive behavior, without labeling the child.	"You put your dishes in the blue tub today. We'll be able to find them easily tomorrow." (Rather than, "You're a good girl for putting your dishes in the right place.")
Tell children what they may do, rather than what they may not do.	"You can roll the truck on the carpet where there is lots of room. If you want to play in the dramatic play area, you will have to put the truck away because it is in the way."
Model appropriate behavior by being polite and respectful at all times.	"Will you please hold my bag for a minute? Thank you."
Encourage children to move their bodies when they seem restless.	"Oanh, you seem full of energy. Would you like to use the tumbling mats or join the children on the climber?"
Individualize rules and limits when needed to meet a child's needs.	"If you don't want to join us for a story you may do puzzles or draw a picture."
Gain control of your own angry feelings before responding to a child's actions. Ask a colleague for help if needed.	"Mr. Lopez, will you please help Aimee pick up the blocks she threw at Leo? I need to calm down before she and I talk about her behavior."

Using positive guidance takes practice. It may take some time before you feel comfortable teaching children in new ways. The children will let you know how much better they feel because of your understanding and caring.

what's next?

Skill-Building Journal, section **10-6** *(Learning Activity B)* and section **10-1** *(Feedback).*

Learning Activities

C. Setting Rules and Limits

In this activity you will learn to

- use positive statements that tell children what to do when reminding children of rules

- individualize rules and limits, as appropriate, to support children's needs

Rules and limits help both children and teachers agree on what behavior is expected. When children feel safe because they know adults have set limits, they are more likely to explore and experiment appropriately.

It's best to have just a few, important rules.

Create just enough rules to keep your classroom working well. If there are too few rules, the children might be unsafe and the environment disorderly. When there are too many rules, however, children are unsure of themselves and can't remember what to do. Children feel a sense of mastery when they can remember and follow a few simple, important rules.

- What are the rules in your classroom?

- How do the rules help children stay safe and learn?

Tell children the reasons why rules are needed.

Children are more likely to follow rules if they know the reasons for them and help to create them. To begin the process of setting rules, talk with children about the consequences of certain actions. "What might happen if someone squirts water on the floor?" Children can answer the question: "When the water spills, the floor gets slippery. Someone might fall and get hurt." Then they can suggest a needed rule: "Keep the water in the water table." (See *Learning Activity D, Helping Children Learn to Take Precautions*, in module 1, *Safe*, for an example of helping children create safety rules.)

State rules in clear, positive terms.

Young children find it easier to remember rules when they are stated clearly and positively. For example, "Walk when you're indoors so you don't hurt yourself," rather than "Don't run indoors," tells children what they can do and why. Children are more likely to internalize the rules when teachers' reminders are positive and delivered in a brief, firm manner.

Positive Statements Help Children Follow Rules

To Respond to This Behavior	Say or Do This
Several children are talking too loudly.	"Use quiet voices inside; you can talk loudly outside."
A child hits another child.	"I can't let you hurt other children. Tell me what happened. Maybe I can help you solve the problem."
A child throws a shovel.	"Use the shovel to dig with; if you want to throw something, you can throw the ball."
A child climbs on the table.	"Keep your feet on the floor. Climb only on the climber."
A child pushes another child on the slide.	"Keep your hands off other children. It's dangerous to push someone on the slide."
A child stands up and gets in the way of the others at story time.	"Please sit down on the rug. I'll hold the book up high so everyone can see."
A child swears at another child.	"Please don't use those words here. I don't want to hear them, and I don't want the other children to learn them."
A child absent-mindedly drips paint on the floor.	"Wipe your brush on the jar, so the paint won't drip."

There are times when it's necessary to change a rule to meet a child's need.

Most of the time, teachers need to apply classroom rules and limits consistently so the children will learn what they are expected to do. In some situations, however, it is appropriate to change a rule to meet a child's needs at a particular time. Consider the following example:

> Rhonda, who is new to the program, shows little interest in most activities but loves painting. Painting seems to allow her to express her feelings and to release tension. One of the classroom rules (to try at least two interest areas a day) is designed to encourage children to try different activities. For example, if a child spends most of the morning in the block area, the teachers help the child make a different choice for the afternoon. Because painting seems to meet Rhonda's emotional needs, a teacher tells her, "I think painting helps you feel comfortable here. When you are ready, you can try other activities. Until then, you may paint for as long as you like." The teachers also explain to the other children, "Rhonda is still getting used to our classroom. She may stick to painting until she feels ready to try other activities."

- What would make you change the rules for a child in your classroom?

- How do you and your colleagues work together to make sure rules are working?

Good rules keep children safe and challenge them to grow.

Rules should reflect children's capabilities at each stage of development. As children grow and mature, they can handle more freedom, activities, and responsibilities. Teachers need to observe carefully to know when individual children or the whole group can handle greater freedom. There is a fine line between keeping children safe and keeping them from growth and independence. The limits set for 4-year-olds in September may need to be adjusted in a few months' time.

what's next?

Skill-Building Journal, section **10-7** *(Learning Activity C)* and section **10-1** *(Feedback).*

Learning Activities

LEARNING
ACTIVITY

D. Teaching Children to Use Problem-Solving Skills

In this activity you will learn to

● recognize why problem-solving is important to self-discipline

● teach children skills they can use to solve problems on their own

Every day the children in your care face problems that require solutions. Some of the problems affect just one individual, such as a child wants to play shoe store and doesn't know how to join the group. Other problems involve two or more children, such as a disagreement about who will look through the microscope in the science area. Some involve most or all of the children in the group, such as the fact that clean-up time has become difficult.

When teachers solve problems, children don't learn problem-solving skills.

Because many young children get frustrated easily, it's tempting for a teacher to solve the problem quickly by suggesting a solution she knows will work: "I'll just put the microscope in the closet." Such a solution doesn't teach children how to solve problems on their own. Learning how to solve problems is an important skill that will benefit children now and throughout their lives. Children who begin to see themselves as problem solvers are more likely to tackle difficult problems when they get older. They are more likely to be successful in school, because they have confidence in their own abilities.

One of the best ways to teach problem-solving skills is to create a classroom community in which this skill is valued. When a problem arises, allow time for children to seek their own solutions with your support and guidance. Here are some suggestions for promoting social problem-solving skills in your classroom.

There are many strategies teachers can use to teach social problem-solving skills.

Be patient. Children may need time and opportunities to try and try again. You can help them by saying, "I can see how hard you are trying," or by asking questions that may prompt a solution that will work.

Accept and respect children's responses. Keep in mind that children think differently from adults. They are more likely to continue to solve problems when they feel that all their ideas are accepted and valued.

Allow time for children to think. Young children may have trouble putting their thoughts into words. It may take time for them to collect their thoughts and express their ideas. If adults are impatient, children will stop trying.

Offer help a little at a time. When the first solution to a problem doesn't work, help the child learn from the experience and think of other ideas. Observing what happens can help them think of a new solution. Mistakes are not failures; they are part of learning to solve problems.

Respond to children's questions by asking questions that stimulate thinking. "How could we . . . ?" "What might happen if . . ." "Do you remember when . . ." "What do you want to happen . . ."

Encourage multiple solutions. This will keep children thinking about new possibilities and options. "Jorge, that was a good idea. Tyrone, do you have another suggestion?"

When a problem arises that affects the whole class, use it as an opportunity to teach the group the steps used to solve a problem. By taking part in this process, children will begin to learn skills they can apply in the future. You will probably do this many times in large and small groups before children become skilled problem solvers. Make and post a chart that explains the process in words and pictures. Children can refer to it when they need a reminder of how to solve a problem.

Here are the steps for problem-solving with two children, a small group, or the whole class. The adult role varies, depending on the situation. Engage children in the process as much as possible.

There are five steps in solving problems.

Tell what happened. The person with the problem (teachers or children) explains what took place. When needed, restate what is said to clarify and make sure all ideas are validated. "So, you think that . . . ."

Define the problem. Explain why the situation needs a solution. Perhaps it is a safety concern, two children both want to use the grater, or the block-builders are getting in the way of the puppeteers.

Think of possible solutions. Invite children to think of solutions. It's important to let children know that there is no one right answer; many solutions might work. Encourage everyone to contribute: "Does anyone have an idea?" Write down all the ideas on paper so the group can discuss each one. Ask children to explain their ideas if they are not clear: "Can you say more about that?"

Agree on a solution. Restate the children's ideas and ask them to think about which one they would like to try. Describe how it would work and make sure everyone has the same understanding. "Here's what I think we decided. See if you agree."

Try the solution and assess the results. Let children know that sometimes an idea doesn't solve the problem. Explain that everyone will try out the plan and observe what happens. Set a time to talk about what happened. Even when it's clear a solution is working, it's a good idea to help children talk about why it solved the problem. Sometimes children want to give up on an idea if it doesn't work out immediately. Encourage them to modify the idea and try again before abandoning it altogether. As needed, help them choose a new solution.

The ability to solve problems, which often requires testing a variety of solutions instead of giving up, is an important life skill. Teachers who are good problem-solvers themselves can inspire children by modeling strategies and giving children opportunities to practice these skills.

what's next?

Skill-Building Journal, section **10-8** *(Learning Activity D)* and section **10-1** *(Feedback).*

Learning Activities

LEARNING
ACTIVITY

E. Responding to Challenging Behavior

In this activity you will learn to

- look for the reasons behind a child's challenging behavior

- work with families to develop a plan for responding to challenging behavior

Some children's behavior may challenge teachers and parents, but they are actually signs of normal development. This behavior gives way to new ones when children move to the next stage of development. For example:

- A 3-year-old pours his own milk at lunch almost every day, spilling some. He wants to do things for himself.

- A 4-year-old is very interested in watching the boys urinate. She is curious about the differences between boys and girls.

- A 5-year-old tells the younger children how to do things, in a bossy way. "Do it this way." He is proud of his skills and likes to teach others.

Some behavior is a challenge for the child and for adults.

Challenging behavior, such as biting or having tantrums, does not give way so easily. This causes problems for the child, for others in the group, and for adults. Challenging behavior prevents children from full participation in the program. It occurs again and again and, unless addressed, can lead to serious problems later in life. In most cases, there is a reason for the child's behavior.

Describe causes for challenging behavior.

Some reasons children might use challenging behavior are described below:[33]

"I don't feel well." Health problems and conditions such as illness, allergies, lack of sleep, poor nutrition, or hunger can be a cause of children's misbehavior. If you suspect a physical problem, talk with the children's families and consider having the child evaluated by a health professional.

"I don't know what I'm supposed to do." Often teachers give children brief instructions: "Clean up." "Get ready." "Use the brush properly." When the child does not comply, the teacher might assume he or she is resisting on purpose. However, many young children don't understand what the teacher is asking. Vague words such as "properly" have no meaning for the child and he is she is not likely to ask what the strange word means. Children often need a teacher to show them what to do and how to do it, for example, how to hold a brush so the paint doesn't drip down the page or onto hands and clothing.

"I want you to notice me." Children need to feel important and valued. When they don't receive enough positive attention, they may seek out negative attention. They have learned that when they act up, adults notice them and spend time with them. Unfortunately, once children are successful in getting attention by misbehaving, they are likely to continue their unacceptable behavior unless the cycle is broken.

"I'm bored." Even in the most interesting and varied environment, some children will be bored because they can't find something to do. Making an extra effort to consider their unique characteristics and interests when planning activities and selecting new materials helps to alleviate boredom and encourage involvement.

"I want more control." Some children have very few opportunities to make decisions or to exercise control over their lives. When children are given choices, such as which materials to use, whom to play with, alternative ways to express strong feelings, they feel more powerful and they begin to develop self-discipline.

"I'm scared." Often the child who is aggressive toward others and challenges adults is a fearful child. To overcome his fears, the child acts as if he is powerful. To help this child, try to find out what his fears are and what is causing them. Make a plan to address them and reassure him that he is safe.

"I'm frustrated." When a child misbehaves often, perhaps the classroom materials and activities do not match his or her developmental skills. An appropriate program can minimize some challenging behavior. Children can feel a sense of accomplishment and success when the classroom materials and activities are interesting and challenging, but do not require skills that they have not yet mastered. For example, a child may not have the fine motor skills needed to thread beads on a string. The teacher can encourage such a child to use toys with large pieces that are easier to hold and manipulate. Teachers can also learn to recognize the signs that a child is getting tired and frustrated and direct the child to a soothing activity such as water or sand play or listening to soft music.

Teachers and families need to work together to help a child with challenging behavior.

When a child uses challenging behavior over a period of time, and positive guidance strategies have not helped, it's time for the adults who care for the child to work together. Reassure the family that there are times when some preschool children behave in this way, but the behavior cannot be allowed at the program. Follow these steps to help the child learn appropriate ways to behave.

Define the behavior. Begin by clearly defining the problem behavior in terms that will be easily understood by all. Use objective, descriptive terms that do not label or judge the child.

Collect information. Next, collect information about when the problem behavior occurs. Observe the child at the program and ask parents to share information about the child's home activities.

Review and analyze the information. Go over the observation notes and other information collected. Try to identify the possible causes for the behavior. A situation at home might be causing the child to feel upset or frustrated. Or, perhaps the classroom environment: the schedule, activities, or room arrangement, does not meet the child's needs.

Develop and implement a plan. Together, you and the family can develop a consistent, written plan for responding to the behavior and teaching the child alternatives ways to express strong feelings. It is very important to tell the child that he or she is still loved and cared for, even if the behavior is not acceptable. Most children want to learn how to behave in acceptable ways because they want you to like them and want to have friends.

Assess progress. Maintain regular contact with the family so you can evaluate how well the plan is working and make adjustments if needed. Change takes time and it takes some children longer than others to learn new ways to express their feelings and meet their needs.

Common Challenging Behavior

Physical aggression. Respond immediately to hitting, scratching, kicking, and other behavior that hurts people. Get down to the child's level and clearly state the rule forbidding this behavior: "I cannot let you hurt people. Use words to say what you want." Involve the child in comforting the child who was hurt (if the hurt child permits this) so she can understand the connection between her actions and the other child's pain. "Please get the ice pack from the freezer so Jose can put it on his shin." Then help both children find something else to do. "Now that you are both feeling calmer, let's see if we can find something to do."

When a child uses physical aggression and is out of control, you may need to hold her until she calms down. Ask a colleague to respond to the hurt child. Children feel scared when they lose control, and your firm arms can help a child feel safe because you have taken charge. It may take a few minutes, but the child will calm down. Then you can discuss what happened: "Do you want to talk about what made you feel so angry? I could see that you were upset." Reassure the child that you want to listen to her feelings.

Let the child recover before discussing alternative ways to handle anger and frustration. Do this during a quiet moment later in the day, or the following day: "Yesterday, when you felt upset, you kicked another child. Next time, what could you do instead?" This discussion can be a rehearsal so that the next time the child begins to lose control, she will have an alternative to lashing out at someone else. "That sounds like a good plan. You could use some playdough until you feel better." Later, when the child has finished in the art area, be sure to offer support: "I noticed that when you felt upset you worked with playdough. Do you want to talk about why you were angry earlier?"

Biting is arguably the most emotionally-charged challenging behavior. Adults tend to have very strong reactions to biting and may overreact, rather than trying to solve the problem. The parents of a child who has been bitten are likely to be horrified, and fear for their child's safety. The parents of the child who did the biting may be embarrassed, ashamed, defensive, and unsure of how to respond. Teachers need to understand what may have caused the child to bite and work with the family to stop this unacceptable behavior.

As with other forms of aggression, respond immediately when one child bites another. State the rule clearly, involve the child who did the biting in comforting the child who was bitten, and help both children find something else to do. In addition, talk with the child and the parents to find out what might be causing this challenging behavior. Some children have great difficulty controlling their urge to bite. It may help to give the child something they are allowed to bite (for example, a clean washcloth) until they learn to control this behavior.

Temper tantrums are a child's way of expressing frustration by screaming, kicking, and crying. Temper tantrums often occur when children have many strong feelings that they can't express through words. During a tantrum, a teacher may need to protect the child, as well as other people and things, by firmly holding the child's arms and legs until the child calms down. The child will recover more quickly from the tantrum if no harm comes to people or objects. Once calm is restored, you can talk about what happened and what the child could do differently in the future. It is important to let children know that you will listen to and accept their feelings.

It's important to remember that children who are withdrawn or overly quiet also deserve our careful attention. They too are not able to fully benefit from the program. Although their behavior does not disrupt others in the group, it can indicate that there is something in the child's life that needs to be addressed. Follow the steps for working with families described above to help such a child become an active member of the group.

what's next?

Skill-Building Journal, section **10-9** *(Learning Activity E)*, section **10-1** *(Feedback)*, and section **10-10** *(Reflecting on Your Learning)*.

11

Families

Overview

Communicating Frequently With Families to Share Information About Their Children and the Program

Offering a Variety of Ways for Families to Participate in the Program

Providing Support to Families

Your Own Views About Families

Learning Activities

A. Building Partnerships With Families

B. Communicating With Families

C. Providing Ways for Families to Participate

D. Planning and Participating in Conferences With Families

E. Providing Support to Families

11.   Families

Families are the most important people in children's lives. They are children's first teachers. Families are therefore your partners in teaching young children.

Positive relationships with families are the basis for partnerships.

Effective preschool programs build positive relationships with families. Some families eagerly participate in programs, but others are reluctant or have responsibilities that prevent active involvement. Perhaps they had experiences that make them uneasy in schools. They may not speak English well and worry that they will not be understood. In a family's culture, parental involvement might be considered interference. To build relationships with all families, you must identify and address these concerns and value all families as teaching partners.

Everyone benefits from a partnership.

Both teachers and families are important to the relationship. Teachers know about child development and learning. They see children in group settings where they interact with other children and materials. Families bring valuable information about their children's interests, strengths, and responses to new experiences. They have dreams and expectations for their children. When families and teachers share information regularly, children are more likely to feel comfortable and thrive.

Learning about each family enables teachers to communicate effectively and offer support.

Every family is unique. A family's attitudes about play, discipline, food, and gender roles are rooted in culture. The more teachers know about children's backgrounds, the better they can communicate with families to meet children's needs. The communication, interaction, and child-rearing practices accepted in your own culture may differ from another's. It's important to be respectful of the differences.

Early childhood programs can help families support their children's development. Also, teachers are often among the first people to recognize when a family is under stress and having difficulty meeting their children's basic needs. Sometimes teachers are also among the first to recognize an individual child's special needs. You can help families find the assistance they need.

You can build partnerships with families by

- communicating frequently to share information about their children and the program

- offering a variety of ways for families to participate in the program

- providing support to families

Communicating Frequently With Families to Share Information About Their Children and the Program

1. **Share information with families on a daily basis.** "I'm glad you told us that Marcus didn't eat breakfast. He was hungry before lunch, so we gave him a snack."

2. **Respond to families' questions and concerns.** "We also noticed the change in Sara's behavior. Why don't we set up a time to talk? What would work best for your schedule?"

3. **Keep families informed about program activities.** "Have you seen our new display of the children's work on their bird study? You can see how much they have learned from their drawings and the photos we took."

4. **Get to know a little about each family.** Find out about their culture, interests, and skills and invite them to make unique contributions to the program.

5. **Tailor communication strategies to meet individual needs.** Offer a variety of ways to communicate: e-mail, phone, notes.

6. **Hold parent-teacher conferences regularly and as needed to share information about children's progress and to plan.** "Here's the folder where we keep samples of Linda's work. You can see how her drawings have changed and how interested she is in writing."

Ms. Kim Withholds the Good News

Ms. Kim has been watching Linda develop the courage to go down the slide. She knows that Linda's father is concerned about his daughter's timidity and fear of trying new activities. Ms. Kim has reassured Mr. Carter that Linda is taking her time but clearly making progress. At first, Linda watched the other children use the slide. Then she climbed up the ladder holding Ms. Kim's hand. Recently she climbed up and down the ladder by herself. Yesterday, for the first time, she climbed to the top of the ladder and went down the slide by herself. Ms. Kim gave her a big hug when she reached the bottom. She decides to say nothing about Linda's accomplishment so Mr. Carter can enjoy the surprise when he sees it for himself. Today Linda and her father arrive a little early. "Watch me, Daddy!" calls Linda as she climbs the ladder and zips down the slide. "Wow!" says Mr. Carter. "That looks like fun!" Ms. Kim smiles and says, "That's a big accomplishment, isn't it? She just needed the time to find out she can do it safely. I'm sure this will give her the confidence to try other new tasks as well."

Offering a Variety of Ways for Families to Participate in the Program

7. **Invite family members to visit the program at any time.** Explain your open-door policy to families when they enroll and in various communications throughout the year.

8. **Make participation in the classroom a positive experience for family members.** "Choose whatever interest area you like. You'll find some suggestions of how to work with the children posted on the wall."

9. **Invite families to share talents, interests, and aspects of their culture.** Take time to learn about each family so you can discover ways they might enjoy contributing to the program.

10. **Offer workshops and resources on topics of interest to families.** "We're having a workshop on challenging behavior. It seems to be a topic lots of parents are eager to discuss."

11. **Hold meetings and events at times that are convenient for most families.** "We know that working parents are very busy, so we're planning a dinner meeting and will provide child care."

12. **Offer a variety of ways for families to contribute to the program.** Family members might keep the program Web site updated, sew doll clothes, make story tapes, or volunteer in the classroom.

Ms. Williams Finds a Way

At the mid-year orientation for new families, Mr. Bradley says to Ms. Williams, "I don't have a lot of time, but I want to be a part of Tyrone's life in the program." Ms. Williams asks Mr. Bradley about his work and interests and discovers his hobby is bird-watching. "You know, I've been wanting to put up some bird feeders in our yard. I thought the children could become interested in watching them and learning about their habits." Mr. Bradley responds, "Tyrone has caught my interest in birds. He could help me build some bird feeders at home, and we could set them up near the classroom windows." Ms. Williams answers, "What a wonderful idea! I'll get some books on birds from the library." Mr. Bradley smiles broadly and says, "I think you'll be surprised to find out how much Tyrone knows about birds. This will be a great project for us to do together."

Providing Support to Families

13. **Maintain confidentiality about children and families.** "Thank you for sharing this information. With your permission, I'll tell the director. We will keep the information private."

14. **Recognize when families are under stress and offer additional support.** Maintain an up-to-date directory of community agencies that provide support services.

15. **Work with families to develop strategies for promoting children's positive behavior.** "Many children go through a phase of using 'bathroom' words. If we ignore them, it usually stops."

16. **Help families understand what their children learn through daily routines and activities.** "Aimee loves building with blocks. When she does, she is learning math and social studies concepts."

17. **Use familiar terms instead of professional jargon when talking with families.** "When children play with the pegboard and beads, they are strengthening the hand and finger muscles they use for drawing and writing."

18. **Provide families with information on child development and typical preschool behavior.** "It's not uncommon for 4-year-olds to be a bit bossy at times, but Tony is learning how to play cooperatively with others."

19. **Notify a supervisor when a family seems to need professional help.** Give factual information to a supervisor if any behavior, conversation, or injury to a child raises concerns.

example

Mr. Lopez Reassures a Concerned Parent

"I don't know what to do," says Ms. Jordan. "Avida's been coming here for a month, and she still cries and clings to me when I leave. How long will this go on?" Mr. Lopez explains, "Some children take a while to get used to being separated from their families. She stops crying and gets involved in activities soon after you leave. Maybe it would help to have goodbye rituals. Could you do a short activity with Avida each morning?" Ms. Jordan responds, "Yes, but I'm not sure it will help." "Well, let's try it," Mr. Lopez responds. "Let's have Avida wave from the window when you leave. We'll call that our *goodbye window*." Ms. Jordan says, "Great. I'll come a little earlier tomorrow. Why don't you tell her about the window idea?" "I sure will," answers Mr. Lopez. "Remember, we work as a team to support Avida."

what's next?

Skill-Building Journal, section **11-2** *(Overview)*, section **11-11** *(Answer Sheets)*, and section **11-1** *(Feedback)*.

Your Own Views About Families

There are many different kinds of families.

What does the word *family* mean to you? Do you think of a mother, father, and children living together? Do you think of different kinds of family relationships? Our experiences influence our views about families and how children should be reared.

The traditional idea of a family as a mother and father with several children does not always apply today. Very few families in the United States typify the traditional model of a mother who works in the home, a father who works outside the home, and their two children. Children may be growing up with a single mother or father or in step-families. They may live with several relatives—their mother, a grandmother, an aunt and her children—or they may live with a grandparent who has legal custody. A family might include children, a parent, and his or her partner of the same or different gender.

Parenting can be a challenging job.

Many of today's families are affected by multiple sources of stress that can make parenting a very difficult job. Some families are struggling to provide for their children's basic needs. They may live in substandard housing, depend on unreliable transportation to get to their jobs, and lack health insurance. These factors, accompanied by violence, drug and alcohol abuse, poverty, and other sources of stress, can leave families with little energy to meet the emotional needs of their children.

It's easy to blame families for their children's problems, especially when you see families who don't behave toward their children as you think they should. If you have difficulty accepting the values and lifestyles of some children and families in your program, examine the source of your negative reactions. Do you expect children's families to conform to your own personal values? Are you willing to learn about different cultural practices and parenting styles? It may help to remember that most families want the best for their children and try hard to be good families. They, too, are guided by their own experiences growing up in a family.

Before you begin the learning activities in this module, spend a few minutes thinking about how your own views and experiences affect the way you work with families.

what's next?

Skill-Building Journal, section **11-3** *(Your Own Views About Families),* section **11-1** *(Feedback),* and section **11-4** *(Pre-Training Assessment)*

LEARNING
ACTIVITY

Learning Activities

A. Building Partnerships With Families

In this activity you will learn to

- think about what makes a good partnership

- use a variety of ways to get to know each family

The two most important worlds in the lives of many young children are home and their child development program or school. Children have to bridge these two worlds each day and adapt to different environments and expectations. When children know that their families and teachers respect one another and communicate in positive ways, they feel more secure and comfortable. The bridge between their two worlds is sturdy. This is why high-quality early childhood programs build partnerships with families.

The Benefits of Partnerships

Strong partnerships benefit everyone involved. Families are assured that their children are safe and nurtured. As they learn more about the program and what their children are learning, they can support their children's development. Families help teachers learn about each child's life experiences, special interests, strengths, and needs. Teachers use this information to help each child feel comfortable in the program and to plan for each child's learning. Children feel secure, knowing that their families and their teachers keep them safe and help them learn. They feel proud of their family's involvement.

Families and teachers share a common concern for children's well-being.

Developing partnerships can be both challenging and time-consuming. Sometimes a child's teacher and family have different views on child rearing. They may even have different ideas about a child's strengths, interests, and needs. A family and teacher might not always understand each other's point of view and may disagree about how to solve a problem. What they almost always have in common, though, is real concern for the child's well-being.

Families know a lot about their children.

Although both the teacher and the family know a great deal about a particular child, this knowledge and information must be combined to create a total picture. Families typically have information about the following areas of a child's life:

Health and growth history. "The pediatrician said that Ben's allergies are under control. Thank you for working with us to coordinate his treatment."

Relationships with other family members. "Janelle has a special relationship with her grandfather, who lives with us. He's taught her how to fish."

Ways the child likes to be comforted. "We found that rubbing his back helps him relax when he has trouble settling down at nap time."

Food preferences and allergies. "Sara is allergic to all kinds of berries. She knows to avoid them but may need your help."

How the child reacts to changes in routines. "As long as I explain what is going to happen, Marcus is okay. He doesn't like changes in his routines that are a surprise."

The child's favorite activities at home. "Amanda loves to help me cook. She especially likes making cookies and creating different shapes."

The child's fears. "Leo is very afraid of dogs. He was once bitten by a neighbor's dog, and now he screams when he sees one."

The family's lifestyle. "We try our best to eat dinner together, but we can't always manage it during the week. On weekends, though, we gather everyone for family dinners."

What happened last night, over the weekend, or on vacation. "Benjamin woke up three times last night with bad dreams. Don't be surprised if he's tired and grumpy today." "Avida collected lots of shells on our beach trip. May she bring them to show the other children?"

Teachers bring a complementary perspective about a child.

Teachers have information about the following areas in the child's life:

Favorite interest areas and materials. "Michelle is a block builder. She is very creative in her building and has inspired other children to build."

What the child is learning. "Leo is very good at hearing the different sounds in words. He's especially good at rhyming words. This is so important for learning to read."

Special abilities. "Maria can really stick with a task once she gets started. She spent a long time taking apart an old clock to find out what was inside."

How the child plays with others. "Marcus likes to watch before he joins the other children. When he's ready, he comes up with such good ideas! The other children enjoy playing with him."

How the child reacts to changes in the environment. "Aimee is very observant. I can always count on her to notice anything new in the classroom."

What the child talks about during the day. "Carlos told us all about visiting his grandparents. He obviously loves them a lot."

What the child did each day. "Jorge really enjoyed cooking today. He grated the cheese for our pizza and thoroughly enjoyed eating it."

As you learn more about each family and share information, you build positive relationships.

Learning About Families to Build Relationships

Conversation, enrollment forms, and observation will help you learn about each child and family.

Just as every child is unique, every family is different. As you get to know a family, you can determine how best to communicate with them and how to make them feel comfortable in your program. Make the most of initial contacts at enrollment time, home visits, and daily exchanges to get to know the families in your program.

Most programs have a system for enrolling children that includes family interviews and forms. This first contact can leave a powerful impression, so you want the experience to be positive. It's also an excellent opportunity to learn about a child and family. Take time to find out how to pronounce the child's full name correctly, because names are very important. It is preferable to verify the child's name before meeting with the family, but, if you are unable to do so, ask the family early in the interview process. Let them know you realize the importance of correct pronunciation and spelling. Ask them how their child's name was chosen, whether, for example, the child is named for someone. You can learn a lot from this conversation and, at the same time, show respect for the family.

In addition to collecting information through your program's enrollment form, allow time for an informal conversation that is adapted for each family. Some families readily share information about themselves, but others are offended if you ask certain kinds of questions or if they think you are singling them out as being different. Asking direct questions is not always the best way to get to know a family. Sometimes it is better to discover a family's preferences and goals for their child by observing and talking over time.

If your questions seem welcome, open-ended questions, such as the following, generate the most information:

- What would you like us to know about your child?

- What are your child's favorite activities?

- Do you have any special concerns that we should know about?

- What are your hopes and dreams for your child?

- What makes your child feel comfortable?

- What makes your child happy?

As you get to know a family through conversation and observation, try to identify the family's special needs and talents. You may also be able to learn something about the family's culture and heritage. Here are some possible questions for which to seek answers, directly or indirectly:

- Will it be difficult to bring your child to and from the program each day? If so, is there anything we can do to help?

- Is there anything we should know about your family that will help us in teaching your child?

- Are there any special traditions or celebrations that are important to your child and your family?

- Would you be willing to share something about your traditions with the class?

Home visits are one of the best ways to learn about a child and family.

Many teachers make home visits before the children begin attending the program. Home visits are an excellent way to begin building a bridge to the program for a child who has never been away from home. The child and family meet you in the environment where they are most comfortable: their home. For families who have unhappy memories of their own school experiences, this opportunity to get to know their child's teacher in their own setting can help them feel more positive. When they find that you are friendly and respectful, they will begin to trust you. For a child who may be fearful on the first day in your classroom, seeing your friendly, familiar face will be very comforting.

Home visits provide teachers with valuable insights about a child's home environment and how family members relate to the child. You might learn, for example, who lives in the home, whether a child shares a room with others, what the child's favorite toys are, and what the child enjoys doing at home. This information will help you to build a relationship with each child and family.

Bring something with you to share on a home visit.

When you visit a child at home, bring something with you. You might bring pictures of your program to share with the child and family so they know a little about what to expect. Bring a toy that will be in the classroom and introduce it to the child. If possible, bring something that you can leave, such as a children's book or paper and crayons. You might invite the child to draw some pictures to bring to class on the first day.

Some families are comfortable in their homes and will welcome a home visit from their children's teacher. Others may not want you to come. Try your best to put families at ease but do not insist if the family resists. If you cannot visit a child at home, try to talk with the family by telephone or arrange to meet in a place where the family might be more comfortable, such as a park or the program facility.

Daily exchanges with families build positive relationships.

The informal conversations you have with families when they bring and pick up their children are excellent opportunities to communicate about the children's experiences and to strengthen partnerships. Family members can tell you about anything unusual that might affect the child's behavior: a sleepless night, a special trip the family is planning, the illness of a family member. You can share with families anything special that is happening in the program, such as a visitor or a planned trip. Most important, say something specific about their child. You might tell them about a new accomplishment, a particularly interesting block structure, a new friend, or how the child solved a problem.

In these daily exchanges, be friendly and respectful. Always greet each parent by name. Let them know through your attitude and tone of voice that they and their children are appreciated. This will go a long way in maintaining positive relationships and building partnerships.

Helping Families and Children Deal With Separation

The first few days and weeks of the program can be very challenging for children, families, and teachers, especially when a child has never been in group care away from home. Separation difficulties involve strong emotions for both children and their families. Children and families need support and guidance from teachers who are sensitive to their needs. When separation problems are handled well, relationships between teachers and families are strengthened.

Explain why it is important to say goodbye.

Because separating can be so painful, some families are tempted to sneak out of the room while their children are looking the other way. Explain to these families that, although leaving without saying goodbye might seem to be the easiest thing to do, they might find it useful to imagine how they would feel if the most important people in their lives disappeared without warning. Point out that saying goodbye gives children the security of knowing they can count on their families to let them know what is happening.

Try to explain to families how their children might be feeling. "I know it's hard to say goodbye to Mark when he has tears rolling down his face. When you give him a hug and reassure him that you will pick him up later, he may still feel sad, but he knows that you love him and will come back for him." Here are some strategies for helping families and children separate:

- Encourage families to stay for a few minutes until their children are involved in activities. Provide comfortable adult-size furniture so family members can sit.

- Display photos of each child and family in the classroom where children can easily see them.

- Have a goodbye window where children may wave to their families as they leave.

- Invite families to send a comfort item for the child from home, such as a stuffed animal or a special blanket.

- Install a telephone in each classroom so family members can call to talk to their children during the day.

- Read story books about going to school and separation.

The end of the day can also be difficult for children.

Like separations, reunions can be easy or difficult. Some days, children run gleefully to greet the family members who are picking them up. They are happy to see them and ready to go home. Other days, they are upset. They may burst into tears, have tantrums about getting their coats on, or complain about something that happened during the day (events they haven't mentioned earlier to teachers). Help families understand that this range of emotions is perfectly normal. Children sometimes save their deepest feelings for their families, the people they trust most.

When initial contacts and experiences in the program are handled well, you begin partnerships with families that will benefit everyone.

what's next?

Skill-Building Journal, section **11-5** *(Learning Activity A)* and section **11-1** *(Feedback).*

Learning Activities

B. Communicating With Families

In this activity you will learn to

- use a variety of ways to communicate with families

- address differences in a positive way

Good communication is essential to building partnerships with families and encouraging their involvement in the program. Families feel more involved when they know what's happening. Some information can be shared when children are brought to the program in the morning or picked up at the end of the day. These times, however, are usually too brief to provide lots of information. Teachers need to communicate in many ways to keep all families informed about the program's current activities and future plans.

Introducing Families to the Program

At the beginning of the year, families are generally eager to know what their children will be doing in the program and what they can expect. This is a good time to orient them and to share resources.

Take families on a tour of the classroom.

When families come to your program to enroll their children, invite them into the classroom. If the program is in session, invite them to observe and talk with you about what they notice. If the program has not yet started, provide a tour of the classroom and explain what they can expect. In either case, you can point out key aspects, such as

- how the room is organized in interest areas to give children choices and what takes place in each area

- what children learn from playing with different materials

- how and why materials are labeled

- the daily schedule and routines

- the books, print, writing tools, and math materials that are available

You might share with families some of the topics the group may be exploring and ask about their child's interests. Invite families to share something from home that could be displayed in the classroom or used by the children.

Give each family a description of the program and your curriculum.

If possible, give families written information about the program. A family handbook is a good way to be sure everyone understands the program's policies, schedules, and procedures. Families are also interested in what their children will be learning and how they can support their learning at home. The publisher of the early childhood curriculum your program has adopted might have a parent booklet to share with families, or your program might develop its own booklet. All written materials should be available in the home languages of the families you serve.

Using a Variety of Ways to Communicate

The more approaches you use to keep families informed, the more likely you will reach everyone. There are many ways to communicate with families. Select the ways that are manageable for you and that will work with the families in your program.

A **program newsletter** can provide general information of interest to all families, as well as specific news about each classroom. It might include news and information about coming events, the month's menus, suggested activities for families and children to do at home, information about community events of interest to families, reviews of children's books, and reviews of books on parenting and related topics. If you have a digital camera, it is easy to add photos to the newsletter.

Weekly class bulletins are brief notes about what happened that week in a particular classroom. They give families a sense of what their children are learning so they can ask specific questions and have conversations at home.

A **mailbox system** gives each family a box or a pocket in a shoebag where you can place flyers about upcoming events, news bulletins, or notes to individual families. When families speak several languages, some programs color code the boxes and paper for each language.

Family journals can be sent home with the child and returned the next day. Teachers can write about noteworthy observations and tuck flyers or notices in the journals. Families, in turn, can write notes back.

A **family bulletin board** can be located in the lobby or inside the classroom near children's cubbies where families will easily see it. Post articles, a calendar of events, reminders of upcoming meetings, the week's menus, and other items of general interest.

Visual displays of what children are learning can include photographs of children involved in activities and studies. Write a brief description of what the children are doing and what they are learning, and include children's artwork and writings.

Pictures of children and their families can be displayed prominently in the classroom along with pictures of the staff. This conveys the message that everyone is part of the classroom community. Include everyone's names so families can identify the children their child talks about at home and begin to get to know the other families.

Telephone calls to each family on a regular basis are a way to maintain communication. You can use these calls to share something about a child's progress, to express concern if a child is sick, or to discuss a problem. This doesn't have to take a lot of time—perhaps just one call a month to every family.

Computers offer many options for communicating if the families in your program have access to them. You can use e-mail to send out general messages and to communicate with individual families. Some programs set up a Web site or an electronic bulletin board to keep families informed. They use digital cameras to post pictures of what the different classes are doing.

Addressing Differences in a Positive Way

Teachers and families do not always see things the same way. They can misunderstand one another and feel annoyed by what another person has said or done. These feelings can get in the way of a partnership unless they are resolved.

Cultural differences can lead to misunderstandings.

Sometimes misunderstandings are caused by cultural differences that have not been recognized and respected. For example, a teacher may misunderstand a mother who insists on taking off her son's coat and hat in the morning and putting them in his cubby. The teacher thinks, "Carlos can take off his own coat and hat and put them away. It's important for children to develop independence and self-help skills." In the family's culture, however, mothers traditionally show their love for their children by doing things for them, even if they can do it themselves. Just before leaving her child for the day, she wants to be sure her son knows he is loved.

A teacher who does not understand this perspective might tell the mother what she is thinking, causing the mother to feel confused, guilty, or uncomfortable about leaving her child in the care of people with different values. However, a teacher who understands the mother's reasoning might say, "I know how much you love your son. He's growing up so fast, isn't he?" The teacher decides not to take this difference on as an issue. She knows that children understand and can live with differences between how things are done at home and at the program, as long as there is mutual respect.

Other differences may conflict with the program's philosophy and goals.

Other differences may go against your program's philosophy. These are often not easy to reconcile and may require time and effort. For example, parents may complain that they only see their children playing at the program. They want their children to be ready for school and want to see concrete examples of academic work, such as worksheets and homework. You think these approaches are not the best way to prepare children for school and may work against that goal. Rather than simply defending your position, use these differences as an opportunity to talk with families and respond to their concerns. Here is how you might do this.

Try to understand the family's position. Ask open-ended questions to gain a better understanding. "What kinds of experiences do you think would help your child? What are you most eager for your child to learn here?"

Respect their concerns and wishes. Let families know that you have heard their concerns and respect their wishes. "We absolutely agree with you that it's important for children to develop the skills they need to be ready for school. I hear you saying that you worry your child isn't learning those skills here."

Explain how your program addresses their concerns and wishes. This is an opportunity to share information. "Many families share your concerns. It's not easy to see how much children are learning through their play, but the objectives of our curriculum include many of the skills you identified as important. The things we do every day help children acquire these skills."

Suggest a way to work together on specific goals. Be open-minded about whether your program might do more. Also think of ways families can be involved. "After talking with you, I realized we can offer the children other experiences here at the center to reinforce skills. And there is nothing more important than what you do with your child at home. Reading books together each day and talking about what happens in the stories is the best way to encourage children to love reading. Here's a booklet, called *Reading Right From the Start,* with lots of good suggestions for families. We also have take-home book packs with a story to read and activities you can do together."

Make a plan to see how parents perceive the partnership. Agree to be in touch again to monitor the child's progress in reaching the goals you and the family identified. "May we set up a time to meet again in a month, to see how our plan is working? I'll be able to share examples of the progress your child has made and what we will be working on."

what's next?

Skill-Building Journal, section **11-6** *(Learning Activity B)* and section **11-1** *(Feedback).*

Learning Activities

LEARNING ACTIVITY

C. Providing Ways for Families to Participate

In this activity you will learn to

- offer a variety of ways for families to be involved in the program

- make participation in classroom activities a positive experience

Most families want to be involved in their children's lives in the program. While some families can arrange their work schedules in order to eat lunch with the children occasionally, go on field trips, or volunteer in the classroom, others are not able to participate in this way. It's important to offer a variety of options that match families' interests, skills, and schedules.

Families can be involved in many ways.

Make it a point to let families know how much you value their participation and how it benefits the program. Families who come on field trips may enjoy themselves so much that they need little or no encouragement to do it again. The parent who sews new curtains for the children's puppet theater, however, may never see the theater in action. In such a case, be sure to send a thank-you note home. Describe how the children are using the theater and enclose a photograph showing them putting on a play. Most important, let families know that there are many ways to contribute to and participate in the program.

Contributing something that benefits the program. Family members who cannot take part in program activities during the day may have talents and skills that the program needs. You may find family members who can contribute by sewing aprons or doll clothes, making audiotapes of favorite stories to go with familiar books, or typing children's stories or a class newsletter.

Collecting beautiful junk. There are lots of throw-away items in every home that the program can use, such as empty food containers; ribbons; wrapping paper; and old keys, buttons, plastic bottle caps, or shells for sorting and classifying. Every family can help collect items like these. You may find that you will get a better response by asking for one or two items at a time, rather than sending a long list of things to collect.

Family members can be important resources for learning activities.

Participating in a study. Before you select topics for a study (see *Learning Activity D*, module 5, *Cognitive*), find out what kinds of work family members do and what their special interests or hobbies are. Does anyone work at a nearby clinic, grocery store, construction site, or farm? Do you know a parent who plays an instrument or works as a car mechanic, a grandparent who is a storyteller, or someone who knows a lot about insects? There are countless ways for families to participate in and contribute to a study.

Joining a field trip. With enough notice, some family members can arrange their schedules to go on a field trip. It's always helpful to have a few extra adults when taking children away from the center. Just as you prepare children for the trip by talking about what they will see and by discussing their questions, let participating family members know the purpose of the trip and how to make it a meaningful learning experience for the children.

Building and landscaping projects. Some family members may have skills or an interest in helping to build a playground structure, prepare a garden plot, or give the walls a new coat of paint. These are projects that can be worked on at odd hours or on a weekend.

A family room. If space is available, consider setting up a family room at your center or school. Provide comfortable places to sit, resources that interest families, and pots with hot water and fresh coffee. One school found that the level of family involvement increased dramatically when they invited family members to use the program's washer and dryer while they visited.

Participating in the Classroom [34]

Some family members may have time to participate in the classroom during the day. With a little planning and preparation, you can make these experiences meaningful for them, helpful to you, and enjoyable for the children. Families can see how you work with children and how much the children are learning through play. Their parenting skills may improve as a result. You gain an extra hand in the classroom to help you offer activities that need adult supervision, such as cooking and woodworking. Children benefit by seeing members of their family become part of the classroom community and more involved in their education.

You may find that some children behave differently when their family members, particularly their parents, participate in the classroom. They may act out more or demand their parents' full attention. It's important to prepare parents for this possibility and reassure them that such behavior is normal. Advise them to give their children extra attention and assure them that such behavior will decrease with time.

Make participation a positive experience by preparing families.

To make classroom participation a positive and meaningful experience, you must orient families. You might prepare a one-page tip sheet (translated if necessary) giving families a few ideas of how to get started. The orientation should offer these suggestions:

- **Observe what children do** and let them know you are interested. You can describe what you see: "I notice you made a pattern with the pegs: red/blue, red/blue." This tells children that their work is important.

- **Follow children's lead** without taking over. For example, you might say, "I'm going to try to make the same pattern you did with the beads and laces." This makes children more aware of what they did and reinforces their learning.

- **Ask open-ended questions** that have more than one right answer. Such questions can help you find out what children are thinking and encourage them to express their ideas in words. Here are some examples: "How did you decide to do it this way?" "How many ways can you use it?" "What will it do?" "What do you like best?"

- **Offer assistance** when it is needed. If you see a child is frustrated, offer to help or make a suggestion. "I see there are no more long blocks. Do you think two of these blocks will work if you put them together?"

You may find it helpful to post charts and displays in the classroom to explain what children are learning. If your curriculum has specific goals and objectives, post them. This helps both teachers and visitors to keep the curriculum objectives in mind as they observe and work with children. You can expand on this concept by taking a photo of the children that illustrates each objective. For example, you might use a photo of children working together for the objective, "Plays well with other children"; a photo of a child looking at a caterpillar with a magnifying glass for the objective, "Observes objects and events with curiosity"; and a photo of a child ordering keys by size for the objective, "Arranges objects in a series." Children looking at books in a library area shows "Enjoys and values reading," and a child writing his name on his artwork represents the objective, "Writes letters and words."

Explain to families how children learn in each interest area and what they can do.

It's very likely that family members will work with children in some of the interest areas in your classroom. To make that experience more meaningful, consider making a chart that describes what children are likely to do in each area and how family volunteers can help.

Meaningful Interest Area Experiences

Interest Area	What Children Do and Learn	How Families Can Help
Blocks	Make creative designs, roads for cars, and buildings like those they see around them. Learn about shapes, sizes, and other symbols.	Talk to children about their buildings. Offer props they can use. Help children find and clean up the blocks.
Dramatic Play	Take on new roles to increase understanding. Learn thinking skills as they pretend.	Join in children's make-believe. Suggest roles and ideas; help children find props.
Toys & Games	Build, sort, classify, and match. Develop math skills; refine small muscles in their hands.	Play games with children. Talk about what they are doing; help a child in need.
Art	Express their ideas and feelings through their artwork. Explore materials and develop their own ideas about how to use them.	Encourage children to experiment with different materials. Ask them about their work and show interest in their answers.
Library	Choose quiet places to look at books, practice writing, and re-enact favorite stories.	Offer to read a book to a child or a small group. Help children who want to write.
Discovery	Explore, experiment, and observe interesting objects, collections, and living things on display.	Show curiosity about the materials. Discuss their findings.
Sand & Water	Run their hands through the materials. Pour, measure, scoop, build, and make discoveries.	Offer props and talk about what children are discovering and doing.
Music & Movement	Make and listen to music. Explore instruments, move, and sing.	Help children use a tape recorder or CD player. Play instruments with children.
Cooking	Follow recipes to create snacks and meals. Learn literacy skills, math skills, and make scientific discoveries as they follow recipes.	Help children follow the recipe cards and remind them of safety rules. Share a favorite recipe with a group of children.
Computers	Work together to choose programs and follow the directions. Interact and create while using computer games.	Assist children in following the procedures for using computers. Play games with children.
Outdoors	Develop large-muscle skills and coordination. Explore nature.	Supervise and play games with children. Take an interest in their discoveries.

what's next?

Skill-Building Journal, section **11-7** *(Learning Activity C)* and section **11-1** *(Feedback).*

Learning Activities

LEARNING ACTIVITY

D. Planning and Participating in Conferences With Families

In this activity you will learn to

- prepare for family conferences by reviewing information you have collected about their children's progress

- share information with families and jointly plan ways to support their children's development and learning

In most early childhood programs, teachers meet two or three times a year with each child's family to review how their child is progressing in all areas of development and to devise a plan to support the child's learning. Conferences are opportunities to focus on one child and family. Although much information about the child is shared daily, conferences allow for in-depth discussions. When they are carefully planned, everyone benefits. Families are assured that the teachers really know their child and that their child is developing and learning as expected. Teachers gain new insights about a child's behavior, interests, culture, and experiences and often receive more support from the family. Children benefit from the stronger partnerships that usually result.

Planning for Conferences

The best preparation for a conference with a family is to review all you know about the child and prepare a summary of the child's progress to share with the family. If you use a systematic approach to assessing children's progress, as described in module 12, you will have a wealth of information about what every child knows and can do in relation to the goals and objectives of your curriculum. You will have observed children and kept records of what you saw and heard. You may have a checklist to keep track of children's progress toward each objective. You will probably also have a portfolio for each child and collected samples of work, such as drawings, writing, and photographs of constructions. When each sample of work is dated and similar samples have been collected over time, a portfolio is concrete evidence of a child's progress.

Review all you know about the child's progress.

Before the conference, examine all of the evidence of the child's developmental progress. Prepare a brief summary of what you want to highlight for families about their child's progress in each developmental area. Organize the work samples you want to share and think about your goals for the child.

Many families are interested in learning how their child gets along in a group setting with peers. They want to know as much as possible about their child's daily experiences in the program: favorite activities, friends, response to daily routines, classroom behavior. Think of examples that will help families picture what their child does in the program and understand how these experiences support development.

Involve families in planning for the conference.

When you schedule conferences, ask families what time would be most convenient for them to attend. If possible, offer several options and provide adequate notice so families can make plans. Allow enough time for the conference so you and the family will not feel rushed. Explain that the conference is an opportunity for each of you to share what you know about the child's progress so all of you can better support the child's development and learning.

Encourage families to consider their goals for the conference. Most importantly, each family will want to know that you understand and like their child. In addition, they may have a specific concern they would like to discuss or a suggestion for how they would like you to work with their child. It is also possible that a parent might have a concern about the program's philosophy and curriculum or a complaint about something you did or didn't do. It is helpful to know about these issues ahead of time so you can respond constructively.

Conducting the Conference

At the beginning of the conference, try to establish a relaxed and comfortable tone. Allow time for social conversation. Offer a snack and confirm how much time you have available. Here's how a conference might proceed.

Discuss how the child has adjusted to the program. You might begin with a question, such "How do you think things are going?" or "Does Amanda seem happy to come to the program?" Then share some examples of your own observations: "Amanda has really started to make friends here. Several other children seek her out and ask her to join activities."

Share some positive examples of the child's work. A good way to illustrate a child's progress is to show samples of work. Photos of block structures or designs, writing, drawings, and dictated stories are concrete examples of what a child can do. Talk about each sample and explain what it shows. "Notice how Amanda was writing her name when she first came in September and what she can do just a few months later. She can recognize and write not only the letters in her name but several other letters as well."

Discuss the child's progress. Review the summary you have prepared to highlight the child's progress in each developmental area. Share your program's goals and objectives and point out what their child is learning. "Amanda can sort and organize objects like bottle caps and shape blocks, and tell us how she did it. These are important math skills and address several of our curriculum objectives, such as classifying objects and arranging objects in a series.

Invite families to share their observations. "What do you think Amanda has learned? Does she do any of these things at home?" Record what you learn from families on the same form you used to summarize the child's progress.

Bring up any concerns. If you have any concerns, be sure to have concrete examples to illustrate what you want to discuss. "We've noticed that, when Amanda looks at a book or draws a picture, she bends very close to it. She also squints her eyes a lot. We think it might be a good idea to have her eyes checked."

Make sure to discuss next steps at school and at home.

Discuss specific goals for the child. Use your curriculum goals and objectives to talk about those you want to focus on next. "We want to encourage Amanda's interest in writing and to build on her ability to sort, compare, and count." Invite their ideas as well: "Do you have any specific goals for your child?"

Agree on some next steps. At the end of the conference, summarize your discussion and identify the actions you have each agreed to take and how you will follow up. "It would be wonderful if Amanda could help you cook and measure the ingredients. That's an excellent way to use her math skills. I'll give you the phone numbers of the children she has started to play with, and you can arrange some play dates for her."

Tips for Family Conferences

Respect culturally based communication practices. Maintain an appropriate physical distance, eye contact, and tone of voice; allow enough time for responses to questions; use or avoid physical contact, as appropriate.

Ask open-ended questions. This often elicits more information.

Confirm the partnership. "It's helpful to know that you sometimes have to repeat directions to be sure Oanh understands what to do. We'll remember to do that here as well."

Take notes during the conference. This is very important if you are discussing a complex or difficult situation. Explain to families that the notes will help you follow up on their concerns and implement their suggestions.

Pay attention to body language. Especially note signs that a parent might feel tense, hurt, disappointed, or angry.

Repeat what you think you heard. Restate their comments and suggestions to make sure you heard them correctly. "You are concerned that Maria is tired when she gets home, so you would like us to make sure she naps every day."

Offer advice when asked. Always offer more than one suggestion. "Some families find it helpful to allow their children to select what clothes to wear. Others offer a choice between two items, for example, the red sweater or the blue one." If you don't know an answer, say you will try to find out and then tell them.

---

what's next?

Skill-Building Journal, section **11-8** *(Learning Activity D)* and section **11-1** *(Feedback).*

Learning Activities

E. Providing Support to Families

In this activity you will learn to

- recognize signs that families are under stress

- provide support to families to prevent or cope with stress

Many families with young children, especially young and first-time parents, have stressful lives. Parents can be overwhelmed, trying to balance the demands of a job and family. They may feel unsure about sharing the care of their children, and they might not understand changes in their children's behavior. Some families feel comfortable voicing their worries and seeking assistance; others do not. Teachers of young children are often in a good position to identify parents who are experiencing overwhelming stress and offer help.

Recognizing When Families Are Under Stress[35]

Stress is a normal part of daily life for many families. Most families can cope with typical frustrations and tension, so stress doesn't interfere with their work and home activities. Some families, however, are affected over a long period of time by significant sources of stress, such as community violence, homelessness, substance abuse, or lack of basic necessities. The stresses are not caused by single events such as divorce, an illness, or accident. Rather, they are routine, unrelenting, and an integral part of daily life. They may be beyond the control of individual families.

There are many sources of long-term stress.

Long-term stress may be caused by

- unemployment

- lack of food, clothing, transportation, and medical care

- living in overcrowded, inadequate, or temporary housing

Other stressful situations for families include

- violence or substance abuse in the home or community

- chronic illness or disability of a child or other family member, along with lack of access to needed services and support

- abuse and neglect of a child, spouse, or other family member

- depression or other mental illness of a child or family member

- learning a new language and adapting to a new culture

There may be other sources of stress that are specific to your community, such as when military personnel are called for duty away from home. Regardless of the cause of high stress in their lives, families tend to have similar concerns, needs, and behavior. When families are overwhelmed, family life suffers and children's behavior is affected.

Stress can overwhelm some families.

If family life is unpredictable, unstable, and chaotic because the family moves frequently, then children must adapt to new child care programs, teachers, and classmates. Children may have difficulty focusing and lack a sense of order and discipline in their lives.

If adult family members are unable to give their children affection and attention, then children may be expected to assume adult responsibilities such as caring for younger siblings. They may come to the program tired.

If children and adult family members have unmet health and nutrition needs because of lack of access to adequate food or needed health care, including immunizations, dental checkups, and counseling, then children may come to the program hungry or sick.

If children receive inconsistent, overly punitive, or little parental discipline, children may not know what to expect or how to behave.

Learn to identify the signs of overwhelming stress on a family.

When a family is under stress, they may seem disorganized, frequently forgetting things such as mittens on a cold day or a child's special blanket. A parent might seem frustrated when a child is slow to get ready to go home. A parent might complain to a teacher about the difficulty of handling the child's growing independence. Families under stress might be unwilling to accept help, or they might be more interested in talking about adult problems than their child's.

When you see signs of stress, it is important not to add to them. This is not the time to discuss a child's inappropriate behavior or changes in the program's vacation schedule. However, it would be appropriate to share information about their child that will help a family get through the evening. For example, you would let a parent know her child has been tired and cranky all afternoon so you can discuss whether the child might be getting sick. When a family knows the reasons for their child's behavior, they are less likely to be frustrated or angered by crankiness and more likely to comfort the child. They are more likely to interact positively with their child and less likely to lose control.

Involve your supervisor if you think a family needs help.

Always notify your supervisor when you think families may need professional help. Do not counsel families or refer them to social services or mental health professionals without first discussing the situation with your supervisor. Your job is to help families get the support they need, not to provide it yourself.

When families do confide in you, it is essential to maintain complete confidentiality. This means you should not discuss a child with anyone other than your colleagues or the child's family. This holds true for information about families as well. You should not share records with anyone who does not have permission to see them, and you should not hold discussions about children or families during times when other children or parents are present. Ask your supervisor about your program's guidelines for maintaining confidentiality.

- What sources of stress might the families in your program experience?

- How does your program provide relief for families who are experiencing these sources of significant stress?

Helping Families Locate Resources

Parents often need to know where they can get help for themselves, their child, or the whole family. Your director can give you information about parent education opportunities. Here are some things you can do to help:

Encourage connections by introducing families who live in the same neighborhood or have children of the same age. "I'm glad you met, because you live near one another and your children are developing a nice friendship."

Develop a classroom directory so families can support one another by sharing responsibilities and errands, such as by carpooling, grocery shopping, and preparing meals. "Several families have joined a food co-op in your neighborhood. I can give you their phone numbers so you can find out more."

Point out resources, articles, workshops, and television or radio shows on children and families. "Next Tuesday at 8:00 p.m., there's a show on Channel 8 about stepparenting and blended families."

Display books on topics that interest families—playground safety, juggling home and work responsibilities, planning quick and healthy meals—and invite families to borrow these resources.

Tell families about services and special programs provided by community groups. Provide as much information as possible: names, phone numbers, locations, and hours of operation.

Sharing Information on Child Growth and Development

You can be a resource for families about the typical development of children.

Families sometimes do not know much about the typical development of young children. As a result, they may expect too much or too little of their children. Here are some things you can do to help:

Invite a parent to observe his or her child with you. Discuss what you see and explain why the child's actions are typical of a particular stage of development.

Provide information about parenting workshops on topics such as supporting emerging literacy, adjusting to a new baby, responding to children's growing independence, and other subjects that would interest families of preschool children.

Include information on child development in newsletters and on the family bulletin board. The charts in other modules will be useful.

Invite families to attend staff workshops about topics of interest.

Establish a parent lending-library of books, magazines, and videotapes about child growth and development.

Introduce families who are dealing with, or have already successfully handled, similar developmental issues and who have expressed their willingness to share information.

Model positive ways to interact with children.

When families are in the classroom, either to participate or just to drop off or pick up their children, you can talk with families and model positive ways to interact with children. In the following exchanges between a teacher and the children in her care, families would witness several positive interactions:

Ms. Thomas encourages Aimee to help put away the beads and laces. She talks and laughs with Leo as she ties his shoes. She also asks Benjamin a question about his painting, "Tell me, how did you make these long, squiggly lines?"

The children's families might comment, "I can't get Aimee to put any of her things away at home." "Leo squirms around so much at home that I just want to get his shoes tied as quickly as possible." "I never know what to say about Benjamin's drawings except that they are nice."

Ms. Thomas uses these comments to begin conversations about

- promoting children's self-help skills ("We find that children clean up better when we label the containers so children know where things go.")

- using routines as times to talk with children ("It might help to make a game out of tying shoes. He probably squirms because he's eager to get going.")

- supporting creativity by asking children about their paintings ("I try to describe what I see to make children more aware of what they have created. I encourage children to describe what they have done and how they did it.")

When you demonstrate positive ways to talk with and support children, you help families improve their interactions with their children.

Often families turn to teachers for advice about frustrating or confusing behavior. When this happens, be sure to respond in a way that acknowledges families' skills and helps them feel confident and capable. Remind families that they know more about their children than anyone else. Asking what approaches they use at home helps families discover or recognize what works for them and their children.

what's next?

Skill-Building Journal, section **11-9** *(Learning Activity E),* section **11-1** *(Feedback),* and section **11-10** *(Reflecting on Your Learning).*

12
Program Management

Overview

> Learning About Each Child

> Working as a Team to Offer an Individualized Program

> Using Information to Evaluate the Program

Managing Your Own Life

Learning Activities

> A. Collecting Information About Each Child

> B. Organizing and Using Portfolios

> C. Meeting Individual Needs and Interests

> D. Working as a Team to Plan and Evaluate the Program

12. Program Management

Teachers plan, conduct, and evaluate the program.

As an early childhood teacher, you play many roles. Your most important role is to keep children safe and healthy and to encourage their development and learning. In addition, you help children build a sense of competence and gain confidence in their abilities. You support families, and, with your colleagues, you use management skills to ensure the smooth operation of the program.

Many teachers do not see themselves as managers. Your program probably has a director who performs management tasks such as preparing budgets, hiring, scheduling, and providing support to teachers. Yet you and your colleagues are also managers. You work as a team to plan a program that meets the needs of each child and the group. You create a supportive learning environment, guide children's learning, and assess their progress.

Teachers use information about each child to plan and evaluate their program.

Effective early childhood programs are developmentally, individually, and culturally appropriate. They are based on child development theories and principles that describe, in general, how most young children develop. In addition, the programs are tailored to respond to the characteristics of each child. This requires teachers and families first to identify each child's skills, needs, and interests. Next, this team of adults works together to plan and implement a responsive program with appropriate challenges that allow each child to progress. Families and teachers regularly share information about each child and work together to offer a program that builds on the child's interests, offers appropriate challenges, and reflects the child's family, language, and culture.

Program evaluations help teachers decide what changes to make.

Teachers plan activities, interactions with children, transitions and routines, and other aspects of the program. As plans are implemented, it is important to review what actually happened during the day, during the week, and over a period of time. Teachers note interest areas and learning materials that are used by many children and those that do not seem to be as popular. Evaluation lets teachers know which approaches are resulting in positive outcomes for children, as well as which children had problems completing activities. Evaluation also lets teachers know where changes need to be made to the environment, interactions, daily schedule, and so on.

You can manage your program effectively by

- learning about each child's culture, language, family, skills, needs, and interests

- working as a team to offer an individualized program

- using information to evaluate the program

Learning About Each Child

1. **Communicate with families often, using a variety of strategies.** Learn about each child's family life, culture, home language, and unique characteristics. Use this information in planning changes to the environment and activities.

2. **Observe each child regularly and use a notation system that is objective, accurate, and avoids labeling.** Notes about what children say and do, families' descriptions of children's play at home, and information from children's portfolios can be analyzed and used to develop summaries of children's progress.

3. **Observe children in different settings and at different times of the day.** "Yesterday I observed Avida playing house with Leo. The next time I'll observe her when she is playing by herself."

4. **Collect examples and photographs of work that document children's skills, interests, and progress.** Portfolios for each child, which contain these examples and photographs of children's work, are useful for documenting each child's progress over time.

5. **Play and talk with children to learn about their interests and abilities.** The best source of information about each child is the child, him- or herself. Use everyday opportunities to find out each child's likes, dislikes, strengths, and needs.

Mr. Lopez Collects and Documents Facts About Benjamin

As Benjamin rips lettuce leaves in half, Mr. Lopez crouches near the table, note pad in hand. "You look ready to make a lettuce roll-up, Benjamin. What do you want to spread on the leaf—cream cheese or peanut butter?" "Peanut butter!" Benjamin answers. He places a leaf in his left hand. Then he picks up a knife, holds it with his fist, and dips it straight down into the peanut butter. He spreads peanut butter partly on the leaf and partly on his palm. "You could lay the leaf on the paper towel to do that," Mr. Lopez says. He demonstrates how to hold the leaf on the paper towel. Benjamin lays the leaf down. Mr. Lopez makes another suggestion, "You might find a more comfortable way to hold the knife." Benjamin experiments with several ways to grip the knife until he finds one that works. He rolls up the lettuce leaf and takes a bite. Mr. Lopez photographs Benjamin eating, then writes on an index card: "Benjamin chose peanut butter, responded positively to my suggestions, tried different ways to hold the knife, and kept trying until he could spread the peanut butter on lettuce."

Working as a Team to Offer an Individualized Program

6. **Meet regularly with colleagues to plan the program.** Weekly meetings provide opportunities to review children's progress, discuss changes to the environment, and plan activities.

7. **Ensure that curriculum goals are the basis for planning experiences for the children.** "Let's look at our curriculum goals in our next teachers' meeting and make sure we're offering opportunities for all children to meet those goals."

8. **Use ongoing assessment information to plan for individual children and the group.** Review and analyze observation notes, portfolio information, and information from families to prepare progress summaries for each child.

9. **Include each family in planning how to encourage their child's development and learning.** Include families in regular planning meetings or provide other opportunities for offering their ideas.

10. **Use creative thinking skills, such as brainstorming, to plan and solve problems.** Team members use these skills to develop short- and long-term plans, strategies for dealing with inappropriate behavior, and other issues.

11. **Appreciate and use the strengths of all team members, including teachers, families, and volunteers.** "In our planning meeting, I want to review our first observation notes about the children, as well as the information families provided at enrollment about their children's interests and strengths."

Ms. Richards and Ms. Kim Update the Outdoor Area

Ms. Richards and Ms. Kim use their Friday meeting time to discuss ways to offer new materials and challenges outdoors. During the week, they take notes about children's outdoor activities. Carlos collects some leaves, Marcus makes a network of roads in the sandbox, and Maria brushes the side of the building with water. Ms. Kim takes photographs of a village several children built from boxes and notes that Sara is the leader of this project. Ms. Richards audiotapes the children and a visiting librarian acting out *Ask Mr. Bear*. On Friday the teachers share the information collected and discuss their ideas. Ms. Kim says, "The children really enjoyed building a village. Let's get some more boxes and building props." Ms. Richards suggests, "We could also read and act out other books." Next they consider ways to build on individual skills and interests. They think Carlos might like to help plant a garden and Marcus would enjoy using small cars in the sandbox. They decide to bring the easels outdoors to support Maria's interest in painting.

Using Information to Evaluate the Program

12. **Use program goals as a component of program evaluation.** Program or curriculum goals guide teachers' planning and help them assess whether children are making progress.

13. **Identify what is working well and what needs to be improved, every day.** "The block area was a busy place today, as usual, but I didn't see any children at the discovery table."

14. **Plan teaching approaches and change the environment, materials, interest areas, routines, and activities in response to what you learn about each child.** "Jamie and Sara have taken quite an interest in bugs this spring. I'll add some Eric Carle books and posters on insects to the library area."

15. **Use information about children's use of materials to determine whether changes are needed.** Lack of interest in or misuse of toys can help teachers determine whether they need to put some toys away, add new ones, or display them differently.

Ms. Williams and Ms. Frilles Evaluate Their Program

example

"We certainly have a lot of information to help us evaluate our program," Ms. Williams says to Ms. Frilles. Let's review our summary forms to see what skills the children are demonstrating." They review the forms and record on a chart the types of skills that children are using, under the headings "Cognitive," Social/Emotional," "Language," and "Physical." Then they list on a second sheet the month's activities that worked well and those that presented problems. "I was sure that Tyrone would do well with the new climber," says Ms. Frilles, "and Oanh surprised me by going all the way to the top on her first try!" Ms. Williams adds, "That day and later in the week, we had to intervene to help some of the children work out problems over taking turns with the trikes." The two teachers continue to review information about the children's activities, successes, and problems. The review helps them plan changes to the outdoor area, the blocks and art areas, and the daily schedule. They also decide to introduce small-group activities after morning choice time. Ms. Williams declares, "I'm excited about our plans for improving the program!"

what's next?

Skill-Building Journal, section **12-2** *(Overview),* section **12-10** *(Answer Sheets),* and section **12-1** *(Feedback).*

Managing Your Own Life

Management skills are used at home.

Many of the things you do at home require management skills. For example, when you plan a trip to the grocery store, you might begin by making a list. You consider how many people will be eating each meal, what foods each person likes, and what ingredients you need. You can do this because you observe each member of your household, include them in planning balanced meals, and follow recipes.

The more orderly and efficient you are in managing your life outside of work, the more time you have to do things other than chores. Think about times when careful management encourages effective use of time and resources:

- You save gas and time by doing all your errands at the same time, rather than making several trips.

- You make sure you have all the tools and materials you need before you start a project, such as painting a room or repairing a bicycle.

- You keep records of all bills and file receipts promptly.

- You keep emergency numbers posted beside the telephone.

- You involve the family in planning a vacation that will interest everyone.

- You borrow a folding table and extra chairs from a neighbor when you are having a crowd over for a special meal or a neighborhood meeting.

- You make a list of what you *must* do (have the car inspected), what you'd *like to do* (get a haircut), and what you *can do later* (shop for new running shoes).

- You remember the importance of relaxation and make time for exercise and spending time with friends and family.

Organizing your time and your environment to work *for* you rather than *against* you helps you manage more effectively.

what's next?

Skill-Building Journal, section **12-3** (*Managing Your Own Life*), section **12-1** (*Feedback*), and section **12-4** (*Pre-Training Assessment*).

LEARNING
ACTIVITY

Learning Activities

A. Collecting Information About Each Child

In this activity you will learn to

- use multiple sources of information to get to know each child

- complete observation records that are objective, accurate, and complete

Program management involves planning an environment, routines, and activities that are appropriate for the group, as well as for individual children. Planning begins with gathering information about each child. Teachers need information about the typical behaviors and interests of preschool children (see *Learning Activity A* in modules 4–10) and about each child's culture, language, family, interests, skills, needs, temperament, and other characteristics.

Assessment information helps you make decisions.

Assessment begins with learning about each child using informal and formal strategies. There are different types of assessment. Each serves a different purpose. Some programs conduct health and developmental screenings at enrollment or soon after. *Screening* results provide useful information about each child's skills and may identify signs of possible developmental concerns. In these instances, teachers and specialists meet as a team to discuss the results and for the necessity of a *health* or *developmental evaluation* to pinpoint the child's strengths and needs. Information from screenings helps the team plan ways to address the child's needs in the classroom, at home, and through other interventions. Teachers also might conduct *initial developmental assessments* to begin planning for each child and the group. The appropriate use of an initial assessment is to get to know each child, that is, to find out what each child knows and is able to do. Then you can adjust the program to match children's skills, interests, and needs.

Different strategies will help you to learn different things about each child.

To keep track of each child's progress and respond to each child's changing skills, interests, and needs, teachers need a system for *ongoing assessment*. There are many ways to get to know each child and his or her progress. Conversations with children's families provide information about a child's unique characteristics. Checklists can also help you to learn about each child. Teachers check off children's accomplishments on a prepared list, such as "builds a tower with at least nine blocks." Samples of children's work, collected over time, also provide useful information about each child's progress. Observations of children's play and activities can tell you about their skills and interests, as well as how they handle frustration, get involved in group play, and cope with separation.

To offer a program that meets individual needs and interests, you need to learn about each child. As you work with children, get information from their families, complete checklists, and analyze your observation notes, you learn a lot about the children. For example, you learn that Aimee is a leader on the playground and during dramatic play, Tony is learning to share, Linda changes best friends several times a day, and Maria's vocabulary is expanding rapidly in both Spanish and English. The assessment process helps you keep up-to-date on how children are growing and changing.

Using your program's curriculum and assessment system will help you plan for each child and the group.

Your program may use a written curriculum to guide the work teachers do with children and families. A developmentally appropriate curriculum will include information about all areas of a child's development: physical, emotional, social, linguistic, aesthetic, and cognitive.[36] The curriculum will also include goals and objectives that are realistic and attainable for most children in the group. It is important that you understand these goals and objectives, as well as how children show that they have met them or are working toward meeting them. You collect information about children's development through conversations with children and their families, watching children throughout the day, and analyzing your observation records. Assessment to support learning works best when it is linked closely to the goals and objectives of your curriculum. Curriculum and assessment go together:

- The *curriculum* provides goals and objectives that help you organize your environment and plan your routines, activities, and instructional strategies, as well as provides a focus for your assessment of children's work.

- *Assessment* helps you know how each child is progressing toward meeting the goals and objectives.

The learning activities in this module focus on the assessment process and how assessment helps you to meet individual and group needs.

Observing and Recording Children's Work

Observations are a useful way to get to know individual children: their likes and dislikes, the level of skills they are developing, and with whom they like to spend time. It helps to focus the observation. For example, you might observe some children to see what they are doing in relation to a curriculum or program goal, such as "Classifies objects." Another time, you might want to learn how different children respond to new materials, explore a new interest area, or solve a problem.

Teachers observe children for a variety of reasons.

To determine each child's interests, strengths, and needs. "Tony likes to organize new items on the science table by sorting collections in egg cartons."

To meet individual needs. "Amanda and Michelle have mastered the puzzles we have. We need to create new challenges."

To document progress. "I took photos to show Sara's use of fine motor skills."

To determine the cause of a challenging behavior. "I reviewed my notes, and it seems that Carlos hits other children when he doesn't know how to enter a group."

To report children's progress to families, colleagues, and specialists. "Ms. White, I'd like to share some of my observations of Mark's ability to solve problems. My notes show how his skills have developed since we last met."

To evaluate the effects of the environment and activities. "Please share your observations of children's use of the reading area so we can discuss what's working well and what we might want to change."

Useful observation notes are complete, accurate, and objective.

The primary purpose of conducting an observation is to collect accurate and useful information about a child. This requires a careful, systematic approach. You and your colleagues need to watch, listen, and write down what children do and say as it happens.

To be complete, *observation notes* must include several facts.

Facts to Include in Observation Notes[37]

- The child's name

- The observer's name

- The date and time of the observation

- The setting (where the activity is taking place and who is involved—for example, "Linda and Maria sit on the floor in the library area looking at books")

- The behavior (what the child you are observing does and says)

- Descriptions of actions

- Quotations of language

- Descriptions of gestures

- Descriptions of facial expressions

- Descriptions of creations

Write only the facts.

Useful observation notes contain just the facts. Interpretations, impressions, assumptions, and judgments should not be included in notes. As you write descriptions of what a child does and says, you are not trying to determine if the child's actions mean that he or she is shy, or aggressive, or creative. Labels such as these will not help you to record the child's actions and statements. At a later time you will use these notes to analyze and evaluate. You record what a child does and says: what you can see and hear, not what you think he wants to do, why she is doing something, or that he will not do something.

Observation is an ongoing process.

A single observation cannot provide a complete picture of a child. Children, like adults, do not behave in the same way all the time. Illness, reactions to events at home or the program, and other factors affect what children do and say. Several brief (5- to 10-minute) observations can provide the information needed to determine a child's interests, skills, and needs. You observe during indoor and outdoor activities over a period of time, as children arrive and leave the program, move from one activity to another, engage in activities, and interact with other children and staff. Children change over time, so observation is an ongoing process. Work with your colleagues to develop a schedule for conducting regular observations of all the children in the class during a variety of activities.

A series of observation notes completed over a period of time should address all areas of a child's development. Each observation note, however, can provide information about several developmental areas at one time. For example, you might observe a child's play with another child, during which he demonstrates cognitive as well as social skills. In another instance, he might demonstrate cognitive as well as physical skills.

When you have collected several notes about a child, you can analyze the information and make comments such as the following:

- "Amanda can retell a familiar story in her own words."

- "Linda can build a tower with the unit and double-unit blocks, balance blocks of different sizes, and use a variety of blocks and unit cubes to add detail to her structures."

- "Oanh can name *red* and *black*, and demonstrates her understanding of cause and effect by intentionally mixing white paint with other colors to make lighter shades."

To draw conclusions such as these, you must be sure that your recordings are objective and accurate. Compare the following notes from an observation of a child at the water table.

Objective and Accurate Recordings

Example 1: Objective and Accurate

Tony moved the water back and forth with the funnel. The water splashed inside and outside the basin. Some fell on other children's shoes. Tony began to giggle.

This note includes only the facts about what Tony did *(moved the water back and forth),* what happened *(the water splashed inside and outside the basin),* and his reaction *(Tony began to giggle).* The facts are recorded in the order they happen. Information is not omitted. Read the following two examples about the same observation.

Example 2: Not Objective

Tony was bad today. He angrily splashed the water on the floor and on other children at the water basin. Then he laughed at them.

This is not an objective recording because it uses a label (bad) and makes judgments *(He angrily splashed the water; he laughed at them).* Given what the teacher saw, he or she could not know why Tony was laughing or whether he acted in anger. The word *bad* doesn't give useful information about Tony's behavior, since *bad* is a word that means different things to different people.

Example 3: Not Accurate

Tony stood at the water basin, looking to see if a teacher was watching him. He giggled and began to splash water on other children.

In this example, a fact is added that was not observed *(looking to see if a teacher was watching him).* A fact is omitted *(Tony moved the water back and forth with the funnel).* A fact is also written out of order *(He giggled and began to splash water.).*

Making an objective and accurate note, such as Example 1, requires practice. Opportunities for taking brief notes are present throughout the day. With practice, you will become skilled at completing observation notes as you work with, and care for young children.

How, When, and What to Observe

Use these tips for recording observations of children.

Observation works best when it is done naturally as you work with children. For example, if several children are reading in the library area, you would note the setting *(the library area)*, who is involved *(Janelle, Avida, and Tony)*, and the date and time. The date will help you to see progress in a child's development across the year. The time will help you to identify patterns that are related to times of the day (such as whether a child's behavior becomes challenging before nap time). Write only what you observe directly. To save time, use short phrases with abbreviations and initials instead of complete sentences.

In the examples below, *Cs* means *children*; *T* means *teacher*; *dr* means *dramatic play*; *J* and *A* represent childrens' names.

3 Cs, A reads Fish Is Fish *to 2 Cs—tells story from pictures and reads some words:* "fish...pond...friends".

You may describe how a child is doing or saying something.
J, laughing while talking, "Fish Is Fish *has funny pictures in it."*)

You may also note how children respond to questions you ask.
T—"Why do you thnk the fish thght that birds look like fish w/ wings?
A—"Because the fish nvr saw a bird before, only other fish & the frog."

Here are other ideas to help you observe and record efficiently:

- Jot down notes and carry a pad and pencil with you.

- Use arrows to indicate movement.

- Make diagrams of the environment showing the child in relation to the setting and to others in the room.

To ensure accuracy, compare your observations with those of colleagues.

Teachers must be sure their observations match those of others. Eyewitness accounts of accidents demonstrate how several people watching the same event relate it differently. Compare your notes to those of a colleague. If they are similar, you are maintaining an accurate record. If they are different, the information may not be useful. Two teachers with different perceptions should observe the child together. They can discuss and compare their notes later, thus ensuring accurate note taking. If the notes still differ greatly, your director or trainer can help.

what's next?

Skill-Building Journal, section **12-5** *(Learning Activity A)* and section **12-1** *(Feedback).*

LEARNING
ACTIVITY

Learning Activities

B. Organizing and Using Portfolios

In this activity you will learn to

- collect work samples and other items in a portfolio to document a child's progress and changing characteristics

- use portfolios to share information with families, meet individual needs, and involve children in self-assessment

An important part of a teacher's management responsibilities is keeping current information about each child's growing skills, changing interests, and experiences that might affect their development and learning. In addition to documenting your observations by keeping written notes, another way to collect information about children over time is to keep a portfolio.

A portfolio is a system for organizing samples of a child's work to document progress over time. It is a purposeful collection with a variety of representative examples of work across the curriculum. The items in a portfolio are concrete illustrations of a child's efforts, achievements, and learning style.

Work samples are records of children's progress.

Work samples are the major component of a portfolio. Typically, teachers save items, such as a series of paintings that show a child's use of new colors or photographs of the child climbing up the ladder to the slide, as records of individual progress. It is important to date each work sample so that, taken together, these materials provide a picture of the child's progress over time. Each sample of a child's work reveals a great deal of information about that child's development. You can write an observation note about a particular work to help you remember details about how it was produced.

THINK

- Is children's work displayed in your classroom?

- What samples of work might you collect to show what children are learning?

The following are some examples of work samples that could be included in a portfolio.[38]

Portfolio Items

Work completed at the program or at home

- drawings, paintings, collages, weavings

- writing (scribbles, labels, letters, names and words, numbers, signs and messages)

- a story dictated to a teacher and/or illustrated by the child

- a book made by the child

- computer printouts

- graphs or drawings of a science experiment

Photographs of a child's work and play activities

- block building or other block structure

- a woodworking construction

- a sculpture made from clay or recyclable materials

- a freshly baked snack

- shells or other natural objects sorted by size and color

- indoor/outdoor murals or other group projects the child has participated in

Photographs showing a child's accomplishments

- standing on the top of the climber

- swinging

- riding a tricycle

- completing a puzzle

Photographs showing a child involved in everyday routines and activities

- using a serving spoon

- brushing teeth

- listening to a story

- cleaning up

Written records of a child's interests

- questions asked or answered during a small group activity

- favorite books

- descriptions of drawings and other work

- comments after a field trip

Video and audio recordings of a child's use of language

- singing, telling a story, or playing with others

- conversing during a family-style meal

- engaging in dramatic play

- identifying a solution to a problem

A child's portfolio creates a balanced picture of development.

Family members can also contribute items, such as scribbles written at home, descriptions of the child playing with a younger sibling, or examples of the child's self-discipline. Make sure you have items that illustrate the child's creativity, interests, and progress toward developing cognitive, physical, social/ emotional, and language skills. The items in the portfolio should present a balanced picture of the child's development through participation in interest areas, indoors and outdoors, and all parts of the daily schedule: routines, transitions, choice time, and group time.

You will need a sufficient variety of work samples in a portfolio to have enough evidence to assess a child's growth, but you don't need a large number of work samples in each portfolio. To show growth, collect similar samples over a period of time, such as a collection of a child's work in writing her name completed in November, January, and April. Another example would be photographs of block structures built by a child during a period of several months. At the beginning of the year, think of two or three items—such as writing samples, children's paintings, or photographs—that would be good for documenting development in particular areas. Set a goal to collect these items 3–5 times throughout the year.

Teachers can use portfolios in several ways:

- Share information with parents. "It's easy to see Jorge's progress when we compare the drawings he made six months ago to the ones he made last week."

- Review a child's progress, set new goals, and plan strategies. "This videotape shows Maria telling an imaginative story with a lot of different plots. We'll help her expand her skills so her stories are easier to follow."

- Help children evaluate their work and recognize their own skills and progress. "Tell me about what you and Michelle are doing here in this photograph."

Create a storage system for portfolios.

You will need containers large enough to hold the items and a system for organizing them. Accordion files, magazine files, empty pizza boxes (unused, donated by a local business), hanging file folders, pocket folders, X-ray folders, or plastic containers with lids can be used. File the portfolio items by date and group them by categories that make sense for your program. For example, you might group them by activity, area of development, or interest area.

what's next?

Skill-Building Journal, section **12-6** *(Learning Activity B)* and section **12-1** *(Feedback).*

Learning Activities

LEARNING
ACTIVITY

C. Meeting Individual Needs and Interests

In this learning activity you will learn to

- analyze information about children to learn about their culture, family, strengths, needs, and interests

- tailor the program to correspond with children's individual characteristics

High-quality early childhood programs reflect and respond to developmental and individual characteristics.

High-quality early childhood programs are based on two understandings: the typical developmental characteristics of children ages 3–5 and the characteristics of individual children. The environment, materials, activities, and interactions between adults and children in such programs reflect and correspond to children's developmental levels and each child's culture, family, strengths, needs, and interests. For example, Ms. Williams and Ms. Frilles use what they know about preschool children and what they know about individual children to prepare for a neighborhood walk.

Preschool children can act without thinking, so the teachers make a group-walk rope to keep the children safe while walking near busy streets. Next, they fill a wagon with large balls, buckets, and shovels. Most preschool children enjoy these items as do the children in their class. They add some items with individual needs, interests, and skills in mind. Amanda and Tyrone like quiet activities, so Ms. Williams puts picture books in the wagon and large chalk for drawing on sidewalks. Several children play games with rules, so Ms. Frilles brings a T-ball stand and plastic bats and balls. Knowing that, even with the rope, Mark and Oanh have difficulty staying with the class, the teachers hold their hands on the walk to and from the park.

Teachers do not have to provide separate materials and activities for each child.

Individualizing the program does not mean you have to provide a separate set of materials or plan one-on-one activities for each child. Instead, you can respond to individual children during your regular activities. To plan this, you and your colleagues review observation notes, examine samples of children's work, reflect on recent events and interactions, and analyze the information you have about each child. You think about what individual children enjoy doing, the materials they use, the skills they are developing, and what is happening in their lives. Here is an example of teachers planning a program that meets individual needs and interests.

Ms. Kim says she has observed 3-year-old Marcus trying to pedal a tricycle. He can only just reach the pedals, so he is having a hard time. Ms. Richards has also noticed Marcus' efforts. They discuss Marcus' learning style. Rather than give up in frustration, Marcus keeps trying to figure out a way to make the pedals work. Ms. Kim reviews the notes she made last month to assess Marcus's physical skills. Her analysis shows that last month Marcus was not using the pedals at all. Ms. Richards tells her that Marcus's house has a long paved driveway. His grandmother has mentioned that there is an old tricycle in their garage that needs to be repaired. The teachers develop a plan.

Background. Marcus has a tricycle at home and a place to ride it. Ms. Kim will tell Marcus's grandmother about his efforts and ask if the tricycle has been repaired. If so, she will suggest encouraging Marcus to ride at home.

Need. At the program, Marcus needs to practice riding on a tricycle that is an appropriate size. Ms. Kim will exchange the larger tricycle with a smaller tricycle from another classroom.

Skill. Marcus is self-motivated and works hard to meet challenges. Everyone will let Marcus know they realize he is working hard to master riding the tricycle.

Interest. Marcus seems to really like riding the trike.

Teachers will continue observing Marcus to see if their plans are effective. When Marcus masters riding the trike, they will build on his skills and interests by offering props such as a firefighter hat, street signs, or cones to ride around.

In the above example, the teachers respond to Marcus by incorporating strategies within their existing approach and schedule. They didn't take Marcus away from the class to teach him to ride. Instead, they planned to offer appropriate equipment, work with his family, offer encouragement, and build on his interests. These are all strategies that help you meet individual needs.

THINK

- When were you able to develop a plan to specifically address a child's need or interest?

- What was the result?

You can meet individual needs in group activities as well as one-on-one.

Teachers can use various teaching strategies to make sure they are supporting each child, even when not working with him or her individually. For example, Ms. Thomas and Mr. Lopez have analyzed their assessment information about the children in their group and know which children show strengths in using different thinking skills. Janelle and Tony respond well to questions that involve recall abilities; Avida and Leo do well with cause-and-effect questions, and Aimee and Benjamin like to share their feelings. After reading *Daisy and the Egg* to these six children in the library area, Ms. Thomas asks the children several questions: "Who can tell me all that you remember about the story?" "Why does sitting on the eggs help them to hatch?" "How would you feel if you were a duck and helped an egg to hatch?" In this way, each child has a chance to participate in the activity at the level that's best for him or her.

Write a summary of development for each child.

An important part of individualizing is identifying each child's developmental level in relation to your curriculum's or program's goals and objectives for children, and then supporting each child's development and learning. Your information from children's families, your reviews of children's portfolios, as well as your observation notes, help you to analyze and evaluate what an individual child might need and make decisions accordingly. This enables you to write summary reports. Many teachers complete these summaries at least three times during the year and use the information for planning. Often, early childhood programs have a system for documenting summaries of information about each child, analyzing the information to understand each child's strengths and needs, and planning for each child and the group. In the example below, Ms. Kim plans for Marcus.

Ms. Kim has information about Marcus's new ability to pedal a tricycle, as well as his skill in walking along the edge of a sandbox, running while moving his arms and legs, climbing the ladder on the low slide, and throwing a ball with both hands. She and Ms. Richards review the information and complete a summary of development that shows Marcus's progress in these gross motor skills. Then they record the objectives he has met on the program's summary form, based on the evidence. The teachers have information about Marcus in other areas of development as well—cognitive, language, social/emotional—and use this information to complete his summary. Of course, they have similar information about all the children in their group, and they use the developmental summaries when they prepare their weekly plans.

Meeting the Needs of Children With Disabilities

Including children with disabilities can be a rewarding experience.

As required by federal legislation, many classrooms include children with disabilities. Disabilities might be developmental, such as mental retardation; physical, such as muscular dystrophy; a health impairment, such as human immunodeficiency virus (HIV) disease or asthma; or a hearing, visual, or speech/language disorder. Teachers, families, health professionals, and administrators work together to identify and respond to the child's skills, needs, and interests.

When successful, including children with disabilities in a child development program is a very rewarding experience for everyone involved. Inclusion provides an environment in which all children can succeed. It helps children with disabilities gain independence and enables all children to develop comfortable, fair relationships with others. It teaches children to resist stereotypes and name-calling. Children with disabilities are children first. They thrive in an environment that accepts differences and where adults strive to meet each child's individual needs.

Consider your own feelings about children with disabilities.

To offer a program for a child with a disability, teachers may need to examine their own attitudes and behaviors toward persons with disabilities. Here are some typical responses toward children with disabilities:

- Avoiding or ignoring the child. "May Carrie be in your group? I never know what to say to her."

- Feeling sad. "Every time I see her walker, my eyes start watering."

- Believing the disability can be fixed. "He'll outgrow his hearing problems."

- Denying the disability. "Lots of children can't pay attention."

Although these are commonly held attitudes and behaviors, they do a disservice to the child. To support the child's development, teachers must take time to identify, acknowledge, and address their personal feelings.

- What are the benefits of inclusion for the child with a disability and for the whole group?

- What are the challenges you face in meeting the needs of a child with a disability?

- How can you get support to overcome these challenges?

Caring for Preschool Children

When a child with a disability enrolls in your program, you need to learn about the child and family as well as the characteristics, effects, and treatment related to the disability. Here are some sources of information:

The child. Make a home visit and invite the child to the classroom. This will help you get to know the child as a person, rather than focusing primarily on the disability.

The child's family. Meet with the parents to learn about the child's favorite activities, over-all level of development, strengths, and interests. Parents are the best source of information about the child's experiences and developmental history, and the best ways to promote the child's development and learning.

Doctors, specialists, and previous teachers. With the parents' written consent, your program may contact professionals who have provided treatment and supported the child's development. The information they provide will contribute to a total picture of the child's characteristics. If addressing the child's needs is beyond your expertise and experience, seek advice from these specialists. You cannot be expected to know about every type of disability.

Professional resources. Use books, journals, and other resources to research the range of abilities and needs that a child with a particular disability might have. Remember that the range of individual differences among children with the same disability is as great as the differences among children in general.

Contact regional and national support groups and clearinghouses. Your director or trainer can help you identify and contact organizations that can provide information to help you work with children in your care who have disabilities. You might want to conduct a search on the World Wide Web for these organizations, using keywords such as *disability* or *inclusion,* or the name of a specific condition, such as *autism.*

Once you have an understanding of the child and the disability, you can meet with your colleagues, the child's parents, and specialists to plan an individualized program. In addition, you may need to make accommodations, such as rearranging the environment to make the pathways wide enough for a wheelchair, creating books of textured fabrics to provide tactile experiences, or providing several large-print versions of books for a child with a visual impairment. Several additional examples of accommodations appear in module 3, *Learning Environment.*

what's next?

Skill-Building Journal, section **12-7** *(Learning Activity C)* and section **12-1** *(Feedback).*

Learning Activities

D. Working as a Team to Plan and Evaluate the Program

In this learning activity you will learn to

- develop daily, weekly, and long-range plans

- evaluate the effectiveness of your plans

Planning helps you prepare well for each day.

Planning involves thinking about what you want to do and how you will do it. When you plan, you are better prepared. You have sufficient materials and are more easily able to involve children in activities suited to their skills and interests. As a result, the program runs more smoothly.

Everyone who cares for and interacts with children at the program—teachers, family members, and volunteers—can be part of the planning team. Many programs regularly include parents and volunteers in planning and implementing the program. The more all team members are involved in planning, the more likely they are to realize the important role they play in carrying out the plans.

Teaching teams often include individuals with particular strengths, interests, and talents. Ideally, each member's skills complement those of others on the team. One teacher might speak several languages; another might be a gifted storyteller. A regular volunteer might be an artist with the ability to share her talent with others. A parent who is a carpenter could bring the program's old equipment back to life. Each member contributes something special to the team.

- Who are the people in your program who can be involved in planning for individual children?

- How can you involve them?

Long-range planning covers a month or more ahead.

Two types of planning are useful for early childhood programs: long-range and weekly. Long-range planning involves thinking ahead—perhaps a month or more—to consider what materials, activities, and experiences you want to offer the children. For example, if you are going to set up a grocery store next to the dramatic play area next month, your plans might include the following tasks:

- Collecting empty food containers and cans, and shopping bags for the store.

- Sending a letter to parents asking them to save these items.

- Getting the cash register and play money from the storage closet.

- Gathering writing materials so children can make signs for the store.

- Calling the local grocery store to schedule a behind-the-scenes tour.

- Asking the librarian to suggest and reserve some books about foods and shopping.

Long-range planning allows you to respond to changing seasons or to arrange a special event such as a trip, a family picnic, or a visit by a special guest. Thinking and planning ahead ensure that special events really happen.

Weekly plans are also needed.

Weekly plans are more detailed than long-range plans. Weekly planning does not have to be a lengthy process, but a planning meeting should be part of the schedule. Teaching staff might hold planning meetings before children arrive, after they leave, or during rest time. Most programs have a standard format to guide planning meetings and to record weekly plans. However, teaching teams frequently find that they must tailor the approach to their own situations.

Weekly planning involves using the information about each child to determine the activities you will conduct, as well as changes to the environment and ways to include children's families and community resources in the program. A good place to start planning is to ask yourself, "What do I need to plan that will help me be a better manager?" The following categories may be useful for you and your colleagues.

Special focus—a study topic related to children's interests and experiences that guides planning for a week or more, depending on children's responses. The team plans a variety of activities and selects materials that are based on the topic. For example, after a trip to a neighborhood pet store, the children explore the topic, fish. The teachers add plastic fish props to the water table, plan a movement activity so children can swim like fish, stock the library area with stories about fish, and drape a net over a corner.

Group time—a 10- to 15-minute meeting when children participate in an adult-led experience, such as reading a story, moving to music, or setting rules for using new playground equipment. Group time activities can build on the study topic or an ongoing project. Group time near the beginning of the day or at the end is also used to discuss the day's activities. Teachers describe the plans for the day, note changes to the schedule, talk about upcoming events, and summarize what the children did. Children talk about what they did at home, their plans for the day, and activities they particularly enjoyed.

Small-group activities—open-ended experiences for 3–6 children at a time, planned and led by teachers. Activities may support the special focus, respond to children's interests, coincide with the time of year, such as a walk during the fall to collect seeds or dried grasses. During small-group time you can also introduce new materials or a new concept, or teach a particular skill.

Changes to the environment—adding or removing props or materials, or changing the arrangement of indoor or outdoor space. Such changes primarily affect children's opportunities during choice time. For example, teachers might add new transportation props to the block area, add a collection of keys to sort and classify in the toys and games area, or move the easels outdoors on warm days.

Outdoor activities—the choices offered in the outdoor space. Including the outdoors as a separate category helps teachers plan for outdoor experiences as thoughtfully as they do for indoor ones.

Teacher responsibilities—the specific tasks each teacher will complete to ensure that the plan can be implemented. For example, if the plan includes blowing bubbles outdoors, someone needs to collect a variety of frames (old eye glasses with lenses removed, berry containers, plastic 6-pack rings) and mix the soap solution. It is important to agree on who will do what and to post a list reminding people of their assignments.

Focus on particular children—individuals with unique skills, needs, or interests whom teachers want to pay particular attention to during a given week. For example, a child whose mother is about to have a baby might need extra one-on-one time and books about new babies and older brothers or sisters. You may also want to list children teachers plan to observe during the week. To ensure confidentiality, do not include this category in the written plan posted on the bulletin board.

An example of a completed planning form for a 4-year-old group follows.[39]

Weekly Planning Form

Planning Changes to the Environment

Week of: May 5-9   Study/Project: Worms (week 3)

Teacher: Ms. Thomas   Assistant: Mr. Lopez:

"To Do" List:
- Permission slips for field visit
- Check w/ Mr. Fox at worm farm
- Ask librarian to locate books about worms

Blocks Add ramps and arches	**Dramatic Play** Offer props (shipping boxes, etc.) children might use to recreate a worm farm	**Toys and Games** Use food and other cards from lotto games to make a new game for the area called, "Can I compost this?"
Art Add wire, wire cutters, pipe cleaners, cardboard, boxes, dirt, clay, playdough and up close photograph of a worm	**Library** Add informational books and storybooks on worms	**Discovery** Have clipboards available for children to record observations of worms Add magnifying glasses
Sand and Water Add variety of sifters and sieves	**Music and Movement** Add sleeping bags for children to crawl around like worms	**Cooking** Make fruit salad: peel carrots (add peelings to compost bin)
Computers Add *One Small Square: Backyard* CD-ROM	**Outdoors** Offer garden tools to begin preparing area to plant vegetables and add worm compost	**Family/Community Involvement** Ask parent volunteers to work with children building the worm viewing area outside.

Planning for Groups

	Monday	Tuesday	Wednesday	Thursday	Friday
Group Time (songs, stories, games, discussions, etc.)	Move like a worm to "Glow Worm" song	Discuss tomorrow's field site visit; write down children's questions	Prepare for field site visit	Discuss field site visit; did we find the answers to our questions	Discuss what we need to do to make our worm farm better
Story Time	*Inch by Inch*	*The Very Hungry Caterpillar*	*Are You My Mother?*	*Wonderful Worms*	*The Empress and the Silkworm*
Small-Group Activities	Animal classification game (Ben's mom will help)	Observe a worm and a caterpillar; record how they are the same and how they are different		Compare samples of dirt children brought from home and compost.	Work with group building outdoor worm viewing area
Special Activities (site visits, special events, etc.)	Have Mrs. Johnson (the science teacher) show how to use and care for the microscope she's lending the class	Teach children how to use disposable cameras	Visit to the worm farm! Take pictures, bring clipboards	Write thank-you letter to Mr. Fox; invite children to draw pictures to include	

Notes *(reminders, changes, children to observe)*

Planning Changes to the Environment

Week of: _____

Teacher: _____

Study/Project: _____

Assistant: _____

Blocks	Dramatic Play	Toys and Games
Art	Library	Discovery
Sand and Water	Music and Movement	Cooking
Computers	Outdoors	Family/Community Involvement

"To Do" List:

Planning for Groups

	Monday	Tuesday	Wednesday	Thursday	Friday
Group Time (songs, stories, games, discussions, etc.)					
Story Time					
Small-Group Activities					
Special Activities (site visits, special events, etc.)					

Notes *(reminders, changes, children to observe)*

Teaching Strategies   © 2002 Teaching Strategies, Inc.

Knowledge of children's individual and developmental characteristics guides the planning process.

Teachers use many tools and strategies to help them plan. First, they know the typical characteristics of children at a given age and stage of development. Second, they have specific knowledge of each child. Information gathered through conversations with families and daily interactions with children guide the planning process. In addition, daily observations provide important clues about teaching strategies to use, what changes are needed in the environment, and other program practices.

Early childhood teachers must be flexible.

Anyone who has worked with young children knows that even the best plans don't always work out as intended. Relax and enjoy the experience when a walk to a neighborhood playground becomes a trip to a construction site where the dirt movers and cranes have captured children's interests. Join in the learning when the children use materials in different ways from what you had planned. Extend the outdoor time when children are fully involved in a project or a dramatic play scenario. Teachers who work with this age group must be very flexible.

Evaluation is the next step in the planning process.

In many early childhood programs, teachers meet at the end of each day to discuss what happened. Questions such as these can guide your discussions:

- What did the children do in each interest area?

- Which materials did the children use?

- What skills did the children demonstrate?

- What worked well? What problems came up?

- Did the children have disagreements, conflicts, or other behavior problems? If so, how were they resolved?

- Which children had problems finding something to do? How did we respond?

- Did we welcome and provide meaningful roles for family members who visited the program?

- What changes are needed in

    the indoor or outdoor environment?

    materials and equipment?

    our interactions with children?

    our interactions with families?

    group time?

    small-group activities?

Plans are modified based on what you learn from evaluation.

Daily evaluation meetings tend to be short but very effective, because the answers to the above questions are fresh in teachers' minds. Planning is an ongoing process; if necessary, the team can change the weekly plan to solve a problem or respond to interests. Here are examples:

Making whole wheat pretzels was a popular activity today. The children really enjoyed the food, and the way the dough changed as it was kneaded made for interesting scientific discoveries. Ms. Thomas and Mr. Lopez will change their plans and have another food preparation activity during choice time later this week.

Linda had a particularly stressful day. She cried when her mother left this morning, which hasn't happened in several months, and she threw a block during choice time. Ms. Kim will spend more one-on-one time with her tomorrow.

Several children had trouble using the new climber. Ms. Kim and Ms. Richards will observe over the next few days to see if the climber continues to be a source of frustration.

Teachers can use a similar evaluation process when meeting to develop weekly and long-range plans. An analysis of observation notes collected over time can be useful. For example, when several children begin to write words, teachers can plan to work with these children to further extend their writing skills by helping them to sound out words. Or, if the same toys have not been used for several weeks, putting some toys away, adding new ones, or changing the location of some items could spark children's interests. Observation also lets teachers know when a plan is not working. For example, if children are unable to complete the puzzles and often leave them out unfinished, the puzzles may be too difficult. Teachers can then provide puzzles with fewer pieces and less complex shapes.

what's next?

Skill-Building Journal, section **12-8** *(Learning Activity D)*, section **12-1** *(Feedback)*, and section **12-9** *(Reflecting on Your Learning)*.

Professionalism

Overview

Striving to Meet the Standards of the Profession

Continuing to Build Your Knowledge and Skills

Acting Responsibly and Ethically in Your Work

Viewing Yourself as a Professional

Learning Activities

A. Striving to Meet the Standards of the Profession

B. Continuing to Gain New Knowledge and Skills

C. Demonstrating Ethical Behavior in Your Work

D. Talking About the Value of Your Work

13. Professionalism

A professional has specialized knowledge and skills.

Teaching young children requires a commitment to providing the very best care and education. It is more than a job; it's a profession with specialized knowledge and skills. The early childhood profession is concerned with the care and education of children from birth through age 8. You work with children at the time when they are developing more quickly than they will at any other period in their lives. You help shape children's views about learning and the world around them. By providing a high-quality early childhood program, you help children learn to see themselves as capable learners and give family members peace of mind.

The early childhood profession sets standards for quality.

Every profession sets standards that guide the practice of its members. There are different types of standards in the early childhood profession. Some address program health, safety, and supervisory requirements and practices. Others define the content and skills that preschool children need to master to be ready for kindergarten. The early childhood profession also takes positions on important topics, and organizations issue position papers that are intended to guide and inform practice. As a professional, you should know what standards are applicable to you so you can be confident that you are working to achieve them.

Professionals have an obligation to act responsibly and ethically at all times. This can be challenging because it's not always easy to know the best decision or course of action in a given situation. A code of ethical conduct gives guidance to early childhood professionals on responsible behavior and how to resolve difficult problems.

Professionals never finish learning.

The early childhood field has grown tremendously over the past decades. There is always new information and research on the importance of these early years to children's development and learning and about how to help children develop to their potential. The more skilled and knowledgeable you become, the more effective you are as a teacher and the more satisfaction you will gain from your work with young children and families.

You can maintain a commitment to professionalism by

- striving to meet the standards of the profession

- continuing to build your knowledge and skills

- acting responsibly and ethically in your work

Striving to Meet the Standards of the Profession

1. **Learn about the standards that define a quality program.** Review the standards that apply to your program, such as the NAEYC Center Accreditation Criteria, your state early learning standards, Head Start Program Performance Standards, or military child development standards.

2. **Use professional standards to assess program effectiveness.** "This checklist will help us evaluate the safety and quality of our outdoor area."

3. **Support the program's efforts to achieve recognition for quality.** Volunteer to serve on a team to help your center prepare for center accreditation, for a program review, or for a monitoring visit.

4. **Work toward a credential and/or teaching degree.** Complete the process of obtaining a CDA credential; enroll in college classes and complete the requirements for certification.

Ms. Frilles Teaches the Value of Content Standards

"Ms. Frilles, look at this cute project I found in an activity book," exclaims Julie, a student teacher. "We take a potato, cut off the top, make a face on it, and then sprinkle grass seed on top. Won't it be fun when the children see the grass grow? It will look like hair!" Ms. Frilles looks at the activity and responds, "It does look cute, but what will children learn from this activity?" Julie answers, "We'd be teaching them science." Ms. Frilles pulls out their curriculum book and looks at the section on science content. She says, "There are many good science topics children can study. The science content standards suggest 'big ideas' children can explore, such as what plants need to grow. I think we can plan some longer-term activities that will enable the children to learn a lot about growing plants from their own experiences." Julie responds, "You mean like having the children plant a garden and use lots of different seeds?" "Exactly," responds Ms. Frilles. "We can start by asking them what they think plants need to grow and see what they know already."

Continuing to Build Your Knowledge and Skills

5. **Analyze your skills to identify areas to strengthen.** Review the *Pre-Training Assessments* in this training program. Discuss the results with a supervisor and trainer to develop a plan to strengthen your skills.

6. **Participate in professional organizations and training opportunities.** "I'd like to attend the state conference next month, to learn more about long-term studies."

7. **Keep up-to-date about appropriate practices for encouraging young children's growth and development.** "May I borrow this position statement, *Learning to Read and Write*? I need ideas for responding to parents who want us to teach reading a certain way."

8. **Talk with and observe colleagues to learn more about caring for young children.** "I'd like to visit your classroom this week to observe how you handle large group meetings. I need some help with my meetings."

9. **Review resources that keep you current with new ideas and research.** Read articles in *Young Children* and other early childhood publications.

Mr. Lopez and Ms. Thomas Learn About Portfolios

During his break, Mr. Lopez sits in the staff lounge, thumbing through a professional journal. An article on using portfolios to document and assess children's progress catches his eye. "This looks really interesting," he says. "It might be a good way to show families how much their children are learning." Before returning to the classroom, he signs out the journal so he can read the article at home. During the next day's planning meeting, he shares what he has learned with Ms. Thomas and asks her to read the article, too. "I've heard about portfolios," she says, "but I don't understand how they are different from what we already do." After reading the article, Ms. Thomas is as enthusiastic about portfolios as Mr. Lopez. They decide to attend a workshop on the topic to learn more about the use of portfolios in documenting children's learning.

Acting Responsibly and Ethically in Your Work

10. **Keep information about children and their families confidential.** "Children's files are confidential, Ms. Robinson. Only the center staff and you and her father may read your daughter's file."

11. **Behave in an honest, reliable, and dependable manner in performing duties.** Come to work on time, be prepared for each day, and communicate with colleagues and families clearly.

12. **Treat each child as an individual and show no bias because of culture, background, abilities, or gender.** Find out about each child's special interests and family practices and traditions. Plan materials and activities that relate to what you learn.

13. **Stand up for practices that are ethical and developmentally appropriate and speak out against those that are not.** "We never use physical punishment when a child misbehaves. We look for the causes and take steps to prevent the behavior from happening again."

14. **Support other teachers when they need assistance.** "When Jorge first joined our class, he had a hard time adjusting. I think I can give you some ideas that will help him adjust to a new classroom."

example

Ms. Kim Acts Professionally and Maintains Confidentiality

Ms. Jones arrives to pick up her child, Sara, at the end of the day. As she walks in, she sees one of the children on top of a table and about to jump off. "Excuse me just a moment, Ms. Jones," says Ms. Kim. She immediately goes over to the table and stops Marcus from jumping. Then she says, "I know you like to climb and jump, Marcus, but it is not safe to jump off the table. You may jump when we go outside. Let me help you down, and we'll find something else to do." When she comes back, Ms. Jones says, "Boy, he's a wild one. He must drive you crazy." Ms. Kim responds, "Marcus really likes climbing and facing new challenges. Now, let me tell you about the building Sara has been working on."

what's next?

Skill-Building Journal, section **13-2** *(Overview),* section **13-10** *(Answer Sheets),* and section **13-1** *(Feedback).*

Viewing Yourself as a Professional

Do you view yourself as a professional? Some people think that preschool teachers are not as professional as those who teach older children. When they see a teacher on the floor talking with a child who is building with blocks, helping a group make playdough, or taking on a pretend role in the dramatic play area, they think that anyone can teach young children. They do not realize that early childhood teachers have specialized knowledge and skills.

Early childhood teachers have specialized skills and knowledge.

Early childhood teachers understand how young children develop and learn, and how to meet diverse needs. You work hard to develop skills. When you appreciate your own growing knowledge and skills, you gain confidence in yourself as a professional. You understand not only how to teach, but why you use certain practices. You can explain to family members and visitors that the child building with blocks is learning about spatial relationships, solving problems, and exploring social studies. When you make playdough with children, you're helping them read a recipe, measure ingredients, and notice how materials change when they are mixed. When you are confident about what you are doing and why, people will recognize that you are a professional.

Each person has special interests and abilities.

Every teacher, like each child, is a unique person. You bring who you are to your work with young children; you bring your personality, temperament, interests, and special talents.

Do you tend to be outgoing and energetic, or quiet and reserved? Would people describe you as fun-loving or serious? Do you like being in a big crowd or with one friend? Do you enjoy a new challenge and jump right in, or do you like to analyze and think about it before responding? Gaining self-awareness will help you recognize how you respond to the children you teach and their families. Think about the children you relate to most easily and those with whom it is more difficult to form a relationship. How do your own personality and style of relating affect your relationships with children and families?

You also bring special interests and talents to your work with young children. Are you musical? Artistic? Do you love animals? Like to cook? Enjoy gardening? What are your special abilities and interests? What do you most enjoy? Think about how you can bring your passions and talents into the classroom to share with young children.

what's next?

Skill-Building Journal, section **13-3** *(Viewing Yourself as a Professional)*, section **13-1** *(Feedback)*, and section **13-4** *(Pre-Training Assessment).*

Learning Activity

A. Striving to Meet the Standards of the Profession

In this activity you will learn to

- become familiar with the standards that guide the early childhood profession

- identify the standards that apply to your program

Many standards apply to your program.

Every profession sets standards that guide program and individual practice. In the early childhood profession, different kinds of standards are developed by different organizations. Many, but not all, will apply to you and your program.

Standards That Define Program Quality

In an effort to improve the quality of early childhood programs and to recognize programs that offer high-quality services, the National Association for the Education of Young Children (NAEYC) has defined the standards for program quality and established a process for programs that want to be accredited. It is a voluntary process, and any early childhood program, regardless of how it is funded, may apply for NAEYC accreditation. In addition to this accreditation process, NAEYC has also clearly defined developmentally appropriate practice. Two resources that early childhood professionals find valuable are:

- *NAEYC Early Childhood Program Standards and Accreditation Criteria: The Mark of Quality in Early Childhood Education* (2005)

- *Developmentally Appropriate Practice in Early Childhood Programs,* Revised ed. (1997)

While the NAEYC standards apply to all programs serving young children, other standards apply to specific programs. Find out what standards apply specifically to your program.

Standards for Teachers

Participating in this training program is helping you to meet standards for teachers.

As you participate in this training program, you are becoming familiar with a set of standards that apply to teacher competencies: the *Child Development Associate (CDA) Competency Standards*. There are 13 functional areas in which early childhood teachers must demonstrate competence. The 13 modules in *Caring for Preschool Children* address these areas. The Council for Professional Recognition is the organization that operates a national credentialing program for early childhood educators. Teachers who demonstrate that they are competent in each of the 13 areas are awarded a CDA credential. This credential is nationally recognized in the field of early childhood education.

Position Statements

Position statements explain an organization's stand on important issues.

In addition to documents that define program quality, NAEYC and other professional organizations publish position statements on issues of central importance to the profession. After identifying a current issue requiring clarification, a group of experts works with the NAEYC staff to develop the statement. The document is then submitted to the Governing Board for review and final approval. Sometimes a joint position statement is developed in collaboration with another organization also concerned about the same issue. Go to the NAEYC Web site (www.naeyc.org) to find all the position statements. Here are a few examples of what you will find:

- *NAEYC Code of Ethical Conduct and Statement of Commitment* (Revised ed.) (1997, 2005)

- *Early Childhood Curriculum, Assessment, and Program Evaluation* (2003)

- *Inclusion* (by the Division for Early Childhood of the Council for Exceptional Children and endorsed by NAEYC) (1993)

- *Learning to Read and Write* (with the International Reading Association, 1998)

- *Prevention of Child Abuse in Early Childhood Programs and the Responsibilities of Early Childhood Professionals to Prevent Child Abuse* (1996)

- *Responding to Linguistic and Cultural Diversity* (1995)

- *School Readiness* (1995)

- *Technology and Young Children—Ages 3 through 8* (1996)

- *Violence in the Lives of Children* (1993, 2006)

Early Learning Standards

Early learning standards describe what preschool children should know and be able to do.

Many school districts have content standards for subjects such as literacy, math, science, the arts, and technology, for kindergarten through 12th grade. In addition, states have developed, or are in the process of developing, early learning standards for preschool children. State Departments of Education Web sites post information about their standards. These standards vary from state to state. Programs that receive federal funds must address these early learning standards. All these standards have been helpful to educators and curriculum developers in defining what preschool children should know and be able to do when they enter kindergarten.

How These Standards Apply to You

As an early childhood professional, it's important to get to know the standards that apply to your program. Your center may already be in the process of gaining accreditation through NAEYC or meeting other program standards. Your involvement in this process will teach you a lot about the standards. The curriculum you use should show how content standards are addressed and help you plan appropriate activities and experiences for children. Take time to find out about standards, position papers, and professional competencies that are of particular importance and interest to you and your work.

what's next?

Skill-Building Journal, section **13-5** *(Learning Activity A)* and section **13-1** *(Feedback).*

Learning Activities

LEARNING ACTIVITY

B. Continuing to Gain New Knowledge and Skills

In this activity you will learn to

- think about your own growth as an early childhood professional

- identify ways that you can continue to learn about your profession

Teachers have four stages of professional development.

In the teaching profession there is always something new to learn, and there is a path of professional development. Lilian Katz, an early childhood educator, has studied how teachers grow professionally. Her research suggests that teachers pass through four different stages of professional development: survival, consolidation, renewal, and maturity. These stages are described in the following paragraphs.[40]

1. Survival

Teachers at the Survival Stage are new to the field and may be insecure. They tend to devote most of their attention to learning the center's routines and to performing assigned tasks. This stage is called *survival,* in part because of the concentrated focus on immediate needs rather than long-range planning. If you are at this stage, you will benefit from a comprehensive orientation to the job and shadowing or observing an experienced teacher. You may want to join a professional association such as your local affiliate of the National Association for the Education of Young Children (NAEYC). Continued training and experience will help you move to the next stage, Consolidation.

2. Consolidation

When teachers reach this stage, they are more confident and begin to look beyond simply completing daily routines. They seek new ways to accomplish routine tasks and to handle problems. If you are at this stage, you will find it useful to exchange ideas with other teachers and become actively involved in a professional association. Informal conversations, group meetings, training sessions, and open discussions will help you grow and move to the next stage, Renewal.

3. Renewal

During the third or fourth year on the job, teachers may begin to be bored with the day's routines. Often their interest drops and enthusiasm falls. Teachers in this stage need renewal, new challenges to rekindle their excitement and commitment to caring for young children. If you are at this stage, try to attend conferences and workshops, take on a leadership role in a professional organization, or pursue a special interest. These professional activities will provide stimulation and help you move to the fourth stage, Maturity.

4. Maturity

Teachers at this stage are committed professionals. They understand the need to seek new ideas and skills and continue to grow professionally. If you are a mature teacher, you can be a mentor for new teachers. You might also gain the skills needed to assume new challenges as a supervisor, trainer, or center administrator.

- What stage of professional development best describes you?

- How can you find the support you need to continue to grow and learn?

Professionals never stop learning.

No matter how many years you've been a teacher or how much you already know, it is important to continue to learn more about your profession. This is true for a number of reasons:

There is always new information to be learned. All professionals need to keep up with the latest developments in their fields. Research and experience often lead to more effective strategies for working with children. You became a teacher because you wanted to help children develop and learn. To do that, it's important to keep up with the latest information and apply it to your teaching practices.

Continual learning helps you evaluate and strengthen your practices. You will have new interests and ideas to bring to the program. When you enjoy learning, you help children enjoy learning, too.

You care about children. Each article or book you read, every discussion you participate in, and every conference you attend can give you new insights or help you solve problems. Because you care about children, you are always alert for new and helpful information about their development. For example, when a child with a disability joins your group, you can use this opportunity to learn new ways to include the child in all program activities in a meaningful way.

You want to grow professionally. A commitment to continual learning can lead to improved performance. Learning may lead to greater confidence, more responsibility, a promotion, and perhaps a salary increase.

Continual learning helps you recognize your strengths as a teacher. Learning tends to affirm the good work you have been doing and the understandings you have already developed. You may rediscover ideas to support children's development and leaning that you have not thought about in a while.

In addition to participating in this training program, there are many other ways you can continue learning.

Join one of the professional organizations.

Professional organizations help you keep up-to-date on the latest information and current issues in the profession. Many have local affiliates that meet regularly. These organizations have Web sites, offer newsletters, books, videotapes, brochures, and other publications with useful information and helpful tips. Attending professional conferences is a way to meet other teachers with similar interests and concerns. The following chart identifies some of the early childhood professional organizations and the services they offer.

Early Childhood Professional Organizations

Organization	Services
Association for Childhood Education International (ACEI) 17904 Georgia Avenue, Suite 215 Olney, MD 20832 301-570-2001 800-423-3563 www.acei.org	Resources and support for meeting the developmental needs of children from birth through early adolescence worldwide *Journals: Childhood Education and Journal of Research in Childhood Education* Annual conference National and international affiliate chapters
Center for the Child Care Workforce, American Federation of Teachers Educational Foundation 555 New Jersey Avenue, NW Washington, DC 20001 202-662-8005 www.ccw.org	Works to improve wages, status, and working conditions of early childhood professionals Publications, articles, papers, and other resources
National Association for Bilingual Education 1313 L Street, NW, Suite 210 Washington, DC 20005 202-898-1829 www.nabe.org	Advocates for language-minority students with a variety of programs to support English language learners Publishes *NABE News, Bilingual Research Journal, and NABE Journal of Research and Practice (NJRP)*
National Association of Child Care Resource and Referral Agencies (NACCRRA) 3101 Wilson Boulevard, Suite 350 Arlington, VA 22201 703-341-4100 www.naccrra.org	A national network of over 800 child care resource and referral centers that help families, child care providers, and communities find, provide, and plan affordable, quality child care Provides training and resources, and promotes national policies and partnerships Annual policy meetings and other events

Organization	Services
National Association for the Education of Young Children (NAEYC) 1313 L Street, NW, Suite 500 Washington, DC 20005 800-424-2460 202-232-8777 www.naeyc.org	Print, video, and Web resources and support on the care and education of children from birth through age eight Journals: *Young Children, Teaching Young Children,* and an online resource, "Beyond the Journal" Holds a national conference and a smaller professional development institute each year Has 100,000 members and 360 affiliates at local, state, and regional levels Also publishes *Early Childhood Research Quarterly* (ECRQ)
National Black Child Development Institute (NBCDI) 1313 L Street, NW, Suite 110 Washington, DC 20005-4110 202-833-2220 800-556-2234 www.nbcdi.org	Advocates on behalf of the growth and development of African-American children Focuses on critical issues in early childhood education, child welfare, and health care Quarterly newsletter includes two issues of *Child Health Talk* Annual conference Affiliate chapters throughout the country
National Child Care Association 2025 M Street, NW, Suite 800 Washington, DC 20036-3309 800-543-7161 www.nccanet.org	A professional trade association focused on the needs of licensed, private childhood care and education programs Quarterly newsletter Annual conference with workshops focused on management issues Credentials for teachers and for administrators
National Head Start Association (NHSA) 1651 Prince Street Alexandria, VA 22314 703-739-0875 www.nhsa.org	Represents Head Start children, families, staff, and programs nationwide Agency and individual memberships Annual training conferences Quarterly journal: *Children and Families*
Southern Early Childhood Association (SECA) P. O. Box 55930 Little Rock, AR 72215-5930 800-305-7322 www.southernearlychildhood.org	Provides a voice on local, state, and federal issues affecting young children Quarterly journal: Dimensions and other resource materials Holds annual conference

Early childhood professionals can continue learning by using the Internet.

The Internet offers a world of information that is just a mouse click away. As you can see from the chart, most national and regional early childhood organizations have Web sites, as do publishers of resources for early childhood professionals. Educational television shows and museums have companion Web sites. Government agencies, such as the Department of Education and the Department of Health and Human Services, share free publications online and offer legislative updates. In addition, government-sponsored clearinghouses and projects, such as the National Child Care Information Center (www.nccic.org), offer research reports and practical strategies online. Every site also has links to other sites, making online sources of information easy to find.

If you are a new to the Internet, you will find helpful guidance on learning to use e-mail, surf the Web, and conduct research at the Community Learning Networks Web site (www.cln.org/guidebooks.html). This site is for K–12 teachers, but the "Beginners Central" provides an excellent orientation on how to use the Internet.

A comprehensive set of links to more than 80 important Web sites for early childhood professionals can be accessed on the Teaching Strategies Web site (www.teachingstrategies.com/pages/page.cfm?pageid=116).

Study groups are an excellent way to continue learning about teaching and caring for young children. They sometimes form to explore a particular topic, such as long-term studies, ongoing assessment, or literacy throughout the day. Members agree to read relevant materials (e.g., an article or a chapter in a book) in preparation for each meeting. A study group might also form to address a situation, such as aggressive behavior in the classroom. In a study group, one person should take the lead in facilitating the meetings, and another member should keep notes so that everyone stays informed about what takes place.

The more convenient the time and location for a study group, the more likely participants will come to each meeting and share ideas. Therefore, consider setting up a study group at your center or school, or at least in the neighborhood. Talk with the director about allocating time during the workday for these meetings, if possible.

Attend professional conferences. The early childhood field offers a wide range of national and local conferences, as illustrated in the chart on professional organizations. At these conferences, you often have an opportunity to hear keynote speeches by well-known educators. You can select from a great variety of workshops on a wide range of topics, visit an exhibit hall to browse and shop, and meet with colleagues from all over the state, the country, and the world.

Participate in training or degree programs. Completing this training program will be a great achievement, but it is not the end. You can continue to take advantage of opportunities to attend workshops and courses in your area. Your local Department of Social Services, public school adult education program, Office of Child Development Services, County Extension Office, and other government agencies in your area may offer workshops. Many colleges offer courses leading to an associate or bachelor's degree or a CDA credential. Individual courses at colleges and universities may also be an option for you. Some courses and seminars are offered through distance learning, via satellite hook-up or Internet-based learning modules.

- What opportunities to continue learning are available to you?

- How can you take advantage of these opportunities?

what's next?

Skill-Building Journal, section **13-6** *(Learning Activity B)* and section **13-1** *(Feedback).*

Learning Activities

LEARNING
ACTIVITY

C. Demonstrating Ethical Behavior in Your Work

In this activity you will learn to

- distinguish between professional and unprofessional behavior

- follow the standards of ethical behavior in the early childhood profession

Some of your decisions require a lot of thought.

Teachers make hundreds of decisions every day. Some decisions require a lot of thought, such as how to set up your classroom, what topics the children can study, and how to teach conflict resolution. You make other decisions quickly, such as deciding whether to intervene or to stand back and observe a child, or deciding how to respond to a parent's request that you not let her child nap. Some decisions involve a lot of soul-searching because they touch on core values and beliefs, such as how to respond to a parent who wants you to give her child worksheets or what to say to a colleague who speaks harshly.

The Early Childhood Code of Ethical Conduct[41]

The early childhood field, like most professions, has developed a code of ethics to provide guidelines for responsible behavior and a way to resolve problems with ethical dimensions. The *NAEYC Code of Ethical Conduct* defines professional responsibilities in four areas.

Ethical responsibilities to children:

> *...to provide care and education in settings that are safe, healthy, nurturing, and responsive for each child. We are committed to supporting children's development and learning; respecting individual differences; and helping children learn to live, play, and work cooperatively. We are also committed to promoting children's self-awareness, competence, self-worth, resiliency, and physical well-being.*

Ethical responsibilities to families:

> *...to bring about communication, cooperation, and collaboration between the home and early childhood program in ways that enhance the child's development.*

Ethical responsibilities to colleagues, including co-workers, employers, and employees:

...to establish and maintain settings and relationships that support productive work and meet professional needs.

Ethical responsibilities to community and society:

...to provide programs that meet the diverse needs of families, to cooperate with agencies and professions that share the responsibility for children, to assist families in gaining access to [them] ...and to assist in the development of community programs that are needed ... As individuals, we acknowledge our responsibility to provide the best possible programs of care and education for children ....and to serve as a voice for young children everywhere.

The following chart identifies some ethical standards for teaching young children and provides several examples of professional versus unprofessional behavior related to each standard.

Guide to Ethical Professional Behavior

Ethics of Teaching	Professional Behavior	Unprofessional Behavior
Treat each child as an individual, avoid comparisons, and show no bias because of culture, background, abilities, or gender.	Comforting a child who is hurt or upset. "It doesn't feel good when the other children won't let you play. I don't think they knew that you were trying to help. Let's show them your idea. It's a good one."	Teasing children when they cry. Comparing one child to another. "Crying isn't going to help. The other children don't want to play with a crybaby."
Base program practices on current knowledge of early childhood education and what you know about each child.	Making sure materials, activities, practices, and routines are developmentally and culturally appropriate. "I think some of the children are getting frustrated because the activity we planned is too difficult. I'll modify the activity and see if that works better."	Having all the children do the same activities at the same time. "Everyone is making pumpkins today. You can build with the blocks when you finish your pumpkin."
Be respectful and positive in communicating with children.	Giving children clear directions that show respect for their work and play. "We have to clean up soon so we can go outside. If you haven't finished, we will save your building until tomorrow so you can keep working on it."	Speaking rudely to children, using harsh words and a negative tone. "Is there something wrong with your ears? How many times do I have to tell you to clean up? Get busy. Now!"

Ethics of Teaching	Professional Behavior	Unprofessional Behavior
Maintain confidentiality about children and their families.	Discussing a child's problem confidentially with another teacher or the supervisor and trying to identify ways to help the child. "He often comes to the center in dirty clothes. I'm concerned because the other children notice it and I can see it makes him feel bad. Let's see what ideas the director has for dealing with the problem in a positive way."	Talking about a particular child in front of the child or with a parent other than the child's. "Yes, we all are very aware of how he comes to school. I'm glad you don't let your child look like this."
Treat families with respect, even during difficult situations.	Talking privately to a parent who often comes late about the problems this causes and discussing possible solutions. "Our center closes at 6:30, and I have to leave to pick up my own child. If you can't get here by that time, could someone else pick up your daughter?"	Getting angry with a parent who is late and demanding that he or she do better. "This is the third time you have been late this week. I need to go home, too, you know! If you're not careful, you'll have to find another place to take your child."
Be honest, reliable, and regular in attendance.	Arriving at work every day on time and ready to perform your assigned duties. "I can't wait to show the children the new game I made over the weekend. I'd like to introduce it to a small group during choice time and see how it goes."	Calling in sick unnecessarily, arriving late, or not doing assigned duties. Talking with colleagues rather than paying attention to children. "I was too busy to get the materials I promised. You should be glad I came to work today."
Dress appropriately for work.	Wearing comfortable, clean clothes suitable for playing with and caring for children, bending and lifting, sitting on the floor, and moving quickly when necessary.	Wearing clothes that hinder movement and are inappropriate for a child care setting.
Maintain accurate, timely, and appropriate records	Completing an injury report immediately after the incident. "Let me tell you exactly what happened on the playground, and you can read the full report on the incident."	Failing to record information about an injury. "No one ever reads these injury reports. I'm not wasting my time filling one out.
Advocate on behalf of children, families, self, and others. Let others know the importance of quality early childhood programs.	Agreeing to talk to a community organization about the program's need for volunteers. "It would mean so much to our children to have other adults and older children come to read books to them at the center. I'd be happy to come and talk about getting a project started."	Belittling child care work as only babysitting. "As soon as I can, I'm going to get a real job."

Caring for Preschool Children

Situations With Ethical Dimensions

Sometimes the right decision or action is not obvious.

Some situations with ethical dimensions present dilemmas that are complex and difficult to resolve. A lot of different issues may be involved that make it difficult to decide how to respond. The following situation was described in NAEYC's journal, *Young Children*.

> *At a staff meeting Marla reports her concern that a family with a daughter in her classroom has asked that she be served her food after male children in the class have been served, as a way to support the family's belief that females should 'learn their proper place' in society.*[42]

If you were Marla, how would you respond? You probably have strong views of your own on this issue. To determine an ethical response, you could turn to The *Code of Ethical Conduct* to learn what guidance it offers.[43] A principle of ethical responsibilities to children is applicable:

> *P-1.3-We shall not participate in practices that discriminate against children by denying benefits, giving special advantages, or excluding them from programs or activities on the basis of their sex, race, national origin, religious beliefs, medical condition, disability, or the marital status/family structure, sexual orientation, or religious beliefs or other affiliations of their families. (Aspects of this principle do not apply in programs that have a lawful mandate to provide services to a particular population of children.)*

After reading this principle in the *Code of Ethical Conduct*, you reassure yourself that it's not ethical to treat boys and girls differently. It's also against your personal values. You don't think you should discriminate against girls, in favor of boys. This seems like an easy decision, until you look further in the *Code*. Under ethical responsibilities to families, you see two statements of ideals that relate to this situation:

> *I-2.5-To respect the dignity and preferences of each family and to make an effort to learn about its structure, culture, language, customs, and beliefs.*

> *I-2.6-To acknowledge families' childrearing values and their right to make decisions for their children.*

This guidance reminds you that families are of primary importance in children's lives and in their development. Does this mean that you must agree to the wishes of these parents? How do you balance these conflicting values and beliefs? Is there a way to show respect for the family's wishes while helping them to understand the reason for program practices? This next principle supports that approach:

P-2.2: We shall inform families of program philosophy, policies, curriculum, assessment system, and personnel qualifications, and explain why we teach as we do—which should be in accordance with our ethical responsibilities to children (see Section I).

To respond to the family respectfully, you must find a way to convey your respect for their beliefs and reassure them that their practices at home will have a profound influence on their child. At the same time, you will have to explain the reasons for the practices you follow at school.

- When did you face an ethical dilemma in your work?

- How did you handle it?

- What approach will you take if it happens again?

what's next?

Skill-Building Journal, section **13-7** *(Learning Activity C)* and section **13-1** *(Feedback).*

Learning Activities

D. Talking About the Value of Your Work

In this activity you will learn to

- share what you know about the needs of young children and the early childhood profession with others

- advocate for high-quality programs for young children

Advocacy is working for change.

It may seem like a lot to expect early childhood professionals to share their knowledge with others and advocate for their profession. Advocacy, you might think, is for others, for people who like to speak before groups and who know how to influence the thinking of politicians and the public.

Advocacy is working for change, and an advocate is someone who works for a cause. Early childhood advocates speak out on issues that affect children and families and on issues related to their own working conditions because they feel very strongly about these issues. Often, decision makers aren't aware of the problems and issues related to providing quality child development programs for preschool children. Without awareness and understanding, change is not possible. As an early childhood professional, you are in a good position to help others understand important issues and concerns.

You know a lot about the value of high-quality care and education.

Think about how much you know about your profession. Having taught for some time, and by working through this training program, you have gained a good understanding of the importance of your work. You understand children's developmental needs and the kind of safe and nurturing early childhood environments that support children's growth and learning. You see firsthand the positive impact you have on young children and their families. You also know that children who attend high-quality programs are more likely to be ready for school and to succeed.

You know a lot about the problems the profession faces.

Advocates are people who see a problem and care deeply about making a difference. You are becoming aware of how many children and families are not able to benefit from living in a nation that is rich in resources. Many children are growing up in poverty, without health insurance, and in families that are experiencing high levels of stress. Early childhood teachers, who provide care and education for children, work long hours and earn low salaries. Some of these teachers leave the profession because they can't make enough to support their families.

Policy makers and the public may care about children, but they don't understand the difference that a high-quality early childhood program can make. As a result, they are not willing to allocate the funds that are needed desperately by so many programs. They need to hear from knowledgeable early childhood professionals.

Choose an approach that is comfortable for you.

You don't have to get up before a group of people and give a speech to be an effective advocate. There are many ways you can share the value of your work and convince others that investing in programs for young children makes sense. You can have informal conversations with people you know. You can write about your experiences or meet with people who are decision makers. Start with an approach that is comfortable for you. Here are a few of the many ways you can talk about the value of your work, advocate for high-quality programs, and avoid making excuses for not taking action.[44]

Share ideas for appropriate practice with other teachers and families (instead of just observing disapprovingly).

Explain to administrators why worksheets are inappropriate learning tools for young children (rather than using them and resenting that you must use practices that are inconsistent with your profession's knowledge base).

Explain to families why children learn best through purposeful and productive play (instead of bemoaning that parents are pushing their children or giving in, yourself, and using inappropriate methods and materials).

Write a letter to the editor of a newspaper or magazine to respond to an article or letter (instead of complaining about how other people don't understand the needs of children, families, or early childhood professionals).

Write to your state or federal legislators about a pending issue and share your experiences as a way to point out needs (rather than just assuming someone else will write).

Meet someone new who is interested in early childhood education and ask her or him to join a professional group such as NAEYC, NBCDI, SECA, or ACEI (instead of just wondering why the person isn't involved).

Ask a friend to go with you to community meetings where issues of concern to children and families will be discussed (instead of staying home because you don't want to go alone).

Volunteer to represent your professional group in a coalition to speak out on the developmental needs of young children (instead of waiting to be asked or declining because you've never done it before).

Agree to serve on a legislative telephone tree (rather than refusing because you don't think your phone call will matter anyway).

Work and learn with others to develop a position statement on a critical issue (instead of saying, "I don't really know much about this topic.").

Volunteer to speak at a school board meeting about how your program complies with professional standards for early childhood education (instead of resigning yourself to the fact that your school system doesn't understand much about early childhood education).

Conduct a local or state survey of salaries in early childhood programs (instead of ignoring the issue because no one has the facts).

Persuade colleagues that it is important to work toward accreditation from NAEYC (rather than just assuming no one wants to improve the program).

what's next?

Skill-Building Journal, section **13-8** *(Learning Activity D)*, section **13-1** *(Feedback)*, and section **13-9** *(Reflecting on Your Learning).*

Glossary

abstract thinking

the ability to think about ideas and concepts without using concrete materials

assessment

The process of observing, recording, and otherwise documenting the work children do and how they do it, and using this information as a basis for a variety of educational decisions that affect the child and the program

body fluids

liquid and semi-liquid substances eliminated by or present in the body, such as blood, lymph, feces, urine, mucus, saliva, digestive juices, and vomit

challenging behavior

behavior, such as recurring biting or temper tantrums, that occurs again and again, causes problems for a child, others in the group, and adults, and interferes with a child's full engagement in the program

classify

to group objects or events on the basis of a similar characteristic or attribute

closed question

a question for which there is only one correct answer

cognitive development

development of the ability to think and reason

communication

the act of expressing and sharing ideas and feelings with others

competence

possessing the knowledge and skills to do something well

consequence

the natural or logical result of any behavior

construct understanding

apply existing knowledge to try to explain and make sense of new observations and experiences

conventional reading and writing

reading and writing that follows standard rules for language use

creativity

the ability to use one's imagination to develop a new idea or product

daily schedule

a plan for the day's activities (The schedule includes the times and the order in which activities will happen.)

diet

the kinds and amounts of food and drink usually consumed, or a special selection of food and drink chosen to promote health

discipline

the ways in which adults teach children acceptable behavior

disinfectant

a cleaning solution that destroys harmful bacteria and viruses

egocentric

the belief that everyone has the same thoughts and feelings as one's own

emergency

an unplanned or unexpected event that calls for immediate action to prevent or redress harm

emerging literacy

the developmental processes through which children gain listening, speaking, reading, and writing skills

environment

the complete makeup of the indoor and outdoor areas used by children (The environment includes the space and how it is arranged and furnished, the schedule and routines, materials and equipment, activities, and the children and adults who are present.)

ethics

a set of principles, standards, or guidelines that direct acceptable behavior and help one decide what is right or good rather than what is quickest or easiest

fine motor skills

movements that involve the use of small muscles, for example, using hands and wrists to pick up puzzle pieces or to cut with a pair of scissors

gross motor skills

movements that involve the use of large muscles, the entire body, or large parts of the body, for example, running, hopping, or climbing

hand-eye coordination

the ability to direct finger, hand, and wrist movements to accomplish a motor task, such as fitting a peg in a hole, piling blocks, or catching a ball

hygiene

practices that preserve good health and prevent disease

limits and rules

guidelines set by teachers and children to define acceptable behavior

maintaining confidentiality

sharing information only with people who have a need to know

networking

spending time with people who perform similar tasks to share ideas, information, and experiences

nonverbal communication

the act of conveying feelings or ideas through gestures and body language

nutrient

a substance in food that nourishes the body

nutritious

nourishing; providing vitamins, minerals, complex carbohydrates, or protein to the body

observation

the act of systematically watching and listening to a child (The information gained from observation is used to plan a program that responds to the child's needs, strengths, interests, and other individual characteristics.)

observation note

a complete, accurate, and objective written account of the setting and of what is said and done during an observation period.

open-ended materials

materials and toys (such as blocks, dramatic play props, and art supplies) that children can use in many different ways

open-ended question

a question that can be answered in a number of different ways

peer

a person who is the same age or at the same developmental level

phonological awareness

the ability to hear and distinguish the different sounds in words

physical development

the gradual gaining of control of large and small muscles

physical environment

the organization of the classroom and outdoor space, including how they are arranged and furnished, the selection of materials and equipment, and the display of materials and children's work

physical fitness

the state of health that includes the individual's level of endurance, strength, flexibility, percentage of body fat, and degree of nutritional balance

portfolio

a collection of items, including work samples, photographs, lists of favorite books, and audio and videotape recordings, that document a child's progress and interests

positive guidance

techniques that help children learn to behave in acceptable ways. These methods help children develop self-discipline

precaution

a step taken to prevent injuries and to ensure safety

predictable books

those with lots of repetition, refrains, and/or cumulative text where one sentence is added on each page and the text is repeated (Such books allow children to anticipate the text that comes next.)

problem solving

the process of considering various aspects of a situation and identifying one or more approaches that are likely to lead to solutions

professionalism

a commitment to gaining and maintaining knowledge and skills in a particular field and to using that knowledge and those skills to provide the highest-quality services possible

prosocial skills

accepted behaviors, such as sharing or taking turns, which children learn and use to get along in society

punishment

control of children's behavior by use of force, fear, or deprivation

repetitive books

those that repeat certain words and phrases

representation

the act of creating a model that stands for something else (e.g., a block building, a drawing, a sculpture, a skit, a written story, or a chart)

routines

scheduled events that happen every day, such as meals, naps, toileting, washing hands, and getting dressed

safety

freedom from danger, harm, or loss

screening

a brief assessment procedure designed to identify possible developmental or learning concerns that require thorough health and/or developmental evaluations by expert diagnosticians

self-discipline

the ability to control one's own behavior, to think before acting on one's feelings

self-esteem

a sense of worth; a feeling about one's abilities and accomplishments (Someone who feels connected to others, respected and valued, and able to do things successfully and independently is likely to have positive self-esteem.)

sense of self

understanding who you are; how you identify yourself in terms of culture, environment, physical attributes, preferences, skills, and experiences (Development of a sense of self begins in infancy and evolves throughout life in response to experiences and interactions with others.)

sensory awareness

seeking information through sight, sound, touch, taste, and smell, for example, by smelling spices or turning in the direction of a voice

sequencing

putting things or events in logical order according to a specific criterion, such as size (large to small), sound (loud to quiet), height (short to tall), or time (first, second, third, and so on)

social development

the gradual process through which children learn to enjoy being with other people and gain skills such as sharing, cooperating, and empathizing

sodium

a mineral normally found in seafood, poultry, and some vegetables; one of the components of table salt

standard language

the form of any language that is usually taught in an educational setting and that follows specific rules for speech and writing (There are many forms of a language (dialects) other than the standard spoken and written forms.)

a study

a project that involves children in an in-depth investigation of a topic that is worth learning about and that interests them; they research answers to their questions and express their growing understanding in a variety of ways

starch

a carbohydrate substance found in such foods as potatoes, rice, corn, wheat, cassava, and many other vegetables

temperament

the nature or disposition of a child; the way a child responds to and interacts with people, materials, and situations

transitions

the in-between times in the daily schedule when children have completed one routine or activity and are moving to the next one

verbal language

a system of words with rules for their use in speaking, listening, reading, and writing

References

1   National Association for the Education of Young Children. (2005). *NAEYC code of ethical conduct and statement of commitment*. (p. 3). Washington, DC: Author.

2   American Academy of Pediatrics & American Public Health Association. (2002). *Caring for our children: National health and safety performance standards: Guidelines for out-of-home child care programs: A joint collaborative project of American Academy of Pediatrics, American Public Health Association, and National Resource Center for Health and Safety in Child Care* (2nd ed.). Elk Grove Village, IL: The Academy.

3   Aronson, S. S. (2002). *Healthy young children: A manual for programs* (4th ed.), (pp. 27–28, 129–130). Washington, DC: National Association for the Education of Young Children.

4   *Ibid* (pp. 32–33).

5   From *Caring for our children: National health and safety performance standards: Guidelines for out-of-home child care programs: A joint collaborative project of American Academy of Pediatrics, American Public Health Association, and National Resource Center for Health and Safety in Child Care* (2nd ed.), (pp. 23, 226, 424), by American Academy of Pediatrics & American Public Health Association, 2002, Elk Grove Village, IL: The Academy. Copyright 2002 by AAP, APHA & NRCHSCC. Adapted (p. 226) / Reprinted (pp. 23, 424) with permission.

6   From *Caring for our children: National health and safety performance standards: Guidelines for out-of-home child care programs: A joint collaborative project of American Academy of Pediatrics, American Public Health Association, and National Resource Center for Health and Safety in Child Care* (2nd ed.), (pp. 97–98), by American Academy of Pediatrics & American Public Health Association, 2002, Elk Grove Village, IL: The Academy. Copyright 2002 by AAP, APHA & NRCHSCC. Adapted with permission.

Aronson, S. (2002). *Healthy young children: A manual for programs*. Washington, DC: National Association for the Education of Young Children.

7   Rings, bugs, and handwashing. (2003, September). *Child Health Alert, 21*.

8   From *Caring for our children: National health and safety performance standards: Guidelines for out-of-home child care programs: A joint collaborative project of American Academy of Pediatrics, American Public Health Association, and National Resource Center for Health and Safety in Child Care* (2nd ed.), (pp. 85, 124–125), by American Academy of Pediatrics & American Public Health Association, 2002, Elk Grove Village, IL: The Academy. Copyright 2002 by AAP, APHA & NRCHSCC. Reprinted with permission.

Aronson, S. (2002) *Healthy young children: A manual for programs* (4th ed.). Washington, DC: National Association for the Education of Young Children.

9   The federal government defines *hazardous exposure to blood* as direct contact by blood or blood-containing body fluids with the employee's eyes, mouth, or non-intact skin. [Occupational Health and Safety Administration Regulations (Standards - 29 CFR, 1910.1030)].

10 Dodge, D. T., & Colker, L. J. (1998). *The Creative Curriculum® for family child care* (pp. 204–207). Washington, DC: Teaching Strategies, Inc.

Dodge, D. T., Colker, L. J., & Heroman, C. (2002). *The Creative Curriculum® for preschool* (4th ed.) (pp. 443–469). Washington, DC: Teaching Strategies, Inc.

11 Wortman, A. M. (2001, July/August). Preventing work-related musculoskeletal injuries. *Child Care Information Exchange, 140*.

12 American Academy of Pediatrics. (1998). *Caring for your baby and child: Birth to age 5* (pp. 349, 360–361). New York, NY: Bantam.

References

13 Dodge, D. T., Colker, L. J., & Heroman, C. (2002). *The Creative Curriculum® for preschool* (4th ed.) (pp. 49–50). Washington, DC: Teaching Strategies, Inc.

14 Sanders, S. (2002). *Active for life: Developmentally appropriate movement programs for young children* (pp. 54–56). Washington, DC: National Association for the Education of Young Children.

15 National Council of Teachers of Mathematics. (2000). *Principles and standards for school mathematics.* Reston, VA: Author.

16 Helm, J. H., & Katz, L. (2001). *Young investigators: The project approach in the early years.* New York: Teachers College Press.

17 Stoeke, J. M. (1996). *Minerva Louise at school.* New York: Dutton Books.

18 American Academy of Pediatrics. (2003, February). Hearing assessment in infants and children: Recommendations beyond neonatal screening. *Pediatrics, 111*(2), 436–440. Retrieved February 20, 2003, from http://www.aap.org/policy/0121.html#table2.

American Speech-Language-Hearing Association. (2004). *How does your child hear and talk?* Retrieved January 15, 2004, from http://www.asha.org/public/speech/development/child_hear_talk.htm.

19 Hart, B., & Risley, T. R. (1995). *Meaningful differences in the everyday experiences of young american children.* Baltimore: Paul H. Brookes Publishing Co.

20 Tabors, P. (1998, November).What early childhood educators need to know: Developing effective programs for linguistically and culturally diverse children and families. *Young Children, 53*(6), 20–26.

21 Koralek, D. G. (2003, March). Reading aloud with children of all ages. Beyond the Journal, *Young Children on the Web.* Retrieved January 2, 2004, from http://www.naeyc.org/resources/journal/2003/ReadingAloud.pdf.

22 Isenberg, J. P., & Jalongo, M. R. (1997). *Creative expression and play in the early childhood curriculum* (2nd ed.) (p. 7). Upper Saddle River, NJ: Merrill.

Kellogg, R. (1970). *Analyzing children's art.* Palo Alto, CA: National Press Books.

23 Koralek, D. G., Dodge, D. T., & Pizzolongo, P. J. (2003). *Caring for preschool children* (2nd ed., Vol. II) (p. 36). Washington, DC: Teaching Strategies, Inc.

24 Erikson, E. H. (1994). *Identity and the life cycle.* New York: W.W. Norton & Company.

25 Kohn, A. (2001). Five reasons to stop saying "Good job!" *Young Children.* 56(5), 24–28.

26 McClellan, D., & Katz, L. G. (1993). Young children's social development: A checklist. *ERIC Digest.* ED356100. Retrieved January 2, 2004, from http://www.ericfacility.net/databases/ERIC_Digests/ed356100.html.

27 National Association of School Psychologists. Development of social skills in young children: Guidelines for parents. *Parenting Perspectives.* Retrieved January 2, 2004, from http://www.teachersandfamilies.com/open/parent/socialskills1.cfm.

28 Paley, V. (1992). *You can't say you can't play.* Cambridge, MA: Harvard University Press.

29 Koralek, D. G. (1999). *Classroom strategies to promote children's social and emotional development* (pp. 35–149). Lewisville, NC: Kaplan Press.

30 Smilansky, S., & Shefatya, L. (1990). *Facilitating play: A medium for promoting cognitive, socio-emotional, and academic development in young children.* Gaithersburg, MD: Psychosocial & Educational Publications.

[31] Bodrova, E., & Leong, D. J. (2003). Chopsticks and counting chips: Do play and foundational skills need to compete for the teacher's attention in an early childhood classroom? *Young Children, 58*(2), 10–17.

[32] Dodge, D. T., Colker, L. J., & Heroman, C. (2002). *The Creative Curriculum® for preschool* (4th ed.) (pp. 107–108). Washington, DC: Teaching Strategies, Inc.

[33] Dodge, D. T., Colker, L. J., & Heroman, C. (2002). *The Creative Curriculum® for preschool* (4th ed.)(pp. 120–121). Washington, DC: Teaching Strategies, Inc.

[34] Dodge, D. T., Colker, L. J., & Heroman, C. (2002). The family's role. *The Creative Curriculum® for preschool* (4th ed.)(pp. 228–231). Washington, DC: Teaching Strategies, Inc.

[35] Koralek, D. G. (1993). *In Responding to children under stress* (pp. 40–42). Washington, DC: Head Start Bureau.

[36] Bredekamp, S., & Copple, C. (Eds.). (1997). *Developmentally appropriate practice in early childhood programs* (pp. 20–21). Washington, DC: National Association for the Education of Young Children.

[37] Dodge, D. T., Colker, L. J., & Heroman, C. (2002). The family's role. *The Creative Curriculum® for preschool* (4th ed.)(pp. 166–168). Washington, DC: Teaching Strategies, Inc.

[38] Dodge, D. T., Colker, L. J., & Heroman, C. (2002). The family's role. *The Creative Curriculum® for preschool* (4th ed.)(pp. 200–203). Washington, DC: Teaching Strategies, Inc.

[39] Dodge, D. T., Colker, L. J., & Heroman, C. (2002). The family's role. *The Creative Curriculum® for preschool* (4th ed.)(pp. 98–99). Washington, DC: Teaching Strategies, Inc.

[40] Katz, L. G. (1995). Teacher's developmental stages. *Talks with teachers of young children* (pp. 7–13). Norwood, NJ: Ablex Publishing Corporation.

[41] National Association for the Education of Young Children. (2005). *NAEYC code of ethical conduct and statement of commitment.* Washington, DC: Author.

[42] Brophy–Herb, H. E., Kostelnik, M. J., and Stein, L.C. (2001). A developmental approach to teaching about ethics using the NAEYC Code of Ethical Conduct. *Young Children, 56,* 80–84.

[43] National Association for the Education of Young Children. (2005). *NAEYC code of ethical conduct and statement of commitment.* Washington, DC: Author.

[44] From *Speaking out: Early childhood advocacy,* (pp. 14–15), by S. G. Goffin & J. Lombardi, 1998, Washington, DC: National Association for the Education of Young Children. Copyright 1998 by NAEYC. Adapted with permission.

Robinson, A., & Stark, D. R. (2002). *Advocates in action: Making a difference for young children.* Washington, DC: National Association for the Education of Young Children.

Resources

It would be impossible to list all of the excellent resources for early childhood professionals. Here are some favorites, both old and new. The first category lists items that are relevant to all modules. Additional materials are listed for specific modules. Many could be listed in more than one category. You can purchase items marked with an asterisk (*) and review additional books and videos at the Teaching Strategies Web site (www.teachingstrategies.com).

General

Ages and Stages: Developmental Descriptions and Activities, Birth Through Eight Years, Karen Miller (Marshfield, MA: TelShare, 2001). This clearly written guide describes the stages children pass through as they develop physically, emotionally, and intellectually. Descriptions of children's behavior are accompanied by suggestions of ways teachers can respond to encourage growth and development.

The Creative Curriculum® for Preschool, 4th edition, Diane Trister Dodge, Laura J. Colker, and Cate Heroman (Washington, DC: Teaching Strategies, Inc., 2002). This is a comprehensive curriculum for preschool. It offers practical strategies based on child development theory for creating a learning environment and promoting learning in eleven interest areas: Blocks, Dramatic Play, Toys and Games, Art, Sand and Water, Library, Discovery, Music and Movement, Cooking, Computers, and Outdoors. It describes the vital role of the teacher in guiding and assessing learning in all content areas.

Developmentally Appropriate Practice in Early Childhood Programs, Revised edition, Sue Bredekamp and Carol Copple, Eds. (Washington, DC: National Association for the Education of Young Children, 1997). This publication expands the core ideas of the influential 1987 edition, defining standards of quality in programs serving children up to age eight. Increased attention is given to issues of curriculum content and assessment as well as strategies teachers can use to support growth and development.

Developmental Profiles: Pre-Birth to Eight, 4th edition, Lynn Marotz and K. Eileen Allen (Albany, NY: Delmar Publishers, Inc., 2003). Included in this helpful book are a discussion of child development principles and concepts and chapters devoted to each age group. The chapter on the preschool child provides separate developmental profiles and growth patterns for 3-, 4-, and 5-year-old children.

Safe and Healthy

The ABCs of Safe and Healthy Child Care, An On-line Handbook for Child Care Providers, U.S. Department of Health and Human Services, Public Health Service, and Centers for Disease Control (Atlanta, GA: Centers for Disease Control, 1996). This publication contains a practical and descriptive list of all major childhood illnesses, how they are spread, and measures for prevention. It is available on the Web (www.cdc.gov/ncidod/abc).

Caring for Our Children: National Health and Safety Performance Standards: Guidelines for Out-of-Home Child Care Programs, 2nd edition, American Academy of Pediatrics and American Public Health Association, Elk Grove Village, IL: American Academy of Pediatrics, 2002). This volume defines the standards and rationale for ensuring children's health and safety in child care programs. It is available on the Web (http://nrc.uchsc.edu).

Cup Cooking: Individual Child-Portion Picture Recipes, Barbara Johnson (Beltsville, MD: Gryphon House, 1998). Children can prepare the single-serving recipes in this book with little assistance from adults. Simple illustrations explain the steps involved in measuring and mixing ingredients.

Healthy Young Children: A Manual for Programs, 4th edition, Susan Aronson, Ed. (Washington, DC: National Association for the Education of Young Children, 2002). This comprehensive manual includes three separate chapters devoted to maintaining a safe environment, promoting transportation safety, and handling emergencies.

Model Child Care Health Policies, 4th edition, American Academy of Pediatrics. (Washington, DC: National Association for the Education of Young Children, 2002. These model policies provide an excellent starting point for writing health policies. The policies are available on a computer disk so that programs can adapt and reproduce them.

Pretend Soup and Other Real Recipes: A Cookbook for Preschoolers and Up, Mollie Katzen (Berkeley, CA: Tricycle Press, 1994). The author of the popular "Moosewood" cookbooks for grown ups provides this collection of colorful picture recipes for young children. An educational supplement includes ideas for making cooking an integral part of the preschool curriculum.

Learning Environment

Caring Spaces, Learning Places: Children's Environments That Work, Jim Greenman (Redmond, WA: Exchange Press Inc., 1988). This book shows how to set up environments that make creative use of space and respond to children's developmental needs. It is richly illustrated with photographs of children using indoor and outdoor spaces.

The Complete Learning Center Book, Rebecca Isbell (Beltsville, MD: Gryphon House Books, 1995). This illustrated guide gives layouts and suggestions for setting up and using 32 learning centers in preschool classrooms.

Hug a Tree, Robert E. Rockwell, Elizabeth A. Sherwood, and Robert A. Williams (Beltsville, MD: Gryphon House, 1983). Readers of this book will learn to make use of the outdoor environment in a variety of ways. Each outdoor learning experience has a suggested age level, a clear description of the activity, and suggestions for follow-up learning.

The Outside Play and Learning Book, Karen Miller (Beltsville, MD: Gryphon House, 1989). A comprehensive and creative collection of outdoor activities, this book offers practical suggestions for making good use of the outdoor environment in all seasons.

The Right Stuff for Children Birth to 8: Selecting Play Materials to Support Development, Martha B. Bronson (Washington, DC: National Association for the Education of Young Children, 1995). This book is a thorough guide to appropriate play materials. The chapter for preschool children describes typical developmental characteristics and suggests materials to encourage different kinds of activities.

Physical

Fit Kids, Kenneth H. Cooper, M.D., M.P.H. (Nashville, TN: Broadman and Holman, 1999). This book on the physical development of school-age children has tips for encouraging children to participate in fitness activities and follow nutritious diets. Menus and recipes are included. Although written for parents, this resource includes useful information for school-age program staff.

Jump for Joy!, Myra K. Thompson (Upper Saddle River, NJ: Prentice Hall, 1992). Teachers will find more than 375 creative, and usually cooperative, movement activities for 3- to 5-year-olds in this book. The selections are organized by the equipment needed, for example, balls, hoops, beanbags, and ribbons.

Woodworking for Young Children, Patsy Skeen, Anita Garner, and Sally Cartwright (Washington, DC: National Association for the Education of Young Children, 1984). This book will help you include woodworking in your classroom, to give children opportunities to create while building their small motor skills and hand-eye coordination.

Cognitive

The Block Book, 3rd edition, E. S. Hirsch, Ed. (Washington, DC: National Association for the Education of Young Children, 1996). This illustrated classic describes how and what children can learn using blocks: math concepts, science, social studies, self-awareness, and more.

*Building Your Baby's Brain: A Parent's Guide to the First Five Years, Diane Trister Dodge and Cate Heroman (Washington, DC: Teaching Strategies, Inc., 1999). The first five years of life are critical for brain development. This clearly written booklet, packed full of illustrations and helpful charts, explains what scientists know about brain development. It shows how parents and teachers can make a big difference.

Earthways: Simple Environmental Activities for Young Children, Carol Petrash (Beltsville, MD: Gryphon House, 1992). Most of the activities presented in this book make use of materials found in nature. Children can learn to understand and value the plants and animals that share their world.

Mudpies to Magnets: A Preschool Science Curriculum and *More Mudpies to Magnets,* Robert A. Williams, Robert E. Rockwell, and Elizabeth A. Sherwood (Beltsville, MD: Gryphon House, 1987 and 1990). Each book describes numerous hands-on science experiments for young children, including clear directions and materials needed.

*Your Child's Growing Mind: A Practical Guide Brain Development and Learning from Birth to Adolescence, Jane M. Healy (New York, NY: Doubleday, 1994). This clear guide translates brain development research into practical information. The author explains in detail how children develop language and memory, and addresses academic learning: reading, writing, spelling, and mathematics. This book provides much solid advice on how to promote (not push) children's readiness, motivation, and problem-solving skills.

Creative

The Big Messy Art Book: But Easy to Clean Up, MaryAnn F. Kohl (Beltsville, MD: Gryphon House, 2000). The activities in this book allow children to express themselves in new and exciting ways. For example, an artist might paint a hanging ball as it swings back and forth.

Growing Up Creative, 2nd ed., Teresa Amabile (Buffalo, NY: Creative Education Foundation, 1992). Written for parents, this book explains Amabile's theories about creativity and offers strategies for encouraging children's creativity.

Kids Create, Laurie Carlson (Charlotte, VT: Williamson Publishing, 1990). This book describes art and craft projects for children ages three through nine. It provides illustrated instructions for a wide variety of activities that allow children to exercise their creativity.

Making Make Believe: Fun Props, Costumes, and Creative Play Ideas, MaryAnn F. Kohl (Beltsville, MD: Gryphon House, Inc., 1999). Read this book to learn how to use inexpensive and throw-away items to create a life-size igloo, build a stage, and make a variety of props and dress-up costumes. The ideas in this book will take children's imaginative play to new heights.

Move Over, Mother Goose! Finger Plays, Action Verses, and Funny Rhymes, Ruth I. Dowell (Beltsville, MD: Gryphon House, 1987). Every preschool classroom needs a resource such as this, filled with words and ideas for singing, chanting, and more.

Mudworks, Creative Clay, Dough, and Modeling Experiences, Mary Ann Kohl (Bellingham, WA: Bright Ring Publishing, 1989). There are over 100 open-ended ways to engage children in modeling experiences described in this book. The clearly written recipes are presented in a format that gives appropriate guidance to adults.

Please Don't Move the Muffin Tins: A Hands-Off Guide to Art for the Young Child, Bev Bos (Roseville, CA: Turn-the-Page Press, 1984). This is a wonderful collection of developmentally appropriate art experiences for young children.

Preschool Art, It's the Process, Not the Product!, Mary Ann Kohl (Beltsville, MD: Gryphon House, 1994). As the title suggests, this book offers a selection of open-ended art activities that allow children to fully experience the process of creating something rather than the product itself.

Communication

Emerging Literacy: Young Children Learn to Read and Write, Dorothy S. Strickland and Lesley Mandel Morrow, Eds. (Newark, DE: International Reading Association, 1989). Each of the 12 chapters in this book was written by a different expert on children's literacy development. Learning literacy is presented as a continuous process that begins when parents and providers expose infants to oral and written language and that continues throughout childhood.

Learning Language and Loving It, Elaine Weitzman (Toronto, Canada: The Hanen Centre, 1992). This practical resource reflects the strategies used to implement an on-site training program for early childhood staff. The author reviews language learning from birth through the preschool years. The examples, illustration, and graphics are extremely clear and readable.

*Learning to Read and Write: Developmentally Appropriate Practices for Young Children, Susan B. Neuman, Carol Copple, and Sue Bredekamp (Washington DC: National Association for the Education of Young Children, 2000). Teachers can be assured that this approach to fostering early literacy development is developmentally appropriate and based on research about the most effective ways to help young children gain language and literacy skills. Strategies are illustrated through numerous photographs and examples of children's work.

Much More Than the ABCs: The Early Stages of Reading and Writing, Judith A. Schickedanz (Washington, DC: National Association for the Education of Young Children, 1998). This updated version of an early literacy classic covers how preschoolers learn about reading and writing. The final chapter offers ideas for organizing an environment that supports children's language and literacy explorations.

Playing with Print, Fostering Emergent Literacy, Carol Ann Bloom (Glenview, IL: Good Year Books, 1997). The practical and diverse ideas in this book are organized in chapters dedicated to the environment, curriculum, dramatic play, and the role of the teacher. Teachers are encouraged to link literacy to all aspects of the curriculum so children can learn about print in meaningful ways.

*Reading Right From the Start, Toni S. Bickart and Diane Trister Dodge (Washington, DC: Teaching Strategies, Inc., 2000). This easy-to-read, richly illustrated booklet shows parents how they can help their children (birth to five) gain the language and literacy knowledge necessary to become readers and writers. Teachers can use this book to help parents feel more confident about what they can do at home.

*Starting Out Right: A Guide to Promoting Children's Reading Success, National Research Council, M. Susan Burns, Peg Griffin, and Catherine E. Snow, Eds. (Washington, DC: National Academy Press, 1999). The practical suggestions for supporting children's literacy development in this book are based on the published findings of a national research panel, *Preventing Reading Difficulties in Young Children*. The appendixes include a glossary and list of literacy-related Internet sites.

Story S-t-r-e-t-c-h-e-r-s: Activities to Expand Children's Favorite Books and *More Story S-t-r-e-t-c-h-e-r-s*, Shirley C. Raines and Robert J. Canady (Beltsville, MD: Gryphon House, 1989 and 1991). Filled with activities teachers can use to extend children's enjoyment of their favorite books. Five active learning experiences are described for each of 90 books.

Self, Social, and Guidance

Alike and Different: Exploring Our Humanity With Young Children, Revised edition, Bonnie Neugebauer, Ed. (Washington, DC: National Association for the Education of Young Children, 1992). The articles collected in this book offer thoughtful advice and approaches to meeting the needs of all children. Also addressed are diversity issues related to staffing, living in a changing world, and resources.

Anti-Bias Curriculum: Tools for Empowering Young Children, Louise Derman-Sparks and the A.B.C. Task Force (Washington, DC: National Association for the Education of Young Children, 1989). This book contains many practical suggestions for helping adults understand how we unintentionally convey biases to children and how to minimize, deal with, and even eliminate those biases.

Beyond Self-Esteem: Developing a Genuine Sense of Human Value, Nancy E. Curry and Carl N. Johnson (Washington, DC: National Association for the Education of Young Children, 1990). Part I of this book describes how children of different ages develop a sense of self and self-esteem. Part II presents strategies for encouraging children to develop strong, positive identities.

Common Sense Discipline, Grace Mitchell and Lois Dewsnap (Marshfield, MA: TelShare Publishing, 1995). Through real-life stories about children, this book demonstrates a developmentally appropriate approach to guidance. The authors look for the reasons for certain behaviors and suggest individualized strategies parents and teachers can use to promote self-discipline.

*Early Violence Prevention, Tools for Teachers of Young Children, Ronald G. Slaby, Wendy C. Roedell, Diana Arezzo, and Kate Hendrix (Washington, DC: National Association for the Education of Young Children, 1995). This book combines research results with teaching guidelines to help prevent violent behaviors in young children. It presents techniques for helping children understand their feelings and provides alternatives to aggression, such as conflict resolution.

*First Feelings, Milestones in the Emotional Development of Your Baby and Child, Stanley Greenspan (New York: Viking Penguin, USA, 1994). Dr. Greenspan, child psychiatrist and author, reviews the stages of normal emotional development for children. He offers suggestions for parents on how to handle typical problems and challenges. Teachers can adapt these strategies in their work with young children.

Meeting the Challenge: Effective Strategies for Challenging Behaviors in Early Childhood Environments, Barbara Kaiser and Judy Rasminsky (Ontario, Canada: Canadian Child Care Federation, 1999). Available from NAEYC, this book provides an overall approach that helps teachers observe and reflect on children's use of challenging behaviors. The authors also provide practical strategies for helping individual children learn appropriate ways to express their strong feelings and learn to behave in acceptable ways.

Roots and Wings: Affirming Culture in Early Childhood Programs, Stacy York (Minneapolis: Redleaf Press, 1991). This resource defines a framework for multicultural education and shows how it is related to quality early childhood programs. The author defines the stages through which children pass as they become aware of differences and develop prejudices. She discusses the effects of prejudice on young children from diverse cultures.

Starting School: From Separation to Independence, Nancy Balaban (New York: Teachers College Press, 1985). This book explains how children experience and cope with separation and provides practical suggestions for supporting children.

There's Gotta Be a Better Way: Discipline That Works! Revised edition, Becky Bailey (Oviedo, FL: Loving Guidance, 1997). This book reminds us that every moment of conflict is a potential teaching opportunity. It provides the strategies teachers need to create a problem-solving community of learners where aggression and power struggles are avoided.

Basic

MATHEMATICS

Concepts

Level E

Master the Basics One Step at a Time

written by
Serena Crompton

edited by
Bearl Brooks
and
Marie-Jose Shaw

Student's Edition

ESP Publishing, Inc.
Largo, Florida 33773

Author: Serena Crompton

Book Design: Bearl Brooks

Editors: Bearl Brooks and Marie-Jose Shaw

Cover Design: Minnie Peek

Graphic Arts Credits: Nancy Baldridge, Rebecca Brown, Barbara K. Heer, Margie Luster, Donna Morrow, Sheila Shockley, Robin Sydorenko, Janet E. Thiel, Judy Warren

Student's Edition

Order number: BMC-E

ISBN 0-8209-0649-2

Published by
ESP Publishing, Inc. Largo, FL 33773

Copyright © 1999

Printed in the United States of America.

The Concept of Place

Learning Objective: *We will learn to identify place within a series of figures.*

Place is the position of a figure in relation to other figures.

EXAMPLE:

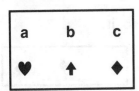

In the box at the left, the ♥ is in the "a" place, the ↑ is in the "b" place, and the ◆ is in the "c" place.

    _a_ ♥   _b_ ↑   _c_ ◆

A Identify the place occupied by each figure in each box.

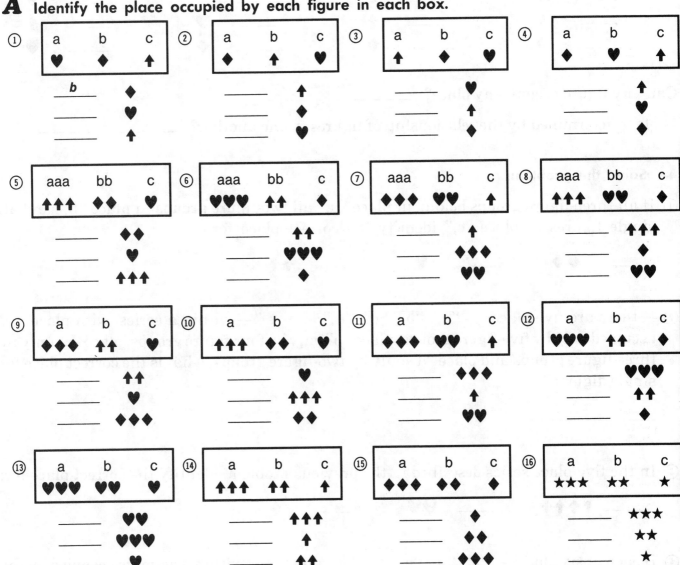

REMINDER: Write the definition of place.

Unit 1 cont'd ☞

Within each series, figures occupy places in relation to one another. Identify the place occupied by each figure within a series. In the series ♥ ♦ ↑ for example, ♥ occupies the "a" place, while ♦ is in the "b" place, and ↑ in the "c" place.

a	b	c
♥	♦	↑

B Complete the following exercise, and answer the questions relating to it.

① ♦ ♥ ↑   ② ↑ ♦ ♥   ③ ♥ ↑ ♦   ④ ↑ ♥ ♦

_____ ♥   _____ ♥   _____ ↑   _____ ♦
_____ ↑   _____ ↑   _____ ♥   _____ ↑
_____ ♦   _____ ♦   _____ ♦   _____ ♥

Can any figure occupy any place? _____

Is place determined by the relationship of figures to one another? _____

C Solve the problems.

① If all three-figure groups belong in place "a," all two-figure groups in place "b," and all single figures in place "c," identify the correct place for:

_____ ♦♦   _____ ♥   _____ ↑↑↑

② If there are five places — "a," "b," "c," "d," and "e" — within a series, with place "a" occupied only by five-figure groups, place "b" only by four-figure groups, place "c" only by three-figure groups and place "d" only by two-figure groups, what is the correct place for single figures?

_____

③ In the five-place series described in the previous problem, identify the correct place for:

_____ ↑↑↑↑   _____ ♥♥   _____ ♦

④ If each of six places — "a," "b," "c," "d," "e," and "f" — within a series is occupied by the same single figure ♦, name the place each ♦ occupies in relation to the other ♦'s.

♦   ♦   ♦   ♦   ♦   ♦

_____   _____   _____   _____   _____   _____

6

The Concept of Direction   Unit 2

Direction is the course along which something is moving, pointing or facing.

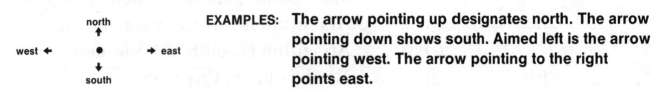

EXAMPLES: **The arrow pointing up designates north. The arrow pointing down shows south. Aimed left is the arrow pointing west. The arrow pointing to the right points east.**

A Study the diagram and mark each statement true or false.

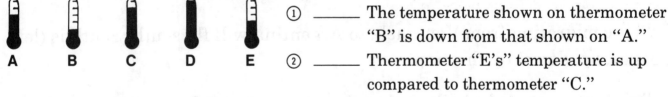

g f e d c b a ● A B C D E F G

① __false__ Point "A" on the scale is to the left of point "a."

② _____ The farthest point to the left of the scale is point "g."

③ _____ All points to the right of the mid-point are labeled with capital letters.

④ _____ Point "e" is directly to the right of point "d."

⑤ _____ Point "E" is directly to the left of point "D."

⑥ _____ Point "B" is three points to the left of point "F."

⑦ _____ Of all the points labeled with small letters, point "a" is the farthest to the right.

⑧ _____ Point "B" is to the right of point "b."

⑨ _____ Point "G" is farthest to the right of all points labeled with capital letters.

⑩ _____ Point "G" is the farthest point to the right of the scale.

B Study the diagram and mark each statement true or false.

A B C D E

① _____ The temperature shown on thermometer "B" is down from that shown on "A."

② _____ Thermometer "E's" temperature is up compared to thermometer "C."

③ _____ Thermometer "D's" temperature is up compared to thermometers "A," "B," "C," and "E."

④ _____ The temperature registered on thermometer "C" is up from that shown on "B," but down from that shown on "D."

⑤ _____ Thermometer "C's" temperature is up compared to all others.

REMINDER: Write the definition of direction.

_____

_____

C Study the map and mark each statement true or false.

① __true__ Venezuela is north of Bolivia.

② _____ Brazil stretches farther east than any other South American country.

③ _____ Argentina is directly west of Chile.

④ _____ Argentina is south of Venezuela.

⑤ _____ North is up on this map.

⑥ _____ Both Columbia and Peru are situated to the east of Brazil.

⑦ _____ Peru is south of Columbia and north of Chile.

⑧ _____ French Guiana is west of both Venezuela and Columbia.

⑨ _____ West is toward the right on this map.

⑩ _____ A line drawn north from Bolivia to Venzuela would first cross Brazil.

D Using diagrams from the previous exercises, underline the correct directions.

① Two South American archaeologists have agreed to meet at a village in French Guiana to discuss a new project. One of the archaeologists lives in French Guiana. The other will travel from Columbia, crossing Venezuela and continuing toward the (north, south, west, east).

② Geese migrating from Venezuela to Argentina will fly south. South is (left, right, up, down) on the map.

③ Two houses are to be built so that they face one another on points "f" and "e" on the scale shown on page 7. The house on point "f" will face (left, right, up, down) on the scale, while the house on point "e" will face (left, right, up, down).

④ The five thermometers on page 7 register five different temperatures. The temperature on the thermometer that is farthest to the right is (up, down, north, south) compared to thermometers "C" and "D."

8

The Concept of Size

Learning Objective: *We will learn to compare and classify objects by size.*

Size is the amount of space which something occupies.

EXAMPLE: The center pizza is not the same size as the other pizzas. The center pizza is smaller.

A Circle the correct answer.

① Circle the mushroom that is taller.

② Circle the tiniest hummingbird.

③ Circle the biggest bird cage.

④ Circle the tie that is narrower.

⑤ Circle the porcupine with longer quills.

⑥ Circle the shortest vase.

⑦ Circle the fattest parrot.

⑧ Circle the man with the thinner mustache.

⑨ Circle the plant with the widest leaves.

⑩ Circle the thickest book.

REMINDER: Write the definition of size.

_____

_____

Unit 3 cont'd ☞

B Match the groups of objects with the correct groups of sizes.

① nails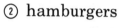

one-penny,
two-penny,
16-penny

④ slacks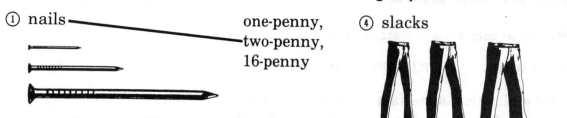

3x5,
5x7,
8x10

② hamburgers

AAA,
AA,
D

⑤ picture frames

small,
medium,
large

③ batteries

single,
double,
triple

⑥ soft drinks

slim,
regular,
husky

C Underline the correct answers.

① Wendy wears size 7AA shoes. Carol wears size 5½A. Sara's size is 8B. (Wendy, Carol, Sara) has the shortest foot. (Wendy, Carol, Sara) wears the narrowest shoe.

② Scott wants a television that he can watch from his bed. The only space for a TV is across the room along the opposite wall. A store clerk suggested that a larger screen would allow Scott to view his favorite programs from a distance. The store sells televisions with screens of three sizes. A (13-inch, 19-inch, 26-inch) screen would offer the biggest picture.

③ When the nursery was remodeled to give Cheryl a room of her own, there was hardly enough space for both a bed and a dresser. Cheryl's mother chose a (twin-size, full-size, queen-size) bed for Cheryl's new room, because that size occupied the least amount of space.

④ While shopping for Christmas presents, David realized he needed to know the correct sizes of certain items. Only one gift that he wanted to buy was not labeled according to size. It was a (belt, picture frame, pair of earrings).

The Concept of Shape

Learning Objective: *We will learn to recognize nine different shapes.*

Shape is a distinct form.

EXAMPLE: Four sides of the same size make a special type of rectangle called a square.

square

A Fill in the blanks with the names of the shapes.

circle

triangle

rectangle

ellipse

semi-circle

hexagon

pentagon

octagon

① A ____triangle____ has three sides that may or may not be the same size.

② Another name for _____ is oval.

③ A _____ looks like a circle that has been cut in two.

④ A _____ has four sides but is not always a square.

⑤ Five sides make a shape called a _____ .

⑥ Two shapes are bounded completely by curved lines. These are the _____ and the _____ .

⑦ A six-sided figure is called a _____ .

⑧ The _____ , bounded by eight straight lines, has more sides than the pentagon or the hexagon.

⑨ The _____ , _____ , _____ , _____ , _____ , _____ , _____ , _____ , or _____ may be any size.

REMINDER: Write the definition of shape.

_____

_____

Unit 4 cont'd ☛

B In each box, circle the shape that is different.

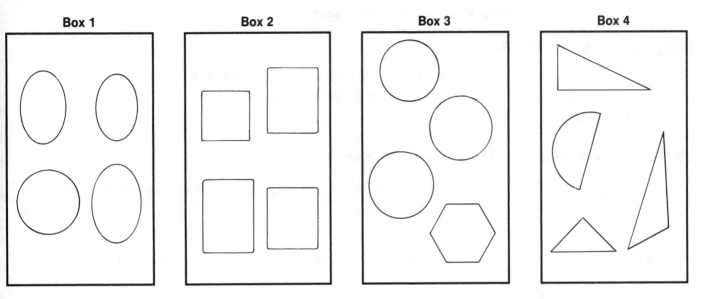

Box 1   Box 2   Box 3   Box 4

C Underline the correct answers.

① Maria's younger sister wants to know how to draw a picture of a house. Maria shows her how to draw the roof with (four, two, six, three) straight lines that form a triangle. The body of the house is a square with (eight, four, five, three) sides of the same size, explains Maria. Maria draws squares for the windows, too, yet the door and the chimney she makes in the shape of rectangles that have (five, six, two, four) sides but are not squares.

② In art class the students learned that an egg has (straight, curved) lines as does an ellipse. An orange has (straight, curved) lines as well, but is shaped like a circle.

③ The building in Washington, D.C., that is called the Pentagon has (three, four, five, six) sides. If it had (three, four, five, six) sides, perhaps it would be called the Hexagon. The Octagon might be a suitable name for a building with (six, five, eight, seven) sides.

④ Some of the nine shapes on page 11 have straight lines and some have curved lines. The (semi-circle, triangle, octagon) is the only shape that has both straight and curved lines.

12

Number Recognition

Learning Objective: *We will learn to recognize numbers and what they mean.*

Numbers are symbols that tell how many.

EXAMPLE: A number tells how many dots are on the domino.

___5___

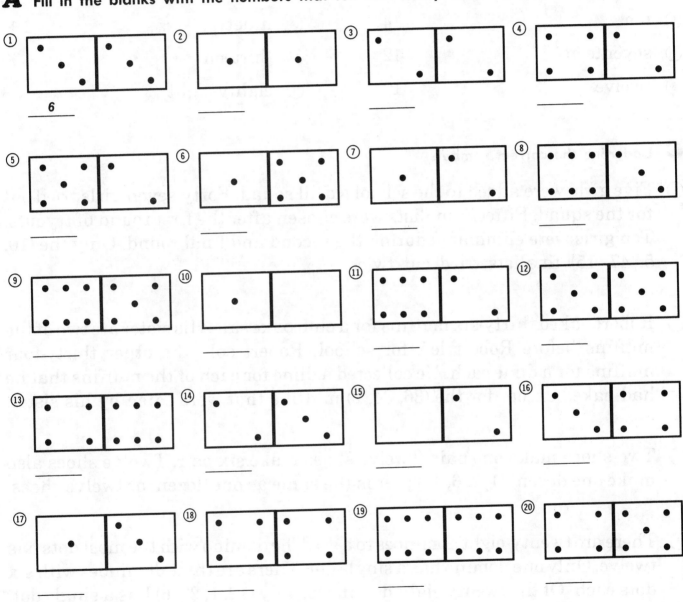

A Fill in the blanks with the numbers that tell how many dots are on the dominoes.

① ___6___

② _____

③ _____

④ _____

⑤ _____

⑥ _____

⑦ _____

⑧ _____

⑨ _____

⑩ _____

⑪ _____

⑫ _____

⑬ _____

⑭ _____

⑮ _____

⑯ _____

⑰ _____

⑱ _____

⑲ _____

⑳ _____

REMINDER: Write the definition of a number.

_____

_____

Unit 5 cont'd ☞

B Match the words with the numbers that have the same meanings.

①	five	8	⑨	four	3
②	eleven	11	⑩	sixty	56
③	twenty	5	⑪	three	60
④	eight	20	⑫	fifty-six	4
⑤	fourteen	17	⑬	one hundred	13
⑥	ten	14	⑭	ninety	100
⑦	seventeen	12	⑮	thirteen	90
⑧	twelve	10	⑯	eighty-eight	88

C Underline the correct numbers.

① Five girls were added to the school's drill squad. Forty-seven girls tried out for the squad. Fifteen finalists were chosen after the first round of tryouts. Ten girls were eliminated during the second and final round. Only the (10, 5, 47, 15) finalists tried out twice.

② Robert baked thirty-six muffins for a club bake sale. His sister ate two of the muffins before Robert left for school. Robert sold the other thirty-four muffins for a dime each. He collected a dime for each of the muffins that he had baked except for the (36, 34, 2) muffins that were eaten by his sister.

③ Two shoes make one pair. Twelve shoes make six pair. Twelve shoes also make one dozen. (1, 2, 6, 12) pair is the same as one dozen, or twelve shoes.

④ There are twenty-eight dominoes to a set. The domino with the most dots has twelve. Only one domino has a single dot. There are three dominoes with six dots each. Of the twenty-eight dominoes, only (12, 1, 28, 6) has a single dot.

⑤ There are nine known planets in our solar system. Earth is one of these. Earth is one of (9, 1, 16) known planets.

Comprehension Check

A Write the numbers that have the same meanings as these word names.

① _400_ four hundred
② _____ ninety-eight
③ _____ twenty-one
④ _____ seventy-seven
⑤ _____ thirty-two
⑥ _____ twelve
⑦ _____ sixty-five
⑧ _____ fifty-six
⑨ _____ five hundred
⑩ _____ four
⑪ _____ fourteen
⑫ _____ forty
⑬ _____ eleven
⑭ _____ one hundred
⑮ _____ ten
⑯ _____ ninety
⑰ _____ nineteen
⑱ _____ nine
⑲ _____ fifty-five
⑳ _____ twenty-five
㉑ _____ thirty
㉒ _____ sixty-one
㉓ _____ sixteen
㉔ _____ six
㉕ _____ eighty-nine
㉖ _____ three hundred
㉗ _____ seventy
㉘ _____ forty-seven
㉙ _____ twenty-three
㉚ _____ seventy-four

B Identify the number that occupies each space in each box.

①

a	b	c
6	4	3

_6_ a
_____ b
_____ c

②

a	b	c
7	5	2

_____ a
_____ b
_____ c

③

a	b	c
8	0	1

_____ a
_____ b
_____ c

④

a	b	c
9	9	9

_____ a
_____ b
_____ c

⑤

aaa	aa	a
1	2	0

_____ aaa
_____ aa
_____ a

⑥

aaa	aa	a
3	8	3

_____ aaa
_____ aa
_____ a

⑦

aaa	aa	a
2	2	5

_____ aaa
_____ aa
_____ a

⑧

aaa	aa	a
4	8	8

_____ aaa
_____ aa
_____ a

⑨

100	10	1
8	6	3

_____ 100
_____ 10
_____ 1

⑩

100	10	1
1	3	4

_____ 100
_____ 10
_____ 1

⑪

100	10	1
5	5	5

_____ 100
_____ 10
_____ 1

⑫

100	10	1
7	2	9

_____ 100
_____ 10
_____ 1

⑬

1000	100	10	1
4	5	8	4

_____ 1000
_____ 100
_____ 10
_____ 1

⑭

1000	100	10	1
7	2	9	6

_____ 1000
_____ 100
_____ 10
_____ 1

⑮

1000	100	10	1
5	0	6	7

_____ 1000
_____ 100
_____ 10
_____ 1

⑯

1000	100	10	1
9	8	8	8

_____ 1000
_____ 100
_____ 10
_____ 1

Test 1 cont'd

C In each row, name the shape and circle the one which is not the same size as the others.

① _____ circle _____

② _____

③ _____

④ _____

⑤ _____

⑥ _____

⑦ _____

⑧ _____

⑨ _____

Write a paragraph explaining where things are located in your classroom. Use directions such as "left," "right," "up," "down," "north," "south," "west," and "east."

_____

_____

_____

_____

_____

_____

_____

_____

_____

Number Sequence 1-25   Unit 6

Learning Objective: *We will learn to place the numbers 1-25 in their proper sequence.*

Sequence is the order in which things follow each other.

EXAMPLE: The number "1" comes before "2." The number "2" is followed by "3."
The sequence is "1, 2, 3."

A Fill in the blanks with the missing numbers.

① 1 2 3 4 __5__   ② 3 ___ 5 6 7   ③ 4 ___ 6 7 8   ④ 5 6 7 8 ___

⑤ 10 11 12 ___   ⑥ 14 15 ___ 17   ⑦ 12 13 ___ 15   ⑧ 16 17 18 ___

⑨ 19 20 ___ 22   ⑩ 21 22 23 ___   ⑪ 22 ___ 24 25   ⑫ ___ 2 3 4

⑬ ___ 8 9 10 11   ⑭ 15 16 ___ 18   ⑮ 9 ___ 11 12 13   ⑯ 11 12 13 ___

⑰ 20 21 ___ 23   ⑱ 17 18 19 ___   ⑲ ___ 7 8 9 10   ⑳ 2 ___ 4 5 6

㉑ 8 9 10 11 ___   ㉒ 13 14 ___ 16   ㉓ 18 ___ 20 21   ㉔ 22 23 24 ___

㉕ ___ 2 3 4 5 6   ㉖ 4 5 6 7 ___   ㉗ 9 10 ___ 12 13   ㉘ 5 6 ___ 8 9

B Fill in the blanks.

① one two _____ four five six _____ eight

② nine _____ eleven twelve _____ fourteen fifteen

③ _____ seventeen eighteen nineteen _____

④ twenty-one twenty-two _____ twenty-four _____

C Write the first twenty-five counting numbers in sequence.

_1_ _____

_____

REMINDER: *Write the definition of sequence.*

_____

_____

D Rearrange these number words in proper sequences.

① eight   five   seven   nine   six

_____ *five   six   seven   eight   nine* _____

② twenty-one   seventeen   nineteen   eighteen   twenty

_____

③ fifteen   thirteen   sixteen   fourteen   twelve

_____

④ twenty-five   twenty-one   twenty-three   twenty-four   twenty-two

_____

⑤ ten   twelve   nine   thirteen   eleven

_____

⑥ three   one   two   four   five

_____

E Write the numbers in sequence.

① After kindergarten, a student enters grade one. If the child progresses at an acceptable rate, he or she moves on to grades two, three, four, and five. The final level of elementary school is grade six. Junior high school customarily begins with grade seven. Before a student can pass on to becoming a high school freshman in grade nine, he or she must also complete grade eight, which follows directly after grade seven. After the freshman year comes grade ten, which is also called the sophomore year. The junior year, or grade 11, follows next. A passing junior will become a senior in grade 12 and will graduate afer this final year in high school. What are the twelve grades in school? _____

_____

② The city zoo is located on 25th Street. Members of the Science Club at Henderson High School need to map the route for an upcoming field trip. To get from the school parking lot to the zoo, a bus will first cross 13th Street, then 14th Street, 15th Street, and all successively numbered streets up to and including 25th Street.
Which numbered streets will the bus cross? _____

_____

18

Number Sequence 1-50

Learning Objective: *We will learn to place the numbers 1-50 in their proper sequence.*

Sequence is the order in which things follow each other.

EXAMPLES: The four numbers following 10 are 11, 12, 13, and 14.
The four numbers following 20 are 21, 22, 23, and 24.
The four numbers following 30 are 31, 32, 33, and 34.

A In sequence, list the four numbers that follow each specified number.

① 6 _7_ _8_ _9_ _10_ ② 25 __ __ __ __ ③ 13 __ __ __ __ ④ 39 __ __ __ __

⑤ 46 __ __ __ __ ⑥ 9 __ __ __ __ ⑦ 19 __ __ __ __ ⑧ 33 __ __ __ __

⑨ 42 __ __ __ __ ⑩ 1 __ __ __ __ ⑪ 16 __ __ __ __ ⑫ 22 __ __ __ __

⑬ 28 __ __ __ __ ⑭ 40 __ __ __ __ ⑮ 11 __ __ __ __ ⑯ 44 __ __ __ __

⑰ 21 __ __ __ __ ⑱ 35 __ __ __ __ ⑲ 3 __ __ __ __ ⑳ 36 __ __ __ __

B Fill in the blanks.

① twenty-six _____ _____ _____ _____

② thirty-one _____ _____ _____ _____

③ thirty-six _____ _____ _____ _____

④ forty-one _____ _____ _____ _____

⑤ forty-six _____ _____ _____ _____

C Write numbers 25-50 in sequence.

_25_ __ __ __ __ __ __ __ __ __ __ __ __

__ __ __ __ __ __ __ __ __ __ __ __ __

REMINDER: Write the definition of sequence.

_____

_____

Unit 7 cont'd ☛

D Rearrange these number words in proper sequences.

① twenty-six   twenty-eight   twenty-five   twenty-seven   twenty-nine
twenty-five _____   _____   _____   _____

② thirty-five   thirty-three   thirty-six   thirty-four   thirty-seven
_____   _____   _____   _____   _____

③ forty-eight   fifty   forty-six   forty-nine   forty-seven
_____   _____   _____   _____   _____

④ twenty-three   twenty-six   twenty-four   twenty-two   twenty-five
_____   _____   _____   _____   _____

⑤ fourteen   eighteen   seventeen   fifteen   sixteen
_____   _____   _____   _____   _____

⑥ six   three   four   two   five
_____   _____   _____   _____   _____

E Write the numbers in sequence.

① After graduating from high school at age 18, Melissa worked as a teller at a local bank. One year later, at age 19, she enrolled at the state university. She spent the next four birthdays as a student at MSU. Birthdays _____, _____, _____, and _____ were spent at college.

② On her first wedding anniversary, Kate received a single red rose from her husband, Phillip. The next year she received two roses, the third year she received three and so on until buying the anniversary roses became quite an expensive gesture. After twelve years of marriage, Phillip decided to limit future anniversary flowers to a dozen roses. From anniversary number 12 through anniversary number 24, Kate received a dozen roses. On the 25th anniversary of her wedding, however, Kate opened the box to find 25 beautiful red roses. For each of the 24 years that followed, Phillip again sent the customary dozen roses. The golden anniversary brought another surprise. To celebrate 50 years of marriage, Phillip sent Kate 50 perfect red roses. On which anniversaries did Phillip send a dozen roses? _____, _____, _____, _____, _____, _____, _____, _____, _____, _____, _____,
_____, _____, _____, _____, _____, _____, _____, _____, _____, _____, _____,
_____, _____, _____, _____, _____, _____, _____, _____, _____, _____, _____,
_____, and _____ .

Number Sequence 1-100

Learning Objective: *We will learn to place the numbers 1-100 in their proper sequence.*

Sequence is the order in which things follow each other.

EXAMPLES: The three numbers between 1 and 5 are 2, 3, and 4.
The three numbers between 41 and 45 are 42, 43, and 44.
The three numbers between 91 and 95 are 92, 93, and 94.

A Fill in the blanks so that the numbers are in sequence.

① 10 *11 12 13* 14   ② 56 __ __ __ 60   ③ 22 __ __ __ 26   ④ 89 __ __ __ 93

⑤ 73 __ __ __ 77   ⑥ 41 __ __ __ 45   ⑦ 64 __ __ __ 68   ⑧ 37 __ __ __ 41

⑨ 8 __ __ __ 12   ⑩ 95 __ __ __ 99   ⑪ 52 __ __ __ 56   ⑫ 15 __ __ __ 19

⑬ 27 __ __ __ 31   ⑭ 69 __ __ __ 73   ⑮ 46 __ __ __ 50   ⑯ 32 __ __ __ 36

⑰ 60 __ __ __ 64   ⑱ 83 __ __ __ 87   ⑲ 4 __ __ __ 8   ⑳ 78 __ __ __ 82

B Fill in the blanks.

① fifty-one ___*fifty-two*___ ___*fifty-three*___ ___*fifty-four*___ fifty-five

② sixty-seven _____ _____ _____ seventy-one

③ eighty-eight _____ _____ _____ ninety-two

④ seventy-three _____ _____ _____ seventy-seven

⑤ ninety-six _____ _____ _____ one hundred

⑥ forty-nine _____ _____ _____ fifty-three

⑦ fifty-five _____ _____ _____ fifty-nine

REMINDER: Write the definition of sequence.

_____

_____

Unit 8 cont'd ☞

C Rearrange in proper sequences.

① seventy-nine   eighty-one   seventy-eight   eighty-two   eighty

_____ _____ _____ _____ _____

② thirty-five   thirty-two   thirty-six   thirty-three   thirty-four

_____ _____ _____ _____ _____

③ sixty-one   sixty-three   sixty   sixty-two   fifty-nine

_____ _____ _____ _____ _____

④ ninety-seven   ninety-nine   ninety-six   one hundred   ninety-eight

_____ _____ _____ _____ _____

D Write numbers 1-100 in sequence.

1 _____

_____

_____

_____

_____

E Write the numbers in sequence.

① Following a serious accident, Willis was confined to a hospital bed. During his stay in the hospital, he learned to knit. His first major knitting project was a sweater for his favorite nurse. Using a pattern from a needlework magazine, Willis started at the neck and increased the number of stitches per row every fifth row until a yoke of 14 rows was completed. Rows 1, _____ , _____ , and 4 had the same number of stitches. Rows 5, _____ , _____ , _____ , and 9 were increased by a few stitches, and rows 10, _____ , _____ , _____ , and 14 were increased by a few more stitches.

② During tryouts for the marching band, contestants were assigned numbers for identification. They competed in groups of 10. One hundred musicians were divided into 10 groups and asked to play a selected piece of music. In the first group were contestants 1, 2, 3, 4, 5, 6, 7, 8, 9, and 10. Competing in the second group were the contestants sequentially numbered 11, 12, 13, 14, 15, 16, 17, 18, 19, and 20. The next group of 10 included contestants 21, _____ , _____ , _____ , _____ , _____ , _____ , _____ , _____ and 30. Contestants 31, _____ , _____ , _____ , _____ , _____ , _____ , _____ , _____ and 40 were in the fourth group, and so the grouping continued through the tenth and final set of contestants numbered 91, _____ , _____ , _____ , _____ , _____ , _____ , _____ , _____ and _____ .

Counting by 1

Learning Objective: *We will learn to count by 1 from 1 to 100.*

Counting is the naming of numbers in the proper order so that we may find the total number of units in a group.

EXAMPLE: There are 10 units in this group.

1	2	3	4	5	6	7	8	9	10

A Circle each unit within a group and write the total number of units in the space provided.

① ___20___

② _____

③ _____

④ _____

⑤ _____

⑥ _____

⑦ _____

⑧ _____

⑨ _____

REMINDER: Write the definition of counting.

_____

_____

Unit 9 cont'd ☞

B Number each unit in a group and write the total number in the space at the left.

① __38__ ⌒ ⌒ ⌒ ⌒ ⌒ ⌒ ⌒ ⌒ ⌒ ⌒ ⌒ ⌒ ⌒ ⌒ ⌒ ⌒ ⌒ ⌒ ⌒
__1__ ___ ___ ___ ___ ___ ___ ___ ___ ___ ___ ___ ___ ___ ___ ___ ___ ___ ___

⌒ ⌒ ⌒ ⌒ ⌒ ⌒ ⌒ ⌒ ⌒ ⌒ ⌒ ⌒ ⌒ ⌒ ⌒ ⌒ ⌒ ⌒
___ ___ ___ ___ ___ ___ ___ ___ ___ ___ ___ ___ ___ ___ ___ ___ ___ ___

② ___ 🚗 🚗 🚗 🚗 🚗 🚗 🚗 🚗 🚗 🚗 🚗 🚗 🚗 🚗 🚗 🚗 🚗 🚗 🚗
___ ___ ___ ___ ___ ___ ___ ___ ___ ___ ___ ___ ___ ___ ___ ___ ___ ___ ___

③ ___ 🚁 🚁 🚁 🚁 🚁 🚁 🚁 🚁 🚁 🚁 🚁 🚁 🚁 🚁
___ ___ ___ ___ ___ ___ ___ ___ ___ ___ ___ ___ ___ ___

④ ___ ☕ ☕ ☕ ☕ ☕ ☕ ☕ ☕ ☕ ☕
___ ___ ___ ___ ___ ___ ___ ___ ___ ___

⑤ ___ ✉ ✉ ✉ ✉ ✉ ✉ ✉ ✉ ✉ ✉ ✉ ✉ ✉ ✉ ✉
___ ___ ___ ___ ___ ___ ___ ___ ___ ___ ___ ___ ___ ___ ___

C Count by 1 to 100 and fill in the missing numbers.

1 2 3 4 __5__ 6 7 ___ 9 10 11 ___ ___ 14 15 16 17 ___ ___ ___ 21

22 23 24 ___ 26 ___ 28 ___ ___ ___ 32 33 34 ___ 36 ___ ___ ___ 39 40 41 ___

43 44 ___ 46 47 48 ___ 50 51 52 ___ 54 55 56 ___ ___ ___ 60 ___ ___ 63

64 65 ___ 67 68 69 70 ___ ___ ___ 74 ___ 76 77 78 79 ___ ___ 82 ___ ___

___ 86 87 88 89 ___ ___ 92 93 ___ 95 ___ ___ ___ 99 ___

D Fill in the blanks with the correct numbers.

① For April's tenth birthday, her mother gave her a bracelet with a gold charm shaped like a four-leaf clover. The next year April received a charm in the shape of a basketball. Birthday number 12 brought a tiny pair of gold ballet slippers to add to the bracelet, and with birthday number 13 came a minature typewriter. At age 14, the year that she won the art award, April was given a replica of an easel for her birthday bracelet. The next year she added a paint brush, and by the next year, when she was given the charm that said "Sweet 16," her bracelet was nearly full. There were _____ charms in all.

② Hank's new pet hen laid an egg every single morning without fail. It laid one on Monday. It laid one on Tuesday. It laid one each morning on Wednesday, Thursday, Friday, Saturday, and Sunday and on the following Monday, Tuesday, Wednesday, Thursday, Friday, Saturday, and Sunday. The next day Hank told all his friends about his very dependable hen and even invited some of his closest comrades to meet the creature eye to eye. The hen was out in the barnyard when Hank and his friends arrived. Hank checked the nest and found no egg. It was nearly noon. They all waited. They waited some more. Finally, Hank's father offered an explanation, "This is Labor Day," he told the boys. "Even farm animals deserve time off." Hank's hen laid _____ eggs in all.

Counting by 2

Learning Objective: *We will learn to count by 2 from 2 to 200.*

Counting is the naming of numbers in the proper order so that we may find the total number of units in a group.

EXAMPLE: There are 12 units in this group.

★★ ★★ ★★ ★★ ★★ ★★

A Circle each pair of units within a group. Write the total number of units in the space at the left.

① ___10___ ★★ ★★ ★★ ★★ ★★

② _____ ★★ ★★ ★★ ★★ ★★ ★★ ★★ ★★ ★★ ★★ ★★

③ _____ ★★ ★★ ★★ ★★ ★★ ★★ ★★ ★★ ★★

④ _____ ★★ ★★ ★★ ★★ ★★ ★★ ★★

⑤ _____ ★★ ★★ ★★ ★★ ★★ ★★ ★★ ★★ ★★ ★★ ★★ ★★ ★★ ★★ ★★

⑥ _____ ★★ ★★ ★★ ★★ ★★ ★★ ★★ ★★

⑦ _____ ★★ ★★ ★★ ★★ ★★ ★★ ★★ ★★ ★★ ★★ ★★ ★★

⑧ _____ ★★ ★★ ★★ ★★ ★★ ★★

⑨ _____ ★★ ★★ ★★ ★★ ★★ ★★ ★★ ★★ ★★ ★★

REMINDER: Write the definition of counting.

_____

_____

Unit 10 cont'd ☞

B Count by two and write the total number in the space at the left.

① _____ ★★ ★★ ★★ ★★ ★★ ★★ ★★ ★★ ★★ ★★ ★★ ★★ ★★ ★★ ★★ ★★

② _____ ★★ ★★ ★★ ★★ ★★ ★★ ★★ ★★ ★★ ★★ ★★ ★★ ★★

③ _____ ★★ ★★ ★★ ★★ ★★ ★★ ★★ ★★ ★★ ★★ ★★ ★★ ★★
           ★★ ★★ ★★ ★★ ★★ ★★ ★★ ★★ ★★ ★★ ★★ ★★

④ _____ ★★ ★★ ★★ ★★ ★★ ★★ ★★ ★★ ★★ ★★ ★★
           ★★ ★★ ★★ ★★ ★★ ★★ ★★ ★★ ★★ ★★ ★★

⑤ _____ ★★ ★★ ★★ ★★ ★★ ★★ ★★ ★★ ★★

C Count by 2 to 200 and fill in the missing numbers.

2 4 **6** 8 10 12 ___ ___ 18 ___ 22 ___ ___ ___ 30 ___ ___ ___ 38

40 42 44 ___ 48 ___ ___ 54 56 ___ ___ 62 64 ___ ___ 70 ___ 74 ___

___ 80 ___ ___ 86 88 90 92 94 ___ 98 ___ ___ ___ 106 ___ ___ 112 ___

___ ___ 120 122 124 ___ ___ 130 ___ ___ 136 138 ___ 142 ___ 146 148 150 152

___ ___ ___ 160 ___ ___ ___ 170 ___ ___ ___ 178 180 ___ ___ 186 188 ___

192 194 196 ___ ___

D Fill in the blanks with the correct numbers.

① Ned sailed around the world. On route, he noted the creatures he saw. Ned was especially fascinated by the whales. He noted two of each species of whales: two bottle-nosed whales, two beluga whales, two killer whales, two pilot whales, two baleen whales, two gray whales, two right whales, two blue whales, and two narwhals. How many whales did Ned see? _____

② George became an uncle to twin boys. For his newborn nephews' birthday, George shopped for two of everything. He bought two hats, two coats, two bottle warmers, two blankets, two rattles, two teddy bears, and two bibs. How many gifts did George buy? _____

③ Alicia invited only couples to her party. She invited Joan and Alan, David and Celia, Marianne and Marc, Lennie and Pat, Rita and Preston, and Janice and Kyle. She also invited Greg and Meredith, Brent and Sharon, Tony and Cecile, Samantha and Irvin, Zachary and Sybil, and Mallory and Lee. How many people did Alicia invite to her party? _____

Comprehension Check

Test 2

A Fill in the blanks with the missing numbers.

① 6 _7_ 8 9 10   ② 34 35 36 37 ___   ③ 81 82 ___ 84 85   ④ 16 17 ___ 19 20

⑤ ___ 93 94 95 96   ⑥ 53 54 ___ 56 57   ⑦ 20 21 22 ___ 24   ⑧ 75 ___ 77 78 79

⑨ 43 ___ ___ ___ 47   ⑩ 7 ___ ___ ___ 11   ⑪ 64 ___ ___ ___ 68   ⑫ 19 ___ ___ ___ 23

⑬ 31 ___ ___ ___ 35   ⑭ 88 ___ ___ ___ 92   ⑮ 2 ___ ___ ___ 6   ⑯ 77 ___ ___ ___ 81

⑰ 1 ___ ___ ___ ___   ⑱ 12 ___ ___ ___ ___   ⑲ 60 ___ ___ ___ ___   ⑳ 96 ___ ___ ___ ___

B Rearrange in proper sequences.

①	seventeen	sixteen	nineteen	fifteen	eighteen
	fifteen				
②	thirty	twenty-seven	twenty-nine	thirty-one	twenty-eight
③	seventy-six	seventy-four	seventy-three	seventy-five	seventy-seven
④	ninety-eight	ninety-five	ninety-seven	ninety-four	ninety-six
⑤	twelve	fourteen	ten	eleven	thirteen
⑥	fifty-four	fifty-two	fifty-three	fifty-six	fifty-five
⑦	seventy-two	seventy	sixty-nine	seventy-one	sixty-eight
⑧	eight	five	six	four	seven
⑨	forty-one	forty-three	thirty-nine	forty-one	forty

Test 2 cont'd ☞

C Number each unit in a group and write the total number in the space at the left.

① ___ ✈ ✈ ✈ ✈ ✈ ✈ ✈ ✈ ✈
  ___ ___ ___ ___ ___ ___ ___ ___ ___

② ___ ♥ ♥ ♥ ♥ ♥ ♥ ♥ ♥ ♥ ♥ ♥ ♥ ♥ ♥ ♥ ♥ ♥ ♥
  ___ ___ ___ ___ ___ ___ ___ ___ ___ ___ ___ ___ ___ ___ ___ ___ ___ ___

③ ___ 🚌 🚌 🚌 🚌 🚌 🚌 🚌 🚌 🚌 🚌 🚌 🚌
  ___ ___ ___ ___ ___ ___ ___ ___ ___ ___ ___ ___

D Circle each pair of units in a group. Write the total number of units in the space.

① _____ ⌐ ⌐   ⌐ ⌐   ⌐ ⌐   ⌐ ⌐   ⌐ ⌐   ⌐ ⌐

② _____ ⍦ ⍦   ⍦ ⍦   ⍦ ⍦   ⍦ ⍦   ⍦ ⍦   ⍦ ⍦   ⍦ ⍦

③ _____ 🚗 🚗   🚗 🚗   🚗 🚗   🚗 🚗

E Count by 1 from 1 to 100.

1 _*2*_ ___ ___ ___ ___ ___ ___ ___ ___ ___ ___ ___ ___ ___ ___ ___ ___ ___ ___ ___

___ ___ ___ ___ ___ ___ ___ ___ ___ ___ ___ ___ ___ ___ ___ ___ ___ ___ ___ ___

___ ___ ___ ___ ___ ___ ___ ___ ___ ___ ___ ___ ___ ___ ___ ___ ___ ___ ___ ___

___ ___ ___ ___ ___ ___ ___ ___ ___ ___ ___ ___ ___ ___ ___ ___ ___ ___ ___ ___

___ ___ ___ _100_

F Count by 2 from 2 to 200.

2 _*4*_ ___ ___ ___ ___ ___ ___ ___ ___ ___ ___ ___ ___ ___ ___ ___ ___ ___ ___ ___

___ ___ ___ ___ ___ ___ ___ ___ ___ ___ ___ ___ ___ ___ ___ ___ ___ ___ ___ ___

___ ___ ___ ___ ___ ___ ___ ___ ___ ___ ___ ___ ___ ___ ___ ___ ___ ___ ___ ___

___ ___ ___ ___ ___ ___ ___ ___ ___ ___ ___ ___ ___ ___ ___ ___ ___ ___ ___ ___

___ ___ ___ _200_

List 10 things that you buy in units of 1.   **List 10 things that you buy in pairs.**

① _____   ① _____
② _____   ② _____
③ _____   ③ _____
④ _____   ④ _____
⑤ _____   ⑤ _____
⑥ _____   ⑥ _____
⑦ _____   ⑦ _____
⑧ _____   ⑧ _____
⑨ _____   ⑨ _____
⑩ _____   ⑩ _____

Counting by 3

Learning Objective: *We will learn to count by 3 from 3 to 300.*

Counting is the naming of numbers in the proper order so that we may find the total number of units in a group.

EXAMPLE: There are 9 units in this group.

★★★   ★★★   ★★★

A Circle every three units within a group. Write the total number of units in the space at the left.

① ___12___ ★★★ ★★★ ★★★ ★★★

② _____ ★★★ ★★★ ★★★ ★★★ ★★★ ★★★

③ _____ ★★★ ★★★

④ _____ ★★★ ★★★ ★★★ ★★★ ★★★ ★★★ ★★★ ★★★

⑤ _____ ★★★ ★★★ ★★★

⑥ _____ ★★★ ★★★ ★★★ ★★★ ★★★

⑦ _____ ★★★ ★★★ ★★★ ★★★ ★★★ ★★★ ★★★

⑧ _____ ★★★

⑨ _____ ★★★ ★★★ ★★★ ★★★ ★★★ ★★★ ★★★ ★★★ ★★★ ★★★

REMINDER: Write the definition of counting.

_____

_____

Unit 11 cont'd 👉

B Count by three and write the total number in the space at the left.

① _____ ◆◆◆ ◆◆◆ ◆◆◆ ◆◆◆ ◆◆◆ ◆◆◆ ◆◆◆
          ◆◆◆ ◆◆◆ ◆◆◆ ◆◆◆ ◆◆◆ ◆◆◆ ◆◆◆

② _____ ◆◆◆ ◆◆◆ ◆◆◆ ◆◆◆ ◆◆◆ ◆◆◆ ◆◆◆ ◆◆◆

③ _____ ◆◆◆ ◆◆◆ ◆◆◆ ◆◆◆ ◆◆◆ ◆◆◆ ◆◆◆
          ◆◆◆ ◆◆◆ ◆◆◆ ◆◆◆ ◆◆◆ ◆◆◆ ◆◆◆

④ _____ ◆◆◆ ◆◆◆ ◆◆◆ ◆◆◆ ◆◆◆ ◆◆◆ ◆◆◆ ◆◆◆ ◆◆◆
          ◆◆◆ ◆◆◆ ◆◆◆ ◆◆◆ ◆◆◆ ◆◆◆ ◆◆◆ ◆◆◆

⑤ _____ ◆◆◆ ◆◆◆ ◆◆◆ ◆◆◆ ◆◆◆ ◆◆◆

C Count by 3 to 300 and fill in the missing numbers.

3 __6__ ____ 12 15 ____ 21 24 27 ____ ____ 36 ____ ____ ____ 48 51 54 ____

____ ____ 66 ____ ____ ____ 78 81 84 87 ____ 93 ____ 99 102 ____ ____ 111 114

117 ____ ____ 126 129 132 ____ ____ 141 144 147 ____ ____ ____ 159 162 165 ____ 171

174 ____ ____ 183 186 189 192 ____ ____ ____ 204 207 210 213 216 ____ 222 225 228

____ ____ 237 ____ 243 ____ ____ 252 255 258 261 ____ ____ 270 ____ 276 279 282 ____

____ 291 294 ____ ____

D Fill in the blanks with the correct numbers.

① For the kindergarten's Easter egg hunt, Ms. Blackwell brought brightly colored eggs. She had dyed three eggs orange, three eggs red, three eggs purple, three eggs blue, three eggs yellow, three eggs pink, three eggs green, and three eggs brown. How many eggs did Ms. Blackwell dye for the hunt? _____

② Several members of the senior class drove to school each day. Three drove convertibles. Three drove pickup trucks. Three drove jeeps. Three more drove vans. How many seniors drove to school? _____

③ The Gardening Club planted trees along the sides of the school building. Club members planted three dogwoods, three maples, three weeping willows, three oaks, three redbuds, three poplars, and three mimosas. How many trees did the club members plant? _____

④ To get to the national competition, Henderson's debate team challenged many different schools. The team defeated three opponents at the local level and went on to win over three more schools at the regional meet. At the state contest, the Henderson team triumphed over the top three teams in Missouri. How many teams did Henderson defeat before the national meet? _____

Counting by 4

Learning Objective: *We will learn to count by 4 from 4 to 400.*

Counting is the naming of numbers in the proper order so that we may find the total number of units in a group.

EXAMPLE: There are 12 units in this group.

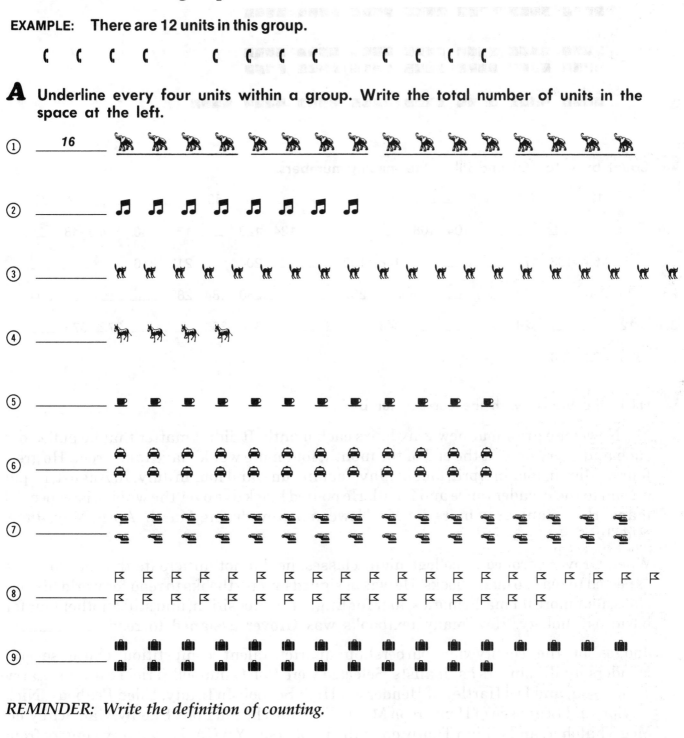

A Underline every four units within a group. Write the total number of units in the space at the left.

① _____16_____

② _____

③ _____

④ _____

⑤ _____

⑥ _____

⑦ _____

⑧ _____

⑨ _____

REMINDER: Write the definition of counting.

Unit 12 cont'd ☞

B Count by four and write the total number in the space at the left.

① __60__ ▪▪▪▪ ▪▪▪▪ ▪▪▪▪ ▪▪▪▪ ▪▪▪▪ ▪▪▪▪ ▪▪▪▪ ▪▪▪▪
               ▪▪▪▪ ▪▪▪▪ ▪▪▪▪ ▪▪▪▪ ▪▪▪▪ ▪▪▪▪ ▪▪▪▪

② _____ ▪▪▪▪ ▪▪▪▪ ▪▪▪▪ ▪▪▪▪ ▪▪▪▪ ▪▪▪▪ ▪▪▪▪ ▪▪▪▪ ▪▪▪▪ ▪▪▪▪ ▪▪▪▪

③ _____ ▪▪▪▪ ▪▪▪▪ ▪▪▪▪ ▪▪▪▪ ▪▪▪▪ ▪▪▪▪ ▪▪▪▪

④ _____ ▪▪▪▪ ▪▪▪▪ ▪▪▪▪ ▪▪▪▪ ▪▪▪▪ ▪▪▪▪ ▪▪▪▪
               ▪▪▪▪ ▪▪▪▪ ▪▪▪▪ ▪▪▪▪ ▪▪▪▪ ▪▪▪▪ ▪▪▪▪

⑤ _____ ▪▪▪▪ ▪▪▪▪ ▪▪▪▪ ▪▪▪▪ ▪▪▪▪ ▪▪▪▪ ▪▪▪▪ ▪▪▪▪

C Count by 4 to 400 and fill in the missing numbers.

4   8   12   _16_   20   24   ___   ___   36   40   44   ___   52   56   ___   ___   ___   72   76

80   ___   ___   ___   ___   ___   104   108   ___   ___   ___   124   128   ___   136   140   144   148   ___

___   ___   164   168   172   ___   ___   184   188   192   ___   ___   204   ___   212   216   ___   ___   ___

232   236   240   ___   248   ___   ___   260   264   268   ___   ___   280   284   288   ___   ___   ___   304

308   312   ___   ___   324   328   ___   ___   340   ___   ___   ___   356   360   ___   ___   ___   372   376   ___

___   388   392   396   ___

D Fill in the blanks with the correct numbers.

① Mr. Newcomb grew four new gray hairs each month. It didn't matter that he pulled out each and every one. At the end of the month, four more would have taken root. He grew four in March, four in April, four in May, four in June, and four in July. In August, he put an end to the invaders once and for all. He poured black dye over the whole disrespectful mane. How many gray hairs did Mr. Newcomb grow during March, April, May, June, and July? _____

② When Grover enrolled in college night classes, he did not anticipate that he would be expected to read so many books. He was assigned four textbooks to read for world history class, four more for mathematics, four for English composition, and still another four for basic psychology. How many textbooks was Grover assigned to read? _____

③ Judges at the countywide barbershop quartet talent competition chose several Hendersonville singers as finalists. Selected were Bob Campbell, Tricia Stevens, Larry Thompson, and Del Hartley of Henderson High School; Jo Brady, Ellen Peabody, Nick Taylor, and Lee Olsen of Henderson Methodist Church; and Polly Shelby, Gail Schuyler, Meg Thatcher, and Lillian Thornton of the Henderson YWCA. How many singers from Hendersonville were chosen as finalists? _____

Counting by 5

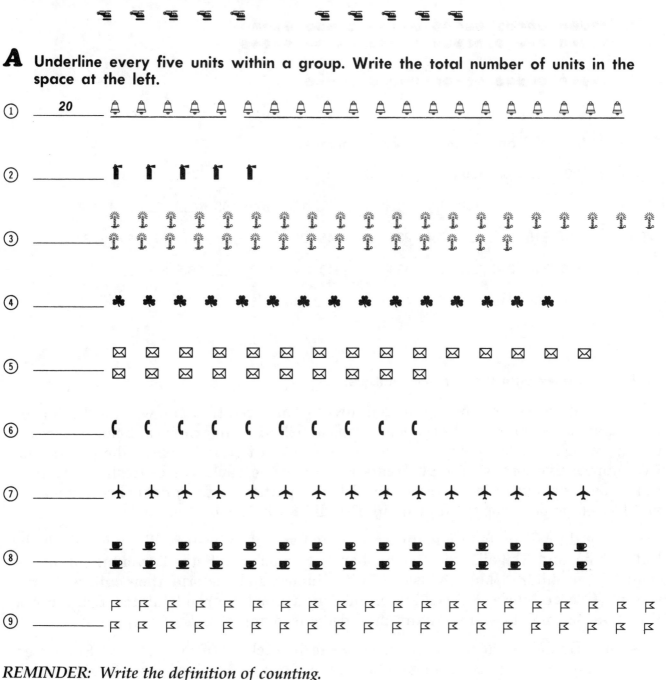

Learning
Objective: *We will learn to count by 5 from 5 to 500.*

Counting is the naming of numbers in the proper order so that we may find the total number of units in a group.

EXAMPLE: There are 10 units in this group.

A Underline every five units within a group. Write the total number of units in the space at the left.

① ___20___

② _____

③ _____

④ _____

⑤ _____

⑥ _____

⑦ _____

⑧ _____

⑨ _____

REMINDER: Write the definition of counting.

_____

_____

B Count by five and write the total number in the blank at the left.

① _____ ••••• ••••• ••••• ••••• ••••• •••••
          ••••• ••••• ••••• ••••• •••••

② _____ ••••• ••••• ••••• ••••• ••••• ••••• •••••

③ _____ ••••• ••••• ••••• ••••• ••••• ••••• ••••• •••••

④ _____ ••••• ••••• ••••• ••••• ••••• •••••
          ••••• ••••• ••••• ••••• ••••• •••••

⑤ _____ ••••• ••••• ••••• ••••• •••••

C Count by 5 to 500 and fill in the missing numbers.

5 _10_ ____ 20 ____ 30 35 ____ 45 50 55 ____ ____ ____ 75 80 85 90 ____

____ 105 110 ____ ____ ____ 130 135 ____ ____ ____ 155 160 165 ____ ____ ____ 185 ____

195 200 ____ 210 215 ____ ____ 230 235 ____ 245 250 ____ ____ ____ 270 275 280 ____

____ ____ 300 305 310 315 ____ ____ 330 ____ 340 345 350 ____ 360 365 ____ ____ ____

385 390 ____ ____ 405 410 ____ 420 425 ____ ____ 440 445 ____ ____ ____ 465 ____ 475

____ ____ 490 ____ ____

D Fill in the blanks with the correct numbers.

① When asked her favorite hobby, Karen always answered that she was a collector. In particular, she would add, she collected tropical fish. Her aquariums at home housed an ever-growing assortment of swimmers. There were five tigerfish, five mollies, five scats, five guppies, five lungfish, five glass cats, and five coolie loaches in the freshwater tanks. In the marine tanks resided five surgeonfish, five pufferfish, five prickly leatherjackets, and five emperor snappers. How many fish did Karen's collection include? _____

② Attending the Wilson family reunion were the five Wilson sisters, Winona, Elizabeth, Ruth, Tillie, and Abigail; their five husbands, Samuel, Eli, Seth, Trevor, and Jim; the couples' five children, May, Winslow, Edith, James, and Victoria; their children's five spouses, George, Maria, Walter, Marge, and Ernest; and five grandchildren, Betsy, Barb, Kitty, Jacob, and Lee. How many attended the reunion? _____

③ Freshman English students were asked to write limericks of five verses each. Submitted the next day were five verses about a talking textbook, five verses about linking verbs, five verses about a telephone that knew too much, five verses about tooth decay, five verses about gym socks that took over a locker, and five verses about a man who misplaced his eyebrows. How many verses were submitted? _____

Counting by 10

Learning
Objective: *We will learn to count by 10.*

Counting is the naming of numbers in the proper order so that we may find the total number of units in a group.

EXAMPLE: There are 20 units in this group.

A Underline every ten units within a group. Write the total number of units in the space at the left.

① ___30___

② _____

③ _____

④ _____

⑤ _____

⑥ _____

⑦ _____

⑧ _____

⑨ _____

REMINDER: Write the definition of counting.

_____

_____

Unit 14 cont'd ☞

B Count by ten and write the total number in the blank at the left.

① _____ ▪▪▪▪▪▪▪▪▪▪ ▪▪▪▪▪▪▪▪▪▪ ▪▪▪▪▪▪▪▪▪▪ ▪▪▪▪▪▪▪▪▪▪ ▪▪▪▪▪▪▪▪▪▪

② _____ ▪▪▪▪▪▪▪▪▪▪ ▪▪▪▪▪▪▪▪▪▪ ▪▪▪▪▪▪▪▪▪▪

③ _____ ▪▪▪▪▪▪▪▪▪▪ ▪▪▪▪▪▪▪▪▪▪ ▪▪▪▪▪▪▪▪▪▪ ▪▪▪▪▪▪▪▪▪▪

④ _____ ▪▪▪▪▪▪▪▪▪▪ ▪▪▪▪▪▪▪▪▪▪

⑤ _____ ▪▪▪▪▪▪▪▪▪▪ ▪▪▪▪▪▪▪▪▪▪ ▪▪▪▪▪▪▪▪▪▪ ▪▪▪▪▪▪▪▪▪▪
▪▪▪▪▪▪▪▪▪▪ ▪▪▪▪▪▪▪▪▪▪

C Count by 10 to 1,000 and fill in the missing numbers.

_10_ ___ ___ 40 50 60 ___ 80 90 ___ ___ ___ 130 140 150 ___ 170 ___ ___

200 210 220 ___ ___ ___ ___ 270 280 290 ___ ___ 320 ___ ___ ___ 360 370 380

___ 400 410 ___ ___ 440 450 ___ ___ ___ 490 500 510 ___ ___ 540 550 ___ ___

580 ___ ___ ___ 620 630 640 650 ___ ___ ___ 690 700 710 ___ ___ ___ 750 760

770 ___ 790 ___ ___ 820 830 ___ ___ 860 870 880 ___ 900 ___ ___ ___ 940 ___

___ 970 980 990 _____

D Fill in the blanks with the correct numbers.

① The cast and crew of the junior play ordered pizzas to go after the last dress rehearsal before opening night. Each pizza was cut into 10 servings or slices. There were 10 slices of sausage pizza, 10 slices of hamburger pizza, 10 slices of mushroom pizza, 10 slices of pepperoni, 10 slices of black olive, 10 slices of cheese and 10 slices of taco pizza. How many slices were ordered? _____

② Trimming the Christmas tree is an activity in which every member of the Stephens family takes part. Around the bottom of the tree are hung 10 silver bells. Just above these belong the 10 candy canes. Continuing up the tree are circles of 10 wooden horses, 10 gold stars, 10 pine cones, 10 red apples, 10 green balls, 10 tiny angels, and 10 minature presents. How many ornaments hang from the Stephens' tree? _____

③ Kurt enrolled in a 10-day summer camp. The day before leaving for camp, Kurt packed 10 changes of clothes. He packed 10 pairs of socks, 10 changes of underwear, 10 T-shirts, 10 pairs of jeans, and 10 sweatshirts. He also packed 10 postcards to send home, 10 postage stamps, 10 candy bars for midnight snacks, 10 books, and 10 razor blades for a fresh shave each morning. How many items did Kurt pack? _____

Patterns in Counting

Learning Objective: *We will learn to recognize patterns of numbers.*

Patterns serve as examples to be imitated.

EXAMPLE: The pattern 1 2 3 1 2 3 1 2 3 1 2 3...
would continue ...1 2 3 1 2 3 1 2 3...

A Study the patterns and fill in the missing numbers.

① 7 8 9 10 7 8 9 10 _7_ 8 9 ___ ___ 8 9 ___

② 3 5 3 5 3 5 ___ ___ 3 5 3 5 3 ___ ___ 5

③ 1 2 8 14 1 2 8 14 1 2 ___ ___ 1 ___ 8 ___

④ 7 7 7 4 7 7 7 4 ___ 7 7 ___ 7 ___ ___ 4

⑤ 8 8 8 2 6 6 6 2 4 4 ___ ___ 2 2 ___ ___

⑥ 2 2 3 5 5 3 8 8 ___ 11 ___ 3 14 ___

⑦ 4 4 0 0 8 8 0 0 10 ___ ___ 0 14 ___ 0 ___

⑧ 1 2 2 2 1 4 4 4 ___ 6 6 ___ 1 ___ 8 ___

⑨ 2 4 6 1 8 10 12 1 14 ___ 18 ___ 20 ___ ___ 1

⑩ 1 3 2 5 7 2 9 11 ___ 13 ___ 2 ___ 19 ___

⑪ 3 6 9 10 12 15 18 19 21 ___ ___ 28 ___ 33 36 ___

⑫ 2 4 8 10 12 16 18 ___ 24 26 28 ___ ___ 36 ___ 42

⑬ 1 3 5 7 9 11 ___ 15 ___ 19 21 23 ___ ___ 29 31

⑭ 7 14 21 28 ___ 42 49 56 63 ___ 77 84 91 ___ 105 ___

⑮ 1 2 3 4 5 ___ 7 8 9 10 11 ___ 13 ___ ___ 16

⑯ 6 9 15 18 24 27 33 36 ___ 45 51 ___ ___ 63 69 ___

⑰ 1 2 3 5 6 7 9 10 ___ 13 14 ___ 17 ___ ___

⑱ 2 4 6 7 8 10 12 13 14 ___ 18 ___ ___ 22 24 ___

⑲ 6 0 6 0 8 0 8 0 ___ 0 10 ___ ___ 0 12 ___

⑳ 1 1 1 2 3 3 3 4 5 ___ 5 ___ 7 ___ ___ 8

㉑ 1 2 3 4 6 8 10 12 15 18 ___ ___ 28 32 ___ ___

㉒ 3 6 9 12 15 18 ___ 24 27 30 33 ___ ___ 42 45 ___

㉓ 0 1 0 1 0 2 0 2 0 ___ ___ 3 0 4 ___ ___

㉔ 10 20 30 35 40 60 80 ___ 90 100 110 ___ 120 ___ ___ 165

㉕ 4 8 12 ___ 20 24 28 32 36 ___ 44 48 52 ___ 60

㉖ 1 3 4 6 7 9 10 12 13 15 ___ 19 ___ 22

㉗ 5 10 20 25 30 40 45 50 60 ___ ___ 80 ___ ___ 100 105

㉘ 8 9 10 18 19 20 28 29 30 ___ 40 ___ ___ 50

REMINDER: Write the definition of a pattern.

_____

_____

Unit 15 cont'd

B Study the patterns and add the missing numbers.

①	20	40	60	80	100	120	140	160	*180*	___	___	___
②	1	2	2	1	1	2	2	1	___	___	___	___
③	2	4	8	10	14	16	20	22	___	___	___	___
④	0	3	0	6	0	9	0	12	___	___	___	___
⑤	10	11	20	21	30	31	40	41	___	___	___	___
⑥	1	1	3	3	5	5	7	7	___	___	___	___
⑦	12	11	10	9	8	7	6	5	___	___	___	___
⑧	7	3	3	3	7	3	3	3	___	___	___	___
⑨	1	2	3	2	1	2	3	2	___	___	___	___
⑩	2	9	16	23	30	37	44	51	___	___	___	___
⑪	50	100	150	200	250	300	350	400	___	___	___	___
⑫	60	1	50	1	40	1	30	1	___	___	___	___
⑬	2	2	6	6	8	8	12	12	___	___	___	___
⑭	30	15	15	30	30	15	15	30	___	___	___	___
⑮	1	2	2	3	4	4	5	6	___	___	___	___
⑯	9	9	0	18	18	0	27	27	___	___	___	___
⑰	23	21	19	17	15	13	11	9	___	___	___	___
⑱	5	5	10	10	20	20	40	40	___	___	___	___

C Fill in the blanks with the correct numbers.

① Brian wanted to cook spaghetti and meatballs for his friends. He tried to remember a recipe for the sauce which his aunt always prepared. The recipe called for 4 pounds of tomatoes and 12 ounces of tomato paste, and he remembered that the seasonings had been listed alphabetically. He was not sure of the specific amounts needed of each seasoning, however. He phoned his aunt and she told him that the amount of each alphabetical listing should be increased by 1 teaspoon. For example, she said, Brian should add 1 teaspoon of basil, 2 teaspoons of garlic powder, and 3 teaspoons of marjoram. Brian figured that the list would continue:

_____ teaspoons of oregano
_____ teaspoons of pepper
_____ teaspoons of rosemary
_____ teaspoons of salt
_____ teaspoons of thyme

② Lucy's mother forgot the combination to the wall safe, where the family records and documents were stored. Lucy reminded her mother that the combination was made up of 10 numbers, beginning with 1. Each number that followed, recalled Lucy, was double the number that preceded it. If the combination began 1, 2, 4, 8, how would it continue?

_____ _____ _____ _____ _____ _____

Comprehension Check

A Underline every three within a group. Write the total number in the blank.

① _____ ▲▲▲▲▲▲▲▲▲▲▲▲▲▲▲▲▲▲▲▲▲▲▲▲▲▲▲▲▲▲▲▲▲▲▲

② _____ ▲▲▲▲▲▲▲▲▲▲▲▲▲▲▲▲▲▲▲▲▲▲▲▲

③ _____ ▲▲

④ _____ ▲▲▲▲▲▲▲▲▲▲▲▲▲▲▲▲▲▲▲▲▲▲▲▲▲▲▲▲▲

B Underline every four within a group. Write the total number in the blank.

① _____ ▲▲

② _____ ▲▲▲▲▲▲▲▲▲▲▲▲▲▲▲▲▲▲▲▲▲▲▲
         ▲▲▲▲▲▲▲▲▲▲▲▲▲▲▲▲▲▲▲▲▲

③ _____ ▲▲▲▲▲▲▲▲▲▲▲▲▲▲▲▲▲▲▲▲▲▲▲▲▲▲▲▲▲▲▲▲

④ _____ ▲▲▲▲▲▲▲▲▲▲▲▲▲▲▲▲▲▲▲▲▲▲▲▲▲▲▲▲▲

C Underline every five within a group. Write the total number in the blank.

① _____ ▲▲▲▲▲▲▲▲▲▲▲▲▲▲▲▲▲▲▲▲▲▲▲▲▲

② _____ ▲▲▲▲▲▲▲▲▲▲▲▲▲▲▲▲▲▲▲▲▲▲▲▲▲▲▲▲▲▲▲▲▲▲▲▲▲

③ _____ ▲▲▲▲▲▲▲▲▲▲▲▲▲▲▲▲▲▲▲▲▲▲▲▲▲▲▲▲▲▲▲▲

④ _____ ▲▲▲▲▲▲▲▲▲▲▲▲▲▲▲▲▲▲▲▲▲▲▲▲▲
         ▲▲▲▲▲▲▲▲▲▲▲▲▲▲▲▲▲▲▲▲▲▲▲

D Underline every ten within a group. Write the total number in the blank.

① _____ ▲▲▲▲▲▲▲▲▲▲▲▲▲▲▲▲▲▲▲▲▲▲▲
         ▲▲▲▲▲▲▲▲▲▲▲▲▲▲▲▲▲▲▲▲▲▲▲

② _____ ▲▲▲▲▲▲▲▲▲▲

③ _____ ▲▲▲▲▲▲▲▲▲▲▲▲▲▲▲▲▲▲▲▲▲▲▲▲▲▲▲▲▲▲▲▲▲▲▲▲▲▲

④ _____ ▲▲▲▲▲▲▲▲▲▲▲▲▲▲▲▲▲▲▲▲▲▲▲▲▲▲▲▲▲

Test 3 cont'd ☞

E Count by 3 from 30 to 90.

30 ____ ____ ____ ____ ____ ____ ____ ____ ____

____ ____ ____ ____ ____ ____ ____ ____ 90

F Count by 4 from 40 to 120.

40 ____ ____ ____ ____ ____ ____ ____ ____ ____

____ ____ ____ ____ ____ ____ ____ ____ 120

G Count by 5 from 50 to 150.

50 ____ ____ ____ ____ ____ ____ ____ ____ ____

____ ____ ____ ____ ____ ____ ____ ____ 150

H Count by 10 from 100 to 300.

100 ____ ____ ____ ____ ____ ____ ____ ____ ____

____ ____ ____ ____ ____ ____ ____ ____ 300

I Study the patterns and fill in the missing numbers.

①	4	5	6	_4_	5	6	4	5	___	4	___	6
②	19	19	19	18	18	18	___	17	17	___		16
③	45	46	47	___	49	50	49	___	47	___	45	
④	81	81	81	18	18	18	___	18	81	81	___	___
⑤	20	20	20	60	15	15	___	45	10	10	___	___
⑥	60	55	50	45	40	35	30	___	20	___		5
⑦	2	2	4	4	6	6	___	8	___	___	12	12
⑧	3	5	7	0	9	11	___	0	15	___	19	___
⑨	11	22	33	___	___	66	77	88	99	___	121	132
⑩	10	1	20	1	30	___	40	1	___	1	___	1
⑪	1	4	7	10	___	16	19	___	25	28	___	34
⑫	1	2	4	___	16	32	16	8	___	2	___	

List things that we find in groups of 3, 4, 5, and 10. For example, there are five vowels: a, e, i, o, and u.

Groups of 3

1. _____
2. _____
3. _____
4. _____

Groups of 5

1. _____
2. _____
3. _____
4. _____

Groups of 4

1. _____
2. _____
3. _____
4. _____

Groups of 10

1. _____
2. _____
3. _____
4. _____

Number Words

Learning Objective: *We will learn to recognize word names for numbers.*

A number word is a word name for a number. A number word also tells how many.

EXAMPLE: Each number has a word name. The word name for 1 is one.
The word name for 2 is two.

A Fill in the blanks with the number words that tell how many dots are on the dominoes.

① _____three_____   ② _____   ③ _____   ④ _____

⑤ _____   ⑥ _____   ⑦ _____   ⑧ _____

B Write the number words that tell how many pictures are in each row.

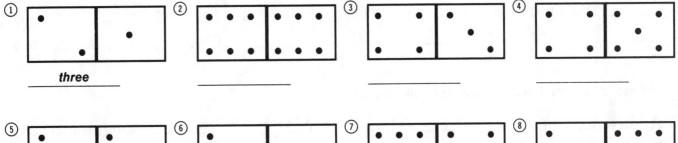

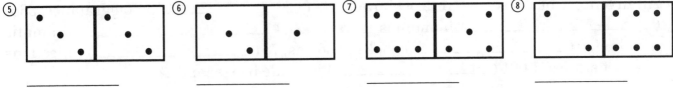

① _____

② _____

③ _____

④ _____

⑤ _____

REMINDER: Write the definition of a number word.

_____

_____

Unit 16 cont'd ☞

C Write the word names for the numbers at the right.

① ___one___ 1   ② _____ 2   ③ _____ 3   ④ _____ 4

⑤ _____ 5   ⑥ _____ 6   ⑦ _____ 7   ⑧ _____ 8

⑨ _____ 9   ⑩ _____ 10   ⑪ _____ 11   ⑫ _____ 12

⑬ _____ 13   ⑭ _____ 14   ⑮ _____ 15   ⑯ _____ 16

⑰ _____ 17   ⑱ _____ 18   ⑲ _____ 19   ⑳ _____ 20

㉑ _____ 30   ㉒ _____ 40   ㉓ _____ 50   ㉔ _____ 60

㉕ _____ 70   ㉖ _____ 80   ㉗ _____ 90   ㉘ _____ 100

㉙ _____ 200   ㉚ _____ 300   ㉛ _____ 400   ㉜ _____ 500

㉝ _____ 600   ㉞ _____ 700   ㉟ _____ 800   ㊱ _____ 900

D Write the word names for the numbers.

① An inventory of the school library showed 542 (___five hundred forty-two___) biographies, 363 (_____) humorous novels, 721 (_____) dramatic novels, 400 (_____) books of poems, 78 (_____) collections of short stories, 1,001 (_____) juvenile books, and 289 (_____) reference books.

② A recipe for stuffed trout serves 6 (_____) people and calls for 6 (_____) small, whole trout, 9 (_____) slices of bacon, 8 (_____) slices of whole wheat bread, 12 (_____) ounces of mushrooms, 4 (_____) green onions, and the juice of 3 (_____) limes. The trout must be baked at a temperature of 350 (_____) degrees for 20 (_____) minutes.

③ Test scores for the American history exam were as follows: 2 (_____) scored 47 (_____) percent, 1 (_____) scored 56 (_____) percent, 6 (_____) scored 83 (_____) percent, 3 (_____) scored 90 (_____) percent, 1 (_____) scored 92 (_____) percent, 11 (_____) scored 95 (_____) percent, and 7 (_____) scored a perfect 100 (_____) percent.

④ At age 12 (_____), Melissa is the shortest girl in her class. Standing 50 (_____) inches tall, she compares with Connie at 52 (_____) inches, Megan at 55 (_____) inches, Amy at 61 (_____) inches, and Phyllis at 64 (_____) inches.

Cardinal and Ordinal Numbers

Learning Objective: *We will learn to recognize cardinal and ordinal numbers.*

Cardinal numbers are used in simple counting to tell us how many there are in a group. Ordinal numbers tell what place the number has in a group.

EXAMPLE:
There are 5 lions in this group. The 5th lion has opened his eyes.

A Fill in the blanks.

① There are _____6_____ wishing wells.
   The _____3rd_____ wishing well has no pail.

② There are _____ sailboats.
   The _____ sailboat has no flag.

③ There are _____ clowns.
   The _____ clown is unhappy.

④ There are _____ cars.
   The _____ car is a convertible.

⑤ There are _____ bird cages.
   The _____ cage has no bird inside.

⑥ There are _____ deer.
   Only the _____ deer has antlers.

⑦ There are _____ candles.
   The _____ candle has no flame.

⑧ There are _____ pitchforks.
   The _____ pitchfork has 3 prongs.

⑨ There are _____ camels.
   The _____ camel has 2 humps.

⑩ There are _____ apples.
   The _____ has been bitten.

REMINDER: Write the definition of cardinal and ordinal numbers.

Unit 17 cont'd ☛

B Match the word names with the ordinal numbers.

① thirtieth   100th   ⑩ eleventh   2,000th

② twenty-first   13th   ⑪ two thousandth   11th

③ one hundredth   30th   ⑫ sixty-eighth   17th

④ thirteenth   21st   ⑬ seventeenth   68th

⑤ forty-seventh   94th   ⑭ second   59th

⑥ third   18th   ⑮ tenth   14th

⑦ ninety-fourth   47th   ⑯ fifty-ninth   2nd

⑧ seventieth   3rd   ⑰ fourteenth   10th

⑨ eighteenth   70th   ⑱ fifth   5th

C Fill in the blanks with the cardinal or ordinal numbers.

① Three (____3____) new cheerleaders were added to the squad. During tryouts, eighty-nine (_____) students competed. Fifteen (_____) semi-finalists were chosen. These were narrowed to five (_____) finalists. Robert Stephens was named fourth (_____) alternate. Tanya Dickens was chosen third (_____) alternate. Second (_____) alternate cheerleader was Margie Elroy. First (_____) alternate was Dave Gray. The three new cheerleaders are Scott Thompson, who scored fifty (_____) out of a possible fifty points; Lana Williamson, who scored second (_____) highest with forty-eight (_____) points; and Louise Lansford, who came in third (_____) with forty-seven (_____) points.

② Several Henderson students performed in a community telethon to raise money for public television. Drew Morrison, a ninth (_____) grader, was the eighth (_____) performer in the telethon. Cameron Mitchell, from the sixth (_____) grade, was the twenty-fourth (_____) performer. A tenth (_____) grader was the thirty-seventh (_____) performer, and thirteen (_____) members of the high school choir performed in the fiftieth (_____) place slot. An eleventh (_____) grader did a tap dance as the sixty-fourth (_____) performer. Three (_____) seniors filled the one hundredth (_____) place slot. A total of one hundred fifty (_____) performers took part in the telethon.

44

Roman Numerals

Learning Objective: *We will learn to recognize the Roman numerals I through M.*

A Roman numeral is part of the system of numbering that was developed by the ancient Romans.

The system of numbering which we generally use is called the Arabic system. The Arabic numeral 1 was written by the ancient Romans as I.

1	I	8	VIII
2	II	9	IX
3	III	10	X
4	IV	50	L
5	V	100	C
6	VI	500	D
7	VII	1000	M

A Write the Arabic numerals that mean the same as the Roman numerals.

① M _1,000_ ② CDL ____ ③ DIV ____ ④ VIII ____ ⑤ XXXIII ____

⑥ D ____ ⑦ IV ____ ⑧ CCC ____ ⑨ XIII ____ ⑩ XXVIII ____

⑪ C ____ ⑫ II ____ ⑬ CXI ____ ⑭ XXII ____ ⑮ CDXLIV ____

⑯ L ____ ⑰ IX ____ ⑱ DLV ____ ⑲ DCXL ____ ⑳ LXXVII ____

㉑ X ____ ㉒ CX ____ ㉓ CMIX ____ ㉔ XXIV ____ ㉕ CCXXII ____

㉖ CC ____ ㉗ DCC ____ ㉘ DXXV ____ ㉙ XCIX ____ ㉚ XLVIII ____

㉛ CM ____ ㉜ CMI ____ ㉝ CDXV ____ ㉞ DCCCV ____ ㉟ LXXXIX ____

㊱ XI ____ ㊲ XCI ____ ㊳ CXLV ____ ㊴ DCVI ____ ㊵ CCCXXX ____

㊶ LX ____ ㊷ VII ____ ㊸ CXXX ____ ㊹ LXXIX ____ ㊺ DCCLXX ____

㊻ VI ____ ㊼ CII ____ ㊽ LXXV ____ ㊾ XCIII ____ ㊿ CCXXXIII ____

51 CD ____ 52 XXV ____ 53 CXVI ____ 54 LXXXI ____ 55 DCCCVI ____

56 XV ____ 57 XXI ____ 58 DXLV ____ 59 CCCIX ____ 60 CMXCIX ____

61 XL ____ 62 XVI ____ 63 XLVI ____ 64 DCCCL ____ 65 DCCLXXX ____

66 DX ____ 67 DXC ____ 68 XVII ____ 69 XXXIX ____ 70 DCCCLXXX ____

REMINDER: Write the definition of a Roman numeral.

_____

_____

Unit 18 cont'd ☛

B Write the Roman numerals that mean the same as the Arabic numerals.

① 65 __LXV__ ② 44 _____ ③ 508 _____ ④ 97 _____ ⑤ 115 _____

⑥ 3 _____ ⑦ 80 _____ ⑧ 10 _____ ⑨ 303 _____ ⑩ 199 _____

⑪ 72 _____ ⑫ 50 _____ ⑬ 940 _____ ⑭ 100 _____ ⑮ 12 _____

⑯ 849 _____ ⑰ 136 _____ ⑱ 717 _____ ⑲ 5 _____ ⑳ 88 _____

㉑ 500 _____ ㉒ 115 _____ ㉓ 14 _____ ㉔ 39 _____ ㉕ 613 _____

㉖ 1 _____ ㉗ 222 _____ ㉘ 426 _____ ㉙ 212 _____ ㉚ 41 _____

㉛ 919 _____ ㉜ 405 _____ ㉝ 47 _____ ㉞ 666 _____ ㉟ 101 _____

㊱ 285 _____ ㊲ 760 _____ ㊳ 55 _____ ㊴ 1,000 _____ ㊵ 59 _____

㊶ 907 _____ ㊷ 341 _____ ㊸ 61 _____ ㊹ 419 _____ ㊺ 830 _____

C Write the Roman numerals that mean the same as the Arabic numerals.

① When the Mitchells considered planting a garden, the entire family discussed what should be grown. It was decided that 36 (____XXXVI____) sweet potato plants, 110 (_____) heads of lettuce, 19 (_____) pepper plants, 44 (_____) tomato plants, 11 (_____) cucumber plants, and 3 (_____) rows of corn should be planted.

② A total of 973 (_____) students are enrolled in the Henderson Public School System. Seventy-four (_____) children attend kindergarten at Henderson. One hundred three (_____) pupils are in the first grade. Enrolled in the second grade are 97 (_____) students while another 119 (_____) children are enrolled in grades 3 (_____), 4 (_____), and 5 (_____). Middle school students total 281 (_____), with 77 (_____) enrolled in grade 6 (_____), 124 (_____) enrolled in grade 7 (_____), and 80 (_____) enrolled in grade 8 (_____). In the four high school classes, 299 (_____) students attend daily. One hundred forty-four (_____) students are in the ninth grade, 26 (_____) are in the tenth grade, 102 (_____) are in the eleventh grade, and 27 (_____) are in grade 12 (_____).

③ There are 26 (_____) letters in the alphabet. Five (_____) of these letters are vowels. Twenty-one (_____) are consonants.

Even Numbers

Learning Objective: *We will learn to recognize even numbers from 2 to 1,000.*

Even numbers are those which can be named by counting by two beginning with the number 2.

EXAMPLES: Two, four, six, eight, and ten are even numbers.

1 <u>2</u> 3 <u>4</u> 5 <u>6</u> 7 <u>8</u> 9 <u>10</u>

A Underline the even numbers.

① 11 12 13 14 15 16 17 18 19 20

② 26 27 28 29 30 31 32 33 34 35

③ 45 46 47 48 49 50 51 52 53 54

④ 101 102 103 104 105 106 107 108 109 110

⑤ 314 315 316 317 318 319 320 321 322 323

⑥ 37 38 39 40 41 42 43 44 45 46

⑦ 798 799 800 801 802 803 804 805 806 807

⑧ 200 201 202 203 204 205 206 207 208 209

⑨ 53 54 55 56 57 58 59 60 61 62

⑩ 418 419 420 421 422 423 424 425 426 427

⑪ 646 647 648 649 650 651 652 653 654 655

⑫ 811 812 813 814 815 816 817 818 819 820

⑬ 259 260 261 262 263 264 265 266 267 268

⑭ 434 435 436 437 438 439 440 441 442 443

⑮ 11 10 9 8 7 6 5 4 3 2

⑯ 333 332 331 330 329 328 327 326 325 324

⑰ 100 99 98 97 96 95 94 93 92 91

⑱ 212 211 210 209 208 207 206 205 204 203

⑲ 622 621 620 619 618 617 616 615 614 613

⑳ 44 43 42 41 40 39 38 37 36 35

㉑ 78 77 76 75 74 73 72 71 70 69

㉒ 555 554 553 552 551 550 549 548 547 546

㉓ 829 828 827 826 825 824 823 822 821 820

㉔ 168 167 166 165 164 163 162 161 160 159

㉕ 24 23 22 21 20 19 18 17 16 15

㉖ 480 479 478 477 476 475 474 473 472 471

㉗ 710 709 708 707 706 705 704 703 702 701

㉘ 999 998 997 996 995 994 993 992 991 990

REMINDER: *Write the definition of an even number.*

_____

_____

Unit 19 cont'd ☞

B Underline the even numbers.

① 1 <u>4</u> 6 8 7 14 34 310 11 47

② 300 286 3 39 87 460 95 44 2 18

③ 12 91 687 318 466 13 58 904 221 35

④ 77 40 899 1000 16 51 63 211 82 19

⑤ 64 28 473 319 21 208 818 611 73 81

⑥ 210 888 33 71 80 727 391 600 17 83

⑦ 97 11 45 314 789 54 650 462 29 146

⑧ 261 485 38 410 43 909 307 72 820 91

⑨ 182 402 64 841 93 807 724 30 93 16

⑩ 701 813 491 377 21 34 45 54 7 37

⑪ 30 601 44 206 442 881 623 420 22 5

⑫ 949 27 390 280 161 821 69 207 248 99

⑬ 78 255 822 32 61 418 661 24 607 42

⑭ 233 845 428 433 31 814 802 49 454 70

⑮ 502 528 268 89 166 111 335 817 301 723

⑯ 481 674 705 299 72 228 470 682 29 261

⑰ 481 263 63 546 147 202 880 485 999 500

⑱ 10 36 610 549 919 208 141 234 987 115

C Place a "✓" beside the even numbers.

① Irene Wilson is mother to five _____ children. Each of her children has children of his/her own. Irene is grandmother to thirteen _____ . Six _____ of Irene's grandchildren are parents. One _____ grandchild has four _____ children. Another has two _____ daughters. Three _____ of Irene's grandchildren have one _____ son each. A sixth grandchild has twins. Irene is great-grandmother to eleven _____ children.

② One _____ commercial airline offers eight _____ flights daily between New York City and San Francisco. Each of the four _____ morning flights carries a maximum of two hundred thirty _____ passengers. Any afternoon flight, however, is limited to one hundred eighty-five _____ passengers.

③ The campus honor society is seeking twenty-four _____ new members. Participants in the group currently number three hundred eighty-one _____ . One hundred ninety-eight _____ freshmen have submitted their applications to be reviewed by society members. Applicants will be judged in three _____ areas: academic achievement, leadership abilities, and community involvement. Fifty _____ semi-finalists will be chosen. Each semi-finalist will be interviewed by a special committee of honor society members. After the interviews have been completed, the two _____ dozen finalists will receive engraved invitations to the club.

Odd Numbers

Learning Objective: *We will learn to recognize odd numbers from 1 to 999.*

Odd numbers are those which can be named by counting by two beginning with the number 1.

EXAMPLE: One, three, five, seven, and nine are odd numbers.

<u>1</u> 2 <u>3</u> 4 <u>5</u> 6 <u>7</u> 8 <u>9</u> 10

A Underline the odd numbers.

① <u>11</u> 12 13 14 15 16 17 18 19 20

② 64 65 66 67 68 69 70 71 72 73

③ 182 183 184 185 186 187 188 189 190 191

④ 30 31 32 33 34 35 36 37 38 39

⑤ 78 79 80 81 82 83 84 85 86 87

⑥ 949 950 951 952 953 954 955 956 957 958

⑦ 261 262 263 264 265 266 267 268 269 270

⑧ 24 25 26 27 28 29 30 31 32 33

⑨ 335 336 337 338 339 340 341 342 343 344

⑩ 690 691 692 693 694 695 696 697 698 699

⑪ 552 553 554 555 556 557 558 559 560 561

⑫ 88 89 90 91 92 93 94 95 96 97

⑬ 428 429 430 431 432 433 434 435 436 437

⑭ 922 923 924 925 926 927 928 929 930 931

⑮ 72 71 70 69 68 67 66 65 64 63

⑯ 208 207 206 205 204 203 202 201 200 199

⑰ 610 609 608 607 606 605 604 603 602 601

⑱ 502 501 500 499 498 497 496 495 494 493

⑲ 418 417 416 415 414 413 412 411 410 409

⑳ 880 879 878 877 876 875 874 873 872 871

㉑ 30 29 28 27 26 25 24 23 22 21

㉒ 91 90 89 88 87 86 85 84 83 82

㉓ 652 651 650 649 648 647 646 645 644 643

㉔ 228 227 226 225 224 223 222 221 220 219

㉕ 475 474 473 472 471 470 469 468 467 466

㉖ 44 43 42 41 40 39 38 37 36 35

㉗ 390 389 388 387 386 385 384 383 382 381

㉘ 822 821 820 819 818 817 816 815 814 813

REMINDER: Write the definition of an odd number.

_____

_____

Unit 20 cont'd ☞

B Underline the odd numbers.

① <u>11</u> 45 314 798 53 12 46 315 799 54

② 14 48 317 801 57 649 262 6 96 619

③ 212 44 555 168 480 423 205 324 71 3

④ 802 58 650 2 617 824 19 707 402 4

⑤ 32 108 45 207 421 64 97 182 30 78

⑥ 300 77 210 261 701 949 233 481 10 93

⑦ 314 904 888 7 485 184 333 111 500 919

⑧ 208 432 161 38 479 813 200 46 822 72

⑨ 818 1000 24 301 441 18 725 829 710 439

⑩ 444 555 820 901 2 877 778 999 19 5

⑪ 502 613 69 821 15 706 546 951 714 160

⑫ 200 433 112 166 75 20 628 27 255 844

⑬ 287 186 626 344 16 201 323 666 98 288

⑭ 845 126 128 891 622 455 477 274 147 114

⑮ 661 416 91 705 998 162 283 221 428 607

⑯ 923 87 330 100 51 148 777 215 92 80

⑰ 99 579 378 722 611 946 540 978 118 912

⑱ 529 796 991 105 178 933 996 499 31 944

C Place a "✓" beside the odd numbers.

① At the beginning of the fall semester, Marjorie bought new school supplies. In addition to buying twelve _____ textbooks, Marjorie purchased seven _____ notebooks, one thousand _____ sheets of notebook paper, three _____ dozen pencils, ten _____ pens, one hundred _____ paper clips, one _____ stapler, and thirteen _____ report binders.

② A sign in the lobby of the county courthouse shows that the sheriff's office is in room number one hundred twenty-three _____ . The county commissioners meet in room one hundred twenty-seven _____ , which is next to the county clerk's office. Circuit court is held in rooms two hundred two _____ , two hundred three _____ , two hundred four _____ , and two hundred five _____ .

③ During the first three _____ months of school, eight hundred forty-eight _____ books were checked out of the high school library. Three hundred sixty-five _____ books were checked out by the freshmen. Another two hundred one _____ books were borrowed by members of the sophomore class. Juniors read a total of one hundred fifty-four _____ library books during the same time period. Seniors checked out the least of the four _____ classes. Only one hundred twenty-eight _____ books were borrowed by twelfth-grade students.

Comprehension Check

A Write the word names for the following numbers.

① 53 _fifty-three_   ② 75 _____   ③ 13 _____   ④ 97 _____

⑤ 110 _____   ⑥ 18 _____   ⑦ 21 _____   ⑧ 64 _____

⑨ 19 _____   ⑩ 49 _____   ⑪ 2,000 _____   ⑫ 15 _____

⑬ 11 _____   ⑭ 88 _____   ⑮ 32 _____   ⑯ 206 _____

⑰ 601 _____   ⑱ 14 _____   ⑲ 40 _____   ⑳ 12 _____

B Write "c" before each cardinal number and "o" before each ordinal number.

① __c__ seventeen   ② _____ eighty-three   ③ _____ sixty-ninth   ④ _____ twelfth

⑤ _____ seventh   ⑥ _____ eightieth   ⑦ _____ forty-one   ⑧ _____ thirty

⑨ _____ thirteen   ⑩ _____ twenty-third   ⑪ _____ seventy-four   ⑫ _____ second

C Make each cardinal number into an ordinal number by adding "st," "nd," "rd," or "th."

① 88 _th_   ② 113 ___   ③ 42 ___   ④ 3 ___   ⑤ 1,000 ___   ⑥ 51 ___   ⑦ 22 ___   ⑧ 107 ___

⑨ 64 ___   ⑩ 336 ___   ⑪ 10 ___   ⑫ 95 ___   ⑬ 20 ___   ⑭ 33 ___   ⑮ 9 ___   ⑯ 271 ___

D Write the Roman numerals for these Arabic numerals.

① 38 _XXXVIII_   ② 16 _____   ③ 143 _____   ④ 709 _____   ⑤ 914 _____

⑥ 95 _____   ⑦ 67 _____   ⑧ 582 _____   ⑨ 74 _____   ⑩ 404 _____

⑪ 15 _____   ⑫ 624 _____   ⑬ 56 _____   ⑭ 219 _____   ⑮ 311 _____

⑯ 75 _____   ⑰ 31 _____   ⑱ 310 _____   ⑲ 540 _____   ⑳ 892 _____

㉑ 412 _____   ㉒ 25 _____   ㉓ 513 _____   ㉔ 1,000 _____   ㉕ 237 _____

㉖ 99 _____   ㉗ 500 _____   ㉘ 105 _____   ㉙ 63 _____   ㉚ 608 _____

㉛ 222 _____   ㉜ 906 _____   ㉝ 8 _____   ㉞ 10 _____   ㉟ 717 _____

㊱ 510 _____   ㊲ 18 _____   ㊳ 77 _____   ㊴ 161 _____   ㊵ 50 _____

Test 4 cont'd ☞

E Write the Arabic numerals for these Roman numerals.

① C _100_ ② LXV ____ ③ DXIV ____ ④ DCCIII ____ ⑤ CCCXIX ____

⑥ II ____ ⑦ DIV ____ ⑧ LVIII ____ ⑨ CCLXIV ____ ⑩ CDXCVIII ____

⑪ CXI ____ ⑫ CDX ____ ⑬ CCXL ____ ⑭ LXXXVI ____ ⑮ CMXCIX ____

⑯ LIX ____ ⑰ XXIV ____ ⑱ DCXXX ____ ⑲ LXXVI ____ ⑳ DCCCVII ____

F Write "e" before each even number and "o" before each odd number.

① _o_ 65 ② __ 44 ③ __ 508 ④ __ 97 ⑤ __ 115 ⑥ __ 3 ⑦ __ 80 ⑧ __ 10

⑨ __ 303 ⑩ __ 199 ⑪ __ 72 ⑫ __ 50 ⑬ __ 940 ⑭ __ 100 ⑮ __ 12 ⑯ __ 849

⑰ __ 136 ⑱ __ 717 ⑲ __ 5 ⑳ __ 88 ㉑ __ 115 ㉒ __ 14 ㉓ __ 39 ㉔ __ 613

㉕ __ 1 ㉖ __ 222 ㉗ __ 426 ㉘ __ 211 ㉙ __ 41 ㉚ __ 919 ㉛ __ 405 ㉜ __ 47

㉝ __ 66 ㉞ __ 101 ㉟ __ 285 ㊱ __ 760 ㊲ __ 53 ㊳ __ 907 ㊴ __ 59 ㊵ __ 1,010

㊶ __ two ㊷ __ seventeen ㊸ __ twenty-eight ㊹ __ seventy-nine

㊺ __ twenty-five ㊻ __ eleven ㊼ __ eighty-one ㊽ __ two hundred

㊾ __ fifteen ㊿ __ four 51 __ forty-eight 52 __ ninety-nine

53 __ three hundred 54 __ sixty-one 55 __ seven 56 __ thirty-two

57 __ one hundred one 58 __ fifty-six 59 __ sixteen 60 __ one hundred ten

Write a short paragraph about yourself. Include your age, your grade in school, your address, how many brothers or sisters you have, how many organizations you have joined, etc. Be sure to include at least one word name for a number, one cardinal and one ordinal number, one Roman numeral, an even number, and an odd number.

_____

_____

_____

_____

_____

_____

_____

_____

Comparisons of Numbers

Unit 21

Learning
Objective: *We will learn to compare types of numbers.*

A comparison is a study of how things are alike or different.

EXAMPLES:

| VII | XVI | CDXV | DCC | CMIX | 569 |

Five of the six numbers shown above are alike because they are Roman numerals. The sixth number is different from the others because it is an Arabic numeral.

A Check the numbers which are alike because they belong in the group named at the beginning of each row.

① even numbers   a. 123   b. XXV   c. 28 ✓   d. 10 ✓   e. three

② cardinal numbers   a. 84   b. 95th   c. second   d. 49   e. 72

③ number words   a. five   b. twenty   c. 1st   d. 13   e. LIX

④ Arabic numerals   a. 84   b. CMV   c. 110   d. 38   e. IV

⑤ 3-digit numbers   a. 22   b. 444   c. 3   d. 397   e. 7

⑥ odd numbers   a. fourth   b. 19   c. 112   d. ten   e. 221

⑦ ordinal numbers   a. 1,000   b. seven   c. 83rd   d. 976   e. thirtieth

⑧ 4-digit numbers   a. 44   b. 8,971   c. 3,233   d. 848   e. 1,000

⑨ Roman numerals   a. six   b. DIV   c. M   d. 17   e. CDIII

REMINDER: Write the definition of a comparison.

B In each row, underline the number that is different.

①   a. 175   b. 3   c. 749   d. 61   e. <u>4</u>   f. 17

②   a. 393   b. 24   c. VI   d. 10   e. 100   f. 63

③   a. 211   b. 323   c. 896   d. 175   e. 12   f. 224

④   a. eighteen   b. ninety   c. 48   d. seven   e. two   f. nine

⑤   a. 310th   b. 912   c. 618   d. 35   e. 406   f. 21

⑥   a. 7   b. 6   c. 5   d. 32   e. 8   f. 1

⑦   a. 290   b. 8   c. 34   d. 661   e. 56   f. 2

⑧   a. 69th   b. 71st   c. first   d. 23rd   e. fifth   f. twenty

C Underline the number which is different from others in the paragraph.

① Marietta lives on 45th Street. Hers is the third house on the left. She is the second oldest of six children and has just completed the 10th grade the day before her 16th birthday.

② Marietta's parents are Homer and Agnes Ralston. They were married 23 years ago, when Agnes was barely 19. Their 6 children range in age from 8 to 21. They have one grandchild, a boy, named Daniel. He is 3 months old.

③ The youngest of the Ralston children is Homer Jr., who will be 9 years old in June. At school, Homer Jr. is the only boy in his class who was named after his father. Since there are 16 other boys in his class, Homer Jr. feels especially honored. Homer says he wants to marry at age 25, as did his father, Homer Sr. Homer also wants 6 children, and he plans to name his son, Homer Ralston III.

④ Sharing with four sisters is sometimes hard for each one of the Ralston daughters. Living with five squabbling girls can also be a challenge for their parents and their only brother. Three of the girls say they want small families after they marry. Marietta and her nine-year-old sister, Abby, insist that they will have only male children.

Numbers That Are Equal

Unit 22

Learning Objective: *We will learn to recognize numbers that have equal values.*

Equal numbers are those that have like values.

EXAMPLE: The Roman numeral V has the same value as the Arabic numeral 5. The Roman numeral V is equal to 5.

A Check the amounts that have the same value as the number of dots at the left.

① [dots]   a. four   b. 12   c. XVIII   d. 16 ✓   e. 8

② [dots]   a. XXII   b. 16   c. 20   d. 30   e. eleven

③ [dots]   a. three   b. four   c. VIII   d. 6   e. twelve

④ [dots]   a. 18   b. IX   c. 17   d. 9   e. eight

⑤ [dots]   a. XII   b. 10   c. XIII   d. 15   e. twelve

⑥ [dots]   a. ten   b. 14   c. 12   d. XV   e. 13

⑦ [dots]   a. 16   b. 21   c. XVI   d. 24   e. thirty

⑧ [dots]   a. 18   b. nine   c. 12   d. XVIII   e. fifteen

⑨ [dots]   a. eight   b. ten   c. 18   d. XII   e. IX

REMINDER: Write the definition of equal numbers.

B In each exercise, underline the two amounts that are equal.

① a. <u>48</u>   b. <u>XLVIII</u>   c. 84   ② a. ten   b. XX   c. 10

③ a. 1,000   b. 100   c. M   ④ a. XXV   b. XXX   c. thirty

⑤ a. 82   b. CXXXIX   c. LXXXII   ⑥ a. 21   b. XI   c. XXI

⑦ a. D   b. 50   c. fifty   ⑧ a. XL   b. forty   c. 150

⑨ a. 16   b. XIV   c. 16   ⑩ a. 39   b. CCCIX   c. 309

⑪ a. XC   b. ninety   c. CM   ⑫ a. DX   b. sixty   c. 510

⑬ a. eleven   b. XII   c. 11   ⑭ a. 120   b. 70   c. LXX

⑮ a. CD   b. DC   c. 600   ⑯ a. 103   b. CM   c. 900

C In each paragraph, underline the two amounts that are equal.

① Susan packed 16 blouses, three sweaters, six pairs of boots, one hat, a dozen handkerchiefs, sixteen skirts, and three coats for her trip to Chicago.

② The plane left gate number 135 at exactly 7:30 a.m. One hundred twenty-five minutes later, Susan was told to fasten her seat belt for landing. A taxi drove more than 25 miles to one hundred thirty-five Garden Avenue, where Susan's grandmother had lived for the past thirty-five years.

③ Susan loved browsing through her grandmother's library, which housed collections written by many of the finest women authors. Susan's favorite collection was the 18-volume set of books that represented the complete works of George Eliot. The first sixteen books that were numbered under the authorship of Eliot were works of fiction. Adam Bede consumed volumes I and II. Felix Holt was to be found in volume number three; Romola in IV and V; Scenes of Clerical Life in VI; Daniel Deronda in VII, VIII, and IX; and so on. The last two volumes, XVII and XVIII, contained Eliot's letters and journals.

Numbers That Are Not Equal

Unit 23

Learning Objective: *We will learn to recognize numbers that have different values.*

Equal numbers are those that have like values. Numbers that are not equal have different values.

EXAMPLE: The Roman numeral V has the same value as the Arabic numeral 5, but has a different value than the Arabic numeral 10. The Roman numeral V is equal to the Arabic numeral 5, but is not equal to 10.

A Place a check (✓) before the amount that has a different value than the number of dots at the beginning of each exercise.

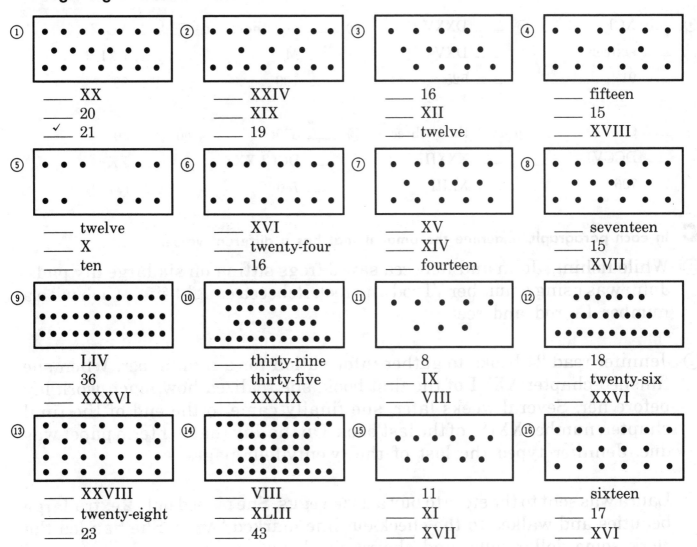

1.
____ XX
____ 20
✓ 21

2.
____ XXIV
____ XIX
____ 19

3.
____ 16
____ XII
____ twelve

4.
____ fifteen
____ 15
____ XVIII

5.
____ twelve
____ X
____ ten

6.
____ XVI
____ twenty-four
____ 16

7.
____ XV
____ XIV
____ fourteen

8.
____ seventeen
____ 15
____ XVII

9.
____ LIV
____ 36
____ XXXVI

10.
____ thirty-nine
____ thirty-five
____ XXXIX

11.
____ 8
____ IX
____ VIII

12.
____ 18
____ twenty-six
____ XXVI

13.
____ XXVIII
____ twenty-eight
____ 23

14.
____ VIII
____ XLIII
____ 43

15.
____ 11
____ XI
____ XVII

16.
____ sixteen
____ 17
____ XVI

REMINDER: Write the definition of numbers that are not equal.

_____

_____

Unit 23 cont'd ☛

B In each exercise, check (✓) the amount that has a different value.

① ___ 379
___ CCCLXXIX
✓ MDIV

② ___ 113
___ XCIII
___ ninety-three

③ ___ 40
___ LX
___ XL

④ ___ DCL
___ 650
___ CD

⑤ ___ III
___ 300
___ CCC

⑥ ___ XXII
___ 211
___ twenty-two

⑦ ___ XI
___ IX
___ nine

⑧ ___ eighty-four
___ 76
___ LXXXIV

⑨ ___ XCI
___ sixteen
___ 91

⑩ ___ DXXV
___ DXV
___ 525

⑪ ___ one thousand
___ M
___ 100

⑫ ___ XCIX
___ CXLV
___ 99

⑬ ___ 607
___ DCCVI
___ 706

⑭ ___ thirty-three
___ XXXIII
___ XLIII

⑮ ___ 870
___ DCCLXXX
___ 780

⑯ ___ 10
___ XX
___ twenty

C In each paragraph, underline the amount that has a different value.

① While fishing, John and Rebecca saw 6 frogs sitting on six large lily pads. John was using a number VI rod and reel. Rebecca caught six catfish with a number IX rod and reel.

② Jennifer read 24 books to gather information for a term paper. When she finished chapter XXVI of the first book, she realized how much work lay before her. Several weeks later, she finally came to the end of the final chapter, number XXIV, of the last book. On the day that her term paper was due, Jennifer typed the last of the twenty-four pages.

③ Laura was sent to the store to buy a dozen eggs. She picked out 12 extra-large beauties and walked to the check-out line marked "VII." She handed the clerk some dollar bills, and she received twelve cents in change.

④ Lennie bought a pattern for a crocheted sweater. The pattern called for eight rows of double crochet with a number XIII needle. This was followed by 8 rows of single crochet using a number VIII needle.

Numbers That Are Greater Than

Unit 24

Learning Objective: *We will learn to recognize numbers that have larger values.*

A number that is greater than another number has a larger value.

EXAMPLE: The number 100 is greater than any of these other numbers. a. <u>100</u> b. 75 c. 46 d. 21

A Underline the number which is greater than the other numbers in each problem.

① a. 44   b. 98   c. <u>210</u>   d. 39

② a. 108   b. 46   c. 208   d. 426

③ a. 11   b. 45   c. 314   d. 53

④ a. 259   b. 100   c. 622   d. 78

⑤ a. 101   b. 37   c. 200   d. 44

⑥ a. 14   b. 48   c. 58   d. 41

⑦ a. 33   b. 212   c. 55   d. 111

⑧ a. 99   b. 880   c. 70   d. 89

⑨ a. 706   b. 607   c. 760   d. 670

⑩ a. 1   b. 10   c. 100   d. 1,000

⑪ a. 810   b. 18   c. 81   d. 180

⑫ a. 4   b. 6   c. 7   d. 5

⑬ a. 701   b. 813   c. 491   d. 397

⑭ a. 72   b. 820   c. 813   d. 724

⑮ a. 314   b. 789   c. 650   d. 462

⑯ a. 44   b. 206   c. 442   d. 420

⑰ a. 528   b. 502   c. 268   d. 166

⑱ a. 546   b. 201   c. 485   d. 500

⑲ a. 335   b. 301   c. 111   d. 481

⑳ a. 841   b. 807   c. 881   d. 822

㉑ a. 17   b. 13   c. 15   d. 19

㉒ a. 777   b. 333   c. 555   d. 666

㉓ a. 315   b. 301   c. 333   d. 233

㉔ a. 71   b. 77   c. 701   d. 710

㉕ a. 288   b. 82   c. 28   d. 280

㉖ a. 991   b. 933   c. 978   d. 996

㉗ a. 477   b. 774   c. 474   d. 747

㉘ a. 287   b. 201   c. 323   d. 283

REMINDER: Write the definition of a number that is greater than another number.

_____

_____

Unit 24 cont'd ☞

B In each row, check (✓) the amount that has the greater value.

① a. 38   b. forty   c. 83   d. XXVIII   e. 79   f. seventy

    ___   ___   ✓   ___   ___   ___

① a. nine   b. 99   c. 19   d. XC   e. CM   f. XIX

    ___   ___   ___   ___   ___   ___

① a. 67   b. seventy-six   c. 60   d. LXXVII   e. 76   f. LXVII

    ___   ___   ___   ___   ___   ___

① a. twelve   b. seven   c. VIII   d. eleven   e. 10   f. IV

    ___   ___   ___   ___   ___   ___

① a. 100   b. forty-nine   c. LXXXVI   d. XCVII   e. ten   f. ninety-four

    ___   ___   ___   ___   ___   ___

① a. CCC   b. D   c. 267   d. LX   e. 76   f. eighty

    ___   ___   ___   ___   ___   ___

C In each paragraph, underline the number which is greater.

① At the produce section of the supermarket, Scott found oranges for 50 cents a pound, apples for 62 cents a pound, red grapes at 99 cents per pound, and grapefruit for only 25 cents per pound.

② Maxine worried about being too short to win a spot on the girls' basketball team. Several of Maxine's friends were also planning to try out for the team. Julie was very quick and measured 68 inches in height. Jasmine, also a good athlete, was sixty-seven inches tall. Maxine's other friends, while not athletically outstanding, ranged from 65 to 72 inches in height. In her track shoes, Maxine measured only 62 inches.

③ To make her prom dress, Christiane brought seven yards of satin, 5 yards of Chantilly lace, two yards of woven interfacing, 15 yards of seam binding, and twenty yards of beaded trim.

④ The Wilsons' average monthly water bill showed a usage of about 500 gallons. One month, however, a leaky pipe caused the amount of water used to jump to nine hundred eighty-four gallons. The next month's usage was 991 gallons. A plumber repaired the leak, and the usage returned to normal.

Numbers That Are Less Than

Unit 25

Learning Objective: *We will learn to recognize numbers that have smaller values.*

A number that is less than another number has a smaller value.

EXAMPLE: The number 30 is less than any of these other numbers. a. 60 b. 50 c. 40 d. <u>30</u>

A Underline the number which is less than the other numbers in each problem.

① a. 53 b. 75 c. <u>13</u> d. 97   ② a. 110 b. 18 c. 21 d. 64

③ a. 19 b. 49 c. 15 d. 51   ④ a. 11 b. 88 c. 32 d. 21

⑤ a. 14 b. 40 c. 41 d. 400   ⑥ a. 17 b. 12 c. 69 d. 83

⑦ a. 70 b. 8 c. 39 d. 19   ⑧ a. 38 b. 95 c. 15 d. 75

⑨ a. 16 b. 67 c. 31 d. 25   ⑩ a. 500 b. 222 c. 35 d. 44

⑪ a. 892 b. 608 c. 717 d. 900   ⑫ a. 10 b. 8 c. 20 d. 6

⑬ a. 17 b. 28 c. 79 d. 11   ⑭ a. 28 b. 48 c. 8 d. 18

⑮ a. 222 b. 211 c. 919 d. 199   ⑯ a. 51 b. 15 c. 150 d. 5

⑰ a. 76 b. 65 c. 58 d. 85   ⑱ a. 20 b. 19 c. 18 d. 170

⑲ a. 42 b. 24 c. 180 d. 61   ⑳ a. 630 b. 703 c. 801 d. 710

㉑ a. 1 b. 101 c. 10 d. 11   ㉒ a. 504 b. 405 c. 540 d. 500

㉓ a. 96 b. 100 c. 69 d. 19   ㉔ a. 85 b. 80 c. 75 d. 90

㉕ a. 285 b. 585 c. 582 d. 258   ㉖ a. 777 b. 666 c. 444 d. 99

㉗ a. 10 b. 9 c. 7 d. 8   ㉘ a. 166 b. 61 c. 160 d. 610

REMINDER: Write the definition of a number that is less than another number.

_____

_____

B In each row, check (✓) the amount that has the lesser value.

① a. DXV   b. 499   c. M   d. 510   e. D   f. 600
    ___   ✓   ___   ___   ___   ___

② a. thirty   b. XXX   c. 30   d. XXVIII   e. 29   f. 9
    ___   ___   ___   ___   ___   ___

③ a. 411   b. ninety   c. 114   d. forty-one   e. 14   f. XVI
    ___   ___   ___   ___   ___   ___

④ a. 399   b. 939   c. 93   d. 390   e. 993   f. XXXIX
    ___   ___   ___   ___   ___   ___

⑤ a. 200   b. two   c. CC   d. 20   e. twelve   f. X
    ___   ___   ___   ___   ___   ___

⑥ a. fourteen   b. XV   c. five   d. 41   e. 10   f. six
    ___   ___   ___   ___   ___   ___

C Study the paragraphs, and answer the questions.

① Of the four Sadler brothers, three decided to diet. The brother who weighed the least continued to eat as he always had. Timothy Sadler weighted 230 pounds the day the diet began. Walker Sadler weighed one hundred forty-five pounds. Jerry Sadler brought the scale to read 302, and Pat brought it to two hundred sixty. Which brother chose not to diet?

_____

② Outside the theater, long lines of people extended from each of the ticket booths. At ticket booth A, 36 shivering customers waited their turns. Fifty people needed tickets at booth B, while twenty-eight more waited at booth C. Lynn and Don took their places at the end of the line with the least number of people. From what booth did Lynn and Don purchase their tickets?

_____

③ By guessing which jar held the least number of jelly beans, children won free rides on the Amusement Park Express. The red jar held 796 jelly beans. The blue jar held 699. The yellow jar contained nine hundred. Jason guessed that the blue jar held the least. Joan said it was the red jar, and Travis agreed. Who won the free ride?

_____

Comprehension Check   Test 5

A Match the numbers that are equal.

① 727	49	⑪ five hundred one	one hundred five
② forty-nine	1,000	⑫ 115	LI
③ LXXII	XCIV	⑬ CV	CXV
④ XCIV	DCCXXVII	⑭ XV	501
⑤ M	seventy-two	⑮ 51	15

⑥ CMXCIX	888	⑯ two	one thousand
⑦ eighty-eight	XC	⑰ 14	DCCC
⑧ 18	999	⑱ 60	sixty
⑨ DCCCLXXXVIII	eighteen	⑲ 800	XIV
⑩ ninety	88	⑳ one thousand	2

B Check the pairs of numbers that are not equal.

① ✓ a. 25	b. XV	⑪ ___ a. sixty-two	b. LVII
② ___ a. three	b. III	⑫ ___ a. 77	b. 77
③ ___ a. 720	b. DCCXX	⑬ ___ a. CDX	b. 125
④ ___ a. 986	b. 896	⑭ ___ a. 69	b. 96
⑤ ___ a. 19	b. XIX	⑮ ___ a. 222	b. CCXXII
⑥ ___ a. XXXIV	b. 314	⑯ ___ a. 81	b. eighty-one
⑦ ___ a. 200	b. 20	⑰ ___ a. 144	b. CXLIV
⑧ ___ a. 500	b. D	⑱ ___ a. XCI	b. 910
⑨ ___ a. CMI	b. 901	⑲ ___ a. eleven	b. XI
⑩ ___ a. eighty	b. 18	⑳ ___ a. CIV	b. one hundred four

63   Test 5 cont'd ☛

C Write "g" before the number that is greater than all others in each row.

① _g_ 473   ___ seventy-four   ___ XLIII   ___ 374   ___ XXXIV

② ___ LXXXVIII   ___ 80   ___ DCCC   ___ 81   ___ eighteen

③ ___ nineteen   ___ 92   ___ XXIX   ___ ninety   ___ 299

④ ___ twenty-eight   ___ 288   ___ 310   ___ CCXC   ___ XXXV

⑤ ___ DXIII   ___ 653   ___ LXVIII   ___ seven hundred   ___ CMII

⑥ ___ 177   ___ XVII   ___ 71   ___ 717   ___ eighty

D Write "l" before the number that is less than all others in each row.

① ___ XXXVIII   ___ 313   ___ 67   _l_ thirty-three   ___ 131

② ___ 54   ___ DIV   ___ 55   ___ LII   ___ sixty

③ ___ 90   ___ 19   ___ nine   ___ eight   ___ IV

④ ___ 46   ___ LXIX   ___ XVI   ___ twenty   ___ 64

⑤ ___ 113   ___ thirty-one   ___ 10   ___ VIII   ___ 100

⑥ ___ 888   ___ 555   ___ 222   ___ LXXXVIII   ___ 333

Fill in the blanks with "equal to," "greater than," or "less than."

The Robinson triplets often swap clothes with one another. Holly wears a size 7 dress, which is ___greater than___ Molly's size 5. Dolly's dress size, however, is _____ Holly's. Dolly wears a size seven. Belts present a different problem for the three sisters. Dolly's size 24 is _____ Molly's XXIV, but is _____ Holly's size twenty-two. All the sisters wear size small blouses and sweaters. While Molly may sometimes borrow Holly's size VIII coat, which is _____ her own size six, Holly cannot wear Molly's coat. Hats and gloves, scarves, and handbags are exchanged freely among the three girls. The one item of clothing that is never borrowed is footwear. Molly's size five shoe is _____ Dolly's size 7, but is _____ Holly's size IV.

Practice with Comparisons

Unit 26

Learning Objective: *We will learn to use symbols in comparisons of numbers.*

A comparison is a study of how things are alike or different.

EXAMPLES: Certain mathematical symbols tell if numbers are alike or different.
5 is equal to 5 may be written 5 = 5.
5 is not equal to 10 is written 5 ≠ 10.
Symbols also tell how numbers are different.
10 is greater than 5 is written 10 > 5.
5 is less than 10 is written 5 < 10.

A Use the symbols = or ≠ to compare the following numbers.

① 13 __≠__ twenty   ② IV ____ 4   ③ XVI ____ nine

④ 793 ____ 397   ⑤ 800 ____ DCCC   ⑥ seventy-one ____ 71

⑦ M ____ three   ⑧ 119 ____ XIX   ⑨ forty ____ 14

⑩ LXX ____ 72   ⑪ 298 ____ 298   ⑫ 326 ____ CCCXXVI

⑬ 95 ____ 59   ⑭ 103 ____ CCCI   ⑮ 301 ____ CIII

⑯ 494 ____ 494   ⑰ seventy-five ____ 57   ⑱ forty-one ____ XLI

⑲ DIX ____ LIX   ⑳ 86 ____ sixty-eight   ㉑ CMXCIX ____ 999

㉒ 88 ____ LXXXVIII   ㉓ twenty-two ____ 22   ㉔ ten ____ X

B Use the symbols > or < to compare the following numbers.

① 89 __<__ 90   ② 710 ____ 107   ③ four ____ three

④ VII ____ eleven   ⑤ 21 ____ XII   ⑥ 843 ____ 856

⑦ 1,000 ____ D   ⑧ fifty-one ____ LXX   ⑨ eighteen ____ XIX

⑩ 46 ____ 64   ⑪ 210 ____ 201   ⑫ XX ____ IX

⑬ XX ____ XL   ⑭ 655 ____ 555   ⑮ 6 ____ 7

⑯ 5 ____ fourteen   ⑰ 309 ____ CCCIV   ⑱ eight ____ eighty

⑲ L ____ C   ⑳ 199 ____ 200   ㉑ 420 ____ 244

㉒ 341 ____ 413   ㉓ 579 ____ LXXIX   ㉔ six ____ fifty

㉕ 619 ____ 691   ㉖ XX ____ XII   ㉗ nineteen ____ 90

㉘ CXV ____ 515   ㉙ 444 ____ 440   ㉚ XC ____ CIX

REMINDER: Write the definition of a comparison.

_____

_____

Unit 26 cont'd ☞

C Use symbols to tell if each two numbers are equal or not equal. If they are not equal, show whether the first number is greater than or less than the second number.

① 53 __≠__ thirteen

      53 > thirteen

② 75 _____ 97

③ 222 _____ twenty-two

④ 563 _____ 563

⑤ LXIV _____ 44

⑥ 710 _____ 801

⑦ DIII _____ 503

⑧ fifty-eight _____ 85

⑨ eleven _____ XI

⑩ 496 _____ 649

⑪ sixty _____ DX

⑫ 50 _____ 401

⑬ 666 _____ CXVI

⑭ 85 _____ LXXXV

⑮ 258 _____ 285

⑯ forty-six _____ 46

⑰ 890 _____ 908

⑱ 371 _____ XXXVIII

⑲ one _____ one

⑳ XIX _____ 109

㉑ 362 _____ 498

D Fill in the blanks with =, >, or <.

① When Vicki and Kate rented their first apartment, they began to share all expenses, including the cost of groceries. At the supermarket, they always look for bargains. A weekly special on soft drinks is one of the best bargains that they find at 98 cents, the cost for a four-liter bottle of soft drink _____ 98 cents for a three-liter bottle that is not on sale.

② Eggs, Vicki and Kate discovered, are priced according to size. A dozen large eggs cost 89 cents, which is _____ 79 cents for medium eggs.

③ At the meat counter, the two young women find that top round steak, at 89 cents per pound _____ 39 cents per pound for chicken, but _____ eighty-nine cents a pound for pork roast.

④ They buy a variety of canned vegetables. A 16-ounce can of green beans for 33 cents _____ the cost of a 33-cent can of corn. Though both women like asparagus and artichoke hearts, they choose the latter because a 15-ounce can is on sale for 79 cents and _____ 99 cents a can for asparagus.

⑤ At the magazine display, Kate picks up a copy of "Stretching Your Food Dollar" for a price of 85 cents, which _____ the cost of large eggs at 89 cents per dozen.

Place Value — Ones

Learning Objective: *We will learn to identify the ones' place in single- and multi-digit numbers.*

Place value is determined by the position of a digit in relation to the other digits of a number.

EXAMPLE: In the number 2,346, the 6 is in the ones' place. This means that the number 2,346 has six ones.

A Underline the digits that occupy the ones' place in the following numbers.

① 1,00<u>1</u>	② 378	③ 922	④ 684	⑤ 7,459
⑥ 73	⑦ 4,888	⑧ 313	⑨ 21	⑩ 400
⑪ 766	⑫ 284	⑬ 8,970	⑭ 3,645	⑮ 48
⑯ 3	⑰ 649	⑱ 555	⑲ 199	⑳ 17
㉑ 1,895	㉒ 7	㉓ 10	㉔ 69	㉕ 312
㉖ 56	㉗ 908	㉘ 541	㉙ 145	㉚ 514
㉛ 415	㉜ 1,094	㉝ 27	㉞ 713	㉟ 9,999
㊱ 5,674	㊲ 206	㊳ 864	㊴ 12	㊵ 79
㊶ 678	㊷ 876	㊸ 786	㊹ 768	㊺ 867
㊻ 687	㊼ 32	㊽ 118	㊾ 93	㊿ 39
51 4	52 6,741	53 1,444	54 2,820	55 3,961
56 8	57 135	58 468	59 5	60 8,045
61 3,013	62 71	63 9,473	64 267	65 4,950
66 35	67 16	68 200	69 7,070	70 9

REMINDER: *Write the definition of place value.*

_____

_____

Unit 27 cont'd ☞

B How many ones are in these numbers?

① 34
<u>   *four*   </u>

② 98
_____

③ 1,083
_____

④ 157
_____

⑤ 755
_____

⑥ 162
_____

⑦ 945
_____

⑧ 302
_____

⑨ 304
_____

⑩ 2,792
_____

⑪ 754
_____

⑫ 234
_____

⑬ 1,433
_____

⑭ 641
_____

⑮ 218
_____

⑯ 1,355
_____

⑰ 856
_____

⑱ 17
_____

⑲ 1,016
_____

⑳ 13
_____

㉑ 428
_____

㉒ 701
_____

㉓ 7,082
_____

㉔ 352
_____

㉕ 1,270
_____

㉖ 849
_____

㉗ 1,176
_____

㉘ 53
_____

㉙ 3,114
_____

㉚ 1
_____

C Fill in the blanks.

① In the number eight thousand, nine hundred sixty-one, the <u>   *one*   </u> is in the ones' place.

② The eight is in the _____ place in the number six thousand, one hundred twenty-eight.

③ There are _____ ones in the number twelve.

④ In the number four hundred, forty-four, the _____ is in the one's place.

⑤ The number three thousand has _____ ones.

⑥ The _____ is in the ones' place in the number six thousand, one hundred three.

⑦ In the number five thousand, thirty, the _____ is in the ones' place

⑧ The number seven thousand, seven hundred, seventy-eight has _____ ones.

68

Place Value — Tens

Learning Objective: *We will learn to identify the tens' place in multi-digit numbers.*

Place value is determined by the position of a digit in relation to the other digits of a number.

EXAMPLE: In the number 2,346, the 4 is in the tens' place. This means that the number 2,346 has four tens.

A Underline the digits that occupy the tens' place in the following numbers.

① <u>9</u>0   ② 594   ③ 5,408   ④ 1,693   ⑤ 39

⑥ 768   ⑦ 79   ⑧ 9,119   ⑨ 415   ⑩ 213

⑪ 17   ⑫ 84   ⑬ 40   ⑭ 9,547   ⑮ 486

⑯ 12   ⑰ 5,463   ⑱ 991   ⑲ 96   ⑳ 541

㉑ 317   ㉒ 21   ㉓ 867   ㉔ 933   ㉕ 282

㉖ 50   ㉗ 762   ㉘ 707   ㉙ 20   ㉚ 3,749

㉛ 864   ㉜ 4,441   ㉝ 811   ㉞ 687   ㉟ 468

㊱ 72   ㊲ 145   ㊳ 10   ㊴ 555   ㊵ 798

㊶ 313   ㊷ 229   ㊸ 873   ㊹ 884   ㊺ 482

㊻ 946   ㊼ 700   ㊽ 809   ㊾ 4,901   ㊿ 602

51 678   52 23   53 1,476   54 531   55 710

56 16   57 3,103   58 80   59 4,000   60 786

61 53   62 876   63 4,765   64 514   65 6,500

66 5,981   67 300   68 667   69 1,001   70 9,724

REMINDER: Write the definition of place value.

B How many tens are in these numbers?

① 100   ② 721   ③ 31   ④ 812   ⑤ 2,972
____*none*____   _____   _____   _____   _____

⑥ 557   ⑦ 751   ⑧ 403   ⑨ 6,101   ⑩ 146

⑪ 253   ⑫ 4,113   ⑬ 53   ⑭ 2,807   ⑮ 72

⑯ 3,341   ⑰ 203   ⑱ 3,801   ⑲ 89   ⑳ 549

㉑ 432   ㉒ 658   ㉓ 107   ㉔ 6,711   ㉕ 948

㉖ 824   ㉗ 5,531   ㉘ 457   ㉙ 261   ㉚ 43

C Fill in the blanks.

① In the number six thousand, nine hundred ninety-six, there are
_____*nine*_____ tens.

② The _____ is in the tens' place in the number eighty-one.

③ There are _____ tens in the number four thousand, three hundred twenty.

④ In the number seven hundred nineteen, the _____ is in the tens' place.

⑤ The zero is in the _____ place in the number two thousand, one hundred five.

⑥ In the number one thousand, nine hundred ninety-four, the _____ is in the tens' place.

⑦ There are three _____ in the number thirty-five.

⑧ In the number four thousand, two hundred seventy, there are _____ tens.

70

Place Value — Hundreds

Unit 29

Learning Objective: ***We will learn to identify the hundreds' place in multi-digit numbers.***

Place value is determined by the position of a digit in relation to the other digits of a number.

EXAMPLE: **In the number 2,346, the 3 is in the hundreds' place. This means that the number 2,346 has three hundreds.**

A **Underline the digits that occupy the hundreds' place in the following numbers.**

① 500	② 672	③ 4,141	④ 351	⑤ 6,754
⑥ 8,202	⑦ 7,007	⑧ 687	⑨ 117	⑩ 667
⑪ 3,009	⑫ 137	⑬ 8,848	⑭ 786	⑮ 7,461
⑯ 451	⑰ 991	⑱ 2,000	⑲ 7,294	⑳ 601
㉑ 6,435	㉒ 229	㉓ 309	㉔ 496	㉕ 3,007
㉖ 102	㉗ 4,597	㉘ 783	㉙ 1,033	㉚ 154
㉛ 846	㉜ 201	㉝ 1,089	㉞ 4,739	㉟ 842
㊱ 4,000	㊲ 840	㊳ 123	㊴ 6,921	㊵ 9,014
㊶ 710	㊷ 133	㊸ 3,200	㊹ 8,915	㊺ 162
㊻ 145	㊼ 7,908	㊽ 6,262	㊾ 906	㊿ 793
(51) 9,631	(52) 702	(53) 1,401	(54) 415	(55) 6,187
(56) 485	(57) 648	(58) 8,150	(59) 1,941	(60) 2,104
(61) 9,540	(62) 876	(63) 2,408	(64) 6,128	(65) 8,831
(66) 900	(67) 181	(68) 4,146	(69) 3,498	(70) 605

REMINDER: Write the definition of place value.

____

____

Unit 29 cont'd

B How many hundreds are in these numbers?

① 4,352   ② 3,603   ③ 865   ④ 4,084   ⑤ 9,305

   three

⑥ 2,700   ⑦ 631   ⑧ 5,425   ⑨ 915   ⑩ 4,036

⑪ 776   ⑫ 261   ⑬ 6,500   ⑭ 2,020   ⑮ 6,740

⑯ 148   ⑰ 2,284   ⑱ 5,041   ⑲ 1,006   ⑳ 9,711

㉑ 286   ㉒ 1,468   ㉓ 2,331   ㉔ 1,147   ㉕ 3,002

㉖ 3,398   ㉗ 8,746   ㉘ 1,423   ㉙ 954   ㉚ 358

C Fill in the blanks.

① The number one thousand, two hundred twelve has _____*two*_____ hundreds.

② _____ is in the hundreds' place in the number four thousand, five hundred forty-six.

③ Three thousand thirty-one has _____ hundreds.

④ Six is in the _____ place in the number six hundred fifty-two.

⑤ There are _____ hundreds in the number six thousand, eight hundred twenty-five.

⑥ In the number eight thousand, one hundred twenty-eight, _____ is in the hundreds' place.

⑦ There are four _____ in the number two thousand, four hundred twenty-three.

⑧ In the number one thousand seventy-seven, the _____ is in the hundreds' place.

Place Value — Thousands

Learning Objective: *We will learn to identify the thousands' place in multi-digit numbers.*

Place value is determined by the position of a digit in relation to the other digits of a number.

EXAMPLE: In the number 2,346, the 2 is in the thousands' place. This means that the number 2,346 has two thousands.

A Underline the digits that occupy the thousands' place in the following numbers.

① 6,466	② 2,592	③ 1,110	④ 1,009	⑤ 6,226
⑥ 7,877	⑦ 8,298	⑧ 2,423	⑨ 7,107	⑩ 3,031
⑪ 8,124	⑫ 4,590	⑬ 6,478	⑭ 9,336	⑮ 8,200
⑯ 7,411	⑰ 1,332	⑱ 4,178	⑲ 9,128	⑳ 1,123
㉑ 6,156	㉒ 1,000	㉓ 1,998	㉔ 4,774	㉕ 5,312
㉖ 2,409	㉗ 8,531	㉘ 6,648	㉙ 1,378	㉚ 6,192
㉛ 3,871	㉜ 6,100	㉝ 9,372	㉞ 7,081	㉟ 7,338
㊱ 8,801	㊲ 2,618	㊳ 3,711	㊴ 6,881	㊵ 8,021
㊶ 2,913	㊷ 3,748	㊸ 2,465	㊹ 1,902	㊺ 8,277
㊻ 3,909	㊼ 3,401	㊽ 4,835	㊾ 8,416	㊿ 2,864
51 1,926	52 4,056	53 4,598	54 7,413	55 5,411
56 7,971	57 7,374	58 5,544	59 4,312	60 3,194
61 8,107	62 6,139	63 3,427	64 7,083	65 9,148
66 4,620	67 1,610	68 9,984	69 2,702	70 6,128

REMINDER: Write the definition of place value.

Unit 30 cont'd 🖝

B How many thousands are in these numbers?

① 8,216   ② 7,207   ③ 2,964   ④ 8,998   ⑤ 6,016

eight _____   _____   _____   _____   _____

⑥ 1,760   ⑦ 2,646   ⑧ 6,841   ⑨ 9,563   ⑩ 8,074

_____   _____   _____   _____   _____

⑪ 6,724   ⑫ 3,369   ⑬ 3,162   ⑭ 6,701   ⑮ 8,164

_____   _____   _____   _____   _____

⑯ 9,130   ⑰ 6,213   ⑱ 4,954   ⑲ 5,473   ⑳ 7,151

_____   _____   _____   _____   _____

㉑ 7,976   ㉒ 5,114   ㉓ 1,474   ㉔ 8,954   ㉕ 3,565

_____   _____   _____   _____   _____

㉖ 4,256   ㉗ 2,911   ㉘ 5,553   ㉙ 4,682   ㉚ 6,148

_____   _____   _____   _____   _____

C Fill in the blanks.

① The number seven thousand, eight hundred ninety-seven has
_____ _seven_ _____ thousands.

② In the number one thousand, three hundred thirty-six, the _____
is in the thousands' place.

③ There are _____ thousands in the number four thousand five.

④ In the number six thousand, seven hundred forty-nine, the six is in
the _____ place.

⑤ The number nine thousand, three hundred fifty-two, has
_____ thousands.

⑥ In the number five thousand, one hundred twelve, the _____
is in the thousands' place.

⑦ There are two _____ in the number two thousand, nine
hundred eighty-one.

⑧ The number six thousand, two hundred eight has _____ thousands.

Comprehension Check

Test 6

A Use symbols to tell if the numbers are equal. If the numbers are not equal, use the appropriate symbols to tell whether the first number in each pair is greater than or less than the second number.

① 428 __=__ CDXXVIII

② 121 _____ CXII

③ 3,141 _____ 3,411

④ XXVI _____ 24

⑤ nineteen _____ 91

⑥ 6,465 _____ 6,465

⑦ XI _____ eleven

⑧ 45 _____ LXV

⑨ 3,140 _____ 314

⑩ 798 _____ DCCXCVIII

⑪ LIII _____ 53

⑫ twelve _____ 21

⑬ 157 _____ 995

⑭ DCXLIII _____ 463

⑮ 831 _____ 1,380

⑯ 260 _____ 99

⑰ XIV _____ XL

⑱ 8,910 _____ 981

⑲ eighty _____ eighteen

⑳ 31 _____ thirty-one

㉑ 7,772 _____ 7,777

㉒ 10 _____ X

㉓ M _____ 100

㉔ 215 _____ twenty-five

㉕ XCLXVI _____ 966

㉖ 169 _____ 238

㉗ 6,228 _____ 6,228

㉘ 9,012 _____ 9,492

㉙ 2,004 _____ 204

㉚ fifty-one _____ 15

㉛ 4,118 _____ 4,118

㉜ XCVIII _____ 98

㉝ DXI _____ DIX

㉞ 1,261 _____ 1,216

㉟ 100 _____ 10

㊱ V _____ 5

㊲ ninety _____ forty

㊳ thirty-five _____ 350

㊴ 1,417 _____ MCDXVII

㊵ 9,781 _____ 9,781

㊶ 1,423 _____ 1,243

㊷ XVII _____ XVII

㊸ 2,558 _____ 8,223

㊹ 1,054 _____ CLIV

㊺ 129 _____ 398

㊻ twenty-six _____ sixty

㊼ 3,018 _____ 5,499

㊽ eleven _____ four

㊾ 1,687 _____ 6,187

㊿ 2,423 _____ 2,423

51 5 _____ 10

Test 6 cont'd ☛

B Fill in the blanks with the correct numbers.

① Six thousands + seven hundreds + eight tens + seven ones = _____ **6,787** _____

② Two thousands + three hundreds + two tens + three ones = _____

③ Seven hundreds + five tens + eight ones = _____

④ One thousand + two hundreds + six tens + nine ones = _____

⑤ Nine thousands + nine ones = _____

⑥ Eight thousands + eight hundreds + two tens + five ones = _____

⑦ Five thousands + three hundreds + nine tens + six ones = _____

⑧ Three thousands + six hundreds + one ten + four ones = _____

⑨ Eight thousands + two tens = _____

⑩ One thousand + four hundreds + five ones = _____

⑪ Seven thousands + eight hundreds + eight tens = _____

⑫ Four thousands + one hundred + three tens + two ones = _____

⑬ Nine tens + nine ones = _____

⑭ Two thousands + seven tens + nine ones = _____

⑮ Eight ones = _____

C Tell how many thousands, hundreds, tens, and ones are in each number.

① 4,748 = _____

② 5,512 = _____

③ 2,072 = _____

④ 6,490 = _____

⑤ 8,804 = _____

The Number Scale   Unit 31

Learning Objective: *We will learn to compare numbers on a number scale.*

A number scale is a line along which numbers are positioned according to their values.

EXAMPLE:
As we move toward the
right on a number scale,
we can see that each
number has a larger value than the number to its left.

0 1 2 3 4 5 6 7 8 9 10 11 12

A Fill in the missing numbers.

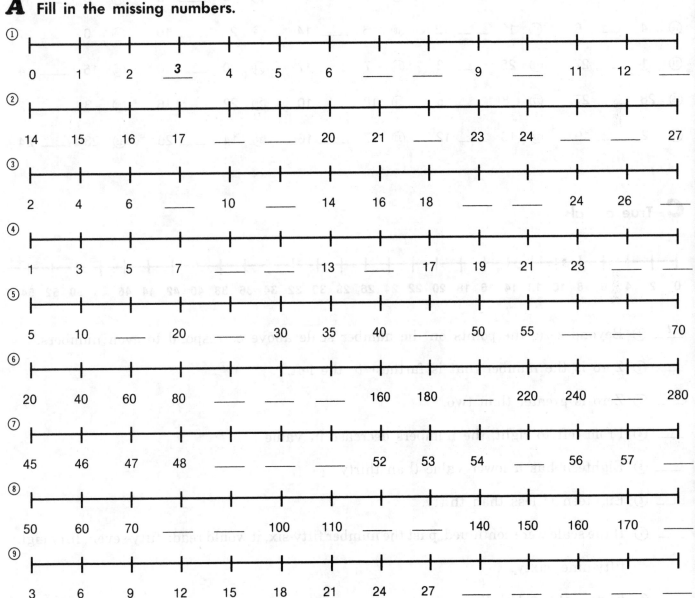

① 0 1 2 *3* 4 5 6 ___ ___ 9 ___ 11 12 ___

② 14 15 16 17 ___ ___ 20 21 ___ 23 24 ___ ___ 27

③ 2 4 6 ___ 10 ___ 14 16 18 ___ ___ 24 26 ___

④ 1 3 5 7 ___ ___ 13 ___ 17 19 21 23 ___ ___

⑤ 5 10 ___ 20 ___ 30 35 40 ___ 50 55 ___ ___ 70

⑥ 20 40 60 80 ___ ___ ___ 160 180 ___ 220 240 ___ 280

⑦ 45 46 47 48 ___ ___ ___ 52 53 54 ___ 56 57 ___

⑧ 50 60 70 ___ ___ 100 110 ___ ___ 140 150 160 170 ___

⑨ 3 6 9 12 15 18 21 24 27 ___ ___ ___ ___ ___

REMINDER: Write the definition of a number scale.

_____

_____

B Study the number scale and tell whether the numbers are greater than (>) or less than (<).

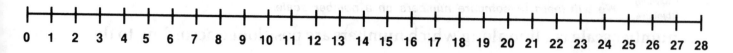

① 1 $\underline{<}$ 2   ② 12 ___ 13   ③ 20 ___ 21   ④ 10 ___ 18   ⑤ 24 ___ 9

⑥ 28 ___ 25   ⑦ 22 ___ 24   ⑧ 11 ___ 25   ⑨ 26 ___ 23   ⑩ 5 ___ 7

⑪ 10 ___ 5   ⑫ 1 ___ 0   ⑬ 9 ___ 18   ⑭ 8 ___ 9   ⑮ 0 ___ 18

⑯ 4 ___ 6   ⑰ 10 ___ 12   ⑱ 16 ___ 14   ⑲ 21 ___ 19   ⑳ 6 ___ 27

㉑ 1 ___ 27   ㉒ 25 ___ 3   ㉓ 7 ___ 17   ㉔ 20 ___ 10   ㉕ 15 ___ 4

㉖ 28 ___ 27   ㉗ 8 ___ 5   ㉘ 18 ___ 10   ㉙ 22 ___ 16   ㉚ 3 ___ 12

㉛ 2 ___ 19   ㉜ 13 ___ 12   ㉝ 17 ___ 16   ㉞ 14 ___ 25   ㉟ 23 ___ 24

C True or False

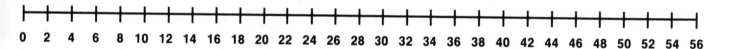

_t_ ① Beyond zero, the points on the number scale above correspond to even numbers.

___ ② Zero is the number that is farthest to the left.

___ ③ Zero is greater than two.

___ ④ From left to right, the numbers decrease in value.

___ ⑤ Eighteen has a lower value than thirty.

___ ⑥ Eighteen is less than thirty.

___ ⑦ If the scale were continued, past the number fifty-six, it would read: fifty-seven, fifty-eight,

  fifty-nine, sixty...

___ ⑧ Forty-eight is less than fifty.

___ ⑨ Forty-eight is to the left of fifty.

___ ⑩ Fifty-six is greater than zero.

Sets

Learning Objective: *We will learn to identify sets.*

A set is a group of things that belong together.

EXAMPLE: These shapes may be grouped into two sets.

▲ △ ▲ △   Set A   Set B
△ ▲ △ ▲   △ △ △ and ▲ ▲ ▲
▲ △ ▲ △   △ △ △   ▲ ▲ ▲

A Make two sets from each group.

		Set A	Set B
①	+ ● + ● + ● + ● + ● + ●	+ + + + +	● ● ● ● ●
②	□ □ □ □ ■ ■ □ □ ■ ■ □ ■		
③	♥ ♥ ↑ ♥ ♥ ↑ ♥ ♥ ↑ ♥ ♥ ↑		
④	✈ ✈ ✈ 🚁 🚁 🚁 ✈ ✈ ✈ 🚁 🚁 🚁		
⑤	⑦ ⑦ ⑦ ⑦ ? ? ? ? ⑦ ⑦ ⑦ ⑦		
⑥	X Y X Y X Y X Y X Y X Y		
⑦	$ $ $ $ $ $ $ $ $ $ $ $		
⑧	1 2 1 2 1 2 1 2 1 2 1 2		
⑨	⇨ ⇨ ⇨ ⇦ ⇦ ⇦ ⇨ ⇨ ⇨ ⇦ ⇦ ⇦		
⑩	🚌 🚌 🚌 🚗 🚗 🚗 🚌 🚗 🚗 🚗 🚗 🚌		
⑪	C C C C M M M C C C M M		
⑫	◆ ◆ ◆ ◆ ♣ ♣ ♣ ♣ ♣ ♣ ♣ ♣		
⑬	1¢ 1¢ 5¢ 1¢ 1¢ 1¢ 5¢ 1¢ 1¢ 1¢ 5¢ 5¢		
⑭	? ? ? ? ? ? ? ? ? ? ? ?		

REMINDER: Write the definition of a set.

_____

_____

Unit 32 cont'd ☞

B Identify the sets to which these numbers belong.

Set A = {all Roman numerals}   Set B = {all even Arabic numerals}   Set C = {all odd Arabic numerals}

C ① 1, 3, 5, 7, 9, 11, 13, 15, 17, 19

___ ② 22, 24, 26, 28, 30, 32, 34, 36, 38, 40

___ ③ I, II, III, IV, V, VI, VII, VIII, IX, X

___ ④ 10, 8, 2, 4, 36, 102, 204, 12, 16, 20

___ ⑤ 27, 41, 33, 15, 7, 3, 95, 101, 13, 209

___ ⑥ D, M, C, V, X, D, M, C, V, X

___ ⑦ 2, 2, 2, 2, 2, 2, 2, 2, 2, 2

___ ⑧ 11, 21, 31, 41, 51, 61, 71, 81, 91, 101

___ ⑨ XL, LX, X, X, X, L, L, L, LX, XL

___ ⑩ 4, 8, 12, 16, 20, 24, 28, 32, 36, 40

___ ⑪ 21, 19, 17, 15, 13, 11, 9, 7, 5, 3

___ ⑫ 99, 49, 99, 49, 99, 49, 99, 49, 99, 49

___ ⑬ 100, 200, 300, 400, 500, 600, 700

___ ⑭ II, IV, VI, VIII, X, XII, XIV, XVI, XVIII, XX

C Fill in the blanks.

① Marissa, Ethan, Johnny, and Elizabeth are freshmen. Pam, Debbie, Cooper, Wayne, Allie, and Sean are sophomores. Julie is a junior. Vicki, Jerry, Bonnie, Barbara, Carol, Rick, Paul, and Harold are seniors. If Set A = {all sophomores}, there are _____ members in Set A.

② At the supermarket, Marge bought ten apples, ten pears, ten oranges, ten bananas, ten peaches, ten grapefruits, ten lemons, and ten limes. If all the fruit is grouped in sets according to type, there will be _____ sets.

③ At the auditions for tap dancers to perform in the spring recital, Emma won a spot in the first line. Her friend, Geneva, was chosen for the second line, while another friend, Mary Ellen, was placed in line six. If Set A = {lines one and two}, Set B = {lines three and four}, and Set C = {lines five and six}, Geneva belongs in Set _____.

④ At her wedding shower, Rebecca received eight dinner plates, six salad plates, six soup bowls, and eight saucers. If a set includes a dinner plate, a salad plate, a soup bowl, and a saucer, Rebecca has _____ complete sets.

80

Subsets

Unit 33

Learning Objective: *We will learn to recognize subsets of larger sets.*

A subset is a group that is made up of certain members of a larger set.

EXAMPLES: B and C are subsets.

A = {♥, ♡, ♥, ♡, ♥, ♡, ♥, ♡, ♥, ♡, ♥, ♡}
B = {♥, ♥, ♥, ♥, ♥, ♥}
C = {♡, ♡, ♡, ♡, ♡, ♡}

A Match the sets and subsets.

① A = {♣, ♧, ♣, ♧, ♣, ♧, ♣, ♧} B = {a, e, i, o, u} C = {b, c, d}

② A = {A, A, A, A, A, B, B, B} B = {△, △, △, △} C = {△, △, △, △}

③ A = {⊠, ⊠, ⊠, △, △, △, ⊠, ⊠} B = {1, 3, 5, 7} C = {2, 4, 6, 8}

④ A = {a, e, i, o, u, b, c, d} B = {A, A, A, A} C = {B, B, B}

⑤ A = {1, 2, 3, 4, 5, 6, 7, 8} B = {♣, ♣, ♣, ♣} C = {♧, ♧, ♧, ♧}

⑥ A = {△, △, △, △, △, △, △, △} B = {10, 20, 30, 40} C = {15, 25, 35, 45}

⑦ A = {10, 15, 20, 25, 30, 35, 40, 45} B = {⊠, ⊠, ⊠, ⊠, ⊠} C = {△, △, △}

⑧ A = {1¢, 5¢, 5¢, 5¢, 1¢, 1¢, 1¢, 1¢} B = {34, 86, 19, 121} C = {57, 48, 64, 70}

⑨ A = {11, 12, 13, 14, XI, XII, XIII, XIV} B = {11, 12, 13, 14} C = {XI, XII, XIII, XIV}

⑩ A = {Beth, Ellen, David, Joe} B = {1¢, 1¢, 1¢, 1¢, 1¢} C = {5¢, 5¢, 5¢}

⑪ A = {34, 86, 19, 121, 57, 48, 64, 70} B = {♤, ♤, ♤, ♤} C = {♠, ♠, ♠, ♠}

⑫ A = {★, ★, ★, ◆, ◆, ★, ◆, ★} B = {Beth, Ellen} C = {David, Joe}

⑬ A = {♤, ♠, ♤, ♠, ♠, ♠, ♤, ♤} B = {13, 23, 33, 43} C = {19, 29, 39, 49}

⑭ A = {13, 19, 23, 29, 33, 39, 43, 49} B = {★, ★, ★, ★, ★} C = {◆, ◆, ◆}

REMINDER: Write the definition of a subset.

81

Unit 33 cont'd

B Study the sets below and mark the following statements true or false.

B ⊆ A	B is a subset of Set A.
△ ∈ A	△ is a member of Set A.
△ ∉ B	△ is not a member of Set B.

① A = {10, 11, 12, 13, 14}
  B = {10, 12, 14}
  C = {11, 13}

② A = {15, 16, 25, 26, 35}
  B = {15, 25, 35}
  C = {16, 26}

③ A = {1, 2, 3, 4, 5}
  B = {1, 2}
  C = {3, 4, 5}

④ A = {a, e, b, c, d}
  B = {a, e}
  C = {b, c, d}

__t__ B ⊆ A
____ A ⊆ B
____ 10 ∉ C

____ C ⊆ A
____ 26 ∈ A
____ 26 ∉ B

____ A ⊆ C
____ 3 ∉ C
____ 1 ∈ B

____ e ∈ A
____ e ∈ B
____ e ∈ C

⑤ A = {△, △, △, □, □, △}
  B = {△, △, △}
  C = {□, □}

⑥ A = {X, X, V, V, V}
  B = {X, X}
  C = {V, V, V}

⑦ A = {6, 7, 8, 9, 10}
  B = {6, 7, 8}
  C = {9, 10}

⑧ A = {10, 15, 20, 25, 30}
  B = {10, 20, 30}
  C = {15, 25}

____ △ ⊆ □
____ B ⊆ C
____ C ∈ B

____ V ⊆ B
____ V ∈ B
____ V ∈ C

____ B ⊆ A
____ B ⊆ C
____ B ∈ C

____ 15 ∉ C
____ 15 ∉ B
____ 15 ∉ A

C Fill in the blanks.

① Set A includes all whole numbers. Set B includes all even numbers. Set C includes all odd numbers. Set B _____ Set A. Set C _____ Set A.

② Set A includes letters a, b, c, d, e, and f. Set B includes letters a, b, and c. Set C includes letters d, e, and f. Letter e _____ Set A. Letter e _____ Set B. Letter e _____ Set C.

③ Set A includes all Roman and Arabic numerals. Set B includes all Roman numerals. Set C includes all Arabic numerals. XVII _____ Set A. XVII _____ Set B. XVII _____ Set C.

④ Set A includes numbers 11 and 12. Set B includes number 11. Set C includes number 12. _____ ∈ Set B. _____ ∈ Set C.

⑤ Set A includes numbers 10, 20, 30, 40, 50, and 60. Set B includes numbers 10 and 20. Set C includes numbers 30 and 40. Set B _____ Set A. Set C _____ Set A. The number 50 _____ Set A. The number 50 _____ Set B. The number 50 _____ Set C. The number 10 _____ Set A. The number 10 _____ Set B. The number 10 _____ Set C. The number 40 _____ Set C. The number 40 _____ Set B. The number 40 _____ Set A.

82

Intersection of Sets

Learning Objective: *We will learn to identify intersections of sets.*

When there are two sets that include like members, a third set made up of those members that are alike is called the intersection of the two sets.

EXAMPLE: Three members are included in both sets A and B. The intersection of A and B is {♦, ♦, ♦}.

$A = \{♦, ◇, ♦, ◇, ♦, ◇\}$

$B = \{♦, ♦, ♦\}$

$A \cap B = \{♦, ♦, ♦\}$

A Underline the members that are included in both sets.

① A = {1, 2, 3, 4, 5}
   B = {1, 3, 5}

② A = {30, 40, 50, 60, 70}
   B = {40, 60, 80, 100}

③ A = {6, 7, 8, 9, 10}
   B = {6, 8, 10, 12, 14}

④ A = {5, 10, 15, 20, 25}
   B = {10, 20}

⑤ A = {a, b, c, d, e}
   B = {a, e}

⑥ A = {I, II, III, IV, V}
   B = {I, III, V}

⑦ A = {3, 6, 9, 12, 15}
   B = {3, 6, 9}

⑧ A = {x, y, z, 4, 5}
   B = {4, 5, 6, 7, 8}

⑨ A = {♣, ♧, ♣, ♧, ♣}
   B = {♣, ♣, ♣}

⑩ A = {0, 1, 2, 3, 4}
   B = {1, 2, 3, 4}

⑪ A = {1, 13, 15, 21, 23}
   B = {13, 15}

⑫ A = {100, 200, 300, 400, 500}
   B = {100, 500}

⑬ A = {10, 9, 8, 7, 6}
   B = {9, 7, 5, 3, 1}

⑭ A = {a, e, i, o, u}
   B = {w, y}

⑮ A = {22, 33, 44, 55, 66}
   B = {22, 44, 66}

⑯ A = {X, V, C, M, D}
   B = {X, V}

⑰ A = {12, 14, 16, 18, 20}
   B = {12, 14, 16, 18, 20}

⑱ A = {6, 7, 8, 9, 0}
   B = {0}

⑲ A = {boys, girls}
   B = {girls}

⑳ A = {⇑, ⇑, ⇑, ⇓, ⇓}
   B = {⇑, ⇑, ⇑, ⇑, ⇑}

㉑ A = {1¢, 1¢, 1¢, 1¢, 1¢}
   B = {5¢}

㉒ A = {61, 71, 81, 91, 101}
   B = {91, 101}

㉓ A = {★, ●, ★, ●, ★}
   B = {●}

㉔ A = {Beth, Amy, Grace}
   B = {Beth, Amy}

㉕ A = {30, 60, 90, 120}
   B = {30, 60, 90, 120}

㉖ A = {◀, ◀, ◀, ◁, ◁}
   B = {◁, ◁}

㉗ A = {M, N, W}
   B = {M, W}

㉘ A = {a, a, a, a, a}
   B = {a, a, b, b, b}

㉙ A = {37, 24, 16, 8, 10}
   B = {24, 16, 8, 10}

㉚ A = {20, 21, 22, 23, 24}
   B = {21, 23, 25, 27}

㉛ A = {4, 5, 6, IV, V}
   B = {4, IV}

㉜ A = {A, B, C, a, b}
   B = {A, B, C, D, E}

㉝ A = {teachers, students}
   B = {principals}

㉞ A = {5, 10, 15, 20, 25}
   B = {5, 10, 15, 20, 25}

㉟ A = {✈, ✈, 🚗, 🚗, 🚗}
   B = {✈}

㊱ A = {2, 14, 36, 12, 9}
   B = {36, 12, 9, 6}

㊲ A = {♤, ♤, ♤, ♤, ♠}
   B = {♤, ♤, ♤, ♤}

㊳ A = {91, 72, 86, 97}
   B = {91, 97}

㊴ A = {u, v, w, x, y}
   B = {x}

㊵ A = {0, 2, 4, 6, 8}
   B = {2, 4, 6, 8}

REMINDER: *Write the definition of an intersection of sets.*

Unit 34 cont'd

B Identify the intersections of the sets.

① A = {10, 9, 8, 7, 6}   ② A = {x, x, x, y, x}   ③ A = {1, 2, 3, 4, 5}   ④ A = {a, b, c, d, e}

  B = {6, 8, 10}   B = {x, y}   B = {2, 4, 6, 8, 10}   B = {u, v, x, y, z}

  A ∩ B = {_**10, 8, 6**_}   A ∩ B = {_____}   A ∩ B = {_____}   A ∩ B = {_____}

⑤ A = {_____}   ⑥ A = {I, II, III, IV, V}   ⑦ A = {10, 20, 30, 40, 50}   ⑧ A = {3, 6, 9, 12, 15}

  B = {_____}   B = {II, IV, VI, VIII}   B = {10, 15, 20, 25, 30}   B = {1, 3, 5, 7, 9}

  A ∩ B = {_____}   A ∩ B = {_____}   A ∩ B = {_____}   A ∩ B = {_____}

⑨ A = {a, b, c, d, e}   ⑩ A = {1, 2, 3, 4, 5}   ⑪ A = {_____}   ⑫ A = {21, 31, 41, 51, 61}

  B = {c, b, a, e, d}   B = {6, 7, 8, 9, 10}   B = {_____}   B = {30, 31, 32, 33, 34}

  A ∩ B = {_____}   A ∩ B = {_____}   A ∩ B = {_____}   A ∩ B = {_____}

⑬ A = {X, XI, XII, XIII}   ⑭ A = {a, b, c, 1, 2, 3}   ⑮ A = {h, i, j, k, l}   ⑯ A = {58, 59, 60, 61}

  B = {XIV, XV, XVI}   B = {2, 4, 6, 8, 10}   B = {l, m, n, o, p}   B = {63, 62, 61, 60}

  A ∩ B = {_____}   A ∩ B = {_____}   A ∩ B = {_____}   A ∩ B = {_____}

C Identify each member of A ∩ B.

① Roger, Johnny, Lynn, Ronald, Bobby, Ramona, Jan, Richard, and Jim are senior members of the marching band. Johnny, Ramona, Jan, Larry, Denise, and Michael are senior members of the choir. A = {senior members of the marching band}. B = {senior members of the choir}.
  A ∩ B = {_____}.

② Oregon, California, Washington, and Nevada are situated in the Pacific time zone. Maine, North Carolina, South Carolina, Florida, Washington, Oregon, and California are coastal states. A = {those Pacific time zone states that are named above}. B = {those coastal states that are named above}.
  A ∩ B = {_____}.

③ January, March, May, July, August, October, and December are months that have 31 days. April, June, September, and October are months that have 30 days. A = {months that have 31 days}. B = {months that have 30 days}.
  A ∩ B = {_____}.

④ Traditional gifts for the ninth wedding anniversary include: pottery, willow, china, glass, and crystal. Traditional gifts for the fifteenth wedding anniversary include glass and crystal. A = {traditional gifts for the 9th anniversary}. B = {traditional gifts for the 15th anniversary}.
  A ∩ B = {_____}.

84

Union of Sets

Learning Objective: *We will learn to form and identify unions of sets.*

When all members of two sets are combined to form a third set, the third set is called the union of the two sets.

EXAMPLE:

All the members of Sets A and B have been combined to form a third set. The Union of Sets A and B is {◇, ◇, ◇, ◇, ◇, ◇, ◆, ◆, ◆, ◆, ◆, ◆}.

A = {◆, ◆, ◆, ◆, ◆, ◆}
B = {◇, ◇, ◇, ◇, ◇, ◇}
A ∪ B = {◇, ◇, ◇, ◇, ◇, ◇, ◆, ◆, ◆, ◆, ◆, ◆}

A Match the sets and their unions.

① A = {7, 8, 9, 10, 11}   B = {12, 13, 14, 15, 16}   C = {5, 10, 15, 20, 25, 30, 35, 40, 45, 50}

② A = {a, b, c, d, e}   B = {A, B, C, D, E}   C = {7, 8, 9, 10, 11, 12, 13, 14, 15, 16}

③ A = {2, 4, 6, 8, 10}   B = {1, 3, 5, 7, 9}   C = {♠, ♠, ♠, ♠, ♤, ♤, ♤, ♤}

④ A = {10, 20, 30, 40, 50}   B = {5, 15, 25, 35, 45}   C = {red, blue, yellow, green}

⑤ A = {♠, ♠, ♠, ♠}   B = {♤, ♤, ♤, ♤}   C = {a, A, b, B, c, C, d, D, e, E}

⑥ A = {V, X, XV, XX}   B = {XXX, XL, L, LX}   C = {1, 2, 3, 4, 5, 6, 7, 8, 9, 10}

⑦ A = {red, blue}   B = {green, yellow}   C = {V, X, XV, XX, XXX, XL, L, LX}

⑧ A = {◄, ◄, ◄, ►, ►}   B = { ▼, ▲, ▲, ▲, ▼}   C = {3, 6, 9, 12, 15, 18, 21, 24, 27, 30}

⑨ A = {a, b, c}   B = {x, y, z}   C = {a, b, c, d, e, f, g, h, i}

⑩ A = {50, 150, 250, 350}   B = {100, 200, 300, 400}   C = {◄, ◄, ◄, ▲, ▲, ▲, ►, ►, ▼, ▼}

⑪ A = {3, 9, 15, 21, 27}   B = {6, 12, 18, 24, 30}   C = {50, 100, 150, 200, 250, 300, 350, 400}

⑫ A = {a, e, i}   B = {b, c, d, f, g, h}   C = {a, b, c, x, y, z}

⑬ A = {X, X, X, X, X}   B = {O, O, O, O, O}   C = {13, 23, 33, 43, 53, 63, 73, 83, 93, 103}

⑭ A = {13, 33, 53, 73, 93}   B = {23, 43, 63, 83, 103}   C = {X, O, X, O, X, O, X, O, X, O}

REMINDER: *Write the definition of a union of sets.*

B Fill in the blank.

① A = {a, b, c}

  B = {a, b, c}

  A ∪ B = { **a, a, b, b, c, c** }

② A = {1, 10, 100}

  B = {1,000}

  A ∪ B = { _____ }

③ A = {9, 18, 27}

  B = {36, 45, 54}

  A ∪ B = { _____ }

④ A = {0}

  B = {2, 4, 6, 8}

  A ∪ B = { _____ }

⑤ A = {🚕, 🚕, 🚕}

  B = {🚕, 🚕, 🚕}

  A ∪ B = { _____ }

⑥ A = {L, C}

  B = {D, M}

  A ∪ B = { _____ }

⑦ A = {22, 44, 66}

  B = {33, 55, 77}

  A ∪ B = { _____ }

⑧ A = {E, F, G, H}

  B = {I, J}

  A ∪ B = { _____ }

⑨ A = {15, 51}

  B = {51, 15}

  A ∪ B = { _____ }

⑩ A = {✈, ✈, ✈, ✈}

  B = {🚌}

  A ∪ B = { _____ }

⑪ A = {2, 22, 222}

  B = {3, 33, 333}

  A ∪ B = { _____ }

⑫ A = {20, 24}

  B = {8, 12, 16}

  A ∪ B = { _____ }

C Identify each member of A ∪ B.

① At the local pharmacy, aspirins, cold remedies, and pain relievers are located on the left side of aisle number one. Toothpastes, mouthwashes, and dental floss may be found on the right side of aisle one.
A = {items on the left side of aisle one}. B = {items on the right side of aisle one}.
A ∪ B ={ _____ }

② The two-story inn offered a dozen guest rooms. On the first floor were rooms 101, 102, 103, 104, and 105. On the second floor were rooms 200, 201, 202, 203, 204, 205, and 206.
A = {guest rooms on the first floor}. B = {guest rooms on the second floor}.
A ∪ B ={ _____ }

③ On Fridays, Baker's Bakery sells all chocolate items at half price. For 50 cents each, chocolate eclairs, chocolate fried pies, and chocolate shortbread may be bought. Chocolate brownies, cupcakes, and doughnuts cost a quarter apiece. Chocolate cookies and fudge squares cost a dime each. Every Friday, Baker's sells more of its expensive items; therefore, fewer chocolate cookies and fudge squares are baked.
A = {50-cent items}. B = {25-cent items}. C = {10-cent items}.
A ∪ B ={ _____ }

Comprehension Check　　　　Test 7

A Study the number scale and mark the following statements true or false.

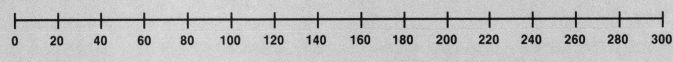

0 20 40 60 80 100 120 140 160 180 200 220 240 260 280 300

____ ① The points on the scale range right to left from 0 to 300.

____ ② If the scale were continued, the number shown to the right of 300 would be 320.

____ ③ 100 < 180.

____ ④ Each number on the scale has a larger value than the number to its right.

____ ⑤ 240 > 260.

B Study the number scale and identify the members of the sets.

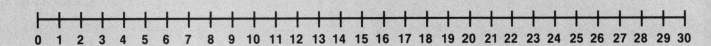

0 1 2 3 4 5 6 7 8 9 10 11 12 13 14 15 16 17 18 19 20 21 22 23 24 25 26 27 28 29 30

① A = {the first four numbers to the right of 0}
A = { _____ *1, 2, 3, 4* _____ }

② B = {all even numbers between 21 and 29}
B = { _____ }

③ C = {all numbers less than 7}
C = { _____ }

④ D = {all numbers that include the digit 6}
D = { _____ }

⑤ E = {all odd numbers between 8 and 16}
E = { _____ }

⑥ F = {all numbers to the right of 22}
F = { _____ }

⑦ G = {all numbers that include 0 as a digit}
G = { _____ }

⑧ H = {all numbers between 12 and 18}
H = { _____ }

⑨ I = {all numbers to the left of 10}
I = { _____ }

⑩ J = {all numbers greater than 25}
J = { _____ }

C Identify the sets to which these members belong.

A = {numbers with 3 as a digit}　　B = {odd numbers}　　C = {numbers with 0 as a digit}

_C_ ① {0, 20, 106, 405, 90, 10, 301}

____ ② {13, 15, 17, 19, 21, 23, 25, 27}

____ ③ {3, 11, 13, 31}

____ ④ {3, 30, 103, 43, 39, 83, 306}

____ ⑤ {3, 300}

____ ⑥ {103, 301, 310, 101, 100}

____ ⑦ {201, 401, 601, 21, 41, 61}

____ ⑧ {31, 33, 13, 83, 38, 103}

87　　　　　　　　　　Test 7 cont'd ☞

D Study the sets and mark the following statements true or false.

① A = {u, v, w, x, y}
　B = {u, w, y}
　C = {v, x}

_____*f*___ A ⊆ B
_____ v ∈ C

② A = {27, 133, 10, 100}
　B = {27, 10}
　C = {133, 100}

_____ B ⊆ A
_____ C ⊆ A

③ A = {0, 2, 4, 6, 8}
　B = {0}
　C = {2, 4, 6, 8}

_____ 4 ∈ C
_____ A ∈ 4

④ A = {5, 15, 53, 25, 58}
　B = {15, 25}
　C = {53, 58}

_____ B ⊆ A
_____ 15 ∉ C

⑤ A = {6, 12, 18, 24, 30}
　B = {6, 12, 24}
　C = {18, 30}

_____ C ⊆ A
_____ 18 ∉ A

⑥ A = {X, X, X, X}
　B = {X, X}
　C = {X, X}

_____ A ⊆ B
_____ A ⊆ C

⑦ A = {10, 20, 30, 40}
　B = {10, 30}
　C = {20, 40}

_____ C ⊄ B
_____ B ⊄ C

⑧ A = {0, 1, 2, 3, 4, 5}
　B = {1, 3, 5}
　C = {2, 4}

_____ 4 ∈ C
_____ 45 ∈ B

E Fill in the blanks.

① A = {24, 26, 28, 30}
　B = {22, 24, 26, 28}

　A ∩ B ={ ___*24, 26, 28*___ }

② A = {a, b, c, d}
　B = {a, e, i, o}

　A ∩ B ={ _____ }

③ A = {1, 2}
　B = {2, 4}

　A ∪ B ={ _____ }

④ A = {z, z, z, z}
　B = {z, z}

　A ∩ B ={ _____ }

⑤ A = {z, z, z, z}
　B = {z, z}

　A ∪ B ={ _____ }

⑥ A = {3, 11, 13, 31}
　B = {3, 13, 31, 113}

　A ∩ B ={ _____ }

⑦ A = {202, 402}
　B = {22, 42}

　A ∪ B ={ _____ }

⑧ A = {a, b, c}
　B = {b, c, d}

　A ∪ B ={ _____ }

⑨ A = {5, 4, 3}
　B = {1, 2, 3}

　A ∪ B ={ _____ }

List the members of three sets. Let Set A include all students in your class. Let Set B include all boys in your class, while Set C includes all girls.

A = { _____ }

B = { _____ }

C = { _____ }

Referring to the sets above, mark the following statements true or false.

_____① B ⊆ A　_____② C ⊆ A　_____③ A ⊆ C　_____④ A ∩ B = C　_____⑤ B ∪ C = A

Definite and Endless Sets

Learning Objective: *We will learn to distinguish between definite and endless sets.*

A definite set is one whose members can be counted. The members of an endless set extend indefinitely; they cannot be counted.

EXAMPLES:

A = {0, 1, 2, 3}   A is the set of whole numbers from 0 to 3.

B = {0, 1, 2, 3...}   B is the endless set of whole numbers.

A is a definite set. B is an endless set.

A Identify each of the following as a definite (d) or endless (e) set.

__d__ ① The set of cities located in the United States and serving as state capitals.

_____ ② The set of years from 1800 to 2000.

_____ ③ The set of all the stars in the universe.

_____ ④ The set of California elementary schools that offered foreign language classes in 1972.

_____ ⑤ The set of all the letters in the English alphabet.

_____ ⑥ The set of counting numbers from 1 to 1,000.

_____ ⑦ The set of all the students enrolled in grades 1 through 12 in your school.

_____ ⑧ The set of counting numbers.

_____ ⑨ The set of even numbers.

_____ ⑩ The set of athletes who have won Olympic gold medals.

_____ ⑪ The set of Arabic numerals from 10 through 10,000.

_____ ⑫ The set of all the years to come after 1986.

_____ ⑬ The set of odd numbers between 1 and 99.

_____ ⑭ The set of ninth-grade math instructors that taught in New York City public schools in 1964.

REMINDER: Write the definition of definite and endless sets.

_____

_____

     Unit 36 cont'd

B Tell how many members are in each set.

| n(A) = 10 | The number of members in Set A is 10. |

① A = {2, 4, 6, 8, 10}
n(A) = ____5____

② B = {1, 2, 3, 4, 5}
n(B) = _____

③ C = {0, 1, 2, 3, 4}
n(C) = _____

④ D = {0, 1, 2, 3...}
n(D) = _____

⑤ E = {a, b, c, d}
n(E) = _____

⑥ F = {a, b, c...z}
n(F) = _____

⑦ G = {1, 2, 3...10}
n(G) = _____

⑧ H = {98, 99, 100}
n(H) = _____

⑨ I = {2, 4, 6, 8...}
n(I) = _____

⑩ J = {Don, Mary}
n(J) = _____

⑪ K = {10, 12, 14, 16}
n(K) = _____

⑫ L = {900, 1,000}
n(L) = _____

⑬ M = {1800, 1900, 1986}
n(M) = _____

⑭ N = {X, X, X}
n(N) = _____

⑮ O = {X, X, X...}
n(O) = _____

⑯ P = {11, 22, 33, 44}
n(P) = _____

⑰ Q = {2, 4, 6...20}
n(Q) = _____

⑱ R = {4, 4, 4, 4, 4, 4}
n(R) = _____

⑲ S = {999}
n(S) = _____

⑳ T = {A, a, B, b}
n(T) = _____

㉑ U = {10, 9, 8}
n(U) = _____

㉒ V = {V, X, L, C, D, M}
n(V) = _____

㉓ W = {9, 9, 9...}
n(W) = _____

㉔ X = {1800, 1801...}
n(X) = _____

C Tell how many members are in each set.

① Set A includes Tom; his father, Harry; his mother, Irene; and his brothers, John, Terry, Randy, and Kevin.
n(A) = _____7_____ .

② Set B includes poets Edna St. Vincent Millay, May Sarton, Nikki Giovanni, Gwendolyn Brooks, Amy Lowell, Elinor Wylie, Marianne Moore, Louise Bogan, Ruth Stone, May Swenson, Shirley Kaufman, Maxine Kumin, Anne Sexton, and Adrienne Rich.
n(B) = _____ .

③ Set C includes babies born in 1986, 1987, 1988, 1989, and every year thereafter.
n(C) = _____ .

④ Set D includes all items in Sharon's wallet: a one-dollar bill, a five-dollar bill, one quarter, a penny, a photograph of her best friend, an identification card, a driver's license, a credit card, a calendar, and a coupon for a free pizza.
n(D) = _____ .

⑤ Set E includes every high school senior who will enroll in college following graduation.
n(E) = _____ .

⑥ Set F includes the months in a year: January, February, March, April, May, June, July, August, September, October, November, and December.
n(F) = _____ .

Basic Addition Facts

Learning
Objective: *We will learn to add by combining sets.*

Addition is the combining of numbers to obtain the total value or sum.

EXAMPLE:

If the 2 members of Set B are added   A = {■, ■, ■}   3
to the 3 members of Set A, the   B = {■, ■}   + 2
resulting set has 5 members.   A ∪ B = {■, ■, ■, ■, ■}   5

A Tell how many members are in each set.

① A = {△, △, △, △, △}   n(A) = __5__   ② A = {●, ●, ●, ●}   n(A) = ____
  B = {△, △, △}   n(B) = + __3__   B = {●, ●, ●, ●}   n(B) = + ____
  A ∪ B = {△, △, △, △,   A ∪ B = {●, ●, ●, ●,
          △, △, △, △}   n(A ∪ B) = __8__   ●, ●, ●, ●}   n(A ∪ B) = ____

③ A = {■, ■, ■, ■, ■, ■}   n(A) = ____   ④ A = {◇, ◇, ◇}   n(A) = ____
  B = {■, ■, ■}   n(B) = + ____   B = {◇, ◇, ◇, ◇}   n(B) = + ____
  A ∪ B = {■, ■, ■, ■, ■,   A ∪ B = {◇, ◇, ◇, ◇,
          ■, ■, ■, ■}   n(A ∪ B) = ____   ◇, ◇, ◇}   n(A ∪ B) = ____

⑤ A = {O, O, O, O, O}   n(A) = ____   ⑥ A = {▲, ▲, ▲, ▲}   n(A) = ____
  B = {O, O, O, O, O}   n(B) = + ____   B = {▲, ▲, ▲, ▲, ▲}   n(B) = + ____
  A ∪ B = {O, O, O, O, O,   A ∪ B = {▲, ▲, ▲, ▲, ▲,
          O, O, O, O, O}   n(A ∪ B) = ____   ▲, ▲, ▲, ▲}   n(A ∪ B) = ____

⑦ A = {♦, ♦, ♦, ♦, ♦}   n(A) = ____   ⑧ A = {◁, ◁}   n(A) = ____
  B = {♦}   n(B) = + ____   B = {◁, ◁, ◁, ◁, ◁, ◁, ◁, ◁} n(B) = + ____
  A ∪ B = {♦, ♦, ♦,   A ∪ B = {◁, ◁, ◁, ◁, ◁,
          ♦, ♦, ♦}   n(A ∪ B) = ____   ◁, ◁, ◁, ◁, ◁}   n(A ∪ B) = ____

⑨ A = {♣, ♣, ♣, ♣, ♣, ♣, ♣}   n(A) = ____   ⑩ A = {⊠, ⊠}   n(A) = ____
  B = {♣, ♣, ♣, ♣}   n(B) = + ____   B = {⊠, ⊠}   n(B) = + ____
  A ∪ B = {♣, ♣, ♣, ♣, ♣, ♣,   A ∪ B = {⊠, ⊠,
          ♣, ♣, ♣, ♣, ♣}   n(A ∪ B) = ____   ⊠, ⊠}   n(A ∪ B) = ____

⑪ A = {✵}   n(A) = ____   ⑫ A = {♤, ♤, ♤, ♤, ♤}   n(A) = ____
  B = {✵, ✵, ✵, ✵}   n(B) = + ____   B = {♤, ♤, ♤, ♤, ♤, ♤}   n(B) = + ____
  A ∪ B = {✵, ✵,   A ∪ B = {♤, ♤, ♤, ♤, ♤, ♤,
          ✵, ✵, ✵}   n(A ∪ B) = ____   ♤, ♤, ♤, ♤, ♤}   n(A ∪ B) = ____

REMINDER: Write the definition of addition.

_____

_____

Unit 37 cont'd 👉

B Tell how many members are in each set.

① A ={△, △, △, △, △, △}   B ={△, △, △, △, △, △}   A ∪ B ={△, △, △, △, △, △, △, △, △, △, △, △}
   n(A) = __6__   +   n(B) = __6__   =   n(A ∪ B) = __12__

② A ={•, •, •, •, •}   B ={•, •, •, •, •, •, •, •}   A ∪ B ={•, •, •, •, •, •, •, •, •, •, •, •, •}
   n(A) = ____   +   n(B) = ____   =   n(A ∪ B) = ____

③ A ={★, ★, ★, ★, ★, ★, ★, ★}   B ={★, ★, ★, ★, ★, ★, ★, ★}   A ∪ B ={★, ★, ★, ★, ★, ★, ★, ★, ★, ★, ★, ★, ★, ★, ★, ★}
   n(A) = ____   +   n(B) = ____   =   n(A ∪ B) = ____

④ A ={○, ○, ○, ○}   B ={○, ○, ○, ○, ○, ○, ○, ○, ○, ○, ○}   A ∪ B ={○, ○, ○, ○, ○, ○, ○, ○, ○, ○, ○, ○, ○, ○, ○}
   n(A) = ____   +   n(B) = ____   =   n(A ∪ B) = ____

⑤ A ={x, x, x, x, x, x, x, x, x}   B ={x, x, x, x, x, x}   A ∪ B ={x, x, x, x, x, x, x, x, x, x, x, x, x, x, x}
   n(A) = ____   +   n(B) = ____   =   n(A ∪ B) = ____

⑥ A ={◁, ◁, ◁, ◁, ◁, ◁, ◁, ◁, ◁, ◁}   B ={◁, ◁}   A ∪ B ={◁, ◁, ◁, ◁, ◁, ◁, ◁, ◁, ◁, ◁, ◁, ◁}
   n(A) = ____   +   n(B) = ____   =   n(A ∪ B) = ____

C Tell how many members are in each set.

① Set A includes 6 red apples. Set B includes 7 green apples.

n(A) = ____6____
n(B) = + __7__
n(A ∪ B) = __13__

② There are 7 cocker spaniels in Set A and 7 beagles in Set B.

n(A) = ____
n(B) = + ____
n(A ∪ B) = ____

③ Nine gymnasts belong to Set A, and 7 belong to Set B.

n(A) = ____
n(B) = + ____
n(A ∪ B) = ____

④ One drummer belongs in Set A. Three drummers belong in Set B.

n(A) = ____
n(B) = + ____
n(A ∪ B) = ____

⑤ There are 2 hamburgers in Set A and 1 cheeseburger in Set B.

n(A) = ____
n(B) = + ____
n(A ∪ B) = ____

⑥ Set A includes 4 rowboats, while Set B includes 9 sailboats.

n(A) = ____
n(B) = + ____
n(A ∪ B) = ____

⑦ There are 3 lanterns in Set A and 2 candles in Set B.

n(A) = ____
n(B) = + ____
n(A ∪ B) = ____

⑧ There are 8 parrots in Set A, while 7 canaries are in Set B.

n(A) = ____
n(B) = + ____
n(A ∪ B) = ____

⑨ There are 7 moths in Set A. Three butterflies are in Set B.

n(A) = ____
n(B) = + ____
n(A ∪ B) = ____

⑩ Set A includes 1 math book. Set B includes 1 English book.

n(A) = ____
n(B) = + ____
n(A ∪ B) = ____

⑪ Six oil paintings are in Set A. Eight ink drawings are in Set B.

n(A) = ____
n(B) = + ____
n(A ∪ B) = ____

⑫ Three carnations belong in Set A. Six roses are in Set B.

n(A) = ____
n(B) = + ____
n(A ∪ B) = ____

Addition on a Number Line

Learning Objective: *We will learn to add with the aid of a number line.*

Addition is the combining of numbers to obtain the total value or sum.

EXAMPLE:

To add 3 and 2, begin at point 3 on the number line and move 2 points to the right. The sum is 5.

The numbers on a number line are positioned, left to right, according to increasing values.

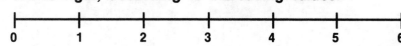

A Use the number line in adding the numbers below.

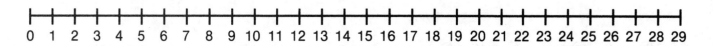

① 2 + 6 = __8__   ② 9 + 10 = _____   ③ 14 + 11 = _____   ④ 12 + 12 = _____

⑤ 7 + 20 = _____   ⑥ 5 + 9 = _____   ⑦ 15 + 13 = _____   ⑧ 0 + 5 = _____

⑨ 1 + 12 = _____   ⑩ 8 + 9 = _____   ⑪ 17 + 6 = _____   ⑫ 23 + 2 = _____

⑬ 3 + 9 = _____   ⑭ 10 + 6 = _____   ⑮ 13 + 8 = _____   ⑯ 11 + 7 = _____

⑰ 3 + 20 = _____   ⑱ 6 + 12 = _____   ⑲ 4 + 2 = _____   ⑳ 0 + 10 = _____

㉑ 20 + 5 = _____   ㉒ 14 + 9 = _____   ㉓ 2 + 18 = _____   ㉔ 12 + 3 = _____

㉕ 1 + 6 = _____   ㉖ 5 + 22 = _____   ㉗ 14 + 3 = _____   ㉘ 19 + 8 = _____

㉙ 27 + 1 = _____   ㉚ 20 + 2 = _____   ㉛ 15 + 9 = _____   ㉜ 10 + 10 = _____

㉝ 11 + 10 = _____ ㉞ 3 + 6 = _____   ㉟ 0 + 23 = _____   ㊱ 15 + 6 = _____

㊲ 13 + 7 = _____   ㊳ 1 + 19 = _____   ㊴ 7 + 18 = _____   ㊵ 19 + 4 = _____

㊶ 26 + 3 = _____   ㊷ 12 + 0 = _____   ㊸ 13 + 4 = _____   ㊹ 4 + 11 = _____

㊺ 9 + 16 = _____   ㊻ 17 + 3 = _____   ㊼ 15 + 2 = _____   ㊽ 16 + 7 = _____

㊾ 23 + 1 = _____   ㊿ 12 + 16 = _____ 51 6 + 23 = _____   52 17 + 0 = _____

REMINDER: Write the definition of addition.

_____

_____

Unit 38 cont'd ☞

B Use the number line in these addition problems.

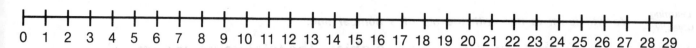

① 1	② 6	③ 11	④ 10	⑤ 3	⑥ 20	⑦ 16	⑧ 14	⑨ 21	⑩ 5
2	12	0	2	7	2	8	3	2	8
+ 3	+ 5	+ 8	+ 2	+ 10	+ 3	+ 2	+ 7	+ 2	+ 0
6									

⑪ 13	⑫ 17	⑬ 5	⑭ 20	⑮ 8	⑯ 2	⑰ 0	⑱ 15	⑲ 22	⑳ 1
3	10	5	5	8	2	8	1	4	5
+ 4	+ 1	+ 5	+ 3	+ 9	+ 2	+ 9	+ 4	+ 2	+ 4

㉑ 7	㉒ 9	㉓ 6	㉔ 19	㉕ 4	㉖ 9	㉗ 12	㉘ 18	㉙ 3	㉚ 8
12	13	4	2	12	2	12	7	8	2
+ 2	+ 7	+ 8	+ 6	+ 7	+ 1	+ 2	+ 2	+ 10	+ 6

C Use the number line in these addition problems.

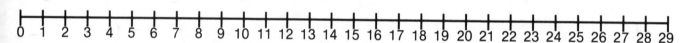

① Melinda, Jason, and Tess entered a pie eating contest. Jason ate 9 fruit pies. Tess ate 7 cream pies. Melinda ate 11 pies of different kinds. How many pies were eaten? **27**

② During the last game of the baseball season, the home team scored in only two innings. One point was scored in the first inning, and three were listed in the ninth. How many points were scored? _____

③ A Fourth of July fishing trip for members of the Outdoor Club netted 14 catfish, 5 large mouth bass, and 10 buffalo fish. How many fish did the club members catch? _____

④ Pottsdam reported a record snowfall during the winter of 1971. In December, 10 inches of snow fell. The next two months brought 11 more inches. How many inches fell that year? _____

⑤ Eighteen seniors attended Career Day at the university. Eight eleventh graders also participated. No members of the sophomore class were present. How many students attended? _____

⑥ Several traffic accidents were reported during the first quarter of 1985. Two accidents occurred in January, 7 in February, and 12 in March. How many accidents were reported? _____

⑦ Six chocolate cakes, 9 angel food cakes, and 5 red velvet cakes were sold during the ninth-grade bake sale at Henderson High School. How many cakes were sold? _____

⑧ During a tour of a wildlife refuge, students saw 4 buffalo near the highway. Two buffalo were seen beside a pond, and 5 were spotted under some trees. How many buffalo were seen? _____

94

Adding One-Digit Numbers

Learning Objective: *We will learn to add single-digit numbers.*

In the Arabic numbering system, 0, 1, 2, 3, 4, 5, 6, 7, 8, and 9 are one-digit numbers.

EXAMPLES:

To add 3, 2, and 5, first find the sum of 3 and 2. Add 5 to this sum.

$$\left.\begin{array}{r} 3 \\ 2 \\ + \ 5 \\ \hline 10 \end{array}\right\}$$

$$\begin{array}{r} 3 \\ + \ 2 = \quad 5 \\ + \ 5 = 10 \end{array}$$

A Add these one-digit numbers.

① 2 + 6 **8**	② 1 + 7	③ 9 + 3	④ 7 + 6	⑤ 3 + 1	⑥ 5 + 2	⑦ 2 + 8	⑧ 4 + 5	⑨ 8 + 9	⑩ 6 + 4
⑪ 7 + 0	⑫ 8 + 3	⑬ 9 + 1	⑭ 5 + 8	⑮ 6 + 9	⑯ 0 + 4	⑰ 5 + 5	⑱ 2 + 1	⑲ 3 + 3	⑳ 9 + 9
㉑ 1 9 + 2	㉒ 8 3 + 5	㉓ 2 2 + 1	㉔ 3 9 + 4	㉕ 7 5 + 3	㉖ 6 5 + 7	㉗ 2 8 + 4	㉘ 9 8 + 1	㉙ 6 0 + 7	㉚ 1 1 + 1
㉛ 2 8 + 1	㉜ 3 9 + 1	㉝ 4 5 + 6	㉞ 6 6 + 0	㉟ 1 7 + 5	㊱ 8 2 + 9	㊲ 3 2 + 0	㊳ 9 2 + 2	㊴ 6 9 + 2	㊵ 1 2 + 1
㊶ 2 6 + 6	㊷ 7 5 + 5	㊸ 4 3 + 8	㊹ 2 6 + 8	㊺ 9 0 + 2	㊻ 7 0 + 7	㊼ 5 5 + 0	㊽ 4 5 + 2	㊾ 3 9 + 0	㊿ 2 5 + 1
51 1 6 + 7	52 4 5 + 9	53 2 6 + 3	54 4 1 + 1	55 1 7 + 8	56 5 3 + 2	57 2 7 + 6	58 7 2 + 2	59 9 3 + 5	60 7 2 + 5

REMINDER: Write the definition of one-digit numbers.

___

Unit 39 cont'd 🖙

B Find the sums.

① 2 + 1 + 2 + 0 = __5__   ② 6 + 2 + 3 + 1 = ___   ③ 9 + 1 + 4 + 2 = ___   ④ 3 + 4 + 2 + 1 = ___

⑤ 7 + 2 + 5 + 4 = ___   ⑥ 3 + 3 + 2 + 5 = ___   ⑦ 5 + 1 + 2 + 1 = ___   ⑧ 4 + 2 + 3 + 8 = ___

⑨ 6 + 1 + 5 + 7 = ___   ⑩ 2 + 7 + 2 + 8 = ___   ⑪ 5 + 2 + 1 + 1 = ___   ⑫ 4 + 7 + 3 + 4 = ___

⑬ 8 + 3 + 6 + 1 = ___   ⑭ 3 + 2 + 4 + 5 = ___   ⑮ 5 + 4 + 2 + 2 = ___   ⑯ 6 + 5 + 1 + 2 = ___

⑰ 7 + 1 + 1 + 1 = ___   ⑱ 6 + 4 + 0 + 6 = ___   ⑲ 5 + 6 + 3 + 2 = ___   ⑳ 1 + 5 + 5 + 8 = ___

㉑ 8 + 2 + 4 + 5 = ___   ㉒ 2 + 5 + 2 + 6 = ___   ㉓ 1 + 9 + 5 + 1 = ___   ㉔ 1 + 0 + 4 + 8 = ___

㉕ 9 + 0 + 2 + 8 = ___   ㉖ 8 + 1 + 1 + 7 = ___   ㉗ 3 + 2 + 8 + 3 = ___   ㉘ 4 + 1 + 5 + 2 = ___

㉙ 2 + 8 + 1 + 4 = ___   ㉚ 5 + 3 + 2 + 7 = ___   ㉛ 5 + 2 + 2 + 1 = ___   ㉜ 2 + 2 + 4 + 2 = ___

㉝ 6 + 3 + 2 + 2 = ___   ㉞ 2 + 0 + 0 + 4 = ___   ㉟ 2 + 6 + 3 + 4 = ___   ㊱ 4 + 3 + 3 + 6 = ___

C Find the sums.

① In a basket of mixed fruit, there were 3 oranges, 8 apples, 2 bananas, and 4 pears. How many fruits were in the basket?

_____17_____

② Four trout swam past the boat. They were followed by 3 bass, 2 catfish, and 1 carp. How many fish swam past the boat?

_____

③ On the dinner table, Lennie placed 4 silver knives, 4 silver forks, 4 silver teaspoons, and 4 silver soup spoons. How many pieces of silver were placed?

_____

④ In a tool box, Blair stored 1 hammer, 3 screwdrivers, 4 wrenches, and 1 saw. How many tools were stored in the tool box?

_____

⑤ The total population of the Davis household includes 2 adults, 2 children, and 2 pets. How many are in the household?

_____

⑥ During summer break, Gina wrote 5 letters to Dan, 6 letters to Rob, and 7 letters to Steve. How many letters did Gina write?

_____

⑦ The spring honor roll included 7 seniors, 2 juniors, 8 sophomores, and 2 freshmen. How many students were named to the list?

_____

⑧ On a 14-day diet, Tom lost 6 pounds in one week. The next week he lost 4 pounds. How many pounds did he lose?

_____

⑨ On Monday, Emily studied 3 hours for a math test. Tuesday she studied 4 hours. How many hours did Emily study?

_____

⑩ Six elephants, 4 lions, 2 tigers, and 1 bear were in the circus parade. How many animals were in the parade?

_____

⑪ In his freshman year, Max was absent from school 2 days in March, 3 days in April, and 3 days in May. How many days was he absent?

_____

⑫ The art exhibit included 5 oil paintings, 5 watercolors, and 4 sculptures. How many items were on display?

_____

Adding Two-Digit Numbers

Learning Objective: *We will learn to add two-digit numbers.*

Two-digit numbers have digits in both the ones' place and the tens' place.

EXAMPLES:

First add the digits in the ones' column. Next add the digits in the tens' column.

$$\begin{array}{r} 13 \\ + 12 \\ \hline 25 \end{array}\Bigg\} \qquad \begin{array}{r} 3 \\ + 2 \\ \hline 5 \\ 10 \\ + 10 \\ \hline 25 \end{array}$$

Carry numbers to the left.

$$\begin{array}{r} 1 \\ 13 \\ 12 \\ + 15 \\ \hline 40 \end{array}\Bigg\} \qquad \begin{array}{r} 3 \\ 2 \\ + 5 \\ \hline 10 \\ 10 \\ 10 \\ + 10 \\ \hline 40 \end{array}$$

A Add these two-digit numbers.

① 14 + 68 = **82**	② 71 + 42	③ 33 + 10	④ 11 + 47	⑤ 23 + 28	⑥ 63 + 39	⑦ 87 + 46	⑧ 95 + 44
⑨ 21 + 81	⑩ 32 + 91	⑪ 68 + 73	⑫ 18 + 46	⑬ 61 + 35	⑭ 89 + 42	⑮ 21 + 35	⑯ 47 + 74
⑰ 89 + 91	⑱ 16 + 51	⑲ 63 + 21	⑳ 11 + 82	㉑ 19 + 64	㉒ 52 + 84	㉓ 47 + 33	㉔ 19 + 21
㉕ 20 88 + 18	㉖ 61 17 + 38	㉗ 16 21 + 88	㉘ 83 37 + 18	㉙ 72 73 + 91	㉚ 60 17 + 83	㉛ 79 71 + 14	㉜ 53 14 + 78
㉝ 95 46 + 50	㉞ 46 22 + 91	㉟ 46 82 + 61	㊱ 48 53 + 84	㊲ 10 43 + 90	㊳ 93 77 + 28	㊴ 20 91 + 91	㊵ 18 24 + 26
㊶ 48 41 + 93	㊷ 80 77 + 24	㊸ 30 93 + 16	㊹ 10 70 + 18	㊺ 13 49 + 13	㊻ 77 21 + 13	㊼ 44 55 + 47	㊽ 37 11 + 30

REMINDER: *Write the definition of two-digit numbers.*

_____

_____

B Find the sums.

① 60 + 14 + 42 + 64 = __180__   ② 42 + 88 + 16 + 23 = _____   ③ 42 + 22 + 51 + 29 = _____

④ 49 + 27 + 39 + 28 = _____   ⑤ 16 + 82 + 16 + 92 = _____   ⑥ 72 + 48 + 99 + 13 = _____

⑦ 78 + 25 + 58 + 22 = _____   ⑧ 32 + 61 + 41 + 86 = _____   ⑨ 61 + 24 + 60 + 74 = _____

⑩ 21 + 42 + 33 + 84 = _____   ⑪ 54 + 28 + 43 + 33 = _____   ⑫ 31 + 81 + 48 + 24 = _____

⑬ 94 + 54 + 70 + 15 = _____   ⑭ 50 + 25 + 28 + 26 = _____   ⑮ 88 + 91 + 66 + 11 = _____

⑯ 13 + 35 + 81 + 73 = _____   ⑰ 17 + 23 + 16 + 48 = _____   ⑱ 16 + 74 + 70 + 52 = _____

⑲ 99 + 72 + 22 + 84 = _____   ⑳ 70 + 68 + 22 + 29 = _____   ㉑ 26 + 11 + 74 + 81 = _____

㉒ 26 + 36 + 35 + 46 = _____   ㉓ 14 + 72 + 28 + 80 = _____   ㉔ 48 + 59 + 99 + 50 = _____

㉕ 18 + 10 + 36 + 61 = _____   ㉖ 54 + 99 + 19 + 20 = _____   ㉗ 81 + 41 + 23 + 49 = _____

C Find the sums.

① In a survey, 21 students listed reading as their favorite pastime. Thirty-two said they would rather watch television, and 54 preferred the radio. Twelve students listed other pastimes. How many were surveyed?
__119__

② At the jewelry store, 14 watches were displayed in the window. Also displayed were 11 necklaces, 16 tie clasps, and 25 engagement rings. How many items were displayed in the store window?
_____

③ Members of the 4-H Club baked cookies for a bake sale. Ten dozen chocolate chip cookies were baked, and 12 dozen peanut butter cookies were baked. How many dozen cookies did club members bake?
_____

④ Thirty members of the senior class planned to enroll in college after high school. Sixteen seniors hoped to find jobs, and 11 were undecided about their plans. How many students were in the senior class?
_____

⑤ Participating in the field trip to the art museum were 48 students, 12 teachers, 10 area artists, and 23 local residents. How many persons visited the art museum?
_____

⑥ Elizabeth counted 19 errors in her first news story. Her second story contained 14 errors, and her third attempt contained 10. How many errors were in the three stories?
_____

⑦ Twenty freshmen ordered the school yearbook. Nineteen sophomores placed orders, as did 38 juniors and 56 seniors. How many students ordered the school yearbook?
_____

⑧ Participants in the bicycle tour through Vermont pedaled 46 miles on Saturday and 32 miles on Sunday. How many miles did they travel during the two days?
_____

Comprehension Check

A Tell how many members are in each set.

① A ={△, △, △, △, △, △, △}   B ={△, △, △, △}   A ∪ B ={△, △, △, △, △, △, △, △, △, △, △}

n(A) = _____   +   n(B) = _____   =   n(A ∪ B) = _____

② A ={A, B, C, D...Z}   B ={a, b, c, d...z}   A ∪ B ={A, a, B, b, C, c, D, d...Z, z}

n(A) = _____   +   n(B) = _____   =   n(A ∪ B) = _____

③ A ={♤, ♤, ♤, ♧, ♧, ♧}   B ={♤, ♧, ♤, ♧, ♤, ♧}   A ∪ B ={♤, ♤, ♤, ♤, ♤, ♤, ♧, ♧, ♧, ♧, ♧, ♧}

n(A) = _____   +   n(B) = _____   =   n(A ∪ B) = _____

④ A ={2, 4, 6, 8...}   B ={1, 3, 5, 7...}   A ∪ B ={1, 2, 3, 4, 5, 6, 7, 8...}

n(A) = _____   +   n(B) = _____   =   n(A ∪ B) = _____

⑤ A ={X, X, X, X, X}   B ={X, X, X, X, X}   A ∪ B ={X, X, X, X, X, X, X, X, X, X}

n(A) = _____   +   n(B) = _____   =   n(A ∪ B) = _____

B Add these one-digit numbers.

① 6	② 3	③ 1	④ 8	⑤ 9	⑥ 0	⑦ 1	⑧ 9	⑨ 5	⑩ 6
+ 7	+ 6	+ 2	+ 5	+ 4	+ 3	+ 8	+ 7	+ 1	+ 5
13									

⑪ 5	⑫ 7	⑬ 4	⑭ 1	⑮ 8	⑯ 9	⑰ 9	⑱ 0	⑲ 6	⑳ 5
1	8	3	4	0	1	4	1	3	9
+ 1	+ 9	+ 2	+ 1	+ 2	+ 9	+ 5	+ 6	+ 0	+ 9

㉑ 5	㉒ 8	㉓ 2	㉔ 7	㉕ 6	㉖ 3	㉗ 6	㉘ 1	㉙ 7	㉚ 2
8	8	0	4	4	6	2	8	1	9
+ 4	+ 2	+ 2	+ 1	+ 5	+ 3	+ 1	+ 4	+ 1	+ 6

㉛ 2	㉜ 7	㉝ 2	㉞ 9	㉟ 7	㊱ 1	㊲ 1	㊳ 8	㊴ 1	㊵ 6
2	4	2	2	4	8	3	8	0	6
8	8	7	5	7	4	2	6	3	1
+ 6	+ 2	+ 9	+ 0	+ 6	+ 6	+ 7	+ 2	+ 7	+ 9

㊶ 8	㊷ 3	㊸ 2	㊹ 5	㊺ 2	㊻ 1	㊼ 3	㊽ 6	㊾ 2	㊿ 5
2	1	0	4	0	8	3	4	3	2
5	1	5	9	8	5	4	2	2	8
+ 2	+ 1	+ 5	+ 4	+ 4	+ 3	+ 8	+ 1	+ 2	+ 7

   Test 8 cont'd ☞

C Add these two-digit numbers.

① 11 +14	② 53 +41	③ 79 +85	④ 31 +24	⑤ 63 +15	⑥ 79 +94	⑦ 21 +44	⑧ 48 +31
25							

⑨ 57 +64	⑩ 92 +62	⑪ 26 +96	⑫ 61 +93	⑬ 21 +24	⑭ 45 +55	⑮ 51 +68	⑯ 32 +53

⑰ 24 71 +34	⑱ 80 25 +86	⑲ 50 26 +17	⑳ 82 41 +97	㉑ 74 24 +53	㉒ 10 84 +52	㉓ 74 64 +97	㉔ 18 23 +78

㉕ 63 77 +21	㉖ 26 17 +19	㉗ 49 23 +34	㉘ 81 10 +93	㉙ 73 14 +90	㉚ 48 88 +74	㉛ 85 18 +43	㉜ 33 11 +15

㉝ 91 98 +20	㉞ 84 32 +16	㉟ 13 87 +49	㊱ 81 13 +20	㊲ 46 82 +27	㊳ 25 98 +18	㊴ 10 24 +30	㊵ 14 41 +18

㊶ 55 + 82 + 90 + 12 = _____   ㊷ 72 + 58 + 29 + 71 = _____   ㊸ 43 + 91 + 44 + 45 = _____

㊹ 87 + 77 + 77 + 78 = _____   ㊺ 99 + 91 + 95 + 11 = _____   ㊻ 50 + 26 + 13 + 69 = _____

㊼ 82 + 11 + 57 + 65 = _____   ㊽ 46 + 95 + 17 + 14 = _____   ㊾ 16 + 12 + 20 + 43 = _____

㊿ 31 + 12 + 16 + 67 = _____   51 52 + 62 + 82 + 72 = _____   52 55 + 84 + 41 + 32 = _____

53 87 + 18 + 66 + 26 = _____   54 34 + 41 + 62 + 13 = _____   55 23 + 66 + 69 + 82 = _____

Write a paragraph which includes an addition problem that can be solved on the number line below.

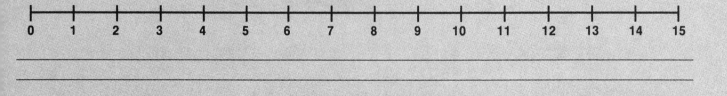

_____

_____

_____

_____

_____

100

Adding Three-Digit Numbers

Learning Objective: *We will learn to add three-digit numbers.*

A three-digit number has digits in the ones' place, in the tens' place, and in the hundreds' place.

EXAMPLE:

When we add three-digit numbers, we sometimes carry to the thousands' column.

```
  111
  333
  222
+ 555
─────
1,110
```

A Add these three-digit numbers.

① 117
+ 235
352

② 476
+ 436

③ 439
+ 750

④ 802
+ 825

⑤ 253
+ 688

⑥ 112
+ 715

⑦ 287
+ 822

⑧ 503
+ 469

⑨ 467
+ 453

⑩ 291
+ 614

⑪ 927
+ 328

⑫ 594
+ 172

⑬ 648
+ 350

⑭ 252
+ 192

⑮ 570
+ 941

⑯ 300
+ 232

⑰ 375
+ 387

⑱ 360
+ 829

⑲ 166
+ 576

⑳ 475
+ 384

㉑ 627
+ 149

㉒ 582
+ 372

㉓ 941
+ 602

㉔ 320
+ 314

㉕ 907
529
+ 703

㉖ 125
207
+ 813

㉗ 467
566
+ 891

㉘ 192
806
+ 378

㉙ 357
372
+ 581

㉚ 893
624
+ 853

㉛ 719
624
+ 258

㉜ 769
716
+ 276

㉝ 345
671
+ 193

㉞ 216
723
+ 242

㉟ 691
735
+ 842

㊱ 639
818
+ 527

㊲ 318
307
+ 672

㊳ 601
796
+ 785

㊴ 202
327
+ 612

㊵ 391
176
+ 504

㊶ 319
847
+ 138

㊷ 692
953
+ 879

㊸ 625
413
+ 484

㊹ 985
697
+ 135

㊺ 132
907
+ 620

㊻ 741
406
+ 788

㊼ 250
152
+ 431

㊽ 452
697
+ 835

REMINDER: Write the definition of a three-digit number.

Unit 41 cont'd ☞

B Find the sums.

① 929 + 683 + 174 + 709 = __2,495__

② 231 + 531 + 796 + 589 = _____

③ 484 + 254 + 105 + 288 = _____

④ 760 + 414 + 730 + 264 = _____

⑤ 713 + 869 + 295 + 387 = _____

⑥ 962 + 541 + 348 + 409 = _____

⑦ 856 + 971 + 351 + 320 = _____

⑧ 907 + 620 + 374 + 140 = _____

⑨ 678 + 825 + 105 + 245 = _____

⑩ 384 + 627 + 149 + 582 = _____

⑪ 372 + 941 + 602 + 320 = _____

⑫ 314 + 907 + 529 + 125 = _____

⑬ 207 + 467 + 566 + 192 = _____

⑭ 806 + 378 + 357 + 361 = _____

⑮ 492 + 732 + 859 + 417 = _____

⑯ 264 + 835 + 252 + 192 = _____

⑰ 570 + 941 + 300 + 232 = _____

⑱ 375 + 387 + 360 + 829 = _____

C Find the sums.

① Smith County coal miners worked 272 days in 1981, 193 days in 1982, and 176 days the following year. In 1984, all miners were laid off. How many days did the miners work during the four years?
__641__

② Three hundred one of Smithton's residences are listed in the phone directory. Another 102 residences have unlisted numbers, and 111 have no phones. How many residences are in the town of Smithton?
_____

③ The day Clark began a new novel, he read 192 pages. The next day he read 103 pages. He completed the book on the third day after reading 151 more pages. How many pages did he read?
_____

④ Jenna collects coins. There are 210 silver dollars in her collection, plus 106 half dollars, 136 quarters, 148 dimes, 120 nickels, and 113 pennies. How many coins are in the collection?
_____

⑤ In one month, the Smith County humane shelter was the temporary home for 116 cats, 218 kittens, 309 dogs, and 493 puppies. How many animals were housed at the shelter during the month?
_____

⑥ A traffic counter placed on a city street tallied 403 vehicles on Monday, 397 on Tuesday, 416 on Wednesday, and 379 on Thursday. How many vehicles were counted during the four days?
_____

⑦ Five hundred ninety people attended the first performance at the community theater. Attendance dropped to 206 the following evening. How many people attended the two performances?
_____

⑧ In 1981, kindergarten enrollment at Smith County Schools was 609. In 1982, enrollment increased to 794. What was the total kindergarten enrollment for the two years?
_____

Adding Four-Digit Numbers

Unit 42

Learning
Objective: *We will learn to add four-digit numbers.*

A four-digit number has digits in the ones' place, the tens' place, the hundreds' place, and in the thousands' place.

EXAMPLE:

When we add four-digit numbers, we sometimes carry to the ten thousands' column.

$$
\begin{array}{r}
1\ 1\ 1\ 1 \\
3{,}333 \\
2{,}222 \\
+\ \ 5{,}555 \\
\hline
11{,}110
\end{array}
$$

A Add these four-digit numbers.

①　8,373　　② 3,718　　③ 6,594　　④ 7,158　　⑤ 6,523　　⑥ 3,265
　+ 5,623　　+ 4,621　　+ 2,842　　+ 4,237　　+ 3,718　　+ 3,738
　13,996

⑦　1,371　　⑧ 1,531　　⑨ 2,594　　⑩ 6,472　　⑪ 2,141　　⑫ 1,311
　+ 3,845　　+ 1,111　　+ 3,612　　+ 3,158　　+ 6,622　　+ 8,725

⑬　2,894　　⑭ 5,080　　⑮ 4,021　　⑯ 4,491　　⑰ 5,117　　⑱ 8,029
　+ 3,643　　+ 3,017　　+ 6,351　　+ 3,994　　+ 2,141　　+ 1,994

⑲　5,016　　⑳ 5,999　　㉑ 2,741　　㉒ 1,847　　㉓ 6,074　　㉔ 5,074
　6,301　　5,840　　6,453　　1,162　　8,222　　7,618
　+ 8,100　　+ 8,820　　+ 6,362　　+ 9,228　　+ 7,992　　+ 4,613

㉕　2,710　　㉖ 1,166　　㉗ 2,520　　㉘ 5,582　　㉙ 6,612　　㉚ 1,423
　3,718　　6,198　　5,511　　2,326　　4,607　　3,845
　+ 5,331　　+ 8,628　　+ 3,782　　+ 1,418　　+ 4,214　　+ 4,284

㉛　3,331　　㉜ 5,470　　㉝ 6,912　　㉞ 3,729　　㉟ 2,432　　㊱ 2,441
　8,148　　9,984　　8,161　　9,492　　6,188　　6,031
　+ 2,494　　+ 2,702　　+ 8,209　　+ 1,522　　+ 2,446　　+ 1,918

REMINDER: Write the definition of a four-digit number.

Unit 42 cont'd ☞

B Find the sums.

①	②	③	④	⑤	⑥
2,402	3,093	1,377	9,711	4,622	8,410
6,484	1,610	2,134	4,531	9,146	4,390
1,938	7,018	4,554	4,789	8,261	9,307
+ 7,724	+ 1,349	+ 7,377	+ 5,465	+ 4,853	+ 7,282
18,548					

⑦	⑧	⑨	⑩	⑪	⑫
9,156	2,088	8,883	1,783	6,613	7,408
4,284	1,861	3,718	3,129	5,890	9,910
7,331	1,738	7,273	1,687	4,221	1,651
+ 1,921	+ 1,621	+ 9,160	+ 3,184	+ 3,547	+ 6,321

⑬	⑭	⑮	⑯	⑰	⑱
1,821	1,147	4,609	6,136	8,181	4,554
9,114	2,300	5,442	9,170	4,216	7,772
6,871	2,863	1,891	2,871	9,517	2,004
+ 4,233	+ 3,987	+ 2,811	+ 5,026	+ 2,013	+ 1,667

C Find the sums.

① A canned good inventory at the supermarket listed 1,279 cans of green beans, 2,860 cans of corn, 1,783 cans of carrots, and 1,043 cans of beets. How many cans were inventoried?

6,965

② During one week, Smith Office Supply sold 1,011 binders, 7,693 boxes of paperclips, 5,481 pencils, and 9,000 sheets of typing paper. How many items were sold during one week?

③ In September, 3,738 ducks passed over the Whittaker Wildlife Refuge. The next month, 4,610 ducks flew over. The November tally was 1,019. How many ducks flew over the refuge during the three-month period?

④ In 1981, the Smith County newspaper claimed 5,064 subscribers. One year later, 1,089 new subscribers were added. The next year brought 1,105 more. How many subscribers were there at the end of 1983?

⑤ Sun lovers flocked to the beach the first day that the temperature climbed past 65 degrees. By 10 a.m., 1,036 people had claimed their spots in the sun. By 2 p.m., 1,104 others had arrived. How many were at the beach that day?

⑥ Smithton College lists 4,186 freshmen among its enrollment statistics. Added to this number are 5,283 sophomores, 6,128 juniors, and 3,986 seniors. What is the college's total enrollment?

Adding Five-Digit Numbers

Learning Objective: *We will learn to add five-digit numbers.*

A five-digit number has digits in the ones' place, the tens' place, the hundreds' place, the thousands' place, and in the ten thousands' place.

EXAMPLE:

When we add five-digit numbers, we sometimes carry to the hundred thousands' column.

```
 111 11
 33,333
 22,222
+ 55,555
───────
111,110
```

A Add these five-digit numbers.

① 11,001
  + 23,783
  ──────
    34,784

② 92,246
  + 84,574

③ 59,673
  + 74,888

④ 83,139
  + 21,104

⑤ 11,766
  + 12,284

⑥ 13,897
  + 14,364

⑦ 51,548
  + 16,317

⑧ 64,918
  + 55,519

⑨ 19,920
  + 17,211

⑩ 89,522
  + 72,310

⑪ 24,692
  + 53,122

⑫ 65,627
  + 90,828

⑬ 54,129
  + 14,530

⑭ 51,431
  + 41,153

⑮ 21,094
  + 33,273

⑯ 47,133
   59,999
  + 41,678

⑰ 47,324
   81,184
  + 68,595

⑱ 99,350
   39,514
  + 35,584

⑲ 52,674
   15,314
  + 44,542

⑳ ,82,055
   39,615
  + 68,571

㉑ 60,804
   56,130
  + 13,627

㉒ 16,394
   73,642
  + 67,654

㉓ 95,066
   35,671
  + 66,820

㉔ 69,707
   70,911
  + 12,378

㉕ 19,025
   94,354
  + 84,169

㉖ 35,396
   76,877
  + 98,911

㉗ 99,415
   10,213
  + 11,171

㉘ 28,413
   40,149
  + 54,715

㉙ 48,616
   12,175
  + 46,318

㉚ 99,119
   96,205
  + 41,213

REMINDER: *Write the definition of a five-digit number.*

Unit 43 cont'd ☞

B Find the sums.

①
```
   17,222
   12,386
   72,493
+  32,528
  _____
  134,629
```

②
```
   22,650
   27,762
   28,707
+  29,203
```

③
```
   37,493
   18,640
   32,444
+  13,381
```

④
```
   13,468
   73,546
   83,672
+  37,145
```

⑤
```
   38,103
   95,554
   79,841
+  31,342
```

⑥
```
   22,943
   87,344
   88,445
+  48,246
```

⑦
```
   94,647
   70,048
   80,949
+  49,490
```

⑧
```
   15,060
   25,167
   85,223
+  53,147
```

⑨
```
   65,453
   15,571
   56,165
+  73,103
```

⑩
```
   58,805
   94,000
   60,786
+  61,536
```

⑪
```
   28,766
   34,765
   64,514
+  65,650
```

⑫
```
   66,598
   16,730
   68,677
+  69,100
```

⑬
```
   17,097
   24,190
   93,539
+  61,480
```

⑭
```
   15,002
   67,234
   14,143
+  51,567
```

⑮
```
   54,682
   27,700
   78,687
+  91,171
```

C Find the sums.

① In the five years that followed the discovery of the Grand Prairie diamond mine, 16,781 gems were found. In the next 10 years, 23,949 more diamonds were taken from the mine. How many were found in 15 years?

40,730

② Most of the population of Smith County lives in three cities. Diego, with a population of 18,232, is the smallest of the cities. The population of Chandler is 27,690, and the population of Douglas is 43,921. What is the combined population of the three cities?

③ Sage Canyon Ranch was built around 32,000 head of cattle. In the years that followed, 11,000 head were added. A partnership with the Silver Dollar Ranch brought another 19,800 to the herd. What was the total count after the partnership?

④ During the first week in October, the Crown Pumpkin Farm harvested 10,986 pumpkins. The next week's harvest was 13,561. Another 27,910 pumpkins were picked during the last two weeks of the month. What was the total harvest?

⑤ The Larado Forest covers 18,000 acres of land. It is near the Pines Resort, which includes another 36,700 acres. The Oak Hill Waterfowl Refuge to the north covers 16,560 acres. What is the total number of acres?

⑥ At the Sunny Brite factory, 87,000 eggs were cleaned and packed in one day. A machine failure caused the next day's total to drop to 61,942. On the third day, 76,893 eggs were processed. How many eggs were cleaned in three days?

106

Finding the Sums

Learning Objective: *We will learn to identify the parts of an addition problem.*

A sum is the combined value of two or more numbers which are called addends.

EXAMPLE: **5,555 is the sum of addends 3,333 and 2,222.**

$$\begin{array}{r} 3,333 \\ +2,222 \\ \hline 5,555 \end{array}$$

A From each group of numbers, determine which are addends and which is the sum. Label each addend "a" and each sum "s." Write the addition problems in the spaces at the right.

① 2,495 _a_   2,495
  2,147 _a_   +2,147
  4,642 _s_   4,642

② 113 ___
  234 ___
  121 ___

③ 682 ___
  264 ___
  946 ___

④ 4,758 ___
  2,498 ___
  2,260 ___

⑤ 20,411 ___
  75,728 ___
  55,317 ___

⑥ 657 ___
  422 ___
  235 ___

⑦ 1,875 ___
  3,307 ___
  1,432 ___

⑧ 1,543 ___
  3,586 ___
  2,043 ___

⑨ 19,022 ___
  50,026 ___
  69,048 ___

⑩ 496 ___
  140 ___
  906 ___
  270 ___

⑪ 1,951 ___
  9,810 ___
  6,415 ___
  1,444 ___

⑫ 9,564 ___
  6,833 ___
  1,136 ___
  1,595 ___

⑬ 13,996 ___
  18,339 ___
  19,436 ___
  51,771 ___

⑭ 11,395 ___
  38,639 ___
  10,241 ___
  17,003 ___

⑮ 5,216 ___
  2,642 ___
  1,206 ___
  9,064 ___

⑯ 680 ___
  196 ___
  308 ___
  176 ___

⑰ 310 ___
  366 ___
  829 ___
  153 ___

⑱ 68,097 ___
  10,372 ___
  96,954 ___
  18,485 ___

REMINDER: Write the definition of a sum.

   Unit 44 cont'd ☞

B Match the addends with their sums.

① 7,258 + 1,002 =   1,370   ⑩ 8,214 + 7,431 =   2,105

② 3,194 + 4,172 =   34,525   ⑪ 1,066 + 1,039 =   31,618

③ 659 + 155 + 556=   8,260   ⑫ 18,548 + 13,070 =   2,028

④ 12,237 + 22,288 =   7,366   ⑬ 15,422 + 24,496 =   15,645

⑤ 17,035 + 11,759 =   10,919   ⑭ 268 + 822 + 938=   39,918

⑥ 932 + 615 + 433=   27,805   ⑮ 8,290 + 3,497 =   2,344

⑦ 9,522 + 1,397 =   28,794   ⑯ 922 + 692 + 730=   11,032

⑧ 15,992 + 11,813 =   1,980   ⑰ 529 + 220 + 391=   11,787

⑨ 318 + 156 + 232=   706   ⑱ 8,320 + 2,712 =   1,140

C Study the paragraphs below. In the space to the right of each paragraph, write the addition problem and label the addends "a" and the sums "s."

① Linda's add-a-pearl necklace was strung with 8 pearls when she entered high school. By the end of her senior year, 4 more pearls had been added. Four more were added during college. How many pearls were there at the end of college?

② Ann drove 4,875 miles the first year after she was licensed. The next year, she drove 6,742 miles. By the next year, she had added 8,460 miles to her record. How many miles did Ann drive during the three years?

③ Freshman English students were asked to learn 100 new words the first week of the fall semester. The next week, they were asked to learn 150 new words, and in week three, they were asked to learn 200 more. How many words did they learn in three weeks?

④ Wilbur earned 300 extra points by turning in additional homework during the first semester of the school year. During the second semester, Wilbur earned 185 extra points. How many extra points did he earn during the year?

An Addition Table

Learning
Objective: *We will learn to add with the aid of an addition table.*

An addition table shows the combined values of given pairs of numbers.

EXAMPLE:
Where row 1 (from left to right) meets with column 1
(from top to bottom) is the number 2. The addition sentence
would be written $1 + 1 = 2$.   2 is the sum of $1 + 1$.

+	0	1	2	3
0	0	1	2	3
1	1	②	3	4
2	2	3	4	5
3	3	4	5	6

A Write the additions sentences shown below.

① $2 + 2 = 4$

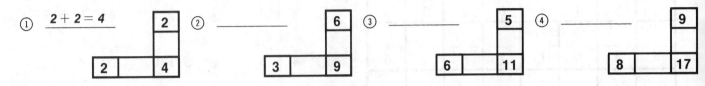

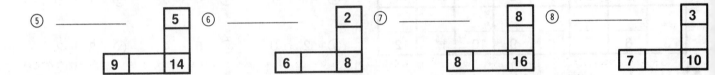

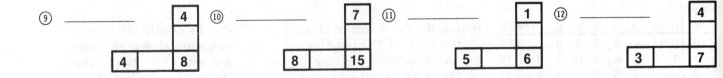

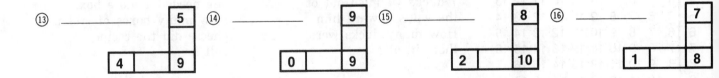

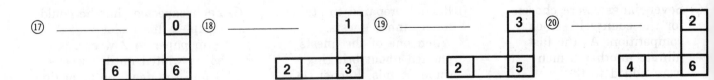

REMINDER: Write the definition of an addition table.

Unit 45 cont'd ☞

B On the addition table to the left, write the letter of each addition problem next to its sum.

+	0	1	2	3	4	5	6
0	D 0	1	2	3	4	5	6
1	1	2	3	4	5	6	7
2	2	3	4	5	6	7	8
3	3	4	5	6	7	8	9
4	4	5	6	7	8	9	10
5	5	6	7	8	9	10	11
6	6	7	8	9	10	11	12

(A) 5 + 2   (B) 6 + 6   (C) 4 + 6

(D) 0 + 0   (E) 3 + 1   (F) 5 + 5

(G) 6 + 3   (H) 2 + 4   (I) 1 + 0

(J) 4 + 1   (K) 5 + 6   (L) 0 + 4

(M) 2 + 6   (N) 1 + 2   (O) 3 + 5

(P) 4 + 3   (Q) 5 + 0   (R) 4 + 4

(S) 1 + 1   (T) 0 + 3   (U) 1 + 6

(V) 2 + 0   (W) 5 + 4   (X) 3 + 2

C Use the addition table to find the sums.

+	0	1	2	3	4	5	6	7	8	9
0	0	1	2	3	4	5	6	7	8	9
1	1	2	3	4	5	6	7	8	9	10
2	2	3	4	5	6	7	8	9	10	11
3	3	4	5	6	7	8	9	10	11	12
4	4	5	6	7	8	9	10	11	12	13
5	5	6	7	8	9	10	11	12	13	14
6	6	7	8	9	10	11	12	13	14	15
7	7	8	9	10	11	12	13	14	15	16
8	8	9	10	11	12	13	14	15	16	17
9	9	10	11	12	13	14	15	16	17	18

① Martin fed 8 ducks at the edge of the pond. As he tore off pieces of bread and scattered them on the ground, another 7 ducks waddled out of the water toward him. How many ducks were there in all?

_____

② Jillian bought 2 boxes of cream cheese to make a strawberry cheesecake. When she checked the recipe, she found that she needed 1 more box. How many boxes of cream cheese did the recipe call for?

_____

③ Seven judges were chosen for the county livestock competition. At the last minute another 2 men were added to the judging panel. How many judges reviewed the county's prize livestock?

_____

④ Rachel prepared the table for 9 dinner guests. When one of the guests phoned about bringing some friends, Rachel set 2 more places at the table. How many guests would be coming to dinner?

_____

⑤ Zach expected that he could complete his biology term paper in 2 weeks, so he waited until 2 weeks before the deadline to begin. His paper was finished 3 weeks after the deadline. How many weeks did he work on the paper?

_____

Comprehension Check

A Add these three-digit numbers.

①	185	②	729	③	348	④	123	⑤	629	⑥	943
	+ 369		+ 336		+ 763		+ 819		+ 584		+ 426
	554										

⑦	741	⑧	539	⑨	630	⑩	214	⑪	337	⑫	306
	+ 123		+ 875		+ 572		+ 381		+ 270		+ 583

⑬	135	⑭	156	⑮	261	⑯	750	⑰	248	⑱	130
	382		112		178		832		848		603
	+ 741		+ 314		+ 449		+ 424		+ 317		+ 911

⑲	473	⑳	153	㉑	869	㉒	661	㉓	613	㉔	231
	890		473		119		288		284		908
	124		574		564		246		979		800
	+ 753		+ 413		+ 984		+ 582		+ 433		+ 729

B Add these four-digit numbers.

①	1,338	②	1,151	③	2,356	④	6,341	⑤	2,616	⑥	1,837
	+ 7,451		+ 3,111		+ 9,142		+ 7,528		+ 4,221		+ 1,215
	8,789										

⑦	2,386	⑧	8,107	⑨	4,349	⑩	1,471	⑪	5,603	⑫	5,589
	9,443		4,603		9,914		8,109		1,061		8,894
	+ 5,300		+ 2,511		+ 5,211		+ 2,994		+ 8,100		+ 2,900

⑬	2,767	⑭	1,198	⑮	6,870	⑯	5,740	⑰	1,669	⑱	8,012
	4,345		1,246		2,972		6,671		2,688		5,215
	6,132		2,728		9,422		1,483		2,535		3,482
	+ 2,357		+ 7,311		+ 3,081		+ 1,681		+ 5,721		+ 1,268

⑲	6,446	⑳	8,224	㉑	9,184	㉒	6,889	㉓	4,529	㉔	4,286
	6,210		8,354		5,924		1,216		2,922		2,611
	1,274		3,823		9,778		2,019		2,624		9,031
	+ 1,344		+ 1,434		+ 4,002		+ 3,917		+ 1,438		+ 1,810

Test 9 cont'd

C Add these five-digit numbers.

① 12,130
  + 70,813
    82,943

② 98,242
  + 54,764

③ 57,946
  + 87,388

④ 82,311
  + 13,094

⑤ 11,127
  + 72,686

⑥ 11,348
  + 39,674

⑦ 51,165
   34,187
  + 65,459

⑧ 51,189
   11,979
  + 22,101

⑨ 87,925
   32,120
  + 25,436

⑩ 19,222
   69,506
  + 82,278

⑪ 51,441
   52,390
  + 54,114

⑫ 13,513
   23,130
  + 29,743

⑬ 45,479
   11,963
   97,398
  + 48,671

⑭ 83,152
   89,445
   93,399
  + 53,555

⑮ 18,044
   51,425
   46,357
  + 71,444

⑯ 83,629
   80,655
   17,551
  + 65,106

⑰ 38,160
   32,407
   17,637
  + 36,694

⑱ 54,249
   36,556
   68,672
  + 67,902

D Label each addend "a" and each sum "s." Write the problems in the spaces at the right.

① 5,290 _a_
  7,493 _s_
  2,203 _a_

    5,290
  + 2,203
    7,493

② 190 ___
  297 ___
  487 ___

③ 37,956 ___
  14,753 ___
  23,203 ___

④ 23,927 ___
  15,997 ___
  74,708 ___
  34,784 ___

⑤ 1,768 ___
  9,425 ___
  4,201 ___
  3,456 ___

⑥ 1,104 ___
  2,432 ___
  2,405 ___
  5,941 ___

⑦ 282 ___
  516 ___
  984 ___
  186 ___

⑧ 9,624 ___
  5,120 ___
  3,373 ___
  1,131 ___

⑨ 161 ___
  238 ___
  540 ___
  141 ___

Fill in the squares on the number table, and write 12 addition sentences using these numbers.

+	0	1	2	3	4	5	6
0							
1							
2							
3							
4							
5							
6							

① _____
② _____
③ _____
④ _____
⑤ _____
⑥ _____
⑦ _____
⑧ _____
⑨ _____
⑩ _____
⑪ _____
⑫ _____

Simple Addition

Learning Objective: *We will learn to add by combining ten thousands, thousands, hundreds, tens, and ones.*

Addition is the combining of numbers to obtain the total value or sum.

EXAMPLE:
Multi-digit numbers may be added by combining ones, tens, hundreds, etc.

$$
\begin{array}{r}
333 \\
222 \\
+\ 555 \\
\hline
1{,}110
\end{array}
\Bigg\}
$$

$$
\begin{array}{r}
300 + 30 + 3 \\
200 + 20 + 2 \\
+\ 500 + 50 + 5 \\
\hline
1{,}000 + 100 + 10 = 1{,}110
\end{array}
$$

A Add these two-digit numbers by combining ones and tens.

①
$$
\begin{array}{r} 67 \\ +\ 83 \\ \hline \end{array}
\qquad
\begin{array}{r} 60 + 7 \\ 80 + 3 \\ \hline 140 + 10 = 150 \end{array}
$$

②
$$
\begin{array}{r} 91 \\ +\ 58 \\ \hline \end{array}
$$

③
$$
\begin{array}{r} 22 \\ +\ 25 \\ \hline \end{array}
$$

④
$$
\begin{array}{r} 59 \\ +\ 68 \\ \hline \end{array}
$$

⑤
$$
\begin{array}{r} 96 \\ +\ 26 \\ \hline \end{array}
$$

⑥
$$
\begin{array}{r} 56 \\ +\ 88 \\ \hline \end{array}
$$

⑦
$$
\begin{array}{r} 13 \\ +\ 82 \\ \hline \end{array}
$$

⑧
$$
\begin{array}{r} 26 \\ +\ 48 \\ \hline \end{array}
$$

⑨
$$
\begin{array}{r} 18 \\ 53 \\ +\ 73 \\ \hline \end{array}
$$

⑩
$$
\begin{array}{r} 14 \\ 42 \\ +\ 34 \\ \hline \end{array}
$$

⑪
$$
\begin{array}{r} 26 \\ 26 \\ +\ 33 \\ \hline \end{array}
$$

⑫
$$
\begin{array}{r} 31 \\ 62 \\ +\ 58 \\ \hline \end{array}
$$

B Add these three-digit numbers by combining ones, tens, and hundreds.

①
$$
\begin{array}{r} 132 \\ +\ 435 \\ \hline \end{array}
\qquad
\begin{array}{r} 100 + 30 + 2 \\ 400 + 30 + 5 \\ \hline 500 + 60 + 7 = 567 \end{array}
$$

②
$$
\begin{array}{r} 512 \\ +\ 135 \\ \hline \end{array}
$$

③
$$
\begin{array}{r} 624 \\ +\ 517 \\ \hline \end{array}
$$

④
$$
\begin{array}{r} 182 \\ +\ 112 \\ \hline \end{array}
$$

⑤
$$
\begin{array}{r} 271 \\ +\ 111 \\ \hline \end{array}
$$

⑥
$$
\begin{array}{r} 517 \\ +\ 178 \\ \hline \end{array}
$$

⑦
$$
\begin{array}{r} 882 \\ 521 \\ +\ 504 \\ \hline \end{array}
$$

⑧
$$
\begin{array}{r} 612 \\ 614 \\ +\ 567 \\ \hline \end{array}
$$

⑨
$$
\begin{array}{r} 291 \\ 651 \\ +\ 481 \\ \hline \end{array}
$$

REMINDER: Write the definition of addition.

Unit 46 cont'd ☛

C Add these four- and five-digit numbers by combining ones, tens, hundreds, thousands, and ten thousands.

①
$$4,986 \qquad 4,000 + 900 + 80 + 6$$
$$+ \ 3,031 \qquad 3,000 \qquad + 30 + 1$$

$$7,000 + 900 + 110 + 7$$
$$= 8,017$$

②
$$6,566$$
$$+ \ 1,010$$

③
$$18,200$$
$$+ \ 13,256$$

④
$$35,871$$
$$+ \ 10,075$$

⑤
$$1,240$$
$$1,542$$
$$+ \ 9,103$$

⑥
$$6,267$$
$$6,371$$
$$+ \ 4,856$$

⑦
$$17,683$$
$$14,581$$
$$+ \ 66,248$$

⑧
$$54,018$$
$$31,702$$
$$+ \ 15,261$$

D Read each problem, then add by combining ones, tens, hundreds, thousands, and ten thousands.

① Alvin collects U.S. postage stamps. In his collection are 14,563 5-cent stamps, 10,910 10-cent stamps, and 22,015 20-cent stamps. How many 5-, 10-, and 20-cent stamps are included in Alvin's collection?

② Irene is a cake decorator. In one month, she decorated 35 wedding cakes, 22 birthday cakes, and 14 anniversary cakes. How many cakes did Irene decorate that month?

③ A biology assignment called for freshmen students to find out their blood types. The results were 109 with type A blood, 157 with type B, and 174 with type O. How many freshman class members participated in the biology exercise?

Addition Problems

Learning Objective: *We will learn to add single- and multi- digit numbers.*

Addition is the combining of numbers to obtain the total value or sum.

EXAMPLE:	Single- and mult-digit numbers may be combined to obtain a sum.	3,333 + 2 3,335

A Find the sums.

(1) 667
+ 11
678

(2) 300
+ 9

(3) 121
+ 37

(4) 138
+ 84

(5) 81
+ 478

(6) 615
+ 74

(7) 61
+ 1

(8) 645
+ 11

(9) 79
+ 9

(10) 118
+ 20

(11) 197
+ 29

(12) 420
+ 60

(13) 121
+ 64

(14) 35
+ 2

(15) 222
+ 92

(16) 33
+ 9

(17) 244
+ 96

(18) 253
+ 7

(19) 261
+ 2

(20) 27
+ 4

(21) 597
+ 28

(22) 78
+ 3

(23) 291
+ 33

(24) 301
+ 54

(25) 31
84
+ 6

(26) 322
1
+ 33

(27) 108
93
+ 44

(28) 73
93
+ 5

(29) 84
236
+ 400

(30) 37
84
+ 1

(31) 233
381
+ 96

(32) 92
14
+ 9

(33) 144
17
+ 10

(34) 421
334
+ 33

(35) 200
4
+ 48

(36) 91
54
+ 5

(37) 16
24
+ 6

(38) 145
4
+ 77

(39) 908
486
+ 62

(40) 624
99
+ 6

(41) 65
7
+ 93

(42) 51
96
+ 1

(43) 32
70
+ 2

(44) 531
401
+ 54

(45) 155
61
+ 87

(46) 64
85
+ 16

(47) 488
81
+ 91

(48) 9
41
+ 60

REMINDER: *Write the definition of addition.*

Unit 47 cont'd ☞

B Find the sums.

①
5,204
4,180
+ 716
10,100

②
4,596
192
+ 5,281

③
97,681
1,680
+ 3,701

④
2,241
41,317
+ 24,079

⑤
99,491
4,764
+ 601

⑥
8,017
118
+ 65

⑦
6,787
6,238
+ 231

⑧
784
2,841
+ 1,862

⑨
3,347
6,112
+ 641

⑩
69,324
4,539
+ 1,799

⑪
41,761
1,874
726
+ 3,815

⑫
67,882
5,396
9,711
+ 156

⑬
71,471
555
897
+ 8,626

⑭
4,420
2,070
1,496
+ 117

⑮
17,923
9,149
328
+ 580

C Find the sums.

① During his two-year stay in Europe, Peter mailed 476 letters, 1,001 post cards, and 49 packages to friends and relatives in the United States. How many items did Peter send to America?

1,526

② Twenty-seven students failed the final history exam. One hundred thirteen students passed the exam. Sixteen students had borderline grades and could pass with extra credit. How many were tested?

③ During a cross-country race, runners completed 413 miles in four days. Another 94 miles was run the fifth day, and 1,035 miles were covered in the 12 days after that. Was was the total number of miles run?

④ Thirty-six planes landed at Smithton Airport on the morning before the pilots' strike. On the same morning, 12 additional planes departed. How many planes flew in and out of the airport that morning?

⑤ On the first day of a new exercise program, Lisa did 25 sit-ups. The next day, she did 50. By the third day, she could manage 75 sit-ups, and on day four she did 100. How man sit-ups did she do in four days?

⑥ In its first month of operation, Frank's Hot Dogs served 10,981 customers. During the second month, 9,738 customers were served. Advertising during the third month brought in 13,046 customers. How many were served during the three months?

116

Addition Practice

Unit 48

Learning Objective: *We will learn to add various combinations of numbers.*

Addition is the combining of numbers to obtain the total value or sum.

EXAMPLE:
Single- and multi-digit numbers may be added in columns or rows. Each problem is made up of two or more addends and a sum.

```
3,333
  222
   50
+   5
_____
3,610
```

$3,333 + 222 + 50 + 5 = 3,610$

A Find the sums.

①	8,211 343 + 58 _____ **8,612**	②	51,102 133 + 139	③	1,021 23 + 141	④	6,496 13 + 15	⑤	612 11 + 8
⑥	6,784 93 + 8,313	⑦	680 40 + 126	⑧	1,161 251 + 38	⑨	23,616 164 + 1,451	⑩	9,115 9 + 189
⑪	18,514 3,198 202 + 68	⑫	182 181 139 + 98	⑬	75,111 14,678 1,801 + 69	⑭	1,441 43 206 + 232	⑮	1,832 20,219 180 + 158
⑯	1,842 3,312 9,256 + 202	⑰	10,421 2,277 189 + 192	⑱	14,319 19,425 6,125 + 192	⑲	19,411 966 2,257 + 9,343	⑳	13,378 25,941 6,455 + 78
㉑	173 65 79 + 121	㉒	1,541 221 54 + 45	㉓	10,011 985 129 + 1,919	㉔	3,220 1,511 146 + 235	㉕	1,191 6,162 106 + 184

REMINDER: *Write the definition of addition.*

117

Unit 48 cont'd 🖝

B Find the sums.

① $177 + 210 + 146 + 59 = \underline{\quad 592 \quad}$

② $2,091 + 32 + 149 + 114 = \underline{\qquad}$

③ $1,551 + 141 + 64 + 73 = \underline{\qquad}$

④ $23,923 + 223 + 319 + 296 = \underline{\qquad}$

⑤ $158 + 215 + 172 + 91 = \underline{\qquad}$

⑥ $1,262 + 268 + 2,121 + 97 = \underline{\qquad}$

⑦ $15,240 + 3,529 + 121 + 189 = \underline{\qquad}$

⑧ $1,627 + 941 + 827 + 1,109 = \underline{\qquad}$

⑨ $972 + 920 + 905 + 1,255 = \underline{\qquad}$

⑩ $766 + 998 + 444 + 1,511 = \underline{\qquad}$

⑪ $5,327 + 621 + 189 + 74 = \underline{\qquad}$

⑫ $2 + 859 + 776 + 9,541 = \underline{\qquad}$

⑬ $543 + 634 + 2,139 + 1,145 = \underline{\qquad}$

⑭ $1,924 + 1,576 + 1,310 + 2 = \underline{\qquad}$

⑮ $3,701 + 601 + 1 + 1,761 = \underline{\qquad}$

⑯ $1 + 209 + 1,181 + 2,268 = \underline{\qquad}$

⑰ $1,984 + 129 + 7 + 2,182 = \underline{\qquad}$

⑱ $114 + 11 + 71 + 1,304 = \underline{\qquad}$

C Find the sums.

① The Crestview Retirement Home has only 1 resident over age 100. There are 12 residents between ages 90 and 100, 58 residents between ages 70 and 90, and 37 residents ages 50-70. How many reside at Crestview?

_____**108**_____

② Members of the senior class ordered 179 yearbooks. Juniors ordered 363. Sophomores ordered a record low of 68 yearbooks, and freshmen ordered a record high of 497. How many high-school yearbooks were ordered?

_____

③ Cynthia, Dale, and Marla were the top three candy salespersons in the band fundraising drive. Cynthia sold 2,868 candy bars. Dale sold 1,077, and Marla sold 998. What was the total number of bars sold by the top three?

_____

④ Kristen's personal library consists of both fiction and nonfiction works by women authors. There are 764 works of nonfiction plus 1,013 works of fiction. In addition, there are 78 biographies of notable women. How many books are in Kristen's library?

_____

⑤ In one day, 1,987 invitations to the community benefit dance were mailed. The next day, another 1,647 were dispatched. On the third day, the last 746 invitations were mailed. What was the total number of invitations that were mailed?

_____

⑥ Attending the junior class play were 1,319 adults, many of whom were parents of members of the junior class. Also in attendance were 3,543 students and 621 children under age 5. How many attended the play?

_____

The Associative Property

Learning Objective: *We will learn to recognize the associative property in addition problems.*

The associative property of addition holds that the sum will be the same regardless of the way in which a series of numbers is combined.

EXAMPLE: □□□ + □□ + □ = □□□□□□

[□□□ + □□] + □ = □□□□□□   □□□ + [□□ + □] = □□□□□□
      5   + 1 =   6   3   +   3   =   6

A Match each addition problem in the left column with the two on the right which demonstrate the associative property.

_**b**_ ① △△△ + [△△△ + △△△] = △△△△△△△△△

___ ② [□□ + □□□] + □□ = □□□□□□□

___ ③ [△△△△ + △] + △ = △△△△△△

a. △△△△ + △△△ + △ =
     △△△△△△△△

___ ④ [△△△△ + △△△] + △ = △△△△△△△△

___ ⑤ △△ + [△△△△△ + △△△△] = △△△△△△△△△△△

b. △△△ + △△△ + △△△ =
     △△△△△△△△△

___ ⑥ [□ + □□□] + □ = □□□□□

c. □□□□ + □□ + □□□□ =
     □□□□□□□□□□

___ ⑦ [△△ + △△△△△] + △△△△ = △△△△△△△△△△△

d. △△△△ + △ + △ =
     △△△△△△

___ ⑧ [△△△ + △△△] + △△△ = △△△△△△△△△

___ ⑨ □□□□ + [□□ + □□□□] = □□□□□□□□□□

e. □□ + □□□ + □□ =
     □□□□□□□

___ ⑩ □ + [□□□ + □] = □□□□□

f. △△ + △△△△△ + △△△△ =
     △△△△△△△△△△△

___ ⑪ △△△△ + [△ + △] = △△△△△△

___ ⑫ △△△△ + [△△△ + △] = △△△△△△△△

g. □ + □□□ + □ =
     □□□□□

___ ⑬ □□ + [□□□ + □□] = □□□□□□□

___ ⑭ [□□□□ + □□] + □□□□ = □□□□□□□□□□

REMINDER: Write the definition of the associative property of addition.

_____

_____

B Match the addends with the sums.

① △△△△△ + [△△△ + △△△△△] =

② [▢▢▢ + ▢▢▢] +▢▢▢▢▢▢ =

③ △△ + [△△△△△△△ + △△△△△] =

④ [▢▢▢▢▢ + ▢▢▢▢▢] + ▢▢▢▢▢ =

⑤ [△△ + △△△△△△△] + △△△△△ =

⑥ ▢▢▢ + [▢▢▢ + ▢▢▢▢▢▢] =

⑦ [△△△△△ + △△△] + △△△△△ =

⑧ ▢▢▢▢▢ + [▢▢▢▢▢ + ▢▢▢▢▢] =

△△△△△△△△△△△△△

△△△△△△△△△△△△△△

▢▢▢▢▢▢▢▢▢▢▢▢▢▢▢

▢▢▢▢▢▢▢▢▢▢▢▢▢

C The day before the senior prom, members of the junior class sold flowers. Working in teams of two, the juniors competed to see who could sell the most. Below are two lists. The list to the left shows individual team sales. Find the total sales for each team and match them with the numbers at right to see who ranked highest in the competition. You will find that teams tied for each of the top three places.

Team Sales

① Rosa sold 12 carnations and 8 mums. Her partner, Ron, sold 5 orchids.

② David sold 13 carnations and 12 roses. His partner, Debra, sold 3 mums.

③ Paul sold 7 roses and 13 carnations. His partner, Bonnie, sold 7 orchids.

④ Rick sold 13 carnations. His partner, Rita, sold 12 roses and 3 mums.

⑤ Ralph sold 7 orchids. His partner, Jerry, sold 13 mums and 7 carnations.

⑥ Carol sold 12 roses. Her partner, Harold, sold 8 carnations and 5 mums.

Total Sales

____ ____ First place trophies were given to the two teams who sold 28 flowers apiece.

____ ____ Second place ribbons were given to the two teams who sold 27 flowers apiece.

____ ____ Third place ribbons were given to the two teams who sold 25 flowers apiece.

Using the Associative Property

Learning
Objective: *We will learn to use the associative property of addition.*

The associative property of addition holds that the sum will be the same regardless of the way in which a series of numbers is combined.

EXAMPLES:

$$[3 + 2] + 1 = 3 + 2 = \underline{}5$$
$$+\ 1$$
$$\overline{6}$$

$$3 + [2 + 1] = \underline{}3$$
$$2 + 1 = +\ 3$$
$$\overline{6}$$

A Below each set of brackets, write the sum of the two numbers within the brackets. Add to this sum the third number and write the answer in the space to the right of each problem.

① [35 + 29] + 12 = ___76___
   ___64___

② 35 + [29 + 12] = _____
   _____

③ 118 + [91 + 62] = _____
   _____

④ [118 + 91] + 62 = _____
   _____

⑤ [794 + 182] + 7,110 = _____
   _____

⑥ 794 + [182 + 7,110] = _____
   _____

⑦ 997 + [2,920 + 9,051] = _____
   _____

⑧ [997 + 2,920] + 9,051 = _____
   _____

⑨ [255 + 7,669] + 9,844 = _____
   _____

⑩ 255 + [7,669 + 9,844] = _____
   _____

⑪ 4,151 + [1,153 + 2,762] = _____
   _____

⑫ [4,151 + 1,153] + 2,762 = _____
   _____

⑬ [1,189 + 742] + 859 = _____
   _____

⑭ 1,189 + [742 + 859] = _____
   _____

⑮ 7,769 + [5,415 + 4,363] = _____
   _____

⑯ [7,769 + 5,415] + 4,363 = _____
   _____

⑰ [4,213 + 3,911] + 4,519 = _____
   _____

⑱ 4,213 + [3,911 + 4,519] = _____
   _____

REMINDER: Write the definition of the associative property of addition.

_____

_____

Unit 50 cont'd 👉

B Study each problem in column A. In column B, write a second problem that demonstrates the associative property of addition. Find the sums for all problems.

Column A	Column B
① [2,415 + 7,613] + 1,023 = __11,051__	__2,415 + [7,613 + 1,023] = 11,051__
② 7,016 + [117 + 6,112] = _____	_____
③ 91 + [1,812 + 2,681] = _____	_____
④ [9,841 + 2,972] + 1,821 = _____	_____
⑤ [1,411 + 711] + 3,042 = _____	_____
⑥ 5,241 + [5,221 + 8,171] = _____	_____
⑦ [6,591 + 35,833] + 931 = _____	_____

C Study the paragraphs below. In the space to the right of each paragraph, write two addition sentences that demonstrate the associative property. Find the sums.

① Barbara collected 387 aluminum cans the first day of the city-wide can collection weekend. On the second day, Barbara collected 596 cans. Barbara also turned in cans collected by her youngest brother, who was not old enough to officially take part in the event. These totaled 212. How many cans did Barbara turn in?

a. _____

b. _____

② When she baked the holiday ham, Celia cooked it for 60 minutes without removing the skin. She let it bake 60 minutes longer with the skin removed, then she smoothed on a brown sugar glaze and baked the ham another 60 minutes. How many minutes did the ham bake?

a. _____

b. _____

③ While hiking, Paula saw 6 deer, 10 wild turkeys, and 23 squirrels. How many animals did she see?

a. _____

b. _____

Comprehension Check

A Add these numbers by combining ones, tens, hundreds, and thousands.

① 565
 + 156

$500 + 60 + 5$
$100 + 50 + 6$
$600 + 110 + 11$
$= 721$

② 8,659
 + 9,258

③ 454
 + 367

④ 1,488
 + 8,101

⑤ 9,710
 + 3,174

⑥ 4,481
 + 1,253

⑦ 190
 + 241

⑧ 130
 + 561

⑨ 1,576
 + 9,019

⑩ 7,557
 + 1,529

⑪ 9,619
 + 7,548

⑫ 2,111
 + 1,841

⑬ 2,089
 + 9,123

⑭ 1,232
 + 7,710

⑮ 7,109
 + 2,365

⑯ 134
  629
 + 108

⑰ 3,221
  1,958
 + 2,078

⑱ 312
  448
 + 402

B Find the sums.

① 11,173
 + 222
 11,395

② 2,234
 + 528

③ 92,263
 + 3,822

④ 3,131
 + 78

⑤ 234
 + 6

⑥ 4,394
 + 483

⑦ 17,830
  337
 + 456

⑧ 9,784
  400
 + 960

⑨ 789
  1,285
 + 662

⑩ 61,570
  5,563
 + 7,601

⑪ 5,966
  835
 + 75

⑫ 52,794
  4,781
 + 808

⑬ 2,366
  8,445
  775
 + 6,661

⑭ 12,960
  7,431
  154
 + 9,938

⑮ 161
  15
  57
 + 410

⑯ 215
  346
  243
 + 7

⑰ 5,279
  4,781
  676
 + 1,808

⑱ 720
  71
  366
 + 84

Test 10 cont'd ☛

C Find the sums.

① $46,978 + 295 + 134 + 178 =$ __47,585__

② $1,785 + 9,721 + 292 + 275 =$ _____

③ $127 + 193 + 6,952 + 2,109 =$ _____

④ $5,196 + 3,061 + 47,946 + 252 =$ _____

⑤ $240 + 40,730 + 8,984 + 362 =$ _____

⑥ $800 + 524 + 457 + 71,260 =$ _____

⑦ $225 + 835 + 224 + 3,696 =$ _____

⑧ $6,511 + 548 + 9,179 + 59 =$ _____

⑨ $514 + 566 + 28,278 + 816 =$ _____

⑩ $887 + 3,103 + 944 + 8,410 =$ _____

⑪ $8,715 + 711 + 5,161 + 123 =$ _____

⑫ $474 + 134 + 59,514 + 999 =$ _____

D Below each set of brackets, write the sum of the two numbers within the brackets. Add to this sum the third addend and write the answer in the space at the right.

① $[152 + 810] + 8,161 =$ __9,123__
   962

② $152 + [810 + 816] =$ _____
   _____

③ $7,871 + [6,060 + 1,821] =$ _____
   _____

④ $[7,871 + 6,060] + 1,821 =$ _____
   _____

⑤ $[3,119 + 2,353] + 2,042 =$ _____
   _____

⑥ $3,119 + [2,353 + 2,042] =$ _____
   _____

⑦ $262 + [2,244 + 2,213] =$ _____
   _____

⑧ $[262 + 2,244] + 2,213 =$ _____
   _____

⑨ $[1,419 + 2,111] + 5,613 =$ _____
   _____

⑩ $1,419 + [2,111 + 5,613] =$ _____
   _____

⑪ $1,212 + [2,751 + 3,219] =$ _____
   _____

⑫ $[1,212 + 2,751] + 3,219 =$ _____
   _____

Write a paragraph that includes a problem with three addends. Using these three addends, write two addition sentences that demonstrate the associative property.

_____
_____
_____
_____
_____
_____
_____

The Commutative Property

Learning Objective: *We will learn to recognize the commutative property in addition problems.*

The commutative property of addition holds that the sum will be the same if the order of the addends is reversed.

EXAMPLE:
Adding on a number line is helpful in demonstrating the commutative property.

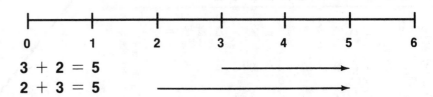

$3 + 2 = 5$
$2 + 3 = 5$

A Draw arrows to demonstrate the commutative property of addition.

①

$4 + 10 = 14$
$10 + 4 = 14$

②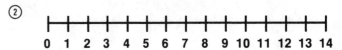

$4 + 8 = 12$
$8 + 4 = 12$

③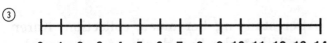

$4 + 6 = 10$
$6 + 4 = 10$

④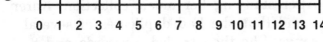

$3 + 5 = 8$
$5 + 3 = 8$

⑤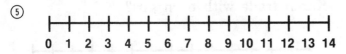

$5 + 6 = 11$
$6 + 5 = 11$

⑥

$7 + 6 = 13$
$6 + 7 = 13$

⑦

$4 + 7 = 11$
$7 + 4 = 11$

⑧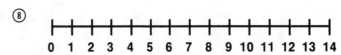

$5 + 8 = 13$
$8 + 5 = 13$

⑨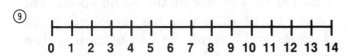

$5 + 7 = 12$
$7 + 5 = 12$

⑩

$3 + 6 = 9$
$6 + 3 = 9$

REMINDER: Write the definition of the commutative property of addition.

_____

_____

Unit 51 cont'd ☞

B Match the addends with the sums.

① ▲ ▲ ▲ ▲ ▲ ▲ ▲ + ▲ ▲ ▲ ▲ ▲ ▲ ▲ ▲ =

② △ △ △ △ △ △ △ △ + △ △ △ △ △ =

③ ▲ ▲ + ▲ ▲ ▲ ▲ ▲ ▲ ▲ ▲ ▲ =

④ △ △ △ △ △ △ △ △ △ △ + △ △ △ =

⑤ △ △ △ △ △ + △ △ △ △ △ △ △ △ =

⑥ ▲ ▲ ▲ ▲ ▲ ▲ ▲ ▲ ▲ + ▲ ▲ =

⑦ ▲ ▲ ▲ ▲ ▲ ▲ ▲ ▲ + ▲ ▲ ▲ ▲ ▲ ▲ =

⑧ △ △ △ + △ △ △ △ △ △ △ △ △ △ =

▲ ▲ ▲ ▲ ▲ ▲ ▲ ▲ ▲ ▲ ▲ ▲

△ △ △ △ △ △ △ △ △ △ △ △ △

▲ ▲ ▲ ▲ ▲ ▲ ▲ ▲ ▲ ▲ ▲ ▲ ▲ ▲ ▲

△ △ △ △ △ △ △ △ △ △ △ △ △ △

C Read each problem and draw arrows to demonstrate the commutative property.

① On the first day of training for the swim team, Lynn swam 4 laps around the pool, rested for 5 minutes, and swam 5 more laps. On the second day, she swam 5 laps, rested, and swam 4 more. How many laps did she swim each day?

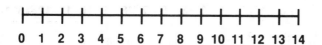

0 1 2 3 4 5 6 7 8 9 10 11 12 13 14

4 + 5 = 9
5 + 4 = 9

② After studying her music collection, Karen found that she had duplicates of several songs. She then traded 3 records and 8 tapes with Elaine. With Maria, she traded 8 records and 3 tapes. How many items did Karen trade with each girl?

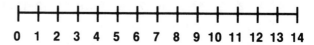

0 1 2 3 4 5 6 7 8 9 10 11 12 13 14

3 + 8 = 11
8 + 3 = 11

③ During the first week that he was at summer camp, Marcus received 8 letters from his friends and 6 letters from his family. During the second week of camp, he received 6 letters from his friends and 8 from his family. How many letters did he get each week?

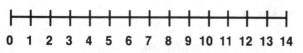

0 1 2 3 4 5 6 7 8 9 10 11 12 13 14

8 + 6 = 14
6 + 8 = 14

④ On a practice exercise, Greg typed 60 words per minute with 3 errors. His second try resulted in 4 errors at the same speed. The next day, he increased his speed, but made 4 errors and 3 errors on two attempts. How many errors did he make each day?

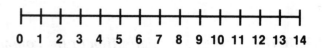

0 1 2 3 4 5 6 7 8 9 10 11 12 13 14

3 + 4 = 7
4 + 3 = 7

126

Using the Commutative Property   Unit 52

Learning Objective: *We will learn to use the commutative property of addition.*

The commutative property of addition holds that the sum will be the same if the order of the addends is reversed.

EXAMPLE:

$$\begin{array}{r} 3,333 \\ +\ 2,222 \\ \hline 5,555 \end{array} \quad = \quad \begin{array}{r} 2,222 \\ +\ 3,333 \\ \hline 5,555 \end{array}$$

A Find the sums.

① 613
+ 113
726

② 113
+ 613

③ 381
+ 629

④ 629
+ 381

⑤ 642
+ 156

⑥ 156
+ 642

⑦ 961
+ 152

⑧ 152
+ 961

⑨ 196
+ 191

⑩ 191
+ 196

⑪ 416
+ 742

⑫ 742
+ 416

⑬ 834
+ 940

⑭ 940
+ 834

⑮ 793
+ 473

⑯ 473
+ 793

⑰ 891
+ 890

⑱ 890
+ 891

⑲ 3,113
+ 2,055

⑳ 2,055
+ 3,113

㉑ 5,509
+ 8,441

㉒ 8,441
+ 5,509

㉓ 8,071
+ 6,238

㉔ 6,238
+ 8,071

㉕ 6,452
+ 3,909

㉖ 3,909
+ 6,452

㉗ 5,815
+ 2,620

㉘ 2,620
+ 5,815

㉙ 8,068
+ 9,445

㉚ 9,445
+ 8,068

㉛ 9,670
+ 3,606

㉜ 3,606
+ 9,670

㉝ 9,347
+ 6,863

㉞ 6,863
+ 9,347

㉟ 4,147
+ 3,484

㊱ 3,484
+ 4,147

㊲ 5,114
+ 362

㊳ 362
+ 5,114

㊴ 693
+ 2,467

㊵ 2,467
+ 693

㊶ 250
+ 4,365

㊷ 4,365
+ 250

REMINDER: Write the definition of the commutative property of addition.

_____

_____

Unit 52 cont'd 📭

B For each problem, write an addition sentence that illustrates the commutative property. Find the sums.

① 6,339 + 1,406 = _**7,745**_ _**1,406 + 6,339 = 7,745**_   ⑩ 7,361 + 199 = _____ _____

② 394 + 5,728 = _____ _____   ⑪ 138 + 1,112 = _____ _____

③ 8,057 + 7,260 = _____ _____   ⑫ 8,958 + 215 = _____ _____

④ 6,961 + 121 = _____ _____   ⑬ 2,735 + 5,120 = _____ _____

⑤ 9,337 + 187 = _____ _____   ⑭ 856 + 2,223 = _____ _____

⑥ 363 + 1,057 = _____ _____   ⑮ 599 + 202 = _____ _____

⑦ 934 + 5,913 = _____ _____   ⑯ 298 + 1,654 = _____ _____

⑧ 224 + 268 = _____ _____   ⑰ 8,929 + 284 = _____ _____

⑨ 6,264 + 7,245 = _____ _____   ⑱ 133 + 629 = _____ _____

C Study each paragraph and write two addition sentences that demonstrate the commutative property.

① For her birthday, Janice received 14 gifts and 7 cards. Her twin sister, Christina, received 7 gifts and 14 cards. What was the total number of gifts and cards received by each girl?

_____**14 + 7 = 21**_____
_____**7 + 14 = 21**_____

② When preparing tuna casserole, Connie allowed 30 minutes baking time with the lid on and 15 minutes with the lid off. Wilbur allowed 15 minutes with the lid on and 30 minutes with the lid off. What was the total minutes allowed by each?

_____
_____

③ During a night of bowling, Ted bowled 10 strikes and 15 spares. His friend, Sam, bowled 15 strikes and 10 spares. What was the combined number of strikes and spares that each boy bowled?

_____
_____

④ On a two-day float trip, the Waterbabies group traveled 18 miles the first day and 16 miles the second. The Tadpoles traveled 16 miles the first day and 18 the next. How many miles did each group travel?

_____
_____

⑤ For display in the school lobby, Martin chose 12 color photographs and 8 black and white prints. Regina selected 8 color prints and 12 black and white prints for display. How many photos did each select?

_____
_____

⑥ In ceramics class, Diane made 6 vases and 2 bowls. Bill made 2 cookie jars and 6 chess sets. How many ceramic items did each of the two students produce?

_____
_____

Basic Subtraction Facts   Unit 53

Learning Objective: *We will learn to subtract by deducting one set from another.*

Subtraction is the deducting of one number from another to find the difference of the two numbers.

EXAMPLE: If the 2 members of set B are deducted from the 5 members of A∪B, the difference is the 3 members of set A.

$$A \cup B = \{\square,\square,\square,\square,\square\} \qquad 5$$
$$B = \{\square,\square\} \qquad -\ 2$$
$$A = \{\square,\square,\square\} \qquad 3$$

A Tell how many members are in each set.

① A∪B = {△,△,△,△,△,△,△,△} n(A∪B) = __8__
  B = {△,△,△} n(B) = − __3__
  A = {△,△,△,△,△} n(A) = __5__

② A∪B = {●,●,●,●,●,●,●,●,●} n(A∪B) = ____
  B = {●,●,●,●} n(B) = − ____
  A = {●,●,●,●} n(A) = ____

③ A∪B = {■,■,■,■,■,■,■,■,■,■} n(A∪B) = ____
  B = {■,■,■,■,■,■,■} n(B) = − ____
  A = {■,■,■} n(A) = ____

④ A∪B = {◇,◇,◇,◇,◇,◇,◇} n(A∪B) = ____
  B = {◇,◇,◇} n(B) = − ____
  A = {◇,◇,◇,◇} n(A) = ____

⑤ A∪B = {O,O,O,O,O,O,O,O,O,O,O} n(A∪B) = ____
  B = {O,O,O,O,O} n(B) = − ____
  A = {O,O,O,O,O,O} n(A) = ____

⑥ A∪B = {▲,▲,▲,▲,▲,▲,▲,▲,▲} n(A∪B) = ____
  B = {▲,▲,▲,▲} n(B) = − ____
  A = {▲,▲,▲,▲,▲} n(A) = ____

⑦ A∪B = {◆,◆,◆,◆,◆,◆} n(A∪B) = ____
  B = {◆,◆,◆,◆,◆} n(B) = − ____
  A = {◆} n(A) = ____

⑧ A∪B = {□,□,□,□,□,□,□,□,□,□,□} n(A∪B) = ____
  B = {□,□,□,□,□,□,□,□,□} n(B) = − ____
  A = {□,□} n(A) = ____

⑨ A∪B = {△,△,△,△,△,△,△,△,△,△,△} n(A∪B) = ____
  B = {△,△,△,△} n(B) = − ____
  A = {△,△,△,△,△,△,△} n(A) = ____

⑩ A∪B = {●,●,●,●} n(A∪B) = ____
  B = {●,●} n(B) = − ____
  A = {●,●} n(A) = ____

⑪ A∪B = {■,■,■,■,■} n(A∪B) = ____
  B = {■} n(B) = − ____
  A = {■,■,■,■} n(A) = ____

⑫ A∪B = {◇,◇,◇,◇,◇,◇,◇,◇,◇,◇,◇,◇} n(A∪B) = ____
  B = {◇,◇,◇,◇,◇,◇,◇} n(B) = − ____
  A = {◇,◇,◇,◇,◇} n(A) = ____

⑬ A∪B = {O,O,O,O,O,O,O,O} n(A∪B) = ____
  B = {O} n(B) = − ____
  A = {O,O,O,O,O,O,O} n(A) = ____

⑭ A∪B = {▲,▲,▲,▲,▲,▲} n(A∪B) = ____
  B = {▲,▲,▲,▲} n(B) = − ____
  A = {▲,▲} n(A) = ____

REMINDER: Write the definition of subtraction.

B Tell how many members are in each set.

① A∪B = {△,△,△,△,△,△,△,△,△,△,△,△}   A = {△,△,△,△,△,△}   B = {△,△,△,△,△,△}
n(A∪B) = __12__   —   n(A) = __6__   =   n(B) = __6__

② A∪B = {●,●,●,●,●,●,●,●,●,●,●,●,●,●}   A = {●,●,●,●,●}   B = {●,●,●,●,●,●,●,●,●}
n(A∪B) = _____   —   n(A) = _____   =   n(B) = _____

③ A∪B = {□,□,□,□,□,□,□,□,□,□,□,□,□,□,□,□,□,□}   A = {□,□,□,□,□,□,□,□,□}   B = {□,□,□,□,□,□,□,□,□}
n(A∪B) = _____   —   n(A) = _____   =   n(B) = _____

④ A∪B = {◇,◇,◇,◇,◇,◇,◇,◇,◇,◇,◇,◇,◇,◇}   A = {◇,◇,◇,◇,◇,◇,◇,◇,◇,◇}   B = {◇,◇,◇,◇}
n(A∪B) = _____   —   n(A) = _____   =   n(B) = _____

⑤ A∪B = {▲,▲,▲,▲,▲,▲,▲,▲,▲,▲,▲,▲,▲,▲,▲}   A = {▲,▲,▲,▲,▲,▲,▲,▲,▲}   B = {▲,▲,▲,▲,▲,▲}
n(A∪B) = _____   —   n(A) = _____   =   n(B) = _____

⑥ A∪B = {■,■,■,■,■,■,■,■,■,■,■}   A = {■,■,■,■}   B = {■,■,■,■,■,■,■,■}
n(A∪B) = _____   —   n(A) = _____   =   n(B) = _____

C Tell how many members are in each set.

① Set A∪B includes 13 bananas. Set B includes seven bananas.

n(A∪B) = __13__
n(B) = − __7__
n(A) = __6__

② There are 14 dogs in set A∪B. Set A has 7 dogs.

n(A∪B) = _____
n(A) = − _____
n(B) = _____

③ Sixteen athletes belong to set A∪B. Set B includes 9 athletes.

n(A∪B) = _____
n(B) = − _____
n(A) = _____

④ Four musicians belong in set A∪B. Set A includes only one musician.

n(A∪B) = _____
n(A) = − _____
n(B) = _____

⑤ There are 3 pizzas in set A∪B. Set B includes 1 pizza.

n(A∪B) = _____
n(B) = − _____
n(A) = _____

⑥ Set A∪B includes 13 trains. There are 4 trains in set A.

n(A∪B) = _____
n(A) = − _____
n(B) = _____

⑦ Set A∪B includes 5 flashlights. Set B has 2 flashlights.

n(A∪B) = _____
n(B) = − _____
n(A) = _____

⑧ There are 15 geese in set A∪B. Set A includes 8 geese.

n(A∪B) = _____
n(A) = − _____
n(B) = _____

⑨ Ten insects belong to set A∪B. Set B includes 3 insects.

n(A∪B) = _____
n(B) = − _____
n(A) = _____

⑩ Two books belong to set A∪B. Set A has only 1 book.

n(A∪B) = _____
n(A) = − _____
n(B) = _____

⑪ Set A∪B includes 14 statues. There are 8 statues in set B.

n(A∪B) = _____
n(B) = − _____
n(A) = _____

⑫ There are 9 flowers in set A∪B. Set A includes 3 flowers.

n(A∪B) = _____
n(A) = − _____
n(B) = _____

Subtraction on a Number Line **Unit 54**

Learning Objective: ***We will learn to subtract with the aid of a number line.***

Subtraction is the deducting of one number from another to find the difference of the two numbers.

EXAMPLE:

To subtract 2 from 5, begin at point 5 on the number line and move 2 spaces to the left. The difference is 3.

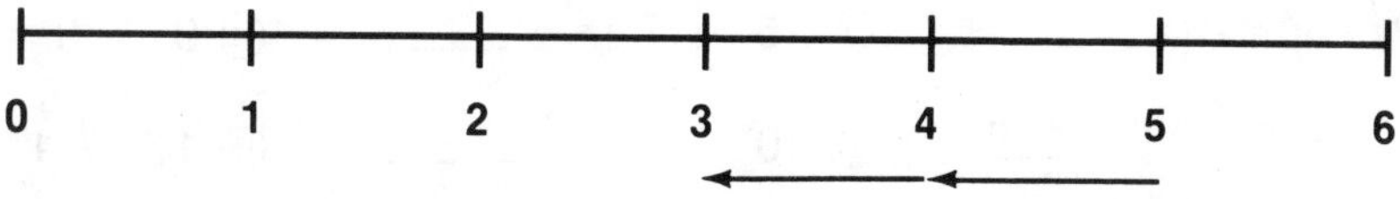

A Use the number line in subtracting the numbers below.

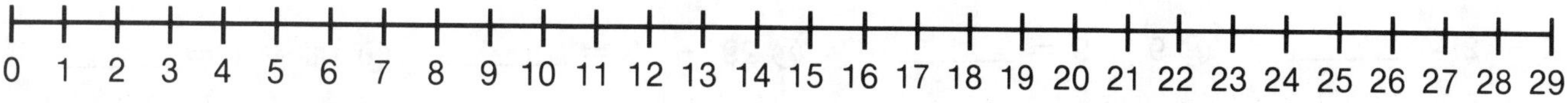

① 23 − 1 = 22	② 28 − 12	③ 29 − 6	④ 17 − 0	⑤ 25 − 9	⑥ 20 − 3	⑦ 17 − 2	⑧ 23 − 7	⑨ 29 − 26	⑩ 12 − 12
⑪ 17 − 4	⑫ 15 − 11	⑬ 20 − 13	⑭ 20 − 1	⑮ 25 − 7	⑯ 23 − 4	⑰ 21 − 10	⑱ 9 − 6	⑲ 23 − 0	⑳ 21 − 15
㉑ 28 − 1	㉒ 22 − 2	㉓ 24 − 9	㉔ 20 − 10	㉕ 7 − 6	㉖ 27 − 5	㉗ 17 − 3	㉘ 27 − 8	㉙ 25 − 5	㉚ 23 − 14
㉛ 20 − 18	㉜ 15 − 12	㉝ 18 − 6	㉞ 6 − 2	㉟ 1 − 1	㊱ 12 − 3	㊲ 16 − 10	㊳ 21 − 13	㊴ 18 − 11	㊵ 13 − 1
㊶ 17 − 8	㊷ 23 − 6	㊸ 25 − 2	㊹ 27 − 20	㊺ 14 − 9	㊻ 28 − 13	㊼ 5 − 4	㊽ 8 − 2	㊾ 19 − 9	㊿ 25 − 14
(51) 24 − 12	(52) 16 − 9	(53) 13 − 4	(54) 22 − 7	(55) 18 − 9	(56) 19 − 4	(57) 12 − 1	(58) 26 − 13	(59) 8 − 8	(60) 24 − 14

REMINDER: Write the definition of subtraction.

____

____

B Use the number line in these subtraction problems.

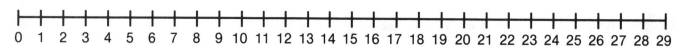

① 7 − 2 = __5__

② 14 − 13 = _____

③ 12 − 4 = _____

④ 25 − 4 = _____

⑤ 13 − 5 = _____

⑥ 14 − 7 = _____

⑦ 11 − 3 = _____

⑧ 13 − 13 = _____

⑨ 9 − 4 = _____

⑩ 15 − 7 = _____

⑪ 9 − 8 = _____

⑫ 17 − 6 = _____

⑬ 23 − 2 = _____

⑭ 10 − 6 = _____

⑮ 17 − 1 = _____

⑯ 27 − 9 = _____

⑰ 15 − 13 = _____

⑱ 22 − 5 = _____

⑲ 15 − 4 = _____

⑳ 14 − 4 = _____

㉑ 19 − 8 = _____

㉒ 16 − 12 = _____

㉓ 18 − 7 = _____

㉔ 23 − 5 = _____

㉕ 14 − 2 = _____

㉖ 9 − 9 = _____

㉗ 29 − 16 = _____

㉘ 11 − 1 = _____

㉙ 28 − 14 = _____

㉚ 24 − 17 = _____

㉛ 19 − 7 = _____

㉜ 26 − 18 = _____

C Draw arrows to illustrate the subtraction process. Write the subtraction sentence next to each arrow.

① There are 24 students in the ninth grade foreign language classes. Thirteen of these students are studying French. The remaining students are studying Spanish. How many ninth-graders are studying Spanish?

② Of the 29 members of the high school honor society, 12 have perfect 4.0 grade point averages. How many honor society members do not have perfect grade point averages?

③ Of the 16 members of the school newspaper staff, 9 have part-time jobs as interns on the area's daily and weekly newspapers. How many school newspaper staff members do not have such part-time employment?

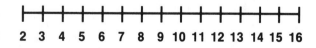

④ Twenty-three students participated in tryouts for the high school debate team. Only 8 students were selected for the team. How many students who competed did not win a spot on the team?

Subtracting One-Digit Numbers   Unit 55

Learning Objective: **We will learn to subtract single-digit numbers.**

In the Arabic numbering system, 0, 1, 2, 3, 4, 5, 6, 7, 8, and 9 are one-digit numbers.

EXAMPLE: A series of subtractions may be completed by finding the
difference of the first two numbers and subtracting the
third number from this difference.

$$\left.\begin{array}{r} 5 \\ 3 \\ -2 \\ \hline 0 \end{array}\right\} \quad \begin{array}{r} 5 \\ -3 = 2 \\ \hline -2 \\ \hline 0 \end{array}$$

A Subtract these one-digit numbers.

① 9 −8 **1**	② 6 −4	③ 3 −0	④ 2 −1	⑤ 1 −1	⑥ 7 −5	⑦ 8 −6	⑧ 5 −3	⑨ 0 −0	⑩ 4 −2
⑪ 2 −0	⑫ 3 −2	⑬ 5 −1	⑭ 6 −2	⑮ 7 −4	⑯ 6 −3	⑰ 8 −3	⑱ 4 −0	⑲ 9 −6	⑳ 7 −1
㉑ 8 −8	㉒ 7 −2	㉓ 6 −5	㉔ 8 −4	㉕ 3 −1	㉖ 2 −2	㉗ 4 −3	㉘ 5 −4	㉙ 9 −9	㉚ 5 −0
㉛ 6 −1	㉜ 1 −0	㉝ 3 −3	㉞ 4 −1	㉟ 5 −5	㊱ 7 −3	㊲ 8 −5	㊳ 9 −7	㊴ 6 −2	㊵ 7 −6
㊶ 7 −0	㊷ 8 −7	㊸ 6 −6	㊹ 5 −2	㊺ 4 −4	㊻ 9 −5	㊼ 6 −0	㊽ 9 −2	㊾ 7 −7	㊿ 9 −3

B Subtract these one-digit numbers and show the series of subtractions as in the sample exercise above.

① 9
4
−2

② 8
7
−0

③ 5
2
−1

④ 6
4
−2

REMINDER: Write the definition of one-digit numbers.

_____

_____

C Subtract these single-digit numbers.

① $9 - 0 - 8 = \underline{\ \ 1\ \ }$ ② $6 - 3 - 2 = \underline{\hspace{1cm}}$ ③ $7 - 1 - 2 = \underline{\hspace{1cm}}$ ④ $8 - 5 - 0 = \underline{\hspace{1cm}}$

⑤ $4 - 1 - 1 = \underline{\hspace{1cm}}$ ⑥ $5 - 1 - 2 = \underline{\hspace{1cm}}$ ⑦ $8 - 4 - 3 = \underline{\hspace{1cm}}$ ⑧ $9 - 5 - 4 = \underline{\hspace{1cm}}$

⑨ $8 - 4 - 1 = \underline{\hspace{1cm}}$ ⑩ $6 - 0 - 3 = \underline{\hspace{1cm}}$ ⑪ $3 - 2 - 0 = \underline{\hspace{1cm}}$ ⑫ $6 - 1 - 5 = \underline{\hspace{1cm}}$

⑬ $4 - 2 - 1 = \underline{\hspace{1cm}}$ ⑭ $2 - 1 - 1 = \underline{\hspace{1cm}}$ ⑮ $6 - 2 - 1 = \underline{\hspace{1cm}}$ ⑯ $5 - 1 - 1 = \underline{\hspace{1cm}}$

⑰ $6 - 3 - 0 = \underline{\hspace{1cm}}$ ⑱ $4 - 2 - 2 = \underline{\hspace{1cm}}$ ⑲ $5 - 4 - 0 = \underline{\hspace{1cm}}$ ⑳ $6 - 4 - 1 = \underline{\hspace{1cm}}$

㉑ $7 - 6 - 0 = \underline{\hspace{1cm}}$ ㉒ $8 - 2 - 5 = \underline{\hspace{1cm}}$ ㉓ $3 - 1 - 1 = \underline{\hspace{1cm}}$ ㉔ $7 - 1 - 3 = \underline{\hspace{1cm}}$

㉕ $9 - 7 - 1 = \underline{\hspace{1cm}}$ ㉖ $6 - 2 - 3 = \underline{\hspace{1cm}}$ ㉗ $4 - 3 - 0 = \underline{\hspace{1cm}}$ ㉘ $8 - 6 - 1 = \underline{\hspace{1cm}}$

㉙ $4 - 1 - 3 = \underline{\hspace{1cm}}$ ㉚ $7 - 4 - 2 = \underline{\hspace{1cm}}$ ㉛ $9 - 4 - 1 = \underline{\hspace{1cm}}$ ㉜ $6 - 2 - 2 = \underline{\hspace{1cm}}$

㉝ $9 - 6 - 2 = \underline{\hspace{1cm}}$ ㉞ $5 - 1 - 4 = \underline{\hspace{1cm}}$ ㉟ $6 - 5 - 0 = \underline{\hspace{1cm}}$ ㊱ $7 - 4 - 3 = \underline{\hspace{1cm}}$

D Solve the problems.

① Kenny sorted the laundry into 8 piles. He washed 2 of the piles on the delicate wash cycle, and he used cold water. The rest of the laundry he washed on the permanent press cycle in warm water. How many piles did he wash in warm water? __6__

② Delores invited 7 friends to drive to the city to see a play. Four of her friends did not like the theater and chose not to go. Another became ill and had to stay at home. How many friends drove with Delores to see the play? ____

③ Ramona wrote 9 poems and submitted these to be published in a national magazine. She later received notice that all but 2 poems had been accepted by the editors of the magazine. How many poems were accepted? ____

④ Ronald picked 9 quarts of strawberries. He gave 4 quarts of the berries to his grandmother. The rest he kept for himself. How many quarts of strawberries did Ronald keep? ____

⑤ During her first semester as a math tutor, Agnes worked with 7 students. Two of the students moved to another city before the semester was complete. Two more stopped attending the tutorial sessions. How many students completed the semester? ____

⑥ Jason ordered 8 roses on St. Valentine's Day. He gave 1 rose to his mother and 1 rose to his grandmother. He gave the remaining roses to his friend, Elizabeth. How many roses did Jason give Elizabeth? ____

Comprehension Check   Test 11

A For each problem, write a second addition sentence to illustrate the commutative property. Find the sums.

① $8,211 + 3,435 =$ __11,646__   __3,435 + 8,211 = 11,646__   ② $8,510 + 2,133 =$ _____ _____

③ $1,391 + 2,123 =$ _____ _____   ④ $1,416 + 4,961 =$ _____ _____

⑤ $1,315 + 6,121 =$ _____ _____   ⑥ $1,806 + 7,849 =$ _____ _____

⑦ $3,831 + 3,680 =$ _____ _____   ⑧ $4,012 + 6,116 =$ _____ _____

⑨ $1,251 + 3,823 =$ _____ _____   ⑩ $6,160 + 1,641 =$ _____ _____

⑪ $4,622 + 8,253 =$ _____ _____   ⑫ $5,343 + 7,791 =$ _____ _____

⑬ $2,441 + 7,793 =$ _____ _____   ⑭ $7,049 + 2,155 =$ _____ _____

⑮ $1,168 + 4,210 =$ _____ _____   ⑯ $4,728 + 3,946 =$ _____ _____

⑰ $4,481 + 9,173 =$ _____ _____   ⑱ $4,635 + 4,235 =$ _____ _____

⑲ $7,491 + 5,121 =$ _____ _____   ⑳ $8,264 + 8,433 =$ _____ _____

B Tell how many members are in each set.

① $A \cup B = \{\triangle,\triangle,\triangle,\triangle,\triangle,\triangle,\triangle,\triangle,\triangle,\triangle,\triangle,\triangle,\triangle\}$ $A = \{\triangle,\triangle,\triangle,\triangle,\triangle,\triangle\}$ $B = \{\triangle,\triangle,\triangle,\triangle,\triangle,\triangle,\triangle\}$
$n(A \cup B) =$ __13__ $-$ $n(A) =$ __6__ $=$ $n(B) =$ __7__

② $A \cup B = \{\bullet,\bullet,\bullet,\bullet,\bullet,\bullet,\bullet,\bullet,\bullet,\bullet,\bullet\}$ $A = \{\bullet,\bullet,\bullet,\bullet,\bullet,\bullet,\bullet,\bullet\}$ $B = \{\bullet,\bullet,\bullet\}$
$n(A \cup B) =$ ____ $-$ $n(A) =$ ____ $=$ $n(B) =$ ____

③ $A \cup B = \{\square,\square,\square,\square,\square,\square,\square,\square,\square,\square,\square,\square\}$ $A = \{\square,\square,\square,\square,\square\}$ $B = \{\square,\square,\square,\square,\square,\square,\square\}$
$n(A \cup B) =$ ____ $-$ $n(A) =$ ____ $=$ $n(B) =$ ____

④ $A \cup B = \{\blacktriangle,\blacktriangle,\blacktriangle,\blacktriangle,\blacktriangle,\blacktriangle,\blacktriangle,\blacktriangle,\blacktriangle,\blacktriangle,\blacktriangle,\blacktriangle,\blacktriangle,\blacktriangle,\blacktriangle\}$ $A = \{\blacktriangle,\blacktriangle,\blacktriangle,\blacktriangle,\blacktriangle,\blacktriangle,\blacktriangle\}$ $B = \{\blacktriangle,\blacktriangle,\blacktriangle,\blacktriangle,\blacktriangle,\blacktriangle,\blacktriangle,\blacktriangle\}$
$n(A \cup B) =$ ____ $-$ $n(A) =$ ____ $=$ $n(B) =$ ____

⑤ $A \cup B = \{O,O,O,O,O,O,O,O,O,O,O,O,O,O,O,O\}$ $A = \{O,O,O,O,O,O,O,O,O\}$ $B = \{O,O,O,O,O,O,O\}$
$n(A \cup B) =$ ____ $-$ $n(A) =$ ____ $=$ $n(B) =$ ____

⑥ $A \cup B = \{\blacksquare,\blacksquare,\blacksquare,\blacksquare,\blacksquare,\blacksquare,\blacksquare,\blacksquare,\blacksquare,\blacksquare,\blacksquare\}$ $A = \{\blacksquare,\blacksquare,\blacksquare\}$ $B = \{\blacksquare,\blacksquare,\blacksquare,\blacksquare,\blacksquare,\blacksquare,\blacksquare,\blacksquare\}$
$n(A \cup B) =$ ____ $-$ $n(A) =$ ____ $=$ $n(B) =$ ____

Test 11 cont'd ☞

C Subtract these one-digit numbers.

| ① 8
− 2
6 | ② 7
− 5 | ③ 9
− 2 | ④ 3
− 0 | ⑤ 5
− 1 | ⑥ 6
− 5 | ⑦ 8
− 8 | ⑧ 7
− 0 | ⑨ 3
− 2 | ⑩ 6
− 1 |

| ⑪ 9
− 6 | ⑫ 8
− 5 | ⑬ 6
− 4 | ⑭ 4
− 1 | ⑮ 9
− 4 | ⑯ 5
− 5 | ⑰ 7
− 4 | ⑱ 6
− 3 | ⑲ 2
− 2 | ⑳ 7
− 3 |

| ㉑ 9
− 7 | ㉒ 4
− 3 | ㉓ 7
− 6 | ㉔ 6
− 2 | ㉕ 8
− 4 | ㉖ 5
− 2 | ㉗ 1
− 1 | ㉘ 9
− 8 | ㉙ 4
− 2 | ㉚ 9
− 5 |

D Subtract these one-digit numbers.

① $9 - 2 - 6 =$ __1__   ② $4 - 1 - 1 =$ _____   ③ $5 - 3 - 0 =$ _____   ④ $7 - 1 - 6 =$ _____

⑤ $8 - 5 - 1 =$ _____   ⑥ $2 - 1 - 0 =$ _____   ⑦ $3 - 2 - 1 =$ _____   ⑧ $6 - 2 - 2 =$ _____

⑨ $9 - 3 - 5 =$ _____   ⑩ $5 - 1 - 1 =$ _____   ⑪ $6 - 3 - 2 =$ _____   ⑫ $8 - 1 - 5 =$ _____

⑬ $8 - 2 - 2 =$ _____   ⑭ $7 - 2 - 3 =$ _____   ⑮ $4 - 2 - 1 =$ _____   ⑯ $9 - 4 - 4 =$ _____

⑰ $4 - 3 - 0 =$ _____   ⑱ $9 - 2 - 1 =$ _____   ⑲ $3 - 3 - 0 =$ _____   ⑳ $5 - 2 - 1 =$ _____

㉑ $7 - 3 - 3 =$ _____   ㉒ $5 - 0 - 5 =$ _____   ㉓ $6 - 1 - 1 =$ _____   ㉔ $8 - 0 - 6 =$ _____

Describe how you would solve each problem on the number line. For example, to subtract 3 from 5, you would start at point 5 on the number line and move to the left 3 points. The answer is 2.

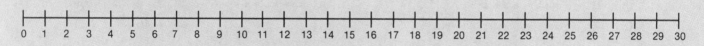

① $24 - 12 - 8 =$ _____   ② $30 - 10 - 5 =$ _____   ③ $18 - 6 - 9 =$ _____   ④ $10 - 8 - 2 =$ _____

_____   _____   _____   _____

_____   _____   _____   _____

_____   _____   _____   _____

_____   _____   _____   _____

_____   _____   _____   _____

_____   _____   _____   _____

_____   _____   _____   _____

Subtracting Two-Digit Numbers

Learning Objective: *We will learn to subtract two-digit numbers.*

Two-digit numbers have digits in both the ones' place and the tens' place.

EXAMPLE: First subtract the digits in the ones'
column. Next subtract the digits in
the tens' column.

$$\begin{array}{r} 55 \\ -\ 33 \\ \hline 22 \end{array}$$

A Subtract these two-digit numbers.

① $\begin{array}{r} 42 \\ -11 \\ \hline 31 \end{array}$ ② $\begin{array}{r} 71 \\ -30 \\ \hline \end{array}$ ③ $\begin{array}{r} 34 \\ -10 \\ \hline \end{array}$ ④ $\begin{array}{r} 66 \\ -23 \\ \hline \end{array}$ ⑤ $\begin{array}{r} 87 \\ -37 \\ \hline \end{array}$ ⑥ $\begin{array}{r} 99 \\ -58 \\ \hline \end{array}$ ⑦ $\begin{array}{r} 21 \\ -10 \\ \hline \end{array}$ ⑧ $\begin{array}{r} 31 \\ -21 \\ \hline \end{array}$

⑨ $\begin{array}{r} 68 \\ -12 \\ \hline \end{array}$ ⑩ $\begin{array}{r} 89 \\ -64 \\ \hline \end{array}$ ⑪ $\begin{array}{r} 29 \\ -15 \\ \hline \end{array}$ ⑫ $\begin{array}{r} 74 \\ -61 \\ \hline \end{array}$ ⑬ $\begin{array}{r} 86 \\ -24 \\ \hline \end{array}$ ⑭ $\begin{array}{r} 47 \\ -10 \\ \hline \end{array}$ ⑮ $\begin{array}{r} 39 \\ -28 \\ \hline \end{array}$ ⑯ $\begin{array}{r} 64 \\ -44 \\ \hline \end{array}$

⑰ $\begin{array}{r} 91 \\ -70 \\ \hline \end{array}$ ⑱ $\begin{array}{r} 18 \\ -13 \\ \hline \end{array}$ ⑲ $\begin{array}{r} 46 \\ -33 \\ \hline \end{array}$ ⑳ $\begin{array}{r} 54 \\ -32 \\ \hline \end{array}$ ㉑ $\begin{array}{r} 75 \\ -43 \\ \hline \end{array}$ ㉒ $\begin{array}{r} 35 \\ -34 \\ \hline \end{array}$ ㉓ $\begin{array}{r} 85 \\ -51 \\ \hline \end{array}$ ㉔ $\begin{array}{r} 33 \\ -21 \\ \hline \end{array}$

㉕ $\begin{array}{r} 39 \\ -12 \\ \hline \end{array}$ ㉖ $\begin{array}{r} 89 \\ -16 \\ \hline \end{array}$ ㉗ $\begin{array}{r} 96 \\ -64 \\ \hline \end{array}$ ㉘ $\begin{array}{r} 56 \\ -23 \\ \hline \end{array}$ ㉙ $\begin{array}{r} 47 \\ -36 \\ \hline \end{array}$ ㉚ $\begin{array}{r} 88 \\ -20 \\ \hline \end{array}$ ㉛ $\begin{array}{r} 38 \\ -17 \\ \hline \end{array}$ ㉜ $\begin{array}{r} 86 \\ -21 \\ \hline \end{array}$

㉝ $\begin{array}{r} 57 \\ -42 \\ \hline \end{array}$ ㉞ $\begin{array}{r} 97 \\ -72 \\ \hline \end{array}$ ㉟ $\begin{array}{r} 83 \\ -60 \\ \hline \end{array}$ ㊱ $\begin{array}{r} 78 \\ -53 \\ \hline \end{array}$ ㊲ $\begin{array}{r} 96 \\ -45 \\ \hline \end{array}$ ㊳ $\begin{array}{r} 82 \\ -61 \\ \hline \end{array}$ ㊴ $\begin{array}{r} 95 \\ -50 \\ \hline \end{array}$ ㊵ $\begin{array}{r} 46 \\ -22 \\ \hline \end{array}$

㊶ $\begin{array}{r} 77 \\ -26 \\ \hline \end{array}$ ㊷ $\begin{array}{r} 26 \\ -24 \\ \hline \end{array}$ ㊸ $\begin{array}{r} 55 \\ -44 \\ \hline \end{array}$ ㊹ $\begin{array}{r} 43 \\ -12 \\ \hline \end{array}$ ㊺ $\begin{array}{r} 84 \\ -53 \\ \hline \end{array}$ ㊻ $\begin{array}{r} 99 \\ -54 \\ \hline \end{array}$ ㊼ $\begin{array}{r} 49 \\ -23 \\ \hline \end{array}$ ㊽ $\begin{array}{r} 78 \\ -25 \\ \hline \end{array}$

㊾ $\begin{array}{r} 29 \\ -22 \\ \hline \end{array}$ ㊿ $\begin{array}{r} 67 \\ -36 \\ \hline \end{array}$ 51 $\begin{array}{r} 48 \\ -41 \\ \hline \end{array}$ 52 $\begin{array}{r} 36 \\ -11 \\ \hline \end{array}$ 53 $\begin{array}{r} 85 \\ -12 \\ \hline \end{array}$ 54 $\begin{array}{r} 94 \\ -83 \\ \hline \end{array}$ 55 $\begin{array}{r} 78 \\ -65 \\ \hline \end{array}$ 56 $\begin{array}{r} 97 \\ -51 \\ \hline \end{array}$

REMINDER: *Write the definition of two-digit numbers.*

Unit 56 cont'd 👉

B Subtract these two-digit numbers.

① 65 − 51 = __14__ ② 89 − 74 = _____ ③ 34 − 21 = _____ ④ 89 − 29 = _____

⑤ 96 − 45 = _____ ⑥ 69 − 35 = _____ ⑦ 88 − 42 = _____ ⑧ 74 − 21 = _____

⑨ 66 − 53 = _____ ⑩ 86 − 24 = _____ ⑪ 79 − 16 = _____ ⑫ 27 − 24 = _____

⑬ 88 − 62 = _____ ⑭ 95 − 70 = _____ ⑮ 29 − 22 = _____ ⑯ 78 − 44 = _____

⑰ 38 − 26 = _____ ⑱ 66 − 41 = _____ ⑲ 78 − 12 = _____ ⑳ 76 − 31 = _____

㉑ 83 − 12 = _____ ㉒ 59 − 24 = _____ ㉓ 45 − 23 = _____ ㉔ 81 − 40 = _____

㉕ 46 − 32 = _____ ㉖ 63 − 22 = _____ ㉗ 59 − 42 = _____ ㉘ 65 − 54 = _____

㉙ 78 − 73 = _____ ㉚ 93 − 61 = _____ ㉛ 53 − 32 = _____ ㉜ 86 − 71 = _____

㉝ 97 − 26 = _____ ㉞ 79 − 65 = _____ ㉟ 64 − 50 = _____ ㊱ 68 − 51 = _____

C Solve the problems.

① Ninety-five students graduated from Smithton High School in 1980. Twelve of these students graduated with honors. How many students in the class of '80 did not graduate with honors?

__83__

② Eighty-eight Smithton graduates applied to the state university in the fall. Of these applicants, 76 were accepted to the university. How many applicants were not accepted?

_____

③ Sixty-five college freshmen held part-time jobs. Forty-four of the freshmen who held jobs lived with their parents. How many employed freshmen did not live with their parents?

_____

④ Fifty-three alumni attended the class of '80 five-year reunion at Smithton High School. Ninety-five students graduated from Smithton in 1980. How many of these graduates did not attend the reunion?

_____

⑤ Of Smithton's 95-member class of 1980, 45 graduates were males. How many members of the graduating class of 1980 were females?

_____

⑥ Seventy-six state university freshmen were initiated into professional organizations in the fall of 1981. There were 97 students in the freshman class that semester. How many did not join professional organizations?

_____

Renaming to Subtract

Learning Objective: *We will learn to borrow in subtraction.*

Renaming is necessary when the value of a digit to be subtracted is greater than the value of the digit to be subtracted from.

EXAMPLE: Three tens and 3 ones are equal to 2 tens and 13 ones.

$$\begin{array}{r} 2\ 13 \\ \cancel{3}\ \cancel{3} \\ -\ 2\ 5 \\ \hline 8 \end{array}$$ }
2 tens, 13 ones
− 2 tens, 5 ones
0 tens, 8 ones = 8

A Show how to rename numbers to perform the subtractions.

① 82 } __7__ ten(s), __12__ one(s)
  − 34   −3 ten(s), 4 one(s)
     __4__ ten(s), __8__ one(s) = __48__

② 66 } ____ ten(s), ____ one(s)
  − 38   −3 ten(s), 8 one(s)
     ____ ten(s), ____ one(s) = ____

③ 92 } ____ ten(s), ____ one(s)
  − 55   −5 ten(s), 5 one(s)
     ____ ten(s), ____ one(s) = ____

④ 43 } ____ ten(s), ____ one(s)
  − 18   −1 ten(s), 8 one(s)
     ____ ten(s), ____ one(s) = ____

⑤ 31 } ____ ten(s), ____ one(s)
  − 22   −2 ten(s), 2 one(s)
     ____ ten(s), ____ one(s) = ____

⑥ 28 } ____ ten(s), ____ one(s)
  − 19   −1 ten(s), 9 one(s)
     ____ ten(s), ____ one(s) = ____

⑦ 34 } ____ ten(s), ____ one(s)
  − 28   −2 ten(s), 8 one(s)
     ____ ten(s), ____ one(s) = ____

⑧ 82 } ____ ten(s), ____ one(s)
  − 74   −7 ten(s), 4 one(s)
     ____ ten(s), ____ one(s) = ____

⑨ 50 } ____ ten(s), ____ one(s)
  − 36   −3 ten(s), 6 one(s)
     ____ ten(s), ____ one(s) = ____

⑩ 62 } ____ ten(s), ____ one(s)
  − 47   −4 ten(s), 7 one(s)
     ____ ten(s), ____ one(s) = ____

⑪ 67 } ____ ten(s), ____ one(s)
  − 58   −5 ten(s), 8 one(s)
     ____ ten(s), ____ one(s) = ____

⑫ 44 } ____ ten(s), ____ one(s)
  − 26   −2 ten(s), 6 one(s)
     ____ ten(s), ____ one(s) = ____

⑬ 55 } ____ ten(s), ____ one(s)
  − 37   −3 ten(s), 7 one(s)
     ____ ten(s), ____ one(s) = ____

⑭ 73 } ____ ten(s), ____ one(s)
  − 29   −2 ten(s), 9 one(s)
     ____ ten(s), ____ one(s) = ____

REMINDER: Write the definition of renaming.

_____

_____

Unit 57 cont'd ☞

B Subtract these two-digit numbers.

① 72 − 13 = __59__   ② 50 − 21 = _____   ③ 40 − 25 = _____   ④ 31 − 24 = _____

⑤ 81 − 26 = _____   ⑥ 93 − 46 = _____   ⑦ 71 − 24 = _____   ⑧ 61 − 38 = _____

⑨ 77 − 49 = _____   ⑩ 84 − 68 = _____   ⑪ 56 − 49 = _____   ⑫ 86 − 48 = _____

⑬ 51 − 35 = _____   ⑭ 82 − 43 = _____   ⑮ 30 − 26 = _____   ⑯ 91 − 89 = _____

⑰ 61 − 22 = _____   ⑱ 94 − 55 = _____   ⑲ 43 − 28 = _____   ⑳ 80 − 54 = _____

㉑ 40 − 28 = _____   ㉒ 78 − 29 = _____   ㉓ 63 − 36 = _____   ㉔ 72 − 48 = _____

㉕ 93 − 76 = _____   ㉖ 44 − 16 = _____   ㉗ 67 − 28 = _____   ㉘ 90 − 33 = _____

㉙ 25 − 16 = _____   ㉚ 71 − 63 = _____   ㉛ 66 − 59 = _____   ㉜ 82 − 26 = _____

㉝ 51 − 44 = _____   ㉞ 95 − 46 = _____   ㉟ 52 − 16 = _____   ㊱ 87 − 28 = _____

C Solve the problems.

① Thirty-seven geese lived on a pond that was situated on Ana's farm. Eighteen of the geese were wild. The other geese were domestic. How many of the geese that lived on the pond were domestic? __19__

② Leon has 42 cousins. Fourteen of his cousins are related to Leon's mother. His other cousins are related to his father. How many of Leon's cousins are related to Leon's father and that side of the family? ____

③ There are 81 students in Mr. Davidson's sophomore English class. Seventy-seven of these students plan to enroll in college after graduating from high school. How many do not plan to enroll in college? ____

④ During an illness, Roberta received 20 deliveries from the local florist. Eleven of these deliveries were flowers. The others were potted plants. How many plants did Roberta receive? ____

⑤ Fifty-eight members of Smithton's junior class have been issued driver's licenses. The other members of the class have not yet passed the driver's examination. Of the 83 juniors, how many do not have driver's licenses? ____

⑥ Seventy-six people attended the marching band's first rehearsal. Forty-nine of these people were fellow students. The others were relatives of band members. How many relatives attended the band rehearsal? ____

140

Subtracting Three-Digit Numbers   Unit 58

Learning
Objective: *We will learn to subtract three-digit numbers.*

A three-digit number has digits in the ones' place, in the tens' place, and in the hundreds' place.

EXAMPLE: When we subtract three-digit
numbers, we may need to
rename numbers in the ones',
tens', or hundreds' place.

$$\begin{array}{r} {\scriptstyle 2\ 12\ 13} \\ \cancel{3}\ \cancel{3}\ \cancel{3} \\ -\ 2\ 5\ 5 \\ \hline 7\ 8 \end{array}$$

2 hundreds, 12 tens, 13 ones
− 2 hundreds,   5 tens,   5 ones
0 hundreds,   7 tens,   8 ones = 78

A Show how to rename numbers to perform the subtractions.

① $\begin{array}{r} 711 \\ -\ 532 \end{array}$ *6 hundreds, 10 tens, 11 ones*
      − 5 hundreds,   3 tens,   2 ones
      1 hundred,   7 tens,   9 ones = 179

② $\begin{array}{r} 674 \\ -\ 639 \end{array}$

③ $\begin{array}{r} 934 \\ -\ 570 \end{array}$

④ $\begin{array}{r} 508 \\ -\ 228 \end{array}$

⑤ $\begin{array}{r} 886 \\ -\ 357 \end{array}$

⑥ $\begin{array}{r} 511 \\ -\ 217 \end{array}$

⑦ $\begin{array}{r} 782 \\ -\ 228 \end{array}$

⑧ $\begin{array}{r} 964 \\ -\ 305 \end{array}$

⑨ $\begin{array}{r} 253 \\ -\ 219 \end{array}$

⑩ $\begin{array}{r} 728 \\ -\ 149 \end{array}$

⑪ $\begin{array}{r} 754 \\ -\ 364 \end{array}$

⑫ $\begin{array}{r} 416 \\ -\ 192 \end{array}$

⑬ $\begin{array}{r} 823 \\ -\ 729 \end{array}$

⑭ $\begin{array}{r} 491 \\ -\ 275 \end{array}$

REMINDER: Write the definition of a three-digit number.

_____

_____

B Subtract these three-digit numbers.

① 846 − 503 = _343_   ② 252 − 219 = _____   ③ 750 − 194 = _____   ④ 235 − 232 = _____

⑤ 783 − 573 = _____   ⑥ 928 − 603 = _____   ⑦ 675 − 661 = _____   ⑧ 574 − 483 = _____

⑨ 941 − 726 = _____   ⑩ 285 − 273 = _____   ⑪ 206 − 149 = _____   ⑫ 413 − 203 = _____

⑬ 925 − 709 = _____   ⑭ 521 − 307 = _____   ⑮ 702 − 318 = _____   ⑯ 764 − 665 = _____

⑰ 198 − 192 = _____   ⑱ 873 − 608 = _____   ⑲ 753 − 273 = _____   ⑳ 398 − 185 = _____

㉑ 426 − 358 = _____   ㉒ 917 − 426 = _____   ㉓ 967 − 852 = _____   ㉔ 672 − 617 = _____

㉕ 543 − 176 = _____   ㉖ 612 − 391 = _____   ㉗ 327 − 242 = _____   ㉘ 537 − 196 = _____

㉙ 936 − 248 = _____   ㉚ 818 − 725 = _____   ㉛ 813 − 703 = _____   ㉜ 276 − 106 = _____

㉝ 697 − 587 = _____   ㉞ 723 − 202 = _____   ㉟ 216 − 193 = _____   ㊱ 671 − 405 = _____

C Solve the problems.

① Robin looked at two sets of draperies. A tan set had 120 pleats. A blue set had 110 pleats. How many more pleats did the tan set have compared to the blue set?
_10_

② Before Wilson began to diet, he weighed 215 pounds. After dieting for more than three months, he weighed 183 pounds. How many pounds did Wilson lose during the time that he dieted? ____

③ There were 250 questions on the mid-term biology exam. Amy did not study for the test and answered 103 questions incorrectly. How many of the 250 questions did Amy answer correctly? ____

④ When Dick hunted deer during the fall firearms season, he was one of 986 successful hunters in Smith county. Only 548 of these hunters recorded more than one kill. How many killed only one deer? ____

⑤ Three hundred ninety-six recipes were submitted for the county's wild game recipe contest. One hundred thirty-seven of these recipes explained different ways of preparing wild turkey. How many recipes told how to cook other game? ____

⑥ During one year, Bob's Supermarket announced 221 winners in the cash sweepstakes. One hundred forty-two of these winners were local residents. The others were visitors to the area. How many winners were from out of town? ____

Subtracting Four-Digit Numbers

Learning Objective: *We will learn to subtract four-digit numbers.*

A four-digit number has digits in the ones' place, in the tens' place, in the hundreds' place, and in the thousands' place.

EXAMPLE: When we subtract four-digit numbers, we may need to rename numbers in the ones', tens', hundreds', or thousands' place.

$$
\begin{array}{r}
\overset{2\ \ 12\ 12\ 13}{3,333} \\
-\ 2,555 \\
\hline
778
\end{array}
$$

2 thousands, 12 hundreds, 12 tens, 13 ones
− 2 thousands, 5 hundreds, 5 tens, 5 ones
0 thousands, 7 hundreds, 7 tens, 8 ones = 778

A Subtract these four-digit numbers.

① 4,131
− 1,381
2,750

② 9,847
− 3,044

③ 9,538
− 2,692

④ 7,925
− 5,244

⑤ 4,134
− 3,625

⑥ 8,415
− 4,224

⑦ 9,856
− 9,713

⑧ 7,451
− 5,181

⑨ 7,620
− 3,290

⑩ 7,674
− 1,659

⑪ 7,881
− 1,406

⑫ 9,354
− 7,250

⑬ 3,183
− 1,524

⑭ 5,269
− 3,484

⑮ 7,835
− 1,984

⑯ 9,296
− 8,317

⑰ 4,709
− 2,495

⑱ 3,179
− 2,315

⑲ 6,589
− 2,147

⑳ 3,484
− 2,541

㉑ 5,288
− 1,131

㉒ 4,760
− 4,147

㉓ 4,216
− 3,026

㉔ 8,571
− 3,869

㉕ 8,722
− 2,953

㉖ 6,469
− 6,254

㉗ 4,092
− 1,348

㉘ 6,788
− 2,609

㉙ 8,251
− 5,245

㉚ 1,853
− 1,038

㉛ 4,627
− 1,495

㉜ 8,217
− 4,211

㉝ 4,160
− 3,729

㉞ 2,320
− 2,235

㉟ 4,907
− 1,231

㊱ 5,291
− 2,518

㊲ 7,513
− 2,074

㊳ 6,192
− 4,675

㊴ 1,480
− 1,432

㊵ 6,378
− 3,573

㊶ 6,119
− 2,154

㊷ 9,273
− 2,859

REMINDER: Write the definition of a four-digit number.

B Subtract these four-digit numbers.

① 5,001 − 4,172 = __829__

② 8,352 − 6,264 = _____

③ 5,219 − 2,154 = _____

④ 7,094 − 3,175 = _____

⑤ 2,322 − 1,300 = _____

⑥ 4,318 − 3,753 = _____

⑦ 8,736 − 8,291 = _____

⑧ 9,511 − 8,373 = _____

⑨ 5,623 − 1,399 = _____

⑩ 6,237 − 1,846 = _____

⑪ 2,183 − 1,139 = _____

⑫ 3,936 − 2,337 = _____

⑬ 8,429 − 5,942 = _____

⑭ 4,364 − 4,237 = _____

⑮ 7,158 − 5,565 = _____

⑯ 7,181 − 2,416 = _____

⑰ 3,738 − 3,265 = _____

⑱ 7,137 − 7,003 = _____

⑲ 5,521 − 1,384 = _____

⑳ 6,815 − 3,111 = _____

㉑ 2,925 − 1,264 = _____

㉒ 9,436 − 1,262 = _____

㉓ 6,106 − 4,723 = _____

㉔ 6,301 − 1,589 = _____

㉕ 1,662 − 1,214 = _____

㉖ 3,131 − 2,876 = _____

㉗ 7,251 − 1,218 = _____

C Solve the problems.

① In 1982, enrollment at Smithton High School was 3,163. In 1983, enrollment at the school dropped to 2,894. How many students did Smithton High School lose between 1982 and 1983? __269__

② One of two mountains in Smith County, Mount Scott, rises 3,643 feet above sea level. The other mountain, Mount Baker, measures 3,017 feet above sea level. How many feet higher is Mount Scott? _____

③ Six thousand, five hundred thirty-seven head of longhorn cattle grazed on the Sierra Wildlife Preserve in 1976. Five years later, the cattle numbered 5,080. How many head of cattle were lost during the five years? _____

④ Wendy reported that 6,351 tickets had been sold for the spring concert that would be sponsored by the student council. A total of 8,485 tickets had been printed for the concert. How many tickets had not been sold? _____

⑤ Eight thousand, ninety-seven duck feathers were stuffed into Sam's favorite pillow. Only 4,021 feathers filled Sam's younger sister's pillow. How many more duck feathers were in Sam's pillow? _____

⑥ Area teenagers had purchased 4,491 hamburgers in one year, announced the manager of Burger Delite. The year before, teens had bought 3,994 burgers. How many more burgers did teenagers buy during the later year? _____

Subtracting Five-Digit Numbers

Learning
Objective: *We will learn to subtract five-digit numbers.*

A five-digit number has digits in the ones' place, in the tens' place, in the hundreds' place, in the thousands' place, and in the ten thousands' place.

EXAMPLE:

$$\begin{array}{r} 2\ \ 12\ \ 12\ \ 12\ \ 13 \\ \cancel{3}\,\cancel{3},\cancel{3}\,\cancel{3}\,\cancel{3} \\ -\ 2\,5,5\,5\,5 \\ \hline 7,7\,7\,8 \end{array}\Bigg\}$$

2 ten thousands, 12 thousands, 12 hundreds, 12 tens, 13 ones
− 2 ten thousands,   5 thousands,   5 hundreds,   5 tens,   5 ones
0 ten thousands,   7 thousands,   7 hundreds,   7 tens,   8 ones = 7,778

A Subtract these five-digit numbers.

① 17,511
− 10,023

7,488

② 72,581
− 72,141

③ 88,029
− 19,941

④ 19,501
− 19,417

⑤ 81,002
− 66,301

⑥ 84,088
− 59,995

⑦ 59,212
− 20,206

⑧ 74,164
− 53,636

⑨ 62,184
− 21,555

⑩ 92,281
− 71,162

⑪ 36,074
− 22,372

⑫ 99,222
− 82,227

⑬ 50,747
− 28,824

⑭ 61,846
− 13,173

⑮ 30,525
− 27,103

⑯ 18,533
− 11,175

⑰ 92,611
− 66,619

⑱ 88,628
− 15,992

⑲ 55,113
− 27,252

⑳ 81,328
− 78,211

㉑ 55,822
− 32,614

㉒ 61,246
− 41,893

㉓ 74,214
− 26,296

㉔ 30,142
− 15,433

㉕ 42,849
− 33,845

㉖ 55,231
− 33,318

㉗ 94,139
− 14,824

㉘ 73,325
− 47,099

㉙ 84,270
− 21,815

㉚ 63,369
− 12,816

㉛ 23,282
− 18,209

㉜ 99,492
− 34,372

㉝ 47,433
− 15,221

㉞ 61,882
− 52,432

㉟ 24,461
− 10,663

㊱ 62,441
− 60,311

㊲ 39,018
− 19,181

㊳ 64,841
− 12,402

㊴ 72,418
− 19,387

㊵ 93,161
− 54,823

㊶ 70,183
− 14,913

㊷ 70,313
− 21,774

REMINDER: Write the definition of a five-digit number.

B Subtract these five-digit numbers.

① 45,547 − 37,715 = __7,832__ ② 71,145 − 44,249 = _____ ③ 95,465 − 31,478 = _____

④ 54,622 − 24,496 = _____ ⑤ 91,468 − 26,148 = _____ ⑥ 88,268 − 85,326 = _____

⑦ 90,930 − 41,043 = _____ ⑧ 93,897 − 72,822 = _____ ⑨ 91,564 − 28,473 = _____

⑩ 33,119 − 21,226 = _____ ⑪ 92,820 − 88,186 = _____ ⑫ 16,217 − 11,738 = _____

⑬ 88,337 − 30,898 = _____ ⑭ 39,160 − 18,727 = _____ ⑮ 29,034 − 10,178 = _____

⑯ 33,129 − 16,873 = _____ ⑰ 83,116 − 18,497 = _____ ⑱ 90,422 − 61,358 = _____

⑲ 20,271 − 13,547 = _____ ⑳ 89,910 − 12,740 = _____ ㉑ 32,125 − 16,516 = _____

㉒ 29,013 − 18,219 = _____ ㉓ 11,468 − 10,954 = _____ ㉔ 71,423 − 32,203 = _____

㉕ 91,411 − 47,230 = _____ ㉖ 28,633 − 15,460 = _____ ㉗ 98,710 − 29,715 = _____

C Solve the problems.

① There are 18,912 residents in the town of Berryville. Berryville's closest neighbor Winston, has a population of 81,114. How many more people reside in Winston than in Berryville?
__62,202__

② A total of 75,316 wild geese flew through Benton county on their southward migration. Hunters claimed 13,691 of these birds. How many of the 75,316 geese were not killed by hunters?
_____

③ With an enrollment of 17,028 students, Smith College is responsible for more than half the population of Smithton. Smithton's total population is 26,232. How many residents are not students at Smith College?
_____

④ The library at Smith College offers 31,781 books on loan. Works of fiction total 14,216. The library's non-fiction collection includes references, how-to books, and textbooks. How many books are included in the nonfiction collection?
_____

⑤ The local telephone company reported that 17,952 long distance phone calls were made by Berryville residents during June. Of these calls, 13,239 were made before 5 p.m. How many long distance calls were placed after 5 p.m.?
_____

⑥ In 1984, the Benton County Sheriff's Department answered 27,455 calls. Of those calls, 16,671 involved citizens within the Berryville city limits. How many calls did not involve citizens in Berryville?
_____

146

Comprehension Check

A Show how to rename these two-digit numbers to perform the subtractions.

① $\begin{array}{r} 23 \\ -14 \end{array}$ } $\begin{array}{l} \text{1 ten, \quad 13 ones} \\ -\text{1 ten, \quad 4 ones} \\ \hline \text{0 tens, \quad 9 ones} = 9 \end{array}$

② $\begin{array}{r} 92 \\ -24 \end{array}$ }

③ $\begin{array}{r} 63 \\ -59 \end{array}$ }

④ $\begin{array}{r} 67 \\ -48 \end{array}$ }

⑤ $\begin{array}{r} 51 \\ -39 \end{array}$ }

⑥ $\begin{array}{r} 76 \\ -68 \end{array}$ }

⑦ $\begin{array}{r} 84 \\ -57 \end{array}$ }

⑧ $\begin{array}{r} 21 \\ -17 \end{array}$ }

⑨ $\begin{array}{r} 82 \\ -19 \end{array}$ }

⑩ $\begin{array}{r} 70 \\ -69 \end{array}$ }

B Rename these three-digit numbers to perform the subtractions.

① $\begin{array}{r} 833 \\ -237 \end{array}$ } $\begin{array}{l} \text{7 hundreds, 12 tens, 13 ones} \\ -\text{2 hundreds, \quad 3 tens, \quad 7 ones} \\ \hline \text{5 hundreds, \quad 9 tens, \quad 6 ones} = 596 \end{array}$

② $\begin{array}{r} 820 \\ -176 \end{array}$ }

③ $\begin{array}{r} 561 \\ -134 \end{array}$ }

④ $\begin{array}{r} 243 \\ -104 \end{array}$ }

⑤ $\begin{array}{r} 832 \\ -161 \end{array}$ }

⑥ $\begin{array}{r} 922 \\ -784 \end{array}$ }

⑦ $\begin{array}{r} 515 \\ -156 \end{array}$ }

⑧ $\begin{array}{r} 810 \\ -148 \end{array}$ }

⑨ $\begin{array}{r} 448 \\ -174 \end{array}$ }

⑩ $\begin{array}{r} 241 \\ -190 \end{array}$ }

Test 12 cont'd ☛

C Subtract these two- and three-digit numbers.

① 129 − 111 = __18__ ② 46 − 22 = _____ ③ 96 − 35 = _____ ④ 73 − 48 = _____

⑤ 951 − 313 = _____ ⑥ 661 − 176 = _____ ⑦ 78 − 23 = _____ ⑧ 574 − 384 = _____

⑨ 84 − 47 = _____ ⑩ 971 − 436 = _____ ⑪ 631 − 151 = _____ ⑫ 843 − 122 = _____

⑬ 156 − 110 = _____ ⑭ 882 − 748 = _____ ⑮ 68 − 17 = _____ ⑯ 428 − 261 = _____

⑰ 61 − 38 = _____ ⑱ 34 − 20 = _____ ⑲ 412 − 110 = _____ ⑳ 75 − 48 = _____

D Subtract these four- and five-digit numbers.

① 6,786 − 5,864 = **922**	② 9,185 − 5,519	③ 91,992 − 10,895	④ 1,721 − 1,371	⑤ 3,110 − 2,723	⑥ 83,211 − 10,161
⑦ 2,469 − 2,126	⑧ 56,271 − 35,412	⑨ 9,145 − 1,431	⑩ 94,531 − 15,210	⑪ 28,145 − 22,908	⑫ 3,041 − 1,533
⑬ 78,141 − 32,737	⑭ 5,651 − 4,543	⑮ 99,258 − 56,865	⑯ 6,716 − 4,713	⑰ 3,174 − 2,674	⑱ 73,241 − 50,195
⑲ 8,993 − 2,082	⑳ 99,811 − 55,599	㉑ 8,439 − 5,141	㉒ 96,154 − 53,143	㉓ 85,953 − 16,786	㉔ 5,584 − 4,454
㉕ 26,857 − 11,488	㉖ 7,103 − 1,019	㉗ 81,125 − 17,444	㉘ 3,019 − 2,412	㉙ 4,221 − 1,608	㉚ 63,942 − 39,506

Write 4 brief paragraphs involving subtraction problems with ① two-digit numbers, ② three-digit numbers, ③ four-digit numbers, and ④ five-digit numbers.

① _____ ② _____ ③ _____ ④ _____

_____ _____ _____ _____

_____ _____ _____ _____

_____ _____ _____ _____

_____ _____ _____ _____

_____ _____ _____ _____

_____ _____ _____ _____

_____ _____ _____ _____

Identifying Problem Parts

Unit 61

Learning Objective: We will learn to identify the minuend, the subtrahend, and the remainder in a subtraction problem.

In a subtraction problem, the minuend is the number to be subtracted from. The subtrahend is the number to be subtracted. The remainder is the difference.

EXAMPLE: In the problem at right, 33,333 is the minuend. The subtrahend is 25,555. The remainder is 7,778.

$$\begin{array}{r} 33,333 \\ -\ 25,555 \\ \hline 7,778 \end{array}$$

A Find the remainders. Label each minuend "m," each subtrahend "s," and each remainder "r."

①
$$\begin{array}{r} 9,707 \quad m \\ -\ 6,246 \quad s \\ \hline 3,461 \quad r \end{array}$$

②
$$\begin{array}{r} 25,561 \ \underline{\quad} \\ -\ 25,190 \ \underline{\quad} \\ \hline \underline{\quad} \end{array}$$

③
$$\begin{array}{r} 64,235 \ \underline{\quad} \\ -\ 13,073 \ \underline{\quad} \\ \hline \underline{\quad} \end{array}$$

④
$$\begin{array}{r} 91,194 \ \underline{\quad} \\ -\ 67,170 \ \underline{\quad} \\ \hline \underline{\quad} \end{array}$$

⑤
$$\begin{array}{r} 67,654 \ \underline{\quad} \\ -\ 66,820 \ \underline{\quad} \\ \hline \underline{\quad} \end{array}$$

⑥
$$\begin{array}{r} 3,627 \ \underline{\quad} \\ -\ 3,541 \ \underline{\quad} \\ \hline \underline{\quad} \end{array}$$

⑦
$$\begin{array}{r} 8,841 \ \underline{\quad} \\ -\ 1,237 \ \underline{\quad} \\ \hline \underline{\quad} \end{array}$$

⑧
$$\begin{array}{r} 69,130 \ \underline{\quad} \\ -\ 56,115 \ \underline{\quad} \\ \hline \underline{\quad} \end{array}$$

⑨
$$\begin{array}{r} 7,690 \ \underline{\quad} \\ -\ 1,975 \ \underline{\quad} \\ \hline \underline{\quad} \end{array}$$

⑩
$$\begin{array}{r} 5,571 \ \underline{\quad} \\ -\ 5,299 \ \underline{\quad} \\ \hline \underline{\quad} \end{array}$$

⑪
$$\begin{array}{r} 6,197 \ \underline{\quad} \\ -\ 5,482 \ \underline{\quad} \\ \hline \underline{\quad} \end{array}$$

⑫
$$\begin{array}{r} 63,539 \ \underline{\quad} \\ -\ 62,799 \ \underline{\quad} \\ \hline \underline{\quad} \end{array}$$

⑬
$$\begin{array}{r} 41,528 \ \underline{\quad} \\ -\ 28,413 \ \underline{\quad} \\ \hline \underline{\quad} \end{array}$$

⑭
$$\begin{array}{r} 29,486 \ \underline{\quad} \\ -\ 16,309 \ \underline{\quad} \\ \hline \underline{\quad} \end{array}$$

⑮
$$\begin{array}{r} 9,119 \ \underline{\quad} \\ -\ 7,687 \ \underline{\quad} \\ \hline \underline{\quad} \end{array}$$

⑯
$$\begin{array}{r} 7,102 \ \underline{\quad} \\ -\ 1,340 \ \underline{\quad} \\ \hline \underline{\quad} \end{array}$$

⑰ $149 - 121 = \underline{\quad}$

⑱ $759 - 620 = \underline{\quad}$

⑲ $89 - 59 = \underline{\quad}$

⑳ $171 - 111 = \underline{\quad}$

㉑ $547 - 154 = \underline{\quad}$

㉒ $63 - 18 = \underline{\quad}$

㉓ $41 - 21 = \underline{\quad}$

㉔ $132 - 118 = \underline{\quad}$

㉕ $71 - 30 = \underline{\quad}$

㉖ $899 - 123 = \underline{\quad}$

㉗ $277 - 107 = \underline{\quad}$

㉘ $92 - 36 = \underline{\quad}$

㉙ $53 - 17 = \underline{\quad}$

㉚ $222 - 117 = \underline{\quad}$

㉛ $650 - 337 = \underline{\quad}$

㉜ $493 - 413 = \underline{\quad}$

REMINDER Write the definition of the minuend, the subtrahend, and the remainder.

B Match minuends and subtrahends with remainders.

① 538 – 468 =   20   ⑩ 448 – 367 =   30

② 123 – 103 =   59   ⑪ 841 – 279 =   81

③ 86 – 27 =   70   ⑫ 52 – 22 =   680

④ 76 – 21 =   55   ⑬ 829 – 203 =   562

⑤ 864 – 735 =   23   ⑭ 813 – 133 =   626

⑥ 555 – 469 =   383   ⑮ 71 – 45 =   72

⑦ 47 – 24 =   129   ⑯ 426 – 313 =   85

⑧ 93 – 28 =   65   ⑰ 94 – 22 =   26

⑨ 707 – 324 =   86   ⑱ 464 – 379 =   113

C Study the paragraphs. Below each, write the subtraction problem and label the minuend (m), the subtrahend (s), and the remainder (r). Solve each problem.

① Juanita drove 729 miles to visit her friend, Leslie. On the return trip, Juanita drove 412 miles, stopped for the night, and drove again the next day. How many miles were left?

  729 – 412 = 317
  ___m___ ___s___ ___r___

② Dennis and Randy are planning a cross-country ski route. The route will be 45 miles long. Twenty miles of the route winds through woodlands. How many miles are clear of woods?

  _____
  ____ ____ ____

③ In April, the Smithton High School senior class will travel to Florida. There are 89 seniors at Smithton. Sixty-three have signed up for the trip. How many have not registered?

  _____
  ____ ____ ____

④ All but 14 of Smithton's concert band members also participate in the marching band. There are 98 concert band members. How many are in the marching band?

  _____
  ____ ____ ____

⑤ Rita planted a pepper garden. She planted 134 plants. Eighty-six of these were banana pepper plants. The rest were bell pepper plants. How many bell peppers did she plant?

  _____
  ____ ____ ____

⑥ Joe hung 210 posters during student council elections. He hung 117 posters in the school. The rest he hung around town. How many posters were hung in town?

  _____
  ____ ____ ____

A Subtraction Table   Unit 62

Learning Objective: *We will learn to subtract with the aid of a subtraction table.*

A subtraction table shows the differences of given pairs of numbers.

EXAMPLE:

A subtraction table is read from the inside out. To subtract 3 − 2, find the minuend 3 on the inside of the chart. Follow the column or row that leads to the subtrahend 2. The other column or row that meets with the minuend will lead to the remainder 1.

	0	1	△2
0	0	1	2
□1	1	2	③
2	2	3	4

A Study the problems below. On each partial subtraction table, circle the minuend, draw a triangle around the subtrahend, and draw a square around the remainder.

① 18 − 8 = 10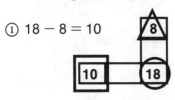

② 18 − 10 = 8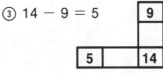

③ 14 − 9 = 5

④ 14 − 5 = 9

⑤ 11 − 2 = 9

⑥ 11 − 9 = 2

⑦ 13 − 7 = 6

⑧ 13 − 6 = 7

⑨ 10 − 3 = 7

⑩ 10 − 7 = 3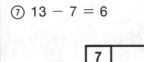

⑪ 16 − 5 = 11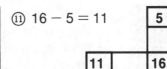

⑫ 16 − 11 = 5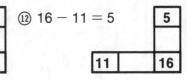

⑬ 12 − 4 = 8

⑭ 12 − 8 = 4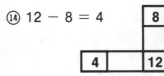

⑮ 17 − 9 = 8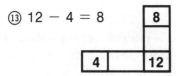

⑯ 17 − 8 = 9

REMINDER: Write the definition of a subtraction table.

B On the table at the right, locate the parts of each problem. Draw a circle around the minuend, place a star beside the subtrahend, and draw a square around the remainder. Label each part with the letter of the problem.

Ⓐ 6 − 3 = 3   Ⓑ 6 − 0 = 6

Ⓒ 6 − 2 = 4   Ⓓ 6 − 1 = 5

−	0	1	2	3	4	5	6
0	0	1	2	3	4	5	6
1	1	2	3	4	5	6	7
2	2	3	4	5	6	7	8
3	3	4	5	6	7	8	9

C Solve the following problems with the aid of the table above.

① 5 − 3 = __2__   ② 2 − 0 = _____   ③ 9 − 3 = _____   ④ 6 − 4 = _____

⑤ 7 − 4 = _____   ⑥ 4 − 1 = _____   ⑦ 8 − 3 = _____   ⑧ 7 − 5 = _____

⑨ 7 − 6 = _____   ⑩ 4 − 2 = _____   ⑪ 1 − 1 = _____   ⑫ 3 − 1 = _____

⑬ 3 − 3 = _____   ⑭ 4 − 3 = _____   ⑮ 6 − 3 = _____   ⑯ 7 − 3 = _____

D Using the table at the left, solve the following problems.

−	0	1	2	3	4	5	6	7	8	9
0	0	1	2	3	4	5	6	7	8	9
1	1	2	3	4	5	6	7	8	9	10
2	2	3	4	5	6	7	8	9	10	11
3	3	4	5	6	7	8	9	10	11	12
4	4	5	6	7	8	9	10	11	12	13
5	5	6	7	8	9	10	11	12	13	14
6	6	7	8	9	10	11	12	13	14	15
7	7	8	9	10	11	12	13	14	15	16
8	8	9	10	11	12	13	14	15	16	17
9	9	10	11	12	13	14	15	16	17	18

① Sharon caught 12 fish while vacationing at Lake Winnepeg. Seven of the fish were too small to keep. She cleaned the remaining fish for supper. How many fish did Sharon clean?

_____

② Lucy entered 10 photographs in the regional amateur photography competition. Three of the photographs won ribbons. The others received no mention. How many photos did not receive ribbons?

_____

③ Lee placed fourth in the national go-cart championship. Thirteen drivers raced in the championship. How many drivers finished behind Lee?

_____

④ Gerald was unit leader to 16 boy scouts at summer camp. Seven of the scouts were 10 years old. The others were between the ages of 11 and 14. How many were in the 11-14 age group?

_____

⑤ Denise mailed 14 applications for summer employment. Seven of the applications resulted in interviews. Denise received no response to the other applications. How many applications resulted in no response?

_____

152

Simple Subtraction

Learning Objective: *We will learn to subtract by deducting ten thousands, thousands, hundreds, tens, and ones.*

Subtraction is the deducting of one number from another to find the difference of the two numbers.

EXAMPLE: **Even when we do not need to rename numbers in subtraction, we may subtract multi-digit numbers by deducting ones, tens, hundreds, etc.**

$$\left.\begin{array}{r} 555 \\ -\,333 \\ \hline 222 \end{array}\right\}$$

5 hundreds, 5 tens, 5 ones
$-$ 3 hundreds, 3 tens, 3 ones
_____
2 hundreds, 2 tens, 2 ones = 222

A Show how to rename numbers to perform the subtractions.

① $\left.\begin{array}{r} 96 \\ -\,54 \end{array}\right\}$ *9 tens, 6 ones*
  $-$ 5 tens, 4 ones
  _____
  4 tens, 2 ones = 42

② $\left.\begin{array}{r} 85 \\ -\,23 \end{array}\right\}$

③ $\left.\begin{array}{r} 77 \\ -\,31 \end{array}\right\}$

④ $\left.\begin{array}{r} 54 \\ -\,13 \end{array}\right\}$

⑤ $\left.\begin{array}{r} 56 \\ -\,24 \end{array}\right\}$

⑥ $\left.\begin{array}{r} 78 \\ -\,15 \end{array}\right\}$

B Subtract these three-digit numbers by deducting ones, tens, and hundreds.

① $\left.\begin{array}{r} 665 \\ -\,311 \end{array}\right\}$ *6 hundreds, 6 tens, 5 ones*
  $-$ 3 hundreds, 1 ten, 1 one
  _____
  3 hundreds, 5 tens, 4 ones = 354

② $\left.\begin{array}{r} 978 \\ -\,246 \end{array}\right\}$

③ $\left.\begin{array}{r} 295 \\ -\,134 \end{array}\right\}$

④ $\left.\begin{array}{r} 597 \\ -\,210 \end{array}\right\}$

⑤ $\left.\begin{array}{r} 695 \\ -\,193 \end{array}\right\}$

⑥ $\left.\begin{array}{r} 275 \\ -\,123 \end{array}\right\}$

REMINDER: Write the definition of subtraction.

_____

_____

                    Unit 63 cont'd ☞

C Subtract these four- and five-digit numbers by deducting ones, tens, hundreds, thousands, and ten thousands.

① 8,059
 − 1,058 }

② 78,615
 − 36,213 }

③ 7,663
 − 1,121 }

④ 47,656
 − 45,144 }

D Study each problem; then subtract by deducting ones, tens, hundreds, thousands, and ten thousands.

① Melissa flew 2,806 miles to visit two cousins. She flew 1,601 miles to visit her cousin, Sheila. From Sheila's home, Melissa flew on to visit her cousin, Earl. How many miles did Melissa fly to visit Earl?

② Scott, Brian, Seth, Adam, and Kyle attended a meeting of future math teachers. Students from all over the United States participated in the meeting. A total of 37,865 students and chaperones were registered at the meeting. From the same state as Scott, Brian, Seth, Adam, and Kyle, 10,223 students and chaperones attended. How many participants came from other states?

Subtraction Practice

Learning Objective: *We will learn to subtract single- and multi-digit numbers.*

Subtraction is the deducting of one number from another to find the difference of the two numbers.

EXAMPLE: **Single- and multi-digit numbers may be subtracted.**

$$533$$
$$-\ 2$$
$$\overline{531}$$

A Find the reminders.

① 224
− 41
183

② 694
− 4

③ 572
− 12

④ 113
− 23

⑤ 41
− 6

⑥ 29
− 8

⑦ 642
− 46

⑧ 422
− 74

⑨ 25
− 9

⑩ 688
− 27

⑪ 505
− 54

⑫ 731
− 21

⑬ 18
− 7

⑭ 642
− 5

⑮ 23
− 7

⑯ 251
− 31

⑰ 834
− 70

⑱ 35
− 2

⑲ 713
− 25

⑳ 50
− 4

㉑ 843
− 63

㉒ 156
− 90

㉓ 900
− 22

㉔ 82
− 6

㉕ 192
− 94

㉖ 760
− 6

㉗ 19
− 6

㉘ 511
− 15

㉙ 54
− 9

㉚ 815
− 36

㉛ 39
− 4

㉜ 365
− 11

㉝ 153
− 89

㉞ 347
− 6

㉟ 933
− 79

㊱ 61
− 3

㊲ 807
− 36

㊳ 209
− 59

㊴ 136
− 52

㊵ 19
− 9

㊶ 262
− 14

㊷ 318
− 90

㊸ 76
− 8

㊹ 634
− 81

㊺ 165
− 26

㊻ 93
− 6

㊼ 86
− 8

㊽ 394
− 97

㊾ 587
− 24

㊿ 624
− 61

51 572
− 58

52 100
− 2

53 82
− 4

54 174
− 31

55 319
− 44

56 661
− 39

REMINDER: Write the definition of subtraction.

_____

_____

B Find the remainders.

① 1,213
  − 298
    915

② 2,423
  − 57

③ 94,648
  − 2,311

④ 5,111
  − 127

⑤ 6,113
  − 348

⑥ 75,116
  − 585

⑦ 85,118
  − 9,987

⑧ 92,510
  − 1,922

⑨ 2,115
  − 1,441

⑩ 12,135
  − 1,334

⑪ 18,711
  − 979

⑫ 3,212
  − 69

⑬ 50,652
  − 390

⑭ 2,313
  − 654

⑮ 59,221
  − 1,254

⑯ 3,682
  − 278

⑰ 5,411
  − 429

⑱ 74,345
  − 4,798

⑲ 31,521
  − 8,044

⑳ 8,362
  − 917

C Find the remainders.

① Seven thousand, five hundred sixteen employees of the Berryville turkey processing plant went on strike. The next day, 474 returned to work. How many continued to strike?
    7,042

② At the end of five years in business, the Gilbraith Company listed 1,429 employees on its payroll. The company started with 371 employees. How many workers has it added over the years?

③ In a local election, 2,987 Berryville citizens voted "yes" or "no" to an increase in sales tax. Supporters of the tax numbered 798. How many voted against the tax?

④ In 1985, 4,291 residents of Benton county were registered to vote. In 1984, the number of countians registered totaled 3,649. How many more registered to vote by 1985?

⑤ Unemployment in Benton county was listed at 11 percent in 1984. Just one year later, the unemployment rate dropped 2 percent. What percentage of unemployment was listed in 1985?

⑥ Six hundred seventy-nine people attend the opening night of the Tarpley Brothers Traveling Circus. Of those attending, only 97 were senior citizens over age 65. How many people under the age of 65 attended?

Subtraction Problems

Learning Objective: *We will learn to subtract various combinations of numbers.*

Subtraction is the deducting of one number from another to find the difference of the two numbers.

EXAMPLE:

Single- and multi-digit numbers may be subtracted in columns or rows. Every subtraction problem has three parts: the minuend, the subtrahend, and the remainder.

minuend ➡   533
subtrahend ➡ − 22
remainder ➡   511

$$533 - 22 = 511$$

A Find the remainders.

①   144
   − 98
    46

② 2,103
  − 910

③ 28,462
    − 8

④   426
 − 311

⑤ 4,531
 − 425

⑥ 9,100
 − 622

⑦   78
 − 51

⑧ 2,004
− 1,037

⑨ 46,144
− 8,584

⑩ 1,733
 − 212

⑪ 55,111
 − 899

⑫   880
 − 89

⑬ 7,097
− 6,607

⑭   760
 − 67

⑮ 10,110
− 1,181

⑯ 1,881
  − 18

⑰ 1,246
  − 75

⑱ 13,701
 − 813

⑲ 49,139
 − 714

⑳ 2,415
 − 314

㉑   462
 − 164

㉒ 72,820
− 8,137

㉓   42
   − 6

㉔ 7,896
  − 50

㉕   442
  − 17

㉖ 5,285
− 2,268

㉗ 16,618
  − 54

㉘ 6,201
 − 485

㉙ 50,019
− 3,353

㉚   301
 − 111

㉛ 48,120
 − 841

㉜   822
 − 211

㉝ 8,078
  − 81

㉞   713
  − 15

㉟ 1,922
 − 777

㊱ 23,315
− 3,013

㊲ 7,770
− 1,710

㊳ 33,233
− 2,471

㊴   252
  − 88

㊵ 28,026
 − 991

㊶   82
  − 28

㊷ 9,339
  − 78

REMINDER: *Write the definition of subtraction.*

_____

_____

B Find the remainders.

① 996 − 274 = __722__

② 7,777 − 44 = _____

③ 2,828 − 72 = _____

④ 2,013 − 232 = _____

⑤ 831 − 449 = _____

⑥ 15,375 − 13 = _____

⑦ 972 − 110 = _____

⑧ 1,821 − 64 = _____

⑨ 3,194 − 915 = _____

⑩ 514 − 11 = _____

⑪ 8,832 − 21 = _____

⑫ 51,440 − 414 = _____

⑬ 617 − 12 = _____

⑭ 69 − 8 = _____

⑮ 3,770 − 839 = _____

⑯ 19,838 − 95 = _____

⑰ 1,575 − 91 = _____

⑱ 667 − 312 = _____

⑲ 510 − 50 = _____

⑳ 2,223 − 544 = _____

㉑ 11,892 − 608 = _____

㉒ 717 − 90 = _____

㉓ 1,210 − 820 = _____

㉔ 613 − 17 = _____

㉕ 2,879 − 11 = _____

㉖ 1,428 − 48 = _____

㉗ 818 − 152 = _____

㉘ 22,211 − 919 = _____

㉙ 1,991 − 651 = _____

㉚ 1,515 − 517 = _____

㉛ 2,879 − 1,114 = _____

㉜ 284 − 88 = _____

㉝ 18,152 − 177 = _____

㉞ 665 − 58 = _____

㉟ 8,518 − 20 = _____

㊱ 1,918 − 170 = _____

C Find the remainders.

① Wilson's Jewelers reduced the prices on 675 watches for a special 3-day sale. During the 3 days, 416 watches were sold at reduced prices. How many of the watches did not sell during the 3 days?

__259__

② There were 94 entries in the Fourth of July Hot-Air Balloon Race. Thirteen balloons never got off the ground. All the others finished the race. How many balloons finished the event?

_____

③ Performing at the Benton County Fair were square dancers from the Berryville Wagon Wheels group. Of the group's 116 members, 47 performed at the fair. How many members did not dance at the fair?

_____

④ Of the 1,066 voting delegates to the Jaycees national convention, 627 voted for the incumbent president. The incumbent ran against 1 opponent. How many delegates voted for the opponent?

_____

⑤ Attending the state business teachers conference were 7,948 instructors. Six hundred thirty-nine instructors taught on the college level. All others taught in high schools. How many taught in high schools?

_____

⑥ Marissa was absent when the teacher changed the week's reading assignment. Marissa had read all but 59 pages of a 250-page assignment when she learned of the change. How many pages had Marissa read?

_____

158

Comprehension Check

A Match minuends and subtrahends with remainders.

① 422 − 41 =   623   ⑪ 8,226 − 278 =   3,454

② 8,061 − 2,063 =   381   ⑫ 11,001 − 2,378 =   8,623

③ 703 − 80 =   8,876   ⑬ 3,922 − 468 =   7,392

④ 1,710 − 211 =   5,998   ⑭ 457 − 59 =   7,948

⑤ 10,101 − 1,225 =   1,499   ⑮ 8,313 − 921 =   398

⑥ 4,405 − 540 =   49,062   ⑯ 10,400 − 1,176 =   9,224

⑦ 50,023 − 961 =   7,985   ⑰ 673 − 74 =   3,369

⑧ 6,919 − 2,485 =   3,865   ⑱ 12,284 − 1,389 =   599

⑨ 8,075 − 90 =   19,430   ⑲ 7,014 − 3,645 =   73

⑩ 25,285 − 5,855 =   4,434   ⑳ 154 − 81 =   10,895

B On the table below, locate the parts of each subtraction problem. Draw a circle around the minuend, a star beside the subtrahend, and a square around the remainder. Label each part with the letter of the problem.

(a) 3 − 3 = 0   (b) 6 − 5 = 1

(c) 8 − 2 = 6   (d) 4 − 0 = 4

__	__0	__1	__2	__3	__4	__5	__6
0	0	1	2	3	4	5	6
1	1	2	3	4	5	6	7
2	2	3	4	5	6	7	8
3	3	4	5	6	7	8	9

C Solve the problems with the aid of the table at right.

① 9 − 6 = *3*   ② 0 − 0 =

③ 4 − 3 =   ④ 7 − 2 =

⑤ 8 − 5 =   ⑥ 5 − 3 =   ⑦ 1 − 0 =   ⑧ 4 − 4 =

⑨ 7 − 1 =   ⑩ 2 − 2 =   ⑪ 7 − 3 =   ⑫ 5 − 4 =

⑬ 3 − 2 =   ⑭ 8 − 6 =   ⑮ 6 − 6 =   ⑯ 5 − 0 =

Test 13 cont'd ☛

D Subtract these numbers by deducting ones, tens, and hundreds.

① 168 } 1 hundred, 6 tens, 8 ones
  − 17 } − 0 hundreds, 1 ten, 7 ones
         1 hundred, 5 tens, 1 one = 151

② 699 }
  − 185 }

③ 59 }
  − 19 }

④ 199 }
  − 27 }

⑤ 298 }
  − 95 }

⑥ 72 }
  − 31 }

E Find the remainders.

① 2,469
  − 253
  ‾‾‾‾‾
  2,216

② 12,265
  − 9,627

③ 828
  − 541

④ 29,145
  − 3,051

⑤ 1,431
  − 153

⑥ 21,094
  − 332

⑦ 7,347
  − 1,335

⑧ 999
  − 365

⑨ 674
  − 37

⑩ 2,063
  − 88

⑪ 64,391
  − 1,240

⑫ 7,941
  − 678

F Find the remainders.

① 4,287 − 643 = **3,644**

② 786 − 44 =

③ 473 − 248 =

④ 11,849 − 9,350 =

⑤ 395 − 145 =

⑥ 26,741 − 531 =

⑦ 4,445 − 428 =

⑧ 2,055 − 396 =

⑨ 1,568 − 571 =

⑩ 355 − 84 =

⑪ 6,859 − 56 =

⑫ 80,456 − 3,013 =

⑬ 62,716 − 394 =

⑭ 7,364 − 267 =

⑮ 65,495 − 66 =

⑯ 356 − 71 =

⑰ 668 − 200 =

⑱ 6,970 − 77 =

Write a paragraph that includes a subtraction problem. Draw a circle around the minuend, a triangle around the subtrahend, and a square around the remainder.

_____

_____

_____

_____

_____

Add or Subtract?

Learning Objective: *We will learn to determine if a problem calls for addition or subtraction.*

Addition is the combining of numbers to obtain the total value or sum. Subtraction is the deducting of one number from another to find the difference or remainder.

EXAMPLE: In problem A, the sum of 333 and 22 is 355. In problem B, the difference of 333 and 22 is 311.

	A	**B**
	333	333
	+ 22	− 22
	355	311

A Find the sums or remainders.

① 841 − 693 = 148

② 539 + 676

③ 8,779 + 8,911

④ 9,941 − 5,102

⑤ 1,311 − 712

⑥ 8,413 + 4,095

⑦ 1,447 + 154

⑧ 8,616 − 121

⑨ 754 + 63

⑩ 18,991 + 1,996

⑪ 20,541 + 21,317

⑫ 222 − 123

⑬ 867 − 249

⑭ 332 + 528

⑮ 226 − 5

⑯ 2,776 − 228

⑰ 7,072 + 920

⑱ 30,374 + 931

⑲ 86,432 − 4,441

⑳ 33,811 + 34

㉑ 3,468 + 7,354

㉒ 683 − 18

㉓ 72,371 − 453

㉔ 810 + 395

㉕ 5,540 + 798

㉖ 413 − 134

㉗ 2,229 + 4,387

㉘ 344 + 884

㉙ 647 + 700

㉚ 45,482 − 469

㉛ 48,809 − 4,940

㉜ 1,506 + 251

㉝ 678 − 52

㉞ 2,353 − 1,476

㉟ 54,531 + 710

㊱ 1,631 − 380

㊲ 4,000 + 786

㊳ 538 + 76

㊴ 4,765 − 514

㊵ 656 + 500

㊶ 5,981 − 300

㊷ 66,710 − 19,724

REMINDER: Write the definition of addition and subtraction.

Unit 66 cont'd ☛

B Fill in the blanks with + or − .

① $500 \underline{\ +\ } 672 = 1,172$
② $4,141 \underline{\quad} 35 = 4,106$
③ $1,567 \underline{\quad} 546 = 2,113$

④ $8,202 \underline{\quad} 770 = 8,972$
⑤ $78 \underline{\quad} 687 = 765$
⑥ $9,117 \underline{\quad} 1,066 = 8,051$

⑦ $113 \underline{\quad} 9 = 122$
⑧ $12,137 \underline{\quad} 138 = 12,275$
⑨ $8,481 \underline{\quad} 478 = 8,003$

⑩ $615 \underline{\quad} 74 = 689$
⑪ $61,164 \underline{\quad} 517 = 61,681$
⑫ $9,911 \underline{\quad} 8,200 = 1,711$

⑬ $197 \underline{\quad} 294 = 491$
⑭ $2,060 \underline{\quad} 1,216 = 844$
⑮ $4,352 \underline{\quad} 2,292 = 2,060$

⑯ $33,092 \underline{\quad} 44 = 33,048$
⑰ $9,625 \underline{\quad} 300 = 9,925$
⑱ $726 \underline{\quad} 1,022 = 1,748$

⑲ $7,459 \underline{\quad} 7,287 = 172$
⑳ $832 \underline{\quad} 2,910 = 3,742$
㉑ $333 \underline{\quad} 154 = 179$

㉒ $3,184 \underline{\quad} 632 = 3,816$
㉓ $20,133 \underline{\quad} 1,089 = 19,044$
㉔ $3,447 \underline{\quad} 39 = 3,408$

㉕ $842 \underline{\quad} 400 = 1,242$
㉖ $1,236 \underline{\quad} 921 = 2,157$
㉗ $4,090 \underline{\quad} 1,441 = 2,649$

㉘ $710 \underline{\quad} 133 = 843$
㉙ $891 \underline{\quad} 3,200 = 4,091$
㉚ $448 \underline{\quad} 915 = 1,363$

㉛ $1,621 \underline{\quad} 457 = 1,164$
㉜ $908 \underline{\quad} 62 = 970$
㉝ $62 \underline{\quad} 49 = 13$

㉞ $90,650 \underline{\quad} 79 = 90,729$
㉟ $396 \underline{\quad} 317 = 713$
㊱ $2,140 \underline{\quad} 1,415 = 3,555$

C Study the paragraphs and identify each as an addition (a) or subtraction (s) problem.

① __s__ Many of Carlisle's residents own satellite receivers which increase the number of television programs that can be viewed. Carlisle has a population of 17,928. There are 610 citizens who are listed as owners of satellite receivers. How many are not owners?

② ____ Happy Hollow Inn recorded a record-breaking business during the Christmas season. In December, 2,842 guests stayed at the inn. The previous December, only 1,089 guests were registered at Happy Hollow. How many more stayed the second year?

③ ____ Yesterday's Treasures is the name of Carlisle's largest antique shop. A store inventory lists 3,975 items for sale. A shipment of additional sale items is expected at any time. What will be the total inventory after the shipment arrives?

④ ____ The number of farm families has decreased in Benton County during the last 5 years. There are 887 farm families today. Five years ago, there were 1,586. How many fewer farm families are there today?

⑤ ____ Land in Benton County sells for an average price of $1,000 per acre. Within 10 years, the price is expected to jump to $2,000 per acre. How much is the price expected to increase within 10 years?

⑥ ____ Businesses located on Main Street numbered 79 in 1960. By 1985, 216 new businesses had opened on Main Street. What was the total number of businesses open by 1985?

Using Addition to Check Subtraction   Unit 67

Learning Objective: We will learn to use addition to prove that subtraction remainders are correct.

Checking is the process of proving correctness.

EXAMPLE: To check a subtraction problem, add
the subtrahend to the remainder.
The sum should be the same as
the minuend.

$$
\begin{array}{rl}
333 & \text{minuend} \\
-\,222 & \text{subtrahend} \\
\hline
111 & \text{remainder} \\
+\,222 & \text{subtrahend} \\
\hline
333 & \text{minuend}
\end{array}
$$

A Use addition to check the following subtraction problems. Place a check (✓) beside each remainder that is correct. Draw an X beside each incorrect remainder.

①
$$
\begin{array}{r}
5,561 \\
-\;875 \\
\hline
4,686 \quad ✓ \\
+\;875 \\
\hline
\mathbf{5,561}
\end{array}
$$

②
$$
\begin{array}{r}
64,855 \\
-\;7,648 \\
\hline
57,207 \;\underline{\quad}
\end{array}
$$

③
$$
\begin{array}{r}
58,815 \\
-\;5,919 \\
\hline
52,904 \;\underline{\quad}
\end{array}
$$

④
$$
\begin{array}{r}
41,602 \\
-\;10,461 \\
\hline
31,141 \;\underline{\quad}
\end{array}
$$

⑤
$$
\begin{array}{r}
95,406 \\
-\;287 \\
\hline
95,218 \;\underline{\quad}
\end{array}
$$

⑥
$$
\begin{array}{r}
6,632 \\
-\;4,086 \\
\hline
2,546 \;\underline{\quad}
\end{array}
$$

⑦
$$
\begin{array}{r}
12,888 \\
-\;3,166 \\
\hline
9,722 \;\underline{\quad}
\end{array}
$$

⑧
$$
\begin{array}{r}
9,001 \\
-\;8,141 \\
\hline
960 \;\underline{\quad}
\end{array}
$$

⑨
$$
\begin{array}{r}
4,634 \\
-\;986 \\
\hline
3,648 \;\underline{\quad}
\end{array}
$$

⑩
$$
\begin{array}{r}
64,662 \\
-\;59,211 \\
\hline
5,451 \;\underline{\quad}
\end{array}
$$

⑪
$$
\begin{array}{r}
10,100 \\
-\;9,622 \\
\hline
488 \;\underline{\quad}
\end{array}
$$

⑫
$$
\begin{array}{r}
67,877 \\
-\;829 \\
\hline
67,056 \;\underline{\quad}
\end{array}
$$

⑬
$$
\begin{array}{r}
82,423 \\
-\;7,107 \\
\hline
75,316 \;\underline{\quad}
\end{array}
$$

⑭
$$
\begin{array}{r}
30,318 \\
-\;12,445 \\
\hline
28,873 \;\underline{\quad}
\end{array}
$$

⑮
$$
\begin{array}{r}
9,064 \\
-\;789 \\
\hline
9,285 \;\underline{\quad}
\end{array}
$$

⑯
$$
\begin{array}{r}
3,368 \\
-\;2,007 \\
\hline
1,361 \;\underline{\quad}
\end{array}
$$

REMINDER: Write the definition of checking.

_____

_____

Unit 67 cont'd ☞

B Use addition to check these subtraction problems. Place a ✓ before each problem that is correct and an X before each incorrect problem.

① ✓ $411 - 171 = 240 + \mathbf{171} = \mathbf{411}$

② ____ $3,321 - 417 = 2,904$

③ ____ $8,199 - 1,282 = 6,917$

④ ____ $1,123 - 615 = 1,508$

⑤ ____ $61,000 - 2,319 = 59,691$

⑥ ____ $9,824 - 4,774 = 5,050$

⑦ ____ $2,553 - 122 = 2,431$

⑧ ____ $40,985 - 312 = 40,673$

⑨ ____ $6,240 - 985 = 4,255$

⑩ ____ $3,128 - 664 = 2,464$

⑪ ____ $829 - 137 = 692$

⑫ ____ $619 - 23 = 586$

⑬ ____ $7,081 - 6,100 = 1,081$

⑭ ____ $937 - 270 = 667$

⑮ ____ $68,801 - 372 = 67,429$

⑯ ____ $4,080 - 2,141 = 1,939$

C Use addition to check each problem. If the problem is incorrect, find the correct answer.

① At the beginning of the play, 503 coats were hung in the cloakroom. At intermission, 76 coats were removed. How many coats were left after intermission?

$$503 - 76 \atop 429$$

② Sixty-two students enrolled in an after-school aerobic dance class, which met once a week for 6 weeks. Only 36 students completed the class. How many dropped out?

$$62 - 36 \atop 36$$

③ The Linn Fire Department has a staff of 18 firefighters. The department hopes to employ a total of 25 firefighters within 5 years. How many additional firefighters would be hired?

$$25 - 18 \atop 7$$

④ Julie's science teacher said that 107 earthquakes had been recorded in the area since 1901. Forty-six of these earthquakes had occurred between 1901 and 1970. How many occurred after that?

$$107 - 46 \atop 151$$

Checking Subtraction Problems

Learning Objective: *We will learn to solve subtraction problems and prove the answers to be correct.*

Checking is the process of proving correctness.

EXAMPLE:

To check a subtraction problem, add the subtrahend to the remainder. The sum should be equal to the minuend.

$$333 - 222 = 111$$
$$111 + 222 = 333$$

$\left. \right\}$ $333 = 333$

A Find the remainders and use addition to check.

①
$$\begin{array}{r} 2,913 \\ -\ 423 \\ \hline \mathbf{2,490} \\ +\ \mathbf{423} \\ \hline \mathbf{2,913} \end{array}$$

②
$$\begin{array}{r} 748 \\ -\ 246 \\ \hline \end{array}$$

③
$$\begin{array}{r} 5,190 \\ -\ 2,827 \\ \hline \end{array}$$

④
$$\begin{array}{r} 73,909 \\ -\ 34,014 \\ \hline \end{array}$$

⑤
$$\begin{array}{r} 835 \\ -\ 84 \\ \hline \end{array}$$

⑥
$$\begin{array}{r} 1,628 \\ -\ 64 \\ \hline \end{array}$$

⑦
$$\begin{array}{r} 192 \\ -\ 65 \\ \hline \end{array}$$

⑧
$$\begin{array}{r} 4,056 \\ -\ 459 \\ \hline \end{array}$$

⑨
$$\begin{array}{r} 87,413 \\ -\ 54,117 \\ \hline \end{array}$$

⑩
$$\begin{array}{r} 971 \\ -\ 737 \\ \hline \end{array}$$

⑪
$$\begin{array}{r} 4,554 \\ -\ 4,431 \\ \hline \end{array}$$

⑫
$$\begin{array}{r} 23,194 \\ -\ 8,107 \\ \hline \end{array}$$

⑬
$$\begin{array}{r} 6,139 \\ -\ 3,427 \\ \hline \end{array}$$

⑭
$$\begin{array}{r} 708 \\ -\ 391 \\ \hline \end{array}$$

⑮
$$\begin{array}{r} 1,484 \\ -\ 620 \\ \hline \end{array}$$

⑯
$$\begin{array}{r} 16,109 \\ -\ 984 \\ \hline \end{array}$$

⑰
$$\begin{array}{r} 270 \\ -\ 261 \\ \hline \end{array}$$

⑱
$$\begin{array}{r} 1,268 \\ -\ 910 \\ \hline \end{array}$$

⑲
$$\begin{array}{r} 191 \\ -\ 41 \\ \hline \end{array}$$

⑳
$$\begin{array}{r} 1,125 \\ -\ 412 \\ \hline \end{array}$$

㉑
$$\begin{array}{r} 1,224 \\ -\ 720 \\ \hline \end{array}$$

㉒
$$\begin{array}{r} 276 \\ -\ 91 \\ \hline \end{array}$$

㉓
$$\begin{array}{r} 41,513 \\ -\ 28,805 \\ \hline \end{array}$$

㉔
$$\begin{array}{r} 5,112 \\ -\ 13 \\ \hline \end{array}$$

㉕
$$\begin{array}{r} 1,089 \\ -\ 171 \\ \hline \end{array}$$

㉖
$$\begin{array}{r} 17,623 \\ -\ 12,232 \\ \hline \end{array}$$

㉗
$$\begin{array}{r} 253 \\ -\ 91 \\ \hline \end{array}$$

㉘
$$\begin{array}{r} 2,106 \\ -\ 1,613 \\ \hline \end{array}$$

㉙
$$\begin{array}{r} 821 \\ -\ 117 \\ \hline \end{array}$$

㉚
$$\begin{array}{r} 18,320 \\ -\ 2,361 \\ \hline \end{array}$$

REMINDER: Write the definition of checking.

_____

_____

Unit 68 cont'd ☛

B Find the remainders and check with addition.

1. $2,181 - 942 = $ _$1,239 + 942 = 2,181$_
2. $6,200 - 1,010 = $ _____
3. $20,525 - 1,491 = $ _____
4. $321 - 82 = $ _____
5. $1,231 - 516 = $ _____
6. $52,227 - 14,317 = $ _____
7. $19,827 - 2,712 = $ _____
8. $8,202 - 2,215 = $ _____
9. $1,102 - 136 = $ _____
10. $92,410 - 10,101 = $ _____
11. $11,372 - 1,192 = $ _____
12. $9,023 - 1,562 = $ _____
13. $718 - 251 = $ _____
14. $13,417 - 4,111 = $ _____
15. $3,291 - 2,012 = $ _____
16. $942 - 326 = $ _____
17. $591 - 62 = $ _____
18. $51,732 - 152 = $ _____

C Solve the problems and use the spaces at the right to check your answers.

1. One hundred sixteen sardines are packed in The Fish Market's biggest tin of sardines in mustard sauce. In the store's smallest tin are 20 sardines. How many more sardines are in the largest tin?

2. Ninety-four singers, dancers, comedians, and other performers took part in a telethon for public television. Only 12 of the performers were amateurs. The others were professional entertainers. How many were professionals?

3. Signatures on a petition to the city board of aldermen numbered 891. Six hundred twenty-two of the petition's signers were city residents. The other signers lived outside the city limits. How many signers were not city residents?

4. At a restaurant, Lana ordered the evening special. She was served 45 popcorn shrimp, a salad, and baked potato. Dorian asked for half an order and was served 15 shrimp, a potato, and salad. How many fewer shrimp were in the half order?

Basic Multiplication Facts

Learning
Objective: *We will learn to multiply by combining sets.*

Multiplication is a shortcut for adding a number to itself.

EXAMPLE:

If there are 3 members in Set A, $A = \{🚗, 🚗, 🚗\}$ $n(A) = 3$

two Set A's would include 3 $2 \times A = \{🚗, 🚗, 🚗\}$ $2 \times n(A) = $ 3

members plus 3 members. $+ \{🚗, 🚗, 🚗\}$ $+\ 3$

                           $\{🚗, 🚗, 🚗, 🚗, 🚗, 🚗\}$ 6

A   Fill in the blanks.

① $B = \{♡, ♡, ♡, ♡, ♡\}$ $n(B) = $ __5__

     $2 \times B = \{♡, ♡, ♡, ♡, ♡\}$ $2 \times n(B) = $ __5__

         $+ \{♡, ♡, ♡, ♡, ♡\}$ $+$ __5__

     $\{♡, ♡, ♡, ♡, ♡, ♡, ♡, ♡, ♡, ♡\}$ __10__

② $C = \{◇, ◇, ◇, ◇\}$ $n(C) = $ ____

     $2 \times C = \{◇, ◇, ◇, ◇\}$ $2 \times n(C) = $ ____

         $+ \{◇, ◇, ◇, ◇\}$ $+$ ____

     $\{◇, ◇, ◇, ◇, ◇, ◇, ◇, ◇\}$ ____

③ $D = \{♣, ♣\}$ $n(D) = $ ____

     $2 \times D = \{♣, ♣\}$ $2 \times n(D) = $ ____

         $+ \{♣, ♣\}$ $+$ ____

     $\{♣, ♣, ♣, ♣\}$ ____

④ $E = \{✈\}$ $n(E) = $ ____

     $2 \times E = \{✈\}$ $2 \times n(E) = $ ____

         $+ \{✈\}$ $+$ ____

     $\{✈, ✈\}$ ____

⑤ $F = \{★, ★, ★, ★, ★\}$ $n(F) = $ ____

     $3 \times F = \{★, ★, ★, ★, ★\}$ $3 \times n(F) = $ ____

             $\{★, ★, ★, ★, ★\}$ ____

         $+ \{★, ★, ★, ★, ★\}$ $+$ ____

             $\{★, ★, ★, ★, ★,$

              $★, ★, ★, ★, ★,$

              $★, ★, ★, ★, ★\}$

⑥ $G = \{🛩, 🛩, 🛩\}$ $n(G) = $ ____

     $3 \times G = \{🛩, 🛩, 🛩\}$ $3 \times n(G) = $ ____

             $\{🛩, 🛩, 🛩\}$ ____

         $+ \{🛩, 🛩, 🛩\}$ $+$ ____

             $\{🛩, 🛩, 🛩,$ ____

               $🛩, 🛩, 🛩,$

               $🛩, 🛩, 🛩\}$

⑦ $H = \{▶, ▶, ▶, ▶\}$ $n(H) = $ ____

     $3 \times H = \{▶, ▶, ▶, ▶\}$ $3 \times n(H) = $ ____

             $\{▶, ▶, ▶, ▶\}$

         $+ \{▶, ▶, ▶, ▶\}$ $+$ ____

             $\{▶, ▶, ▶, ▶, ▶, ▶,$ ____

              $▶, ▶, ▶, ▶, ▶, ▶\}$

⑧ $I = \{♠, ♠\}$ $n(I) = $ ____

     $3 \times I = \{♠, ♠\}$ $3 \times n(I) = $ ____

             $\{♠, ♠\}$ ____

         $+ \{♠, ♠\}$ $+$ ____

             $\{♠, ♠, ♠, ♠, ♠, ♠\}$ ____

REMINDER: Write the definition of multiplication.

_____

_____

           Unit 69 cont'd ☞

B Fill in the blanks.

① A = {●, ●, ●, ●, ●, ●} × 2 = {●, ●, ●, ●, ●, ●} + {●, ●, ●, ●, ●, ●} = {●, ●, ●, ●, ●, ●, ●, ●, ●, ●, ●, ●}

n(A) = _____   × 2 = _____   +   _____   = _____

② B = {◇, ◇, ◇, ◇} × 4 = {◇, ◇, ◇, ◇} + {◇, ◇, ◇, ◇} + {◇, ◇, ◇, ◇} + {◇, ◇, ◇, ◇}

n(B) = _____   × 4 = _____   +   _____   +   _____   +   _____

= {◇, ◇, ◇, ◇, ◇, ◇, ◇, ◇, ◇, ◇, ◇, ◇, ◇, ◇, ◇, ◇}

= _____

③ C = {▲, ▲, ▲, ▲, ▲} × 3 = {▲, ▲, ▲, ▲, ▲} + {▲, ▲, ▲, ▲, ▲} + {▲, ▲, ▲, ▲, ▲}

n(C) = _____   × 3 = _____   +   _____   +   _____

= {▲, ▲, ▲, ▲, ▲, ▲, ▲, ▲, ▲, ▲, ▲, ▲, ▲, ▲, ▲}

= _____

④ D = {□, □} × 5 = {□, □} + {□, □} + {□, □} + {□, □} + {□, □} = {□, □, □, □, □, □, □, □, □, □}

n(D) = _____ × 5 = _____ + _____ + _____ + _____ + _____ = _____

⑤ E = {♣, ♣, ♣, ♣, ♣, ♣, ♣, ♣, ♣, ♣, ♣, ♣, ♣} × 1 = {♣, ♣, ♣, ♣, ♣, ♣, ♣, ♣, ♣, ♣, ♣, ♣, ♣}

n(E) = _____   × 1 = _____

C Study the problems and fill in the blanks.

① Eggs are packed in sets of 12 to a carton. Two cartons were used in making meringue pies for the lunch rush at Margaret's Diner. How many eggs were used?

1 set = 12

2 sets =   12
         + 12
         ─────
2 × 12 = **24**

② Michael bought a set of 8 glasses. He liked them so well that he bought 2 more sets for friends. How many glasses were in the 3 sets that he bought?

1 set = 8

3 sets =   8
            8
         + 8
         ─────
3 × 8 =

③ Amanda bites her fingernails. She recently purchased 4 sets of fake nails in different colors. There are 10 nails to a set. How many nails did she buy?

1 set = 10

4 sets =   10
            10
            10
         + 10
         ─────
4 × 10 =

④ There are 18 volumes to a set of encyclopedias. The library has 2 sets. How many volumes does the library have?

1 set = 18

2 sets =   18
         + 18
         ─────
2 × 18 =

⑤ File folders may be bought in sets of 10. Amy bought 3 sets. How many folders did she buy?

1 set = 10

3 sets =   10
            10
         + 10
         ─────
3 × 10 =

⑥ Ties are packaged in sets of 7. Randy bought 2 packages. How many ties did Randy buy?

1 set = 7

2 sets =   7
         + 7
         ─────
2 × 7 =

168

Multiplication as Repeated Addition   Unit 70

Learning Objective: *We will learn to multiply by repeated adding of numbers.*

Multiplication is a shortcut for adding a number to itself.

EXAMPLE: The result of multiplying 2 times $3 + 3 = 2 \times 3 = 6$
3 is equal to the sum of 3 plus 3.

A Complete the multiplication sentences that produce the same results as the addition problems.

① $8 + 8 + 8 + 8 + 8 =$ ___5___ $\times$ ___8___ $=$ ___40___

② $5 + 5 + 5 + 5 =$ _____ $\times$ _____ $=$ _____

③ $7 + 7 + 7 + 7 + 7 + 7 =$ _____ $\times$ _____ $=$ _____

④ $2 + 2 + 2 + 2 + 2 + 2 + 2 + 2 =$ _____ $\times$ _____ $=$ _____

⑤ $100 + 100 + 100 =$ _____ $\times$ _____ $=$ _____

⑥ $1 + 1 + 1 + 1 + 1 + 1 + 1 =$ _____ $\times$ _____ $=$ _____

⑦ $0 + 0 + 0 + 0 + 0 + 0 =$ _____ $\times$ _____ $=$ _____

⑧ $12 + 12 + 12 + 12 + 12 =$ _____ $\times$ _____ $=$ _____

⑨ $3 + 3 + 3 + 3 + 3 + 3 + 3 =$ _____ $\times$ _____ $=$ _____

⑩ $6 + 6 + 6 + 6 + 6 =$ _____ $\times$ _____ $=$ _____

⑪ $4 + 4 + 4 + 4 + 4 =$ _____ $\times$ _____ $=$ _____

⑫ $10 + 10 + 10 + 10 + 10 + 10 =$ _____ $\times$ _____ $=$ _____

⑬ $25 + 25 + 25 + 25 =$ _____ $\times$ _____ $=$ _____

⑭ $11 + 11 + 11 + 11 + 11 + 11 + 11 + 11 =$ _____ $\times$ _____ $=$ _____

⑮ $9 + 9 + 9 + 9 + 9 + 9 + 9 =$ _____ $\times$ _____ $=$ _____

⑯ $2 + 2 + 2 + 2 + 2 + 2 =$ _____ $\times$ _____ $=$ _____

⑰ $1 + 1 + 1 + 1 + 1 + 1 + 1 + 1 + 1 + 1 =$ _____ $\times$ _____ $=$ _____

⑱ $15 + 15 + 15 + 15 + 15 =$ _____ $\times$ _____ $=$ _____

⑲ $22 + 22 + 22 + 22 =$ _____ $\times$ _____ $=$ _____

⑳ $0 + 0 + 0 + 0 + 0 + 0 + 0 + 0 =$ _____ $\times$ _____ $=$ _____

㉑ $40 + 40 + 40 =$ _____ $\times$ _____ $=$ _____

㉒ $500 + 500 + 500 + 500 =$ _____ $\times$ _____ $=$ _____

㉓ $9 + 9 + 9 + 9 + 9 =$ _____ $\times$ _____ $=$ _____

㉔ $13 + 13 + 13 =$ _____ $\times$ _____ $=$ _____

㉕ $1,500 + 1,500 =$ _____ $\times$ _____ $=$ _____

REMINDER: Write the definition of multiplication.

_____

_____

B Complete the addition sentences that produce the same results as the multiplication problems.

① 4 × 9 = ___9 + 9 + 9 + 9___ = __36__

② 8 × 3 = _____ = _____

③ 5 × 10 = _____ = _____

④ 3 × 75 = _____ = _____

⑤ 7 × 2 = _____ = _____

⑥ 4 × 6 = _____ = _____

⑦ 6 × 5 = _____ = _____

⑧ 7 × 11 = _____ = _____

⑨ 2 × 1,000 = _____ = _____

⑩ 6 × 8 = _____ = _____

⑪ 8 × 7 = _____ = _____

⑫ 2 × 16 = _____ = _____

⑬ 3 × 15 = _____ = _____

⑭ 5 × 0 = _____ = _____

⑮ 7 × 4 = _____ = _____

⑯ 4 × 20 = _____ = _____

⑰ 8 × 4 = _____ = _____

⑱ 6 × 1 = _____ = _____

C For each problem, write an addition sentence and a multiplication sentence.

① Elizabeth bought 6 books of specially issued "Women in History" postage stamps. Each book contained 20 stamps bearing the likenesses of famous women. How many stamps did she buy?
_20 + 20 + 20 + 20 + 20 + 20 = 120_
_6 × 20 = 120_

② In Marlena's Girl Scout unit, there were 6 girls to a tent during summer camp. There were 6 tents in each unit. How many girls were in Marlena's unit?

_____

_____

③ All freshmen at Smithton High School are required to take an achievement test. The test is divided into 4 sections. Each section contains 100 questions. How many questions are on the test?

_____

_____

④ A recipe for Mexican cornbread calls for 3 cups of yellow cornmeal. Daniel will make 5 times the recipe for a family reunion. How many cups of yellow cornmeal will Daniel need?

_____

_____

⑤ On the first day of the fall firearms season for hunting deer, 5 hunters in Benton County killed their limit of 2 deer apiece. How many deer did the hunters kill?

_____

_____

⑥ For a grammar and composition course, Bill bought 3 notebooks. Each notebook contained 500 sheets of paper. How many sheets of paper were in the 3 notebooks?

_____

_____

170

Comprehension Check

A Add or subtract.

① 22,469 − 4,572 **17,897**	② 4,229 − 2,568	③ 11,341 + 29,642	④ 8,505 + 7,311	⑤ 864 − 223	⑥ 2,518 + 834
⑦ 1,569 − 82	⑧ 35,713 + 50,843	⑨ 1,927 + 19	⑩ 6,027 + 511	⑪ 54,815 − 39,365	⑫ 1,533 + 479
⑬ 572 − 100	⑭ 6,593 + 8,639	⑮ 3,361 + 8,072	⑯ 821 − 743	⑰ 9,136 + 19,262	⑱ 31,876 − 6,341
⑲ 19,661 + 41,412	⑳ 236 − 8	㉑ 84,674 − 927	㉒ 5,421 + 757	㉓ 31,702 − 25,463	㉔ 4,587 + 624
㉕ 9,022 − 6,946	㉖ 6,159 + 36,411	㉗ 896 + 793	㉘ 14,908 − 8,126	㉙ 3,659 + 529	㉚ 68,975 + 82,461

B Use addition to check the subtraction problems. Place a check (✓) beside each remainder that is correct and an (X) beside each incorrect remainder.

① 5,824 − 3,144 2,680 ✓ + **3,144** **5,824**	② 39,183 − 690 38,493 ____	③ 637 − 16 621 ____	④ 56,090 − 35,215 20,885 ____
⑤ 96,348 − 1,666 95,682 ____	⑥ 4,336 − 884 3,452 ____	⑦ 14,517 − 1,011 13,506 ____	⑧ 220 − 76 144 ____
⑨ 433 − 57 386 ____	⑩ 87,876 − 9,875 78,001 ____	⑪ 6,884 − 6,780 104 ____	⑫ 4,134 − 964 3,170 ____

Test 14 cont'd ☞

C Find the remainders. Use addition to check your answers.

① 5,779 − 353 = <u>**5,426** + **353** = **5,779**</u> ② 410 − 248 = _____

③ 45,877 − 11,508 = _____ ④ 54,643 − 4,185 = _____

⑤ 2,286 − 855 = _____ ⑥ 829 − 75 = _____

⑦ 63,563 − 5,149 = _____ ⑧ 3,139 − 877 = _____

D Fill in the blanks.

① A = {♡, ♡, ♡, ♡, ♡} × 4 = {♡, ♡, ♡, ♡, ♡} + {♡, ♡, ♡, ♡, ♡} + {♡, ♡, ♡, ♡, ♡} + {♡, ♡, ♡, ♡, ♡}

 n(A) = _____ × 4 = _____ + _____ + _____ + _____

      = {♡, ♡, ♡, ♡, ♡, ♡, ♡, ♡, ♡, ♡, ♡, ♡, ♡, ♡, ♡, ♡, ♡, ♡, ♡, ♡}

      = _____

② B = {♣, ♣, ♣, ♣, ♣, ♣} × 3 = {♣, ♣, ♣, ♣, ♣, ♣} + {♣, ♣, ♣, ♣, ♣, ♣} + {♣, ♣, ♣, ♣, ♣, ♣}

 n(B) = _____ × 3 = _____ + _____ + _____

      = {♣, ♣, ♣, ♣, ♣, ♣, ♣, ♣, ♣, ♣, ♣, ♣, ♣, ♣, ♣, ♣, ♣, ♣}

      = _____

③ C = {♠, ♠, ♠, ♠, ♠, ♠, ♠} × 2 = {♠, ♠, ♠, ♠, ♠, ♠, ♠} + {♠, ♠, ♠, ♠, ♠, ♠, ♠}

 n(C) = _____ × 2 = _____ + _____

      = {♠, ♠, ♠, ♠, ♠, ♠, ♠, ♠, ♠, ♠, ♠, ♠, ♠, ♠}

      = _____

④ D = {◇, ◇, ◇} × 3 = {◇, ◇, ◇} + {◇, ◇, ◇} + {◇, ◇, ◇} = {◇, ◇, ◇, ◇, ◇, ◇, ◇, ◇, ◇}

 n(D) = _____ × 3 = _____ + _____ + _____ = _____

⑤ E = {□, □, □, □} × 2 = {□, □, □, □} + {□, □, □, □} = {□, □, □, □, □, □, □, □}

 n(E) = _____ × 2 = _____ + _____ = _____

E Complete the addition or multiplication sentences.

① 8 + 8 + 8 + 8 + 8 + 8 = <u>**6**</u> × 8 = <u>**48**</u> ② 1 + 1 + 1 + 1 + 1 = _____ × 1 = _____

③ 4 × 15 = _____ + _____ + _____ + _____ = _____ ④ 3 × 400 = _____ + _____ + _____ = _____

⑤ 11 + 11 + 11 + 11 = _____ × 11 = _____ ⑥ 9 + 9 + 9 + 9 + 9 + 9 = _____ × 9 = _____

⑦ 7 × 10 = _____ + _____ + _____ + _____ + _____ + _____ + _____ = _____

⑧ 8 × 0 = _____ + _____ + _____ + _____ + _____ + _____ + _____ + _____ = _____

Write a paragraph that includes a multiplication problem. Write an addition sentence and a multiplication sentence for the problem.

_____

_____

_____

_____

_____

Multiplication Tables for 1, 2, 3, & 4   Unit 71

Learning Objective: *We will learn to multiply 1, 2, 3, & 4 times the numerals 0 - 12.*

Multiplication is a shortcut for adding a number to itself.

EXAMPLE: 2 times 1 is equal to 1 plus 1.
3 times 1 is equal to 1 plus 1 plus 1.
4 times 1 is equal to 1 plus 1 plus 1 plus 1.
Memorizing multiplication tables allows us to skip time-consuming addition.

$$2 \times 1 = 1 + 1 = 2$$
$$3 \times 1 = 1 + 1 + 1 = 3$$
$$4 \times 1 = 1 + 1 + 1 + 1 = 4$$

A Multiply.

① $1 \times 1 =$ __1__   ② $2 \times 1 =$ ____   ③ $3 \times 1 =$ ____   ④ $4 \times 1 =$ ____

⑤ $1 \times 2 =$ ____   ⑥ $2 \times 2 =$ ____   ⑦ $3 \times 2 =$ ____   ⑧ $4 \times 2 =$ ____

⑨ $1 \times 3 =$ ____   ⑩ $2 \times 3 =$ ____   ⑪ $3 \times 3 =$ ____   ⑫ $4 \times 3 =$ ____

⑬ $1 \times 4 =$ ____   ⑭ $2 \times 4 =$ ____   ⑮ $3 \times 4 =$ ____   ⑯ $4 \times 4 =$ ____

⑰ $1 \times 5 =$ ____   ⑱ $2 \times 5 =$ ____   ⑲ $3 \times 5 =$ ____   ⑳ $4 \times 5 =$ ____

㉑ $1 \times 6 =$ ____   ㉒ $2 \times 6 =$ ____   ㉓ $3 \times 6 =$ ____   ㉔ $4 \times 6 =$ ____

㉕ $1 \times 7 =$ ____   ㉖ $2 \times 7 =$ ____   ㉗ $3 \times 7 =$ ____   ㉘ $4 \times 7 =$ ____

㉙ $1 \times 8 =$ ____   ㉚ $2 \times 8 =$ ____   ㉛ $3 \times 8 =$ ____   ㉜ $4 \times 8 =$ ____

㉝ $1 \times 9 =$ ____   ㉞ $2 \times 9 =$ ____   ㉟ $3 \times 9 =$ ____   ㊱ $4 \times 9 =$ ____

㊲ $1 \times 10 =$ ____   ㊳ $2 \times 10 =$ ____   ㊴ $3 \times 10 =$ ____   ㊵ $4 \times 10 =$ ____

㊶ $1 \times 11 =$ ____   ㊷ $2 \times 11 =$ ____   ㊸ $3 \times 11 =$ ____   ㊹ $4 \times 11 =$ ____

㊺ $1 \times 12 =$ ____   ㊻ $2 \times 12 =$ ____   ㊼ $3 \times 12 =$ ____   ㊽ $4 \times 12 =$ ____

B 0 multiplied by any number is equal to 0. Solve the following problems and write an addition sentence for each.

① $1 \times 0 =$ _____   ② $2 \times 0 =$ _____

③ $3 \times 0 =$ _____   ④ $4 \times 0 =$ _____

REMINDER: Write the definition of multiplication.

_____

Unit 71 cont'd ☞

C Fill in the blanks.

① $2 \times 2 = \underline{4}$ ② $4 \times \underline{} = 12$ ③ $\underline{} \times 5 = 5$ ④ $3 \times 1 = \underline{}$

⑤ $\underline{} \times 7 = 7$ ⑥ $1 \times 8 = \underline{}$ ⑦ $3 \times \underline{} = 9$ ⑧ $\underline{} \times 4 = 16$

⑨ $2 \times 0 = \underline{}$ ⑩ $1 \times \underline{} = 1$ ⑪ $2 \times 5 = \underline{}$ ⑫ $2 \times \underline{} = 24$

⑬ $3 \times \underline{} = 18$ ⑭ $2 \times 3 = \underline{}$ ⑮ $4 \times \underline{} = 32$ ⑯ $1 \times 0 = \underline{}$

⑰ $\underline{} \times 9 = 9$ ⑱ $4 \times \underline{} = 44$ ⑲ $\underline{} \times 4 = 8$ ⑳ $3 \times \underline{} = 6$

㉑ $4 \times \underline{} = 0$ ㉒ $\underline{} \times 3 = 3$ ㉓ $2 \times \underline{} = 16$ ㉔ $\underline{} \times 2 = 2$

㉕ $\underline{} \times 10 = 10$ ㉖ $3 \times \underline{} = 36$ ㉗ $3 \times 4 = \underline{}$ ㉘ $4 \times \underline{} = 36$

㉙ $4 \times \underline{} = 4$ ㉚ $2 \times 11 = \underline{}$ ㉛ $\underline{} \times 7 = 14$ ㉜ $2 \times 10 = \underline{}$

㉝ $1 \times 6 = \underline{}$ ㉞ $\underline{} \times 8 = 24$ ㉟ $4 \times \underline{} = 48$ ㊱ $\underline{} \times 7 = 28$

D Fill in the blanks.

① While she was vacationing in Florida, Jessica bought 4 envelopes so that she could mail letters to friends back home. Each envelope cost 12 cents. How much money did Jessica spend for envelopes?

     $4 \times 12 = 48$ cents

② All juniors at Berryville High School are required to include American History on their schedule of classes. To pass the course each student must give 4 oral reports. One student gave no reports. How many reports were not given?

_____

③ For a spring concert, the Berryville High School choir members walked onto the stage and divided themselves into 3 rows. Eleven choir members stood in each row. How many choir members performed in the spring concert?

_____

④ Some Berryville seniors attended evening classes at the local university in addition to their high-school classes. Three seniors attended 2 college classes each. What was the total number of college classes attended by seniors?

_____

⑤ Each of the top 2 winners in a school-sponsored dance marathon were given $10 gift certificates. All other money raised by the marathon went to a charity. How much prize money was awarded?

_____

⑥ There were 4 passengers to each seat in the van that was driven to the regional science fair. The van held 4 seats. How many people traveled in the van to the regional science fair?

_____

Multiplication Tables for 5, 6, and 7   Unit 72

Learning Objective: *We will learn to multiply 5, 6, and 7 times the numerals 0-12.*

Multiplication is a shortcut for adding a number to itself.

EXAMPLE:
1 times 1 is equal to 1.
2 times 1 is equal to $1 + 1$.
3 times 1 is equal to $1 + 1 + 1$.
0 multiplied by any number
is equal to 0.

$1 \times 1 = 1$	$1 \times 0 = 0$
$2 \times 1 = 1 + 1 = 2$	$2 \times 0 = 0 + 0 = 0$
$3 \times 1 = 1 + 1 + 1 = 3$	$3 \times 0 = 0 + 0 + 0 = 0$

A Multiply. Use the blank space for repeated addition, if necessary.

① $5 \times 1 = 5$ ② $6 \times 1 =$ ③ $7 \times 1 =$

④ $5 \times 2 =$ ⑤ $6 \times 2 =$ ⑥ $7 \times 2 =$

⑦ $5 \times 3 =$ ⑧ $6 \times 3 =$ ⑨ $7 \times 3 =$

⑩ $5 \times 4 =$ ⑪ $6 \times 4 =$ ⑫ $7 \times 4 =$

⑬ $5 \times 5 =$ ⑭ $6 \times 5 =$ ⑮ $7 \times 5 =$

⑯ $5 \times 6 =$ ⑰ $6 \times 6 =$ ⑱ $7 \times 6 =$

⑲ $5 \times 7 =$ ⑳ $6 \times 7 =$ ㉑ $7 \times 7 =$

㉒ $5 \times 8 =$ ㉓ $6 \times 8 =$ ㉔ $7 \times 8 =$

㉕ $5 \times 9 =$ ㉖ $6 \times 9 =$ ㉗ $7 \times 9 =$

㉘ $5 \times 10 =$ ㉙ $6 \times 10 =$ ㉚ $7 \times 10 =$

㉛ $5 \times 11 =$ ㉜ $6 \times 11 =$ ㉝ $7 \times 11 =$

㊱ $5 \times 12 =$ ㉟ $6 \times 12 =$ ㊱ $7 \times 12 =$

B Solve the problems and write an addition sentence for each.

① $5 \times 0 =$

② $6 \times 0 =$

③ $7 \times 0 =$

REMINDER: Write the definition of multiplication.

_____

_____

C Fill in the blanks.

① __5__ × 2 = 10 ② 5 × ___ = 25 ③ 6 × 0 = ___ ④ 7 × ___ = 35

⑤ ___ × 6 = 36 ⑥ 5 × 11 = ___ ⑦ 7 × ___ = 7 ⑧ ___ × 4 = 20

⑨ 6 × ___ = 12 ⑩ ___ × 6 = 30 ⑪ 7 × 9 = ___ ⑫ ___ × 4 = 28

⑬ 6 × 11 = ___ ⑭ ___ × 10 = 50 ⑮ ___ × 11 = 77 ⑯ 6 × 3 = ___

⑰ 5 × ___ = 45 ⑱ ___ × 1 = 5 ⑲ ___ × 10 = 70 ⑳ 6 × ___ = 54

㉑ 5 × 1 = ___ ㉒ ___ × 8 = 56 ㉓ ___ × 12 = 60 ㉔ 6 × ___ = 24

㉕ 5 × ___ = 15 ㉖ 7 × 7 = ___ ㉗ 7 × ___ = 0 ㉘ 6 × ___ = 42

㉙ 7 × ___ = 84 ㉚ 5 × 8 = ___ ㉛ 6 × 8 = ___ ㉜ ___ × 12 = 60

㉝ 6 × ___ = 60 ㉞ 5 × 4 = ___ ㉟ ___ × 1 = 6 ㊱ 7 × ___ = 42

㊲ ___ × 7 = 35 ㊳ 6 × ___ = 72 ㊴ 7 × 2 = ___ ㊵ ___ × 5 = 30

D Multiply 5, 6, and 7 times themselves.

① _____ ② _____ ③ _____

E Solve the problems. Write a multiplication sentence for each.

① There are 7 members on the Henderson High School Board of Education. On any official action taken by the board, each member is allowed to cast 1 vote. What is the total number of votes allowed on any action?
_7 × 1 = 7_
_____

② At one school board meeting, 6 teachers asked for extra pay for teaching evening classes for adults. Each of the teachers taught 2 evening classes. How many evening classes were taught by the 6 teachers?
_____

③ School board members discussed eliminating 5 stops on one of the bus routes. It was reported that 3 students boarded the bus at each of the stops in question. How many students would be affected by the board's decision?
_____

④ During the 1985-86 term, some school board members attended district, regional, and state meetings. Six members attended 9 meetings apiece. What was the total number of meetings attended by the 6 board members?
_____

⑤ School board members talked with state legislators about the need for higher salaries for teachers. Each of the 7 board members placed 3 phone calls to legislators. What was the total number of phone calls?
_____

⑥ Because of school closings during the severe winter, the board voted that students should attend classes during the summer. It was decided that classes would be held for 5 hours for each of 4 days. How many hours would classes be held?
_____

Multiplication Tables for 8, 9, and 10   Unit 73

Learning Objective: *We will learn to multiply 8, 9, and 10 times the numerals 0-12.*

Multiplication is a shortcut for adding a number to itself.

EXAMPLE: 4 times 1 is equal to 1 plus 1 plus 1 plus 1.
          4 times 2 is equal to 2 plus 2 plus 2 plus 2.
          4 times 3 is equal to 3 plus 3 plus 3 plus 3.

$$4 \times 1 = 1 + 1 + 1 + 1 = 4$$
$$4 \times 2 = 2 + 2 + 2 + 2 = 8$$
$$4 \times 3 = 3 + 3 + 3 + 3 = 12$$

A Multiply. Use the blank space for repeated addition, if necessary.

① $8 \times 1 = 8$ ② $9 \times 1 =$ ③ $10 \times 1 =$

④ $8 \times 2 =$ ⑤ $9 \times 2 =$ ⑥ $10 \times 2 =$

⑦ $8 \times 3 =$ ⑧ $9 \times 3 =$ ⑨ $10 \times 3 =$

⑩ $8 \times 4 =$ ⑪ $9 \times 4 =$ ⑫ $10 \times 4 =$

⑬ $8 \times 5 =$ ⑭ $9 \times 5 =$ ⑮ $10 \times 5 =$

⑯ $8 \times 6 =$ ⑰ $9 \times 6 =$ ⑱ $10 \times 6 =$

⑲ $8 \times 7 =$ ⑳ $9 \times 7 =$ ㉑ $10 \times 7 =$

㉒ $8 \times 8 =$ ㉓ $9 \times 8 =$ ㉔ $10 \times 8 =$

㉕ $8 \times 9 =$ ㉖ $9 \times 9 =$ ㉗ $10 \times 9 =$

㉘ $8 \times 10 =$ ㉙ $9 \times 10 =$ ㉚ $10 \times 10 =$

㉛ $8 \times 11 =$ ㉜ $9 \times 11 =$ ㉝ $10 \times 11 =$

㉞ $8 \times 12 =$ ㉟ $9 \times 12 =$ ㊱ $10 \times 12 =$

B Solve the problems and write an addition sentence for each.

① $8 \times 0 =$

② $9 \times 0 =$

③ $10 \times 0 =$

REMINDER: *Write the definition of multiplication.*

_____

_____

C Fill in the blanks.

① 10 × 12 = __120__

② ___ × 1 = 9

③ 8 × ___ = 40

④ 9 × 0 = ___

⑤ 10 × ___ = 30

⑥ ___ × 6 = 54

⑦ ___ × 2 = 16

⑧ 10 × ___ = 90

⑨ ___ × 5 = 45

⑩ ___ × 4 = 40

⑪ 8 × 3 = ___

⑫ 9 × ___ = 9

⑬ 10 × ___ = 0

⑭ 8 × 8 = ___

⑮ 9 × ___ = 36

⑯ 8 × ___ = 80

⑰ ___ × 7 = 63

⑱ 10 × 5 = ___

⑲ 9 × 10 = ___

⑳ ___ × 12 = 96

㉑ ___ × 8 = 80

㉒ ___ × 3 = 27

㉓ 10 × 2 = ___

㉔ 8 × ___ = 56

㉕ ___ × 3 = 24

㉖ 10 × ___ = 60

㉗ 8 × ___ = 8

㉘ 10 × 10 = ___

㉙ 8 × ___ = 0

㉚ 9 × 4 = ___

㉛ 9 × ___ = 99

㉜ ___ × 9 = 72

㉝ ___ × 11 = 110

㉞ 9 × ___ = 72

㉟ ___ × 1 = 10

㊱ ___ × 11 = 88

㊲ 8 × 12 = ___

㊳ 10 × ___ = 70

㊴ 9 × ___ = 18

㊵ ___ × 6 = 48

D Multiply 8, 9, and 10 times 10.

① _____

② _____

③ _____

E Solve the problems. Write a multiplication sentence for each.

① Nine reporters are on the staff of the Berryville school newspaper. Each reporter is required to write 3 articles per week. How many articles are written by reporters each week?

    9 × 3 = 27

② Eight student council candidates were photographed for the newspaper. The student photographer snapped 5 shots of each candidate. What was the total number of photographs taken of student council candidates?

_____

③ Berryville High School's newspaper staff attended the regional and state meetings for student journalists. Ten staff members went to the regional meeting and 10 more went to the state meet. How many in all attended?

_____

④ There are 8 pages to each section of the school newspaper. The paper is divided into 2 sections. How many pages are contained in both sections of the newspaper?

_____

⑤ During one year, the newspaper was entered in 10 different competitions. It won 6 awards in each of the competitions. How many awards did the newspaper win that year?

_____

⑥ There are 9 months to each school term. The newspaper is published 4 times each month. How many times is the newspaper published during the entire school term?

_____

Simple Multiplication

Learning Objective: *We will learn to multiply two-digit numbers and to carry.*

Multiplication is a shortcut for adding a number to itself.

EXAMPLE: To multiply 25 by 2, first multiply 2 times 5 ones. From the multiplication tables, we know 2 × 5 is 10. Write down the 0 and carry the 1 to the tens' column. Multiply 2 times 2 tens. The answer is 4. Add the 1 that you carried and write down 5.
$2 \times 25 = 50.$ $25 + 25 = 50.$

$$
\begin{array}{r}
25 \\
\times 2
\end{array} \Big\}
\qquad
\begin{array}{r}
\overset{1}{} \text{2 tens, 5 ones} \\
\times 2 \\
\hline
\text{5 tens, 0 ones} =
\end{array}
\qquad
\begin{array}{r}
25 \\
+25 \\
\hline
50
\end{array}
$$

A Multiply ones, then tens. If you like, check your answers with addition.

①
$$
\begin{array}{r}
13 \\
\times 2
\end{array} \Big\}
\qquad
\begin{array}{r}
\textit{1 ten, 3 ones} \\
\times 2 \\
\hline
\textit{2 tens, 6 ones} = 26
\end{array}
$$

②
$$
\begin{array}{r}
35 \\
\times 1
\end{array} \Big\}
$$

③
$$
\begin{array}{r}
18 \\
\times 4
\end{array} \Big\}
$$

④
$$
\begin{array}{r}
12 \\
\times 9
\end{array} \Big\}
$$

⑤
$$
\begin{array}{r}
74 \\
\times 8
\end{array} \Big\}
$$

⑥
$$
\begin{array}{r}
90 \\
\times 4
\end{array} \Big\}
$$

⑦
$$
\begin{array}{r}
83 \\
\times 5
\end{array} \Big\}
$$

⑧
$$
\begin{array}{r}
61 \\
\times 6
\end{array} \Big\}
$$

⑨
$$
\begin{array}{r}
42 \\
\times 3
\end{array} \Big\}
$$

⑩
$$
\begin{array}{r}
14 \\
\times 8
\end{array} \Big\}
$$

⑪
$$
\begin{array}{r}
24 \\
\times 6
\end{array} \Big\}
$$

⑫
$$
\begin{array}{r}
40 \\
\times 5
\end{array} \Big\}
$$

⑬
$$
\begin{array}{r}
68 \\
\times 7
\end{array} \Big\}
$$

⑭
$$
\begin{array}{r}
71 \\
\times 9
\end{array} \Big\}
$$

REMINDER: Write the definition of multiplication.

_____

_____

Unit 74 cont'd ☞

B Multiply.

① 15
×5
75

② 56
×1

③ 26
×4

④ 85
×5

⑤ 35
×8

⑥ 81
×4

⑦ 54
×6

⑧ 12
×5

⑨ 95
×4

⑩ 66
×6

⑪ 32
×7

⑫ 12
×8

⑬ 88
×8

⑭ 90
×9

⑮ 46
×3

⑯ 78
×7

⑰ 71
×3

⑱ 22
×4

⑲ 33
×8

⑳ 59
×6

㉑ 17
×4

㉒ 50
×2

㉓ 67
×3

㉔ 41
×4

㉕ 13
×5

㉖ 16
×7

㉗ 54
×8

㉘ 20
×2

㉙ 70
×7

㉚ 63
×7

㉛ 30
×9

㉜ 76
×4

C Multiply. Use the blank space to work each problem.

① Members of the Stuart High School drill squad performed 13 to a row, 9 rows deep. How many members performed?

13
× 9
117

② Marianne's aquarium is stocked with 15 species of fish. There are 2 of each species. How many fish are there?

③ During the first 18 weeks of his senior year, Wade was absent 1 day per week. How many days was he absent?

④ There were 79 students in each of the freshman, sophomore, junior, and senior classes. How many students were in all 4 classes?

⑤ All students who failed the mid-term exam in American Literature were required to write 5 book reports. Fourteen students failed the exam. How many book reports were written?

⑥ There was a three-way tie in pedaling the most miles at the Student Council Bike-a-thon. Three students biked 56 miles apiece. What was the total number of miles?

⑦ After a competition, members of the junior and senior swim teams ordered hamburgers. Twenty swimmers ordered 3 burgers apiece. How many burgers were ordered?

⑧ Four yards of fabric were used to make each of the 83 robes for school choir members. How many yards of fabric were used in all?

⑨ Statewide, 47 traffic accidents were reported on each day of a 3-day weekend. What was the total number of accidents reported?

Identifying Problem Parts

Unit 75

*Learning
Objective:* *We will learn to identify the multiplicand, the multiplier, and the product in a multiplication problem.*

In a multiplication problem, the multiplicand is the number to be multiplied by
another. The multiplier is the number by which the multiplicand is multiplied. The
product is the result.

EXAMPLE: In the problem at right, 25 is the multiplicand, which
is multiplied by the multiplier 2. The product of the
multiplication is 50.

```
  25 multiplicand
× 2 multiplier
  50 product
```

A Identify each multiplicand (md), each multiplier (mr), and each product (p).

① 18 _md_
× 3 _mr_
54 _p_

② 73 ___
× 5 ___
365 ___

③ 62 ___
× 3 ___
186 ___

④ 13 ___
× 9 ___
117 ___

⑤ 96 ___
× 2 ___
192 ___

⑥ 37 ___
× 1 ___
37 ___

⑦ 84 ___
× 6 ___
504 ___

⑧ 21 ___
× 8 ___
168 ___

⑨ 33 ___
× 9 ___
297 ___

⑩ 36 ___
× 5 ___
180 ___

⑪ 42 ___
× 8 ___
336 ___

⑫ 92 ___
× 9 ___
828 ___

⑬ 44 ___
× 3 ___
132 ___

⑭ 64 ___
× 7 ___
448 ___

⑮ 15 ___
× 8 ___
120 ___

⑯ 23 ___
× 7 ___
161 ___

⑰ 41 ___
× 1 ___
41 ___

⑱ 39 ___
× 5 ___
195 ___

B Which is the product of the other two numbers? Label each product "p."

① 5 ___
56 ___
280 _p_

② 3 ___
69 ___
23 ___

③ 71 ___
8 ___
568 ___

④ 2 ___
20 ___
10 ___

⑤ 246 ___
41 ___
6 ___

⑥ 6 ___
32 ___
192 ___

⑦ 53 ___
7 ___
371 ___

⑧ 38 ___
266 ___
7 ___

⑨ 39 ___
3 ___
13 ___

⑩ 3 ___
71 ___
213 ___

⑪ 84 ___
5 ___
420 ___

⑫ 15 ___
3 ___
45 ___

⑬ 104 ___
4 ___
26 ___

⑭ 29 ___
58 ___
2 ___

⑮ 4 ___
59 ___
236 ___

⑯ 61 ___
122 ___
2 ___

⑰ 10 ___
60 ___
6 ___

⑱ 94 ___
47 ___
2 ___

REMINDER: Write the definition of the multiplicand, the multiplier, and the product.

181   **Unit 75 cont'd** ☛

C Match the multipliers and multiplicands with the products.

① 5 × 31 =	534		⑩ 7 × 25 =		144
② 6 × 89 =	30		⑪ 3 × 61 =		178
③ 1 × 30 =	155		⑫ 2 × 89 =		183
④ 4 × 21 =	96		⑬ 4 × 36 =		175
⑤ 6 × 16 =	84		⑭ 3 × 53 =		776
⑥ 8 × 22 =	441		⑮ 7 × 14 =		98
⑦ 7 × 63 =	88		⑯ 5 × 80 =		159
⑧ 2 × 13 =	176		⑰ 3 × 17 =		400
⑨ 8 × 11 =	26		⑱ 8 × 97 =		51

D Underline the product in each paragraph. Write a multiplication sentence for each.

① Marching 9 to a row, 36 rows deep, the 324 members of the Stuart High School Marching Warriors led the Christmas parade.

9 × 36 = 324

② One hundred thirty juniors and seniors protested the school's absentee policy. In each of the 2 classes, 65 students signed a petition to change the policy.

_____

③ On a class trip, seniors traveled 4 days to get to their destination. The traveled 425 miles each day for a total of 1,700 miles.

_____

④ The 3 sections of the senior class unanimously voted for a class trip. There are 45 students in each section. The vote was 135 to 0.

_____

⑤ Each foreign language student is required to clock 5 hours per week in the lab. A total of 45 hours is required in a 9-week period.

_____

⑥ In a choral program, 6 students sang 3 solos apiece. Total solo performances was 18.

_____

⑦ Five displays, each containing 24 items, made up the art exhibit. There were 120 items in all.

_____

⑧ For 9 days, the daily rainfall measured 2 inches. Eighteen inches of rain fell during the 9-day period.

_____

⑨ The 224 participants in the state business student conference traveled in 4 buses each carrying 56 persons.

_____

Comprehension Check

A Multiply 1, 2, 3, 4, and 5 times 0-12.

<u>1 ×</u>	<u>2 ×</u>	<u>3 ×</u>	<u>4 ×</u>	<u>5 ×</u>
① $1 \times 0 = 0$				
②				
③				
④				
⑤				
⑥				
⑦				
⑧				
⑨				
⑩				
⑪				
⑫				
⑬				

B Multiply 6, 7, 8, 9, and 10 times 0-5.

<u>6 ×</u>	<u>7 ×</u>	<u>8 ×</u>	<u>9 ×</u>	<u>10 ×</u>
① $6 \times 0 = 0$				
②				
③				
④				
⑤				
⑥				

Test 15 cont'd 🖝

C Multiply 6, 7, 8, 9, and 10 times 6-12.

	6 ×	**7 ×**	**8 ×**	**9 ×**	**10 ×**
①	$6 \times 6 = 36$				
②					
③					
④					
⑤					
⑥					
⑦					

D Multiply. Identify the multiplicands (md), multipliers (mr), and products (p).

① 40 _md_
×2 _mr_
80 _p_

② 16 ____
×3 ____
____

③ 51 ____
×1 ____
____

④ 37 ____
×2 ____
____

⑤ 44 ____
×9 ____
____

⑥ 84 ____
×8 ____
____

⑦ 55 ____
×7 ____
____

⑧ 29 ____
×9 ____
____

⑨ 99 ____
×4 ____
____

⑩ 21 ____
×4 ____
____

⑪ 17 ____
×2 ____
____

⑫ 13 ____
×9 ____
____

⑬ 94 ____
×2 ____
____

⑭ 58 ____
×8 ____
____

⑮ 35 ____
×6 ____
____

⑯ 63 ____
×8 ____
____

⑰ 19 ____
×4 ____
____

⑱ 59 ____
×9 ____
____

⑲ 65 ____
×9 ____
____

⑳ 82 ____
×2 ____
____

㉑ 95 ____
×8 ____
____

㉒ 27 ____
×4 ____
____

㉓ 64 ____
×5 ____
____

㉔ 36 ____
×3 ____
____

㉕ 55 ____
×5 ____
____

㉖ 71 ____
×6 ____
____

㉗ 48 ____
×2 ____
____

㉘ 22 ____
×8 ____
____

㉙ 40 ____
×8 ____
____

㉚ 76 ____
×7 ____
____

Write a paragraph that includes a multiplication problem. Write the multiplication sentence.

_____

_____

_____

_____

_____

Multiplication Practice

Learning Objective: *We will learn to multiply with two-digit numbers.*

Multiplication is a shortcut for adding a number to itself.

EXAMPLE: To multiply by a two-digit number, multiply first by the digit in the ones' column, then by the digit in the tens' column. Add the results.

$$
\begin{array}{r}
250 \\
\times\ 22 \\
\hline
500 \\
500 \\
\hline
5500
\end{array}
\Bigg\}
\qquad
\begin{array}{r}
250 \\
\times\ 2 \\
\hline
500
\end{array}
\ +\
\begin{array}{r}
250 \\
\times\ 20 \\
\hline
5000
\end{array}
= 5{,}500
$$

A Multiply.

①
$$
\begin{array}{r}
822 \\
\times\ 27 \\
\hline
5754 \\
1644 \\
\hline
22{,}194
\end{array}
$$

②
$$
\begin{array}{r}
992 \\
\times\ 22 \\
\hline
\end{array}
$$

③
$$
\begin{array}{r}
288 \\
\times\ 51 \\
\hline
\end{array}
$$

④
$$
\begin{array}{r}
747 \\
\times\ 61 \\
\hline
\end{array}
$$

⑤
$$
\begin{array}{r}
184 \\
\times\ 13 \\
\hline
\end{array}
$$

⑥
$$
\begin{array}{r}
173 \\
\times\ 52 \\
\hline
\end{array}
$$

⑦
$$
\begin{array}{r}
710 \\
\times\ 37 \\
\hline
\end{array}
$$

⑧
$$
\begin{array}{r}
185 \\
\times\ 33 \\
\hline
\end{array}
$$

⑨
$$
\begin{array}{r}
111 \\
\times\ 75 \\
\hline
\end{array}
$$

⑩
$$
\begin{array}{r}
619 \\
\times\ 88 \\
\hline
\end{array}
$$

⑪
$$
\begin{array}{r}
992 \\
\times\ 25 \\
\hline
\end{array}
$$

⑫
$$
\begin{array}{r}
628 \\
\times\ 15 \\
\hline
\end{array}
$$

⑬
$$
\begin{array}{r}
205 \\
\times\ 51 \\
\hline
\end{array}
$$

⑭
$$
\begin{array}{r}
137 \\
\times\ 82 \\
\hline
\end{array}
$$

⑮
$$
\begin{array}{r}
118 \\
\times\ 13 \\
\hline
\end{array}
$$

⑯
$$
\begin{array}{r}
911 \\
\times\ 66 \\
\hline
\end{array}
$$

⑰
$$
\begin{array}{r}
558 \\
\times\ 22 \\
\hline
\end{array}
$$

⑱
$$
\begin{array}{r}
326 \\
\times\ 14 \\
\hline
\end{array}
$$

⑲
$$
\begin{array}{r}
189 \\
\times\ 32 \\
\hline
\end{array}
$$

⑳
$$
\begin{array}{r}
666 \\
\times\ 12 \\
\hline
\end{array}
$$

㉑
$$
\begin{array}{r}
460 \\
\times\ 74 \\
\hline
\end{array}
$$

㉒
$$
\begin{array}{r}
214 \\
\times\ 15 \\
\hline
\end{array}
$$

㉓
$$
\begin{array}{r}
433 \\
\times\ 14 \\
\hline
\end{array}
$$

㉔
$$
\begin{array}{r}
542 \\
\times\ 95 \\
\hline
\end{array}
$$

㉕
$$
\begin{array}{r}
333 \\
\times\ 18 \\
\hline
\end{array}
$$

㉖
$$
\begin{array}{r}
148 \\
\times\ 24 \\
\hline
\end{array}
$$

㉗
$$
\begin{array}{r}
233 \\
\times\ 84 \\
\hline
\end{array}
$$

㉘
$$
\begin{array}{r}
494 \\
\times\ 39 \\
\hline
\end{array}
$$

㉙
$$
\begin{array}{r}
735 \\
\times\ 47 \\
\hline
\end{array}
$$

㉚
$$
\begin{array}{r}
984 \\
\times\ 56 \\
\hline
\end{array}
$$

REMINDER: Write the definition of multiplication.

Unit 76 cont'd ☞

B

To multiply by two-digit numbers with 0 as a digit, write the 0 in the one's column, then multiply by the digit in the ten's column.

	Step 1	Step 2
	250	250
	× 50	× 50
	0	12,500

① 691
  × 20
  13,820

② 816
  × 10

③ 232
  × 80

④ 994
  × 90

⑤ 215
  × 20

⑥ 147
  × 40

⑦ 324
  × 30

⑧ 261
  × 80

⑨ 820
  × 90

⑩ 611
  × 60

⑪ 163
  × 90

⑫ 111
  × 80

⑬ 240
  × 60

⑭ 624
  × 40

⑮ 548
  × 30

⑯ 237
  × 20

⑰ 484
  × 90

⑱ 724
  × 80

⑲ 931
  × 60

⑳ 387
  × 70

㉑ 103
  × 90

㉒ 824
  × 40

㉓ 107
  × 30

㉔ 181
  × 40

C Use the blank spaces to work the problems.

① On a cross-country tour, Keith drove 202 miles per day for 15 days. How many miles did he travel during the 15-day tour?

202
× 15
1010
202
3,030

3,030

② For each book report that he turned in, Mike earned 50 extra points. He turned in 13 book reports during the entire term. How many extra points did he earn?

_____

③ During her first semester at college, Pam phoned home 20 times. Each time she talked 105 minutes. How many minutes did she talk during the semester?

_____

④ For 12 years, 875 tickets were issued for the annual visit by the traveling circus. All tickets were sold each year. How many people attended in 12 years?

_____

⑤ Each of the 11 floats in the homecoming parade measured 15 feet in length. End to end, how many feet of space did the 11 floats fill?

_____

⑥ The total number of entries in Stuart High School's first essay contest was 18. Three years later, the contest attracted 10 times the number of entries. How many entries were there three years later?

_____

The Associative Property Unit 77

Learning Objective: *We will learn to recognize the associative property in multiplication problems.*

The associative property of multiplication holds that the product will be the same regardless of the way in which a series of numbers is grouped.

EXAMPLE:

If we multiply the product of
1×2 by 3, the result is equal
to that of multiplying 1 times
the product of 2×3.

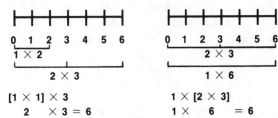

$[1 \times 1] \times 3$ $1 \times [2 \times 3]$
$2 \quad \times 3 = 6$ $1 \times \quad 6 \quad = 6$

A Match the number lines that illustrate the associative property of multiplication.

①
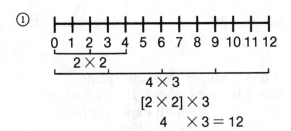

$[2 \times 2] \times 3$
$4 \quad \times 3 = 12$

$3 \times [3 \times 1]$
$3 \times \quad 3 \quad = 9$

②
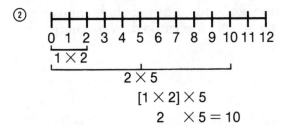

$[1 \times 2] \times 5$
$2 \quad \times 5 = 10$

$2 \times [2 \times 3]$
$2 \times \quad 6 \quad = 12$

③
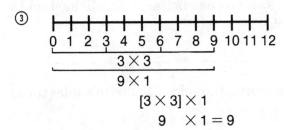

$[3 \times 3] \times 1$
$9 \quad \times 1 = 9$

$1 \times [3 \times 4]$
$1 \times \quad 12 \quad = 12$

④
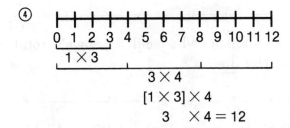

$[1 \times 3] \times 4$
$3 \quad \times 4 = 12$

$1 \times [2 \times 5]$
$1 \times \quad 10 \quad = 10$

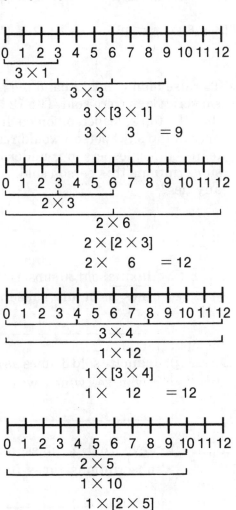

REMINDER: Write the definition of the associative property of multiplication.

B Match the multiplication sentences that illustrate the associative property.

① [3 × 5] × 2 = 30   4 × [6 × 3] = 72   ⑩ [1 × 9] × 7 = 63   4 × [5 × 6] = 120

② [4 × 6] × 3 = 72   3 × [5 × 2] = 30   ⑪ [3 × 4] × 5 = 60   8 × [1 × 3] = 24

③ [2 × 5] × 5 = 50   2 × [4 × 9] = 72   ⑫ [8 × 1] × 3 = 24   1 × [9 × 7] = 63

④ [2 × 4] × 9 = 72   2 × [5 × 5] = 50   ⑬ [4 × 5] × 6 = 120   3 × [4 × 5] = 60

⑤ [6 × 8] × 7 = 336   8 × [7 × 3] = 168   ⑭ [9 × 9] × 2 = 162   2 × [9 × 1] = 18

⑥ [8 × 7] × 3 = 168   2 × [8 × 1] = 16   ⑮ [2 × 9] × 1 = 18   9 × [9 × 2] = 162

⑦ [2 × 4] × 2 = 16   6 × [8 × 7] = 336   ⑯ [3 × 3] × 2 = 18   2 × [3 × 8] = 48

⑧ [2 × 4] × 8 = 64   2 × [4 × 2] = 16   ⑰ [2 × 3] × 8 = 48   8 × [3 × 4] = 96

⑨ [2 × 8] × 1 = 16   2 × [4 × 8] = 64   ⑱ [8 × 3] × 4 = 96   3 × [3 × 2] = 18

C To raise money for 12 band members to attend the state music competition, magazine subscriptions were sold. The 12 band members were assigned to sales teams. It was decided that the top salesperson on each team would attend the state meet with all expenses paid. The overall top salesperson would receive a trophy as well. Study the list below. The name of each team's top salesperson is underlined. Write a multiplication sentence that tells how many subscriptions this person sold. At left, show how each top salesperson ranked. Were there any ties?

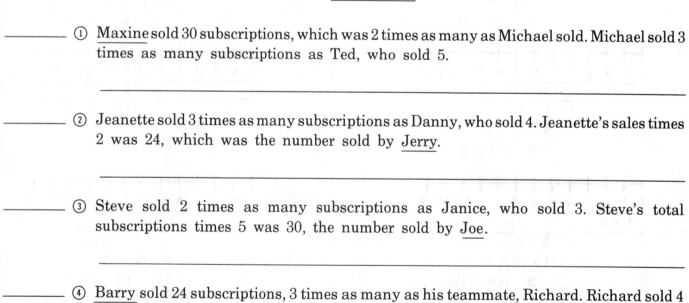

Rank   Team Sales

_____ ① Maxine sold 30 subscriptions, which was 2 times as many as Michael sold. Michael sold 3 times as many subscriptions as Ted, who sold 5.

_____ ② Jeanette sold 3 times as many subscriptions as Danny, who sold 4. Jeanette's sales times 2 was 24, which was the number sold by Jerry.

_____ ③ Steve sold 2 times as many subscriptions as Janice, who sold 3. Steve's total subscriptions times 5 was 30, the number sold by Joe.

_____ ④ Barry sold 24 subscriptions, 3 times as many as his teammate, Richard. Richard sold 4 times as many as James, who sold 2 subscriptions.

Using the Associative Property

Learning Objective: *We will learn to use the associative property of multiplication.*

The associative property of multiplication holds that the product will be the same regardless of the way in which a series of numbers is grouped.

EXAMPLE:

Multiply the numbers in the brackets first. Multiply this product and the third numbers.

$$[1 \times 2] \times 3 \quad = \quad 1 \times [2 \times 3]$$
$$2 \quad \times 3 = 6 \qquad 1 \times \quad 6 \quad = 6$$

A Below each set of brackets, write the product of the two numbers within the brackets. Multiply this product and the third number.

① $[2 \times 6] \times 3 =$ ___36___ ② $2 \times [6 \times 3] =$ _____ ③ $[3 \times 8] \times 4 =$ _____ ④ $3 \times [8 \times 4] =$ _____
   ___12___

⑤ $[9 \times 3] \times 2 =$ _____ ⑥ $9 \times [3 \times 2] =$ _____ ⑦ $[7 \times 9] \times 8 =$ _____ ⑧ $7 \times [9 \times 8] =$ _____

⑨ $[5 \times 6] \times 1 =$ _____ ⑩ $5 \times [6 \times 1] =$ _____ ⑪ $[4 \times 2] \times 7 =$ _____ ⑫ $4 \times [2 \times 7] =$ _____

⑬ $[3 \times 5] \times 5 =$ _____ ⑭ $3 \times [5 \times 5] =$ _____ ⑮ $[1 \times 6] \times 9 =$ _____ ⑯ $1 \times [6 \times 9] =$ _____

⑰ $[7 \times 7] \times 2 =$ _____ ⑱ $7 \times [7 \times 2] =$ _____ ⑲ $[2 \times 5] \times 8 =$ _____ ⑳ $2 \times [5 \times 8] =$ _____

㉑ $[6 \times 4] \times 9 =$ _____ ㉒ $6 \times [4 \times 9] =$ _____ ㉓ $[3 \times 6] \times 6 =$ _____ ㉔ $3 \times [6 \times 6] =$ _____

㉕ $[1 \times 2] \times 4 =$ _____ ㉖ $1 \times [2 \times 4] =$ _____ ㉗ $[8 \times 8] \times 5 =$ _____ ㉘ $8 \times [8 \times 5] =$ _____

㉙ $[9 \times 5] \times 2 =$ _____ ㉚ $9 \times [5 \times 2] =$ _____ ㉛ $[6 \times 1] \times 7 =$ _____ ㉜ $6 \times [1 \times 7] =$ _____

㉝ $[4 \times 8] \times 8 =$ _____ ㉞ $4 \times [8 \times 8] =$ _____ ㉟ $[5 \times 7] \times 2 =$ _____ ㊱ $5 \times [7 \times 2] =$ _____

REMINDER: Write the definition of the associative property of multiplication.

_____

_____

Unit 78 cont'd ☛

B Study each problem in column A. In column B, write a second problem that demonstrates the associative property of multiplication. Find the products for all problems.

	A	B		A	B
①	[12 × 2] × 4 = ___96___	12 × [2 × 4] = 96	⑨	50 × [2 × 5] = _____	_____
②	[3 × 10] × 5 = _____	_____	⑩	6 × [12 × 3] = _____	_____
③	[4 × 11] × 8 = _____	_____	⑪	3 × [25 × 1] = _____	_____
④	[6 × 7] × 20 = _____	_____	⑫	11 × [2 × 2] = _____	_____
⑤	[10 × 10] × 1 = _____	_____	⑬	4 × [2 × 20] = _____	_____
⑥	[8 × 5] × 40 = _____	_____	⑭	12 × [3 × 3] = _____	_____
⑦	[15 × 3] × 2 = _____	_____	⑮	7 × [10 × 8] = _____	_____
⑧	[1 × 90] × 5 = _____	_____	⑯	2 × [6 × 40] = _____	_____

C Write a multiplication sentence for each problem. Match the multiplication sentences that illustrate the associative property.

① Roberta writes mystery stories. In her first story, there were 6 clues to the mystery. There were 4 times as many clues in the next story. The third story contained 2 times as many clues as the second. How many clues were in the third story?

[6 × 4] × 2 = 48

② Two times as many girls entered the third marathon as had run in the second. Two times as many ran in the second race as had in the first. Three ran in the first. How many ran in the third?

③ Frieda found 5 four-leaf clovers on a hillside. Her friend, Marco, found 2 times as many. Grace found 3 times as many as Marco. How many four-leaf clovers did Grace find?

④ At Palmer's Point, 2 sharks were spotted offshore. The next day, 2 times as many were seen. Three times as many were seen the third day as the second. How many sharks were seen the third day?

⑤ Albert made 5 times as many mistakes on his first typing test as he did on his second test. On the second test, he made 2 times the mistakes that he made on the third. He made 3 mistakes on the third test. How many mistakes did he make on the first?

⑥ Six times as many voters said yes to shorter school terms as said no. Four times as many voted no as had no opinion. Two had no opinion. How many voted yes?

The Commutative Property

Learning Objective: *We will learn to recognize the commutative property in multiplication problems.*

The commutative property of multiplication holds that the product will be the same regardless of the order in which the numbers are multiplied.

EXAMPLES:

Multiply the 1 in the outer column times the 2 in the upper row. Then multiply the 2 in the outer column by the 1 in the upper row. The product is the same.

×	1	2
1	1	②
2	②	4

The commutative property of multiplication can be demonstrated on a number line.

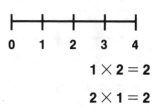

$1 \times 2 = 2$

$2 \times 1 = 2$

A Study the pairs of multiplication problems. Find the products in the table at the right. Label the products with the letters of the problems.

Ⓐ $3 \times 8 =$
$8 \times 3 =$

Ⓑ $6 \times 4 =$
$4 \times 6 =$

Ⓒ $5 \times 7 =$
$7 \times 5 =$

Ⓓ $1 \times 8 =$
$8 \times 1 =$

Ⓔ $6 \times 9 =$
$9 \times 6 =$

Ⓕ $6 \times 5 =$
$5 \times 6 =$

Ⓖ $7 \times 3 =$
$3 \times 7 =$

Ⓗ $4 \times 8 =$
$8 \times 4 =$

Ⓘ $1 \times 5 =$
$5 \times 1 =$

Ⓙ $9 \times 2 =$
$2 \times 9 =$

×	1	2	3	4	5	6	7	8	9
1	1	2	3	*M* 4	5	6	7	8	9
2	2	4	6	8	10	12	14	16	18
3	3	6	9	12	15	18	21	24	27
4	4	8	12	16	20	24	28	32	36
5	5	10	15	20	25	30	35	40	45
6	6	12	18	24	30	36	42	48	54
7	7	14	21	28	35	42	49	56	63
8	8	16	24	32	40	48	56	64	72
9	9	18	27	36	45	54	63	72	81

Ⓚ $3 \times 6 =$
$6 \times 3 =$

Ⓛ $7 \times 8 =$
$8 \times 7 =$

Ⓜ $4 \times 1 =$
$1 \times 4 =$

Ⓝ $8 \times 5 =$
$5 \times 8 =$

Ⓞ $9 \times 3 =$
$3 \times 9 =$

Ⓟ $8 \times 2 =$
$2 \times 8 =$

Ⓠ $4 \times 7 =$
$7 \times 4 =$

Ⓡ $8 \times 9 =$
$9 \times 8 =$

Ⓢ $1 \times 6 =$
$6 \times 1 =$

Ⓣ $5 \times 4 =$
$4 \times 5 =$

Ⓤ $6 \times 7 =$
$7 \times 6 =$

Ⓥ $3 \times 5 =$
$5 \times 3 =$

Ⓦ $6 \times 2 =$
$2 \times 6 =$

Ⓧ $4 \times 9 =$
$9 \times 4 =$

Ⓨ $9 \times 7 =$
$7 \times 9 =$

REMINDER: Write the definition of the commutative property of multiplication.

_____

_____

Unit 79 cont'd ☛

B Use the number lines to demonstrate the commutative property of multiplication.

①
0 1 2 3 4 5 6 7 8 9 10 11 12 13 14

1 × 3 = 3

3 × 1 = 3

②
0 1 2 3 4 5 6 7 8 9 10 11 12 13 14

2 × 4 = 8

4 × 2 = 8

③
0 1 2 3 4 5 6 7 8 9 10 11 12 13 14

1 × 9 = 9

9 × 1 = 9

④
0 1 2 3 4 5 6 7 8 9 10 11 12 13 14

2 × 5 = 10

5 × 2 = 10

⑤
0 1 2 3 4 5 6 7 8 9 10 11 12 13 14

2 × 3 = 6

3 × 2 = 6

⑥
0 1 2 3 4 5 6 7 8 9 10 11 12 13 14

1 × 7 = 7

7 × 1 = 7

⑦
0 1 2 3 4 5 6 7 8 9 10 11 12 13 14

3 × 4 = 12

4 × 3 = 12

⑧
0 1 2 3 4 5 6 7 8 9 10 11 12 13 14

2 × 7 = 14

7 × 2 = 14

C Write a multiplication sentence for each problem. Write a second sentence that demonstrates the commutative property.

① Eight science students from Hickman High School entered projects in the state science fair. Six times as many students entered from other high schools. Hickman faced 48 opponents.

$8 \times 6 = 48$

$6 \times 8 = 48$

② Five times as many fish were caught near Pointer's Creek as were hooked on the Muddy River. Nine fish were caught from the river. Forty-five were caught near Pointer's Creek.

_____

_____

③ Three times as many freshmen attended the Homecoming football game as went to the dance afterward. Twelve freshmen went to the dance. Thirty-six were at the ball game.

_____

_____

④ Six teachers were on staff when Hickman School opened in 1913. Twenty-five years later, 10 times that many were employed at the school. Sixty teachers were on staff in 1938.

_____

_____

⑤ Seven times as many points were scored in the ninth inning of the baseball game as were scored in the first. One point was scored during the first inning. Seven were scored during the ninth.

_____

_____

⑥ Four tornadoes were sighted in Orange County in May. In June, 4 times that many were seen. Sixteen tornadoes were sighted during the month of June.

_____

_____

192

Using the Commutative Property   Unit 80

The commutative property of multiplication holds that the product will be the same regardless of the order in which the numbers are multiplied.

EXAMPLE:

$$
\begin{array}{r}
61 \\
\times\, 31 \\
\hline
61 \\
183 \\
\hline
1{,}891
\end{array}
\qquad
\begin{array}{r}
31 \\
\times\, 61 \\
\hline
31 \\
186 \\
\hline
1{,}891
\end{array}
$$

A Multiply.

①
$$\begin{array}{r} 72 \\ \times\,13 \\ \hline 216 \\ 72 \\ \hline 936 \end{array}$$
②
$$\begin{array}{r} 13 \\ \times\,72 \\ \hline \end{array}$$
③
$$\begin{array}{r} 38 \\ \times\,16 \\ \hline \end{array}$$
④
$$\begin{array}{r} 16 \\ \times\,38 \\ \hline \end{array}$$
⑤
$$\begin{array}{r} 29 \\ \times\,10 \\ \hline \end{array}$$
⑥
$$\begin{array}{r} 10 \\ \times\,29 \\ \hline \end{array}$$
⑦
$$\begin{array}{r} 64 \\ \times\,21 \\ \hline \end{array}$$
⑧
$$\begin{array}{r} 21 \\ \times\,64 \\ \hline \end{array}$$

⑨
$$\begin{array}{r} 56 \\ \times\,79 \\ \hline \end{array}$$
⑩
$$\begin{array}{r} 79 \\ \times\,56 \\ \hline \end{array}$$
⑪
$$\begin{array}{r} 96 \\ \times\,11 \\ \hline \end{array}$$
⑫
$$\begin{array}{r} 11 \\ \times\,96 \\ \hline \end{array}$$
⑬
$$\begin{array}{r} 63 \\ \times\,87 \\ \hline \end{array}$$
⑭
$$\begin{array}{r} 87 \\ \times\,63 \\ \hline \end{array}$$
⑮
$$\begin{array}{r} 42 \\ \times\,58 \\ \hline \end{array}$$
⑯
$$\begin{array}{r} 58 \\ \times\,42 \\ \hline \end{array}$$

⑰
$$\begin{array}{r} 83 \\ \times\,49 \\ \hline \end{array}$$
⑱
$$\begin{array}{r} 49 \\ \times\,83 \\ \hline \end{array}$$
⑲
$$\begin{array}{r} 74 \\ \times\,17 \\ \hline \end{array}$$
⑳
$$\begin{array}{r} 17 \\ \times\,74 \\ \hline \end{array}$$
㉑
$$\begin{array}{r} 66 \\ \times\,12 \\ \hline \end{array}$$
㉒
$$\begin{array}{r} 12 \\ \times\,66 \\ \hline \end{array}$$
㉓
$$\begin{array}{r} 89 \\ \times\,18 \\ \hline \end{array}$$
㉔
$$\begin{array}{r} 18 \\ \times\,89 \\ \hline \end{array}$$

㉕
$$\begin{array}{r} 55 \\ \times\,20 \\ \hline \end{array}$$
㉖
$$\begin{array}{r} 20 \\ \times\,55 \\ \hline \end{array}$$
㉗
$$\begin{array}{r} 62 \\ \times\,38 \\ \hline \end{array}$$
㉘
$$\begin{array}{r} 38 \\ \times\,62 \\ \hline \end{array}$$
㉙
$$\begin{array}{r} 84 \\ \times\,35 \\ \hline \end{array}$$
㉚
$$\begin{array}{r} 35 \\ \times\,84 \\ \hline \end{array}$$
㉛
$$\begin{array}{r} 44 \\ \times\,11 \\ \hline \end{array}$$
㉜
$$\begin{array}{r} 11 \\ \times\,44 \\ \hline \end{array}$$

㉝
$$\begin{array}{r} 94 \\ \times\,80 \\ \hline \end{array}$$
㉞
$$\begin{array}{r} 80 \\ \times\,94 \\ \hline \end{array}$$
㉟
$$\begin{array}{r} 39 \\ \times\,50 \\ \hline \end{array}$$
㊱
$$\begin{array}{r} 50 \\ \times\,39 \\ \hline \end{array}$$
㊲
$$\begin{array}{r} 28 \\ \times\,23 \\ \hline \end{array}$$
㊳
$$\begin{array}{r} 23 \\ \times\,28 \\ \hline \end{array}$$
㊴
$$\begin{array}{r} 98 \\ \times\,55 \\ \hline \end{array}$$
㊵
$$\begin{array}{r} 55 \\ \times\,98 \\ \hline \end{array}$$

REMINDER: Write the definition of the commutative property of multiplication.

_____

_____

B Study each problem in column A. In column B, write a second problem that demonstrates the commutative property of multiplication. Find the products for all problems.

	A	B		A	B		A	B		A	B
①	46 × 22 92 92 1,012	**22** **× 46** **132** **88** **1,012**	②	94 × 57		③	21 × 78		④	97 × 42	

	A	B		A	B		A	B		A	B
⑤	29 × 25		⑥	68 × 16		⑦	61 × 11		⑧	34 × 12	

C Write a multiplication sentence for each problem. Write a second sentence that demonstrates the commutative property. Use the blank space to work the problem.

① Fifteen seniors attended Careers Day at Smithton State College. Eighteen times as many attended in all. How many attended Careers Day?

_____

_____

② Twenty-four votes were cast in opposition to a new free lunch program at Smithton Elementary School. Forty times as many votes supported the program. How many votes supported it?

_____

_____

③ Fifty-one roses bloomed along one wall of Margaret Phearson's flower garden. Thirty-nine times as many tulips bloomed in the garden. How many tulips were in bloom?

_____

_____

④ Sixty-three students took part in a doctor-approved "Diet for Fitness" program. Eighteen times as many pounds were lost among the participants. How many pounds were lost?

_____

_____

Comprehension Check

Test 16

A Multiply.

① 964
   × 24
   ___
   3856
   1928
   ___
   23,136

② 573
   × 11

③ 158
   × 16

④ 864
   × 22

⑤ 713
   × 50

⑥ 518
   × 83

⑦ 433
   × 52

⑧ 148
   × 73

⑨ 843
   × 86

⑩ 461
   × 60

⑪ 556
   × 19

⑫ 271
   × 91

⑬ 192
   × 62

⑭ 653
   × 48

⑮ 983
   × 85

⑯ 153
   × 93

⑰ 100
   × 47

⑱ 615
   × 40

⑲ 491
   × 36

⑳ 338
   × 17

㉑ 479
   × 20

㉒ 232
   × 33

㉓ 125
   × 72

㉔ 721
   × 14

B Label the multiplication sentences that illustrate the associative property (a) and those that illustrate the commutative property (c). Find the products.

① __a__ [2 × 8] × 3 = __48__   2 × [8 × 3] = __48__

② ____ 7 × 66 = ____   66 × 7 = ____

③ ____ [2 × 5] × 5 = ____   2 × [5 × 5] = ____

④ ____ [1 × 3] × 8 = ____   1 × [3 × 8] = ____

⑤ ____ 3 × 41 = ____   41 × 3 = ____

⑥ ____ 98 × 3 = ____   3 × 98 = ____

⑦ ____ [9 × 6] × 6 = ____   9 × [6 × 6] = ____

⑧ ____ 35 × 10 = ____   10 × 35 = ____

⑨ ____ 6 × 73 = ____   73 × 6 = ____

⑩ ____ [3 × 7] × 4 = ____   3 × [7 × 4] = ____

⑪ ____ 31 × 70 = ____   70 × 31 = ____

⑫ ____ 9 × 78 = ____   78 × 9 = ____

⑬ ____ [4 × 5] × 8 = ____   4 × [5 × 8] = ____

⑭ ____ [1 × 9] × 2 = ____   1 × [9 × 2] = ____

195

Test 16 cont'd ☞

C Study each problem in column A. In column B, write a second problem that demonstrates the associative property. Find the products.

A	B	A	B
① $2 \times [91 \times 3] = $ ___546___	$[2 \times 91] \times 3 = 546$	② $[42 \times 3] \times 2 = $ _____	_____
③ $[74 \times 4] \times 2 = $ _____	_____	④ $3 \times [63 \times 7] = $ _____	_____
⑤ $46 \times [50 \times 2] = $ _____	_____	⑥ $[39 \times 2] \times 3 = $ _____	_____
⑦ $[9 \times 14] \times 3 = $ _____	_____	⑧ $8 \times [9 \times 50] = $ _____	_____
⑨ $[3 \times 5] \times 8 = $ _____	_____	⑩ $51 \times [9 \times 1] = $ _____	_____
⑪ $47 \times [5 \times 1] = $ _____	_____	⑫ $[28 \times 2] \times 7 = $ _____	_____

D Study each problem in column A. In column B, write a second problem that demonstrates the commutative property. Find the products.

	A	B		A	B		A	B		A	B
①	16 × 28 — 128 32 — 448		②	45 × 93		③	59 × 78		④	74 × 13	
⑤	40 × 56		⑥	64 × 15		⑦	11 × 73		⑧	29 × 65	
⑨	51 × 92		⑩	97 × 17		⑪	45 × 54		⑫	31 × 23	

Write a paragraph that includes a simple multiplication problem. Write a multiplication sentence for the problem. Write a second sentence that demonstrates the commutative property.

_____

_____

_____

_____

_____

196

Basic Division Facts

Learning
Objective: *We will learn to divide sets.*

Division is the method by which we determine how many times one number contains another number.

EXAMPLE: If set A contains 6 members, how many subsets of 3 members does it contain?

Two subsets of 3 are contained in set A.

$A = \{\Box, \Box, \Box, \Box, \Box, \Box\} \div 3 = \{\underline{\Box, \Box, \Box}, \underline{\Box, \Box, \Box}\}$

$n(A) = 6 \qquad \div 3 = \qquad 2$

$2 \times \{\Box, \Box, \Box\} = \{\Box, \Box, \Box, \Box, \Box, \Box\}$

A Within each set, underline subsets of 2 members. Tell how many subsets are contained in the set.

① $B = \{\underline{\blacktriangle, \blacktriangle}, \underline{\blacktriangle, \blacktriangle}, \underline{\blacktriangle, \blacktriangle}, \underline{\blacktriangle, \blacktriangle}, \underline{\blacktriangle, \blacktriangle}\}$

　$\underline{\ 5\ } \times \{\blacktriangle, \blacktriangle\} = \blacktriangle, \blacktriangle, \blacktriangle, \blacktriangle, \blacktriangle, \blacktriangle, \blacktriangle, \blacktriangle, \blacktriangle, \blacktriangle$

② $C = \{\bullet, \bullet, \bullet, \bullet, \bullet, \bullet, \bullet, \bullet\}$

　$\underline{\qquad} \times \{\bullet, \bullet\} = \{\bullet, \bullet, \bullet, \bullet, \bullet, \bullet, \bullet, \bullet\}$

③ $D = \{\Box, \Box, \Box, \Box\}$

　$\underline{\qquad} \times \{\Box, \Box\} = \{\Box, \Box, \Box, \Box\}$

④ $E = \{\Diamond, \Diamond\}$

　$\underline{\qquad} \times \{\Diamond, \Diamond\} = \{\Diamond, \Diamond\}$

⑤ $F = \{O, O, O, O, O, O, O, O, O, O, O, O, O, O\}$

　$\underline{\qquad} \times \{O, O\} = \{O, O, O, O, O, O, O, O, O, O, O, O, O, O\}$

⑥ $G = \{\blacktriangle, \blacktriangle, \blacktriangle, \blacktriangle, \blacktriangle, \blacktriangle\}$

　$\underline{\qquad} \times \{\blacktriangle, \blacktriangle\} = \{\blacktriangle, \blacktriangle, \blacktriangle, \blacktriangle, \blacktriangle, \blacktriangle\}$

B Fill in the blanks.

① $B = \{\underline{\blacktriangle, \blacktriangle}, \underline{\blacktriangle, \blacktriangle}, \underline{\blacktriangle, \blacktriangle}, \underline{\blacktriangle, \blacktriangle}, \underline{\blacktriangle, \blacktriangle}\}$

　$B \div 2 = \underline{\ 5\ }$

② $C = \{\bullet, \bullet, \bullet, \bullet, \bullet, \bullet, \bullet, \bullet\}$

　$C \div 2 = \underline{\qquad}$

③ $D = \{\Box, \Box, \Box, \Box\}$

　$D \div 2 = \underline{\qquad}$

④ $E = \{\Diamond, \Diamond\}$

　$E \div 2 = \underline{\qquad}$

⑤ $F = \{O, O, O, O, O, O, O, O, O, O, O, O, O, O\}$

　$F \div 2 = \underline{\qquad}$

⑥ $G = \{\blacktriangle, \blacktriangle, \blacktriangle, \blacktriangle, \blacktriangle, \blacktriangle\}$

　$G \div 2 = \underline{\qquad}$

REMINDER: Write the definition of division.

_____

_____

C Fill in the blanks.

① A = {●, ●, ●, ●, ●, ●, ●, ●, ●, ●, ●, ●, ●, ●} ÷ 7 = {●,●,●,●,●,●,●, ●,●,●,●,●,●,●}

        n (A) = ____   ÷ 7 =   ___

② B = {◇, ◇, ◇, ◇, ◇, ◇, ◇, ◇, ◇, ◇, ◇, ◇, ◇, ◇, ◇} ÷ 5 = {◇,◇,◇,◇,◇, ◇,◇,◇,◇,◇, ◇,◇,◇,◇,◇}

        n (A) = ____   ÷ 5 =   ___

③ C = {▲, ▲, ▲, ▲, ▲, ▲, ▲, ▲, ▲, ▲, ▲, ▲, ▲, ▲} ÷ 2 = {▲,▲, ▲,▲, ▲,▲, ▲,▲, ▲,▲, ▲,▲, ▲,▲}

        n (A) = ____   ÷ 2 =   ___

④ D = {□, □, □, □, □, □, □, □, □, □, □, □, □, □, □} ÷ 3 = {□,□,□, □,□,□, □,□,□, □,□,□, □,□,□}

        n (A) = ____   ÷ 3 =   ___

D Match the problems with the division sentences.

① There are 30 students in second-year Spanish. These students are assigned to discussion groups of 3 students each. There are 10 discussion groups.

        24 ÷ 12 = 2

② Sixteen dancers will perform in an upcoming musical. The dancers will perform in 4 rows. Four dancers will dance in each row.

        18 ÷ 3 = 6

        30 ÷ 3 = 10

③ Jennifer bought 24 colored pencils. The pencils were packaged in sets of 12. Jennifer bought 2 packages.

④ Fifty-five business club members formed five committees to talk about goals for the year. Each committee consisted of 11 members.

        16 ÷ 4 = 4

        55 ÷ 5 = 11

⑤ Eighteen students traveled in 3 cars to a ball game. There were 6 students in each car.

Identifying Problem Parts   Unit 82

Learning
Objective: We will learn to identify the dividend, the divisor, and the quotient in a division problem.

In a division problem, the dividend is the number to be divided. The divisor is the number by which the dividend is divided. The quotient is the result.

EXAMPLE: In the division problems below, 6 is the dividend, 3 is the divisor, and 2 is the quotient. There are 2 3's in 6. $2 \times 3 = 6$ $6 \div 3 = 2$

A
2 quotient
divisor 3)6 dividend

B
$\rightarrow 6 \div 3 = 2 \leftarrow$ quotient
dividend   divisor

A Divide. Label each dividend (d), each divisor (v), and each quotient (q).

① v 1)0 (0 q / d)   ② 2)0   ③ 3)0   ④ 4)0   ⑤ 5)0

⑥ 6)0   ⑦ 7)0   ⑧ 8)0   ⑨ 9)0   ⑩ 1)1

⑪ 2)2   ⑫ 3)3   ⑬ 4)4   ⑭ 5)5   ⑮ 6)6

⑯ 7)7   ⑰ 8)8   ⑱ 9)9   ⑲ 1)2   ⑳ 2)4

㉑ 4)8   ㉒ 5)10   ㉓ 6)12   ㉔ 7)14   ㉕ 8)16

㉖ 9)18   ㉗ 1)3   ㉘ 2)6   ㉙ 3)9   ㉚ 4)12

㉛ 5)15   ㉜ 6)18   ㉝ 7)21   ㉞ 8)24   ㉟ 9)27

㊱ 1)4   ㊲ 2)8   ㊳ 3)12   ㊴ 4)16   ㊵ 5)20

㊶ 6)24   ㊷ 7)28   ㊸ 8)32   ㊹ 9)36   ㊺ 1)5

㊻ 2)10   ㊼ 3)15   ㊽ 4)20   ㊾ 5)25   ㊿ 6)30

51 7)35   52 8)40   53 9)45   54 1)6   55 2)12

REMINDER: *Write the definition of the dividend, the divisor, and the quotient.*

_____

_____

B Divide. Label each dividend (d), each divisor (v), and each quotient (q).

① $48 \div 8 = 6$
    d   v   q

② $54 \div 9 =$ ___ ___ ___

③ $7 \div 1 =$ ___ ___ ___

④ $14 \div 2 =$ ___ ___ ___

⑤ $21 \div 3 =$ ___ ___ ___

⑥ $28 \div 4 =$ ___ ___ ___

⑦ $35 \div 5 =$ ___ ___ ___

⑧ $42 \div 6 =$ ___ ___ ___

⑨ $49 \div 7 =$ ___ ___ ___

⑩ $56 \div 8 =$ ___ ___ ___

⑪ $63 \div 9 =$ ___ ___ ___

⑫ $8 \div 1 =$ ___ ___ ___

⑬ $16 \div 2 =$ ___ ___ ___

⑭ $24 \div 3 =$ ___ ___ ___

⑮ $32 \div 4 =$ ___ ___ ___

⑯ $40 \div 5 =$ ___ ___ ___

⑰ $48 \div 6 =$ ___ ___ ___

⑱ $56 \div 7 =$ ___ ___ ___

⑲ $64 \div 8 =$ ___ ___ ___

⑳ $72 \div 9 =$ ___ ___ ___

㉑ $9 \div 1 =$ ___ ___ ___

㉒ $18 \div 2 =$ ___ ___ ___

㉓ $27 \div 3 =$ ___ ___ ___

㉔ $36 \div 4 =$ ___ ___ ___

㉕ $45 \div 5 =$ ___ ___ ___

㉖ $54 \div 6 =$ ___ ___ ___

㉗ $63 \div 7 =$ ___ ___ ___

㉘ $72 \div 8 =$ ___ ___ ___

㉙ $81 \div 9 =$ ___ ___ ___

㉚ $10 \div 1 =$ ___ ___ ___

㉛ $20 \div 2 =$ ___ ___ ___

㉜ $30 \div 3 =$ ___ ___ ___

㉝ $40 \div 4 =$ ___ ___ ___

㉞ $50 \div 5 =$ ___ ___ ___

㉟ $60 \div 6 =$ ___ ___ ___

㊱ $70 \div 7 =$ ___ ___ ___

C Study the problems. Within each paragraph underline the dividend once, and the divisor twice. Write a division sentence for each problem.

① Twenty-seven students joined the "March Against Hunger" to raise money to feed starving people world-wide. The students marched in groups of 3. How many groups of students marched?

    $27 \div 3 = 9$

② Forty assorted soft drinks were delivered to the class picnic site. There were 8 soft drinks to each carton. How many cartons of drinks were delivered?

_____

③ Thirty-six singers participated in a barbershop quartet competition. As there were 4 singers in each group, how many groups took part in the event?

_____

④ Eight parents chaperoned the junior-senior prom. Two parents chaperoned each hour. How many hours did the prom last?

_____

⑤ Fifty shares of stock were held by members of the advertising company's board of directors. Each board member held 10 shares. How many members were on the board of directors?

_____

⑥ Guests slept 2 to a room during the Raven's Nest Inn's mystery weekend. There were 20 guests staying at the inn during the mystery weekend. How many rooms were filled?

_____

200

Simple Division

Learning Objective: *We will learn to divide by one-digit divisors.*

Division is the method by which we determine how many times one number contains another.

EXAMPLE: To divide 264 by 6, first determine how many 6's are in 26.
From the multiplication tables, we know that 4 ÷ 6 = 24.
Subtract 24 from 26. The answer is 2. Bring the last number of
the dividend down and divide 24 by 6. Again, there are 4 6's
in 24.   264 ÷ 6 = 44.

$$\begin{array}{r} 44 \\ 6\overline{)264} \\ \underline{24} \\ 24 \\ \underline{24} \end{array}$$

A Divide.

① $\begin{array}{r} 15 \\ 5\overline{)75} \\ \underline{5} \\ 25 \\ \underline{25} \end{array}$

② $4\overline{)104}$

③ $8\overline{)280}$

④ $6\overline{)396}$

⑤ $7\overline{)224}$

⑥ $9\overline{)117}$

⑦ $3\overline{)138}$

⑧ $4\overline{)68}$

⑨ $7\overline{)546}$

⑩ $2\overline{)192}$

⑪ $5\overline{)425}$

⑫ $8\overline{)704}$

⑬ $3\overline{)201}$

⑭ $6\overline{)504}$

⑮ $9\overline{)297}$

⑯ $4\overline{)236}$

⑰ $5\overline{)180}$

⑱ $8\overline{)352}$

⑲ $6\overline{)354}$

⑳ $8\overline{)336}$

㉑ $4\overline{)96}$

㉒ $7\overline{)112}$

㉓ $2\overline{)58}$

㉔ $9\overline{)396}$

㉕ $4\overline{)380}$

㉖ $7\overline{)441}$

㉗ $9\overline{)828}$

㉘ $6\overline{)192}$

㉙ $5\overline{)365}$

㉚ $8\overline{)432}$

㉛ $3\overline{)54}$

㉜ $9\overline{)162}$

㉝ $3\overline{)141}$

㉞ $2\overline{)94}$

㉟ $6\overline{)210}$

REMINDER: *Write the definition of division.*

B Sometimes, we may use a shortened form of division. To divide 810 by 9, we know that $9 \times 9 = 81$ and $9 \times 0 = 0$. No subtraction is needed. Divide the following problems.

$$\frac{90}{9)810}$$

① $4\overline{)88}$ $\frac{22}{}$

② $2\overline{)100}$

③ $4\overline{)164}$

④ $2\overline{)40}$

⑤ $7\overline{)490}$

⑥ $9\overline{)270}$

⑦ $8\overline{)168}$

⑧ $3\overline{)69}$

⑨ $6\overline{)246}$

⑩ $5\overline{)205}$

⑪ $2\overline{)124}$

⑫ $3\overline{)213}$

⑬ $4\overline{)328}$

⑭ $3\overline{)621}$

⑮ $7\overline{)630}$

⑯ $6\overline{)654}$

⑰ $2\overline{)840}$

⑱ $3\overline{)336}$

⑲ $9\overline{)729}$

⑳ $5\overline{)155}$

㉑ $8\overline{)640}$

㉒ $2\overline{)144}$

㉓ $6\overline{)366}$

㉔ $4\overline{)412}$

㉕ $1\overline{)987}$

㉖ $7\overline{)735}$

㉗ $8\overline{)568}$

㉘ $4\overline{)208}$

㉙ $2\overline{)488}$

㉚ $9\overline{)549}$

㉛ $3\overline{)150}$

㉜ $5\overline{)500}$

㉝ $2\overline{)210}$

㉞ $9\overline{)999}$

㉟ $3\overline{)390}$

㊱ $6\overline{)480}$

㊲ $8\overline{)968}$

㊳ $7\overline{)280}$

㊴ $5\overline{)455}$

㊵ $4\overline{)440}$

㊶ $2\overline{)112}$

㊷ $3\overline{)276}$

C Divide. Use the blank space to work the problems.

① In one season of operation, 810 guests stayed at the Lakeside Resort Inn. During each month that the inn was open, an equal number of guests registered The inn was open 6 months How many guests stayed each month?

② Ninety waiters and waitresses are employed by the Lobster Lake Restaurant. An equal number of waiters and waitresses works each of 5 shifts. How many work during each shift?

③ Four hundred eighty-three toys were distributed to 7 orphanages in a three-county area. Each orphanage received an equal number of toys. How many toys were distributed to each orphanage?

④ Eight hundred twenty-eight votes were cast by convention delegates. Each delegate cast 3 votes. How many delegates attended the convention?

202

Division Practice

Unit 84

Learning Objective: *We will learn to divide by two-digit divisors.*

Division is the method by which we determine how many times one number contains another.

$$22\overline{)5,500}$$
$$250$$

EXAMPLE: To divide 5,500 by 22, first determine how many 22's are in 55.
$2 \times 22 = 44$. Subtract 44 from 55. The remainder is 11. Bring down the next number of the dividend. Divide 110 by 22.
$5 \times 22 = 110$. Bring down the last number of the dividend. There are 0 22's in 0. $5,500 \div 22 = 250$

$$\begin{array}{r} 250 \\ 22\overline{)5,500} \\ 44 \\ \hline 110 \\ 110 \\ \hline 0 \\ 0 \\ \hline 0 \end{array}$$

A Divide.

①
$$\begin{array}{r} 147 \\ 40\overline{)5,880} \\ 40 \\ \hline 188 \\ 160 \\ \hline 280 \\ 280 \\ \hline \end{array}$$

② $30\overline{)9,720}$

③ $13\overline{)2,392}$

④ $52\overline{)8,996}$

⑤ $33\overline{)6,105}$

⑥ $75\overline{)8,325}$

⑦ $15\overline{)9,420}$

⑧ $40\overline{)7,240}$

⑨ $82\overline{)11,234}$

⑩ $32\overline{)6,048}$

⑪ $20\overline{)4,740}$

⑫ $14\overline{)4,564}$

⑬ $12\overline{)7,992}$

⑭ $51\overline{)10,455}$

⑮ $80\overline{)8,880}$

⑯ $18\overline{)5,994}$

⑰ $13\overline{)1,534}$

⑱ $24\overline{)3,552}$

⑲ $90\overline{)9,270}$

⑳ $20\overline{)2,100}$

㉑ $15\overline{)3,210}$

㉒ $11\overline{)165}$

㉓ $14\overline{)6,062}$

㉔ $30\overline{)3,210}$

REMINDER: Write the definition of division.

B Divide.

① $15 \overline{)3,030}$ **202**   ② $11 \overline{)2,277}$ ③ $72 \overline{)1,440}$ ④ $85 \overline{)765}$ ⑤ $67 \overline{)268}$ ⑥ $34 \overline{)6,800}$

⑦ $71 \overline{)213}$ ⑧ $26 \overline{)7,852}$ ⑨ $13 \overline{)650}$ ⑩ $42 \overline{)3,360}$ ⑪ $38 \overline{)1,140}$ ⑫ $66 \overline{)462}$

⑬ $87 \overline{)3,480}$ ⑭ $31 \overline{)9,331}$ ⑮ $29 \overline{)2,320}$ ⑯ $12 \overline{)9,660}$ ⑰ $25 \overline{)5,075}$ ⑱ $56 \overline{)2,240}$

⑲ $16 \overline{)8,096}$ ⑳ $35 \overline{)210}$ ㉑ $44 \overline{)4,488}$ ㉒ $20 \overline{)1,800}$ ㉓ $19 \overline{)950}$ ㉔ $45 \overline{)9,000}$

㉕ $29 \overline{)261}$ ㉖ $64 \overline{)1,920}$ ㉗ $21 \overline{)1,260}$ ㉘ $75 \overline{)150}$ ㉙ $53 \overline{)265}$ ㉚ $70 \overline{)4,900}$

㉛ $79 \overline{)4,740}$ ㉜ $18 \overline{)3,618}$ ㉝ $30 \overline{)1,500}$ ㉞ $80 \overline{)5,600}$ ㉟ $13 \overline{)3,926}$ ㊱ $93 \overline{)7,440}$

C Divide. Use the blank space to work the problems.

① A busy law firm divided all its cases equally among its 18 staff lawyers. The firm handled 2,052 cases in one year. How many cases did each of the 18 staff lawyers handle during the same time period?

② Six thousand forty-eight constituents attended a fundraising dinner that featured Senator Reuben as guest speaker. The attend-ees. were seated at 56 tables. How many persons were seated at each table?

③ Farm Fresh Corporation processes 8,316 head of cattle each day. An equal number of cattle are processed at each of the company's 12 plants. How many head of cattle are processed each day at each plant?

④ Farm Fresh transports its livestock via trucks to the various plants. If each truck holds 63 head of cattle, how many trucks are required to transport 693 head of cattle to one plant?

Division Problems

Learning Objective: *We will learn to divide by both one- and two-digit divisors.*

Division is the method by which we determine how many times one number contains another.

EXAMPLE:

$$264 \div 6 = 44$$
$$5,500 \div 22 = 250$$

```
        44
   6)264
       24
       24
       24
```

```
         250
   22)5,500
        44
        110
        110
          0
          0
```

A Divide.

① 64)1,344 = 21
```
   64)1,344
      128
       64
       64
```

② 35)6,965

③ 56)4,424

④ 11)6,303

⑤ 4)1,700

⑥ 24)5,856

⑦ 22)7,898

⑧ 9)702

⑨ 20)9,580

⑩ 6)522

⑪ 17)5,746

⑫ 3)294

⑬ 16)2,528

⑭ 2)5,618

⑮ 33)7,656

⑯ 7)462

⑰ 45)8,325

⑱ 72)9,000

⑲ 13)936

⑳ 8)504

㉑ 16)608

㉒ 10)290

㉓ 7)441

㉔ 96)1,056

REMINDER: Write the definition of division.

Unit 85 cont'd ☞

B Divide.

① $\overset{30}{70\overline{)2,100}}$ ② $3\overline{)123}$ ③ $24\overline{)480}$ ④ $6\overline{)546}$ ⑤ $9\overline{)459}$ ⑥ $45\overline{)3,600}$

⑦ $57\overline{)285}$ ⑧ $47\overline{)4,700}$ ⑨ $9\overline{)2,763}$ ⑩ $4\overline{)84}$ ⑪ $22\overline{)2,266}$ ⑫ $69\overline{)6,210}$

⑬ $21\overline{)1,470}$ ⑭ $13\overline{)104}$ ⑮ $64\overline{)128}$ ⑯ $2\overline{)1,286}$ ⑰ $42\overline{)3,780}$ ⑱ $6\overline{)6,306}$

⑲ $90\overline{)7,200}$ ⑳ $35\overline{)1,050}$ ㉑ $59\overline{)236}$ ㉒ $63\overline{)315}$ ㉓ $25\overline{)1,000}$ ㉔ $18\overline{)1,260}$

㉕ $85\overline{)1,700}$ ㉖ $8\overline{)4,872}$ ㉗ $40\overline{)120}$ ㉘ $14\overline{)112}$ ㉙ $57\overline{)399}$ ㉚ $31\overline{)279}$

㉛ $7\overline{)2,156}$ ㉜ $16\overline{)1,440}$ ㉝ $12\overline{)6,012}$ ㉞ $68\overline{)340}$ ㉟ $5\overline{)3,525}$ ㊱ $71\overline{)4,260}$

C Divide. Use the blank space to work the problems.

① There are 2,400 seats in the Goldberg Auditorium in Smithton. An equal number of seats is situated in each of the auditorium's 3 sections. How many seats are in each section?

_____

② Marla Wilson, a dentist, will consult 84 patients during the coming week. If she sees an equal number of patients each of 6 days, how many patients will she see each day?

_____

③ The Westport Trading Company orders 9,380 bamboo bird cages each year. Thirty-five cages are packaged in each crate that is ordered. How many crates does the company order each year?

_____

④ The Marchland Express has a sleeping capacity of 2,140. A maximum of 4 occupants can sleep in each of the train's berths. How many berths are on the train?

_____

Comprehension Check

A Underline the subsets and fill in the blanks.

① A = {O, O, O, O, O, O, O, O, O, O, O, O, O, O, O, O}   n (A) = __16__ ÷ 4 = __4__

② B = {▲, ▲, ▲, ▲, ▲, ▲, ▲, ▲, ▲, ▲, ▲, ▲, ▲, ▲, ▲, ▲, ▲, ▲}   n (B) = ____ ÷ 3 = ____

③ C = {■, ■, ■, ■, ■, ■, ■, ■, ■, ■, ■, ■}   n (C) = ____ ÷ 6 = ____

④ D = {◇, ◇, ◇, ◇, ◇, ◇, ◇, ◇, ◇, ◇, ◇, ◇, ◇, ◇, ◇, ◇, ◇, ◇}   n (D) = ____ ÷ 2 = ____

⑤ E = {▲, ▲, ▲, ▲, ▲, ▲, ▲, ▲, ▲, ▲, ▲ }   n (E) = ____ ÷ 11 = ____

⑥ F = {●, ●, ●, ●, ●, ●, ●, ●, ●}   n (F) = ____ ÷ 3 = ____

⑦ G = {O, O, O, O, O, O, O, O, O, O}   n (G) = ____ ÷ 2 = ____

⑧ H = {□, □, □, □, □, □, □, □, □, □, □, □, □}   n (H) = ____ ÷ 1 = ____

B Divide. Label the dividends (d), the divisors (v), and the quotients (q).

① __10__ _q_   ② ____   ③ 48 ÷ 6 =   ④ 0 ÷ 1 =   ⑤ ____
  _d_ 1)10 _v_   __ 7)63 __   __ __ __   __ __ __   __ 3)27 __

⑥ 27 ÷ 9 =   ⑦ 3 ÷ 1 =   ⑧ ____   ⑨ 28 ÷ 7 =   ⑩ 4 ÷ 4 =
  __ __ __   __ __ __   __ 5)40 __   __ __ __   __ __ __

⑪ ____   ⑫ 45 ÷ 9 =   ⑬ 21 ÷ 7 =   ⑭ ____   ⑮ 30 ÷ 6 =
  __ 4)36 __   __ __ __   __ __ __   __ 6)54 __   __ __ __

⑯ ____   ⑰ 4 ÷ 2 =   ⑱ ____   ⑲ 15 ÷ 3 =   ⑳ ____
  __ 9)63 __   __ __ __   __ 2)16 __   __ __ __   __ 9)72 __

㉑ 6 ÷ 2 =   ㉒ ____   ㉓ 24 ÷ 6 =   ㉔ ____   ㉕ 25 ÷ 5 =
  __ __ __   __ 9)81 __   __ __ __   __ 8)56 __   __ __ __

㉖ ____   ㉗ 36 ÷ 12 =   ㉘ ____   ㉙ 20 ÷ 5 =   ㉚ ____
  __ 7)49 __   __ __ __   __ 6)60 __   __ __ __   __ 9)54 __

㉛ 0 ÷ 8 =   ㉜ 9 ÷ 9 =   ㉝ ____   ㉞ 44 ÷ 4 =   ㉟ 14 ÷ 7 =
  __ __ __   __ __ __   __ 4)28 __   __ __ __   __ __ __

Test 17 cont'd ☞

C Divide.

① 35)1,960   quotient 56
```
   56
35)1,960
   175
   ---
    210
    210
```

② 44)5,852

③ 2)1,378

④ 78)8,736

⑤ 64)9,408

⑥ 5)3,490

⑦ 46)9,982

⑧ 16)9,072

⑨ 50)3,150

⑩ 3)291

⑪ 32)8,160

⑫ 9)3,204

⑬ 6)2,742

⑭ 25)900

⑮ 85)9,435

⑯ 55)1,815

⑰ 19)8,588

⑱ 4)348

D Divide.

① 4)8,012   quotient 2,003

② 50)4,500

③ 91)9,191

④ 16)128

⑤ 6)3,612

⑥ 96)384

⑦ 71)2,130

⑧ 46)3,220

⑨ 65)520

⑩ 5)3,060

⑪ 54)270

⑫ 7)7,497

⑬ 2)6,148

⑭ 33)1,320

⑮ 80)7,200

⑯ 9)1,080

⑰ 75)675

⑱ 37)2,960

Write a paragraph that includes a division problem. Underline the dividend within the paragraph. Circle the divisor. Write a division sentence for the problem.

_____

_____

_____

_____

_____

Having a Remainder

Learning Objective: *We will learn to recognize remainders through the division of sets.*

A remainder is the final undivided part of a division problem.

EXAMPLE:
There are 2 subsets of 4 members each in Set A. There is also 1 remaining member in Set A. $9 \div 4 = 2$ with a remainder of 1.

A = {♥, ♥, ♥, ♥, ♥, ♥, ♥, ♥, ♥} ÷ 4 = {♥, ♥, ♥, ♥   ♥, ♥, ♥, ♥   ♥}

      n(A) = 9   ÷ 4 =   **2**   **R 1**

A In each set, underline the subsets of 3 members each. Write the number of subsets and the number of remaining members in the space to the right.

① B = {⚱, ⚱, ⚱, ⚱, ⚱, ⚱, ⚱, ⚱, ⚱, ⚱, ⚱, ⚱, ⚱, ⚱} ÷ 3 = __4__ R __2__

② C = {♠, ♠, ♠, ♠, ♠, ♠, ♠} ÷ 3 = _____ R _____

③ D = {♣, ♣, ♣, ♣, ♣, ♣, ♣, ♣, ♣, ♣, ♣, ♣} ÷ 3 = _____ R _____

④ E = {♡, ♡, ♡, ♡, ♡, ♡, ♡, ♡} ÷ 3 = _____ R _____

⑤ F = {$, $, $, $, $, $, $, $, $, $, $, $, $, $, $} ÷ 3 = _____ R _____

⑥ G = {🚗, 🚗, 🚗, 🚗, 🚗, 🚗, 🚗, 🚗, 🚗, 🚗, 🚗, 🚗, 🚗} ÷ 3 = _____ R _____

⑦ H = {★, ★, ★, ★, ★, ★, ★, ★, ★, ★} ÷ 3 = _____ R _____

⑧ I = {🚁, 🚁, 🚁, 🚁, 🚁} ÷ 3 = _____ R _____

⑨ J = {✈, ✈, ✈, ✈} ÷ 3 = _____ R _____

⑩ K = {✉, ✉, ✉, ✉, ✉, ✉, ✉, ✉, ✉, ✉, ✉, ✉, ✉, ✉, ✉, ✉} ÷ 3 = _____ R _____

B Match the problems and solutions.

① {◇, ◇, ◇, ◇, ◇, ◇, ◇, ◇, ◇} ÷ 2 =   {■, ■, ■, ■, ■, ■, ■, ■, ■, ■, ■} = 2 R 1

② {■, ■, ■, ■, ■, ■, ■, ■, ■, ■, ■, ■} ÷ 5 =   {○, ○, ○, ○, ○, ○, ○, ○, ○, ○, ○, ○, ○, ○, ○, ○, ○, ○, ○} = 3 R 3

③ {○, ○} ÷ 4 =   {◇, ◇, ◇, ◇, ◇, ◇, ◇, ◇, ◇} = 4 R 1

④ {▲, ▲, ▲, ▲, ▲, ▲, ▲} ÷ 2 =   {▲, ▲, ▲, ▲, ▲, ▲, ▲} = 3 R 1

⑤ {□, □, □, □, □, □, □, □, □, □, □, □, □, □, □, □} ÷ 6 =   {△, △, △, △, △, △, △, △, △, △, △, △, △, △, △, △} = 2 R 4

⑥ {◆, ◆, ◆, ◆, ◆, ◆, ◆} ÷ 4 =   {●, ●, ●, ●, ●, ●, ●, ●, ●, ●} = 1 R 4

⑦ {△, △, △, △, △, △, △, △, △, △, △, △, △, △, △, △} ÷ 6 =   {□, □, □, □, □, □, □, □, □, □, □, □, □, □, □, □} = 2 R 2

⑧ {●, ●, ●, ●, ●, ●, ●, ●, ●, ●} ÷ 5 =   {◆, ◆, ◆, ◆, ◆, ◆, ◆} = 1 R 3

REMINDER: Write the definition of a remainder.

_____

_____

C Fill in the blanks.

① A = {O, O, O, O, O, O, O, O, O, O, O, O, O, O, O, O, O, O, O, O, O, O} ÷ 5 =

n(A) = _____   ÷ 5 =

{O, O, O, O, O, O, O, O, O, O, O, O, O, O, O, O, O, O, O, O, O, O}

_____ R _____

② B = {▲, ▲, ▲, ▲, ▲, ▲, ▲, ▲, ▲, ▲, ▲, ▲, ▲, ▲, ▲, ▲, ▲, ▲} ÷ 7 =

n(B) = _____   ÷ 7 =

{▲, ▲, ▲, ▲, ▲, ▲, ▲, ▲, ▲, ▲, ▲, ▲, ▲, ▲, ▲, ▲, ▲, ▲}

_____ R _____

③ C = {□, □, □, □, □, □, □, □, □, □, □, □, □, □, □} ÷ 6 =

n(C) = _____   ÷ 6 =

{□, □, □, □, □, □, □, □, □, □, □, □, □, □, □}

_____ R _____

④ D = {●, ●, ●, ●, ●, ●, ●, ●, ●, ●, ●, ●, ●, ●, ●, ●, ●} ÷ 8 =

n(D) = _____   ÷ 8 =

{●, ●, ●, ●, ●, ●, ●, ●, ●, ●, ●, ●, ●, ●, ●, ●, ●}

_____ R _____

D Write a division sentence for each problem.

① At rehearsal, 24 dancers were told to arrange themselves in 5 equal lines. The result was 5 lines made up of 4 dancers each. The remaining 4 dancers stood to the side and watched.

$$24 \div 5 = 4 \quad R\ 4$$

② While working part-time in a department store, Ann was told to fold sweaters and stack them 3 to a stack. Ann folded 19 sweaters in all. After stacking them in 6 equal stacks, she found that she had 1 sweater remaining.

③ The 39 students who attended the poetry workshop were grouped into smaller discussion circles. It had been expected that each circle would include 12 students. However, there were 3 students remaining after 3 circles had been formed.

④ It was required that the Madison Volunteer Fire Department be staffed by 2 full crews. With a current staff of 27 firefighters, the department has its 2 full crews of 12 each. In addition, 3 extra firefighters serve as alternates.

⑤ The 79 sophomores at Hickman High School were divided into 3 classes of 26 students each. A coin was then flipped to determine in what class the 1 remaining sophomore should be placed.

⑥ Ninety-eight pages of math problems were separated into stacks of 4 pages, stapled, and given to freshmen math students. There were enough hand-outs for 24 students. Two pages were left over.

Problems With Remainders

Learning Objective: *We will learn to work division problems that have remainders.*

A remainder is the final undivided part of a division problem.

EXAMPLE: A remainder is always less than the divisor. After dividing 69 by 2, there is a remainder of 1.

$$\begin{array}{r} 34 \\ 2\overline{)69} \\ \underline{6} \\ 9 \\ \underline{8} \\ ① \end{array}$$

$69 \div 2 = 34$ **R1**

A Divide. Circle the remainders.

① $3\overline{)751}$ = 250
$$\begin{array}{r} 250 \\ 3\overline{)751} \\ \underline{6} \\ 15 \\ \underline{15} \\ 1 \\ \underline{0} \\ ① \end{array}$$

② $3\overline{)971}$

③ $10\overline{)1,824}$

④ $64\overline{)3,194}$

⑤ $9\overline{)1,551}$

⑥ $18\overline{)8,322}$

⑦ $5\overline{)1,446}$

⑧ $14\overline{)4,831}$

⑨ $7\overline{)1,269}$

⑩ $8\overline{)3,770}$

⑪ $16\overline{)6,731}$

⑫ $25\overline{)5,222}$

⑬ $20\overline{)1,086}$

⑭ $9\overline{)1,938}$

⑮ $35\overline{)4,411}$

⑯ $17\overline{)879}$

⑰ $5\overline{)1,577}$

⑱ $8\overline{)926}$

⑲ $13\overline{)172}$

⑳ $28\overline{)791}$

㉑ $11\overline{)142}$

㉒ $8\overline{)489}$

㉓ $85\overline{)222}$

㉔ $21\overline{)919}$

REMINDER: *Write the definition of a remainder.*

Unit 87 cont'd ☛

B Divide.

① $199 \div 19 =$ __10 R 9__ ② $165 \div 4 =$ _____ ③ $517 \div 5 =$ _____ ④ $76 \div 25 =$ _____

⑤ $1,820 \div 9 =$ _____ ⑥ $170 \div 8 =$ _____ ⑦ $61 \div 30 =$ _____ ⑧ $42 \div 5 =$ _____

⑨ $307 \div 3 =$ _____ ⑩ $801 \div 40 =$ _____ ⑪ $1,918 \div 19 =$ _____ ⑫ $85 \div 12 =$ _____

⑬ $710 \div 60 =$ _____ ⑭ $115 \div 10 =$ _____ ⑮ $211 \div 3 =$ _____ ⑯ $225 \div 11 =$ _____

⑰ $440 \div 7 =$ _____ ⑱ $206 \div 5 =$ _____ ⑲ $554 \div 9 =$ _____ ⑳ $5,023 \div 50 =$ _____

㉑ $58 \div 9 =$ _____ ㉒ $9,610 \div 3 =$ _____ ㉓ $65 \div 8 =$ _____ ㉔ $691 \div 7 =$ _____

㉕ $807 \div 20 =$ _____ ㉖ $590 \div 8 =$ _____ ㉗ $99 \div 12 =$ _____ ㉘ $1,180 \div 80 =$ _____

㉙ $2,418 \div 12 =$ _____ ㉚ $399 \div 6 =$ _____ ㉛ $1,011 \div 10 =$ _____ ㉜ $53 \div 6 =$ _____

㉝ $985 \div 9 =$ _____ ㉞ $97 \div 3 =$ _____ ㉟ $109 \div 20 =$ _____ ㊱ $200 \div 11 =$ _____

C Divide. Use the blank space to work the problems. Circle the remainders.

① Laura planned to drive 8 hours per day to visit her aunt, Lucinda. Laura estimated that the total driving time would be 29 hours. How much time would it take Laura to drive to her aunt's house?

_____ days + ___ hours

② Shelley bought a basket of 38 oranges. She divided the oranges equally among the 7 other members of her family. She kept the left over oranges for herself. How many oranges did the other family members get? _____ Shelley? _____

③ There were 87 students in the square dance class. On the first day of class, the group was divided into couples. How many couples were in the class? _____ How many square dancers did not have a partner? _____

④ The percussion section of the band was divided into 2 sections, each with an equal number of members. One section included snare drummers, and the other bass drummers. There were 49 percussionists in the band. How many were in each section? _____ How many were left over? _____

212

Divide or Multiply?

Learning Objective: *We will learn to determine if a problem calls for division or multiplication.*

Division is the method by which we determine how many times one number contains another. Multiplication is a shortcut for adding a number to itself.

EXAMPLE: In problem A, the quotient of 500 divided by 5 is 100. In problem B, the product of 500 times 5 is 2,500.

$$\underset{\textstyle A}{500 \div 5 = 100} \qquad \underset{\textstyle B}{500 \times 5 = 2{,}500}$$

A Divide or multiply.

①
$$\begin{array}{r} 623 \\ \times\ 13 \\ \hline \mathit{1{,}869} \\ \mathit{623} \\ \hline \mathit{8{,}099} \end{array}$$

② $9\overline{)9{,}637}$

③
$$\begin{array}{r} 4{,}621 \\ \times\ 18 \\ \hline \end{array}$$

④ $28\overline{)4{,}294}$

⑤
$$\begin{array}{r} 3{,}647 \\ \times\ 58 \\ \hline \end{array}$$

⑥ $14\overline{)2{,}371}$

⑦
$$\begin{array}{r} 139 \\ \times\ 55 \\ \hline \end{array}$$

⑧ $6\overline{)5{,}233}$

⑨
$$\begin{array}{r} 7{,}181 \\ \times\ 24 \\ \hline \end{array}$$

⑩ $53\overline{)1{,}326}$

⑪
$$\begin{array}{r} 8{,}700 \\ \times\ 73 \\ \hline \end{array}$$

⑫ $61\overline{)2{,}620}$

⑬
$$\begin{array}{r} 3{,}713 \\ \times\ 71 \\ \hline \end{array}$$

⑭ $38\overline{)4{,}552}$

⑮
$$\begin{array}{r} 1{,}615 \\ \times\ 31 \\ \hline \end{array}$$

⑯ $26\overline{)1{,}111}$

⑰
$$\begin{array}{r} 2{,}642 \\ \times\ 92 \\ \hline \end{array}$$

⑱ $59\overline{)4{,}361}$

⑲ $83\overline{)735}$

⑳
$$\begin{array}{r} 339 \\ \times\ 8 \\ \hline \end{array}$$

㉑ $36\overline{)294}$

㉒
$$\begin{array}{r} 6{,}472 \\ \times\ 3 \\ \hline \end{array}$$

㉓ $96\overline{)158}$

㉔
$$\begin{array}{r} 1{,}121 \\ \times\ 3 \\ \hline \end{array}$$

REMINDER: *Write the definition of division and multiplication.*

Unit 88 cont'd ☞

B **Determine if the answers are a result of division or multiplication. Fill in the blanks with the correct symbols: ÷ or ×.**

① 416 _×_ 62 = 25,792   ② 287 ___ 7 = 41   ③ 63 ___ 12 = 756   ④ 1,311 ___ 3 = 437

⑤ 725 ___ 5 = 145   ⑥ 613 ___ 89 = 54,557   ⑦ 4,364 ___ 4 = 1,091   ⑧ 3,654 ___ 9 = 406

⑨ 3,714 ___ 5 = 18,570   ⑩ 8,032 ___ 8 = 1,004   ⑪ 1,030 ___ 5 = 206   ⑫ 178 ___ 97 = 17,266

⑬ 4,021 ___ 6 = 24,126   ⑭ 351 ___ 10 = 3,510   ⑮ 3,624 ___ 4 = 906   ⑯ 491 ___ 39 = 19,149

⑰ 948 ___ 3 = 316   ⑱ 851 ___ 7 = 5,957   ⑲ 5,418 ___ 6 = 903   ⑳ 1,172 ___ 2 = 586

㉑ 1,417 ___ 2 = 2,834   ㉒ 258 ___ 18 = 4,644   ㉓ 29,190 ___ 30 = 973   ㉔ 9,612 ___ 12 = 801

㉕ 3,195 ___ 9 = 355   ㉖ 166 ___ 3 = 498   ㉗ 8,100 ___ 90 = 90   ㉘ 4,172 ___ 5 = 20,860

㉙ 5,999 ___ 7 = 857   ㉚ 5,840 ___ 8 = 730   ㉛ 8,820 ___ 20 = 441   ㉜ 206 ___ 59 = 12,154

㉝ 4,164 ___ 6 = 694   ㉞ 5,363 ___ 6 = 32,178   ㉟ 215 ___ 55 = 11,825   ㊱ 2,127 ___ 3 = 709

C **Write either a division sentence or a multiplication sentence for each problem.**

① At an antique shop, Rosalind found 4 lace collars. Each collar was made up of 17 rows of hand-crocheted lace. In all of the collars, there were 68 rows of crocheted lace.

   4 × 17 = 68

② Three hundred sixty-eight pieces of antique silver were equally divided and displayed in 8 compartments of a glass case. There were 46 pieces of silver in each compartment.

_____

③ Old and rare books lined one entire wall of the antique shop. There were 6 large bookcases, each containing 500 books. There were 3,000 books in all.

_____

④ The store advertised its collection of antique watches. These could be seen on 3 shelves of a jeweler's display case. There were 125 watches on each shelf. The collection included a total of 375 watches.

_____

⑤ The china display included 564 hand-painted plates. The plates were divided equally among 4 antique china cabinets. Each china cabinet contained 141 plates.

_____

⑥ Rosalind bought 12 wooden picture frames, which she planned to present as birthday gifts to relatives and friends. Each frame was priced at $25. Rosalind spent a total of $300 for the frames.

_____

Multiplication to Check Division   Unit 89

Learning
Objective: *We will learn to use multiplication to prove the correctness of division quotients.*

Checking is the process of proving correctness.

EXAMPLE: To check a division problem, multiply the divisor and the quotient. The product of these two numbers should be equal to the dividend.

$$
\begin{array}{r} 100 \\ \times\,5 \\ \hline 500 \end{array}
$$

$$5\,)\overline{500} =$$

$$500 \div 5 = 100 \times 5 = 500$$

A Use multiplication to check the division problems. Place a check (✓) beside each quotient that is correct. Draw an X beside each incorrect quotient.

① 166 ✓
  7)1,162
    7
   46
   42
    42
    42

   166
  × 7
 1,162

② 461 ___
  2)922
    8
   12
   12
    2
    2

③ 396 ___
  6)2,376
   18
   57
   54
   36
   36

④ 624 ___
 12)7,488
   72
   28
   24
   48
   48

⑤ 948 ___
  4)3,782
   36
   18
   16
   22
   22

⑥ 346 ___
  5)1,730
   15
   23
   20
   30
   30

⑦ 137 ___
  9)1,173
    9
   27
   21
   63
   63

⑧ 253 ___
  9)2,277
   18
   47
   45
   27
   27

⑨ 485 ___
 11)5,335
   44
   93
   88
   55
   55

⑩ 62 ___
  9)558
   54
   18
   18

⑪ 22 ___
 11)232
   22
   22
   22

⑫ 42 ___
 15)630
   60
   30
   30

REMINDER: Write the definition of checking.

_____

_____

Unit 89 cont'd ☞

B Use multiplication to check division. Place a ✓ before each problem that is correct and an X before each that is incorrect.

___✓___ ① 6,321 ÷ 21 = 301 × *21 = 6,321*   _____ ② 1,167 ÷ 3 = 389

_____ ③ 7,428 ÷ 14 = 602   _____ ④ 847 ÷ 7 = 121

_____ ⑤ 3,718 ÷ 9 = 402   _____ ⑥ 6,612 ÷ 6 = 1,122

_____ ⑦ 6,189 ÷ 3 = 2,063   _____ ⑧ 2,613 ÷ 13 = 201

_____ ⑨ 1,438 ÷ 4 = 392   _____ ⑩ 2,252 ÷ 4 = 563

_____ ⑪ 812 ÷ 4 = 203   _____ ⑫ 825 ÷ 11 = 65

_____ ⑬ 2,725 ÷ 25 = 109   _____ ⑭ 5,075 ÷ 25 = 203

_____ ⑮ 759 ÷ 3 = 253   _____ ⑯ 2,628 ÷ 12 = 219

_____ ⑰ 9,326 ÷ 18 = 518   _____ ⑱ 1,599 ÷ 3 = 533

C Use multiplication to check division. If the problem is incorrect, find the correct quotient.

① Two hundred fifty-two people took part in a community-wide hunt for a hidden treasure. The participants were assigned to 6-man teams. How many teams took part in the event?

$$\overset{42}{6\,\overline{)252}}$$

② One hundred twenty clues were equally divided among 12 stops along the treasure hunt route. How many clues were placed at each of the 12 stops?

$$\overset{10}{12\,\overline{)120}}$$

③ The 120 clues were found by members of only 30 of the participating teams. Each of the 30 teams found an equal number of clues. How many clues did each team discover?

$$\overset{40}{30\,\overline{)120}}$$

④ A chest filled with $2,250 in silver coins became the property of the team that found it. The money was divided equally among the 6 members of the winning team. How much money did each team member win?

$$\overset{465}{6\,\overline{)2,250}}$$

216

Checking Division Problems

Learning
Objective: *We will learn to solve and check all division problems.*

Checking is the process of proving correctness.

EXAMPLE: To check a division problem that has a remainder, multiply the divisor and the quotient. To this product add the remainder. The sum should be equal to the dividend.

```
    10          10
5 )52         × 5        52 ÷ 5 = 10 R2
    5          50        [5 × 10] + 2
    2         + 2        50 + 2 = 52
    0          52
   R2
```

A Divide. Check your answers with multiplication.

①
```
      112        112
55 )6,187       × 55
     55          560
     68          560
     55        6,160
    137        + 27
    110        6,187
    R27
```

② 64)8,557

③ 48)5,881

④ 91)1,941

⑤ 60)4,620

⑥ 11)9,540

⑦ 6)2,874

⑧ 32)4,086

⑨ 12)8,880

⑩ 3)1,669

⑪ 18)1,414

⑫ 86)6,349

⑬ 6)466

⑭ 2)192

⑮ 11)605

⑯ 9)622

REMINDER: Write the definition of checking.

_____

_____

Unit 90 cont'd 👉

B Divide and check.

① $678 \div 7 = $ **96 R6**
   [7 × 96] + 6
   672 + 6 = 678

② $824 \div 2 = $

③ $237 \div 10 = $

④ $730 \div 3 = $

⑤ $1,812 \div 4 = $

⑥ $782 \div 9 = $

⑦ $459 \div 6 = $

⑧ $336 \div 8 = $

⑨ $200 \div 7 = $

⑩ $411 \div 17 = $

⑪ $3,324 \div 4 = $

⑫ $819 \div 9 = $

⑬ $1,272 \div 6 = $

⑭ $702 \div 13 = $

⑮ $477 \div 9 = $

⑯ $1,120 \div 7 = $

⑰ $615 \div 15 = $

⑱ $2,321 \div 11 = $

⑲ $9,824 \div 16 = $

⑳ $477 \div 3 = $

C Divide and check.

① The bus traveled 220 miles to the football game. It traveled at a steady speed of 55 miles per hour and made no stops along the way. How many hours did the trip take? _____

② Two hundred seventy-six acres of woodland were cleared, surveyed, divided into 12 parcels of equal size, and sold as farm property. How many acres of land were in each parcel? _____

③ State revenues totaling $9,897 were divided equally among 9 county school districts. Any remaining dollars were put into the county's general fund. How much did each school district receive? _____ How much remained in the general fund? _____

④ The election for county treasurer resulted in a 4-way tie. A total of 8,936 votes were cast for the 4 candidates for treasurer. How many votes did each candidate receive?
_____

Comprehension Check

A Match the problems and solutions.

① {O, O, O, O, O, O, O, O, O, O, O, O, O, O, O, O, O} ÷ 10 =

{▲, ▲, ▲, ▲, ▲, ▲, ▲, ▲, ▲, ▲, ▲, ▲, ▲, ▲, ▲, ▲, ▲} = 2 R1

② {▲, ▲, ▲, ▲, ▲, ▲, ▲, ▲, ▲, ▲, ▲, ▲, ▲, ▲, ▲, ▲} ÷ 8 =

{♦, ♦, ♦, ♦, ♦, ♦, ♦, ♦, ♦, ♦, ♦, ♦, ♦, ♦, ♦, ♦, ♦, ♦, ♦, } = 2 R4

③ {□, □, □, □, □, □, □, □, □, □, □, □, □, □, □, □} ÷ 5 =

{O, O, O, O, O, O, O, O, O, O, O, O, O, O, O, O} = 1 R4

④ {♦, ♦, ♦, ♦, ♦, ♦, ♦, ♦, ♦, ♦, ♦, ♦, ♦, ♦, ♦, ♦, ♦, ♦} ÷ 7 =

{□, □, □, □, □, □, □, □, □, □, □, □, □, □, □, □} = 3 R1

⑤ {△, △, △, △, △, △, △, △, △, △, △, △, △, △, △} ÷ 6 =

{◇, ◇, ◇, ◇, ◇, ◇, ◇, ◇, ◇, ◇, ◇} = 3 R2

⑥ {●, ●, ●, ●, ●, ●, ●, ●, ●, ●, ●, ●, ●} ÷ 2 =

{△, △, △, △, △, △, △, △, △, △, △, △, △, △, △} = 2 R3

⑦ {◇, ◇, ◇, ◇, ◇, ◇, ◇, ◇, ◇, ◇, ◇ } ÷ 3 =

{●, ●, ●, ●, ●, ●, ●, ●, ●, ●, ●, ●, ●} = 6 R1

⑧ {□, □, □, □, □, □, □, □, □, □, □, □, □, □, □, □, □} ÷ 9 =

{O, O, O, O, O, O, O, O, O, O, O, O, O, O, O, O, O, O, O, O, O} = 4 R3

⑨ {O, O, O, O, O, O, O, O, O, O, O, O, O, O, O, O, O, O, O, O, O} ÷ 4 =

{▲, ▲, ▲, ▲, ▲, ▲, ▲, ▲, ▲, ▲, ▲, ▲, ▲} = 1 R6

⑩ {▲, ▲, ▲, ▲, ▲, ▲, ▲, ▲, ▲, ▲, ▲, ▲, ▲} ÷ 7 =

{□, □, □, □, □, □, □, □, □, □, □, □, □, □, □, □, □} = 1 R7

B Divide. Check your answers with multiplication.

① 416 ÷ 8 = **52**
    8 × 52 = 416

② 935 ÷ 3 =

③ 768 ÷ 7 =

④ 8,811 ÷ 11 =

⑤ 994 ÷ 15 =

⑥ 102 ÷ 3 =

⑦ 134 ÷ 9 =

⑧ 1,284 ÷ 12 =

⑨ 111 ÷ 7 =

⑩ 8,616 ÷ 12 =

⑪ 175 ÷ 6 =

⑫ 514 ÷ 4 =

⑬ 318 ÷ 6 =

⑭ 722 ÷ 7 =

⑮ 9,911 ÷ 9 =

⑯ 123 ÷ 6 =

⑰ 867 ÷ 3 =

⑱ 2,054 ÷ 50 =

⑲ 1,213 ÷ 12 =

⑳ 249 ÷ 8 =

Test 18 cont'd ☞

C Divide. Check your answers with multiplication.

①
```
        433          433
18 ) 7,794      ×     18
      72          3,464
      59            433
      54          7,794
      54
      54
```

② 23) 1,100

③ 17) 8,392

④ 24) 6,845

⑤ 57) 4,596

⑥ 73) 7,488

⑦ 13) 455

⑧ 83) 921

⑨ 10) 4,117

⑩ 66) 9,042

⑪ 40) 1,228

⑫ 7) 1,389

D Fill in the blanks with ÷ or ×.

① 143 __×__ 6 = 858

② 451 ___ 5 = 2,255

③ 548 ___ 4 = 137

④ 1,631 ___ 7 = 233

⑤ 132 ___ 11 = 12

⑥ 649 ___ 8 = 5,192

⑦ 199 ___ 2 = 398

⑧ 8,952 ___ 8 = 1,119

⑨ 272 ___ 3 = 816

⑩ 1,024 ___ 4 = 256

⑪ 6,925 ___ 25 = 277

⑫ 312 ___ 6 = 1,872

⑬ 265 ___ 6 = 1,590

⑭ 2,790 ___ 9 = 310

⑮ 555 ___ 9 = 4,995

⑯ 1,012 ___ 5 = 5,060

Write two paragraphs, one including a division problem and the other including a multiplication problem. Write a mathematical sentence for each problem.

① _____

_____

_____

_____

② _____

_____

_____

_____

Four Basic Operations

Learning Objective: *We will practice adding, subtracting, dividing, and multiplying.*

The four basic mathematical operations are addition, subtraction, multiplication and division.

EXAMPLES: a. $6 + 2 = 8$ b. $6 - 2 = 4$ c. $6 \times 2 = 12$ d. $6 \div 2 = 3$

a. $\{\Box, \Box, \Box, \Box, \Box, \Box\} + \{\Box, \Box\} = \{\Box, \Box, \Box, \Box, \Box, \Box, \Box, \Box\}$

b. $\{\Box, \Box, \Box, \Box, \Box, \Box\} - \{\Box, \Box\} = \{\Box, \Box, \Box, \Box\}$

c. $\{\Box, \Box, \Box, \Box, \Box, \Box\} \times 2 = \{\Box, \Box, \Box, \Box, \Box, \Box, \Box, \Box, \Box, \Box, \Box, \Box\}$

d. $\{\Box, \Box, \Box, \Box, \Box, \Box\} \div 2 = \{\underline{\Box, \Box,}\ \underline{\Box, \Box,}\ \underline{\Box, \Box}\}$

A Match the problems and solutions.

① $\{●, ●, ●, ●, ●, ●, ●, ●, ●, ●, ●\} \times 2 =$

② $\{△, △, △, △, △, △, △\} + \{△, △, △, △, △, △, △\} =$

③ $\{■, ■, ■, ■, ■, ■, ■, ■, ■, ■, ■, ■\} \div 4 =$

④ $\{◇, ◇, ◇, ◇, ◇, ◇, ◇, ◇, ◇, ◇, ◇, ◇, ◇\} - \{◇, ◇, ◇\} =$

⑤ $\{▲, ▲, ▲, ▲, ▲, ▲, ▲, ▲, ▲, ▲, ▲, ▲, ▲, ▲, ▲, ▲, ▲, ▲\} \div 9 =$

⑥ $\{○, ○, ○, ○, ○, ○, ○, ○, ○, ○, ○, ○\} + \{○, ○, ○, ○, ○, ○, ○, ○\} =$

⑦ $\{◆, ◆, ◆, ◆, ◆, ◆, ◆, ◆\} \times 3 =$

⑧ $\{\Box, \Box, \Box, \Box, \Box, \Box, \Box, \Box\} \times 4 =$

⑨ $\{●, ●, ●, ●, ●, ●, ●\} + \{●, ●, ●, ●\} =$

⑩ $\{△, △, △, △, △, △, △, △, △, △, △, △\} - \{△, △, △\} =$

⑪ $\{■, ■, ■, ■, ■, ■, ■, ■, ■, ■\} \div 2 =$

⑫ $\{◇, ◇, ◇, ◇, ◇, ◇, ◇, ◇, ◇, ◇\} + \{◇, ◇, ◇, ◇, ◇, ◇, ◇, ◇, ◇\} =$

⑬ $\{▲, ▲, ▲, ▲, ▲, ▲, ▲, ▲, ▲\} - \{▲, ▲, ▲, ▲, ▲, ▲, ▲, ▲, ▲\} =$

⑭ $\{○, ○, ○, ○, ○, ○, ○, ○, ○, ○, ○, ○, ○\} \div \{○, ○, ○, ○, ○, ○, ○, ○\} =$

Solutions:

$\{△, △, △, △, △, △, △, △, △, △, △, △, △, △\}$

$\{◇, ◇, ◇, ◇, ◇, ◇, ◇, ◇, ◇, ◇, ◇\}$

$\{●, ●\}$

$\{\underline{■, ■, ■,}\ \underline{■, ■, ■,}\ \underline{■, ■, ■,}\ ■, ■, ■\}$

$\{○, ○, ○, ○, ○, ○, ○, ○, ○, ○, ○, ○, ○, ○, ○, ○, ○, ○, ○, ○\}$

$\{●, ●, ●, ●, ●, ●, ●, ●, ●, ●, ●\}$

$\{\Box, \Box, \Box, \Box, \Box, \Box, \Box, \Box, \Box, \Box, \Box, \Box, \Box, \Box, \Box, \Box,$
$\Box, \Box, \Box, \Box, \Box, \Box, \Box, \Box, \Box, \Box, \Box, \Box, \Box, \Box, \Box, \Box\}$

$\{\underline{▲, ▲, ▲, ▲, ▲, ▲, ▲, ▲, ▲, ▲, ▲, ▲,}\ \underline{▲, ▲, ▲, ▲, ▲, ▲, ▲, ▲, ▲, ▲, ▲, ▲}\}$

$\{◆, ◆, ◆, ◆, ◆, ◆, ◆, ◆, ◆, ◆, ◆, ◆,$
$◆, ◆, ◆, ◆, ◆, ◆, ◆, ◆, ◆, ◆, ◆, ◆\}$

$\{◇, ◇, ◇, ◇, ◇, ◇, ◇, ◇, ◇, ◇, ◇, ◇, ◇, ◇, ◇, ◇, ◇, ◇, ◇\}$

$\{■, ■, ■, ■, ■, ■, ■, ■, ■\}$

$\{△, △, △, △, △, △, △, △, △\}$

$\{\underline{○, ○, ○, ○, ○, ○,}\ ○, ○, ○, ○, ○, ○\}$

$\{\ \ \}$

REMINDER: What are the four basic mathematical operations?

Unit 91 cont'd ☞

B Fill in the blanks with +, −, ×, or ÷.

① {O, O, O, O, O} __+__ {O, O, O, O, O} = {O, O, O, O, O, O, O, O, O, O}

② {■, ■, ■, ■, ■, ■, ■} ____ 3 = {■, ■, ■, ■, ■, ■, ■}

③ {▲, ▲, ▲, ▲} ____ 4 = {▲, ▲, ▲, ▲, ▲, ▲, ▲, ▲, ▲, ▲, ▲, ▲, ▲, ▲, ▲, ▲}

④ {◇, ◇, ◇, ◇, ◇, ◇, ◇, ◇, ◇} ____ {◇, ◇} = {◇, ◇, ◇, ◇, ◇, ◇, ◇}

⑤ {●, ●, ●, ●, ●, ●, ●, ●, ●, ●} ____ 5 = {●, ●, ●, ●, ●, ●, ●, ●, ●, ●}

⑥ {□, □, □, □} ____ {□, □, □, □} = {□, □, □, □, □, □, □, □}

⑦ {△, △, △, △, △, △, △, △, △, △} ____ {△, △, △, △, △, △} = {△, △, △, △}

⑧ {◆, ◆, ◆, ◆, ◆, ◆, ◆} ____ 2 = {◆, ◆, ◆, ◆, ◆, ◆, ◆, ◆, ◆, ◆, ◆, ◆, ◆, ◆}

⑨ {■, ■, ■, ■, ■, ■, ■} ____ {■, ■, ■} = {■, ■, ■, ■, ■, ■, ■, ■, ■, ■}

⑩ {O, O, O, O, O, O, O, O} ____ 2 = {O, O, O, O, O, O, O, O}

⑪ {◇, ◇, ◇, ◇, ◇, ◇, ◇, ◇, ◇} ____ {◇} = {◇, ◇, ◇, ◇, ◇, ◇, ◇, ◇}

⑫ {▲, ▲, ▲} ____ 5 = {▲, ▲, ▲, ▲, ▲, ▲, ▲, ▲, ▲, ▲, ▲, ▲, ▲, ▲, ▲}

⑬ {O, O} ____ {O, O, O, O, O} = {O, O, O, O, O, O, O}

⑭ {□, □, □, □} ____ {□, □, □, □} = { }

⑮ {△, △, △, △} ____ 4 = {△}

⑯ {◆, ◆} ____ 8 = {◆, ◆, ◆, ◆, ◆, ◆, ◆, ◆, ◆, ◆, ◆, ◆, ◆, ◆, ◆, ◆}

⑰ {■, ■, ■, ■, ■, ■, ■} ____ {■, ■, ■} = {■, ■, ■, ■}

⑱ {O, O, O, O, O} ____ 4 = {O, O, O, O, O}

C Study the paragraphs and identify the mathematical operation: (A) addition, (B) subtraction, (C) multiplication, and (D) division.

① __D__ Bernice purchased 80 pieces of china, which completed 16 place settings. A cup, soup bowl, salad plate, saucer, and dinner plate were included in each place setting. There were 5 pieces in each place setting.

② ____ For his special Valentine, Roger bought 12 boxes of candy. Each box contained 45 assorted chocolates. Roger's Valentine received a total of 540 chocolates.

③ ____ Members of the Foreign Language Club earned $1,086 that was to be spent on a trip to Europe. The school board contributed $2,000 toward the trip, and parents gave a total of $3,647 more. In all $6,733 was collected for the trip.

④ ____ Of 7,497 college freshmen, only 3,243 had decided upon a specific area of study. Four thousand two hundred fifty-four freshmen were classified as undecided.

⑤ ____ When a film production company chose Benton as the site for the filming of a movie, 793 local residents auditioned for various acting jobs. Only 27 local people were hired to act in the movie. The remaining 766 were turned away.

⑥ ____ For 18 days, Eynard's Market recorded daily sales of $1,846. The grocery's total income during the 18-day period was $33,228.

Which Operation Produced Result?

Learning Objective: *We will learn to determine if a solution is the result of addition, subtraction, multiplication or division.*

The four basic mathematical operations are addition, subtraction, multiplication, and division.

EXAMPLE:

A	**B**	**C**	**D**
300	300	300	10
+ 30	− 30	× 30	30)300
330	270	9,000	

A Identify the mathematical operations: (A) addition, (B) subtraction, (C) multiplication, and (D) division.

① __A__
61,311
33,816
29,642
124,769

② ____
64
15)960
90
60
60

③ ____
15,219
6,191
9,028

④ ____
4,167
42
8,334
16,668
175,014

⑤ ____
83,494
79,347
4,147

⑥ ____
3,891
89
35,019
31,128
346,299

⑦ ____
42
31)1,320
124
80
62
R18

⑧ ____
55,550
98,441
153,991

⑨ ____
9,844
18
9,862

⑩ ____
7,162
38
57,296
21,486
272,156

⑪ ____
6,452
3
19,356

⑫ ____
9,095
81
9,014

⑬ ____
524
5)2,620
25
12
10
20
20

⑭ ____
8,068
94
8,162

⑮ ____
4,596
7
32,172

⑯ ____
3,606
90
324,540

⑰ ____
2
34)76
68
R8

⑱ ____
3
86)341
258
R83

⑲ ____
1,473
484
1,957

⑳ ____
5,114
362
4,752

REMINDER: What are the four basic mathematical operations?

Unit 92 cont'd ☛

B Fill in the blanks with +, −, ×, or ÷.

① $633 \underline{\times} 91 = 57,603$ ② $4,067 \underline{} 7 = 581$ ③ $7,451 \underline{} 40 = 7,411$ ④ $6,633 \underline{} 9 = 737$

⑤ $7,745 \underline{} 73 = 7,818$ ⑥ $611 \underline{} 99 = 60,489$ ⑦ $756 \underline{} 19 = 775$ ⑧ $9,736 \underline{} 17 = 9,719$

⑨ $560 \underline{} 39 = 521$ ⑩ $457 \underline{} 28 = 12,796$ ⑪ $6,122 \underline{} 57 = 6,179$ ⑫ $2,839 \underline{} 4 = 11,356$

⑬ $61,221 \underline{} 3 = 20,407$ ⑭ $8,111 \underline{} 212 = 7,899$ ⑮ $501 \underline{} 11 = 5,511$ ⑯ $2,138 \underline{} 12 = 2,150$

⑰ $5,080 \underline{} 4 = 1,270$ ⑱ $577 \underline{} 26 = 15,002$ ⑲ $153 \underline{} 177 = 330$ ⑳ $2,608 \underline{} 4 = 652$

㉑ $5,715 \underline{} 3 = 1,905$ ㉒ $3,178 \underline{} 2 = 6,356$ ㉓ $9,582 \underline{} 15 = 9,567$ ㉔ $917 \underline{} 32 = 885$

㉕ $158 \underline{} 9 = 167$ ㉖ $9,589 \underline{} 17 = 9,572$ ㉗ $3,696 \underline{} 12 = 308$ ㉘ $1,708 \underline{} 12 = 1,696$

㉙ $169 \underline{} 61 = 10,309$ ㉚ $70 \underline{} 8,227 = 8,297$ ㉛ $355 \underline{} 12 = 4,260$ ㉜ $7,855 \underline{} 5 = 1,571$

㉝ $1,202 \underline{} 73 = 1,275$ ㉞ $578 \underline{} 55 = 523$ ㉟ $933 \underline{} 3 = 311$ ㊱ $718 \underline{} 7 = 5,026$

C Write a mathematical sentence for each problem.

① The band "Time Travelers" recorded a total of 463 songs in a 3-year period. Only 16 of these songs were listed among the top 25 on the pop music chart. The other 447 songs never became "hits."
$$463 - 16 = 447$$

② Hair Pro Styling Salon offered a monthly special on haircuts. During the month, 849 customers had their hair cut at the salon. Two hundred more haircuts were given that month than the month before. Haircuts given the previous month totaled 649.

_____

③ At the district meeting of agriculture students and teachers, 369 were in attendance. Twelve times as many students and teachers attended the group's state convention. There were 4,428 in attendance at the state meeting.

_____

④ Journalism students were required to write 5 news stories per week for an entire school term. There were 36 weeks in the school term. Each journalism student wrote 180 stories during this period.

_____

⑤ Three hundred twenty-two musicians gathered at a university-sponsored workshop. During the workshop, musicians played in 7-member bands. The 322 attendees were divided into 46 bands.

_____

⑥ During the first session of training camp, 695 cheerleaders attended. During the second session, 755 cheerleaders came to the camp. Total attendance for the two sessions was 1,450.

_____

Four Operations

Learning Objective: *We will learn to determine if a problem calls for addition, subtraction, multiplication, or division.*

The four basic mathematical operations are addition, subtraction, multiplication, and division.

EXAMPLE: The sum of 300 plus 30 is 330. The remainder of 300 minus 30 is 270. The product of 300 times 30 is 9,000. The quotient of 300 divided by 30 is 10.

A	**B**	**C**	**D**
$300 + 30 = 330$	$300 - 30 = 270$	$300 \times 300 = 9,000$	$300 \div 30 = 10$

A Add, subtract, divide, or multiply.

①
$$\begin{array}{r} 12,130 \\ -\ 9,824 \\ \hline \mathit{2,306} \end{array}$$

②
$$\begin{array}{r} 2,579 \\ \times\ 46 \\ \hline \end{array}$$

③ $82\overline{)3,111}$

④
$$\begin{array}{r} 1,127 \\ 1,134 \\ +\ 8,511 \\ \hline \end{array}$$

⑤
$$\begin{array}{r} 6,551 \\ \times\ 18 \\ \hline \end{array}$$

⑥
$$\begin{array}{r} 9,879 \\ -\ 2,519 \\ \hline \end{array}$$

⑦
$$\begin{array}{r} 22,211 \\ 51,441 \\ +\ 12,135 \\ \hline \end{array}$$

⑧
$$\begin{array}{r} 1,370 \\ \times\ 81 \\ \hline \end{array}$$

⑨
$$\begin{array}{r} 7,648 \\ -\ 738 \\ \hline \end{array}$$

⑩ $6\overline{)354}$

⑪
$$\begin{array}{r} 8,130 \\ +\ 94 \\ \hline \end{array}$$

⑫
$$\begin{array}{r} 7,268 \\ \times\ 6 \\ \hline \end{array}$$

⑬
$$\begin{array}{r} 3,967 \\ +\ 4,829 \\ \hline \end{array}$$

⑭
$$\begin{array}{r} 4,315 \\ \times\ 30 \\ \hline \end{array}$$

⑮
$$\begin{array}{r} 6,145 \\ \times\ 33 \\ \hline \end{array}$$

⑯
$$\begin{array}{r} 4,058 \\ -\ 38 \\ \hline \end{array}$$

⑰ $9\overline{)495}$

⑱
$$\begin{array}{r} 1,351 \\ 2,234 \\ 187 \\ +\ 65 \\ \hline \end{array}$$

⑲ $7\overline{)119}$

⑳ $4\overline{)932}$

㉑
$$\begin{array}{r} 506 \\ \times\ 52 \\ \hline \end{array}$$

㉒
$$\begin{array}{r} 390 \\ -\ 23 \\ \hline \end{array}$$

㉓
$$\begin{array}{r} 13,045 \\ +\ 922 \\ \hline \end{array}$$

㉔ $13\overline{)1,227}$

㉕
$$\begin{array}{r} 854 \\ \times\ 11 \\ \hline \end{array}$$

㉖
$$\begin{array}{r} 4,297 \\ \times\ 40 \\ \hline \end{array}$$

㉗ $19\overline{)126}$

㉘
$$\begin{array}{r} 1,185 \\ 2,691 \\ +\ 454 \\ \hline \end{array}$$

㉙
$$\begin{array}{r} 8,171 \\ -\ 6,157 \\ \hline \end{array}$$

㉚ $94\overline{)566}$

REMINDER: *What are the four basic mathematical operations?*

_____

_____

Unit 93 cont'd 👉

B Add, subtract, divide, or multiply.

1. $1,012 \div 4 =$ **253**
2. $1,922 + 211 =$
3. $51,441 - 1,213 =$
4. $5,133 \times 4 =$
5. $3,187 + 119 =$
6. $7,932 - 120 =$
7. $695 \times 6 =$
8. $5,239 \div 13 =$
9. $2,313 - 654 =$
10. $592 \div 8 =$
11. $2,101 + 2,543 =$
12. $682 - 278 =$
13. $5,411 \times 4 =$
14. $5,436 \div 9 =$
15. $297 \times 40 =$
16. $3,150 \div 50 =$
17. $811 + 7,526 =$
18. $9,145 - 4,811 =$
19. $7,100 \times 6 =$
20. $1,579 + 456 =$
21. $6,386 - 4,547 =$
22. $990 \div 15 =$
23. $1,508 \div 4 =$
24. $218 + 4,416 =$
25. $8,362 - 1,738 =$
26. $1,618 + 542 =$
27. $4,911 \times 9 =$
28. $6,381 \div 9 =$
29. $4,455 \times 4 =$
30. $2,580 \div 6 =$
31. $5,532 - 4,073 =$
32. $5,569 + 739 =$
33. $893 + 3,994 =$
34. $6,357 \times 7 =$
35. $486 \times 7 =$
36. $7,144 \div 8 =$

C Write a mathematical sentence for each problem. Solve the problems. Use blank space, if necessary.

1. Tickets to a football game sold for $5 apiece. A total of 547 tickets were sold. What was the income from ticket sales?

   _____

2. Two hundred twelve singers auditioned for the part of Patsy Montana in a school musical. An equal number auditioned each of 4 days. How many auditioned each day?

   _____

3. During a period of high unemployment, 974 applicants competed for 59 state jobs. How many applicants were not hired for one of these state jobs?

   _____

4. The college museum held on display a total of 1,897 artifacts. After the death of one of the founders of the college, 149 items were added to the collection. What was the total?

   _____

226

Writing Fractions

Learning Objective: **We will learn to write fractions.**

A fraction is a numerical representation of some portion of a whole.

EXAMPLES: Figure A represents 1 of 2 equal portions, or 1/2 of the whole.
Figure B represents 2 of 2 equal portions, or the whole.

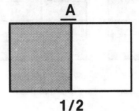   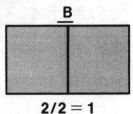

1/2   2/2 = 1

A Fill in the blanks with the correct fractions.

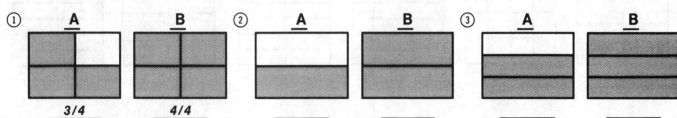

① A **3/4**   B **4/4**   ② A ____ B ____   ③ A ____ B ____

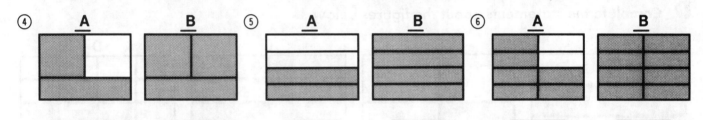

④ A ____ B ____   ⑤ A ____ B ____   ⑥ A ____ B ____

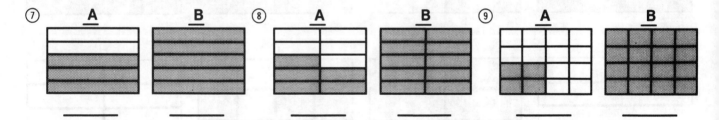

⑦ A ____ B ____   ⑧ A ____ B ____   ⑨ A ____ B ____

B Which fractions are represented by these figures?

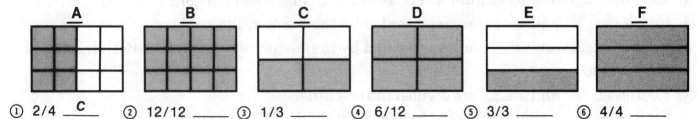

A   B   C   D   E   F

① 2/4 __C__   ② 12/12 ____   ③ 1/3 ____   ④ 6/12 ____   ⑤ 3/3 ____   ⑥ 4/4 ____

REMINDER: Write the definition of a fraction.

_____

_____

Unit 94 cont'd ☞

C Write fractions that represent the shaded portions of the figures below. Circle all fractions that represent the whole, or one.

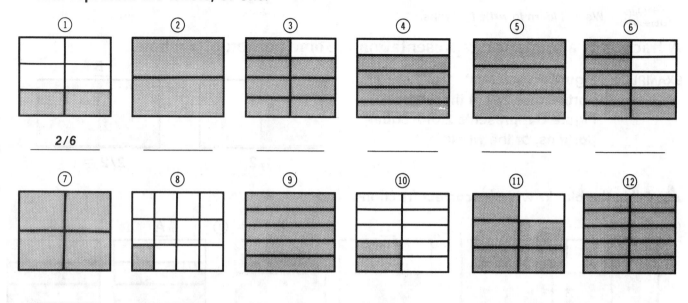

①
__2/6__

②
_____

③
_____

④
_____

⑤
_____

⑥
_____

⑦
_____

⑧
_____

⑨
_____

⑩
_____

⑪
_____

⑫
_____

D Complete the statements about the figures below.

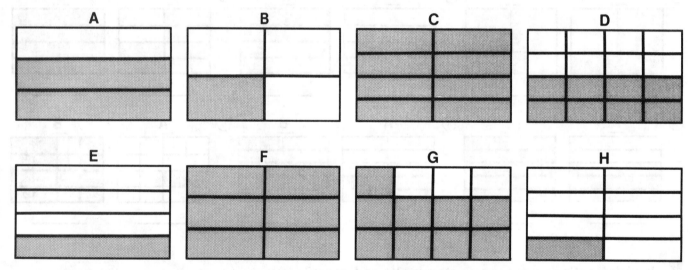

① The shaded portions of figure A represent ___2___ of 3 equal portions.

② Figures _____ and _____ are represented by the fraction 1/4.

③ Figures _____ and _____ are represented by the fractions 8/8 and 6/6. Both fractions are equal to 1.

④ Figures _____ and _____ are divided into eighths.

⑤ Eight of _____ equal portions of figure D are shaded. This is represented by the fraction _____ .

⑥ Figure _____ is represented by the fraction 9/12. Nine of _____ equal portions are shaded.

The Fraction 1/2 Unit 95

Learning
Objective: *We will learn to recognize the fraction 1/2 and its equivalents.*

A fraction is a numerical representation of some portion of a whole.

EXAMPLES: The fraction 1/2 represents 1 of
2 equal portions, or one-half of
the whole. Figure B shows that
2/4 also equals 1/2 of the whole.

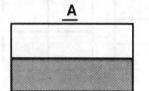 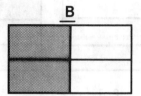

A The first figure in each row represents the whole, or 1. Place a check (✓) beneath each
shaded figure that represents 1/2 of the whole.

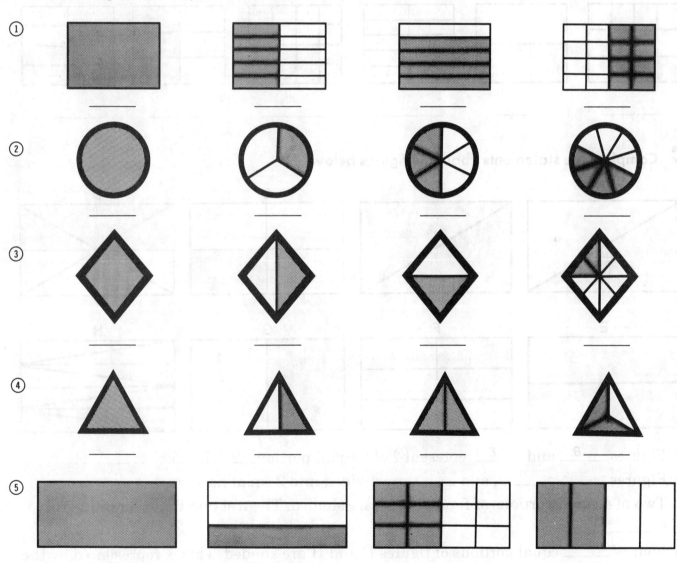

REMINDER: Write the definition of a fraction.

Unit 95 cont'd ☞

B Write the fractions that represent the shaded portions of the figures below. Circle all fractions that are equal to 1/2 of the whole.

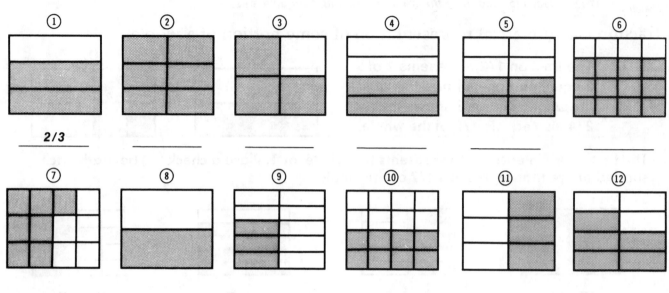

① 2/3 ② _____ ③ _____ ④ _____ ⑤ _____ ⑥ _____

⑦ _____ ⑧ _____ ⑨ _____ ⑩ _____ ⑪ _____ ⑫ _____

C Complete the statements about the figures below.

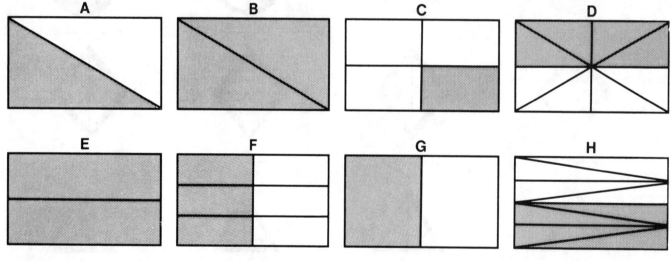

① Figures __B__ and __E__ represent 2 of 2 equal portions. 2/2 is equal to __1__ .

② Figures _____ , _____ , and _____ are divided into 2 equal halves.

③ Two of 4 equal portions of figure _____ are shaded. The fraction that represents this is _____ .

④ Four of _____ equal portions of figures D and H are shaded. This is represented by the fraction _____ .

⑤ Figure F is divided into _____ equal portions. _____ of these portions are shaded. Figure F is represented by the fraction _____ .

⑥ In figures _____ , _____ , _____ , _____ , and _____ , one-half of the whole is shaded.

230

Comprehension Check

A Fill in the blanks with $+$, $-$, $\times$, or $\div$.

① $\{O, O, O, O, O\} \underline{\times} 2 = \{O, O, O, O, O, O, O, O, O, O\}$

② $\{\blacktriangle, \blacktriangle, \blacktriangle, \blacktriangle, \blacktriangle\} \underline{\hspace{1cm}} 2 = \{\blacktriangle, \blacktriangle, \blacktriangle, \blacktriangle, \blacktriangle\}$

③ $\{\square, \square, \square, \square, \square, \square\} \underline{\hspace{1cm}} \{\square, \square, \square\} = \{\square, \square, \square\}$

④ $\{\blacklozenge, \blacklozenge, \blacklozenge, \blacklozenge, \blacklozenge, \blacklozenge\} \underline{\hspace{1cm}} 3 = \{\blacklozenge, \blacklozenge, \blacklozenge, \blacklozenge, \blacklozenge, \blacklozenge\}$

⑤ $\{\bullet, \bullet, \bullet, \bullet, \bullet, \bullet, \bullet\} \underline{\hspace{1cm}} \{\bullet, \bullet, \bullet, \bullet, \bullet, \bullet, \bullet\} = \{\hspace{1cm}\}$

⑥ $\{\blacksquare, \blacksquare, \blacksquare, \blacksquare, \blacksquare\} \underline{\hspace{1cm}} \{\blacksquare, \blacksquare\} = \{\blacksquare, \blacksquare, \blacksquare, \blacksquare, \blacksquare, \blacksquare, \blacksquare\}$

⑦ $\{\diamond, \diamond, \diamond, \diamond, \diamond\} \underline{\hspace{1cm}} \{\diamond, \diamond\} = \{\diamond, \diamond, \diamond\}$

⑧ $\{\bullet, \bullet, \bullet, \bullet, \bullet, \bullet, \bullet\} \underline{\hspace{1cm}} 3 = \{\bullet, \bullet, \bullet, \bullet, \bullet, \bullet, \bullet, \bullet, \bullet, \bullet,$
$\bullet, \bullet, \bullet, \bullet, \bullet, \bullet, \bullet, \bullet, \bullet, \bullet, \bullet\}$

⑨ $\{\triangle, \triangle, \triangle, \triangle, \triangle, \triangle\} \underline{\hspace{1cm}} \{\triangle, \triangle, \triangle\} =$
$\{\triangle, \triangle, \triangle, \triangle, \triangle, \triangle, \triangle, \triangle, \triangle\}$

⑩ $\{\square, \square, \square, \square, \square, \square, \square\} \underline{\hspace{1cm}} 7 = \{\square\}$

B Fill in the blanks with $+$, $-$, $\times$, or $\div$.

① $8,099 \underline{\div} 13 = 623$

② $4,131 \underline{\hspace{1cm}} 984 = 3,147$

③ $795 \underline{\hspace{1cm}} 3 = 2,385$

④ $8,792 \underline{\hspace{1cm}} 2,541 = 6,251$

⑤ $34,841 \underline{\hspace{1cm}} 5,138 = 39,979$

⑥ $13 \underline{\hspace{1cm}} 442 = 5,746$

⑦ $7,645 \underline{\hspace{1cm}} 55 = 139$

⑧ $6,925 \underline{\hspace{1cm}} 25 = 277$

⑨ $4,436 \underline{\hspace{1cm}} 2,542 = 1,894$

⑩ $2,498 \underline{\hspace{1cm}} 567 = 3,065$

⑪ $451 \underline{\hspace{1cm}} 762 = 1,213$

⑫ $2,712 \underline{\hspace{1cm}} 8 = 339$

⑬ $7,881 \underline{\hspace{1cm}} 935 = 8,816$

⑭ $756 \underline{\hspace{1cm}} 12 = 63$

⑮ $4,971 \underline{\hspace{1cm}} 3,518 = 1,453$

⑯ $1,329 \underline{\hspace{1cm}} 6 = 7,974$

⑰ $5,957 \underline{\hspace{1cm}} 7 = 851$

⑱ $591 \underline{\hspace{1cm}} 406 = 185$

C Add, subtract, divide, or multiply.

①
$$7\overline{)3,402} \quad \mathbf{486}$$
$$\underline{28}$$
$$60$$
$$\underline{56}$$
$$42$$
$$\underline{42}$$

②
$$3,183$$
$$\underline{\times 52}$$

③
$$69,783$$
$$\underline{-59,296}$$

④
$$47,093$$
$$17,915$$
$$\underline{+24,348}$$

⑤
$$8,419$$
$$\underline{\times 8}$$

⑥
$$17\overline{)483}$$

⑦
$$2,495$$
$$317$$
$$9,152$$
$$\underline{+2,434}$$

⑧
$$9\overline{)657}$$

⑨
$$348$$
$$\underline{\times 45}$$

⑩
$$6\overline{)4,170}$$

⑪
$$288$$
$$47$$
$$\underline{+604}$$

⑫
$$2,168$$
$$\underline{\times 57}$$

⑬
$$12\overline{)4,260}$$

⑭
$$4,092$$
$$\underline{\times 6}$$

⑮
$$26\overline{)1,872}$$

⑯
$$78,882$$
$$\underline{-51,185}$$

⑰
$$7\overline{)5,026}$$

⑱
$$3,295$$
$$362$$
$$5,413$$
$$\underline{+4,826}$$

Test 19 cont'd ☞

D Write fractions that represent the shaded portions of the figures below. Circle all fractions that represent the whole, or 1.

① ② ③ ④ ⑤ ⑥

3/4 ___ ___ ___ ___ ___ ___

⑦ ⑧ ⑨ ⑩ ⑪ ⑫

___ ___ ___ ___ ___ ___

E Write fractions that represent the shaded portions of the figures below. Circle all fractions that equal 1/2.

① ② ③ ④ ⑤ ⑥

2/2 ___ ___ ___ ___ ___ ___

⑦ ⑧ ⑨ ⑩ ⑪ ⑫

___ ___ ___ ___ ___ ___

Write a paragraph that includes 1 of the 4 basic mathematical operations.

_____

_____

_____

_____

The Fraction 1/3

Learning Objective: *We will learn to recognize the fraction 1/3 and its equivalents.*

A fraction is a numerical representation of some portion of a whole.

EXAMPLE:
The fraction 1/3 represents 1 of 3 equal portions, or one-third of the whole. Figure B shows that 2/6 also equals 1/3 of the whole.

A   B

A The first figure in each row represents the whole, or 1. Place a check (✓) beneath the figures that represent 1/3 of the whole.

①

②

③          

④

REMINDER: Write the definition of a fraction.

Unit 96 cont'd ☞

B Write the fractions that represent the shaded portions of the figures below. Circle all fractions that are equal to 1/3 of the whole.

① ② ③ ④ ⑤ ⑥ ⑦

___3/3___ _____ _____ _____ _____ _____ _____

⑧ ⑨ ⑩ ⑪ ⑫ ⑬ ⑭

_____ _____ _____ _____ _____ _____ _____

C Complete the statements about the figures below.

A   B   C   D   E   F   G

① Three of three equal portions are shaded in figure _____**A**_____ . 3/3 is equal to _____**1**_____ .

② Figures _____ and _____ are divided into 3 equal thirds.

③ Two of three equal portions are shaded in figure _____ . The fraction that represents this is _____ .

④ Four of six equal portions are shaded in figure _____ . The fraction that represents this is _____ , which is equal to 2/3.

⑤ Figure D is divided into _____ equal portions. _____ of these portions are shaded. Figure D is represented by the fraction _____ , which equals 2/3.

⑥ Figures F and G are divided into _____ equal portions. Only in figure _____ is one-third of the whole shaded. The fraction _____ represents figure G.

The Fraction 1/4

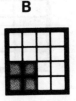

Learning Objective: *We will learn to recognize the fraction 1/4 and its equivalents.*

A fraction is a numerical representation of some portion of a whole.

EXAMPLE:
The fraction 1/4 represents 1 of 4 equal portions, or one-fourth of the whole. Figure B shows that 4/16 also equals 1/4 of the whole.

A   B

A The first figure in each row represents the whole, or 1. Place a check (✓) beneath the figures that represent 1/4 of the whole.

①

_____   _____   _____

②

_____   _____   _____

③          

_____   _____   _____

④

_____   _____   _____

REMINDER: Write the definition of a fraction.

_____

_____

B Write the fractions that represent the shaded portions of the figures below. Circle all fractions that are equal to 1/4 of the whole.

① ② ③ ④ ⑤ ⑥ ⑦

__1/2__   _____   _____   _____   _____   _____   _____

⑧ ⑨ ⑩ ⑪ ⑫ ⑬ ⑭

_____   _____   _____   _____   _____   _____   _____

C Complete the statements about the figures below.

A   B   C   D   E   F   G

① Four of ____4____ equal portions are shaded in figure A.

② Figures _____ , _____ , _____ , and _____ are divided into 4 equal fourths.

③ Four of _____ equal portions are shaded in figure B. Figure B is represented by the fraction _____ , which is equal to 2/4 and 1/2.

④ Three of 4 equal portions are shaded in figure _____ . This is represented by the fraction _____ , which is equal to 9/12 and 6/8.

⑤ Only in figure _____ is one-fourth of the whole shaded.

⑥ In figure C, _____ of _____ equal portions are shaded. The fraction that represents this is _____ .

236

Fractions

Learning Objective: *We will learn to identify the parts of a fraction.*

The denominator is the number below the line and represents the total number of portions into which a unit has been divided. The numerator, or the number above the line, represents the number of portions being considered.

EXAMPLE: In the figure at the right, 3 of a total of 4 portions have been shaded. The shaded area is 3/4 of the whole. 3 is the numerator. 4 is the denominator.

A Study each figure and fill in the blanks with (a) the numerator, (b) the denominator, and (c) the fraction that represents the shaded area.

① a. _1_
b. _4_
c. _1/4_

② a. ____
b. ____
c. ____

③ a. ____
b. ____
c. ____

④ a. ____
b. ____
c. ____

⑤ a. ____
b. ____
c. ____

⑥ a. ____
b. ____
c. ____

⑦ a. ____
b. ____
c. ____

⑧ a. ____
b. ____
c. ____

⑨ a. ____
b. ____
c. ____

⑩ a. ____
b. ____
c. ____

⑪ a. ____
b. ____
c. ____

⑫ a. ____
b. ____
c. ____

⑬ a. ____
b. ____
c. ____

⑭ a. ____
b. ____
c. ____

⑮ a. ____
b. ____
c. ____

⑯ a. ____
b. ____
c. ____

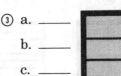

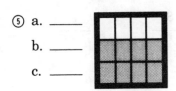

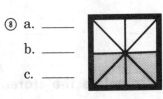

B Circle the fractions that equal 1/2.

3/8 2/4 4/6 2/3 10/10 3/6 1/8 8/16 12/24

C Circle the fractions that equal 1/4.

2/8 8/12 3/5 4/16 2/3 1/4 5/8 8/16 2/2

REMINDER: Write the definition of the denominator and the numerator.

Unit 98 cont'd ☛

D Study the figures below. Fill in the blanks with the correct denominators. Shade the number of portions represented by the numerators.

① ② ③ ④ ⑤ ⑥ ⑦

$$\frac{3}{4} \qquad \frac{1}{\quad} \qquad \frac{3}{\quad} \qquad \frac{2}{\quad} \qquad \frac{1}{\quad} \qquad \frac{3}{\quad} \qquad \frac{3}{\quad}$$

⑧ ⑨ ⑩ ⑪ ⑫ ⑬ ⑭

$$\frac{4}{\quad} \qquad \frac{5}{\quad} \qquad \frac{3}{\quad} \qquad \frac{8}{\quad} \qquad \frac{9}{\quad} \qquad \frac{8}{\quad} \qquad \frac{2}{\quad}$$

E Complete the statements about the figures below.

A   B   C   D   E   F   G

① The fractions that represent the shaded portions of figures _____**B**_____ and _____**F**_____ share a common numerator, 2.

② Figures A and E are each divided into a total of _____ portions.

③ Only one of the total number of portions is shaded in Figures _____ , _____ , and _____ .

④ Figures _____ and _____ show that the fractions 3/4 and 6/8 are equal.

⑤ Figures C and F show that the fractions _____ and _____ are equal.

⑥ The fraction that represents the shaded portion of figure _____ has a denominator of 4.

⑦ Only figure _____ is represented by the denominator 6.

238

Adding Fractions

Learning Objective: *We will learn to add fractions that share common denominators.*

A fraction is a numerical representation or some portion of a whole.

EXAMPLE: If two or more fractions share a common denominator, they can be added. One numerator is added to another. The denominators remain unchanged.

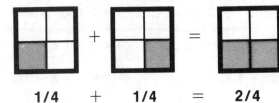

1/4 + 1/4 = 2/4

A Write an addition sentence for each trio of figures.

① +  =

    1/3 + 2/3 = 3/3

② + =

    _____ + _____ = _____

③ +  =

    _____ + _____ = _____

④ + =

    _____ + _____ = _____

⑤ +  =

    _____ + _____ = _____

⑥ + =

    _____ + _____ = _____

⑦  + =

    _____ + _____ = _____

⑧ + =

    _____ + _____ = _____

REMINDER: Write the definition of a fraction.

_____

Unit 99 cont'd ☞

B Add these fractions.

① 1/3 + 1/3 + 1/3 = __3/3__   ② 4/12 + 3/12 + 1/12 = _____   ③ 3/8 + 2/8 + 2/8 = _____

④ 3/10 + 1/10 + 4/10 = _____   ⑤ 8/16 + 1/16 + 5/16 = _____   ⑥ 9/24 + 6/24 + 4/24 = _____

⑦ 4/9 + 2/9 + 1/9 = _____   ⑧ 3/7 + 1/7 + 2/7 = _____   ⑨ 1/5 + 2/5 + 1/5 = _____

⑩ 5/10 + 2/10 + 1/10 = _____   ⑪ 4/6 + 1/6 + 1/6 = _____   ⑫ 6/18 + 5/18 + 6/18 = _____

⑬ 9/12 + 1/12 + 1/12 = _____   ⑭ 2/8 + 1/8 + 3/8 = _____   ⑮ 2/16 + 7/16 + 3/16 = _____

⑯ 2/5 + 1/5 + 2/5 = _____   ⑰ 7/18 + 3/18 + 5/18 = _____   ⑱ 3/6 + 1/6 + 1/6 = _____

⑲ 2/10 + 3/10 + 3/10 = _____   ⑳ 3/24 + 3/24 + 3/24 = _____   ㉑ 5/9 + 1/9 + 2/9 = _____

㉒ 6/12 + 3/12 + 2/12 = _____   ㉓ 3/16 + 4/16 + 5/16 = _____   ㉔ 1/7 + 3/7 + 1/7 = _____

㉕ 1/8 + 2/8 + 2/8 = _____   ㉖ 2/18 + 4/18 + 3/18 = _____   ㉗ 1/4 + 1/4 + 1/4 = _____

㉘ 4/10 + 1/10 + 5/10 = _____   ㉙ 11/24 + 3/24 + 4/24 = _____   ㉚ 6/9 + 1/9 + 1/9 = _____

㉛ 7/12 + 3/12 + 2/12 = _____   ㉜ 2/16 + 9/16 + 4/16 = _____   ㉝ 2/4 + 1/4 + 1/4 = _____

㉞ 8/24 + 10/24 + 2/24 = _____   ㉟ 3/18 + 3/18 + 1/18 = _____   ㊱ 3/9 + 3/9 + 3/9 = _____

C Write an addition sentence for each problem.

① One-fifth of the senior class at Whitman High School enrolled in college immediately following graduation. Three-fifths of the class found jobs after graduating. What portion of the class either enrolled in college or found employment after graduation?

__1/5 + 3/5 = 4/5__

② When a new factory began hiring employees, 7/10 of the job applicants were turned away without interviews. Another 2/10 of the applicants were interviewed but not hired. What portion of the applicants were not hired?

_____

③ Only 3/8 of the county's registered voters went to the polls during the last presidential election. Another 1/8 of the registered voters voted by absentee ballots. What portion of those registered to vote exercised the privilege during the presidential election?

_____

④ The owners of Baker's Market say that 5/7 of the store's sales are made in the meat department. Another 1/7 of the sales, say the owners, are produce items. What portion of the store's sales are either meat or produce?

_____

⑤ During the first game of the season, only 1/6 of the Wildcats team members were allowed to play. During the second game, the athletes who played during the first game plus another 1/6 of the team went on the field. What portion played during the second game?

_____

⑥ On September 1, 7/12 of the tenants at the Lakeshore Apartments paid their monthly rent. Another 2/12 of the tenants paid their rent between September 2 and September 5. What portion of the tenants paid the rent by September 5?

_____

Subtracting Fractions

Unit 100

Learning Objective: *We will learn to subtract fractions that share common denominators.*

A fraction is a numerical representation or some portion of a whole.

EXAMPLE: We can subtract fractions that share a common denominator. Subtract the smaller numerator from the larger one.

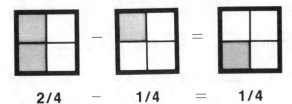

2/4   –   1/4   =   1/4

A Write a subtraction sentence for each trio of figures.

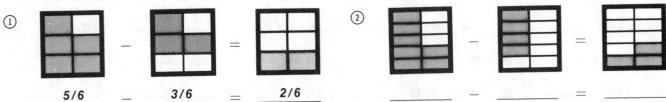

①   5/6   –   3/6   =   2/6   ②

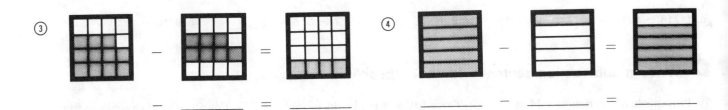

③   ___ – ___ = ___   ④   ___ – ___ = ___

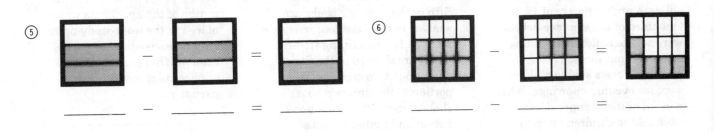

⑤   ___ – ___ = ___   ⑥

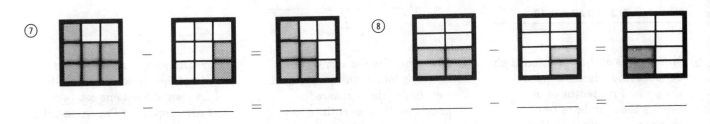

⑦   ___ – ___ = ___   ⑧   ___ – ___ = ___

REMINDER: Write the definition of a fraction.

Unit 100 cont'd ☞

B Subtract these fractions.

① 4/12 − 3/12 = _1/12_   ② 14/16 − 5/16 = _____   ③ 6/24 − 4/24 = _____   ④ 7/9 − 2/9 = _____

⑤ 3/7 − 1/7 = _____   ⑥ 8/10 − 6/10 = _____   ⑦ 2/5 − 1/5 = _____   ⑧ 9/18 − 5/18 = _____

⑨ 6/6 − 2/6 = _____   ⑩ 12/16 − 3/16 = _____   ⑪ 11/12 − 9/12 = _____   ⑫ 6/8 − 3/8 = _____

⑬ 15/18 − 7/18 = _____   ⑭ 3/6 − 1/6 = _____   ⑮ 8/12 − 1/12 = _____   ⑯ 8/10 − 4/10 = _____

⑰ 9/24 − 3/24 = _____   ⑱ 8/9 − 5/9 = _____   ⑲ 11/12 − 6/12 = _____   ⑳ 12/16 − 5/16 = _____

㉑ 5/7 − 1/7 = _____   ㉒ 9/18 − 2/18 = _____   ㉓ 19/24 − 10/24 = _____   ㉔ 3/4 − 1/4 = _____

㉕ 10/10 − 7/10 = _____   ㉖ 3/3 − 2/3 = _____   ㉗ 18/24 − 4/24 = _____   ㉘ 8/9 − 7/9 = _____

㉙ 5/5 − 2/5 = _____   ㉚ 15/16 − 9/16 = _____   ㉛ 17/18 − 3/18 = _____   ㉜ 16/24 − 8/24 = _____

㉝ 2/9 − 1/9 = _____   ㉞ 8/16 − 3/16 = _____   ㉟ 7/12 − 5/12 = _____   ㊱ 5/10 − 4/10 = _____

㊲ 6/7 − 2/7 = _____   ㊳ 11/18 − 10/18 = _____   ㊴ 5/10 − 2/10 = _____   ㊵ 4/12 − 2/12 = _____

㊶ 4/9 − 1/9 = _____   ㊷ 12/12 − 6/12 = _____   ㊸ 20/24 − 6/24 = _____   ㊹ 3/10 − 2/10 = _____

㊺ 11/16 − 8/16 = _____   ㊻ 6/18 − 3/18 = _____   ㊼ 7/7 − 3/7 = _____   ㊽ 4/16 − 3/16 = _____

C Write a subtraction sentence for each problem.

① Two-thirds of the tickets sold at the Winslow Cinema during the summer of 1985 were purchased by children under the age of 12. One third of the summer tickets were sold to children attending afternoon matinees. The remaining tickets sold to children were for evening showings. What portion of the summer tickets were sold to children attending evening showings?

_____ 2/3 − 1/3 = 1/3 _____

② Three-fifths of the books in the Smith County Public Library are housed on the first floor. One-fifth of the library's books are shelved in the first-floor reference section. The remaining first-floor books are shelved in the fiction and non-fiction sections. What portion of the library's books are shelved in the first-floor non-fiction and fiction sections?

_____

③ Four-ninths of the college freshmen who applied for financial aid were granted assistance. Three-ninths of the applicants were placed in the work-study program. Others received full or partial grants. What portion of the applicants received full or partial grants?

_____

④ Nine-tenths of the Smithton High School senior class attended the prom. Five-tenths of the seniors brought dates from other schools. What portion of the class attended, but did not bring dates from other schools?

_____

⑤ Attending the District V Honor Society's fourth annual banquet were 6/7 of the registered members. Two-sevenths of the members helped to organize and attended the event. What portion attended, but did not help organize the banquet?

_____

⑥ A recent survey revealed that 7/16 of the households of Collier City own at least one set of encyclopedias. Two-sixteenths of the households own two or more sets of encyclopedias. What portion of the households own only one set of encyclopedias?

_____

Comprehension Check

A Write the fractions that represent the shaded portions of the figures below. Circle all fractions that are equal to 1/3.

① ② ③ ④ ⑤ ⑥ ⑦

3/3 ____ ____ ____ ____ ____ ____

B Write the fractions that represent the shaded portions of the figures below. Circle all fractions that are equal to 1/4.

① ② ③ ④ ⑤ ⑥ ⑦

3/12 ____ ____ ____ ____ ____ ____

C Complete the statements about the figures below.

A   B   C   D   E   F   G

① Figures ___**B**___ , ___**C**___ , and ___**E**___ are each divided into a total of 3 portions.

② Three portions of the whole are shaded in figures _____ , _____ , and _____ . The common numerator for these three figures is _____ .

③ Six of a total of _____ portions are shaded in figure G. This is represented by the fraction _____ . The numerator of this fraction is _____ . The denominator is _____ .

④ Although the fractions that represent figures _____ , _____ , and _____ share the common denominator 3, they have different numerators.

⑤ Two of a total of 2 portions are shaded in figure _____ . The numerator for this fraction is _____ . The denominator is _____ .

⑥ Figures _____ and _____ show that the fractions 3/4 and 6/8 are equal.

Test 20 cont'd 🖙

D Write an addition or subtraction sentence for each trio of figures.

①  + =   ② − =

$$\underline{\textbf{7/12}} + \underline{\textbf{3/12}} = \underline{\textbf{10/12}}$$

_____ − _____ = _____

③ − =   ④ + =

_____ − _____ = _____

_____ + _____ = _____

⑤ + =    ⑥ − 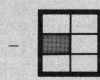 =

_____ + _____ = _____

_____ − _____ = _____

E Add or subtract.

① $3/10 + 5/10 + 1/10 = \underline{\textbf{9/10}}$ ② $9/24 − 2/24 = $ _____   ③ $11/16 − 8/16 = $ _____

④ $1/5 + 1/5 + 2/5 = $ _____   ⑤ $9/9 − 5/9 = $ _____   ⑥ $2/8 + 3/8 + 1/8 = $ _____

⑦ $3/12 + 2/12 + 3/12 = $ _____   ⑧ $7/18 + 3/18 + 4/18 = $ _____   ⑨ $4/5 − 1/5 = $ _____

⑩ $10/16 − 3/16 = $ _____   ⑪ $4/9 + 3/9 + 1/9 = $ _____   ⑫ $8/10 − 3/10 = $ _____

⑬ $7/7 − 4/7 = $ _____   ⑭ $11/24 + 9/24 + 1/24 = $ _____   ⑮ $7/8 − 1/8 = $ _____

⑯ $3/16 + 3/16 + 4/16 = $ _____   ⑰ $1/12 + 8/12 + 2/12 = $ _____   ⑱ $14/18 − 6/18 = $ _____

⑲ $3/7 + 2/7 + 1/7 = $ _____   ⑳ $8/12 − 4/12 = $ _____   ㉑ $1/8 + 1/8 + 1/8 = $ _____

Write two short paragraphs. Include in paragraph 1 a problem in which fractions are to be added. In paragraph 2, include a problem in which fractions are to be subtracted. Write a mathematical sentence for each problem.

① _____   ② _____

_____   _____

_____   _____

_____   _____

_____   _____

_____   _____

244

Remainders in Fractions

*Learning
Objective:* *We will learn to write as fractions the remainders of division problems.*

A remainder is the final undivided part of a division problem.

EXAMPLE: The fraction $^1/_3$ may also be read 1 divided by 3. Remembering that the remainder is always less than the divisor, we may write the remainder as a fraction.

$$\begin{array}{r} 8 \\ 3\overline{)25} \\ 24 \\ \hline R1 \end{array}$$

$$25 \div 3 = 8 \, ^1/_3$$

A Divide. Find the quotients and remainders, then include the remainder in the quotient by writing the remainder as a fraction.

①
$$\begin{array}{r} 118 \\ 6\overline{)713} \\ 6 \\ \hline 11 \\ 6 \\ \hline 53 \\ 48 \\ \hline R5 \end{array}$$
$713 \div 6 = \underline{\quad 118 \, ^5/_6 \quad}$

② $3\overline{)382}$ $382 \div 3 = \underline{\qquad}$

③ $6\overline{)926}$ $926 \div 6 = \underline{\qquad}$

④ $7\overline{)967}$ $967 \div 7 = \underline{\qquad}$

⑤ $4\overline{)519}$ $519 \div 4 = \underline{\qquad}$

⑥ $6\overline{)908}$ $908 \div 6 = \underline{\qquad}$

⑦ $4\overline{)761}$ $761 \div 4 = \underline{\qquad}$

⑧ $5\overline{)842}$ $842 \div 5 = \underline{\qquad}$

⑨ $3\overline{)413}$ $413 \div 3 = \underline{\qquad}$

REMINDER: Write the definition of a remainder.

_____

_____

Unit 101 cont'd ☞

B Find the quotients. Write all remainders as fractions.

① $3,265 \div 8 = $ ___**408 $^1/_8$**___ ② $4,579 \div 9 = $ _____ ③ $3,614 \div 3 = $ _____ ④ $4,274 \div 7 = $ _____

⑤ $3,684 \div 9 = $ _____ ⑥ $2,843 \div 4 = $ _____ ⑦ $1,265 \div 2 = $ _____ ⑧ $5,559 \div 5 = $ _____

⑨ $4,041 \div 8 = $ _____ ⑩ $3,057 \div 5 = $ _____ ⑪ $9,814 \div 9 = $ _____ ⑫ $6,482 \div 8 = $ _____

⑬ $1,465 \div 7 = $ _____ ⑭ $8,137 \div 9 = $ _____ ⑮ $4,613 \div 2 = $ _____ ⑯ $5,429 \div 6 = $ _____

⑰ $2,468 \div 6 = $ _____ ⑱ $6,325 \div 3 = $ _____ ⑲ $1,835 \div 6 = $ _____ ⑳ $9,095 \div 9 = $ _____

㉑ $2,026 \div 5 = $ _____ ㉒ $8,086 \div 4 = $ _____ ㉓ $2,719 \div 9 = $ _____ ㉔ $4,546 \div 5 = $ _____

㉕ $7,351 \div 7 = $ _____ ㉖ $6,062 \div 3 = $ _____ ㉗ $3,285 \div 4 = $ _____ ㉘ $3,285 \div 6 = $ _____

㉙ $8,647 \div 2 = $ _____ ㉚ $2,483 \div 8 = $ _____ ㉛ $1,537 \div 5 = $ _____ ㉜ $4,541 \div 9 = $ _____

C Write a division sentence for each problem. Write all remainders as fractions. Use the blank space to work the problems.

① The Equine Club's annual trail ride is a 14-day event. During these 14 days, club members travel an equal number of miles per day on horseback. Total miles traveled is 276. How many miles are traveled each day?

_____

② The Lion's Mane styling salon advertised longer business hours during its 7-day grand opening. The total number of hours during which the shop was open in those 7 days was 110. If the business hours were the same each day, how many hours was the shop open?

_____

③ A total of 50 reams of typing paper were distributed to students in the advanced typing class. Each of the 27 students received an equal amount of paper. How many reams of paper did each student receive?

_____

④ Cafeteria cooks prepared a total of 97 doughnuts for one noon meal. If 41 persons were served lunch that day, how many doughnuts or portions of doughnuts were available for each person?

_____

246

Mixed Numbers

Learning Objective: *We will learn to write improper fractions as mixed numbers.*

A mixed number is made up of both a whole number and a fraction.

EXAMPLE: An improper fraction has a numerator that is larger than its denominator. We may write an improper fraction as a mixed number.

$$^5/_2 = 5 \div 2 = 2\,^1/_2$$

A Write these improper fractions as mixed numbers.

① $^{19}/_2 = \underline{19 \div 2 = 9\ ^1/_2}$ ② $^9/_5 = \underline{\hspace{3cm}}$ ③ $^4/_3 = \underline{\hspace{3cm}}$

④ $^8/_6 = \underline{\hspace{3cm}}$ ⑥ $^{13}/_9 = \underline{\hspace{3cm}}$ ⑥ $^{15}/_{10} = \underline{\hspace{3cm}}$

⑦ $^{17}/_{11} = \underline{\hspace{3cm}}$ ⑧ $^5/_3 = \underline{\hspace{3cm}}$ ⑨ $^{47}/_9 = \underline{\hspace{3cm}}$

⑩ $^{15}/_4 = \underline{\hspace{3cm}}$ ⑪ $^{63}/_8 = \underline{\hspace{3cm}}$ ⑫ $^9/_6 = \underline{\hspace{3cm}}$

⑬ $^{22}/_{21} = \underline{\hspace{3cm}}$ ⑭ $^{41}/_5 = \underline{\hspace{3cm}}$ ⑮ $^{23}/_8 = \underline{\hspace{3cm}}$

⑯ $^{27}/_7 = \underline{\hspace{3cm}}$ ⑰ $^{33}/_4 = \underline{\hspace{3cm}}$ ⑱ $^{17}/_5 = \underline{\hspace{3cm}}$

⑲ $^7/_6 = \underline{\hspace{3cm}}$ ⑳ $^{20}/_3 = \underline{\hspace{3cm}}$ ㉑ $^{74}/_9 = \underline{\hspace{3cm}}$

㉒ $^{29}/_5 = \underline{\hspace{3cm}}$ ㉓ $^9/_4 = \underline{\hspace{3cm}}$ ㉔ $^{13}/_2 = \underline{\hspace{3cm}}$

㉕ $^{44}/_{33} = \underline{\hspace{3cm}}$ ㉖ $^{55}/_9 = \underline{\hspace{3cm}}$ ㉗ $^{31}/_7 = \underline{\hspace{3cm}}$

㉘ $^{79}/_8 = \underline{\hspace{3cm}}$ ㉙ $^{22}/_4 = \underline{\hspace{3cm}}$ ㉚ $^8/_7 = \underline{\hspace{3cm}}$

㉛ $^{19}/_9 = \underline{\hspace{3cm}}$ ㉜ $^{12}/_8 = \underline{\hspace{3cm}}$ ㉝ $^{89}/_{44} = \underline{\hspace{3cm}}$

㉞ $^{93}/_{45} = \underline{\hspace{3cm}}$ ㉟ $^3/_{45} = \underline{\hspace{3cm}}$ ㊱ $^{18}/_{16} = \underline{\hspace{3cm}}$

㊲ $^{101}/_{25} = \underline{\hspace{3cm}}$ ㊳ $^{13}/_4 = \underline{\hspace{3cm}}$ ㊴ $^{62}/_5 = \underline{\hspace{3cm}}$

REMINDER: Write the definition of a mixed number.

B Match the improper fractions with the mixed numbers of equal value.

① $^{43}/_9$ $9\,^2/_5$ ⑨ $^{58}/_7$ $2\,^5/_9$ ⑰ $^{31}/_4$ $2\,^1/_6$ ㉕ $^{47}/_3$ $16\,^1/_2$

② $^{13}/_2$ $4\,^7/_9$ ⑩ $^{23}/_9$ $3\,^1/_6$ ⑱ $^{55}/_6$ $8\,^3/_7$ ㉖ $^{24}/_5$ $9\,^5/_9$

③ $^{47}/_5$ $5\,^1/_4$ ⑪ $^{19}/_6$ $8\,^2/_7$ ⑲ $^{13}/_6$ $9\,^1/_6$ ㉗ $^{86}/_9$ $15\,^2/_3$

④ $^{21}/_4$ $6\,^1/_2$ ⑫ $^{33}/_8$ $4\,^1/_8$ ⑳ $^{59}/_7$ $7\,^3/_4$ ㉘ $^{33}/_2$ $4\,^4/_5$

⑤ $^{67}/_6$ $5\,^1/_{10}$ ⑬ $^{41}/_8$ $5\,^2/_3$ ㉑ $^{79}/_9$ $12\,^1/_4$ ㉙ $^{43}/_8$ $8\,^1/_6$

⑥ $^7/_2$ $4\,^2/_5$ ⑭ $^{17}/_3$ $9\,^4/_7$ ㉒ $^{49}/_4$ $8\,^7/_9$ ㉚ $^{20}/_9$ $1\,^3/_4$

⑦ $^{51}/_{10}$ $11\,^1/_6$ ⑮ $^{43}/_7$ $5\,^1/_8$ ㉓ $^{39}/_9$ $5\,^3/_{10}$ ㉛ $^{49}/_6$ $5\,^3/_8$

⑧ $^{22}/_5$ $3\,^1/_2$ ⑯ $^{67}/_7$ $6\,^1/_7$ ㉔ $^{53}/_{10}$ $4\,^3/_9$ ㉜ $^7/_4$ $2\,^2/_9$

C Solve the problems. Write all improper fractions as mixed numbers.

① A recipe for Chinese egg rolls calls for oil to be added three times during the preparation. Three-eights cup of oil is used to fry the filling. To flavor the filling, ⅛ cup of sesame oil is added. The egg rolls are finally deep-fried in ⅞ cup of oil. How many cups of oil are used?

$^3/_8 + ^1/_8 + ^7/_8 = {}^{11}/_8 = 1\,^3/_8$

_____

② During Christmas vacation from school, Rodney gained weight. He gained $^3/_{10}$ of a pound during the first week of vacation. In the second week, he gained another $^7/_{10}$ of a pound. The third week of vacation, Rodney gained $^9/_{10}$ of a pound. How many pounds did he gain?

_____

③ Liz baked three pies for a family reunion. After the reunion, $^1/_6$ of the apple pie was left. Three-sixths of the pecan pie was uneaten, as was $^5/_6$ of the pumpkin pie. How much pie did Liz take home following the reunion?

_____

④ Between his 15th and 16th birthdays, Dalton grew $^{11}/_{16}$ of an inch. Between birthdays 16 and 17, he grew $^7/_{16}$ of an inch. During the following year, he grew another, $^9/_{16}$ of an inch. How many inches did he grow in the 3 years?

_____

⑤ When she started jogging for exercise, Rhea ran $^5/_{10}$ of a mile on the first day. The next day, she ran $^8/_{10}$ of a mile. On the third day, Rhea increased the run to $^9/_{10}$ of a mile. How many miles did she run in the three days?

_____

⑥ At the beginning of summer, Jan cut $^{11}/_{12}$ of an inch off her long hair. One week later, she cut $^9/_{12}$ of an inch. Less than a month later, Jan cut another $^7/_{12}$ of an inch off her hair. How many inches did she cut in all?

_____

One as a Factor   Unit 103

Learning Objective: *We will learn to recognize 1 as a factor of all counting numbers.*

A factor is a multiplier that, when multiplied with another factor forms a product.

EXAMPLE: One is a factor of all counting numbers. $1 \times 2 = 2$ "One" and "two" are factors of 2. If the order of the factors is reversed, the product is the same.

$1 \times 1 = 1$	$1 \times 1 = 1$
$1 \times 2 = 2$	$2 \times 1 = 2$
$1 \times 3 = 3$	$3 \times 1 = 3$

A Find the missing factors.

① $1 \times \underline{\quad 6 \quad} = 6$　② $1 \times \underline{\quad} = 13$　③ $1 \times \underline{\quad} = 9$　④ $1 \times \underline{\quad} = 25$　⑤ $1 \times \underline{\quad} = 94$

⑥ $1 \times \underline{\quad} = 40$　⑦ $1 \times \underline{\quad} = 8$　⑧ $1 \times \underline{\quad} = 16$　⑨ $1 \times \underline{\quad} = 33$　⑩ $1 \times \underline{\quad} = 67$

⑪ $1 \times \underline{\quad} = 77$　⑫ $1 \times \underline{\quad} = 99$　⑬ $1 \times \underline{\quad} = 11$　⑭ $1 \times \underline{\quad} = 15$　⑮ $1 \times \underline{\quad} = 10$

⑯ $1 \times \underline{\quad} = 117$　⑰ $1 \times \underline{\quad} = 12$　⑱ $1 \times \underline{\quad} = 84$　⑲ $1 \times \underline{\quad} = 47$　⑳ $1 \times \underline{\quad} = 161$

㉑ $1 \times \underline{\quad} = 54$　㉒ $1 \times \underline{\quad} = 63$　㉓ $1 \times \underline{\quad} = 18$　㉔ $1 \times \underline{\quad} = 91$　㉕ $1 \times \underline{\quad} = 19$

㉖ $1 \times \underline{\quad} = 31$　㉗ $1 \times \underline{\quad} = 22$　㉘ $1 \times \underline{\quad} = 710$　㉙ $1 \times \underline{\quad} = 50$　㉚ $1 \times \underline{\quad} = 79$

㉛ $1 \times \underline{\quad} = 111$　㉜ $1 \times \underline{\quad} = 51$　㉝ $1 \times \underline{\quad} = 86$　㉞ $1 \times \underline{\quad} = 72$　㉟ $1 \times \underline{\quad} = 39$

㊱ $\underline{\quad} \times 1 = 5$　㊲ $\underline{\quad} \times 1 = 26$　㊳ $\underline{\quad} \times 1 = 300$　㊴ $\underline{\quad} \times 1 = 88$　㊵ $\underline{\quad} \times 1 = 53$

㊶ $\underline{\quad} \times 1 = 48$　㊷ $\underline{\quad} \times 1 = 14$　㊸ $\underline{\quad} \times 1 = 95$　㊹ $\underline{\quad} \times 1 = 415$　㊺ $\underline{\quad} \times 1 = 24$

㊻ $\underline{\quad} \times 1 = 64$　㊼ $\underline{\quad} \times 1 = 46$　㊽ $\underline{\quad} \times 1 = 92$　㊾ $\underline{\quad} \times 1 = 110$　㊿ $\underline{\quad} \times 1 = 56$

51) $\underline{\quad} \times 1 = 29$　52) $\underline{\quad} \times 1 = 98$　53) $\underline{\quad} \times 1 = 82$　54) $\underline{\quad} \times 1 = 23$　55) $\underline{\quad} \times 1 = 242$

56) $\underline{\quad} \times 1 = 42$　57) $\underline{\quad} \times 1 = 107$　58) $\underline{\quad} \times 1 = 34$　59) $\underline{\quad} \times 1 = 93$　60) $\underline{\quad} \times 1 = 820$

61) $\underline{\quad} \times 1 = 97$　62) $\underline{\quad} \times 1 = 133$　63) $\underline{\quad} \times 1 = 28$　64) $\underline{\quad} \times 1 = 216$　65) $\underline{\quad} \times 1 = 44$

66) $\underline{\quad} \times 1 = 27$　67) $\underline{\quad} \times 1 = 500$　68) $\underline{\quad} \times 1 = 62$　69) $\underline{\quad} \times 1 = 303$　70) $\underline{\quad} \times 1 = 57$

REMINDER: Write the definition of a factor.

_____

_____

Unit 103 cont'd ☛

B Match the products in columns A with their factors in columns B.

A	B	A	B	A	B	A	B
① 90	75, 1	⑨ 41	59, 1	⑰ 87	1, 89	㉕ 55	1, 45
② 75	83, 1	⑩ 59	1, 60	⑱ 30	1, 87	㉖ 73	1,55
③ 21	1, 90	⑪ 60	41, 1	⑲ 89	30, 1	㉗ 45	80, 1
④ 83	1, 21	⑫ 96	1, 96	⑳ 42	1, 42	㉘ 80	1, 73
⑤ 52	1, 43	⑬ 70	69, 1	㉑ 58	58, 1	㉙ 85	1, 49
⑥ 68	74, 1	⑭ 20	1, 38	㉒ 71	1, 37	㉚ 32	1, 76
⑦ 43	52, 1	⑮ 69	1, 20	㉓ 37	1, 65	㉛ 76	1, 32
⑧ 74	1, 68	⑯ 38	70, 1	㉔ 65	71, 1	㉜ 49	85, 1

C Underline the correct answers.

① If 1 is multiplied with another factor, the product is always equal to (1, the other factor, 1 plus the other factor).

② One and (47, 36, 24) are factors of 47.

③ The commutative property of multiplication holds that 1×95 forms the same product as $(1 + 95, 95 \div 1, 95 \times 1)$.

④ One and 59 are (products, factors, quotients) of 59.

⑤ One times 100 is (equal to, greater than, less than) 100 times 1.

⑥ Because 68×1 is equal to 68, 68 and 1 are (factors, quotients, products) of 68.

⑦ Factors are (products, dividends, multipliers).

⑧ Seventy-seven has as factors (1 and 70, 10 and 7, 77 and 1).

⑨ If the order of two factors is reversed, the product is (greater, the same, less).

Two as a Factor

Learning Objective: *We will learn to recognize 2 as a factor of all even numbers.*

A factor is a multiplier that, when multiplied with another factor, forms a product.

EXAMPLE: Two is a factor of all even numbers. To find what factor multiplied with 2 forms a certain product, divide the product by 2.

$2 \times 1 = 2$	$2 \div 2 = 1$
$2 \times 2 = 4$	$4 \div 2 = 2$
$2 \times 3 = 6$	$6 \div 2 = 3$

A Find the missing factors.

① $2 \times \underline{\ 9\ } = 18 \div 2$ ② $2 \times \underline{\quad} = 100 \div 2$ ③ $2 \times \underline{\quad} = 48 \div 2$ ④ $2 \times \underline{\quad} = 26 \div 2$

⑤ $2 \times \underline{\quad} = 140 \div 2$ ⑥ $2 \times \underline{\quad} = 54 \div 2$ ⑦ $2 \times \underline{\quad} = 184 \div 2$ ⑧ $2 \times \underline{\quad} = 70 \div 2$

⑨ $2 \times \underline{\quad} = 22 \div 2$ ⑩ $2 \times \underline{\quad} = 152 \div 2$ ⑪ $2 \times \underline{\quad} = 14 \div 2$ ⑫ $2 \times \underline{\quad} = 200 \div 2$

⑬ $2 \times \underline{\quad} = 106 \div 2$ ⑭ $2 \times \underline{\quad} = 10 \div 2$ ⑮ $2 \times \underline{\quad} = 32 \div 2$ ⑯ $2 \times \underline{\quad} = 88 \div 2$

⑰ $2 \times \underline{\quad} = 176 \div 2$ ⑱ $2 \times \underline{\quad} = 46 \div 2$ ⑲ $2 \times \underline{\quad} = 118 \div 2$ ⑳ $2 \times \underline{\quad} = 192 \div 2$

㉑ $2 \times \underline{\quad} = 64 \div 2$ ㉒ $2 \times \underline{\quad} = 38 \div 2$ ㉓ $2 \times \underline{\quad} = 126 \div 2$ ㉔ $2 \times \underline{\quad} = 8 \div 2$

㉕ $2 \times \underline{\quad} = 146 \div 2$ ㉖ $2 \times \underline{\quad} = 198 \div 2$ ㉗ $2 \times \underline{\quad} = 162 \div 2$ ㉘ $2 \times \underline{\quad} = 80 \div 2$

㉙ $\underline{\quad} \times 2 = 28 \div 2$ ㉚ $\underline{\quad} \times 2 = 112 \div 2$ ㉛ $\underline{\quad} \times 2 = 156 \div 2$ ㉜ $\underline{\quad} \times 2 = 94 \div 2$

㉝ $\underline{\quad} \times 2 = 40 \div 2$ ㉞ $\underline{\quad} \times 2 = 74 \div 2$ ㉟ $\underline{\quad} \times 2 = 166 \div 2$ ㊱ $\underline{\quad} \times 2 = 142 \div 2$

㊲ $\underline{\quad} \times 2 = 98 \div 2$ ㊳ $\underline{\quad} \times 2 = 30 \div 2$ ㊴ $\underline{\quad} \times 2 = 110 \div 2$ ㊵ $\underline{\quad} \times 2 = 58 \div 2$

㊶ $\underline{\quad} \times 2 = 44 \div 2$ ㊷ $\underline{\quad} \times 2 = 116 \div 2$ ㊸ $\underline{\quad} \times 2 = 190 \div 2$ ㊹ $\underline{\quad} \times 2 = 104 \div 2$

㊺ $\underline{\quad} \times 2 = 36 \div 2$ ㊻ $\underline{\quad} \times 2 = 60 \div 2$ ㊼ $\underline{\quad} \times 2 = 52 \div 2$ ㊽ $\underline{\quad} \times 2 = 128 \div 2$

㊾ $\underline{\quad} \times 2 = 134 \div 2$ ㊿ $\underline{\quad} \times 2 = 92 \div 2$ 51 $\underline{\quad} \times 2 = 68 \div 2$ 52 $\underline{\quad} \times 2 = 72 \div 2$

53 $\underline{\quad} \times 2 = 170 \div 2$ 54 $\underline{\quad} \times 2 = 148 \div 2$ 55 $\underline{\quad} \times 2 = 96 \div 2$ 57 $\underline{\quad} \times 2 = 34 \div 2$

REMINDER: Write the definition of a factor.

Unit 104 cont'd ☛

B Match the products in columns A with their factors in columns B.

A	B	A	B	A	B	A	B
① 16	77, 2	⑨ 164	2, 41	⑰ 42	61, 2	㉕ 194	97, 2
② 50	2, 8	⑩ 82	54, 2	⑱ 122	2, 28	㉖ 76	43, 2
③ 182	25, 2	⑪ 108	92, 2	⑲ 174	21, 2	㉗ 102	2, 38
④ 154	2, 91	⑫ 184	2, 82	⑳ 56	87, 2	㉘ 86	51, 2
⑤ 186	33, 2	⑬ 120	84, 2	㉑ 132	2, 94	㉙ 20	2, 57
⑥ 172	2, 69	⑭ 144	2, 60	㉒ 124	80, 2	㉚ 114	31, 2
⑦ 66	93, 2	⑮ 78	72, 2	㉓ 160	66, 2	㉛ 62	10, 2
⑧ 138	86, 2	⑯ 168	2, 39	㉔ 188	2, 62	㉜ 84	2, 42

C Underline the correct answers.

① Two is a factor of all (counting, <u>even</u>, whole) numbers.

② Two and (12, 6, 24) are factors of 12.

③ If the order of two (dividends, quotients, factors) is reversed, the product is the same.

④ Forty-eight is the (product, quotient, sum) of 2 and 24.

⑤ To find an unknown factor, divide the (remainder, sum, product) by the known factor.

⑥ Ninety has as its factors, (2 and 20, 45 and 2, 2 and 180).

⑦ The product of 79×2 is equal to that of $(2 + 79, 79 \div 2, 2 \times 79)$.

⑧ Two times 68 is equal to $(68 \div 2, 136 \div 2, 68 \div 1)$.

⑨ Two and (70, 280, 45) are factors of 140.

⑩ The commutative property of (division, addition, multiplication) holds that 2×89 is equal to 89×2.

Three as a Factor

Learning
Objective: *We will learn to recognize 3 as a factor of some counting numbers.*

A factor is a multiplier that, when multiplied with another factor, forms a product.

EXAMPLE: If the sum of all digits
of a number is divisible
by 3, then 3 is a factor
of that number.

$$12\} \; 1 + 2 = 3 \div 3 = 1$$
$$3 \times \underline{4} = 12 \quad 12 \div 3 = \underline{4}$$

The sum of the digits of the number 12 is
divisible by 3. Three is a factor of 12.

A Determine whether 3 is a factor of the following numbers. If 3 is a factor, what other factor
multiplied with 3 forms each of the given products? If 3 is not a factor, draw an X across the
entire problem.

① $84\} \; 8 + 4 = \underline{12} \div 3 = \underline{4}$
  $3 \times \underline{28} = 84 \div 3$

② $15\} \; 1 + 5 = \underline{} \div 3 = \underline{}$
  $3 \times \underline{} = 15 \div 3$

③ $141\} \; 1 + 4 + 1 = \underline{} \div 3 = \underline{}$
  $3 \times \underline{} = 141 \div 3$

④ $32\} \; 3 + 2 = \underline{} \div 3 = \underline{}$
  $3 \times \underline{} = 32 \div 3$

⑤ $186\} \; 1 + 8 + 6 = \underline{} \div 3 = \underline{}$
  $3 \times \underline{} = 186 \div 3$

⑥ $75\} \; 7 + 5 = \underline{} \div 3 = \underline{}$
  $3 \times \underline{} = 75 \div 3$

⑦ $210\} \; 2 + 1 + 0 = \underline{} \div 3 = \underline{}$
  $3 \times \underline{} = 210 \div 3$

⑧ $42\} \; 4 + 2 = \underline{} \div 3 = \underline{}$
  $3 \times \underline{} = 42 \div 3$

⑨ $64\} \; 6 + 4 = \underline{} \div 3 = \underline{}$
  $3 \times \underline{} = 64 \div 3$

⑩ $57\} \; 5 + 7 = \underline{} \div 3 = \underline{}$
  $3 \times \underline{} = 57 \div 3$

⑪ $273\} \; 2 + 7 + 3 = \underline{} \div 3 = \underline{}$
  $3 \times \underline{} = 273 \div 3$

⑫ $180\} \; 1 + 8 + 0 = \underline{} \div 3 = \underline{}$
  $3 \times \underline{} = 180 \div 3$

⑬ $111\} \; 1 + 1 + 1 = \underline{} \div 3 = \underline{}$
  $3 \times \underline{} = 111 \div 3$

⑭ $13\} \; 1 + 3 = \underline{} \div 3 = \underline{}$
  $3 \times \underline{} = 13 \div 3$

⑮ $252\} \; 2 + 5 + 2 = \underline{} \div 3 = \underline{}$
  $3 \times \underline{} = 252 \div 3$

⑯ $45\} \; 4 + 5 = \underline{} \div 3 = \underline{}$
  $3 \times \underline{} = 45 \div 3$

⑰ $129\} \; 1 + 2 + 9 = \underline{} \div 3 = \underline{}$
  $3 \times \underline{} = 129 \div 3$

⑱ $150\} \; 1 + 5 + 0 = \underline{} \div 3 = \underline{}$
  $3 \times \underline{} = 150 \div 3$

⑲ $291\} \; 2 + 9 + 1 = \underline{} \div 3 = \underline{}$
  $3 \times \underline{} = 291 \div 3$

⑳ $48\} \; 4 + 8 = \underline{} \div 3 = \underline{}$
  $3 \times \underline{} = 48 \div 3$

㉑ $95\} \; 9 + 5 = \underline{} \div 3 = \underline{}$
  $3 \times \underline{} = 95 \div 3$

㉒ $87\} \; 8 + 7 = \underline{} \div 3 = \underline{}$
  $3 \times \underline{} = 87 \div 3$

㉓ $132\} \; 1 + 3 + 2 = \underline{} \div 3 = \underline{}$
  $3 \times \underline{} = 132 \div 3$

㉔ $201\} \; 2 + 0 + 1 = \underline{} \div 3 = \underline{}$
  $3 \times \underline{} = 201 \div 3$

㉕ $100\} \; 1 + 0 + 0 = \underline{} \div 3 = \underline{}$
  $3 \times \underline{} = 100 \div 3$

㉖ $30\} \; 3 + 0 = \underline{} \div 3 = \underline{}$
  $3 \times \underline{} = 30 \div 3$

㉗ $222\} \; 2 + 2 + 2 = \underline{} \div 3 = \underline{}$
  $3 \times \underline{} = 222 \div 3$

REMINDER: Write the definition of a factor.

_____

_____

Unit 105 cont'd ☞

B Match the products in columns A with their factors in columns B.

A	B	A	B	A	B	A	B
① 147	86, 3	⑨ 78	77, 3	⑰ 135	33, 3	㉕ 216	53, 3
② 258	3, 73	⑩ 192	64, 3	⑱ 168	3, 58	㉖ 159	72, 3
③ 81	49, 3	⑪ 231	3, 26	⑲ 174	3, 56	㉗ 90	61, 3
④ 219	3, 27	⑫ 279	3, 93	⑳ 99	45, 3	㉘ 183	3, 30
⑤ 126	42, 3	⑬ 120	32, 3	㉑ 255	3, 85	㉙ 234	3, 75
⑥ 93	100, 3	⑭ 63	3, 34	㉒ 69	41, 3	㉚ 171	78, 3
⑦ 300	3, 63	⑮ 102	40, 3	㉓ 123	3, 39	㉛ 72	3, 57
⑧ 189	3, 31	⑯ 96	21, 3	㉔ 117	23, 3	㉜ 225	24, 3

C Underline the correct answers.

① Three is a factor of (97, <u>114</u>, 49).

② If the (sum, product, quotient) of the digits of a number is divisible by 3, then 3 is a factor of that number.

③ To find what factor multiplied with 3 forms a certain product, divide the product by (itself, 1, 3).

④ Nine has as its factors (3 and 2, 3 and 3, 3 and 4).

⑤ Three and 6 are factors of (141, 36, 18).

⑥ Three times 81 is (equal to, less than, greater than) 81 times 3.

⑦ Because 3×59 is equal to 177, 3 and 59 are (products, factors, quotients) of 177.

⑧ Forty-two is the product of (3 and 12, 4 and 2, 14 and 3).

⑨ Statement number 6 in this exercise illustrates the (associative, distributive, commutative) property of multiplication.

Comprehension Check

A Find the quotients. Write all remainders as fractions.

① 507 ÷ 2 = **253 ½** ② 2,879 ÷ 7 = _____ ③ 3,669 ÷ 6 = _____ ④ 4,041 ÷ 5 = _____

⑤ 4,555 ÷ 9 = _____ ⑥ 7,528 ÷ 25 = _____ ⑦ 6,049 ÷ 12 = _____ ⑧ 1,289 ÷ 4 = _____

⑨ 2,489 ÷ 8 = _____ ⑩ 8,046 ÷ 10 = _____ ⑪ 8,195 ÷ 9 = _____ ⑫ 3,218 ÷ 16 = _____

⑬ 4,827 ÷ 24 = _____ ⑭ 5,675 ÷ 7 = _____ ⑮ 3,245 ÷ 3 = _____ ⑯ 9,005 ÷ 10 = _____

⑰ 3,571 ÷ 7 = _____ ⑱ 2,057 ÷ 5 = _____ ⑲ 5,493 ÷ 9 = _____ ⑳ 5,677 ÷ 8 = _____

B Write these improper fractions as mixed numbers.

① $50/7$ = 50 ÷ 7 = **7 ¹/₇** ② $26/8$ = 26 ÷ 8 = _____ ③ $11/5$ = 11 ÷ 5 = _____

④ $37/12$ = 37 ÷ 12 = _____ ⑤ $30/4$ = 30 ÷ 4 = _____ ⑥ $67/9$ = 67 ÷ 9 = _____

⑦ $66/7$ = 66 ÷ 7 = _____ ⑧ $88/12$ = 88 ÷ 12 = _____ ⑨ $78/25$ = 78 ÷ 25 = _____

⑩ $82/9$ = 82 ÷ 9 = _____ ⑪ $100/11$ = 100 ÷ 11 = _____ ⑫ $57/16$ = 57 ÷ 16 = _____

⑬ $40/3$ = 40 ÷ 3 = _____ ⑭ $75/6$ = 75 ÷ 6 = _____ ⑮ $69/8$ = 69 ÷ 8 = _____

C Match the products in columns A with their factors in columns B.

A	B	A	B	A	B	A	B
① 41	74, 1	⑨ 96	1, 61	⑰ 65	87, 1	㉕ 19	1, 25
② 74	13, 1	⑩ 24	1, 96	⑱ 14	98, 1	㉖ 25	1, 80
③ 13	1, 41	⑪ 61	47, 1	⑲ 87	1, 14	㉗ 80	1, 19
④ 34	1, 34	⑫ 47	24, 1	⑳ 98	65, 1	㉘ 44	44, 1
⑤ 20	63, 1	⑬ 79	84, 1	㉑ 53	1, 53	㉙ 36	1, 72
⑥ 89	1, 45	⑭ 84	1, 79	㉒ 76	1, 46	㉚ 97	1, 97
⑦ 63	1, 89	⑮ 62	90, 1	㉓ 18	76, 1	㉛ 72	36, 1
⑧ 45	20, 1	⑯ 90	62, 1	㉔ 46	18, 1	㉜ 55	55, 1

Test 21 cont'd ☛

D Find the missing factors by dividing the products by 2.

① $2 \times \underline{\mathbf{56}} = 112 \div 2$ ② $2 \times \underline{} = 78 \div 2$ ③ $\underline{} \times 2 = 94 \div 2$ ④ $2 \times \underline{} = 146 \div 2$

⑤ $\underline{} \times 2 = 64 \div 2$ ⑥ $\underline{} \times 2 = 118 \div 2$ ⑦ $2 \times \underline{} = 144 \div 2$ ⑧ $\underline{} \times 2 = 98 \div 2$

⑨ $2 \times \underline{} = 88 \div 2$ ⑩ $\underline{} \times 2 = 158 \div 2$ ⑪ $\underline{} \times 2 = 200 \div 2$ ⑫ $2 \times \underline{} = 198 \div 2$

⑬ $\underline{} \times 2 = 46 \div 2$ ⑭ $2 \times \underline{} = 37 \div 2$ ⑮ $2 \times \underline{} = 18 \div 2$ ⑯ $2 \times \underline{} = 26 \div 2$

⑰ $\underline{} \times 2 = 186 \div 2$ ⑱ $\underline{} \times 2 = 108 \div 2$ ⑲ $2 \times \underline{} = 168 \div 2$ ⑳ $\underline{} \times 2 = 92 \div 2$

E Determine whether 3 is a factor of the following numbers. Place a check (✓) before each number that has 3 as a factor.

① $\underline{\checkmark}$ 33} $3 + 3 = \underline{\mathbf{6}} \div 3 = \underline{\mathbf{2}}$ ② $\underline{}$ 60} $6 + 0 = \underline{} \div 3 = \underline{}$

③ $\underline{}$ 52} $5 + 2 = \underline{} \div 3 = \underline{}$ ④ $\underline{}$ 78} $7 + 8 = \underline{} \div 3 = \underline{}$

⑤ $\underline{}$ 63} $6 + 3 = \underline{} \div 3 = \underline{}$ ⑥ $\underline{}$ 42} $4 + 2 = \underline{} \div 3 = \underline{}$

⑦ $\underline{}$ 59} $5 + 9 = \underline{} \div 3 = \underline{}$ ⑧ $\underline{}$ 21} $2 + 1 = \underline{} \div 3 = \underline{}$

⑨ $\underline{}$ 45} $4 + 5 = \underline{} \div 3 = \underline{}$ ⑩ $\underline{}$ 69} $6 + 9 = \underline{} \div 3 = \underline{}$

F Underline the correct answers.

① (Quotients, Products, Factors) are multipliers.

② Factors multiplied together form a (sum, product, quotient).

③ (One, Two, Three) is a factor only of even numbers.

④ Three times 14 is equal to (3×42, 14×3, 4×13).

⑤ One times 89 is equal to (89×1, 8×9, $9 \div 8$).

Write the definitions of a mixed number and a factor.

_____

_____

_____

_____

Five as a Factor

Learning Objective: *We will learn to recognize 5 as a factor of counting numbers ending with 0 or 5.*

A factor is a multiplier that, when multiplied with another factor, forms a product.

EXAMPLE: Five is a factor of all counting numbers that end with the digits 0 or 5.

$5 \times 2 = 10$
$5 \times 3 = 15$
$5 \times 4 = 20$

A Place a check (✓) before the numbers that have a 5 as a factor.

✓ ① 15   ___ ② 57   ___ ③ 354   ___ ④ 440   ___ ⑤ 195   ___ ⑥ 159   ___ ⑦ 460   ___ ⑧ 55

___ ⑨ 310   ___ ⑩ 295   ___ ⑪ 258   ___ ⑫ 204   ___ ⑬ 380   ___ ⑭ 400   ___ ⑮ 84   ___ ⑯ 288

___ ⑰ 279   ___ ⑱ 160   ___ ⑲ 75   ___ ⑳ 490   ___ ㉑ 500   ___ ㉒ 261   ___ ㉓ 102   ___ ㉔ 245

___ ㉕ 796   ___ ㉖ 845   ___ ㉗ 913   ___ ㉘ 641   ___ ㉙ 100   ___ ㉚ 105   ___ ㉛ 311   ___ ㉜ 42

___ ㉝ 270   ___ ㉞ 78   ___ ㉟ 551   ___ ㊱ 631   ___ ㊲ 222   ___ ㊳ 190   ___ ㊴ 45   ___ ㊵ 20

B Find the missing factors by dividing the products by 5.

① $5 \times \underline{\ 11\ } = 55 \div 5$ ② $5 \times \underline{\ \ \ } = 300 \div 5$ ③ $5 \times \underline{\ \ \ } = 140 \div 5$ ④ $5 \times \underline{\ \ \ } = 225 \div 5$

⑤ $5 \times \underline{\ \ \ } = 280 \div 5$ ⑥ $5 \times \underline{\ \ \ } = 390 \div 5$ ⑦ $5 \times \underline{\ \ \ } = 415 \div 5$ ⑧ $5 \times \underline{\ \ \ } = 210 \div 5$

⑨ $5 \times \underline{\ \ \ } = 30 \div 5$ ⑩ $5 \times \underline{\ \ \ } = 170 \div 5$ ⑪ $5 \times \underline{\ \ \ } = 285 \div 5$ ⑫ $5 \times \underline{\ \ \ } = 165 \div 5$

⑬ $5 \times \underline{\ \ \ } = 150 \div 5$ ⑭ $5 \times \underline{\ \ \ } = 65 \div 5$ ⑮ $5 \times \underline{\ \ \ } = 200 \div 5$ ⑯ $5 \times \underline{\ \ \ } = 495 \div 5$

⑰ $\underline{\ \ \ } \times 5 = 360 \div 5$ ⑱ $\underline{\ \ \ } \times 5 = 275 \div 5$ ⑲ $\underline{\ \ \ } \times 5 = 185 \div 5$ ⑳ $\underline{\ \ \ } \times 5 = 90 \div 5$

㉑ $\underline{\ \ \ } \times 5 = 25 \div 5$ ㉒ $\underline{\ \ \ } \times 5 = 145 \div 5$ ㉓ $\underline{\ \ \ } \times 5 = 350 \div 5$ ㉔ $\underline{\ \ \ } \times 5 = 465 \div 5$

㉕ $\underline{\ \ \ } \times 5 = 340 \div 5$ ㉖ $\underline{\ \ \ } \times 5 = 435 \div 5$ ㉗ $\underline{\ \ \ } \times 5 = 445 \div 5$ ㉘ $\underline{\ \ \ } \times 5 = 250 \div 5$

㉙ $\underline{\ \ \ } \times 5 = 35 \div 5$ ㉚ $\underline{\ \ \ } \times 5 = 355 \div 5$ ㉛ $\underline{\ \ \ } \times 5 = 315 \div 5$ ㉜ $\underline{\ \ \ } \times 5 = 235 \div 5$

REMINDER: Write the definition of a factor.

_____

_____

Unit 106 cont'd ☞

C Match the products in columns A and their factors in columns B.

A	B	A	B	A	B	A	B
① 385	5, 58	⑨ 80	5, 22	⑰ 120	24, 5	㉕ 480	14, 5
② 290	5, 82	⑩ 330	5, 16	⑱ 320	5, 19	㉖ 115	5, 23
③ 410	25, 5	⑪ 215	66, 5	⑲ 265	5, 64	㉗ 70	5, 96
④ 125	77, 5	⑫ 110	43, 5	⑳ 95	53, 5	㉘ 255	51, 5
⑤ 155	61, 5	⑬ 135	94, 5	㉑ 175	5, 91	㉙ 450	5, 44
⑥ 305	31, 5	⑭ 365	5, 73	㉒ 325	35, 5	㉚ 220	74, 5
⑦ 430	5, 36	⑮ 230	5, 27	㉓ 455	5, 69	㉛ 485	5, 90
⑧ 180	5, 86	⑯ 470	46, 5	㉔ 345	65, 5	㉜ 370	5, 97

D Underline the correct answers.

① (Two, Three, <u>Five</u>) and 85 are factors of 425.

② Five is a factor of (all even numbers, all counting numbers ending with 0 or 5, all odd numbers).

③ To determine what factor multiplied with 5 results in the product 260, (divide, multiply, decrease) 260 by 5.

④ Five is a factor of (357, 508, 420).

⑤ Five times 26 equals 130. Twenty-six times 5 equals (265, 130, 310).

⑥ Because 5 multiplied with 79 forms a product, 5 and 79 are (sums, remainders, factors) of that product.

⑦ Eighty-five has as factors (8 and 5, 5 and 8, 17 and 5).

⑧ The commutative property of multiplication is illustrated by statement number (7, 5, 3) in this exercise.

⑨ The product of 5 and any other counting number (always, sometimes, never) ends with the digits 0 or 5.

Nine and Ten as Factors

Learning Objective: *We will learn to recognize 9 and 10 as factors of certain counting numbers.*

A factor is a multiplier that, when multiplied with another factor, forms a product.

EXAMPLES: If the sum of all digits of a number is divisible by 9, then 9 is a factor of that number.

$$36\} \; 3 + 6 = 9 \div 9 = 1 \qquad 9 \times 4 = 36$$

Ten is a factor of all counting numbers that end with the digit 0.

$$10 \times 2 = 20 \qquad 10 \times 3 = 30 \qquad 10 \times 4 = 40$$

A

Determine whether 9 is a factor of the following numbers. If 9 is a factor, find the second factor that forms each product. Draw an X across the problem if 9 is not a factor.

① $45\} \; 4 + 5 = \underline{\;9\;} \div 9 = \underline{\;1\;}$
   $9 \times \underline{\;5\;} = 45 \div 9$

② $90\} \; 9 + 0 = \underline{\quad} \div 9 = \underline{\quad}$
   $9 \times \underline{\quad} = 90 \div 9$

③ $81\} \; 8 + 1 = \underline{\quad} \div 9 = \underline{\quad}$
   $9 \times \underline{\quad} = 81 \div 9$

④ $135\} \; 1 + 3 + 5 = \underline{\quad} \div 9 = \underline{\quad}$
   $9 \times \underline{\quad} = 135 \div 9$

⑤ $199\} \; 1 + 9 + 9 = \underline{\quad} \div 9 = \underline{\quad}$
   $9 \times \underline{\quad} = 199 \div 9$

⑥ $270\} \; 2 + 7 + 0 = \underline{\quad} \div 9 = \underline{\quad}$
   $9 \times \underline{\quad} = 270 \div 9$

⑦ $495\} \; 4 + 9 + 5 = \underline{\quad} \div 9 = \underline{\quad}$
   $9 \times \underline{\quad} = 495 \div 9$

⑧ $216\} \; 2 + 1 + 6 = \underline{\quad} \div 9 = \underline{\quad}$
   $9 \times \underline{\quad} = 216 \div 9$

⑨ $324\} \; 3 + 2 + 4 = \underline{\quad} \div 9 = \underline{\quad}$
   $9 \times \underline{\quad} = 324 \div 9$

⑩ $108\} \; 1 + 0 + 8 = \underline{\quad} \div 9 = \underline{\quad}$
   $9 \times \underline{\quad} = 108 \div 9$

⑪ $225\} \; 2 + 2 + 5 = \underline{\quad} \div 9 = \underline{\quad}$
   $9 \times \underline{\quad} = 225 \div 9$

⑫ $145\} \; 1 + 4 + 5 = \underline{\quad} \div 9 = \underline{\quad}$
   $9 \times \underline{\quad} = 145 \div 9$

B

Find the missing factors.

① $10 \times \underline{\;11\;} = 110 \div 10$
② $10 \times \underline{\quad} = 480 \div 10$
③ $10 \times \underline{\quad} = 700 \div 10$
④ $10 \times \underline{\quad} = 540 \div 10$

⑤ $10 \times \underline{\quad} = 620 \div 10$
⑥ $10 \times \underline{\quad} = 250 \div 10$
⑦ $10 \times \underline{\quad} = 60 \div 10$
⑧ $10 \times \underline{\quad} = 510 \div 10$

⑨ $10 \times \underline{\quad} = 270 \div 10$
⑩ $\underline{\quad} \times 10 = 310 \div 10$
⑪ $\underline{\quad} \times 10 = 850 \div 10$
⑫ $\underline{\quad} \times 10 = 790 \div 10$

⑬ $\underline{\quad} \times 10 = 340 \div 10$
⑭ $\underline{\quad} \times 10 = 200 \div 10$
⑮ $\underline{\quad} \times 10 = 140 \div 10$
⑯ $\underline{\quad} \times 10 = 460 \div 10$

⑰ $\underline{\quad} \times 10 = 750 \div 10$
⑱ $\underline{\quad} \times 10 = 940 \div 10$
⑲ $\underline{\quad} \times 10 = 590 \div 10$
⑳ $\underline{\quad} \times 10 = 370 \div 10$

C

Place an "n" before numbers that have 9 as a factor and a "t" before numbers that have 10 as a factor.

$\underline{\;t\;}$ ① 440 $\underline{\quad}$ ② 297 $\underline{\quad}$ ③ 830 $\underline{\quad}$ ④ 910 $\underline{\quad}$ ⑤ 648 $\underline{\quad}$ ⑥ 117 $\underline{\quad}$ ⑦ 918 $\underline{\quad}$ ⑧ 660

REMINDER: Write the definition of a factor.

Unit 107 cont'd ☛

D Match the products in columns A with their factors in columns B.

A	B	A	B	A	B	A	B
① 860	9, 80	⑨ 288	9, 32	⑰ 410	9, 18	㉕ 306	9, 81
② 720	10, 86	⑩ 690	87, 10	⑱ 162	10, 99	㉖ 729	10, 80
③ 153	64, 9	⑪ 870	81, 9	⑲ 640	41, 10	㉗ 800	34, 9
④ 576	17, 9	⑫ 729	69, 10	⑳ 990	10, 64	㉘ 790	10, 79
⑤ 710	10, 92	⑬ 320	40, 9	㉑ 630	10, 35	㉙ 280	9, 100
⑥ 920	24, 10	⑭ 144	10, 32	㉒ 350	9, 70	㉚ 207	28, 10
⑦ 198	71, 10	⑮ 360	58, 10	㉓ 170	20, 9	㉛ 650	10, 65
⑧ 240	22, 9	⑯ 580	16, 9	㉔ 180	17, 10	㉜ 900	9, 23

E Underline the correct answers.

① Nine is a factor of (306, 418, 339).

② The product 873 has as factors (8 and 10, 7 and 3, 9 and 97).

③ Ten is a factor of (all counting numbers that end with 0 or 5, all counting numbers, all counting numbers that end in 0).

④ The products of 9 × 53 and 53 × 9 are (different, the same, 376).

⑤ Six hundred twelve has as one of its factors (10, 5, 9).

⑥ Because 10 × 93 is equal to 930, (10 and 93, 1 and 9, 3 and 9) are factors of 930.

⑦ If the order of two factors is reversed, their (quotient, sum, product) is the same.

⑧ Ten times 63 and 9 times 70 have products that are (equal, unequal, fractions).

⑨ Nine is a factor of all counting numbers that have digits adding up to a sum that is divisible by (3, 6, 9).

Finding Factors

Learning Objective: *We will learn to find all factors of numbers.*

A factor is a multiplier that, when multiplied with another factor, forms a product.

EXAMPLE: **A number may have many factors.** $1 \times 16 = 16$ $2 \times 8 = 16$ $4 \times 4 = 16$

One, 2, 4, 8, and 16 are factors of 16. 16: 1, 2, 4, 8, 16

A Complete the multiplication sentences and list all the factors of the following numbers.

① $\underline{\textbf{1}} \times 15 = 15$
$3 \times \underline{\textbf{5}} = 15$
15: $\underline{\textbf{1}}$, $\underline{\textbf{3}}$, $\underline{\textbf{5}}$, $\underline{\textbf{15}}$

② $1 \times \underline{\hspace{1cm}} = 8$
$\underline{\hspace{1cm}} \times 4 = 8$
8: $\underline{\hspace{1cm}}$, $\underline{\hspace{1cm}}$, $\underline{\hspace{1cm}}$, $\underline{\hspace{1cm}}$

③ $1 \times 25 = \underline{\hspace{1cm}}$
$5 \times \underline{\hspace{1cm}} = 25$
25: $\underline{\hspace{1cm}}$, $\underline{\hspace{1cm}}$, $\underline{\hspace{1cm}}$

④ $1 \times \underline{\hspace{1cm}} = 12$
$2 \times \underline{\hspace{1cm}} = 12$
$\underline{\hspace{1cm}} \times 4 = 12$
12: $\underline{\hspace{1cm}}$, $\underline{\hspace{1cm}}$, $\underline{\hspace{1cm}}$, $\underline{\hspace{1cm}}$,
$\underline{\hspace{1cm}}$, $\underline{\hspace{1cm}}$

⑤ $\underline{\hspace{1cm}} \times 20 = 20$
$2 \times \underline{\hspace{1cm}} = 20$
$4 \times \underline{\hspace{1cm}} = 20$
12: $\underline{\hspace{1cm}}$, $\underline{\hspace{1cm}}$, $\underline{\hspace{1cm}}$, $\underline{\hspace{1cm}}$,
$\underline{\hspace{1cm}}$, $\underline{\hspace{1cm}}$

⑥ $1 \times \underline{\hspace{1cm}} = 44$
$2 \times \underline{\hspace{1cm}} = 44$
$\underline{\hspace{1cm}} \times 11 = 44$
12: $\underline{\hspace{1cm}}$, $\underline{\hspace{1cm}}$, $\underline{\hspace{1cm}}$, $\underline{\hspace{1cm}}$,
$\underline{\hspace{1cm}}$, $\underline{\hspace{1cm}}$

⑦ $1 \times \underline{\hspace{1cm}} = 18$
$\underline{\hspace{1cm}} \times 9 = 18$
$3 \times \underline{\hspace{1cm}} = 18$
18: $\underline{\hspace{1cm}}$, $\underline{\hspace{1cm}}$, $\underline{\hspace{1cm}}$, $\underline{\hspace{1cm}}$,
$\underline{\hspace{1cm}}$, $\underline{\hspace{1cm}}$

⑧ $\underline{\hspace{1cm}} \times 32 = 32$
$2 \times \underline{\hspace{1cm}} = 32$
$\underline{\hspace{1cm}} \times 8 = 32$
32: $\underline{\hspace{1cm}}$, $\underline{\hspace{1cm}}$, $\underline{\hspace{1cm}}$, $\underline{\hspace{1cm}}$,
$\underline{\hspace{1cm}}$, $\underline{\hspace{1cm}}$

⑨ $1 \times 63 = \underline{\hspace{1cm}}$
$\underline{\hspace{1cm}} \times 21 = 63$
$7 \times \underline{\hspace{1cm}} = 63$
63: $\underline{\hspace{1cm}}$, $\underline{\hspace{1cm}}$, $\underline{\hspace{1cm}}$, $\underline{\hspace{1cm}}$,

⑩ $\underline{\hspace{1cm}} \times 30 = 30$
$2 \times \underline{\hspace{1cm}} = 30$
$\underline{\hspace{1cm}} \times 10 = 30$
$5 \times \underline{\hspace{1cm}} = 30$
30: $\underline{\hspace{1cm}}$, $\underline{\hspace{1cm}}$, $\underline{\hspace{1cm}}$, $\underline{\hspace{1cm}}$,
$\underline{\hspace{1cm}}$, $\underline{\hspace{1cm}}$, $\underline{\hspace{1cm}}$, $\underline{\hspace{1cm}}$

⑪ $1 \times \underline{\hspace{1cm}} = 66$
$2 \times \underline{\hspace{1cm}} = 66$
$\underline{\hspace{1cm}} \times 22 = 66$
$6 \times \underline{\hspace{1cm}} = 66$
66: $\underline{\hspace{1cm}}$, $\underline{\hspace{1cm}}$, $\underline{\hspace{1cm}}$, $\underline{\hspace{1cm}}$,

⑫ $\underline{\hspace{1cm}} \times 24 = 24$
$2 \times \underline{\hspace{1cm}} = 24$
$3 \times \underline{\hspace{1cm}} = 24$
$\underline{\hspace{1cm}} \times 6 = 24$
24: $\underline{\hspace{1cm}}$, $\underline{\hspace{1cm}}$, $\underline{\hspace{1cm}}$, $\underline{\hspace{1cm}}$,
$\underline{\hspace{1cm}}$, $\underline{\hspace{1cm}}$

⑬ $1 \times \underline{\hspace{1cm}} = 48$
$\underline{\hspace{1cm}} \times 24 = 48$
$3 \times \underline{\hspace{1cm}} = 48$
$\underline{\hspace{1cm}} \times 12 = 48$
$6 \times \underline{\hspace{1cm}} = 48$
48: $\underline{\hspace{1cm}}$, $\underline{\hspace{1cm}}$, $\underline{\hspace{1cm}}$, $\underline{\hspace{1cm}}$,
$\underline{\hspace{1cm}}$, $\underline{\hspace{1cm}}$, $\underline{\hspace{1cm}}$, $\underline{\hspace{1cm}}$,
$\underline{\hspace{1cm}}$, $\underline{\hspace{1cm}}$

⑭ $\underline{\hspace{1cm}} \times 70 = 70$
$2 \times \underline{\hspace{1cm}} = 70$
$\underline{\hspace{1cm}} \times 14 = 70$
$7 \times \underline{\hspace{1cm}} = 70$
70: $\underline{\hspace{1cm}}$, $\underline{\hspace{1cm}}$, $\underline{\hspace{1cm}}$, $\underline{\hspace{1cm}}$,
$\underline{\hspace{1cm}}$, $\underline{\hspace{1cm}}$, $\underline{\hspace{1cm}}$, $\underline{\hspace{1cm}}$

⑮ $\underline{\hspace{1cm}} \times 64 = 64$
$2 \times \underline{\hspace{1cm}} = 64$
$\underline{\hspace{1cm}} \times 16 = 64$
$8 \times \underline{\hspace{1cm}} = 64$
64: $\underline{\hspace{1cm}}$, $\underline{\hspace{1cm}}$, $\underline{\hspace{1cm}}$, $\underline{\hspace{1cm}}$,
$\underline{\hspace{1cm}}$, $\underline{\hspace{1cm}}$, $\underline{\hspace{1cm}}$

REMINDER: Write the definition of a factor.

Unit 108 cont'd ☞

B List all factors of each number.

① 40: _1, 2, 4, 5, 8, 10, 20, 40_   ② 99: _____

③ 110: _____   ④ 56: _____

⑤ 35: _____   ⑥ 96: _____

⑦ 27: _____   ⑧ 2: _____

⑨ 90: _____   ⑩ 100: _____

⑪ 42: _____   ⑫ 54: _____

⑬ 33: _____   ⑭ 9: _____

⑮ 108: _____   ⑯ 88: _____

⑰ 77: _____   ⑱ 49: _____

⑲ 10: _____   ⑳ 81: _____

㉑ 1: _____   ㉒ 55: _____

㉓ 22: _____   ㉔ 80: _____

㉕ 4: _____   ㉖ 50: _____

C Underline the correct answers.

① One, 2, 3, and 6 are factors of (9, 6, 10).

② Every counting number has (itself, 5, 2) as a factor.

③ (Two, Five, One) has only itself as a factor.

④ Six and (8, 12, 15) share four of the same factors.

⑤ Five has a total of (1, 2, 5) factors.

⑥ Every counting number has (1, 2, 5) as a factor.

⑦ If the sum of the digits of a number are divisible by 3, (3, 5, 9) is always a factor of that number.

⑧ A number has 5 as a factor if it ends with the digits (1 or 5, 5 or 2, 0 or 5).

⑨ (Two, Three, Four) is a factor of all even numbers.

⑩ (Two, Five, Ten) is a factor only of numbers that end with 0.

Common Factors

Learning Objective: *We will learn to recognize common factors shared by more than one number.*

A common factor is a multiplier that is shared by two or more products.

EXAMPLE: **Nine and 33 share two common factors.**   **A**   **B**

9: <u>1</u>, <u>3</u>, 9   33: <u>1</u>, <u>3</u>, 11, 33

A Underline the common factors of the numbers in columns A and B.

A	B
(1) 15: <u>1</u>, 3, <u>5</u>, 15	25: <u>1</u>, <u>5</u>, 25
(2) 6: 1, 2, 3, 6	8: 1, 2, 4, 8
(3) 49: 1, 7, 49	77: 1, 7, 11, 77
(4) 22: 1, 2, 11, 22	88: 1, 2, 4, 8, 11, 22, 44, 88
(5) 40: 1, 2, 4, 5, 8, 10, 20, 40	50: 1, 2, 5, 10, 25, 50
(6) 10: 1, 2, 5, 10	20: 1, 2, 4, 5, 10, 20
(7) 27: 1, 3, 9, 27	81: 1, 3, 9, 27, 81
(8) 33: 1, 3, 11, 33	99: 1, 3, 9, 11, 33, 99
(9) 35: 1, 5, 7, 35	45: 1, 3, 5, 9, 15, 45
(10) 18: 1, 2, 3, 6, 9, 18	63: 1, 3, 7, 9, 21, 63
(11) 4: 1, 2, 4	9: 1, 3, 9
(12) 11: 1, 11	33: 1, 3, 11, 33
(13) 77: 1, 7, 11, 77	99: 1, 3, 9, 11, 33, 99
(14) 20: 1, 2, 4, 5, 10, 20	32: 1, 2, 4, 8, 16, 32
(15) 12: 1, 2, 3, 4, 6, 12	18: 1, 2, 3, 6, 9, 18
(16) 44: 1, 2, 4, 11, 22, 44	22: 1, 2, 11, 22
(17) 28: 1, 2, 4, 7, 14, 28	21: 1, 3, 7, 21
(18) 15: 1, 3, 5, 15	45: 1, 3, 5, 9, 15, 45
(19) 10: 1, 2, 5, 10	50: 1, 2, 5, 10, 25, 50
(20) 7: 1, 7	27: 1, 3, 9, 27

REMINDER: Write the definition of a common factor.

_____

_____

B Study each number. Determine if it has as a factor: 2, 3, 5, 9, or 10. List any of these factors beside the number.

① 76: _____2_____

② 225: _____

③ 189: _____

④ 650: _____

⑤ 210: _____

⑥ 340: _____

⑦ 484: _____

⑧ 510: _____

⑨ 124: _____

⑩ 380: _____

⑪ 252: _____

⑫ 495: _____

⑬ 138: _____

⑭ 990: _____

⑮ 540: _____

⑯ 306: _____

⑰ 270: _____

⑱ 96: _____

⑲ 300: _____

⑳ 115: _____

㉑ 150: _____

㉒ 144: _____

㉓ 288: _____

㉔ 1,000: _____

㉕ 156: _____

㉖ 475: _____

㉗ 411: _____

㉘ 290: _____

㉙ 255: _____

㉚ 180: _____

㉛ 400: _____

㉜ 52: _____

C Underline the correct answers.

① Any two or more counting numbers will share (<u>1</u>, 2, 3) as a common factor.

② Six, 27, and 33 share (3, 6, 9) as a common factor.

③ All even numbers share the common factor (2, 3, 10).

④ Because 10, 20, 30, and 40 end with 0, we know they share (0, 3, 10) as a common factor.

⑤ Because the sum of the digits of the number 45 is divisible by both 3 and 9, we know that 3 and 9 are included in the list of (products, factors, quotients) of 45.

⑥ Both 756 and 882 share the common factors (2, 5, and 10; 3, 9, and 10; 2, 3, and 9).

⑦ Both (20 and 500, 575 and 1,000, 25 and 75) share 5 and 10 as common factors.

⑧ If a counting number ends in 0 or 5, then (2, 5, 10) is always a factor of that number.

Factoring

Learning Objective: *We will learn to find the prime factors of numbers.*

Factoring is the process of finding the prime factors of a product.

EXAMPLE:

To find the prime factors of 36, divide 36 by its smallest prime factor. (A prime factor is divisible by 2 numbers: itself and 1.) Divide the quotient obtained by its smallest prime factor. Repeat the process until the quotient obtained is a prime number. The prime factorization of 36 is 2 × 2 × 3 × 3. The prime factors are 2 and 3.

$$\begin{array}{c} 18 \\ 2\overline{)36} \end{array} \qquad \begin{array}{c} 9 \\ 2\overline{)18} \end{array} \qquad \begin{array}{c} 3 \\ 3\overline{)9} \end{array} \qquad\qquad 2 \times 2 \times 3 \times 3 = 36$$

A Write a prime factorization for each problem. List the prime factors beside each number that has been factored.

① $\begin{array}{c} 25 \\ 2\overline{)50} \end{array}$ $\begin{array}{c} 5 \\ 5\overline{)25} \end{array}$

50 = ___**2 × 5 × 5**___
50: ___**2, 5**___

② $\begin{array}{c} 9 \\ 3\overline{)27} \end{array}$ $\begin{array}{c} 3 \\ 3\overline{)9} \end{array}$

27 = _____
27: _____

③ $\begin{array}{c} 21 \\ 3\overline{)63} \end{array}$ $\begin{array}{c} 7 \\ 3\overline{)21} \end{array}$

63 = _____
63: _____

④ $\begin{array}{c} 9 \\ 2\overline{)18} \end{array}$ $\begin{array}{c} 3 \\ 3\overline{)9} \end{array}$

18 = _____
18: _____

⑤ $\begin{array}{c} 22 \\ 2\overline{)44} \end{array}$ $\begin{array}{c} 11 \\ 2\overline{)22} \end{array}$

44 = _____
44: _____

⑥ $\begin{array}{c} 45 \\ 2\overline{)90} \end{array}$ $\begin{array}{c} 15 \\ 3\overline{)45} \end{array}$ $\begin{array}{c} 5 \\ 3\overline{)15} \end{array}$

90 = _____
90: _____

⑦ $\begin{array}{c} 27 \\ 3\overline{)81} \end{array}$ $\begin{array}{c} 9 \\ 3\overline{)27} \end{array}$ $\begin{array}{c} 3 \\ 3\overline{)9} \end{array}$

81 = _____
81: _____

⑧ $\begin{array}{c} 27 \\ 2\overline{)54} \end{array}$ $\begin{array}{c} 9 \\ 3\overline{)27} \end{array}$ $\begin{array}{c} 3 \\ 3\overline{)9} \end{array}$

54 = _____
54: _____

⑨ $\begin{array}{c} 10 \\ 2\overline{)20} \end{array}$ $\begin{array}{c} 5 \\ 2\overline{)10} \end{array}$

20 = _____
20: _____

⑩ $\begin{array}{c} 22 \\ 3\overline{)66} \end{array}$ $\begin{array}{c} 11 \\ 2\overline{)22} \end{array}$

66 = _____
66: _____

⑪ $\begin{array}{c} 21 \\ 2\overline{)42} \end{array}$ $\begin{array}{c} 7 \\ 3\overline{)21} \end{array}$

42 = _____
42: _____

⑫ $\begin{array}{c} 28 \\ 2\overline{)56} \end{array}$ $\begin{array}{c} 14 \\ 2\overline{)28} \end{array}$ $\begin{array}{c} 7 \\ 2\overline{)14} \end{array}$

56 = _____
56: _____

⑬ $\begin{array}{c} 20 \\ 2\overline{)40} \end{array}$ $\begin{array}{c} 10 \\ 2\overline{)20} \end{array}$ $\begin{array}{c} 5 \\ 2\overline{)10} \end{array}$

40 = _____
40: _____

⑭ $\begin{array}{c} 25 \\ 3\overline{)75} \end{array}$ $\begin{array}{c} 5 \\ 5\overline{)25} \end{array}$

75 = _____
75: _____

⑮ $\begin{array}{c} 55 \\ 2\overline{)110} \end{array}$ $\begin{array}{c} 11 \\ 5\overline{)55} \end{array}$

110 = _____
110: _____

The 15 smallest prime numbers are: 2, 3, 5, 7, 11, 13, 17, 19, 23, 29, 31, 37, 41, 43, and 47.

REMINDER: *Write the definition of factoring.*

_____
_____

Unit 110 cont'd ☞

_B_ Factor the following numbers. Use the blank space for division.

① 68 = _2 × 2 × 17_ ② 84 = _____ ③ 46 = _____
68: _2, 17_ 84: _____ 46: _____

$$\begin{array}{r} 34 \\ 2\overline{)68} \end{array} \qquad \begin{array}{r} 17 \\ 2\overline{)34} \end{array}$$

④ 57 = _____ ⑤ 93 = _____ ⑥ 39 = _____
57: _____ 93: _____ 39: _____

⑦ 60 = _____ ⑧ 26 = _____ ⑨ 72 = _____
60: _____ 26: _____ 72: _____

⑩ 120 = _____ ⑪ 85 = _____ ⑫ 51 = _____
120: _____ 85: _____ 51: _____

_C_ Underline the correct answers.

① Two, 3, 5, 7, and 11 are (even numbers, odd numbers, <u>prime numbers</u>).

② With the exception of 0 and 1, if a whole number is not a prime number, it is a composite number. (Nine, 13, 37) is a composite number.

③ A prime number is divisible only by (itelf, 2, itself and 1).

④ (Multiplying, Factoring, Weighing) is the process of finding the prime factors of a product.

⑤ Factoring is accomplished through repeated (addition, division, multiplication).

⑥ The (prime factors, products, factorization) of 76 is 2 × 2 × 19.

⑦ The (prime factors, products, factorization) of 76 are 2 and 19.

⑧ When factoring, divide first by the (smallest, greatest, even) prime factor of the number being factored.

⑨ Twenty has as prime factors 2 and 5. The prime factors of 110 are 2, 5, and 11. Twenty and 110 share (no, one, two) common prime factors.

Comprehension Check

A Study each number and determine if its list of factors includes 2, 3, 5, 9, or 10.

① 57: __3__   ② 222: _____   ③ 136: _____   ④ 855: _____

⑤ 270: _____   ⑥ 501: _____   ⑦ 87: _____   ⑧ 243: _____

⑨ 972: _____   ⑩ 390: _____   ⑪ 162: _____   ⑫ 48: _____

⑬ 830: _____   ⑭ 402: _____   ⑮ 120: _____   ⑯ 435: _____

⑰ 450: _____   ⑱ 175: _____   ⑲ 852: _____   ⑳ 330: _____

B Complete the multiplication sentences and list all factors of the following numbers.

① $1 \times$ __27__ $= 27$
__3__ $\times 9 = 27$
27: __1__, __3__,
__9__, __27__

② _____ $\times 77 = 77$
$7 \times$ _____ $= 77$
77: _____, _____,
_____, _____

③ $1 \times 4 =$ _____
$2 \times$ _____ $= 4$
4: _____, _____,
_____

④ $1 \times$ _____ $= 35$
_____ $\times 7 = 35$
35: _____, _____,
_____, _____

⑤ _____ $\times 9 = 9$
_____ $\times 3 = 9$
9: _____, _____,
_____

⑥ $1 \times$ _____ $= 46$
_____ $\times 23 = 46$
46: _____, _____,
_____, _____

⑦ _____ $\times 93 = 93$
$3 \times$ _____ $= 93$
93: _____, _____,
_____, _____

⑧ $1 \times 49 =$ _____
$7 \times$ _____ $= 49$
49: _____, _____,
_____

⑨ $1 \times 85 =$ _____
_____ $\times 17 = 85$
85: _____, _____,
_____, _____

⑩ _____ $\times 57 = 57$
$3 \times$ _____ $= 57$
57: _____, _____,
_____, _____

⑪ $1 \times$ _____ $= 21$
_____ $\times 7 = 21$
21: _____, _____,
_____, _____

⑫ _____ $\times 15 = 15$
_____ $\times 5 = 15$
15: _____, _____,
_____, _____

⑬ _____ $\times 72 = 72$
$2 \times$ _____ $= 72$
$3 \times$ _____ $= 72$
_____ $\times 18 = 72$
_____ $\times 12 = 72$
$8 \times$ _____ $= 72$
72: _____, _____, _____,
_____, _____, _____,
_____, _____, _____

⑭ $1 \times 108 =$ _____
_____ $\times 54 = 108$
$3 \times$ _____ $= 108$
_____ $\times 27 = 108$
$6 \times$ _____ $= 108$
_____ $\times 12 = 108$
108: _____, _____, _____, _____,
_____, _____, _____,
_____, _____, _____

⑮ $1 \times$ _____ $= 96$
$2 \times$ _____ $= 96$
_____ $\times 32 = 96$
$4 \times$ _____ $= 96$
_____ $\times 16 = 96$
$8 \times$ _____ $= 96$
96: _____, _____, _____, _____,
_____, _____, _____, _____,
_____, _____, _____, _____

⑯ $1 \times$ _____ $= 90$
$2 \times$ _____ $= 90$
_____ $\times 30 = 90$
$5 \times$ _____ $= 90$
_____ $\times 15 = 90$
$9 \times$ _____ $= 90$
90: _____, _____, _____, _____,
_____, _____, _____,
_____, _____, _____

⑰ _____ $\times 490 = 490$
$2 \times$ _____ $= 490$
$5 \times$ _____ $= 490$
_____ $\times 70 = 490$
_____ $\times 49 = 490$
$14 \times$ _____ $= 490$
490: _____, _____, _____, _____,
_____, _____, _____,
_____, _____, _____

⑱ $1 \times 350 =$ _____
_____ $\times 175 = 350$
$5 \times$ _____ $= 350$
_____ $\times 50 = 350$
$10 \times$ _____ $= 350$
350: _____, _____, _____, _____,
_____, _____, _____,
_____, _____

Test 22 cont'd ☛

C Underline the common factors of the numbers in columns A and B.

A

① 18: <u>1</u>, <u>2</u>, 3, 6, 9, 18
② 25: 1, 5, 25
③ 44: 1, 2, 4, 11, 22, 44
④ 32: 1, 2, 4, 8, 16, 32
⑤ 63: 1, 3, 7, 9, 21, 63
⑥ 45: 1, 3, 5, 9, 15, 45
⑦ 20: 1, 2, 4, 5, 10, 20
⑧ 81: 1, 3, 9, 27, 81
⑨ 12: 1, 2, 3, 4, 6, 12
⑩ 64: 1, 2, 4, 8, 16, 32, 64

B

16: <u>1</u>, <u>2</u>, 4, 8, 16
50: 1, 2, 5, 10, 25, 50
66: 1, 2, 3, 6, 11, 22, 33, 66
28: 1, 2, 4, 7, 14, 28
99: 1, 3, 9, 11, 33, 99
30: 1, 2, 3, 5, 9, 15, 30
28: 1, 2, 4, 7, 14, 28
18: 1, 2, 3, 6, 9, 18
36: 1, 2, 3, 4, 6, 9, 12, 18, 36
16: 1, 2, 4, 8, 16

D Factor the following numbers. Use the blank space for division.

① 66 = *2 × 3 × 11*
66: *2, 3, 11*

$$\begin{array}{r} 33 \\ 2\overline{)66} \end{array} \qquad \begin{array}{r} 11 \\ 3\overline{)33} \end{array}$$

② 32 = _____
32: _____

③ 24 = _____
24: _____

④ 30 = _____
30: _____

⑤ 70 = _____
70: _____

⑥ 44 = _____
44: _____

⑦ 18 = _____
18: _____

⑧ 28 = _____
28: _____

⑨ 81 = _____
81: _____

⑩ 63 = _____
63: _____

⑪ 20 = _____
20: _____

⑫ 45 = _____
45: _____

Explain how to determine if a number has 5, 9, or 10 as a factor.

_____
_____
_____
_____
_____

Calendars

Learning Objective: *We will learn to read calendars and to write dates.*

A calendar marks the time that is required for the earth to make a complete revolution around the sun; it tells us when one year ends and a new year begins.

EXAMPLE: The calendar that we generally use is called the Gregorian calendar. It tells us what year it is, what month of the year, what week of the month, what day of the month, and what day of the week.

1985

JANUARY	MARCH	MAY	JULY	SEPTEMBER	NOVEMBER
S M T W T F S	S M T W T F S	S M T W T F S	S M T W T F S	S M T W T F S	S M T W T F S
1 2 3 4 5	1 2	1 2 3 4	1 2 3 4 5 6	1 2 3 4 5 6 7	1 2
6 7 8 9 10 11 12	3 4 5 6 7 8 9	5 6 7 8 9 10 11	7 8 9 10 11 12 13	8 9 10 11 12 13 14	3 4 5 6 7 8 9
13 14 15 16 17 18 19	10 11 12 13 14 15 16	12 13 14 15 16 17 18	14 15 16 17 18 19 20	15 16 17 18 19 20 21	10 11 12 13 14 15 16
20 21 22 23 24 25 26	17 18 19 20 21 22 23	19 20 21 22 23 24 25	21 22 23 24 25 26 27	22 23 24 25 26 27 28	17 18 19 20 21 22 23
27 28 29 30 31	24 25 26 27 28 29 30	26 27 28 29 30 31	28 29 30 31	29 30	24 25 26 27 28 29 30
	31				

FEBRUARY	APRIL	JUNE	AUGUST	OCTOBER	DECEMBER
		1			
1 2	1 2 3 4 5 6	2 3 4 5 6 7 8	1 2 3	1 2 3 4 5	1 2 3 4 5 6 7
3 4 5 6 7 8 9	7 8 9 10 11 12 13	9 10 11 12 13 14 15	4 5 6 7 8 9 10	6 7 8 9 10 11 12	8 9 10 11 12 13 14
10 11 12 13 14 15 16	14 15 16 17 18 19 20	16 17 18 19 20 21 22	11 12 13 14 15 16 17	13 14 15 16 17 18 19	15 16 17 18 19 20 21
17 18 19 20 21 22 23	21 22 23 24 25 26 27	23 24 25 26 27 28 29	18 19 20 21 22 23 24	20 21 22 23 24 25 26	22 23 24 25 26 27 28
24 25 26 27 28	28 29 30	30	25 26 27 28 29 30 31	27 28 29 30 31	29 30 31

A Study the calendar above and complete the following statements.

① This calendar is for the year ___ *1985* ___ .

② The year is divided into 12 _____ .

③ The year begins with the month _____ .

④ The month _____ ends the year.

⑤ January _____ is the first day of the year.

⑥ Only the month of _____ has 28 days.

⑦ December _____ is the last day of the year.

⑧ All months have _____ as the beginning date.

⑨ March _____ is the last day of that month.

⑩ June _____ is the last day of that month.

⑪ _____ is the ninth month of the year.

⑫ Except for February, all months have either 30 or _____ days.

REMINDER: Write the definition of a calendar.

_____

_____

Unit 111 cont'd ☞

B Columns A and B show two different ways to write dates. Match the dates that have the same meaning.

	A	B		A	B
①	March 16, 1954	3-17-35	⑨	July 4, 1976	9-1-72
②	December 9, 1981	6-4-53	⑩	September 1, 1972	8-1-80
③	March 17, 1935	12-9-81	⑪	November 23, 1964	7-4-76
④	June 4, 1953	3-16-54	⑫	August 1, 1980	11-23-64
⑤	February 27, 1928	4-27-53	⑬	October 31, 1914	3-6-20
⑥	January 16, 1932	2-22-75	⑭	March 6, 1955	5-9-11
⑦	April 27, 1953	2-27-28	⑮	May 9, 1911	3-6-55
⑧	February 22, 1975	1-16-32	⑯	March 6, 1920	10-31-14

C Underline the correct answers. Refer to the calendar on the previous page when necessary.

① The last day of 1985 would be written (January 1, 1985; December 1, 1985; <u>December 31, 1985</u>).

② November 27, 1985 is on a (Sunday, Monday, Wednesday).

③ December 25, 1985 falls within the (first, fourth, fifth) week of the month.

④ The first day of April, 1985 is on a (Sunday, Monday, Tuesday).

⑤ June is the (first, third, sixth) month of the year.

⑥ (August, September, November) has 31 days.

⑦ If the calendar were divided into fourths, or quarters, May would fall in the (first, second, third) quarter of the year.

⑧ Each month represents (1/3, 1/4, 1/12) of the year.

⑨ Another way of writing February 19, 1985 is (11-19-85, 2-19-85, 2-1985).

270

Days and Weeks

Unit 112

Learning Objective: *We will learn to read calendars and to convert units of time.*

A week is a time period that is made up of 7 24-hour days.

EXAMPLES: If there are 30 days in one month, that month is made up of 4 weeks and 2 days.

$$7\overline{)30}$$
$$\underline{28}$$
$$R2$$

There are 720 hours in 4 weeks, 2 days.

$$24$$
$$\times 30$$
$$720$$

```
───────────────── 1986 ─────────────────

S M T W T F S    S M T W T F S    S M T W T F S    S M T W T F S    S M T W T F S    S M T W T F S
JANUARY          MARCH       1    MAY              JULY             SEPTEMBER        NOVEMBER      1
      1  2  3  4  2  3  4  5  6  7  8        1  2  3        1  2  3  4  5  1  2  3  4  5  6  2  3  4  5  6  7  8
 5  6  7  8  9 10 11  9 10 11 12 13 14 15  4  5  6  7  8  9 10  6  7  8  9 10 11 12  7  8  9 10 11 12 13  9 10 11 12 13 14 15
12 13 14 15 16 17 18 16 17 18 19 20 21 22 11 12 13 14 15 16 17 13 14 15 16 17 18 19 14 15 16 17 18 19 20 16 17 18 19 20 21 22
19 20 21 22 23 24 25 23 24 25 26 27 28 29 18 19 20 21 22 23 24 20 21 22 23 24 25 26 21 22 23 24 25 26 27 23 24 25 26 27 28 29
26 27 28 29 30 31    30 31             25 26 27 28 29 30 31 27 28 29 30 31       28 29 30          30
FEBRUARY         APRIL            JUNE             AUGUST      1  2 OCTOBER         DECEMBER
            1        1  2  3  4  5  1  2  3  4  5  6  7  3  4  5  6  7  8  9       1  2  3  4  1  2  3  4  5  6
 2  3  4  5  6  7  8  6  7  8  9 10 11 12  8  9 10 11 12 13 14 10 11 12 13 14 15 16  5  6  7  8  9 10 11  7  8  9 10 11 12 13
 9 10 11 12 13 14 15 13 14 15 16 17 18 19 15 16 17 18 19 20 21 17 18 19 20 21 22 23 12 13 14 15 16 17 18 14 15 16 17 18 19 20
16 17 18 19 20 21 22 20 21 22 23 24 25 26 22 23 24 25 26 27 28 24 25 26 27 28 29 30 19 20 21 22 23 24 25 21 22 23 24 25 26 27
23 24 25 26 27 28    27 28 29 30       29 30             31             26 27 28 29 30 31 28 29 30 31
```

A Study the calendar above and complete the following statements.

① On the calendar above, the first day of each week is ___Sunday___ .

② _____ is the last day of each week.

③ The first day of April, 1986 is a _____ .

④ There are four full weeks and _____ days in June, 1986.

⑤ September and _____ , 1986 begin on Monday.

⑥ _____ is the only month in 1986 that ends on Thursday.

⑦ On the above calendar, "T" is the abbreviation for _____ and _____ .

⑧ In 1986, June _____ begins week number three of that month.

⑨ February, March, and _____ , 1986 begin on Saturday.

⑩ Week number _____ of June, 1986 includes days 8-14 of that month.

REMINDER: Write the definition of a week.

_____

_____

Unit 112 cont'd ☞

B Fill in the blanks.

① 75 days = __10__ weeks, __5__ days
   75 ÷ 7 = __10__ R __5__

⑦ 8 weeks, 4 days = _____ hours
   60 × 24 = _____

② 110 days = _____ weeks, _____ days
   110 ÷ 7 = _____ R _____

⑧ 52 weeks, 1 day = _____ hours
   365 × 24 = _____

③ 28 days = _____ weeks, _____ days
   28 ÷ 7 = _____ R _____

⑨ 12 weeks, 6 days = _____ hours
   90 × 24 = _____

④ 90 days = _____ weeks, _____ days
   90 ÷ 7 = _____ R _____

⑩ 4 weeks = _____ hours
   28 × 24 = _____

⑤ 365 days = _____ weeks, _____ days
   365 ÷ 7 = _____ R _____

⑪ 15 weeks, 5 days = _____ hours
   110 × 24 = _____

⑥ 60 days = _____ weeks, _____ days
   60 ÷ 7 = _____ R _____

⑫ 10 weeks, 5 days = _____ hours
   75 × 24 = _____

C Underline the correct answers. Refer to the calendar on the previous page when necessary.

① The year 1986 begins and ends on a (Monday, Tuesday, <u>Wednesday</u>).

② There are 30 days, or (300, 720, 210) hours, in April, June, September, and November.

③ October 17 is one week past (October 10, October 6, October 1).

④ There are (one, two, three) weeks between December 6 and December 27 of the same year.

⑤ If December, 1986 ends on a Wednesday, January, 1987 will begin on a (Tuesday, Wednesday, Thursday).

⑥ December, 1985 ends on a (Tuesday, Wednesday, Thursday).

⑦ If June ends on a Monday, July begins on (Monday, Tuesday, Wednesday).

⑧ July 26, 1986 is (one, two, three) weeks past July 12.

⑨ April 24 is (seven, ten, fourteen) days past April 17.

272

Weeks and Months

Learning Objective: *We will learn to read a calendar and to recognize calendar weeks as well as non-specific 7-day time periods.*

A month is roughly 1/12 of a year and is made up of 28-31 days.

EXAMPLE: **Any 7-day period is considered one week. A week may also be one of the specific 7-day divisions on a calendar — beginning with a Sunday and ending with the following Saturday. A calendar week may begin in one month and end in another month.**

1987

	JAN		MAR		MAY		JULY		SEPT		NOV

```
       1987
      JAN                MAR               MAY                JULY              SEPT               NOV
S M T W T F S      S M T W T F S     S M T W T F S     S M T W T F S     S M T W T F S     S M T W T F S
        1 2 3      1 2 3 4 5 6 7              1 2            1 2 3 4      1 2 3 4 5     1 2 3 4 5 6 7
4 5 6 7 8 9 10     8 9 10 11 12 13 14   3 4 5 6 7 8 9    5 6 7 8 9 10 11   6 7 8 9 10 11 12   8 9 10 11 12 13 14
11 12 13 14 15 16 17   15 16 17 18 19 20 21   10 11 12 13 14 15 16   12 13 14 15 16 17 18   13 14 15 16 17 18 19   15 16 17 18 19 20 21
18 19 20 21 22 23 24   22 23 24 25 26 27 28   17 18 19 20 21 22 23   19 20 21 22 23 24 25   20 21 22 23 24 25 26   22 23 24 25 26 27 28
25 26 27 28 29 30 31   29 30 31          24 25 26 27 28 29 30   26 27 28 29 30 31   27 28 29 30      29 30
                                     31
      FEB                APR               JUNE               AUG               OCT               DEC
1 2 3 4 5 6 7              1 2 3 4     1 2 3 4 5 6                   1         1 2 3     1 2 3 4 5
8 9 10 11 12 13 14   5 6 7 8 9 10 11   7 8 9 10 11 12 13   2 3 4 5 6 7 8   4 5 6 7 8 9 10   6 7 8 9 10 11 12
15 16 17 18 19 20 21   12 13 14 15 16 17 18   14 15 16 17 18 19 20   9 10 11 12 13 14 15   11 12 13 14 15 16 17   13 14 15 16 17 18 19
22 23 24 25 26 27 28   19 20 21 22 23 24 25   21 22 23 24 25 26 27   16 17 18 19 20 21 22   18 19 20 21 22 23 24   20 21 22 23 24 25 26
                   26 27 28 29 30   28 29 30          23 24 25 26 27 28 29   25 26 27 28 29 30 31   27 28 29 30 31
                                                       30 31
```

A Study the calendar above and complete the following statements.

① In 1987, _____February_____ is the only month which has no partial calendar weeks.

② There are six weeks between October 14, 1987 and November _____ , 1987.

③ The first calendar week of 1987 is a partial one, beginning on a _____ instead of a Sunday.

④ There are five calendar weeks in September, 1987. Only _____ of the five weeks are partial calendar weeks.

⑤ The calendar week that begins on Sunday, June 28 ends the following Saturday, July _____ .

⑥ In 1987, January, February, and _____ end with full calendar weeks.

⑦ February, March, and _____ of 1987 begin with full calendar weeks.

⑧ There are _____ weeks between May 26, 1987 and June 9 of the same year.

REMINDER: Write the definition of a month.

_____

_____

Unit 113 cont'd ☞

B **Study the calendar below and complete the following exercise.**

① Underline the four full calendar weeks of December, 1985.

② Draw a circle around each date that falls on a Sunday.

③ Draw a square around each date that falls on a Saturday.

④ Draw an X across each date that falls within the one-week period, December 5 through December 11.

⑤ Draw a ✓ across each date that falls within the two-week period, December 13 through December 26.

						DECEMBER
						1985
S	M	T	W	T	F	S
1	2	3	4	5	6	7
8	9	10	11	12	13	14
15	16	17	18	19	20	21
22	23	24	25	26	27	28
29	30	31				

C **Underline the correct answers. Refer to the calendar on the previous page or the calendar above when necessary.**

① There are a total of 91 days in the three months, April, May, and June. Ninety-one days equals (16, 13, 10) weeks.

② The year 1988 begins with a (full, partial) calendar week.

③ The year 1986 begins with a (full, partial) calendar week.

④ There are (three, five, seven) days in the final calendar week of 1985.

⑤ A full week always has (three, five, seven) days.

⑥ August 4 through 10, 1987 is (a calendar week, a one-week period, a partial week).

⑦ The first calendar weeks of September and December, 1987 begin on (Tuesday, Wednesday, Thursday).

⑧ There are 365 days in 1987. This is equal to (61 full weeks, 48 full weeks, 52 full weeks plus 1 day).

⑨ November, 1985 ends with a (full, partial) calendar week.

Years, Decades, and Centuries   Unit 114

Learning Objective: *We will learn to recognize and to convert units of time.*

A decade is made up of 10 years. A century is made up of 100 years, or 10 decades.

EXAMPLES:
a. 1 century = 100 years
   $1 \times 100 = 100$

b. 1 decade = 10 years
   $1 \times 10 = 10$

c. 1 century = 10 decades
   $1 \times 10 = 10$

d. 100 years = 1 century
   $100 \div 100 = 1$

e. 10 years = 1 decade
   $10 \div 10 = 1$

f. 10 decades = 1 century
   $10 \div 10 = 1$

A Convert the following units of time.

① 5 centuries = __500__ years
   $5 \times 100 = $ __500__

② 10 decades = _____ years
   $10 \times 10 = $ _____

③ 2 centuries = _____ decades
   $2 \times 10 = $ _____

④ 700 years = _____ centuries
   $700 \div 100 = $ _____

⑤ 40 years = _____ decades
   $40 \div 10 = $ _____

⑥ 50 decades = _____ centuries
   $50 \div 10 = $ _____

⑦ 17 decades = _____ years
   $17 \times 10 = $ _____

⑧ 44 centuries = _____ years
   $44 \times 100 = $ _____

⑨ 300 years = _____ decades
   $300 \div 10 = $ _____

⑩ 2,200 decades = _____ centuries
   $2,200 \div 10 = $ _____

⑪ 12 centuries = _____ decades
   $12 \times 10 = $ _____

⑫ 75,000 years = _____ centuries
   $75,000 \div 100 = $ _____

⑬ 1,900 years = _____ decades
   $1,900 \div 10 = $ _____

⑭ 72 decades = _____ years
   $72 \times 10 = $ _____

⑮ 960 decades = _____ centuries
   $960 \div 10 = $ _____

⑯ 141 centuries = _____ decades
   $141 \times 10 = $ _____

⑰ 5,700 years = _____ centuries
   $5,700 \div 100 = $ _____

⑱ 19 centuries = _____ years
   $19 \times 100 = $ _____

⑲ 67 centuries = _____ years
   $67 \times 100 = $ _____

⑳ 67 centuries = _____ decades
   $67 \times 10 = $ _____

㉑ 670 decades = _____ years
   $670 \times 10 = $ _____

㉒ 6,700 years = _____ centuries
   $6,700 \div 100 = $ _____

㉓ 670 decades = _____ centuries
   $670 \div 10 = $ _____

㉔ 6,700 years = _____ decades
   $6,700 \div 10 = $ _____

㉕ 37 centuries = _____ decades
   $37 \times 10 = $ _____

㉖ 950 years = _____ decades
   $950 \div 10 = $ _____

REMINDER: *Write the definition of a decade and a century.*

_____

_____

Unit 114 cont'd ☛

B Convert the following units of time.

① 123 centuries = __12,300__ years ② 392 centuries = _____ decades

③ 2,300 years = _____ centuries ④ 170 decades = _____ years

⑤ 1,920 years = _____ decades ⑥ 1,590 decades = _____ centuries

⑦ 1,953 centuries = _____ decades ⑧ 8,170 years = _____ decades

⑨ 928 centuries = _____ years ⑩ 7,200 years = _____ centuries

⑪ 4,230 decades = _____ centuries ⑫ 202 decades = _____ years

⑬ 820 centuries = _____ decades ⑭ 1,510 years = _____ decades

⑮ 625 centuries = _____ years ⑯ 4,200 years = _____ decades

⑰ 1,240 years = _____ decades ⑱ 567 centuries = _____ decades

⑲ 88 centuries = _____ years ⑳ 88 decades = _____ years

㉑ 1,100 years = _____ centuries ㉒ 9,180 centuries = _____ decades

㉓ 1,981 decades = _____ years ㉔ 34 decades = _____ years

㉕ 272 decades = _____ years ㉖ 918 centuries = _____ decades

C Underline the correct answers.

① The period from 1900 through 1999 is one (decade, <u>century</u>, year).

② When people mention the twenties, fifties, or sixties, they are referring to specific (decades, centuries, years).

③ There are 5 (decades, centuries, years) in the period 1850 to 1900.

④ Fifteen decades is equal to (150, 1,500, 15,000) years.

⑤ There are 20 (decades, centuries, years) in the period 1750 to 1770.

⑥ A century is (10, 100, 1,000) times as long as a year.

⑦ A decade is (1/2, 1/10, 1/100) of a century.

⑧ A (month, year, century) is 1/10 of a decade.

⑨ To determine how many years are in 25 centuries, (divide, increase, multiply) 25 by 100.

⑩ To convert decades to centuries, divide by (1, 10, 100).

Clocks

Learning Objective: *We will learn to distinguish between a.m. and p.m.*

Ante meridian, which is abbreviated a.m., is the period of each day that begins at midnight and lasts until noon. Post meridian, or p.m., begins at noon and lasts until midnight.

EXAMPLES: Clocks measure the 12-hour periods known as a.m. and p.m. The time that passes between 12 a.m. (midnight) and 12 p.m. (noon) is 12 hours. In other words, 12 a.m. plus 12 hours brings us to 12 p.m.

a.m.  **p.m.**

A A beginning time is circled on each of the problems below. Add the number of hours specified and circle the correct ending time on either the a.m. or p.m. clock.

① **a.m.**  **p.m.** ② **a.m.**  **p.m.**  ③ **a.m.**  **p.m.**

2 a.m. + 12 hours   6 a.m. + 6 hours   12 a.m. + 6 hours

④ **a.m.** **p.m.** ⑤ **a.m.**  **p.m.**  ⑥ **a.m.**  **p.m.**

10 a.m. + 3 hours   4 a.m. + 5 hours   8 a.m. + 8 hours

⑦ **a.m.**  **p.m.** ⑧ **a.m.**  **p.m.**  ⑨ **a.m.**  **p.m.**

11 a.m. + 24 hours   9 a.m. + 3 hours   5 a.m. + 14 hours

B Add 12 hours to each of these times.

① 7 a.m. _____ ② 10 p.m. _____ ③ 8 p.m. _____ ④ 11 a.m. _____ ⑤ 3 p.m. _____

REMINDER: *Write the definition of a.m. and p.m.*

_____

_____

C On each of the problems below, a beginning time is circled on the a.m. clock, and an ending time is circled on the p.m. clock. Complete the addition sentence for each problem.

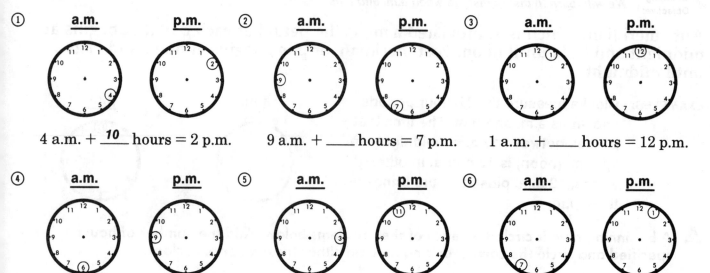

① a.m.   p.m.   ② a.m.   p.m.   ③ a.m.   p.m.

4 a.m. + _10_ hours = 2 p.m.   9 a.m. + ____ hours = 7 p.m.   1 a.m. + ____ hours = 12 p.m.

④ a.m.   p.m.   ⑤ a.m.   p.m.   ⑥ a.m.   p.m.

6 a.m. + ____ hours = 9 p.m.   3 a.m. + ____ hours = 11 p.m.   7 a.m. + ____ hours = 1 p.m.

D Underline the correct answers.

① Another way of writing "noon" is (12 a.m., <u>12 p.m.</u>).

② A clock measures time in (6-hour, 12-hour, 24-hour) periods known as a.m. and p.m.

③ One o'clock in the morning is the same as (1 a.m., 1 p.m.).

④ Ante meridian begins at midnight and lasts until (noon, midnight, 12 a.m.).

⑤ If you were to begin school at 8 a.m. and stay for 7 hours, you would remain at school until (12 p.m., 3 p.m., 5 p.m.).

⑥ (Noon, midnight) is the same as 12 a.m.

⑦ (Post meridian, ante meridian) includes the afternoon hours.

⑧ Persons who report to work at 9 a.m. and close their workday at 5 p.m., spend (4, 8, 14) hours on the job, including breaks.

⑨ There are (12, 24, 48) hours in each day.

278

Comprehension Check

A Match the dates that have the same meanings.

<u>A</u>

① January 19, 1947   2-3-76
② February 3, 1976   10-10-10
③ July 14, 1963   1-19-47
④ October 10, 1910   7-14-63

⑤ April 16, 1952   3-23-47
⑥ May 10, 1917   4-16-52
⑦ March 23, 1947   4-4-34
⑧ April 4, 1934   5-10-17

<u>B</u>

⑨ August 31, 1980   2-1-13
⑩ June 30, 1945   9-1-72
⑪ February 1, 1913   6-30-45
⑫ September 1, 1972   8-31-80

⑬ November 6, 1922   10-2-42
⑭ January 15, 1911   11-6-22
⑮ October 2, 1942   1-15-11
⑯ March 7, 1927   3-7-27

B Convert the following units of time.

① 46 days = __6__ weeks, __4__ days

② 7 weeks, 2 days = _____ hours

③ 450 centuries = _____ decades

④ 190 years = _____ decades

⑤ 710 decades = _____ centuries

⑥ 4,700 years = _____ centuries

⑦ 92 days = _____ weeks, _____ days

⑧ 14 centuries = _____ years

⑨ 230 decades = _____ years

⑩ 40 days = _____ hours

⑪ 2,900 years = _____ centuries

⑫ 916 days = _____ weeks, _____ days

⑬ 85 centuries = _____ decades

⑭ 85 centuries = _____ years

⑮ 100 years = _____ decades

⑯ 6 weeks, 5 days = _____ hours

⑰ 710 years = _____ decades

⑱ 5 decades = _____ years

⑲ 50 decades = _____ centuries

⑳ 1,000 years = _____ centuries

㉑ 72 days = _____ weeks, _____ days

㉒ 200 years = _____ centuries

㉓ 1,200 years = _____ decades

㉔ 16 decades = _____ years

㉕ 47 centuries = _____ decades

㉖ 6 centuries = _____ years

㉗ 3 weeks, 1 day = _____ hours

㉘ 1 century = _____ decades

㉙ 9 decades = _____ years

㉚ 60 days = _____ weeks, _____ days

㉛ 11 centuries = _____ years

㉜ 175 decades = _____ years

㉝ 9 weeks, 6 days = _____ hours

㉞ 28 days = _____ weeks, _____ days

㉟ 31 days = _____ weeks, _____ days

㊱ 365 days = _____ weeks, _____ days

Test 23 cont'd ☞

C **Underline the correct answers.**

① Each (day, week, <u>month</u>) represents 1/12 of a year.

② (April, May, November) is the fifth month of the year.

③ All months have 30 or 31 days except for (January, February, December).

④ December 21 is two weeks past (December 7, December 14, December 28).

⑤ If December, 1987 ends on Friday, January, 1988 begins on (Monday, Friday, Saturday).

⑥ If there are three days in the final calendar week of June, there are (three, four, seven) days in the first calendar week of July.

⑦ There are six (years, decades, centuries) in the period 1730 to 1790.

⑧ A year is (1/12, 1/10, 1/100) of a century. A century is (10, 12, 100) times as long as one decade.

⑨ (Ante meridian, post meridian) includes the evening hours.

⑩ Lunch is usually eaten at (12 a.m., 12 p.m.), or noon.

⑪ A meeting that begins at 11 a.m. and ends at 3 p.m. lasts (two, three, four) hours.

D **Complete the addition sentences.**

①   a.m.   p.m.   ②   a.m.   p.m.

8 a.m. + _____ = 10 p.m.   6 a.m. + _____ = 9 p.m.

③   a.m.   p.m.   ④   a.m.   p.m.

10 a.m. + _____ = 2 p.m.   4 a.m. + _____ = 12 p.m.

Complete the calendar for the current month and year. Then complete the exercise.

① Underline each full calendar week.

② Draw a circle around the date that begins the month.

③ Draw a square around the date that ends the month.

	M	T	W	T	F	S

280

Hours

Learning Objective: *We will learn to write and calculate time.*

An hour is 1/24 of a day.

EXAMPLE: It takes one hour for a clock's short hand to travel one number. One o'clock plus one hour is 2 o'clock or 2:00.

A For each problem below, the hand on the first clock shows the beginning time. On the second clock, draw a hand to show the ending time.

①

4 o'clock + 4 hours

②

12 o'clock + 6 hours

③

9 o'clock + 5 hours

④

7 o'clock + 2 hours

⑤

2 o'clock + 7 hours

⑥

11 o'clock + 12 hours

⑦

3 o'clock + 3 hours

⑧

8 o'clock + 24 hours

⑨

5 o'clock + 9 hours

B 8 o'clock and 8:00 are two ways of writing time. Write these times a second way.

① 7 o'clock _____   ② 11 o'clock _____   ③ 12 o'clock _____   ④ 5 o'clock _____

REMINDER: Write the definition of an hour.

_____

_____

C On each of the problems below, a beginning time is marked on the a.m. clock, and an ending time is marked on the p.m. clock. Complete the addition sentences.

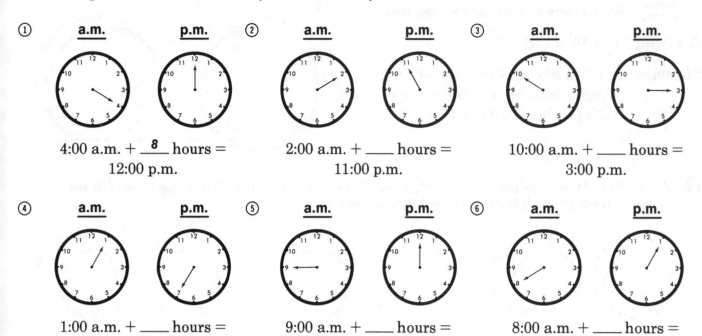

① **a.m.**   **p.m.**

4:00 a.m. + __8__ hours =
12:00 p.m.

② **a.m.**   **p.m.**

2:00 a.m. + ____ hours =
11:00 p.m.

③ **a.m.**   **p.m.**

10:00 a.m. + ____ hours =
3:00 p.m.

④ **a.m.**   **p.m.**

1:00 a.m. + ____ hours =
7:00 p.m.

⑤ **a.m.**   **p.m.**

9:00 a.m. + ____ hours =
12:00 p.m.

⑥ **a.m.**   **p.m.**

8:00 a.m. + ____ hours =
1:00 p.m.

D Underline the correct answers.

① If an hour is 1/24 of a day, there are (12, <u>24</u>, 42) hours in each day.

② The (short, long, second) hand of a clock tells the hour of the day.

③ A six-hour canoe trip that begins at 8:00 a.m. will end at (2:00 a.m., 3:00 p.m., 2:00 p.m.).

④ Three days are equal to (36 hours, <u>72 hours</u>, 48 hours).

⑤ Another way of writing 3 o'clock is (3:00, 3.0, .300).

⑥ If a bus travels 12 hours on each of four days, the total travel time is (24, 48, 60) hours.

⑦ Seven hours past 4 o'clock is (11:00, 3:00, 9:00).

⑧ If a workshop begins at 10:00 in the morning and lasts four hours, it will end at (2:00 a.m., 2:00 p.m., 6:00 a.m.).

⑨ A concert that begins at 7:00 p.m. and ends at 10:00 p.m., lasts a total of (15, 3, 17) hours.

Minutes

Learning Objective: *We will learn to write and calculate time.*

A minute is 1/60 of an hour.

EXAMPLE: It takes five minutes for the clock's long hand to travel one number. Two o'clock plus five minutes is 2:05.

A For each problem below, the hands on the first clock show the beginning time. On the second clock, draw hands to show the ending time.

①

4:15 + 15 minutes

②

12:00 + 30 minutes

③

10:10 + 30 minutes

④

7:00 + 20 minutes

⑤

9:50 + 10 minutes

⑥

3:45 + 15 minutes

⑦

5:25 + 20 minutes

⑧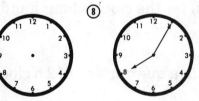

8:05 + 5 minutes

⑨

11:55 + 5 minutes

B A quarter past 4 o'clock is the same as 4:15. Write the equivalents of these times.

① half past one o'clock   ② three-quarters past noon   ③ a quarter until six o'clock

_____   _____   _____

REMINDER: Write the definition of a minute.

_____

_____

Unit 117 cont'd ☞

C On each of the problems below, a beginning time is marked on the first clock, and an ending time is marked on the second clock. Complete the addition sentences.

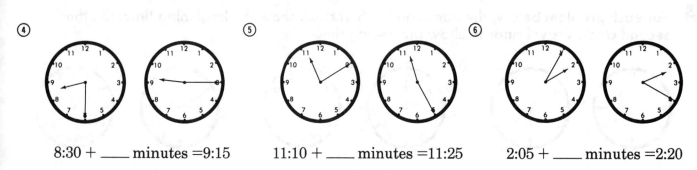

① 5:00 + __35__ minutes = 5:35

② 2:50 + ____ minutes = 3:00

③ 9:15 + ____ minutes = 9:45

④ 8:30 + ____ minutes =9:15

⑤ 11:10 + ____ minutes =11:25

⑥ 2:05 + ____ minutes =2:20

D Underline the correct answers.

① If a minute is 1/60 of an hour, there are (10, 16, 60) minutes in one hour.

② If the clock's long hand points to the number one, it is (one minute past, five minutes past, five minutes before) the hour.

③ It takes (one hour, one minute, five minutes) for the clock's long hand to travel from the number six to the number seven.

④ (Midnight + 15 minutes, a quarter past noon, a quarter until 12 o'clock) is the same as 12:15 p.m.

⑤ If a plane lands at 7:55 after a 45-minute flight, departure time was (8:40, 7:10, 8:50).

⑥ If a movie lasts 120 minutes, it is (1, 2, 12) hours in duration.

⑦ Twenty-four hours, or one day, is equal to (4, 60, 1,440) minutes.

⑧ To convert hours to minutes, (divide, multiply, increase) by 60.

⑨ To convert minutes to hours, (divide, multiply, increase) by 60.

Digital Time

Learning
Objective: *We will learn to write and calculate time.*

A digital clock shows the time in the form of numbers.

EXAMPLES:

A clock with hands would show
2 o'clock as this.

A digital clock face would show
2 o'clock as this.

2:00

A Study the clocks below and write the equivalent digital times.

①

②

③

④

⑤

⑥

_4:00_

⑦

⑧

⑨

⑩

⑪

⑫

⑬

⑭

⑮

⑯

⑰

⑱

B Write the equivalent digital times.

① _____ fifteen minutes past 8 o'clock

② _____ forty-four minutes past eleven

③ _____ twelve minutes until two

④ _____ a quarter until midnight

REMINDER: Write the definition of a digital clock.

_____

_____

Unit 118 cont'd ☞

C To calculate the amount of time that has passed, subtract the beginning time from the ending time.

①

6:15 − 2:10 =
___4___ hours, ___5___ minutes

②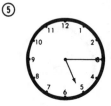

9:30 − 5:05 =
_____ hours, _____ minutes

③

11:55 − 8:20 =
_____ hours, _____ minutes

④

4:10 − 1:00 =
_____ hours, _____ minutes

⑤

8:15 − 5:15 =
_____ hours, _____ minutes

⑥

10:20 − 7:00 =
_____ hours, _____ minutes

D Underline the correct answers.

① If a clock's long hand points to the number four and its short hand points to the number seven, the digital time equivalent would be (4:07, 7:20, 7:04).

② If a train departs a station at 8:47 and arrives at its destination 3 hours and 10 minutes later, its arrival time would be (5:37, 5:57, 11:57).

③ (Two hours, 6 minutes; 18 hours, 40 minutes; 2 hours, 40 minutes) is the duration of a play that begins at 8:17 p.m. and ends at 10:23 p.m.

④ In digital time, the numeral or numerals to the left of the colon tell the (hour, minute, second).

⑤ (Twelve minutes until 3 o'clock, 31 minutes until two, twelve past three) is the same as 3:12.

⑥ In digital time, the numerals to the right of the colon tell the (hour, minute, second).

⑦ In one hour, the (short, long, second) hand of a clock travels one number.

⑧ On a digital clock, the number to the (left, right) of the colon changes every hour.

286

Recognizing Coins

Learning
Objective: *We will learn to identify a penny, nickel, dime, and quarter.*

A coin is a piece of metal that is issued by the government as money.

EXAMPLES:
The U.S. government
issues coins of different
sizes and values.

penny	nickel	dime	quarter
1¢	5¢	10¢	25¢

A Match the sets with their descriptions.

① Set A =

Two nickels, two dimes,
and three pennies.

② Set B =

Two quarters, two nickels,
and three dimes.

③ Set C =

One quarter, one dime, two
nickels, and two pennies.

④ Set D =

Five pennies, one nickel,
and two dimes.

⑤ Set E =

Five dimes, one quarter,
and two nickels.

REMINDER: Write the definition of a coin.

_____

_____

Unit 119 cont'd ☛

B Identify the value of each coin. At the end of each row, total the values.

①

___25___ ¢ + ___5___ ¢ + ___10___ ¢ = ___40___ ¢

②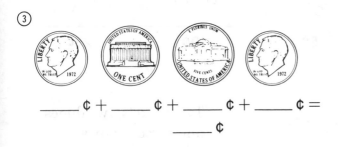

_____ ¢ + _____ ¢ + _____ ¢ = _____ ¢

③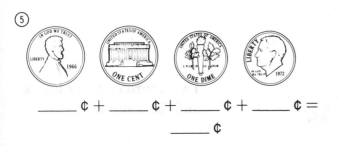

_____ ¢ + _____ ¢ + _____ ¢ + _____ ¢ =

_____ ¢

④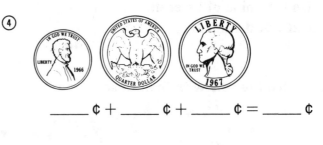

_____ ¢ + _____ ¢ + _____ ¢ = _____ ¢

⑤

_____ ¢ + _____ ¢ + _____ ¢ + _____ ¢ =

_____ ¢

⑥

_____ ¢ + _____ ¢ + _____ ¢ = _____ ¢

C Underline the correct answers.

① (George Washington, Abraham Lincoln, Benjamin Franklin) is pictured on the U.S. 25-cent piece.

② A nickel is (larger than, smaller than, the same size as) a dime.

③ The value of a nickel is (greater than, less than, the same as) the value of a dime.

④ A quarter, a penny, and a (nickel, dime, quarter) equals 36¢.

⑤ If one person has a dime, another has a penny, and another has a nickel, the person with the (dime, penny, nickel) has the most money.

⑥ Franklin D. Roosevelt is pictured on a (dime, penny, nickel).

⑦ If a person has two coins totaling 30¢ and one of the coins is a nickel, the other coin is a (penny, dime, quarter).

⑧ A (penny, nickel, dime) is a different color than other U.S. coins.

⑨ The combined value of two nickels is equal to the value of one (penny, dime, quarter).

Recognizing Bills

Learning Objective: *We will learn to identify a $1, $5, $10, and $20 bill.*

A bill is a piece of paper that is issued by the government as money.

EXAMPLES: The U.S. government issues bills of different values.

$1 $5 $10 $20

A Match the sets with their descriptions.

① Set A

Three $5 bills, two $20 bills, and one $10 bill.

_____

② Set B

Two $1 bills, one $5 bill, and two $10 bills.

_____

③ Set C

One $20 bill, two $10 bills, and two $1 bills.

_____

④ Set D

Three $10 bills, two $5 bills, and one $1 bill.

_____

⑤ Set E

Two $10 bills, one $20 bill, and two $1 bills.

_____

REMINDER: Write the definition of a bill.

_____

_____

B Identify the value of each bill. At the end of each row, total the values.

①

$ __10__ + $ __5__ + $ __5__ + $ __1__ =
$ __21__

②

$ ____ + $ ____ + $ ____ + $ ____ =
$ ____

③

$ ____ + $ ____ + $ ____ + $ ____ =
$ ____

④

$ ____ + $ ____ + $ ____ + $ ____ =
$ ____

⑤

$ ____ + $ ____ + $ ____ + $ ____ =
$ ____

⑥

$ ____ + $ ____ + $ ____ + $ ____ =
$ ____

C Underline the correct answers.

① (George Washington, <u>Andrew Jackson</u>, Abraham Lincoln) is pictured on a $20 bill.

② The value of two $10 bills is equal to (one $20 bill, three $5 bills, five $1 bills).

③ If a person has two bills totaling $30, that person has (a $5 bill and a $10 bill, two $10 bills, a $10 bill and a $20 bill).

④ A $20 bill has four times the value of (two $1 bills, a $5 bill, a $10 bill).

⑤ George Washington is pictured on a ($1 bill, $5 bill, $20 bill).

⑥ A ($1 bill, $5 bill, $10 bill) has the least value of any paper money that is issued by the U.S. government.

⑦ The value of three $5 bills is (greater than, less than, equal to) the value of two $10 bills.

⑧ If an item costs $44, (four $10 bills and one $5 bill, two $20 bills and four $1 bills, four $5 bills and four $1 bills) would cover the expense exactly.

Comprehension Check

Test 24

A For each problem below, the hand on the first clock shows the beginning hour. On the second clock, draw a hand to show the ending hour.

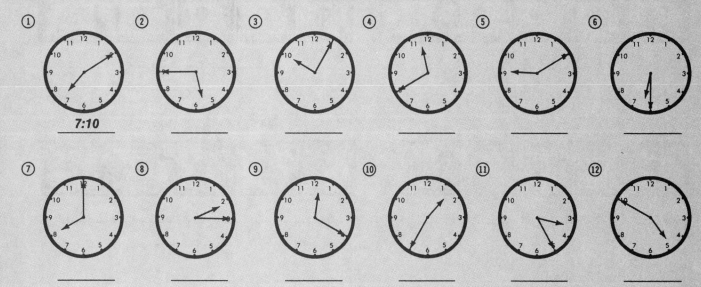

① **a.m.** **p.m.**
5 o'clock + 8 hours

② **a.m.** **p.m.**
9 o'clock + 6 hours

③ **a.m.** **p.m.**
11 o'clock + 1 hour

④ **a.m.** **p.m.**
2 o'clock + 12 hours

⑤ **a.m.** **p.m.**
4 o'clock + 16 hours

⑥ **a.m.** **p.m.**
8 o'clock + 9 hours

B Study the clocks and write the equivalent digital times.

① ② ③ ④ ⑤ ⑥

7:10 _____ _____ _____ _____ _____

⑦ ⑧ ⑨ ⑩ ⑪ ⑫

_____ _____ _____ _____ _____ _____

C For each problem, write a subtraction sentence to calculate the time that has passed.

① From 8:35 a.m. to 11:52 a.m.
  11:52 − 8:35 = 3 hours, 17 minutes

② From 9:02 p.m. to 10:27 p.m.
  _____

③ From 2:13 p.m. to 7:45 p.m.
  _____

④ From 3:05 p.m. to 9:50 p.m.
  _____

⑤ From 1:36 a.m. to 6:41 a.m.
  _____

⑥ From 5:17 a.m. to 8:25 a.m.
  _____

Test 24 cont'd ☞

D Identify the value of each coin. At the end of each row, total the values.

①

_____ ¢ + _____ ¢ + _____ ¢ + _____ ¢ =
_____ ¢

②

_____ ¢ + _____ ¢ + _____ ¢ + _____ ¢ =
_____ ¢

③

_____ ¢ + _____ ¢ + _____ ¢ + _____ ¢ =
_____ ¢

④

_____ ¢ + _____ ¢ + _____ ¢ + _____ ¢ =
_____ ¢

E Identify and total the values of the following bills.

①

$ _____ + $ _____ + $ _____ + $ _____ =
$ _____

②

$ _____ + $ _____ + $ _____ + $ _____ =
$ _____

③

$ _____ + $ _____ + $ _____ + $ _____ =
$ _____

④

$ _____ + $ _____ + $ _____ + $ _____ =
$ _____

F Fill in the blanks.

① In digital time, the hour and the minute are separated by a _____ .

② To convert hours to minutes, _____ by 60.

③ Seven days are equal to _____ hours.

④ The digital time for half past two is _____ .

Write the definitions of (a) an hour, (b) a minute, (c) a coin, and (d) a bill.

(a) _____

(b) _____

(c) _____

(d) _____

Pennies

Learning Objective: *We will learn to add, subtract, and multiply cents and to convert to dollars.*

A penny, or one cent, is a coin that is issued by the U.S. government and that has a value of 1/100 of one dollar.

EXAMPLE: One hundred pennies equal one dollar.

100 × =

A Complete the addition sentences.

①

____¢ + ____¢ = ____¢

②

____¢ + ____¢ = ____¢

③

____¢ + ____¢ + ____¢ = ____¢

④

____¢ + ____¢ = ____¢

B Complete the subtraction sentences.

①

____¢ – ____¢ = ____¢

②

____¢ – ____¢ = ____¢

③

____¢ – ____¢ = ____¢

④

____¢ – ____¢ = ____¢

C Complete the multiplication sentences.

① 7 × = ____¢

② 15 × = ____¢

③ 10 × = ____¢

④ 25 × = ____¢

REMINDER: Write the definition of a penny.

Unit 121 cont'd ☞

D Add, subtract, or multiply.

①		②		③		④		⑤		⑥		⑦		⑧	
	10¢		75¢		12¢		18¢		61¢		13¢		56¢		13¢
+	30¢	−	34¢	×	2	×	3	−	42¢	+	27¢	+	18¢	−	11¢
	40¢														

⑨		⑩		⑪		⑫		⑬		⑭		⑮		⑯	
	46¢		22¢		84¢		12¢		31¢		16¢		77¢		89¢
+	37¢	×	3	−	71¢	×	3	×	2	×	4	−	44¢	−	60¢

⑰		⑱		⑲		⑳		㉑		㉒		㉓		㉔	
	39¢		39¢		91¢		5¢		49¢		64¢		19¢		14¢
+	39¢	×	2	−	87¢	+	6¢	×	2	+	29¢	−	12¢	×	6

E Convert cents to dollars and cents.

① 106¢ = ___*$1.06*___   ② 221¢ = _____   ③ 416¢ = _____   ④ 921¢ = _____

⑤ 367¢ = _____   ⑥ 199¢ = _____   ⑦ 555¢ = _____   ⑧ 618¢ = _____

F Underline the correct answers.

① There are (867, <u>768</u>, 7.68) cents in $7.68.

② One cent plus one cent plus one cent plus one cent is equal to ($1, 1¢ − 1¢, 4 × 1¢).

③ If an item costs $5.99, (59, 599, 99 × 5) pennies would be needed to purchase the item.

④ If you found a penny each day for (36, 65, 365) days, you would find a total of $3.65.

⑤ An overdue fine at the library is 12¢. You search your pockets but only find 8¢. You need (20, 4, 96) more pennies to pay the fine.

⑥ For bank deposits, pennies are packaged in rolls of 50. If four rolls of pennies are deposited, the total deposit is ($4.50, 5,000¢, $2.00).

⑦ A piece of bubble gum costs 2¢. A soda costs 50¢. A small bag of potato chips cost 26¢. Total cost of all items is ($25.25, 78¢, $7.80).

⑧ A penny is another name for (one cent, one dollar, one nickel).

Nickels

Learning Objective: *We will learn to add, subtract, multiply and divide dollars and cents.*

A nickel is a U.S. coin that has a value of 5 cents or 1/20 of one dollar.

EXAMPLE: Twenty nickels equal one dollar.

20 ×  =

A Complete the addition sentences.

①

_____¢ + _____¢ + _____¢ + _____¢ = _____¢

②

_____¢ + _____¢ = _____¢

B Complete the subtraction sentences.

①

_____¢ − _____¢ = _____¢

②

_____¢ − _____¢ = _____¢

C Complete the multiplication sentences.

①

 × 3 = _____¢

②

 × 2 = _____¢

D Complete the division sentences.

①  ÷ 2 = _____¢

②  ÷ 5 = _____¢

REMINDER: Write the definition of a nickel.

_____

_____

Unit 122 cont'd ☞

E Add, subtract, divide, or multiply.

① $.75 − $.30 = $ __.45__ , or __9__ nickels   ② $2.25 ÷ 9 = $ _____ , or _____ nickels

③ $.20 + $.15 = $ _____ , or _____ nickels   ④ $.80 × 3 = $ _____ , or _____ nickels

⑤ $3.50 ÷ 7 = $ _____ , or _____ nickels   ⑥ $.80 + $.30 = $ _____ , or _____ nickels

⑦ $.90 + $.65 = $ _____ , or _____ nickels   ⑧ $3.00 − $2.45 = $ _____ , or _____ nickels

⑨ 4 × $3.15 = $ _____ , or _____ nickels   ⑩ 6 × $1.10 = $ _____ , or _____ nickels

⑪ $5.60 ÷ 8 = $ _____ , or _____ nickels   ⑫ $4.45 − $.85 = $ _____ , or _____ nickels

⑬ 100 × $.15 = $ _____ , or _____ nickels   ⑭ $.25 + $.60 = $ _____ , or _____ nickels

⑮ $6.85 − $3.25 = $ _____ , or _____ nickels   ⑯ $1.90 + $2.15 = $ _____ , or _____ nickels

⑰ $9.00 − $6.85 = $ _____ , or _____ nickels   ⑱ $.40 × 8 = $ _____ , or _____ nickels

F Underline the correct answers.

① To find the number of nickels required to purchase an item that costs $2.45, divide 245 by (5, 10, 20).

② When money amounts are written in numeric form, a (colon, comma, decimal) separates dollars and cents.

③ Forty-five nickels equal (22, 25, 225) cents, or $2.25.

④ Suppose a postage stamp costs 5 nickels, an envelope costs 10 nickels, and a pen costs 20 nickels. The total cost of all items is ($1.75, 70¢, 35¢).

⑤ If you save one nickel each day until you have saved a total of $9.00, you have saved for (90, 180, 45) days.

⑥ (Ten, Five, Two) pennies have the same value as one nickel.

⑦ If a bank contains 100 nickels and 50 nickels are removed, ($1.00, 50¢, $2.50) remains.

⑧ One nickel plus one nickel plus one nickel plus one nickel plus one nickel equals ($5, 5 × 1¢, 5 × 5¢).

Dimes

Learning Objective: *We will learn to add, subtract, multiply and divide dollars and cents.*

A dime is a U.S. coin that has a value of 10 cents or 1/10 of one dollar.

EXAMPLE: Ten dimes equal one dollar.

10 × =

A Complete the addition sentences.

①

___**10**___ ¢ + _____ ¢ + _____ ¢ + _____ ¢ = _____ ¢

②

_____ ¢ + _____ ¢ = _____ ¢

B Complete the subtraction sentences.

①

_____ ¢ − _____ ¢ = _____ ¢

②

_____ ¢ − _____ ¢ = _____ ¢

C Complete the multiplication sentences.

①  × 2 = _____ ¢

②  × 3 = _____ ¢

D Complete the division sentences.

① ÷ 25 = _____ ¢

② ÷ 2 = _____ ¢

REMINDER: Write the definition of a dime.

_____

_____

E Add, subtract, divide, or multiply.

① $.80 + $.20 = $ __1.00__, or __10__ dimes

② $5.00 ÷ 5 = $ _____, or _____ dimes

③ $.60 − $.40 = $ _____, or _____ dimes

④ 3 × $.10 = $ _____, or _____ dimes

⑤ $.40 + $.30 + $.10 = $ _____, or _____ dimes

⑥ $1.70 + $.80 = $ _____, or _____ dimes

⑦ $8.00 ÷ 4 = $ _____, or _____ dimes

⑧ $2.50 × 2 = $ _____, or _____ dimes

⑨ $7.20 − $5.50 = $ _____, or _____ dimes

⑩ $.10 + $.10 + $.10 = $ _____, or _____ dimes

⑪ 4 × $.60 = $ _____, or _____ dimes

⑫ $2.00 ÷ 5 = $ _____, or _____ dimes

⑬ $.90 − $.30 = $ _____, or _____ dimes

⑭ $1.10 ÷ 11 = $ _____, or _____ dime

⑮ $3.60 ÷ 9 = $ _____, or _____ dimes

⑯ 4 × $.30 = $ _____, or _____ dimes

⑰ $.80 + $.50 = $ _____, or _____ dimes

⑱ $2.20 − $1.00 = $ _____, or _____ dimes

F Underline the correct answers.

① The symbol for dollars is (<u>$</u>, ¢, %).

② A dime has (one, two, three) times the value of a nickel.

③ If a local telephone call costs two dimes, one call each day for one week would cost ($.70, $.20, $1.40).

④ If you paid $5.00 for an item that cost only $4.40, you might receive (four dimes, five dimes, six dimes) in change.

⑤ To find the number of dimes required to purchase an item that costs $2.30, divide 230 by (5, 10, 20).

⑥ One dime plus one dime plus one dime equals (3¢, 3 × $10, 3 × 10¢).

⑦ (George Washington, Franklin D. Roosevelt, Benjamin Franklin) is pictured on the U.S. dime.

⑧ One dime has the value of (one, five, ten) pennies.

⑨ The value of ten dimes is equal to twenty (pennies, nickels, dollars).

Quarters

Learning
Objective: *We will learn to add, subtract, multiply, and divide dollars and cents.*

A quarter is a U.S. coin that has a value of 25 cents or 1/4 of one dollar.

EXAMPLE: Four quarters equal one dollar.

4 ×  =

A Complete the addition sentences.

①

____¢ + ____¢ + ____¢ = ____¢

②

____¢ + ____¢ = ____¢

B Complete the subtraction sentences.

①

____¢ − ____¢ = ____¢

②

____¢ − ____¢ = ____¢

C Complete the multiplication sentences.

①

× 1 = ____¢

②

× 2 = ____¢

D Complete the division sentences.

①

÷ 5 = ____¢

②

÷ 2 = ____¢

REMINDER: Write the definition of a quarter.

_____

_____

Unit 124 cont'd ☞

E Add, subtract, divide, or multiply.

① $.75 + $.75 = $ _1.50_, or _6_ quarters

② $2.00 − $1.00 = $ _____, or _____ quarters

③ $.50 × 5 = $ _____, or _____ quarters

④ $3.00 ÷ 2 = $ _____, or _____ quarters

⑤ $.25 + $.50 + $1.00 = $ _____, or _____ quarters

⑥ $3.50 − $.50 = $ _____, or _____ quarters

⑦ $5.00 − $3.50 = $ _____, or _____ quarters

⑧ $5.00 ÷ 2 = $ _____, or _____ quarters

⑨ 3 × $1.25 = $ _____, or _____ quarters

⑩ $1.50 + $2.00 = $ _____, or _____ quarters

⑪ $.25 × 8 = $ _____, or _____ quarters

⑫ $10.00 ÷ 5 = $ _____, or _____ quarters

⑬ $2.25 − $.50 = $ _____, or _____ quarters

⑭ 4 × $.50 = $ _____, or _____ quarters

⑮ $.25 + $1.50 + $.75 = $ _____, or _____ quarters

⑯ $4.75 − $3.25 = $ _____, or _____ quarters

⑰ $3.50 − $3.00 = $ _____, or _____ quarters

⑱ $2.25 × 3 = $ _____, or _____ quarters

F Underline the correct answers.

① The value of a quarter is (greater than, less than, the same as) the combined value of a dime, a nickel, and a penny.

② To find the number of quarters required to purchase an item that costs $8.00, (decrease, divide, multiply) 800 by 25.

③ At a coin-operated laundry, the cost of operating a washer is 60¢ per load. Each load requires two quarters and one dime. (Six, twelve, eighteen) quarters would be required to wash six loads of laundry.

④ (George Washington, Abraham Lincoln, Benjamin Franklin) is pictured on a U.S. quarter.

⑤ One quarter has the value of (five, ten, twenty-five) pennies.

⑥ A quarter has five times the value of one (nickel, dime, dollar).

⑦ The combined value of (two dimes and one nickel, four nickels, two dimes and ten pennies) is equal to one quarter.

⑧ One quarter plus one quarter plus one quarter plus one quarter equals ($2.50, 25¢ ÷ 4, 25¢ × 4).

Making Change With Coins

Unit 125

Learning Objective: *We will learn to calculate change by subtraction and addition.*

Change is the money that is returned when the amount paid is more than the amount due.

EXAMPLE: Change can be calculated by two methods: (1) Subtract the amount due from the amount paid, or (2) add to the amount due until the sum equals the amount paid.

(1)				(2)		
Amount Paid	–	Amount Due	= Change	Amount Due	+ Change	= Amount Paid
75¢		65¢	10¢	65¢	10¢	75¢

A Calculate the amount of change for each problem below; then list 3 ways in which you could make change.

① Amount Paid – Amount Due = Change

25¢ – 12¢ = **13¢**

	25¢	10¢	5¢	1¢	Total
a		1		3	13¢
b			2	3	13¢
c				13	13¢

② Amount Paid – Amount Due = Change

50¢ – 35¢ = _____

	25¢	10¢	5¢	1¢	Total
a					
b					
c					

③ Amount Paid – Amount Due = Change

75¢ – 52¢ = _____

	25¢	10¢	5¢	1¢	Total
a					
b					
c					

④ Amount Paid – Amount Due = Change

$1.00 – 75¢ = _____

	25¢	10¢	5¢	1¢	Total
a					
b					
c					

⑤ Amount Paid – Amount Due = Change

$3.25 – $3.15¢ = _____

	25¢	10¢	5¢	1¢	Total
a					
b					
c					

⑥ Amount Paid – Amount Due = Change

$2.00 – $1.83 = _____

	25¢	10¢	5¢	1¢	Total
a					
b					
c					

⑦ Amount Paid – Amount Due = Change

$5.50 – $5.18 = _____

	25¢	10¢	5¢	1¢	Total
a					
b					
c					

⑧ Amount Paid – Amount Due = Change

$8.00 – $7.12¢ = _____

	25¢	10¢	5¢	1¢	Total
a					
b					
c					

⑨ Amount Paid – Amount Due = Change

$1.75 – $1.55 = _____

	25¢	10¢	5¢	1¢	Total
a					
b					
c					

REMINDER: Write the definition of change.

301

Unit 125 cont'd ☞

B Match the change with the correct problem.

① $2.14 + \underline{\quad?\quad} = \$2.25$ 2 pennies, 1 nickel   ⑨ $3.11 + \underline{\quad?\quad} = \$3.50$ 4 pennies, 1 dime, 1 quarter

② $97¢ + \underline{\quad?\quad} = \$1.00$ 1 penny, 1 dime   ⑩ $2.74 + \underline{\quad?\quad} = \$2.80$ 1 nickel, 1 dime

③ $33¢ + \underline{\quad?\quad} = 40¢$ 1 dime   ⑪ $1.10 + \underline{\quad?\quad} = \$1.25$ 1 penny, 2 dimes

④ $5.60 + \underline{\quad?\quad} = \$5.70$ 3 pennies   ⑫ $29¢ + \underline{\quad?\quad} = 50¢$ 1 penny, 1 nickel

⑤ $66¢ + \underline{\quad?\quad} = 75¢$ 4 pennies, 2 dimes   ⑬ $6.52 + \underline{\quad?\quad} = \$6.75$ 3 pennies, 1 nickel

⑥ $1.59 + \underline{\quad?\quad} = \$1.75$ 3 pennies, 1 quarter   ⑭ $44¢ + \underline{\quad?\quad} = \$1.00$ 3 pennies, 2 dimes

⑦ $4.76 + \underline{\quad?\quad} = \$5.00$ 4 pennies, 1 nickel   ⑮ $8.17 + \underline{\quad?\quad} = \$8.25$ 1 dime, 3 quarters

⑧ $72¢ + \underline{\quad?\quad} = \$1.00$ 1 penny, 1 nickel, 1 dime   ⑯ $1.15 + \underline{\quad?\quad} = \$2.00$ 1 penny, 1 nickel, 2 quarters

C Underline the correct answers.

① Paula bought a photograph album at a cost of $11.53, including sales tax. Paula gave the store cashier $12.00. In change, Paula received (2 quarters; 4 dimes and 3 pennies; 2 pennies, 2 dimes, and 1 quarter).

② After buying a theater ticket for $3.50, Tom walked to the concession stand to spend the change he had received from the four $1-bills that he had given the ticket salesperson. He found that, for exactly the amount of money which remained, he could buy (two candy bars for 1 quarter apiece, six pieces of bubblegum at a dime each, four licorice sticks for a nickel apiece).

③ The Henderson High School Student Council sold homecoming mums for $2.55 each. Ralph gave the salesperson two $1-bills and three quarters for one mum. Steve bought his mum with three $1-bills. (Ralph, Steve) received more in change.

④ When she handed the sales clerk $1 for a 12¢ purchase, Lillian asked to receive all quarters for change. The sales clerk replied that what Lillian asked was not possible. Instead of all quarters, the clerk gave Lillian (2 pennies and 1 dime; 3 pennies, 1 dime, and 3 quarters; 2 dimes and 2 quarters).

Comprehension Check

A Convert cents to dollars and cents.

① 809¢ = _____   ② 113¢ = _____   ③ 254¢ = _____   ④ 677¢ = _____

B Convert dollars and cents to cents.

① $3.97 = _____   ② $4.71 = _____   ③ $7.23 = _____   ④ $9.07 = _____

C Add, subtract, divide, or multiply.

① 75¢ ÷ 3 = _**25¢**_, or _**5**_ nickels

② 42¢ − 13¢ = _____, or _____ pennies

③ 28¢ + 47¢ = _____, or _____ quarters

④ $1.20 ÷ 4 = _____, or _____ dimes

⑤ 12¢ × 5 = _____, or _____ dimes

⑥ 14¢ + 26¢ = _____, or _____ nickels

⑦ 66¢ ÷ 11 = _____, or _____ pennies

⑧ $2.75 − $.25 = _____, or _____ quarters

⑨ $3.16 − $1.96 = _____, or _____ dimes

⑩ 69¢ × 5 = _____, or _____ pennies

⑪ $7.00 + $.50 = _____, or _____ quarters

⑫ $2.40 ÷ 4 = _____, or _____ nickels

⑬ 45¢ × 2 = _____, or _____ dimes

⑭ $3.78 + $.22 = _____, or _____ quarters

⑮ $9.10 − $8.00 = _____, or _____ pennies

⑯ $2.90 × 3 = _____, or _____ dimes

D Underline the correct answers.

① One (dime, quarter, dollar) has the value of 25 pennies or 5 nickels.

② One (penny, dime, quarter) has the value of 2 nickels or 1/10 of a dollar.

③ (Four, Eight, Twenty) quarters are required to buy four sodas at a cost of 50¢ apiece.

④ To wash three loads of laundry at 60¢ apiece, (2 quarters, 1 dime; 6 quarters, 6 dimes; 6 quarters, 3 dimes) are required.

⑤ (Abraham Lincoln, George Washinton, Benjamin Franklin) is pictured on a U.S. penny.

⑥ The combined value of (5 pennies and 1 nickel, 3 nickels, 1 penny and 1 quarter) is equal to one dime.

⑦ If you had 15¢ but lost a nickel, a (penny, nickel, dime) would remain.

Test 25 cont'd ☛

E Calculate the amount of change for each problem; then list 3 ways to make change for that problem.

① Amount   Amount
Paid – Due = Change

75¢ – 54¢ = _____21¢_____

	25¢	10¢	5¢	1¢	Total
a		2		1	21¢
b		1	2	1	21¢
c			4	1	21¢

② Amount   Amount
Paid – Due = Change

25¢ – 11¢ = _____

	25¢	10¢	5¢	1¢	Total
a					
b					
c					

③ Amount   Amount
Paid – Due = Change

50¢ – 31¢ = _____

	25¢	10¢	5¢	1¢	Total
a					
b					
c					

④ Amount   Amount
Paid – Due = Change

$1.00 – 70¢ = _____

	25¢	10¢	5¢	1¢	Total
a					
b					
c					

⑤ Amount   Amount
Paid – Due = Change

$2.50 – $2.05 = _____

	25¢	10¢	5¢	1¢	Total
a					
b					
c					

⑥ Amount   Amount
Paid – Due = Change

$5.25 – $5.01 = _____

	25¢	10¢	5¢	1¢	Total
a					
b					
c					

F Match the change with the correct problem.

① $9.24 + __?__ = $9.50   1 penny, 1 nickel

② 9¢ + __?__ = 15¢   1 penny, 1 dime

③ $4.98 + __?__ = $5.00   1 penny, 1 quarter

④ 89¢ + __?__ = $1.00   2 pennies

⑤ $3.70 + __?__ = $4.00   1 dime, 2 quarters

⑥ 52¢ + __?__ = 60¢   1 nickel, 1 quarter

⑦ 37¢ + __?__ = 50¢   3 pennies, 1 dime

⑧ $2.40 + __?__ = $3.00   3 pennies, 1 nickel

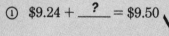

List 8 ways in which you can make change totaling 64¢.

① _____   ② _____

③ _____   ④ _____

⑤ _____   ⑥ _____

⑦ _____   ⑧ _____

Making Change with Bills

Learning Objective: *We will learn to calculate change by subtraction and addition.*

Change is the money that is returned when the amount paid is more than the amount due.

EXAMPLES:

Change in bills is calculated by the same methods as change in coins.

①

Amount Paid	−	Amount Due	=	Change
$5	−	$3	=	$2

②

Amount Due	+	Change	=	Amount Paid
$3	+	$2	=	$5

A Calculate the amount of change for each problem below, then list 3 ways in which you could make change. (Note for teachers: Other combinations of bills are possible.)

①

Amount Paid	−	Amount Due	=	Change
$50	−	$20	=	*$30*

	$20	$10	$5	$1	Total
a	1	1			$30
b	1			2	$30
c		3			$30

②

Amount Paid	−	Amount Due	=	Change
$20	+	$4	=	

	$20	$10	$5	$1	Total
a					
b					
c					

③

Amount Paid	−	Amount Due	=	Change
$40	−	$21	=	

	$20	$10	$5	$1	Total
a					
b					
c					

④

Amount Paid	−	Amount Due	=	Change
$80	−	$65	=	

	$20	$10	$5	$1	Total
a					
b					
c					

⑤

Amount Paid	−	Amount Due	=	Change
$100	+	$14	=	

	$20	$10	$5	$1	Total
a					
b					
c					

⑥

Amount Paid	−	Amount Due	=	Change
$50	−	$12	=	

	$20	$10	$5	$1	Total
a					
b					
c					

⑦

Amount Paid	−	Amount Due	=	Change
$200	−	$127	=	

	$20	$10	$5	$1	Total
a					
b					
c					

⑧

Amount Paid	−	Amount Due	=	Change
$160	+	$149	=	

	$20	$10	$5	$1	Total
a					
b					
c					

⑨

Amount Paid	−	Amount Due	=	Change
$320	−	$306	=	

	$20	$10	$5	$1	Total
a					
b					
c					

REMINDER: Write the definition of change.

_____

_____

B Match the change with the correct problem.

① $11 + ___?___ = $15   3 $1-bills, 1 $5-bill   ⑨ $505 + ___?___ = $550   1 $5-bill, 2 $20-bills

② $2 + ___?___ = $10   4 $1-bills, 1 $5-bill   ⑩ $227 + ___?___ = $230   2 $1-bills, 1 $5-bill

③ $61 + ___?___ = $70   4 $1-bills   ⑪ $115 + ___?___ = $130   3 $1-bills

④ $137 + ___?___ = $150   3 $1-bills, 1 $10-bill   ⑫ $3 + ___?___ = $10   1 $5-bill, 1 $10-bill

⑤ $17 + ___?___ = $100   2 $1-bills, 4 $10-bills   ⑬ $714 + ___?___ = $720   1 $1-bill, 1 $10-bill

⑥ $48 + ___?___ = $60   3 $1-bills, 4 $20-bills   ⑭ $422 + ___?___ = $433   1 $1-bill, 1 $5-bill

⑦ $8 + ___?___ = $50   2 $1-bills, 1 $10-bill   ⑮ $608 + ___?___ = $650   3 $1-bills, 1 $20-bill

⑧ $22 + ___?___ = $40   3 $1-bills, 3 $5-bills   ⑯ $77 + ___?___ = $100   2 $1-bills, 2 $20-bills

C Underline the correct answers.

① Samantha and Edgar went together to buy a clock that cost $42, including tax. Samantha gave a $10-bill and a $20-bill to the sales clerk. Edgar gave the clerk a $1-bill and a $20-bill. The clerk returned (4 $1-bills and 1 $5-bill; 2 $5-bills; 2 $1-bills and 1 $10-bill) in change.

② Members of the Union High School marching band undertook a fund-raising project to earn money for new uniforms. Each member pledged to sell 10 candy bars at $2.00 apiece. The band was guaranteed that $1 of every $2 earned would be returned by the candy company to the school. Thirty band members sold their pledged number of candy bars. The candy company returned to the school ($100, $300, $600).

③ Robert earned $100 per month mowing lawns during the three-month summer vacation from school. With the money earned he bought clothes at Wesley's Department Store. He purchased five pairs of slacks, five shirts, a jacket, and a pair of shoes at a total cost of $279. Robert gave the cashier all the money that he had earned during the summer. In change, Robert received (5 $5-bills; 4 $1-bills, 1 $5-bill, and 1 $20-bill; 1 $1-bill and 1 $20-bill).

④ Rachel withdrew $200 from her savings account to pay for registration at a poetry workshop. Cost of registration was $164. Rachel received (2 $20-bills; 1 $1-bill, 1 $5-bill, and 3 $10-bills; 4 $1-bills and 1 $20-bill) in change.

Buying

Learning Objective: *We will learn to calculate change by subtraction and addition.*

Change is the money that is returned when the amount paid is more than the amount due.

EXAMPLES:

Change can be calculated by two methods.

①

Amount Paid	–	Amount Due	=	Change
$20.00	–	$11.85	=	$8.15

②

Amount Due	+	Change	=	Amount Paid
$11.85	+	$8.15	=	$20.00

A Calculate the amount of change for each problem below, then list 3 ways in which change could be made.

① Amount Paid — Amount Due = Change

$5.00 — $3.76 = **$1.24**

	$20	$10	$5	$1	25¢	10¢	5¢	1¢	Total
a				1		2		4	$1.24
b				1		1	2	4	$1.24
c					4		4	4	$1.24

② Amount Paid — Amount Due = Change

$10.00 — $8.22 = _____

	$20	$10	$5	$1	25¢	10¢	5¢	1¢	Total
a									
b									
c									

③ Amount Paid — Amount Due = Change

$15.00 — $12.37 = _____

	$20	$10	$5	$1	25¢	10¢	5¢	1¢	Total
a									
b									
c									

④ Amount Paid — Amount Due = Change

$50.00 — $24.85 = _____

	$20	$10	$5	$1	25¢	10¢	5¢	1¢	Total
a									
b									
c									

⑤ Amount Paid — Amount Due = Change

$100.00 — $36.99 = _____

	$20	$10	$5	$1	25¢	10¢	5¢	1¢	Total
a									
b									
c									

⑥ Amount Paid — Amount Due = Change

$30.00 — $9.18 = _____

	$20	$10	$5	$1	25¢	10¢	5¢	1¢	Total
a									
b									
c									

REMINDER: Write the definition of change.

_____

_____

Unit 127 cont'd ☞

B Match the change with the correct problem.

① $44.65 + ___?___ = $100.00

3 pennies, 2 dimes, 1 quarter, 3 $1-bills, 1 $20-bill

② $6.84 + ___?___ = $60.00

1 nickel, 3 dimes, 1 $5-bill, 1 $10-bill, 2 $20-bills

③ $26.52 + ___?___ = $50.00

1 penny, 1 nickel, 1 dime, 3 $1-bills, 3 $10-bills, 1 $20-bill

④ 44¢ + ___?___ = $20.00

4 pennies, 2 quarters, 1 $5-bill, 1 $10-bill, 4 $20-bills

⑤ $16.47 + ___?___ = $80.00

6 pennies, 2 quarters, 4 $1-bills, 1 $5-bill, 1 $10-bill

⑥ $4.46 + ___?___ = $100.00

1 penny, 3 dimes, 2 quarters, 4 $1-bills, 3 $5-bills

⑦ $148.80 + ___?___ = $200.00

2 dimes, 1 $1-bill, 1 $10-bill, 2 $20-bills

⑧ $30.19 + ___?___ = $50.00

3 pennies, 2 quarters, 3 $1-bills, 3 $20-bills

C Underline the correct answers.

① Christiane and Daniel shared the cost of dinner at a restaurant. Christiane's food and beverage cost $8.95. Daniel's bill totaled $6.73. Together they gave the cashier $20.00. The ($4.32, $2.22, $11.05) that they received in change they left as a tip for the waiter.

② Cathy and Denise registered for college classes at the same time. Cathy's fees and tuition totaled $1,374.62. Denise, who was only a part-time student, paid $652.13 in tuition and fees. Cathy gave the registration clerk $1,500.00. Denise gave the clerk 7 $100-bills. (Cathy, Denise) received more in change.

③ Terri wrote a check for $125.25 and took it to the bank. She then deposited $100 of the money in a savings account. The teller gave Terri a receipt for the amount of the deposit and (1 $20-bill, 1 $5-bill, and 1 quarter; 5 $20-bills and 3 quarters) in change.

④ Richard purchased a dictionary at a total cost of $24.87. He gave the bookstore cashier 2 $20-bills and said that he wanted as many $1-bills as possible in change. Richard received (13, 15, 24) $1-bills in change.

⑤ In the year 1986, Sean pledged $19.86 to a charity. When a representative of the charity came to collect the pledge, Sean only had a $50-bill. Sean received (5 $10-bills; 4 pennies and 1 dime; 4 pennies, 1 dime, and 3 $10-bills) in change.

Inches

Learning Objective: *We will learn to identify, add, and subtract inches and fractions of inches.*

An inch is a standard unit of measurement equaling 1/12 of one foot or 1/36 of one yard.

EXAMPLE:
A ruler is a tool for measurement. It is marked in inches and fractions of inches. The arrow above the ruler at the right is 1 1/8 inches in length.

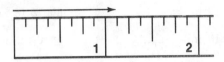

A Draw an arrow to equal the length specified above each ruler.

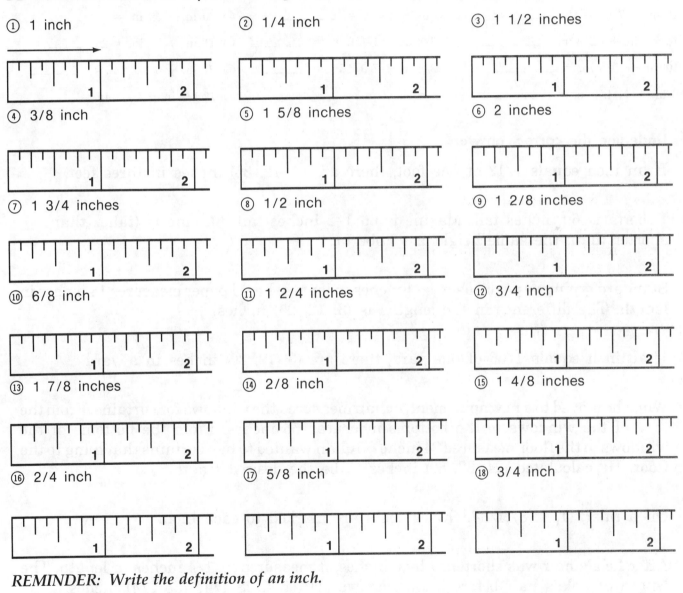

① 1 inch

② 1/4 inch

③ 1 1/2 inches

④ 3/8 inch

⑤ 1 5/8 inches

⑥ 2 inches

⑦ 1 3/4 inches

⑧ 1/2 inch

⑨ 1 2/8 inches

⑩ 6/8 inch

⑪ 1 2/4 inches

⑫ 3/4 inch

⑬ 1 7/8 inches

⑭ 2/8 inch

⑮ 1 4/8 inches

⑯ 2/4 inch

⑰ 5/8 inch

⑱ 3/4 inch

REMINDER: Write the definition of an inch.

B Add or subtract.

① 3 in. + 2 in. = __5 in.__   ② 3 in. − 2 in. = _____   ③ 1 3/4 in. + 2 in. = _____

④ 3 7/8 in. − 2 2/8 in. = _____   ⑤ 10 1/2 in. + 11 in. = _____   ⑥ 7 5/8 in. + 3 in. = _____

⑦ 12 1/8 in. − 6 1/8 in. = _____   ⑧ 10 3/4 in. − 4 1/4 in. = _____   ⑨ 6 7/8 in. − 3 5/8 in. = _____

⑩ 9 3/4 in. − 7 2/4 in. = _____   ⑪ 5 1/4 in. + 5 1/4 in. = _____   ⑫ 21 3/8 in. + 6 3/8 in. = _____

⑬ 36 in. − 12 in. = _____   ⑭ 15 in. + 11 1/2 in. = _____   ⑮ 2 1/2 in. + 9 in. = _____

⑯ 17 in. − 13 in. = _____   ⑰ 6 in. + 6 in. = _____   ⑱ 24 in. + 12 in. = _____

⑲ 16 2/4 in. − 4 1/4 in. = _____   ⑳ 9 1/2 in. − 7 in. = _____   ㉑ 72 in. − 12 in. = _____

㉒ 14 1/4 in. − 7 in. = _____   ㉓ 30 in. + 2 3/8 in. = _____   ㉔ 22 2/4 in. + 1/4 in. = _____

㉕ 19 in. + 7 in. = _____   ㉖ 47 in. − 18 in. = _____   ㉗ 60 in. − 30 in. = _____

㉘ 16 5/8 in. + 2 2/8 in. = _____   ㉙ 4 3/8 in. − 1 1/8 in. = _____   ㉚ 11 in. + 24 in. = _____

㉛ 100 in. + 5/8 in. = _____   ㉜ 3 3/4 in. + 7 3/4 in. = _____   ㉝ 21 in. + 6 1/4 in. = _____

㉞ 2 in. + 44 1/4 in. = _____   ㉟ 56 in. + 13 in. = _____   ㊱ 17 1/2 in. − 4 1/2 in. = _____

C Underline the correct answers.

① If an inch equals 1/12 of one foot, there are (3, 12, <u>36</u>) inches in three feet.

② Roberta is 60 inches tall. Maxine is 66 1/2 inches tall. Maxine is (taller than, shorter than, the same height as) Roberta.

③ Standard typing paper measures 11 inches in length. Legal paper measures 14 inches in length. The difference in the lengths is (3, 12, 25) inches.

④ If an inch equals 1/36 of one yard, there are (3, 12, 36) inches in a yard.

⑤ When he moved to a new apartment, Julian measured the windows for curtains. From the tops of the windows to the bottoms measured 56 inches. From the bottoms of the windows to the floor measured 24 inches. Julian wanted to buy curtains that hung to the floor. He calculated (24, 32, 80) inches to be the desired length.

⑥ On a ruler, (1, 4, 8) 1/8-inch segments are marked to each inch.

⑦ After Lela's hair was shortened by 6 inches, it measured 22 1/4 inches in length. The length of Lela's hair before it was cut was (16 1/4, 28 1/4, 133 2/4) inches.

⑧ Four (quarter-inches, half-inches, eighth-inches) equals 2 inches.

Feet

Learning Objective: *We will learn to convert inches to feet and feet to inches.*

A foot is a standard unit of measurement equaling 12 inches or 1/3 yard.

EXAMPLE: A ruler is usually 1 foot in length. An inch is 1/12 foot.

1/12 foot

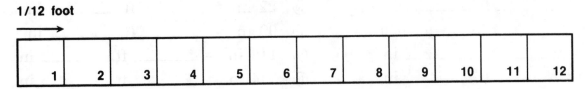

A Draw an arrow to equal the length specified for each ruler.

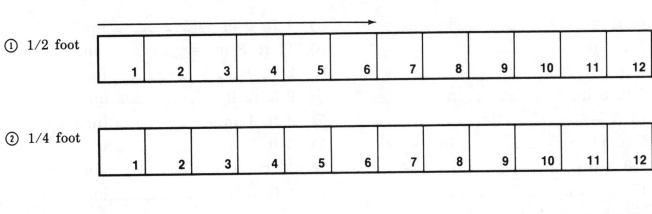

① 1/2 foot

② 1/4 foot

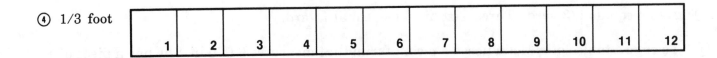

③ 1/6 foot

④ 1/3 foot

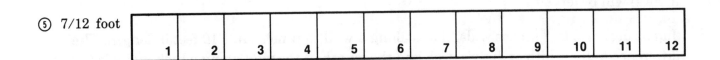

⑤ 7/12 foot

⑥ 3/4 foot

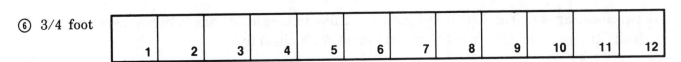

REMINDER: Write the definition of a foot.

Unit 129 cont'd ☞

B Give each measurement in feet and inches.

① 25 in. = ___2___ ft. ___1___ in.   ② 47 in. = _____ ft. _____ in.
③ 39 in. = _____ ft. _____ in.   ④ 74 in. = _____ ft. _____ in.
⑤ 102 in. = _____ ft. _____ in.   ⑥ 19 in. = _____ ft. _____ in.
⑦ 86 in. = _____ ft. _____ in.   ⑧ 52 in. = _____ ft. _____ in.
⑨ 68 in. = _____ ft. _____ in.   ⑩ 22 in. = _____ ft. _____ in.
⑪ 130 in. = _____ ft. _____ in.   ⑫ 99 in. = _____ ft. _____ in.
⑬ 14 in. = _____ ft. _____ in.   ⑭ 118 in. = _____ ft. _____ in.
⑮ 72 in. = _____ ft. _____ in.   ⑯ 144 in. = _____ ft. _____ in.

C Give each measurement in inches.

① 16 ft. 2 in. = ___194___ in.   ② 4 ft. 9 in. = _____ in.
③ 7 1/2 ft. = _____ in.   ④ 11 ft. 3 in. = _____ in.
⑤ 5 ft. 4 1/2 in. = _____ in.   ⑥ 2 ft. 7 in. = _____ in.
⑦ 6 ft. 8 in. = _____ in.   ⑧ 9 5/12 ft. = _____ in.
⑨ 13 ft. = _____ in.   ⑩ 8 ft. 1 in. = _____ in.
⑪ 5 ft. 11 in. = _____ in.   ⑫ 3 ft. 7 in. = _____ in.
⑬ 1 3/4 ft. = _____ in.   ⑭ 10 ft. 2 in. = _____ in.
⑮ 15 ft. 4 in. = _____ in.   ⑯ 1 ft. 5 in. = _____ in.

D Underline the correct answers.

① Sean is 79 inches tall. Richard is 6 ft. 4 in. tall. Randy is 6 1/4 ft. tall. (Sean, Richard, <u>Randy</u>) is the shortest.

② A foot equals 1/3 yard. (Three, six, nine) feet equal 1 yard.

③ To edge a tablecloth, Mona needs a piece of trim that measures 6 ft. 6 in. She has a piece of fringe that is 90 inches long. If she uses the fringe to trim the tablecloth, (6 inches, 1 foot, 24 inches) will be left over.

④ Judy's desk is 3 ft. 8 inches wide. It sits along a wall that measures 10 feet in length. The difference in the width of Judy's desk and the length of the wall along which it sits is (7 feet, 76 inches, 164 inches).

⑤ Between the ages of 9 and 16, Steve grew 1 1/2 feet in height. At age 9, Steve measured 4 ft. 5 in. tall. At age 16, he is (4 ft. 6 1/2 in., 66 inches, 71 inches) tall.

⑥ A ruler is usually 1 foot in length and 1/3 as long as a yardstick. A yardstick is (12, 24, 36) inches long.

⑦ Three feet plus 1/2 foot plus 1/6 foot equals (17, 44, 36 4/6) inches.

Yards

Learning Objective: *We will learn to convert inches and feet to yards and yards to inches and feet.*

A yard is a standard unit of measurement equaling 36 inches or 3 feet.

EXAMPLE: The arrow represents 24 inches, or 2 feet, which is equal to 2/3 yard.

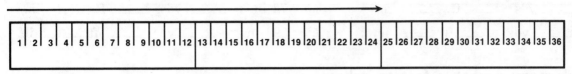

A Draw an arrow to equal the length specified for each ruler.

① 1/3 yd.

② 2 ft. 7 in.

③ 7/36 yd.

④ 1/2 yd.

⑤ 3/4 yd.

⑥ 1 ft. 11 in.

REMINDER: Write the definition of a yard.

B Give each measurement in yards, feet, and inches.

1. 79 in. = __2__ yds. __0__ ft. __7__ in.
2. 320 in. = _____ yds. _____ ft. _____ in.
3. 48 in. = _____ yds. _____ ft. _____ in.
4. 218 in. = _____ yds. _____ ft. _____ in.
5. 613 in. = _____ yds. _____ ft. _____ in.
6. 92 in. = _____ yds. _____ ft. _____ in.
7. 165 in. = _____ yds. _____ ft. _____ in.
8. 480 in. = _____ yds. _____ ft. _____ in.
9. 59 in. = _____ yds. _____ ft. _____ in.
10. 72 in. = _____ yds. _____ ft. _____ in.
11. 501 in. = _____ yds. _____ ft. _____ in.
12. 393 in. = _____ yds. _____ ft. _____ in.

C Give each measurement in feet or inches.

1. 16 yds. = __48__ ft.
2. 44 yds. = _____ ft.
3. 12 yds. = _____ in.
4. 7 1/2 yds. = _____ in.
5. 10 1/4 yds. = _____ in.
6. 19 1/3 yds. = _____ ft.
7. 31 yds. = _____ ft.
8. 17 yds. = _____ in.
9. 6 11/36 yds. = _____ in.
10. 27 yds. = _____ in.
11. 92 yds. = _____ ft.
12. 8 yds. = _____ ft.
13. 19 yds. = _____ in.
14. 77 2/3 yds. = _____ ft.
15. 49 yds. = _____ in.
16. 11 yds. = _____ ft.

D Underline the correct answers.

1. If three poles, each measuring 67 inches in length, are placed end to end, from the outer end of the first pole to the outer end of the third pole is (5 ft. 7 in., 5 yds. 1 ft. 9 in., 201 ft.).

2. The combined height of two bookcases is 2 yds. 1 ft. 5 in. One of the two cases is 1 yd. 1 ft. 2 in. tall. The other is (39, 50, 89) inches tall.

3. One room in Mary's house is 12 feet wide. Another room is 4 yds. 2 ft. wide. The difference in the width of the two rooms is (8 ft. 2 in., 146 in., 2 ft.).

4. A yard is (3, 12, 36) times as long as an inch.

5. A yardstick is (3, 12, 36) times as long as a ruler.

6. Barbara and Ned needed 5/6 yard of piping to complete a science project. Leon loaned them 18 inches of piping. Another (1 ft., 1/6 yd., 9 in.) of piping is still needed for the project.

7. In district competition, Ronald threw a discus 120 yards. Jim's throw measured 300 ft. 7 in. Alvin threw the discus a distance of 3,348 inches. (Ronald, Jim, Alvin) threw the discus the farthest.

Comprehension Check

A Match the change with the correct problem.

① $16 + ___?___ = $50
② $71 + ___?___ = $100
③ $52 + ___?___ = $60
④ $154 + ___?___ = $200
⑤ $13 + ___?___ = $20
⑥ $401 + ___?___ = $410
⑦ $68 + ___?___ = $80
⑧ $84 + ___?___ = $100
⑨ $260 + ___?___ = $300
⑩ $312 + ___?___ = $350

4 $1-bills, 1 $5-bill, 2 $10-bills
4 $1-bills, 3 $10-bills
1 $1-bill, 1 $5-bill, 2 $20-bills
4 $1-bills, 1 $5-bill
3 $1-bills, 1 $5-bill
2 $1-bills, 1 $5-bill
2 $1-bills, 1 $10-bill
2 $20-bills
3 $1-bills, 1 $5-bill, 3 $10-bills
1 $1-bill, 1 $5-bill, 1 $10-bill

B Calculate the amount of change for each problem. List 3 ways of making change for each.

① Amount Paid — Amount Due = Change
$50.00 — $20.67 = __$29.33__

	$20	$10	$5	$1	25¢	10¢	5¢	1¢	Total
a	1		1	4		3		3	$29.33
b		2		9			6	3	$29.33
c			5	4		2	2	3	$29.33

② Amount Paid — Amount Due = Change
$10.00 — $6.57 = _____

	$20	$10	$5	$1	25¢	10¢	5¢	1¢	Total
a									
b									
c									

③ Amount Paid — Amount Due = Change
$40.00 — $36.21 = _____

	$20	$10	$5	$1	25¢	10¢	5¢	1¢	Total
a									
b									
c									

④ Amount Paid — Amount Due = Change
$70.00 — $51.79 = _____

	$20	$10	$5	$1	25¢	10¢	5¢	1¢	Total
a									
b									
c									

⑤ Amount Paid — Amount Due = Change
$100.00 — $19.99 = _____

	$20	$10	$5	$1	25¢	10¢	5¢	1¢	Total
a									
b									
c									

⑥ Amount Paid — Amount Due = Change
$15.00 — $11.18 = _____

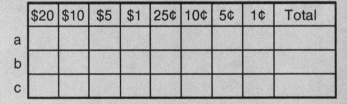

	$20	$10	$5	$1	25¢	10¢	5¢	1¢	Total
a									
b									
c									

Test 26 cont'd ☞

C Draw an arrow to equal the length specified for each ruler.

① 7/8 inch ② 1 1/8 inches ③ 1 1/4 inches

④ 1/2 inch ⑤ 2 inches ⑥ 1 3/8 inches

D Give each measurement in feet and inches.

① 97 in. = __8__ ft. __1__ in.   ② 185 in. = _____ ft. _____ in.
③ 20 in. = _____ ft. _____ in.   ④ 201 in. = _____ ft. _____ in.
⑤ 41 in. = _____ ft. _____ in.   ⑥ 74 in. = _____ ft. _____ in.
⑦ 15 in. = _____ ft. _____ in.   ⑧ 62 in. = _____ ft. _____ in.

E Give each measurement in inches.

① 1 ft. 2 in. = __14__ in.   ② 6 ft. 8 in. = _____ in.
③ 8 ft. 5 in. = _____ in.   ④ 11 ft. 3 in. = _____ in.
⑤ 7 ft. 1 in. = _____ in.   ⑥ 10 ft. 9 in. = _____ in.
⑦ 2 1/2 ft. = _____ in.   ⑧ 3 3/4 ft. = _____ in.

F Give each measurement in yards, feet, and inches.

① 95 in. = __2__ yds. __1__ ft. __11__ in.   ② 84 in. = ____ yds. ____ ft. ____ in.
③ 316 in. = ____ yds. ____ ft. ____ in.   ④ 61 in. = ____ yds. ____ ft. ____ in.
⑤ 105 in. = ____ yds. ____ ft. ____ in.   ⑥ 231 in. = ____ yds. ____ ft. ____ in.

G Give each measurement in feet or inches.

① 52 yds. = __156__ ft.   ② 74 yds. = _____ ft.
③ 25 yds. = _____ in.   ④ 17 yds. = _____ in.
⑤ 31 3/4 yds. = _____ in.   ⑥ 22 1/2 yds. = _____ in.
⑦ 74 1/3 yds. = _____ ft.   ⑧ 100 yds. = _____ ft.

Write a brief paragraph describing in yards, in feet, and in inches the height of each member of your family.

_____

_____

_____

_____

_____

Miles

Learning Objective: *We will learn to convert miles to yards and feet.*

A mile is a standard unit of measurement equaling 5,280 feet or 1,760 yards.

EXAMPLE: Thirty miles is equal to 52,800 yards (30 × 1,760) or 158,400 feet (30 × 5,280).

Miles - 30
Yards - 52,800
Feet - 158,400

A Convert miles to yards.

① 10 mi. × 1,760 = __17,600__ yds.   ② 2 mi. × 1,760 = _____ yds.

③ 56 mi. × 1,760 = _____ yds.   ④ 19 mi. × 1,760 = _____ yds.

⑤ 25 mi. × 1,760 = _____ yds.   ⑥ 94 mi. × 1,760 = _____ yds.

⑦ 8 mi. × 1,760 = _____ yds.   ⑧ 35 mi. × 1,760 = _____ yds.

⑨ 40 mi. × 1,760 = _____ yds.   ⑩ 67 mi. × 1,760 = _____ yds.

⑪ 51 mi. × 1,760 = _____ yds.   ⑫ 12 mi. × 1,760 = _____ yds.

⑬ 86 mi. × 1,760 = _____ yds.   ⑭ 49 mi. × 1,760 = _____ yds.

B Convert miles to feet.

① 41 mi. × 5,280 = __216,480__ ft.   ② 11 mi. × 5,280 = _____ ft.

③ 93 mi. × 5,280 = _____ ft.   ④ 84 mi. × 5,280 = _____ ft.

⑤ 68 mi. × 5,280 = _____ ft.   ⑥ 34 mi. × 5,280 = _____ ft.

⑦ 77 mi. × 5,280 = _____ ft.   ⑧ 46 mi. × 5,280 = _____ ft.

⑨ 21 mi. × 5,280 = _____ ft.   ⑩ 53 mi. × 5,280 = _____ ft.

⑪ 17 mi. × 5,280 = _____ ft.   ⑫ 99 mi. × 5,280 = _____ ft.

⑬ 28 mi. × 5,280 = _____ ft.   ⑭ 72 mi. × 5,280 = _____ ft.

REMINDER: *Write the definition of a mile.*

_____

_____

C Convert miles to yards and feet.

① mi. 24 yds. **42,240** ft. _____

② mi. 95 yds. _____ ft. _____

③ mi. 82 yds. _____ ft. _____

④ mi. 47 yds. _____ ft. _____

⑤ mi. 58 yds. _____ ft. _____

⑥ mi. 20 yds. _____ ft. _____

⑦ mi. 65 yds. _____ ft. _____

⑧ mi. 71 yds. _____ ft. _____

⑨ mi. 14 yds. _____ ft. _____

⑩ mi. 39 yds. _____ ft. _____

⑪ mi. 90 yds. _____ ft. _____

⑫ mi. 63 yds. _____ ft. _____

⑬ mi. 36 yds. _____ ft. _____

⑭ mi. 55 yds. _____ ft. _____

⑮ mi. 74 yds. _____ ft. _____

⑯ mi. 42 yds. _____ ft. _____

D Underline the correct answers.

① There are (two, <u>three</u>, six) times as many feet per mile as there are yards per mile.

② Jeannie walked a total of 1 mile per day to school and back. She walked 5,280 feet altogether, or (one-fourth, one-third, one-half) as many yards.

③ The distance between Washington, D.C., and Baltimore, Maryland, is 37 miles. This is equal to 65,120 (inches, feet, yards).

④ The number of inches per mile is 12 times the number of feet and (3, 10, 36) times the number of yards per mile.

⑤ The distance between New York City, New York, and Philadelphia, Pennsylvania, is 5 miles less than the distance between Philadelphia and Baltimore. The distance between Philadelphia and Baltimore is 95 miles. There is a distance of (475,200; 158,400; 501,600) feet between Philadelphia and New York City.

⑥ By air, the distance between Detroit, Michigan, and Cleveland, Ohio is 95 miles. The road distance between Detroit and Cleveland is 165 miles. The difference in the road distance and the air distance between the two cities is (167,200; 123,200; 369,600) yards.

Centimeters

Learning Objective: *We will learn to convert centimeters and millimeters and to compare each with inches.*

A centimeter is a unit of the metric measurement system equaling approximately 2/5 of one inch.

EXAMPLE:

A metric ruler is marked in centimeters and millimeters. There are 10 millimeters to a centimeter.

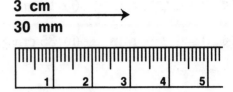

A Draw an arrow equal to the length specified for each ruler.

① 2 cm

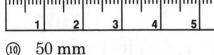

② 20 mm

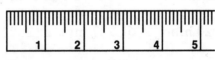

③ 4½ cm

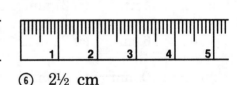

④ 45 mm

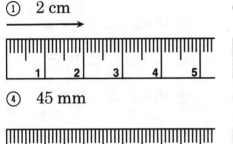

⑤ 25 mm

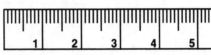

⑥ 2½ cm

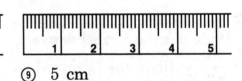

⑦ 1 cm

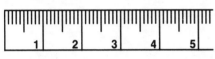

⑧ 10 mm

⑨ 5 cm

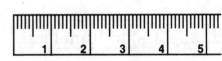

⑩ 50 mm

⑪ ½ cm

⑫ 5 mm

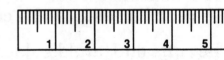

⑬ 15 mm

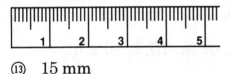

⑭ 1½ cm

⑮ 35 mm

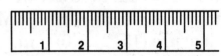

⑯ 3½ cm

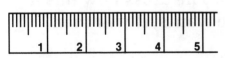

⑰ 4 cm

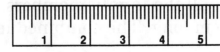

⑱ 40 mm

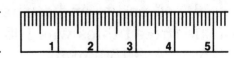

REMINDER: Write the definition of a centimeter.

_____

_____

B Convert centimeters to millimeters.

① 10 cm × 10 = __100__ mm   ② 22 cm × 10 = __220__ mm   ③ 99 cm × 10 = __990__ mm

④ 47 cm × 10 = __470__ mm   ⑤ 8 cm × 10 = __80__ mm   ⑥ 51 cm × 10 = __510__ mm

⑦ 84 cm × 10 = __840__ mm   ⑧ 17 cm × 10 = __170__ mm   ⑨ 111 cm × 10 = __1,110__ mm

⑩ 62 cm × 10 = __620__ mm   ⑪ 35 cm × 10 = __350__ mm   ⑫ 73 cm × 10 = __730__ mm

C Fill in the blanks with the symbols < or >.

① 1 cm __<__ 1 in.   ② 10 mm __<__ 1 in.   ③ 20 mm __>__ 1 cm   ④ 6 cm __>__ 55 mm

⑤ 41 mm __<__ 4 in.   ⑥ 37 mm __>__ 3 cm   ⑦ 3 in. __>__ 3 cm   ⑧ 12 cm __>__ 12 mm

⑨ 63 mm __>__ 6 cm   ⑩ 2 in. __>__ 20 mm   ⑪ 237 mm __<__ 24 cm   ⑫ 10 mm __<__ 10 in.

⑬ 50 cm __>__ 50 mm   ⑭ 98 mm __<__ 10 cm   ⑮ 7 in. __>__ 70 mm   ⑯ 16 cm __<__ 16 in.

D Underline the correct answers.

① One millimeter is equal to (<u>1/10</u>, 1/4, 1/2) of one centimeter.

② A metric ruler is marked in centimeters and (inches, kilometers, <u>millimeters</u>).

③ To convert millimeters to centimeters (increase, multiply, <u>divide</u>) by 10.

④ If a pencil measures 18½ cm in length, it is (<u>185</u>, 1/8, 181) mm long.

⑤ The cuffs on Harold's slacks have a width of 50 mm, or (<u>5</u>, 15, 500) cm.

⑥ Marla wants to lower the hem of her dress by 25 mm. The dress now has a hem measuring 4 cm. If Marla lowers the hem as she wants, it will then measure (<u>15</u>, 21, 40) mm.

⑦ When the Henson family went out for a Sunday dinner, three tables had to be placed end to end so that all the family members could be seated. Each of the three tables was 105 cm long. The combined length of the tables was (315; 10½; <u>3,150</u>) mm.

⑧ No more than 24 encyclopedias, each having a thickness of 50 mm, will fit on Delores' bookshelf. The bookshelf will hold encyclopedias with a combined thickness of (<u>120</u>; 500; 1,200) cm.

Meters

Learning
Objective: *We will learn to convert meters, centimeters, and millimeters and to compare each with yards.*

A meter is a unit of metric measurement that is equal to 100 centimeters; 1,000 millimeters; or approximately 1 1/10 yards.

EXAMPLE: Thirty meters is equal to 3,000 centimeters (30 × 100) or 30,000 millimeters (30 × 1,000). To convert centimeters to meters, divide by 100. To convert millimeters to meters, divide by 1,000.

A Convert meters to centimeters and millimeters.

① m 37
cm ___3,700___
mm ___37,000___

② m 94
cm _____
mm _____

③ m 28
cm _____
mm _____

④ m 77
cm _____
mm _____

⑤ m 63
cm _____
mm _____

⑥ m 49
cm _____
mm _____

⑦ m 92
cm _____
mm _____

⑧ m 13
cm _____
mm _____

⑨ m 56
cm _____
mm _____

⑩ m 81
cm _____
mm _____

⑪ m 33
cm _____
mm _____

⑫ m 52
cm _____
mm _____

⑬ m 96
cm _____
mm _____

⑭ m 15
cm _____
mm _____

⑮ m 75
cm _____
mm _____

⑯ m 24
cm _____
mm _____

⑰ m 50
cm _____
mm _____

⑱ m 39
cm _____
mm _____

⑲ m 8
cm _____
mm _____

⑳ m 106
cm _____
mm _____

㉑ m 119
cm _____
mm _____

㉒ m 2
cm _____
mm _____

㉓ m 225
cm _____
mm _____

㉔ m 88
cm _____
mm _____

㉕ m 26
cm _____
mm _____

㉖ m 132
cm _____
mm _____

㉗ m 20
cm _____
mm _____

㉘ m 11
cm _____
mm _____

REMINDER: *Write the definition of a meter.*

_____

_____

Unit 133 cont'd ☞

B Fill in the blanks with the symbols < or >.

① 1 m __>__ 1 yd.

② 100 cm ____ 1 yd.

③ 1,000 mm ____ 1 yd.

④ 900 cm ____ 8 m

⑤ 4 m ____ 5,000 mm

⑥ 3 m ____ 3 yd.

⑦ 7 yds. ____ 700 cm

⑧ 6 m ____ 950 cm

⑨ 8,000 mm ____ 8 yd.

⑩ 6,000 mm ____ 7 m

⑪ 910 cm ____ 10 m

⑫ 18 yd. ____ 18 m

⑬ 27 m ____ 2,500 cm

⑭ 11 yd. ____ 1,100 cm

⑮ 320 cm ____ 5 m

⑯ 737 cm ____ 6 m

⑰ 19,000 mm ____ 20 m

⑱ 4,636 mm ____ 5 m

⑲ 80 yd. ____ 80,000 mm

⑳ 212 cm ____ 2 m

㉑ 13,472 ____ 15 m

㉒ 9 m ____ 9,460 mm

㉓ 28 m ____ 28 yd.

㉔ 47 yd. ____ 4,700 cm

㉕ 436 cm ____ 4 m

㉖ 213,001 mm ____ 213 m

㉗ 39 yd. ____ 39,000 mm

㉘ 122 cm ____ 1 m

㉙ 3 m ____ 17,000 mm

㉚ 1,122 mm ____ 1 m

㉛ 2,190 mm ____ 2 yd.

㉜ 1,316 cm ____ 13 yd.

㉝ 4 yd. ____ 412 cm

㉞ 18 m ____ 12,920 mm

㉟ 2 yd. ____ 2,506 mm

㊱ 6 m ____ 910 cm

C Underline the correct answers.

① A centimeter is equal to (1/10; 1/100; 1/1,000) of one meter.

② A millimeter is equal to (1/10; 1/100; 1/1,000) of one meter.

③ To convert meters to millimeters (increase; multiply; divide) by 1,000.

④ To convert meters to centimeters (increase; multiply; divide) by 100.

⑤ Louise purchased 12 meters of fabric for kitchen curtains. She purchased an equal amount of fabric to make into curtains for the bathroom. For the bathroom curtains, Louise purchased (12; 120; 1,200) centimeters of fabric.

⑥ The distance from the Winslow High School gymnasium to the parking lot is 74,000 millimeters. The distance from the gym to the parking lot and back again is (74; 148; 148,000) meters.

⑦ Each section of the walkway between the school library and the cafeteria is 1,600 centimeters long. The walkway has five sections. The combined length of all sections is (16; 80; 8,000) meters.

⑧ To determine the number of meters that equal 15,700 (millimeters; yards; centimeters), divide 15,700 by 100.

322

Kilometers

Unit 134

Learning Objective: *We will learn to convert centimeters, meters, and kilometers, and to compare each to miles.*

A kilometer is a unit of metric measurement equaling 1,000 meters; 100,000 centimeters; or approximately 3/5 of one mile.

EXAMPLE: Thirty kilometers is equal to 30,000 meters (30 × 1,000) or 3,000,000 centimeters (30 × 100,000).

kilometers - 30
meters - 30,000
centimeters - 3,000,000

A Convert meters to centimeters and millimeters.

① km 16
m __16,000__
cm __1,600,000__

② km 3
m _____
cm _____

③ km 80
m _____
cm _____

④ km 9
m _____
cm _____

⑤ km 24
m _____
cm _____

⑥ km 2
m _____
cm _____

⑦ km 6
m _____
cm _____

⑧ km 19
m _____
cm _____

⑨ km 42
m _____
cm _____

⑩ km 71
m _____
cm _____

⑪ km 12
m _____
cm _____

⑫ km 4
m _____
cm _____

⑬ km 5
m _____
cm _____

⑭ km 8
m _____
cm _____

⑮ km 10
m _____
cm _____

⑯ km 11
m _____
cm _____

⑰ km 37
m _____
cm _____

⑱ km 15
m _____
cm _____

⑲ km 49
m _____
cm _____

⑳ km 7
m _____
cm _____

㉑ km 25
m _____
cm _____

㉒ km 18
m _____
cm _____

㉓ km 14
m _____
cm _____

㉔ km 52
m _____
cm _____

㉕ km 61
m _____
cm _____

㉖ km 33
m _____
cm _____

㉗ km 98
m _____
cm _____

㉘ km 75
m _____
cm _____

REMINDER: *Write the definition of a kilometer.*

_____

_____

Unit 134 cont'd ☞

B Fill in the blanks with the symbols < or >.

① 1 km ___<___ 1 mi. ② 1 mi. ___ 1,000 m ③ 100,000 cm ___ 1 mi.

④ 4,000 m ___ 5 km ⑤ 3 mi. ___ 3,000 m ⑥ 8 km ___ 900,000 cm

⑦ 9 mi. ___ 9 km ⑧ 205,008 cm ___ 3 km ⑨ 412 m ___ 4 km

⑩ 19 mi. ___ 19,000 m ⑪ 4,704,980 cm ___ 47 km ⑫ 100 km ___ 10,000 m

⑬ 1,100 mi. ___ 1,100 km ⑭ 92 km ___ 90,000 m ⑮ 40,110 m ___ 400 km

⑯ 86 mi. ___ 86 km ⑰ 2,908 m ___ 3 km ⑱ 109,000 cm ___ 1 km

⑲ 1,300,000 cm ___ 13 mi. ⑳ 99 km ___ 9,900 m ㉑ 111 km ___ 111 mi.

㉒ 300,000 cm ___ 3 mi. ㉓ 213,812 cm ___ 3 km ㉔ 11,001 m ___ 11 km

㉕ 13 mi. ___ 13,000 m ㉖ 2,200 m ___ 22 km ㉗ 312 km ___ 31,200 cm

㉘ 10 km ___ 100,000 cm ㉙ 627,000 m ___ 650 km ㉚ 915 mi. ___ 915 km

㉛ 123 km ___ 1,230 m ㉜ 111,620 cm ___ 1 km ㉝ 426 km ___ 402,600 cm

㉞ 216,000 cm ___ 2 km ㉟ 97 mi. ___ 97 km ㊱ 219 mi. ___ 219,000 m

C Underline the correct answers.

① A kilometer is (greater than; equal to; <u>less than</u>) a mile.

② To convert centimeters to kilometers, (multiply; divide; reduce) by 100,000.

③ To convert meters to kilometers, divide by (10; 1,000; 10,000).

④ The distance between Atlanta, Georgia, and Chicago, Illinois, is 715 miles. In kilometers, the distance between these two cities is (greater than; equal to; less than) 715.

⑤ The number of centimeters per kilometer is (10; 100; 1,000) times the number of meters per kilometer.

⑥ The distance between Little Rock, Arkansas, and St. Louis, Missouri, is 48 kilometers less than the distance between Little Rock and Kansas City, Missouri. The distance between Little Rock and Kansas City is 600,000 meters. Therefore, the distance between Little Rock and St. Louis is (552 kilometers; 599,952 meters; 600,048 meters).

⑦ The distance of 877 kilometers between the cities of Louisville, Kentucky, and Buffalo, New York, is (greater than; equal to; less than) the distance of 87,700,000 centimeters between Memphis, Tennessee, and Chicago, Illinois.

Units of Length

Unit 135

Learning Objective: *We will learn to convert and compare units of length.*

A unit of length includes any unit of measurement; such as the inch, foot, yard, mile, millimeter, centimeter, meter, and kilometer; which tells how long.

EXAMPLE: A foot is 12 times as long as an inch. A yard is 3 times as long as a foot. A mile is 1,760 times as long as a yard. A centimeter is 10 times as long as a millimeter. A meter is 100 times as long as a centimeter. A kilometer is 1,000 times as long as a meter. A centimeter is shorter than an inch. A meter is longer than a yard. A kilometer is shorter than a mile.

A Complete each problem with equivalent measurements.

① yds. 36
  ft. **108**
  in. **1,296**

② mi. 22
  yds. _____
  ft. _____

③ m 11
  cm _____
  mm _____

④ km 18
  m _____
  cm _____

⑤ mi. _____
  yds. 5,280
  ft. _____

⑥ m _____
  cm 700
  mm _____

⑦ km _____
  m 9,000
  cm _____

⑧ yds. _____
  ft. 396
  in. _____

⑨ km _____
  m _____
  cm 1,200,000

⑩ yds. _____
  ft. _____
  in. 540

⑪ mi. _____
  yds. _____
  ft. 211,200

⑫ m _____
  cm _____
  mm 28,000

⑬ m 97
  cm _____
  mm _____

⑭ km 49
  m _____
  cm _____

⑮ yds. 110
  ft. _____
  in. _____

⑯ mi. 78
  yds. _____
  ft. _____

⑰ yds. _____
  ft. 267
  in. _____

⑱ mi. _____
  yds. 144,320
  ft. _____

⑲ m _____
  cm 8,900
  mm _____

⑳ km _____
  m 147,000
  cm _____

㉑ mi. _____
  yds. _____
  ft. 84,480

㉒ m _____
  cm _____
  mm 14,000

㉓ km _____
  m _____
  cm 4,500,000

㉔ yds. _____
  ft. _____
  in. 2,808

㉕ km 19
  m _____
  cm _____

㉖ yds. 181
  ft. _____
  in. _____

㉗ mi. 39
  yds. _____
  ft. _____

㉘ m 77
  cm _____
  mm _____

REMINDER: Write the definition of a unit of length.

_____

_____

325

Unit 135 cont'd ☞

B Fill in the blanks with the symbols < or >.

① 318 ft. $\underline{<}$ 3,900 in.   ② 12 in. _____ 12 cm   ③ 18 km _____ 18 mi.

④ 290 yds. _____ 900 ft.   ⑤ 48 yds. _____ 48 m   ⑥ 32,180 mm _____ 30 m

⑦ 9,700 in. _____ 270 yds.   ⑧ 1,818 yds. _____ 1 mi.   ⑨ 200 mm _____ 20 in.

⑩ 96 mi. _____ 96,000 m   ⑪ 729 km _____ 718,000 m   ⑫ 24 mi. _____ 45,000 yds.

⑬ 111 ft. _____ 36 yds.   ⑭ 920,000 m _____ 920 mi.   ⑮ 12 mi. _____ 1,200,000 cm

⑯ 89 in. _____ 7 ft.   ⑰ 13,000 m _____ 13 mi.   ⑱ 600 cm _____ 6 yds.

⑲ 990 mm _____ 99 in.   ⑳ 36,000 mm _____ 36 yds.   ㉑ 72 km _____ 7,500 m

㉒ 813 yds. _____ 275 ft.   ㉓ 496 ft. _____ 710 in.   ㉔ 11 mi. _____ 58,000 ft.

㉕ 2,987 cm _____ 29 m   ㉖ 900 ft. _____ 299 yds.   ㉗ 8,020 m _____ 8 km

㉘ 928 km _____ 928 mi.   ㉙ 811 mi. _____ 811,000 m   ㉚ 621 mi. _____ 621 m

㉛ 22,800 yds. _____ 13 mi.   ㉜ 87 in. _____ 2 yds.   ㉝ 417 yds. _____ 417 m

㉞ 72,000 m _____ 75 km   ㉟ 900 cm _____ 9 yds.   ㊱ 222 ft. _____ 75 yds.

C Underline the correct answers.

① Richard sawed three pieces of wood from one long piece. One of the three pieces was 12 inches long. Another was 2 feet in length. The third piece of wood was 1 yard long. The piece of wood that Richard sawed into three pieces was (15 inches, 3 feet, 2 yards) long.

② The distance around Rosemary's house is 96 feet. The distance around Kyle's house is 32 meters. Kyle's house is (larger than, smaller than, the same size as) Rosemary's house.

③ Gerald is 6 centimeters taller than Cynthia and 6 inches taller than Laura. Cynthia is (taller than, shorter than, the same height as) Laura.

④ Linda drives 8 miles to school each day. After school, she drives 8,000 meters further to work. The distance between Linda's home and school is (greater than, less than, equal to) the distance between school and work.

⑤ A dress pattern calls for a 3 centimeter hem. This is (greater than, less than, equal to) a 3 inch hem.

⑥ The distance between Tampa and Miami, Florida is 435,000 meters. To determine the equal number of kilometers, divide by (10; 100; 1,000).

Comprehension Check

Test 27

A Draw an arrow to equal the length specified above each ruler.

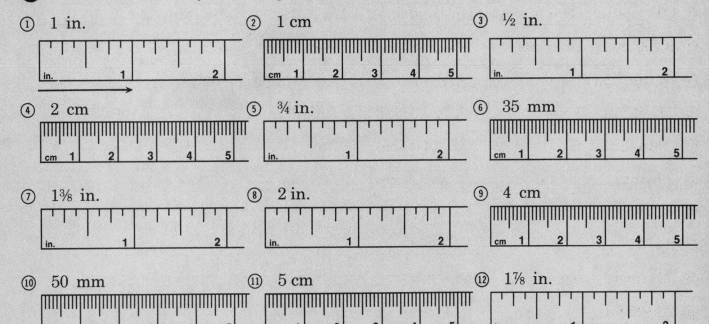

B Fill in the blanks.

① 37 km × __*100,000*__ = 3,700,000 cm

② 289 mi. _____ 1,760 = 508,640 yds.

③ 18 mi. × _____ = 95,040 ft.

④ 13,000 mm _____ 1,000 = 13 m

⑤ 137,280 yds. _____ 1,760 = 78 mi.

⑥ 406,560 ft. ÷ _____ = 77 mi.

⑦ 11,000,000 cm ÷ _____ = 110 km

⑧ 92,000 mm ÷ _____ = 92 m

⑨ 98 yds. _____ 36 = 3,528 in.

⑩ 4,965 yds. × _____ = 14,895 ft.

⑪ 44 km × _____ = 44,000 m

⑫ 536,000 cm _____ 100 = 5,360 m

⑬ 39 m _____ 1,000 = 39,000 mm

⑭ 4,180 cm × _____ = 41,800 mm

⑮ 6,468 ft. _____ 3 = 2,156 yds.

⑯ 96,000 m _____ 1,000 = 96 km

⑰ 312 ft. × _____ = 3,744 in.

⑱ 6,516 in. ÷ _____ = 181 yds.

⑲ 68,470 mm _____ 10 = 6,847 cm

⑳ 1,296 in. ÷ _____ = 108 ft.

㉑ 700,000 cm _____ 100,000 = 7 km

㉒ 8,523 m × _____ = 852,300 cm

Test 27 cont'd ☛

C Complete the problems with equivalent measurements.

① yd. 45
ft. _135_
in. _____

② mi. 32
yd. _____
ft. _____

③ m 54
cm _____
mm _____

④ km 25
m _____
cm _____

⑤ mi. _____
yd. 130,240
ft. _____

⑥ m _____
cm 3,100
mm _____

⑦ km _____
m 147,000
cm _____

⑧ yd. _____
ft. 123
in. _____

⑨ km _____
m _____
cm 6,300,000

⑩ yd. _____
ft. _____
in. 2,088

⑪ mi. _____
yd. _____
ft. 322,080

⑫ m _____
cm _____
mm 49,000

⑬ m 89
cm _____
mm _____

⑭ km 51
m _____
cm _____

⑮ yd. 10
ft. _____
in. _____

⑯ mi. 66
yd. _____
ft. _____

D Fill in the blanks with the symbols < or >.

① 695 ft. __>__ 231 yd.

② 1,300 cm ____ 13 yd.

③ 14,675 m ____ 14 km

④ 211 yd. ____ 21 m

⑤ 27 mi. ____ 27,000 m

⑥ 39,960 yd. ____ 21 mi.

⑦ 9,612 in. ____ 270 yd.

⑧ 4,392 km ____ 4,392 mi.

⑨ 3,125 cm ____ 32 m

⑩ 216 ft. ____ 2,500 in.

⑪ 28 mi. ____ 149,750 ft.

⑫ 29,000 mm ____ 29 yd.

⑬ 460 mm ____ 46 in.

⑭ 7 mi. ____ 700,000 cm

⑮ 835 km ____ 799,000 m

⑯ 92 mi. ____ 92,000 m

⑰ 410 mm ____ 41 in.

⑱ 1,911 yd. ____ 1,911 m

⑲ 1,465 mm ____ 2 m

⑳ 1,215 in. ____ 33 yd.

㉑ 297 in. ____ 297 cm

㉒ 450 cm ____ 49 m

㉓ 9,417 yd. ____ 5 mi.

㉔ 9,207 km ____ 9,207 mi.

㉕ 2,172 cm ____ 21,750 mm

㉖ 4,013 m ____ 4,013 yd.

㉗ 2,966 in. ____ 248 ft.

Write a brief paragraph comparing units of length. (i.e., A yard is 3 times as long as a foot.)

_____
_____
_____
_____
_____
_____

Ounces

Learning
Objective: *We will learn to recognize an ounce as a fraction of a pound.*

An ounce is a standard unit of weight equaling 1/16 of one pound.

EXAMPLE:

Sixteen ounces equal one pound.

A On each scale below, draw a needle pointing to the correct weight.

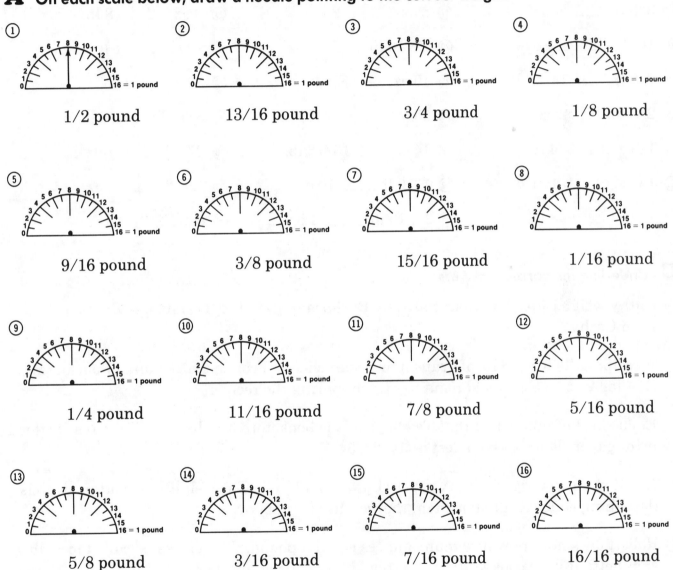

① 1/2 pound   ② 13/16 pound   ③ 3/4 pound   ④ 1/8 pound

⑤ 9/16 pound   ⑥ 3/8 pound   ⑦ 15/16 pound   ⑧ 1/16 pound

⑨ 1/4 pound   ⑩ 11/16 pound   ⑪ 7/8 pound   ⑫ 5/16 pound

⑬ 5/8 pound   ⑭ 3/16 pound   ⑮ 7/16 pound   ⑯ 16/16 pound

REMINDER: Write the definition of an ounce.

_____

_____

Unit 136 cont'd 🖝

B Fill in the blanks with the symbols <, >, or =.

① 13 oz. _≤_ 7/8 lb. ② 2 oz. ___ 1/8 lb. ③ 9/16 lb. ___ 9 oz.

④ 4/8 lb. ___ 8 oz. ⑤ 15/16 lb. ___ 1 lb. ⑥ 11 oz. ___ 5/8 lb.

⑦ 5/8 lb. ___ 5 oz. ⑧ 3/4 lb. ___ 13/16 lb. ⑨ 3 oz. ___ 3/16 lb.

⑩ 8/16 lb. ___ 1/2 lb. ⑪ 6 oz. ___ 1/2 lb. ⑫ 8 oz. ___ 1/8 lb.

⑬ 1/2 lb. ___ 14 oz. ⑭ 9 oz. ___ 1/2 lb. ⑮ 3/8 lb. ___ 3 oz.

⑯ 3/8 lb. ___ 5 oz. ⑰ 8 oz. ___ 1/2 lb. ⑱ 3 oz. ___ 1/8 lb.

⑲ 16/16 lb. ___ 16 oz. ⑳ 13/16 lb. ___ 11 oz. ㉑ 12 oz. ___ 1 lb.

㉒ 7/8 lb. ___ 14/16 lb. ㉓ 10 oz. ___ 5/8 lb. ㉔ 1 oz. ___ 1 lb.

㉕ 2/8 lb. ___ 2 oz. ㉖ 15 oz. ___ 1/2 lb. ㉗ 3/16 lb. ___ 6/8 lb.

㉘ 11 oz. ___ 3/4 lb. ㉙ 14 oz. ___ 13/16 lb. ㉚ 2/4 lb. ___ 7 oz.

㉛ 13 oz. ___ 1/16 lb. ㉜ 1/10 lb. ___ 10 oz. ㉝ 1/4 lb. ___ 4 oz.

㉞ 12 oz. ___ 6/8 lb. ㉟ 11/16 lb. ___ 14 oz. ㊱ 6 oz. ___ 3/8 lb.

C Underline the correct answers.

① Cathy weighs 4 oz. less than Barbara. Barbara is (1/8, 1/4, 1/2) lb. heavier than Cathy.

② A recipe calls for 1/8 lb. of grated parmesan cheese. From a 6-oz. chunk of parmesan, (1/4 lb., 2 oz., 5 oz.) would remain after preparing the recipe.

③ Each sheet of note paper that Ted buys at the bookstore weighs 1 oz. Ted pays 32¢ for 1 lb. of paper. The cost per sheet is (1¢, 2¢, 3¢).

④ A cotton swab weighs 1 oz. A paper clip weighs 1/8 lb. The weight of a cotton swab is (less than, equal to, greater than) the weight of a paper clip.

⑤ Robert does not know how many ounces equal a pound. When a recipe called for 1 lb. of spaghetti, Robert cooked 10 oz. He should have added another (1/8 lb., 1/4 lb., 3/8 lb.) of spaghetti to the pot.

⑥ Seven silk flowers were shipped to Rosemond's Floral Shop. Each flower weighed 2 oz. Shipping cost was 50¢ per pound. Rosemond paid (less than 50¢, more than 50¢, 50¢) for her order of silk flowers.

Pounds

Learning Objective: *We will learn to convert pounds and ounces.*

A pound is a standard unit of weight equaling 16 ounces or 1/2,000 of one ton.

EXAMPLES: To convert pounds to ounces, multiply by 16.   3 lb. $\times$ 16 = 48 oz.
To convert ounces to pounds, divide by 16.   48 oz. $\div$ 16 = 3 lb.

A Convert pounds to ounces.

① 11 lb. = *176 oz.*   ② 56 lb. =   ③ 92 lb. =   ④ 7 lb. =

⑤ 16 lb. =   ⑥ 79 lb. =   ⑦ 12 lb. =   ⑧ 66 lb. =

⑨ 14 lb. =   ⑩ 77 lb. =   ⑪ 8 lb. =   ⑫ 19 lb. =

⑬ 25 lb. =   ⑭ 9 lb. =   ⑮ 43 lb. =   ⑯ 84 lb. =

⑰ 39 lb. =   ⑱ 99 lb. =   ⑲ 61 lb. =   ⑳ 137 lb. =

㉑ 47 lb. =   ㉒ 108 lb. =   ㉓ 22 lb. =   ㉔ 40 lb. =

㉕ 80 lb. =   ㉖ 212 lb. =   ㉗ 88 lb. =   ㉘ 354 lb. =

B Convert ounces to pounds.

① 656 oz. = *41 lb.*   ② 1,040 oz. =   ③ 1,552 oz. =   ④ 464 oz. =

⑤ 336 oz. =   ⑥ 544 oz. =   ⑦ 768 oz. =   ⑧ 2,768 oz. =

⑨ 1,456 oz. =   ⑩ 64 oz. =   ⑪ 1,776 oz. =   ⑫ 3,744 oz. =

⑬ 1,360 oz. =   ⑭ 2,064 oz. =   ⑮ 288 oz. =   ⑯ 7,392 oz. =

⑰ 2,896 oz. =   ⑱ 6,512 oz. =   ⑲ 4,096 oz. =   ⑳ 624 oz. =

㉑ 2,352 oz. =   ㉒ 8,256 oz. =   ㉓ 4,528 oz. =   ㉔ 12,816 oz. =

㉕ 160 oz. =   ㉖ 5,264 oz. =   ㉗ 2,176 oz. =   ㉘ 1,136 oz. =

REMINDER: Write the definition of a pound.

Unit 137 cont'd ☞

C Give each weight in pounds and ounces.

① 27 oz. = _1_ lb. _11_ oz.　　② 35 oz. = ___ lb. ___ oz.　　③ 72 oz. = ___ lb. ___ oz.

④ 139 oz. = ___ lb. ___ oz.　　⑤ 976 oz. = ___ lb. ___ oz.　　⑥ 2,476 oz. = ___ lb. ___ oz.

⑦ 97 oz. = ___ lb. ___ oz.　　⑧ 179 oz. = ___ lb. ___ oz.　　⑨ 58 oz. = ___ lb. ___ oz.

⑩ 1,017 oz. = ___ lb. ___ oz.　　⑪ 516 oz. = ___ lb. ___ oz.　　⑫ 3,011 oz. = ___ lb. ___ oz.

D Fill in the blanks with the symbols <, >, or =.

① 90 lb. _>_ 1,400 oz.　　② 25 oz. ___ 16 lb.　　③ 943 oz. ___ 60 lb.

④ 54 lb. ___ 864 oz.　　⑤ 84 oz. ___ 5 lb.　　⑥ 169 oz. ___ 10 lb.

⑦ 22 lb. ___ 353 oz.　　⑧ 96 oz. ___ 6 lb.　　⑨ 56 lb. ___ 911 oz.

⑩ 1,632 oz. ___ 102 lb.　　⑪ 768 oz. ___ 50 lb.　　⑫ 17 lb. ___ 275 oz.

⑬ 779 lb. ___ 779 oz.　　⑭ 82 lb. ___ 1,311 oz.　　⑮ 25 lb. ___ 415 oz.

E Underline the correct answers.

① Walter weighs 145 lb. 8 oz. His friend, Victor, weighs 212 lb. 10 oz. Victor weighs (69 oz.; 1,000 oz.; <u>67 lb. 2 oz.</u>) more than Walter.

② To determine how many ounces are in 166 lb., (multiply, divide, increase) by 16.

③ At birth, Christy weighed 9 lb. 4 oz. Kim weighed 121 oz. Christy's weight at birth was (less than, equal to, greater than) Kim's birth weight.

④ To find the number of pounds that are equivalent to 2,048 oz., (multiply, divide, increase) by 16.

⑤ A 5-lb. bag of potatoes costs 80¢. The price of potatoes per ounce is (1¢, 5¢, 25¢).

⑥ A pound is always (less than, equal to, greater than) an ounce.

⑦ If a pound is 1/2,000 of one ton, there are (12; 100; 2,000) pounds in each ton.

⑧ Sean borrowed 80 oz. of sugar from a neighbor. He returned 2 lb. of sugar the next day. He still owed his neighbor (32, 48, 78) oz. of sugar.

Tons

Learning
Objective: *We will learn to convert tons and pounds.*

A ton is a standard unit of weight equaling 2,000 pounds.

EXAMPLES: To convert tons to pounds, multiply by 2,000. 3 T. × 2,000 = 6,000 lb.
To convert pounds to tons, divide by 2,000. 6,000 lb. ÷ 2,000 = 3 T.

A Convert tons to pounds.

① 71 T. = *142,000 lb.* ② 80 T. =   ③ 39 T. =   ④ 46 T. =

⑤ 23 T. =   ⑥ 17 T. =   ⑦ 29 T. =   ⑧ 97 T. =

⑨ 84 T. =   ⑩ 56 T. =   ⑪ 11 T. =   ⑫ 31 T. =

⑬ 6 T. =   ⑭ 92 T. =   ⑮ 65 T. =   ⑯ 74 T. =

⑰ 40 T. =   ⑱ 100 T. =   ⑲ 9 T. =   ⑳ 13 T. =

㉑ 52 T. =   ㉒ 7 T. =   ㉓ 20 T. =   ㉔ 87 T. =

㉕ 79 T. =   ㉖ 25 T. =   ㉗ 44 T. =   ㉘ 4 T. =

B Convert pounds to tons.

① 4,000 lb. = *2 T.* ② 102,000 lb. =   ③ 30,000 lb. =   ④ 48,000 lb. =

⑤ 168,000 lb. =   ⑥ 16,000 lb. =   ⑦ 10,000 lb. =   ⑧ 66,000 lb. =

⑨ 42,000 lb. =   ⑩ 38,000 lb. =   ⑪ 56,000 lb. =   ⑫ 74,000 lb. =

⑬ 60,000 lb. =   ⑭ 24,000 lb. =   ⑮ 98,000 lb. =   ⑯ 126,000 lb. =

⑰ 178,000 lb. =   ⑱ 108,000 lb. =   ⑲ 52,000 lb. =   ⑳ 100,000 lb. =

㉑ 20,000 lb. =   ㉒ 32,000 lb. =   ㉓ 94,000 lb. =   ㉔ 150,000 lb. =

㉕ 132,000 lb. =   ㉖ 84,000 lb. =   ㉗ 28,000 lb. =   ㉘ 70,000 lb. =

REMINDER: *Write the definition of a ton.*

_____

_____

   Unit 138 cont'd ☞

C Give each weight in tons and pounds

① 13,579 lb. = __6__ T. __1,579__ lb.   ② 11,131 lb. = ____ T. _____ lb.   ③ 51,617 lb. = ____ T. ____ lb.

④ 18,192 lb. = ____ T. _____ lb.   ⑤ 2,122 lb. = ____ T. ____ lb.   ⑥ 23,242 lb. = ____ T. ____ lb.

⑦ 52,627 lb. = ____ T. _____ lb.   ⑧ 28,293 lb. = ____ T. _____ lb.   ⑨ 3,132 lb. = ____ T. ____ lb.

⑩ 33,343 lb. = ____ T. _____ lb.   ⑪ 7,389 lb. = ____ T. _____ lb.   ⑫ 40,414 lb. = ____ T. _____ lb.

D Fill in the blanks with the symbols <, >, or =.

① 76 T. __>__ 150,000 lb.   ② 116,000 lb. ____ 60 T.   ③ 199,999 lb. ____ 100 T.

④ 27 T. ____ 54,000 lb.   ⑤ 9,837 lb. ____ 9 T.   ⑥ 13 T. ____ 1,300 lb.

⑦ 47 T. ____ 95,000 lb.   ⑧ 26,000 lb. ____ 31 T.   ⑨ 88 T. ____ 176,000 lb.

⑩ 6,394 lb. ____ 12 T.   ⑪ 54 T. ____ 19,000 lb.   ⑫ 81,000 lb. ____ 40 T.

⑬ 11,197 lb. ____ 10 T.   ⑭ 79 T. ____ 79,000 lb.   ⑮ 64,000 lb. ____ 32 T.

E Underline the correct answers.

① Building materials for a new hospital wing weigh 74,000 lb. Freight cost for materials is $302 for the first 25 tons. An additional $10 per ton freight expense is charged for any weight over 25 tons. Total freight cost for all building materials is ($120, $422, $792).

② George's father owns a dump truck that carries a full load of 40,000 lb. of gravel. If his father hauls 4 full loads of gravel in one day, he will transport a total of (80 T., 160 T., 400 T.).

③ To find the number of pounds that equal 710 T., (multiply, divide, increase) by 2,000.

④ Hydraulic jacks were used to move a 12,000-ton ship, section by section. Each ship section weighed 8,000,000 lb. The ship was moved in (2, 3, 6) sections.

⑤ Some large cranes can lift up to 15,000 tons. Such a crane (could, could not) be used to lift a rocket weighing 12,000,000 lb.

⑥ To determine the number of tons that are equivalent to 184,000 lb., (multiply, divide, increase) by 2,000.

Grams

Learning
Objective: *We will learn to recognize a gram as a fraction of a kilogram and to compare grams to ounces.*

A gram is a unit of metric weight equaling 1/1,000 of a kilogram or approximately 35/1,000 of one ounce.

EXAMPLE:

One thousand grams equal one kilogram.

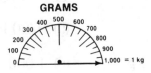

A On each scale below, draw a needle pointing to the correct weight.

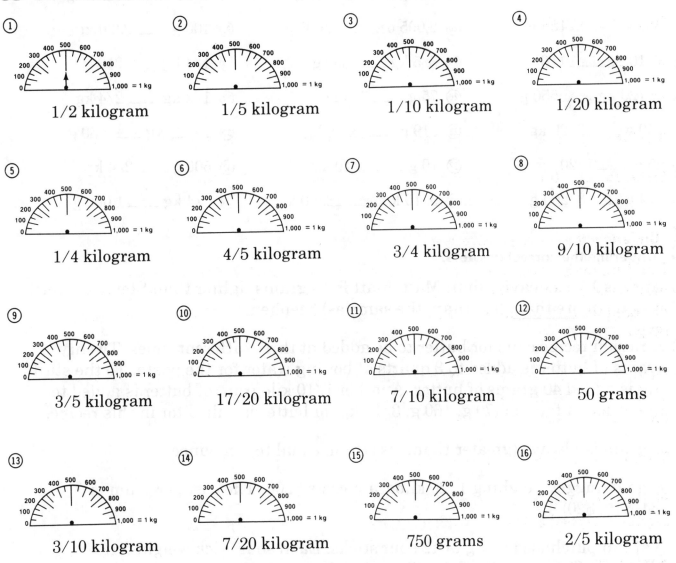

① 1/2 kilogram

② 1/5 kilogram

③ 1/10 kilogram

④ 1/20 kilogram

⑤ 1/4 kilogram

⑥ 4/5 kilogram

⑦ 3/4 kilogram

⑧ 9/10 kilogram

⑨ 3/5 kilogram

⑩ 17/20 kilogram

⑪ 7/10 kilogram

⑫ 50 grams

⑬ 3/10 kilogram

⑭ 7/20 kilogram

⑮ 750 grams

⑯ 2/5 kilogram

REMINDER: *Write the definition of a gram.*

Unit 139 cont'd 🐾

B Fill in the blanks with the symbols <, >, or =.

① 325 g __>__ 3/10 kg   ② 1 kg ____ 1,000 g   ③ 1 g ____ 1 oz.

④ 75 g ____ 1/20 kg   ⑤ 105 oz. ____ 105 g   ⑥ 910 g ____ 9/10 kg

⑦ 4/5 kg ____ 875 g   ⑧ 5/5 kg ____ 1 kg   ⑨ 640 g ____ 13/20 kg

⑩ 1 g ____ 1 kg   ⑪ 9/20 kg ____ 450 g   ⑫ 777 g ____ 4/5 kg

⑬ 5/10 kg ____ 1/2 kg   ⑭ 1,000 g ____ 1,000 oz.   ⑮ 3/10 kg ____ 212 g

⑯ 40 g ____ 1/20 kg   ⑰ 957 g ____ 19/20 kg   ⑱ 6/10 kg ____ 3/5 kg

⑲ 800 g ____ 8/10 kg   ⑳ 2,095 oz. ____ 2,095 g   ㉑ 100 g ____ 2/20 kg.

㉒ 1/10 kg ____ 116 g   ㉓ 3/5 kg ____ 599 g   ㉔ 1/4 kg ____ 210 g

㉕ 11/20 kg ____ 550 g   ㉖ 75 g ____ 3/4 kg   ㉗ 1/2 kg ____ 2/4 kg

㉘ 150 g ____ 3/20 kg   ㉙ 819 g ____ 8/10 kg   ㉚ 19/20 kg ____ 950 g

㉛ 65 g ____ 1/20 kg   ㉜ 10 g ____ 1/10 kg   ㉝ 500 g ____ 2/4 kg

㉞ 114 g ____ 3/20 kg   ㉟ 9/10 kg ____ 18/20 kg   ㊱ 4/4 kg ____ 1,000 g

C Underline the correct answers.

① April is 15 oz. heavier than Matt. Matt is 15 grams lighter than Stephen. April weighs (<u>more than</u>, less than, the same as) Stephen.

② A ravioli recipe calls for butter to be added at three different times. Twenty grams of butter is added to 3 quarts of boiling water for the pasta. To the stuffing is added 40 grams of butter. Another 1/10 kilogram of butter is added to the sauce. A total of (70 g, 160 g, 3/10 kg) of butter is called for in this recipe.

③ A gram is always (greater than, less than, equal to) an ounce.

④ A gold nugget weighing 1/20 kilogram costs $200. The cost per gram is ($4, $10, $20).

⑤ Nathan purchased a bag of 12 sour sticks. Each sour stick weighed 1/10 kilogram. Total weight of the 12 sour sticks was (120 g, 1 kg, 1,200 g).

⑥ When comparing grams and kilograms, the Henderson sophomore chemistry students remembered that "kilo" means 1,000. In other words 1 kilogram is 1,000 times (lighter, heavier, longer) than 1 gram.

Kilograms

Learning Objective: *We will learn to convert kilograms and grams and to compare kilograms with pounds.*

A kilogram is a unit of metric weight equaling 1,000 grams or approximately 2 1/5 pounds.

EXAMPLES: To convert kilograms to grams, multiply by 1,000.   3 kg $\times$ 1,000 = 3,000 g
To convert grams to kilograms, divide by 1,000.   3000 g $\div$ 1,000 = 3 kg

A Convert kilograms to grams.

① 11 kg = *11,000 g*   ② 17 kg =   ③ 6 kg =   ④ 25 kg =

⑤ 63 kg =   ⑥ 92 kg =   ⑦ 47 kg =   ⑧ 112 kg =

⑨ 89 kg =   ⑩ 614 kg =   ⑪ 72 kg =   ⑫ 51 kg =

⑬ 256 kg =   ⑭ 791 kg =   ⑮ 4 kg =   ⑯ 192 kg =

⑰ 866 kg =   ⑱ 105 kg =   ⑲ 914 kg =   ⑳ 10 kg =

㉑ 77 kg =   ㉒ 3 kg =   ㉓ 40 kg =   ㉔ 304 kg =

㉕ 144 kg =   ㉖ 220 kg =   ㉗ 13 kg =   ㉘ 100 kg =

B Convert grams to kilograms.

① 1,000 g = *1 kg*   ② 31,000 g =   ③ 22,000 g =   ④ 441,000 g =

⑤ 501,000 g =   ⑥ 7,000 g =   ⑦ 618,000 g =   ⑧ 197,000 g =

⑨ 912,000 g =   ⑩ 15,000 g =   ⑪ 149,000 g =   ⑫ 27,000 g =

⑬ 416,000 g =   ⑭ 98,000 g =   ⑮ 36,000 g =   ⑯ 74,000 g =

⑰ 29,000 g =   ⑱ 403,000 g =   ⑲ 211,000 g =   ⑳ 52,000 g =

㉑ 71,000 g =   ㉒ 656,000 g =   ㉓ 354,000 g =   ㉔ 16,000 g =

㉕ 99,000 g =   ㉖ 81,000 g =   ㉗ 625,000 g =   ㉘ 200,000 g =

REMINDER: Write the definition of kilograms.

Unit 140 cont'd ☛

C   Give each weight in kilograms and grams.

① 4,107 g = __4__ kg __107__ g   ② 19,012 g = _____ kg _____ g   ③ 11,001 g = _____ kg _____ g

④ 102,109 g = _____ kg _____ g   ⑤ 7,110 g = _____ kg _____ g   ⑥ 9,336 g = _____ kg _____ g

⑦ 410,971 g = _____ kg _____ g   ⑧ 14,908 g = _____ kg _____ g   ⑨ 56,006 g = _____ kg _____ g

⑩ 2,916 g = _____ kg _____ g   ⑪ 39,400 g = _____ kg _____ g   ⑫ 47,700 g = _____ kg _____ g

D   Fill in the blanks with the symbols <, >, or =.

① 16 kg __<__ 16,001 g   ② 27 kg _____ 27 lb   ③ 244,000 g _____ 244 kg

④ 1,500 g _____ 15 kg   ⑤ 11,586 g _____ 12 kg   ⑥ 62 kg _____ 620 g

⑦ 710 kg _____ 710 g   ⑧ 409 lb. _____ 409 kg   ⑨ 12 lb. _____ 12,000 g

⑩ 114 kg _____ 12,000 g   ⑪ 2,600 g _____ 250 kg   ⑫ 111 g _____ 111,000 kg

⑬ 47,000 g _____ 470 kg   ⑭ 59,000 g _____ 59 kg   ⑮ 16,000 kg _____ 160 g

E   Underline the correct answers.

① Jake's cat weighs 8 lb. His dog weighs 8 kg. Jake's cat weighs (more than, <u>less than</u>, the same as) Jake's dog.

② Lana mailed four Christmas packages. One package weighed 12 kg. Another package weighed 8,000 g. A third package weighed 17,000 g, and the fourth weighed 2 kg. Total weight of all packages was (39 kg, 48 kg, 39,000 kg).

③ To find out how many grams are in 97 kilograms, (multiply, divide, increase) by 1,000.

④ A kilogram is always (greater than, less than, equal to) a pound.

⑤ After dieting, Larry weighed 87 kg. Before dieting, he weighed 100 kg. Larry lost (13 g, 13,000 g, 187,000 g) while dieting.

⑥ One airline requires that passengers limit their luggage to 25 lb. If a passenger's luggage weighs 25 (grams, ounces, kilograms), that passenger will have to pay an excess baggage fee.

⑦ If an object weighs 3,000 g, (multiply, divide, increase) by 1,000 to determine its weight in kilograms.

Comprehension Check

A Convert pounds to ounces.

① 41 lb. = **656 oz.**   ② 111 lb. =   ③ 85 lb. =   ④ 100 lb. =

⑤ 407 lb. =   ⑥ 18 lb. =   ⑦ 129 lb. =   ⑧ 5 lb. =

B Convert ounces to pounds.

① 144 oz. = **9 lb.**   ② 688 oz. =   ③ 752 oz. =   ④ 400 oz. =

⑤ 96 oz. =   ⑥ 2,048 oz. =   ⑦ 1,632 oz. =   ⑧ 48 oz. =

C Convert tons to pounds.

① 30 T. = **60,000 lb.**   ② 88 T. =   ③ 19 T. =   ④ 54 T. =

⑤ 49 T. =   ⑥ 5 T. =   ⑦ 66 T. =   ⑧ 10 T. =

D Convert pounds to tons.

① 158,000 lb. = **79 T.**   ② 144,000 lb. =   ③ 80,000 lb. =   ④ 26,000 lb. =

⑤ 14,000 lb. =   ⑥ 78,000 lb. =   ⑦ 112,000 lb. =   ⑧ 194,000 lb. =

E Convert kilograms to grams.

① 500 kg = **500,000 g**   ② 14 kg =   ③ 405 kg =   ④ 30 kg =

⑤ 910 kg =   ⑥ 37 kg =   ⑦ 350 kg =   ⑧ 194 kg =

F Convert grams to kilograms.

① 12,000 g = **12 kg**   ② 79,000 g =   ③ 416,000 g =   ④ 291,000 g =

⑤ 612,000 g =   ⑥ 44,000 g =   ⑦ 171,000 g =   ⑧ 98,000 g =

G Fill in the blanks.

① 112 lb. $\times$ __**16**__ = 1,792 oz.   ② 88,000 lb. $\div$ _____ = 44 T.

③ 666,000 g _____ 1,000 = 666 kg   ④ 8,256 oz. _____ 16 = 516 lb.

⑤ 65 T. _____ 2,000 = 130,000 lb.   ⑥ 21 kg $\times$ _____ = 21,000 g

Test 28 cont'd ☞

H Give each weight in pounds and ounces.

① 375 oz. = __23__ lb. __7__ oz.   ② 1,171 oz. = ____ lb. ____ oz.   ③ 201 oz. = ____ lb. ____ oz.

④ 4,910 oz. = ____ lb. ____ oz.   ⑤ 513 oz. = ____ lb. ____ oz.   ⑥ 977 oz. = ____ lb. ____ oz.

I Give each weight in tons and pounds.

① 25,912 lb. = __12__ T. __1,912__ lb.   ② 8,014 lb. = ____ T. ____ lb.   ③ 12,002 lb. = ____ T. ____ lb.

④ 17,154 lb. = ____ T. ____ lb.   ⑤ 36,901 lb. = ____ T. ____ lb.   ⑥ 42,128 lb. = ____ T. ____ lb.

J Give each weight in kilograms and grams.

① 9,196 g = __9__ kg __196__ g   ② 16,054 g = ____ kg ____ g   ③ 54,912 g = ____ kg ____ g

④ 84,365 g = ____ kg ____ g   ⑤ 43,179 g = ____ kg ____ g   ⑥ 99,016 g = ____ kg ____ g

K Fill in the blanks with $<$, $>$, or $=$.

① 1/10 kg __=__ 100 g   ② 15 oz. ____ 15/16 lb.   ③ 2,000 g ____ 4 kg

④ 1/2 lb. ____ 7 oz.   ⑤ 1,000 lb. ____ 1 T.   ⑥ 454 kg ____ 454 lb.

⑦ 260 g ____ 1/4 kg   ⑧ 77 T. ____ 77 g   ⑨ 11,046 g ____ 11,046 lb.

⑩ 1 kg ____ 1 T.   ⑪ 12 oz. ____ 1 lb.   ⑫ 90 lb. ____ 90,000 g

⑬ 7/8 lb. ____ 14 oz.   ⑭ 500 g ____ 1/2 kg   ⑮ 10 oz. ____ 3/4 lb.

⑯ 800 g ____ 9/10 kg   ⑰ 16/16 lb. ____ 16 oz.   ⑱ 2,000 T. ____ 20 lb.

⑲ 1/8 lb. ____ 2 oz.   ⑳ 3,000 g ____ 30 kg   ㉑ 4 oz. ____ 1/4 lb.

㉒ 247 oz. ____ 247 g   ㉓ 15,000 kg ____ 15 g   ㉔ 1/20 kg ____ 50 g

Define these terms.

① ounce _____

_____

② pound _____

_____

③ ton _____

_____

④ gram _____

_____

⑤ kilogram _____

_____

Metric Tons

Learning Objective: *We will learn to convert metric tons and kilograms and to compare metric tons with U.S. tons.*

A metric ton is a unit of weight equaling 1,000 kilograms or approximately 1 $\frac{1}{10}$ standard U.S. tons.

EXAMPLE: To convert metric tons to kilograms, multiply by 1,000. $3 \text{ t} \times 1,000 = 3,000 \text{ kg.}$
To convert kilograms to metric tons, divide by 1,000. $3,000 \div 1,000 = 3 \text{ t.}$

A Convert metric tons to kilograms.

① 37 t = __37,000 kg__   ② 212 t = _____   ③ 6 t = _____   ④ 11 t = _____

⑤ 78 t = _____   ⑥ 53 t = _____   ⑦ 174 t = _____   ⑧ 310 t = _____

⑨ 10 t = _____   ⑩ 114 t = _____   ⑪ 41 t = _____   ⑫ 26 t = _____

⑬ 628 t = _____   ⑭ 7 t = _____   ⑮ 66 t = _____   ⑯ 4 t = _____

⑰ 16 t = _____   ⑱ 27 t = _____   ⑲ 299 t = _____   ⑳ 500 t = _____

㉑ 75 t = _____   ㉒ 450 t = _____   ㉓ 150 t = _____   ㉔ 170 t = _____

㉕ 98 t = _____   ㉖ 166 t = _____   ㉗ 9 t = _____   ㉘ 129 t = _____

B Convert kilograms to metric tons.

① 17,000 kg = __17 t__   ② 3,000 kg = ____   ③ 88,000 kg = ____   ④ 73,000 kg = ____

⑤ 312,000 kg = ____   ⑥ 589,000 kg = ____   ⑦ 13,000 kg = ____   ⑧ 987,000 kg = ____

⑨ 510,000 kg = ____   ⑩ 65,000 kg = ____   ⑪ 432,000 kg = ____   ⑫ 2,000 kg = ____

⑬ 100,000 kg = ____   ⑭ 33,000 kg = ____   ⑮ 51,000 kg = ____   ⑯ 92,000 kg = ____

⑰ 148,000 kg = ____   ⑱ 946,000 kg = ____   ⑲ 23,000 kg = ____   ⑳ 48,000 kg = ____

㉑ 540,000 kg = ____   ㉒ 60,000 kg = ____   ㉓ 628,000 kg = ____   ㉔ 326,000 kg = ____

㉕ 8,000 kg = ____   ㉖ 700,000 kg = ____   ㉗ 499,000 kg = ____   ㉘ 90,000 kg = ____

REMINDER: Write the definition of a metric ton.

C Give each weight in metric tons and kilograms.

① 467,891 kg = _467_ t _891_ kg   ② 32,900 kg = ___ t ___ kg   ③ 307,109 kg = ___ t ___ kg

④ 5,245 kg = ___ t ___ kg   ⑤ 197,006 kg = ___ t ___ kg   ⑥ 16,161 kg = ___ t ___ kg

⑦ 89,061 kg = ___ t ___ kg   ⑧ 21,155 kg = ___ t ___ kg   ⑨ 500,909 kg = ___ t ___ kg

⑩ 313,197 kg = ___ t ___ kg   ⑪ 74,462 kg = ___ t ___ kg   ⑫ 9,086 kg = ___ t ___ kg

D Fill in the blanks with <, >, or =.

① 75,000 t _>_ 75 kg   ② 3 t ___ 3 T.   ③ 1,900 kg ___ 1 t   ④ 2,500 T. ___ 2,500 t

⑤ 348,000 kg ___ 348 t   ⑥ 472 t ___ 4,720 kg   ⑦ 46,000 kg ___ 46 T.   ⑧ 999 t ___ 999,000 kg

⑨ 52 t ___ 52 kg   ⑩ 77 T. ___ 77 t   ⑪ 16 t ___ 1,600 kg   ⑫ 64,000 kg ___ 643 t

⑬ 89 kg ___ 89 T.   ⑭ 146 t ___ 146,000 kg   ⑮ 309 t ___ 3,009 kg   ⑯ 988 T. ___ 988,000 kg

E Underline the correct answers.

① The cost of steel beams increases according to the weight of the beams. The cost per metric ton is $2,000. The cost per standard U.S. ton would be (greater than, <u>less than</u>, equal to) $2,000.

② Twelve metric tons is (10; 100; 1,000) times heavier than 12 kilograms.

③ To determine how many kilograms are equal to 676 t, (multiply, divide, increase) by 1,000.

④ One train car weighs 2,000 metric tons. Ten cars would weigh (20,000 kg; 2,000,000 kg; 20,000,000 kg).

⑤ Wilson Construction Company received one shipment of materials weighing a total of 13 metric tons. Another shipment weighed 18,056 kilograms. Total weight of the two shipments was (18,069; 5 t, 56 kg; 31 t, 56 kg).

⑥ The Hanson Corporation pledged to send 50 t of grain to underdeveloped nations. At the end of 1985, the company had shipped 15,000 kg of grain to India, 22 t of grain to Africa, and 7,000 kg to southeast Asia. The remainder of the pledged grain was sent to Central America. (6 t; 94 t; 6,000 t) of grain was shipped to Central America.

Units of Weight

Learning Objective: *We will learn to convert and compare units of weight.*

A unit of weight; including the ounce, pound, ton, gram, kilogram, and metric ton; tells how heavy.

EXAMPLE: A pound is 16 times as heavy as an ounce. A ton is 2,000 times as heavy as a pound. A kilogram is 1,000 times as heavy as a gram. A metric ton is 1,000 times as heavy as a kilogram. A gram is lighter than an ounce. A kilogram is heavier than a pound. A metric ton is heavier than a standard U.S. ton.

A Complete the problems with equivalent measurements.

① T. _6_
  lb. _12,000_
  oz. _192,000_

② T. _11_
  lb. ___
  oz. ___

③ T. _14_
  lb. ___
  oz. ___

④ T. _20_
  lb. ___
  oz. ___

⑤ t _40_
  kg ___
  g ___

⑥ t _9_
  kg ___
  g ___

⑦ t _32_
  kg ___
  g ___

⑧ t _18_
  kg ___
  g ___

⑨ T. ___
  lb. _8,000_
  oz. ___

⑩ T. ___
  lb. _2,000_
  oz. ___

⑪ T. ___
  lb. _20,000_
  oz. ___

⑫ T. ___
  lb. _16,000_
  oz. ___

⑬ t ___
  kg _12,000_
  g ___

⑭ t ___
  kg _25,000_
  g ___

⑮ t ___
  kg _3,000_
  g ___

⑯ t ___
  kg _52,000_
  g ___

⑰ T. ___
  lb. ___
  oz. _224,000_

⑱ T. ___
  lb. ___
  oz. _1,248,000_

⑲ T. ___
  lb. ___
  oz. _480,000_

⑳ T. ___
  lb. ___
  oz. _576,000_

㉑ t ___
  kg ___
  g _16,000,000_

㉒ t ___
  kg ___
  g _72,000,000_

㉓ t ___
  kg ___
  g _7,000,000_

㉔ t ___
  kg ___
  g _68,000,000_

REMINDER: Write the definition of a unit weight.

_____

_____

Unit 142 cont'd ☞

B Fill in the blanks with <, >, or =.

① 16 g $\leq$ 16 oz.　　② 16 g ____ 1 lb.　　③ 1 lb. ____ 1 kg

④ 16 oz. ____ 1 kg　　⑤ 1 T. ____ 2,000 lb.　　⑥ 1 T. ____ 1 t

⑦ 2,000 lb. ____ 1 t　　⑧ 1 t ____ 1,000 kg　　⑨ 1,000 kg ____ 1,000,000 g

⑩ 1 t ____ 1,000,000 g　　⑪ 1 T. ____ 1,000,000 g　　⑫ 1,000,000 g ____ 1,000,000 oz.

⑬ 1 t ____ 1,000,000 oz.　　⑭ 1,000,000 oz. ____ 1 T.　　⑮ 1,000,000 oz. ____ 2,000 lb.

C Fill in the blanks.

① 1 kg × _**1,000**_ = 1,000 g　　② 10 lb. × _____ = 160 oz.

③ 100 t × _____ = 100,000 kg　　④ 1,000 T. × _____ = 2,000,000 lb.

⑤ 10,000 kg ÷ _____ = 10 t　　⑥ 100,000 lb. ÷ _____ = 50 T.

⑦ 1,000,000 g ÷ _____ = 1,000 kg　　⑧ 16,000,000 oz. ÷ _____ = 1,000,000 lb.

D True or False

① _**T**_ Of the gram, ounce, pound, ton, kilogram, and metric ton, the gram is the smallest unit of weight.

② ____ To convert metric tons to kilograms or to convert U.S. tons to pounds, multiply by 1,000.

③ ____ Of the units of weight studied in this lesson, the kilogram is the greatest.

④ ____ It takes 2,000 lb. or 2,000,000 oz. to equal a U.S. ton.

⑤ ____ A pound is greater than a gram but less than a kilogram.

⑥ ____ To convert ounces to pounds, multiply by 16.

⑦ ____ A gram is less than an ounce but greater than a kilogram.

⑧ ____ Divide by 2,000 to convert pounds to ounces.

⑨ ____ A U.S. ton is 1,000 times heavier than a pound.

⑩ ____ A gram is 1/10 of one kilogram.

344

Cups

Learning Objective: *We will learn to convert and compare cups and ounces.*

A cup is a standard unit of volume equaling 8 liquid ounces or ½ pint.

EXAMPLE: To convert cups to ounces, multiply by 8.   3 c. × 8 = 24 oz.
To convert ounces to cups, divide by 8.   24 oz. ÷ 8 = 3 c.

A Convert cups to ounces.

① 6 c. = __48 oz.__   ② 11 c. = _____   ③ 17 c. = _____   ④ 23 c. = _____

⑤ 19 c. = _____   ⑥ 32 c. = _____   ⑦ 84 c. = _____   ⑧ 62 c. = _____

⑨ 10 c. = _____   ⑩ 100 c. = _____   ⑪ 39 c. = _____   ⑫ 77 c. = _____

⑬ 41 c. = _____   ⑭ 89 c. = _____   ⑮ 1,000 c. = _____   ⑯ 27 c. = _____

⑰ 125 c. = _____   ⑱ 584 c. = _____   ⑲ 28 c. = _____   ⑳ 15 c. = _____

㉑ 2 c. = _____   ㉒ 54 c. = _____   ㉓ 98 c. = _____   ㉔ 1 c. = _____

㉕ 45 c. = _____   ㉖ 18 c. = _____   ㉗ 119 c. = _____   ㉘ 207 c. = _____

B Convert ounces to cups.

① 7,288 oz. = __911 c.__   ② 1,704 oz. = _____   ③ 744 oz. = _____   ④ 384 oz. = _____

⑤ 208 oz. = _____   ⑥ 3,896 oz. = _____   ⑦ 5,616 oz. = _____   ⑧ 648 oz. = _____

⑨ 576 oz. = _____   ⑩ 2,072 oz. = _____   ⑪ 400 oz. = _____   ⑫ 296 oz. = _____

⑬ 408 oz. = _____   ⑭ 568 oz. = _____   ⑮ 2,208 oz. = _____   ⑯ 4,168 oz. = _____

⑰ 1,800 oz. = _____   ⑱ 656 oz. = _____   ⑲ 504 oz. = _____   ⑳ 112 oz. = _____

㉑ 3,376 oz. = _____   ㉒ 3,000 oz. = _____   ㉓ 3,312 oz. = _____   ㉔ 728 oz. = _____

㉕ 5,216 oz. = _____   ㉖ 3,880 oz. = _____   ㉗ 792 oz. = _____   ㉘ 480 oz. = _____

REMINDER: Write the definition of a cup.

_____

C Study the box and fill in the blanks with >, <, or = .

> 8 oz. = 1 cup
> 6 oz. = ¾ cup
> 4 oz. = ½ cup
> 2 oz. = ¼ cup
> 1 oz. = ⅛ cup

① ½ c. __<__ 8 oz. ② 8 oz. ____ 1 c. ③ ¼ c. ____ 4 oz.

④ 3 oz. ____ ³⁄₈ c. ⑤ 6 oz. ____ ¼ c. ⑥ ²⁄₈ c. ____ ¼ c. ⑦ 5 oz. ____ ⁷⁄₈ c.

⑧ 2 ½ c. ____ 16 oz. ⑨ 4 c. ____ 12 oz. ⑩ ¾ c. ____ 6 oz. ⑪ 4 oz. ____ ²⁄₄ c.

⑫ ⅛ c. ____ 1 oz. ⑬ ⁸⁄₈ c. ____ 16 oz. ⑭ 1 ¼ c. ____ 12 oz. ⑮ 11 oz. ____ 1 ³⁄₈ c.

⑯ 2 ⅝ c. ____ 21 oz. ⑰ ⅞ c. ____ 7 oz. ⑱ 3 ⅝ c. ____ 24 oz. ⑲ 2 oz. ____ ¼ c.

⑳ 1 ¼ c. ____ 18 oz. ㉑ 5 ½ c. ____ 45 oz. ㉒ 4 oz. ____ ½ c. ㉓ 10 ⅛ c. ____ 41 oz.

㉔ 32 oz. ____ 4 c. ㉕ ²⁄₄ c. ____ ½ c. ㉖ 14 oz. ____ 2 c. ㉗ 30 oz. ____ 3 ¾ c.

㉘ 6 ¾ c. ____ 48 oz. ㉙ 1 ⅛ c. ____ 18 oz. ㉚ ⅞ c. ____ 13 oz. ㉛ ¾ c. ____ ⁶⁄₈ c.

㉜ ⅝ c. ____ 5 oz. ㉝ 22 oz. ____ 3 c. ㉞ 9 oz. ____ 1 ⅛ c. ㉟ 15 oz. ____ 2 c.

D Underline the correct answers.

① A recipe calls for 2½ c. of milk. If only 14 oz. of milk is on hand, (2 oz., 6 oz., 34 oz.) more is needed.

② Regina poured 3 c. of water into a large pan. She then added 48 oz. more water. This brought the total amount of water to (45 oz., 51 oz., 72 oz.).

③ To find how many ounces are in 12 c., (multiply, divide, increase) by eight.

④ At a family picnic, Jennifer set out three pitchers of lemonade. Each pitcher contained 64 oz. of liquid. After the picnic was over, 12 oz. of lemonade remained in one pitcher. Seven ounces remained in another pitcher, and the third pitcher was empty. A total of (45 oz., 173 oz., 180 oz.) of lemonade was drunk at the picnic.

⑤ At breakfast, Daryl placed 6-oz. juice glasses beside each plate. Each glass could hold up to (½ c., ¾ c., 6 c.) of juice.

⑥ A cup is a unit of (length, weight, volume).

⑦ (Multiply, Divide, Increase) by 8 to determine the number of cups that equal 128 oz.

Pints and Quarts

Learning Objective: *We will learn to convert quarts, pints, cups, and ounces.*

A pint is a standard unit of volume equaling 2 cups or ½ quart.
A quart is a standard unit of volume equaling 2 pints or ¼ gallon.

EXAMPLE: Three quarts equals 6 pints (3 × 2), 12 cups (3 × 4), or 96 ounces (3 × 32).

qt. __3__
pt. __6__
c. __12__
oz. __96__

A Complete the problems with equivalent volumes.

① qt. __1__   ② qt. __5__   ③ qt. __12__   ④ qt. __16__   ⑤ qt. __21__
  pt. __2__   pt. _____   pt. _____   pt. _____   pt. _____
  c. __4__   c. _____   c. _____   c. _____   c. _____
  oz. __32__   oz. _____   oz. _____   oz. _____   oz. _____

⑥ qt. __10__   ⑦ qt. __50__   ⑧ qt. __75__   ⑨ qt. __37__   ⑩ qt. __8__
  pt. _____   pt. _____   pt. _____   pt. _____   pt. _____
  c. _____   c. _____   c. _____   c. _____   c. _____
  oz. _____   oz. _____   oz. _____   oz. _____   oz. _____

⑪ qt. __19__   ⑫ qt. __33__   ⑬ qt. __48__   ⑭ qt. __15__   ⑮ qt. __28__
  pt. _____   pt. _____   pt. _____   pt. _____   pt. _____
  c. _____   c. _____   c. _____   c. _____   c. _____
  oz. _____   oz. _____   oz. _____   oz. _____   oz. _____

⑯ qt. __4__   ⑰ qt. __56__   ⑱ qt. __9__   ⑲ qt. __40__   ⑳ qt. __63__
  pt. _____   pt. _____   pt. _____   pt. _____   pt. _____
  c. _____   c. _____   c. _____   c. _____   c. _____
  oz. _____   oz. _____   oz. _____   oz. _____   oz. _____

㉑ qt. __11__   ㉒ qt. __24__   ㉓ qt. __100__ ㉔ qt. __6__   ㉕ qt. __72__
  pt. _____   pt. _____   pt. _____   pt. _____   pt. _____
  c. _____   c. _____   c. _____   c. _____   c. _____
  oz. _____   oz. _____   oz. _____   oz. _____   oz. _____

㉖ qt. __13__   ㉗ qt. __4__   ㉘ qt. __85__   ㉙ qt. __28__   ㉚ qt. __2__
  pt. _____   pt. _____   pt. _____   pt. _____   pt. _____

REMINDER: Write the definition of a pint and a quart.

_____

_____

Unit 144 cont'd ☞

B Convert cups to pints.

1. 42 c. = ___21 pt.___ 2. 30 c. = _____ 3. 18 c. = _____ 4. 82 c. = _____

5. 78 c. = _____ 6. 66 c. = _____ 7. 22 c. = _____ 8. 54 c. = _____

9. 14 c. = _____ 10. 58 c. = _____ 11. 46 c. = _____ 12. 10 c. = _____

13. 6 c. = _____ 14. 102 c. = _____ 15. 34 c. = _____ 16. 98 c. = _____

C Convert pints to quarts.

1. 14 pt. = ___7 qt.___ 2. 52 pt. = _____ 3. 34 pt. = _____ 4. 68 pt. = _____

5. 90 pt. = _____ 6. 28 pt. = _____ 7. 102 pt. = _____ 8. 84 pt. = _____

9. 118 pt. = _____ 10. 36 pt. = _____ 11. 148 pt. = _____ 12. 40 pt. = _____

13. 46 pt. = _____ 14. 130 pt. = _____ 15. 60 pt. = _____ 16. 78 pt. = _____

D Underline the correct answers.

1. To determine how many quarts equal 544 oz., divide by (2, 4, <u>32</u>).

2. Jennifer needed to prepare half as much cornbread as a recipe would make. The recipe called for 1 qt. of milk. To make half a recipe, Jennifer used only (2 pts., 2 c., 12 oz.) of milk.

3. To find how many ounces are in 11 pt., (multiply, divide, increase) by 16.

4. Robin measured and poured 4 c. of peanut oil into a large pan. He poured the oil from a bottle containing 64 oz. After Robin used the 4 c. of oil, (1 pt., 16 c., 60 oz.) of oil remained in the bottle.

5. (Multiply, Divide, Increase) by 16 to determine how many pints equal 112 oz.

6. In 8 weeks, the Richardsons used 4 bottles of window cleaning fluid. Each bottle contained 1 qt. of cleaner. The Richardsons used an average of (2 pt., 4 c., 16 oz.) of cleaning fluid each week.

7. Margaret divided 2 qt. of punch equally among 7 guests and herself. Each person received (1 pt., 2 c., 8 oz.) of punch.

Gallons

Learning Objective: *We will learn to convert gallons, quarts, pints, cups, and ounces.*

A gallon is a standard unit of volume equaling 4 quarts, 8 pints, 16 cups, or 128 ounces.

EXAMPLE: Three gallons equal 12 quarts (3 × 4), 24 pints (3 × 8), 48 cups (3 × 16), or 384 ounces (3 × 128).

gallons   _3_
quarts   _12_
pints   _24_
cups   _48_
ounces   _384_

A Complete the problems with equivalent volumes.

① gal. _6_
   qt. _24_
   pt. _48_
   c. _96_
   oz. _768_

② gal. _15_
   qt. ___
   pt. ___
   c. ___
   oz. ___

③ gal. _31_
   qt. ___
   pt. ___
   c. ___
   oz. ___

④ gal. _7_
   qt. ___
   pt. ___
   c. ___
   oz. ___

⑤ gal. _19_
   qt. ___
   pt. ___
   c. ___
   oz. ___

⑥ gal. _24_
   qt. ___
   pt. ___
   c. ___
   oz. ___

⑦ gal. _41_
   qt. ___
   pt. ___
   c. ___
   oz. ___

⑧ gal. _73_
   qt. ___
   pt. ___
   c. ___
   oz. ___

⑨ gal. _80_
   qt. ___
   pt. ___
   c. ___
   oz. ___

⑩ gal. _100_
   qt. ___
   pt. ___
   c. ___
   oz. ___

⑪ gal. _93_
   qt. ___
   pt. ___
   c. ___
   oz. ___

⑫ gal. _9_
   qt. ___
   pt. ___
   c. ___
   oz. ___

⑬ gal. _53_
   qt. ___
   pt. ___
   c. ___
   oz. ___

⑭ gal. _45_
   qt. ___
   pt. ___
   c. ___
   oz. ___

⑮ gal. _66_
   qt. ___
   pt. ___
   c. ___
   oz. ___

⑯ gal. _77_
   qt. ___
   pt. ___
   c. ___
   oz. ___

⑰ gal. _28_
   qt. ___
   pt. ___
   c. ___
   oz. ___

⑱ gal. _89_
   qt. ___
   pt. ___
   c. ___
   oz. ___

⑲ gal. _113_
   qt. ___
   pt. ___
   c. ___
   oz. ___

⑳ gal. _35_
   qt. ___
   pt. ___
   c. ___
   oz. ___

㉑ gal. _81_
   qt. ___

㉒ gal. _2_
   pt. ___

㉓ gal. _92_
   c. ___

㉔ gal. _11_
   oz. ___

㉕ gal. _50_
   qt. ___

REMINDER: Write the definition of a gallon.

_____

_____

Unit 145 cont'd 👉

B Convert to gallons.

① 128 oz. = __1__ gal.   ② 752 c. = ____ gal.   ③ 104 pt. = ____ gal.   ④ 220 qt. = ____ gal.

⑤ 1,648 c. = ____ gal.   ⑥ 1,024 oz. = ____ gal.   ⑦ 316 qt. = ____ gal.   ⑧ 304 pt. = ____ gal.

⑨ 160 pt. = ____ gal.   ⑩ 348 qt. = ____ gal.   ⑪ 5,632 oz. = ____ gal.   ⑫ 272 c. = ____ gal.

⑬ 364 qt. = ____ gal.   ⑭ 464 pt. = ____ gal.   ⑮ 400 c. = ____ gal.   ⑯ 7,936 oz. = ____ gal.

⑰ 512 oz. = ____ gal.   ⑱ 528 c. = ____ gal.   ⑲ 560 pt. = ____ gal.   ⑳ 440 qt. = ____ gal.

㉑ 664 pt. = ____ gal.   ㉒ 256 oz. = ____ gal.   ㉓ 48 qt. = ____ gal.   ㉔ 512 c. = ____ gal.

㉕ 88 qt. = ____ gal.   ㉖ 80 pt. = ____ gal.   ㉗ 3,712 qt. = ____ gal.   ㉘ 80 c. = ____ gal.

㉙ 536 pt. = ____ gal.   ㉚ 84 qt. = ____ gal.   ㉛ 688 c. = ____ gal.   ㉜ 2,304 oz. = ____ gal.

㉝ 3,840 oz. = ____ gal.   ㉞ 1,584 c. = ____ gal.   ㉟ 608 c. = ____ gal.   ㊱ 204 qt. = ____ gal.

C Underline the correct answers.

① In 16 gal., there are (2, <u>4</u>, 8) times as many cups as there are quarts.

② Monica purchases 1 gal. of milk per week at the local grocery. Jeff buys 5 gal. per week for his large family. Jeff buys (6 gal., 16 qt., 80 c.) more milk per week than Monica.

③ To determine the number of ounces in 17 gal., (multiply, divide, increase) by 128.

④ Divide by 8 to determine how many (cups, pints, quarts) equal 79 gal.

⑤ On a hot summer afternoon, Linda brewed and iced a gallon of tea and set it in the refrigerator. A short time later, her brother poured himself a full 16 oz. glass of the tea. He poured 2 more 16 oz. glasses for his friends. Linda's father filled a quart thermos with tea before he left on a fishing trip. Only (2 qt., 3 pt., 64 oz.) of tea was left from the gallon that Linda brewed.

⑥ At the beginning of summer, Luke bought an 8 oz. bottle of tanning lotion. By the end of the season, he had used half a gallon of lotion. Luke used (8, 12, 16) 8 oz. bottles of tanning lotion during the summer.

Comprehension Check

A Convert metric tons to kilograms.

① 487 t = _**487,000 kg**_ ② 92 t = _____ ③ 34 t = _____ ④ 112 t = _____

⑤ 73 t = _____ ⑥ 206 t = _____ ⑦ 55 t = _____ ⑧ 8 t = _____

⑨ 60 t = _____ ⑩ 81 t = _____ ⑪ 29 t = _____ ⑫ 319 t = _____

B Convert kilograms to metric tons.

① 42,000 kg = _**42 t**_ ② 513,000 kg = _____ ③ 1,000 kg = _____ ④ 78,000 kg = _____

⑤ 83,000 kg = _____ ⑥ 67,000 kg = _____ ⑦ 90,000 kg = _____ ⑧ 26,000 kg = _____

⑨ 12,000 kg = _____ ⑩ 341,000 kg = _____ ⑪ 119,000 kg = _____ ⑫ 15,000 kg = _____

C Complete the problems with equivalent weights.

① T. _12_ ② T. _____ ③ T. _____ ④ T. _8_
  lb. _**24,000**_ lb. _42,000_ lb. _____ lb. _____
  oz. _**384,000**_ oz. _____ oz. _1,632,000_ oz. _____

⑤ t _87_ ⑥ t _____ ⑦ t _____ ⑧ t _23_
  kg _____ kg _58,000_ kg _____ kg _____
  g _____ g _____ g _9,000,000_ g _____

⑨ T. _____ ⑩ T. _____ ⑪ t _____ ⑫ t _____
  lb. _80,000_ lb. _____ kg _48,000_ kg _____
  oz. _____ oz. _512,000_ g _____ g _108,000,000_

D Complete the problems with equivalent volumes.

① gal. _84_ ② gal. _____ ③ gal. _____ ④ gal. _____ ⑤ gal. _____
  qt. _336_ qt. _64_ qt. _____ qt. _____ qt. _____
  pt. _672_ pt. _____ pt. _232_ pt. _____ pt. _____
  c. _1,344_ c. _____ c. _____ c. _128_ c. _____
  oz. _10,752_ oz. _____ oz. _____ oz. _____ oz. _6,912_

⑥ gal. _22_ ⑦ gal. _____ ⑧ gal. _____ ⑨ gal. _____ ⑩ gal. _____
  qt. _____ qt. _156_ qt. _____ qt. _____ qt. _____
  pt. _____ pt. _____ pt. _336_ pt. _____ pt. _____
  c. _____ c. _____ c. _____ c. _1,456_ c. _____
  oz. _____ oz. _____ oz. _____ oz. _____ oz. _1,664_

Test 29 cont'd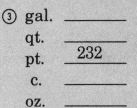

E Convert to pints.

① 96 c. = _48_ pt. ② 464 oz. = ____ pt. ③ 2 c. = ____ pt. ④ 1,824 oz. = ____ pt.

⑤ 864 oz. = ____ pt. ⑥ 1,072 oz. = ____ pt. ⑦ 528 oz. = ____ pt. ⑧ 150 c. = ____ pt.

⑨ 36 c. = ____ pt. ⑩ 48 oz. = ____ pt. ⑪ 168 c. = ____ pt. ⑫ 1,472 oz. = ____ pt.

F Convert to quarts.

① 288 oz. = _9_ qt. ② 136 pt. = ____ qt. ③ 144 c. = ____ qt. ④ 352 oz. = ____ qt.

⑤ 180 c. = ____ qt. ⑥ 672 oz. = ____ qt. ⑦ 30 pt. = ____ qt. ⑧ 356 c. = ____ qt.

⑨ 226 pt. = ____ qt. ⑩ 292 c. = ____ qt. ⑪ 1,824 oz. = ____ qt. ⑫ 60 pt. = ____ qt.

G Convert to gallons.

① 16 c. = _1_ gal. ② 272 pt. = ____ gal. ③ 360 qt. = ____ gal. ④ 2,944 oz. = ____ gal.

⑤ 472 pt. = ____ gal. ⑥ 1,360 c. = ____ gal. ⑦ 7,168 oz. = ____ gal. ⑧ 388 qt. = ____ gal.

⑨ 3,328 oz. = ____ gal. ⑩ 168 qt. = ____ gal. ⑪ 544 pt. = ____ gal. ⑫ 1,136 c. = ____ gal.

H Identify each as (w) a unit of weight or (v) a unit of volume.

① _w_ metric ton ② ____ quart ③ ____ pound ④ ____ cup ⑤ ____ gram

⑥ ____ kilogram ⑦ ____ ton ⑧ ____ gallon ⑨ ____ half gallon ⑩ ____ pint

Write a brief paragraph comparing units of weight. (i.e., A pound is 16 times as heavy as an ounce.)

_____

_____

_____

_____

_____

Milliliters and Centiliters

Unit 146

Learning Objective: *We will learn to convert milliliters and centiliters and to compare each to ounces.*

A milliliter is a metric unit of volume equaling 1/1,000 of a liter or 1/10 of a centiliter or approximately 3/100 ounce. A centiliter equals 1/100 liter, 10 centiliters, or 3/10 ounce.

EXAMPLES:

To convert centiliters to milliliters, multiply by 10. 30 cl × 10 = 300 ml

To convert milliliters to centiliters, divide by 10. 300 ml ÷ 10 = 30 cl

A Convert centiliters to milliliters.

① 2 cl = _____ **20 ml** _____   ② 39 cl = _____   ③ 27 cl = _____

④ 51 cl = _____   ⑤ 18 cl = _____   ⑥ 46 cl = _____

⑦ 63 cl = _____   ⑧ 104 cl = _____   ⑨ 75 cl = _____

⑩ 672 cl = _____   ⑪ 58 cl = _____   ⑫ 890 cl = _____

⑬ 466 cl = _____   ⑭ 67 cl = _____   ⑮ 88 cl = _____

⑯ 341 cl = _____   ⑰ 112 cl = _____   ⑱ 325 cl = _____

⑲ 905 cl = _____   ⑳ 279 cl = _____   ㉑ 7 cl = _____

㉒ 501 cl = _____   ㉓ 249 cl = _____   ㉔ 1,000 cl = _____

㉕ 887 cl = _____   ㉖ 121 cl = _____   ㉗ 392 cl = _____

B Convert milliliters to centiliters.

① 60 ml = _____ **6 cl** _____   ② 1,070 ml = _____   ③ 340 ml = _____

④ 7,120 ml = _____   ⑤ 830 ml = _____   ⑥ 470 ml = _____

⑦ 4,190 ml = _____   ⑧ 530 ml = _____   ⑨ 5,250 ml = _____

⑩ 620 ml = _____   ⑪ 2,030 ml = _____   ⑫ 1,350 ml = _____

⑬ 3,490 ml = _____   ⑭ 4,060 ml = _____   ⑮ 150 ml = _____

⑯ 590 ml = _____   ⑰ 110 ml = _____   ⑱ 3,750 ml = _____

⑲ 960 ml = _____   ⑳ 410 ml = _____   ㉑ 6,020 ml = _____

㉒ 240 ml = _____   ㉓ 1,270 ml = _____   ㉔ 740 ml = _____

㉕ 770 ml = _____   ㉖ 5,000 ml = _____   ㉗ 560 ml = _____

REMINDER: Write the definition of a milliliter and a centiliter.

_____

_____

Unit 146 cont'd 🖝

C Fill in the blanks with >, <, or =.

① 4 cl __<__ 4 oz. ② 560 ml _____ 87 cl ③ 109 oz. _____ 109 ml

④ 1,010 cl _____ 101 ml ⑤ 820 ml _____ 82,000 cl ⑥ 1,057 ml _____ 105 cl

⑦ 100,000 cl _____ 100 ml ⑧ 7,060 ml _____ 76 cl ⑨ 222 cl _____ 2,220 ml

⑩ 987 ml _____ 98 cl ⑪ 361 cl _____ 163 ml ⑫ 99 ml _____ 990 cl

⑬ 419 cl _____ 4,090 ml ⑭ 1,212 ml _____ 130 cl ⑮ 246 cl _____ 862 ml

⑯ 975 cl _____ 9,750 ml ⑰ 19 oz. _____ 19 cl ⑱ 19 oz. _____ 190 ml

⑲ 2,910 cl _____ 29,000 ml ⑳ 416 cl _____ 40 ml ㉑ 2,110 ml _____ 211 cl

㉒ 4 cl _____ 40 ml ㉓ 4 oz. _____ 40 ml ㉔ 900 ml _____ 9 cl

㉕ 1,119 cl _____ 2,000 ml ㉖ 49 cl _____ 49 oz. ㉗ 5,055 ml _____ 600 cl

㉘ 9,720 oz. _____ 9,720 cl ㉙ 357 cl _____ 753 oz. ㉚ 607 cl _____ 6,070 ml

㉛ 908 ml _____ 90 cl ㉜ 3,060 ml _____ 306 oz. ㉝ 1,767 ml _____ 100 cl

㉞ 9,755 ml _____ 10 cl ㉟ 25 cl _____ 25 oz. ㊱ 140 cl _____ 1,400 ml

D Underline the correct answers.

① A centiliter is (10, 100, 1,000) times as great as a milliliter.

② In 1 liter, there are (50, 900, 1,000) more milliliters than there are centiliters.

③ Millie's favorite perfume costs $25 per ounce. The cost per centiliter would be (more than, less than, the same as) $25.

④ A cookie recipe calls for 350 ml of vanilla flavoring. To double the recipe, (7 cl, 35 cl, 70 cl) of vanilla would be needed.

⑤ To determine how many centiliters equal 7,200 ml, (multiply, divide, increase) by 10.

⑥ When selecting a cologne, Janet compared prices and volume. One cologne sold at $28 for a 50 cl bottle. A 250 ml bottle of another cologne also sold for $28. Janet found that she could get more for the price if she bought the (50 cl, 250 ml) bottle.

⑦ (Multiply, Divide, Increase) by 10 to determine the number of milliliters in 96 cl.

Liters

Learning Objective: *We will learn to convert liters, centiliters, and milliliters.*

A liter is a metric unit of volume equaling 100 centiliters; 1,000 milliliters; or approximately 1 liquid quart.

EXAMPLE: Three liters is equal to 300 centiliters
(3 × 100) or 3,000 milliliters (3 × 1,000).

liters	3
centiliters	300
milliliters	3,000

A Complete the charts with equivalent volumes.

① l 29
cl **2,900**
ml **29,000**

② l 40
cl _____
ml _____

③ l 13
cl _____
ml _____

④ l 5
cl _____
ml _____

⑤ l 71
cl _____
ml _____

⑥ l 101
cl _____
ml _____

⑦ l 57
cl _____
ml _____

⑧ l 82
cl _____
ml _____

⑨ l 331
cl _____
ml _____

⑩ l 767
cl _____
ml _____

⑪ l 90
cl _____
ml _____

⑫ l 308
cl _____
ml _____

⑬ l 912
cl _____
ml _____

⑭ l 9
cl _____
ml _____

⑮ l 653
cl _____
ml _____

⑯ l 522
cl _____
ml _____

⑰ l 117
cl _____
ml _____

⑱ l 60
cl _____
ml _____

⑲ l 383
cl _____
ml _____

⑳ l 212
cl _____
ml _____

㉑ l 85
cl _____
ml _____

㉒ l 44
cl _____
ml _____

㉓ l 151
cl _____
ml _____

㉔ l 34
cl _____
ml _____

㉕ l 194
cl _____
ml _____

㉖ l 516
cl _____
ml _____

㉗ l 76
cl _____
ml _____

㉘ l 400
cl _____
ml _____

REMINDER: Write the definition of a liter.

_____

_____

Unit 147 cont'd ☛

B Convert to liters.

① 8,000 ml = __8 l__   ② 49,200 cl = _____   ③ 237,000 ml = _____   ④ 6,900 cl = _____

⑤ 2,300 cl = _____   ⑥ 52,000 ml = _____   ⑦ 58,800 cl = _____   ⑧ 412,000 ml = _____

⑨ 37,000 ml = _____   ⑩ 1,700 cl = _____   ⑪ 375,000 ml = _____   ⑫ 6,500 cl = _____

⑬ 90,200 cl = _____   ⑭ 183,000 ml = _____   ⑮ 9,800 cl = _____   ⑯ 288,000 ml = _____

⑰ 710,000 ml = _____   ⑱ 11,600 cl = _____   ⑲ 49,000 ml = _____   ⑳ 9,500 cl = _____

C Fill in the blanks.

① 3,890 cl __×__ 10 = 38,900 ml

② 800,000 ml _____ 1,000 = 800 l

③ 215 l × _____ = 215,000 ml

④ 9,180 ml ÷ _____ = 918 cl

⑤ 862 l × _____ = 86,200 cl

⑥ 23,600 cl ÷ _____ = 236 l

D Underline the correct answers.

① In 966 liters, there are 869, 400 (more, <u>fewer</u>) centiliters than milliliters.

② To determine the number of liters in 7,100 centiliters, (multiply, divide, increase) by 100.

③ The cost of a 4 l bottle of soft drink is $2.59. The cost of a 2 l bottle is $1.89. The (2 l, 4 l) bottle is the best buy.

④ A 3-qt. saucepan will hold about the same amount of water as will a (3 l, 3 ml, 3 cl) pitcher.

⑤ (Multiply, Divide, Increase) by 1,000 to convert liters to milliliters.

⑥ To determine how many (centiliters, milliliters) are in 562 liters, multiply by 1,000.

⑦ The number of centiliters in a 2 l carton of milk is (greater than, less than, equal to) 100.

⑧ It takes (17, 170, 1,700) 100 ml containers full of liquid to fill a 17 l tub.

Units of Volume

Learning Objective: *We will learn to convert and compare units of volume.*

A unit of volume; including the ounce, cup, pint, quart, gallon, milliliter, centiliter, and liter; tells how much is contained.

EXAMPLES: **A cup contains 8 times as much as an ounce. A pint contains twice as much as a cup. A quart contains twice as much as a pint. A gallon contains 4 times as much as a quart. A centiliter contains 10 times as much as a milliliter. A liter contains 100 times as much as a centiliter. Both a milliliter and a centiliter contain less than an ounce. A liter contains about the same amount as a quart.**

A Complete the charts with equivalent volumes.

① gal. 5
    qt. **20**
    pt. **40**
    c. **80**
    oz. **640**

② gal. _____
    qt. 120
    pt. _____
    c. _____
    oz. _____

③ gal. _____
    qt. _____
    pt. 168
    c. _____
    oz. _____

④ gal. _____
    qt. _____
    pt. _____
    c. 1,200
    oz. _____

⑤ gal. 17
    qt. _____
    pt. _____
    c. _____
    oz. _____

⑥ gal. _____
    qt. 44
    pt. _____
    c. _____
    oz. _____

⑦ gal. _____
    qt. _____
    pt. 80
    c. _____
    oz. _____

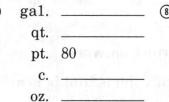

⑧ gal. _____
    qt. _____
    pt. _____
    c. 1,312
    oz. _____

⑨ l 4
    cl _____
    ml _____

⑩ l _____
    cl 1,000
    ml _____

⑪ l _____
    cl _____
    ml 108,000

⑫ l 500
    cl _____
    ml _____

⑬ l _____
    cl 3,800
    ml _____

⑭ l _____
    cl _____
    ml 201,000

⑮ l 45
    cl _____
    ml _____

⑯ l _____
    cl 38,200
    ml _____

⑰ l _____
    cl _____
    ml 94,000

⑱ l 26
    cl _____
    ml _____

⑲ 45 _____
    cl 15,900
    ml _____

⑳ l _____
    cl _____
    ml 54,000

REMINDER: Write the definition of a unit of volume.

_____

_____

Unit 148 cont'd ☞

B Fill in the blanks.

① 3,000 ml = __300__ cl   ② 240 oz. = _____ c.   ③ 1,200 cl = _____ l

④ 50 c. = _____ pt.   ⑤ 288 qt. = _____ gal.   ⑥ 84,000 ml = _____ l

⑦ 112 oz. = _____ pt.   ⑧ 25,000 ml = _____ cl   ⑨ 13,100 cl = _____ l

⑩ 688 oz. = _____ pt.   ⑪ 195,000 ml = _____ l   ⑫ 62 pt. = _____ qt.

⑬ 19,000 ml = _____ cl   ⑭ 194 pt. = _____ qt.   ⑮ 64 oz. = _____ c.

⑯ 229,000 ml = _____ l   ⑰ 672 oz. = _____ qt.   ⑱ 282 c. = _____ pt.

⑲ 42,000 ml = _____ cl   ⑳ 4,800 cl = _____ l   ㉑ 224 c. = _____ gal.

㉒ 36,300 cl = _____ l   ㉓ 1,568 oz. = _____ qt.   ㉔ 104 qt. = _____ gal.

㉕ 8,600 cl = _____ l   ㉖ 1,000 ml = _____ l   ㉗ 396 c. = _____ qt.

㉘ 102,000 ml = _____ cl   ㉙ 318,000 ml = _____ l   ㉚ 9,472 oz. = _____ gal.

㉛ 55,000 ml = _____ l   ㉜ 204 qt. = _____ gal.   ㉝ 116 c. = _____ qt.

㉞ 64,000 ml = _____ cl   ㉟ 86 pt. = _____ qt.   ㊱ 29,700 cl = _____ l

C Underline the correct answers.

① The metric unit of volume that is nearly equal to the U.S. quart is the (centiliter, milliliter, liter).

② Multiply by 10 to convert centiliters to (milliliters, liters, quarts).

③ When making a grocery list Dan lifted the gallon container of bleach to see if more was needed. Two quarts and 3 c. of the bleach had been used. Only (20, 40, 80) oz. remained.

④ To convert smaller units of volume, such as the ounce or cup, to larger units of volume, such as the pint of quart, (multiply, divide, subtract).

⑤ (Multiply, Divide, Subtract) to convert larger units of volume to smaller units of volume.

⑥ A unit of volume tells (how long, how heavy, how much is contained).

⑦ In 12 liters, there are (1,080, 10,800, 108,000) more milliliters than centiliters.

⑧ A pint is (greater than, less than, equal to) a liter.

358

Thermometers

Learning Objective: *We will learn to read a thermometer and to calculate increases and decreases in temperature.*

A thermometer is an instrument for determining temperature.

EXAMPLE: The liquid inside a thermometer rises or falls when the temperature changes. It is compared to marks on a scale that is much like a number line; however, the numbers on a thermometer increase from bottom to top, rather than left to right. Temperature is measured in units that are called degrees. The symbol for degrees is °.

A Study the partial thermometers below and fill in the blanks with the correct temperatures.

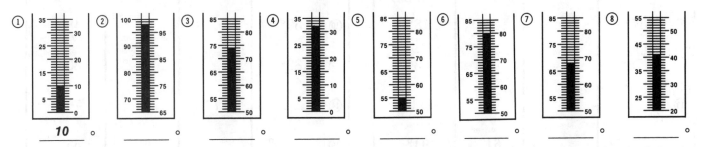

① __10__ ° ② ____ ° ③ ____ ° ④ ____ ° ⑤ ____ ° ⑥ ____ ° ⑦ ____ ° ⑧ ____ °

B Fill in each blank with the difference in temperatures A and B.

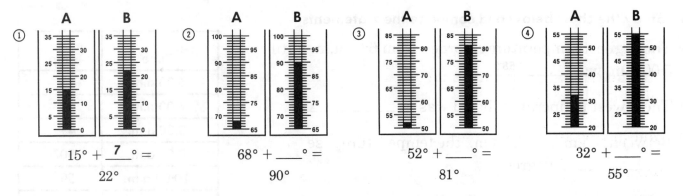

① $15° + \underline{7}° =$
22°

② $68° + \underline{\quad}° =$
90°

③ $52° + \underline{\quad}° =$
81°

④ $32° + \underline{\quad}° =$
55°

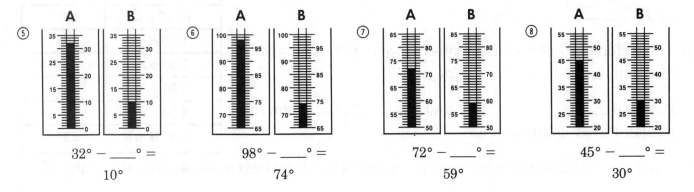

⑤ $32° - \underline{\quad}° =$
10°

⑥ $98° - \underline{\quad}° =$
74°

⑦ $72° - \underline{\quad}° =$
59°

⑧ $45° - \underline{\quad}° =$
30°

REMINDER: Write the definition of a thermometer.

_____

_____

Unit 149 cont'd ☞

C Fill in the blanks.

	Temperature	+ Increase /	Decrease =	New Temperature
①	16°	28°		44°
③	35°		11°	___°
⑤	72°	___°		108°
⑦	97°	___°		133°
⑨	37°		___°	18°
⑪	178°		___°	73°
⑬	___°	78°		111°
⑮	___°		64°	94°

	Temperature	+ Increase /	Decrease =	New Temperature
②	110°	15°		___°
④	86°		41°	___°
⑥	47°	___°		85°
⑧	212°	___°		260°
⑩	59°		___°	48°
⑫	82°		___°	30°
⑭	___°	27°		76°
⑯	___°		49°	53°

D Study the chart below and complete the statements.

① The highest temperature recorded from 6:00 a.m. until 5:00 p.m. was ___ 68° ___ .

② The lowest temperature listed was _____ .

③ Between 6 a.m. and 10 a.m., the temperature rose _____ degrees.

④ A 50° temperature was recorded at _____ a.m. and _____ a.m.

⑤ The difference between the temperature at 6:00 a.m. and 5:00 p.m. was _____ degrees.

⑥ Between _____ p.m. and _____ p.m. the temperature remained at 68°.

Time	Temp.
6:00 a.m.	45°
7:00 a.m.	48°
8:00 a.m.	49°
9:00 a.m.	50°
10:00 a.m.	50°
11:00 a.m.	53°
12:00 p.m.	57°
1:00 p.m.	60°
2:00 p.m.	65°
3:00 p.m.	68°
4:00 p.m.	68°
5:00 p.m.	65°

⑦ The largest temperature increase from one hour to the next was between the hours of _____ and _____ .

⑧ The difference between the lowest temperature and the highest temperature from 6:00 a.m. until 5:00 p.m. was _____ degrees.

Temperature in Fahrenheit Unit 150

Learning Objective: *We will learn to read a Fahrenheit thermometer and to calculate changes in temperature.*

Fahrenheit is the method of temperature measurement that was developed by Gabriel D. Fahrenheit.

EXAMPLES: Water boils at 212 degrees Fahrenheit or 212° F.
Water freezes at 32 degrees Fahrenheit or 32° F.

A Study the partial Fahrenheit thermometers below and fill in the blanks with the correct temperatures. Circle any temperature that is above the boiling point.

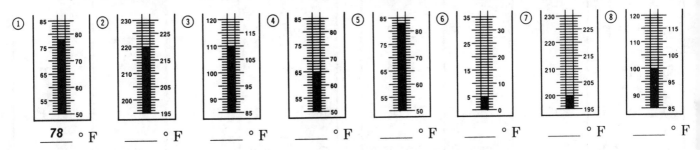

B Fill in each blank with the difference in temperatures A and B.

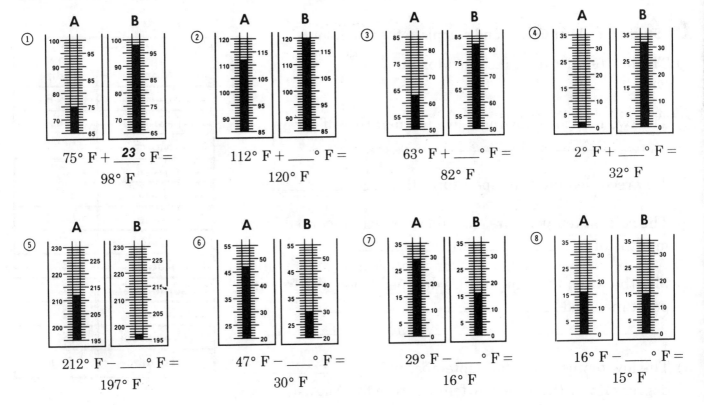

REMINDER: *Write the definition of Fahrenheit.*

_____

C Fill in the blanks.

	Temperature	+ Increase /	− Decrease =	New Temperature
①	79° F	37° F		116 ° F
③	50° F		50° F	____° F
⑤	128° F	____° F		197° F
⑦	216° F	____° F		235° F
⑨	199° F		____° F	12° F
⑪	74° F		____° F	21° F
⑬	____° F	29° F		95° F
⑮	____° F		6° F	139° F

	Temperature	+ Increase /	− Decrease =	New Temperature
②	115° F	92° F		____° F
④	30° F		9° F	____° F
⑥	88° F	____° F		100° F
⑧	43° F	____° F		107° F
⑩	265° F		____° F	232° F
⑫	56° F		____° F	25° F
⑭	____° F	60° F		127°F
⑯	____° F		102° F	8° F

D Study the chart below and complete the statements.

Month	Low Temp.
January	0° F
February	2° F
March	25° F
April	35° F
May	50° F
June	50° F
July	62° F
August	64° F
September	47° F
October	32° F
November	15° F
December	0° F

① The low temperature recorded for the year was ____0____° F.

② The two months showing a low temperature of 50° were _____ and _____ .

③ July recorded lower temperatures than _____ .

④ The coldest temperatures for the year were recorded in the months of _____ and _____ .

⑤ Months when the temperature dropped below the freezing point included _____ , _____ , _____ , _____ , and _____ .

⑥ The low temperature for September was _____ degrees lower than the low temperature for August.

⑦ The low temperature for _____ was exactly at the freezing point.

⑧ Between November and December, the low temperature dropped _____ degrees.

Comprehension Check

A Complete the charts with equivalent volumes.

① l 21
cl *2,100*
ml *21,000*

② l _____
cl 6,800
ml _____

③ l _____
cl _____
ml 122,000

④ l 319
cl _____
ml _____

⑤ l _____
cl 25,200
ml _____

⑥ l _____
cl _____
ml 105,000

⑦ l 370
cl _____
ml _____

⑧ l _____
cl 3,200
ml _____

⑨ l _____
cl _____
ml 43,000

⑩ l 189
cl _____
ml _____

⑪ l _____
cl 7,800
ml _____

⑫ l _____
cl _____
ml 91,000

⑬ qt. 3
pt. _____
c. _____
oz. _____

⑭ qt. _____
pt. 34
c. _____
oz. _____

⑮ qt. _____
pt. _____
c. 204
oz. _____

⑯ qt. _____
pt. _____
c. _____
oz. 224

⑰ qt. 23
pt. _____
c. _____
oz. _____

⑱ gal. 1
qt. _____
pt. _____
c. _____
oz. _____

⑲ gal. _____
qt. 48
pt. _____
c. _____
oz. _____

⑳ gal. _____
qt. _____
pt. _____
c. 1,136
oz. _____

㉑ gal. _____
qt. _____
pt. _____
c. _____
oz. 5,504

㉒ gal. 95
qt. _____
pt. _____
c. _____
oz. _____

B Fill in the blanks.

① 300 cl × __*10*__ = 3,000 ml

② 3,000 ml ÷ _____ = 300 cl

③ 300 l × _____ = 30,000 cl

④ 30,000 cl ÷ _____ = 300 l

⑤ 300 l × _____ = 300,000 ml

⑥ 300,000 ml ÷ _____ = 300 l

⑦ 300 c. × _____ = 2,400 oz.

⑧ 2,400 oz. ÷ _____ = 300 c.

⑨ 300 pt. × _____ = 600 c.

⑩ 600 c. ÷ _____ = 300 pt.

⑪ 300 pt. × _____ = 4,800 oz.

⑫ 4,800 oz. ÷ _____ = 300 pt.

⑬ 300 qt. × _____ = 1,200 c.

⑭ 1,200 c. ÷ _____ = 300 qt.

⑮ 300 qt. × _____ = 9,600 oz.

⑯ 9,600 oz. ÷ _____ = 300 qt.

⑰ 300 gal. × _____ = 38,400 oz.

⑱ 38,400 oz. ÷ _____ = 300 gal.

Test 30 cont'd ☞

C Fill in each blank with the difference in temperatures A and B.

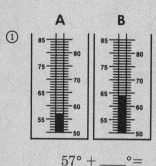

① 57° + ___° = 64°

② 89° + ___° = 97°

③ 211° − ___° = 199°

④ 21° − ___° = 7°

D Study the partial Fahrenheit thermometers below and fill in the blanks with the correct temperatures. Circle any temperature that is below the freezing point.

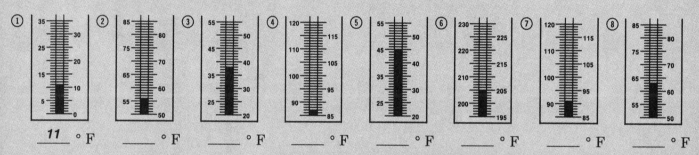

① ___11___ ° F   ② ___ ° F   ③ ___ ° F   ④ ___ ° F   ⑤ ___ ° F   ⑥ ___ ° F   ⑦ ___ ° F   ⑧ ___ ° F

E Calculate changes in temperature.

① 221°F − 30° = *191° F*   ② 26° F − 26° =   ③ 49° F + 110° =

④ 58° F + 50° =   ⑤ 0° F + 74° =   ⑥ 99° F + 2° =

⑦ 144° F − 31° =   ⑧ 36° F − 12° =   ⑨ 62° F − 39° =

⑩ 115° F − 76° =   ⑪ 220° F + 8° =   ⑫ 107° F + 5° =

⑬ 35° F + 3° =   ⑭ 77° F + 18° =   ⑮ 9° F − 8° =

Write a paragraph comparing units of volume. (i.e., A cup contains 8 times as much as an ounce.)

_____

_____

_____

_____

_____

_____

_____

_____

Temperature in Celsius   Unit 151

Learning Objective: *We will learn to read a Celsius thermometer and to calculate changes in temperature.*

Celsius is the method of temperature measurement that was developed by Anders Celsius.

EXAMPLES: Water boils at 100 degrees Celsius or 100° C.
Water freezes at 0 degrees Celsius or 0° C.

A Study the partial Celsius thermometers below and fill in the blanks with the correct temperatures. Circle any temperature that is above the boiling point.

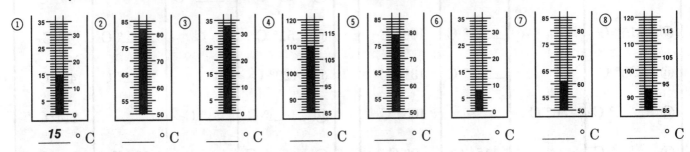

① __*15*__ ° C ② _____ ° C ③ _____ ° C ④ _____ ° C ⑤ _____ ° C ⑥ _____ ° C ⑦ _____ ° C ⑧ _____ ° C

B Fill in each blank with the difference in temperatures A and B.

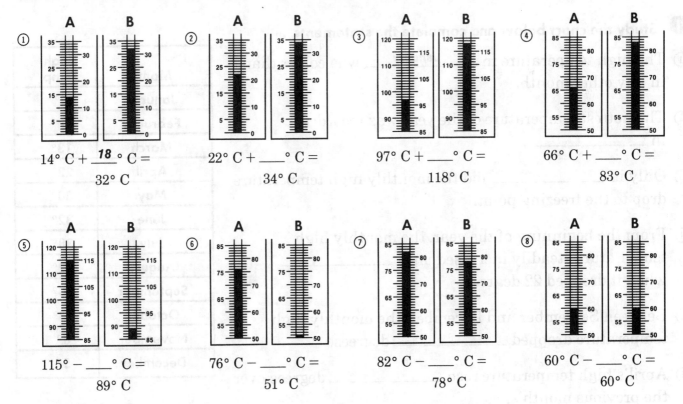

① 14° C + __*18*__ ° C = 32° C

② 22° C + ____ ° C = 34° C

③ 97° C + ____ ° C = 118° C

④ 66° C + ____ ° C = 83° C

⑤ 115° − ____ ° C = 89° C

⑥ 76° C − ____ ° C = 51° C

⑦ 82° C − ____ ° C = 78° C

⑧ 60° C − ____ ° C = 60° C

REMINDER: Write the definition of Celsius.

_____

_____

Unit 151 cont'd ☛

C Fill in the blanks.

	Temperature	+ Increase /	− Decrease =	New Temperature
①	54° C	76° C		<u>130</u> ° C
③	32° C		6° C	____° C
⑤	4° C	____° C		111° C
⑦	12° C	____° C		78° C
⑨	316° C		____° C	100° C
⑪	228° C		____° C	131° C
⑬	____° C	36° C		105° C
⑮	____° C		115° C	0° C

	Temperature	+ Increase /	− Decrease =	New Temperature
②	81° C	25° C		____° C
④	19° C		11° C	____° C
⑥	63° C	____° C		210° C
⑧	20° C	____° C		59° C
⑩	51° C		____° C	7° C
⑫	129° C		____° C	42° C
⑭	____° C	73° C		214°C
⑯	____° C		27° C	94° C

D Study the chart below and complete the statements.

Month	High Temp.
January	0°
February	5°
March	13°
April	22°
May	30°
June	32°
July	38°
August	42°
September	20°
October	16°
November	8°
December	5°

① The high temperature in _____<u>January</u>_____ was colder than in any other month.

② The hottest temperature of the year was recorded in _____ .

③ Only in _____ did the monthly high temperature drop to the freezing point.

④ From the beginning of the year, the monthly high temperature steadily increased until _____, when it dropped 22 degrees.

⑤ Between September and December, the monthly high temperature dropped _____ degrees.

⑥ April's high temperature rose _____ degrees over the previous month's.

⑦ In the first 6 months of the year, the high temperature rose _____ degrees.

⑧ _____ and _____ showed high temperatures of 5° C.

366

Comparison of Fahrenheit and Celsius Unit 152

Learning Objective: *We will learn to compare Fahrenheit and Celsius thermometers.*

Fahrenheit and Celsius are two methods of measuring temperature, each of which is named for its inventor.

EXAMPLES: The boiling point of water is 212° F and 100° C.
The freezing point of water is 32° F and 0° C.

> Temperatures below 0° are preceded by the − symbol.

A Study the thermometer at right and fill in the blanks with the correct temperatures.

① 194° F = __90__ ° C   ② 20° C = ____° F   ③ 23° F = ____° C

④ 60° C = ____° F   ⑤ 185° F = ____° C   ⑥ 75° C = ____° F

⑦ 113° F = ____° C   ⑧ 10° C = ____° F   ⑨ 122° F = ____° C

⑩ 65° C = ____° F   ⑪ −4° F = ____° C   ⑫ 25° C = ____° F

⑬ 203° F = ____° C   ⑭ 40° C = ____° F   ⑮ 14° F = ____° C

°F	°C
212°	100°
203°	95°
194°	90°
185°	85°
176°	80°
167°	75°
158°	70°
149°	65°
140°	60°
131°	55°
122°	50°
113°	45°
104°	40°
95°	35°
86°	30°
77°	25°
68°	20°
59°	15°
50°	10°
41°	5°
32°	0°
23°	-5°
14°	-10°
5°	-15°
-4°	-20°

B Fill in the blanks with <, >, or =.

① 100° C __>__ 100° F   ② 86° F ____ 40° C   ③ 15° C ____ 77° F

④ 131° F ____ 55° C   ⑤ 80° C ____ 135° F   ⑥ 206° F ____ 100° C

⑦ −15° C ____ −4° F   ⑧ 109° F ____ 62° C   ⑨ 27° C ____ 51° F

⑩ 172° F ____ 85° C   ⑪ 3° C ____ 23° F   ⑫ 60° F ____ 30° C

⑬ 18° C ____ 75° F   ⑭ 158° F ____ 70° C   ⑮ 47° C ____ 105° F

⑯ 77° F ____ 24° C   ⑰ 58° C ____ 108° F   ⑱ 133° F ____ 62° C   ⑲ 68° C ____ 140° F

⑳ 98° F ____ 32° C   ㉑ 13° C ____ 64° F   ㉒ 22° F ____ 0° C   ㉓ 51° C ____ 150° F

㉔ 45° F ____ 54° C   ㉕ 72° C ____ 123° F   ㉖ 176° F ____ 80° C   ㉗ 9° C ____ 99° F

REMINDER: Write the definition of Fahrenheit and Celsius.

Unit 152 cont'd ☛

C Fill in the blanks.

	Temperature °F	Temperature °C	Increase / +	Decrease = −	Temperature °F	Temperature °C
①	158		18		_176_	80
②		70	25		203	____
③	194			54	____	60
④		55		40	59	____
⑤	59		90		149	____
⑥		−5	35		____	30
⑦	113			36	77	____
⑧		90		45	____	45
⑨	77		____		131	55
⑩		30	____		203	95
⑪	41			____	5	−15
⑫		65		____	68	20

D Complete the chart below and mark each statement true or false.

false ① The lowest temperature recorded was 0° F.

_____ ② At 12:30 p.m., the temperature was 77° F.

_____ ③ The temperature dropped 9 Fahrenheit degrees between 9:30 a.m. and 10:30 a.m.

_____ ④ Freezing temperatures were recorded at 5:30 a.m.

_____ ⑤ Between 8:30 a.m. and 11:30 a.m., the temperature rose 5 Celsius degrees.

_____ ⑥ The hottest temperature recorded was 40° C.

_____ ⑦ Between 7:30 a.m. and 9:30 a.m., the temperature increased.

_____ ⑧ At both 10:30 a.m. and 11:30 a.m., the temperature was 20° C.

_____ ⑨ At 2:30 p.m., the temperature began to drop for the first time since 5:30 a.m.

_____ ⑩ The high temperature was recorded at 3:30 p.m. and 4:30 p.m.

Time	° F	° C
5:30 a.m.	32	0
6:30 a.m.		5
7:30 a.m.	59	
8:30 a.m.		15
9:30 a.m.	59	
10:30 a.m.		20
11:30 a.m.	68	
12:30 p.m.		25
1:30 p.m.	86	
2:30 p.m.		35
3:30 p.m.	104	
4:30 p.m.		40

Review of U.S. Units of Measure

Learning Objective: *We will learn to recognize and utilize U.S. units of measure.*

The U.S. units of measure include those units of length, weight, and volume which are commonly used in the United States.

EXAMPLE: U.S. units of length include inches, feet, yards, and miles. U.S. units of weight include ounces, pounds, and tons. U.S. units of volume include ounces, cups, pints, quarts, and gallons.

A Write the abbreviations for these units of measurement.

oz. ① ounce _____ ② inch _____ ③ cup _____ ④ ton

_____ ⑤ mile _____ ⑥ pound _____ ⑦ foot _____ ⑧ pint

_____ ⑨ gallon _____ ⑩ yard _____ ⑪ quart

B Write the symbol (+ or ÷) for the mathematical operation used to convert one unit of measure to another.

÷ ① inches to feet _____ ② pints to quarts _____ ③ cups to ounces

_____ ④ miles to yards _____ ⑤ pounds to tons _____ ⑥ gallons to pints

_____ ⑦ ounces to pounds _____ ⑧ yards to inches _____ ⑨ quarts to gallons

_____ ⑩ pints to ounces _____ ⑪ tons to pounds _____ ⑫ ounces to gallons

_____ ⑬ feet to yards _____ ⑭ cups to quarts _____ ⑮ ounces to tons

_____ ⑯ gallons to ounces _____ ⑰ pounds to ounces _____ ⑱ feet to inches

_____ ⑲ tons to ounces _____ ⑳ yards to feet _____ ㉑ cups to gallons

_____ ㉒ quarts to pints _____ ㉓ ounces to cups _____ ㉔ miles to feet

_____ ㉕ gallons to cups _____ ㉖ feet to miles _____ ㉗ gallons to quarts

_____ ㉘ quarts to ounces _____ ㉙ pints to gallons _____ ㉚ cups to pints

REMINDER: Write the definition of U.S. units of measure.

_____

_____

C Fill in the blanks.

① 1 ft. = __12__ in.   ② 1 lb. = _____ oz.   ③ 1 c. = _____ oz.

④ 1 pt. = _____ c.   ⑤ 1 T. = _____ lb.   ⑥ 1 mi. = _____ yd.

⑦ 1 qt. = _____ pt.   ⑧ 1 gal. = _____ qt.   ⑨ 1 qt. = _____ c.

⑩ 1 gal. = _____ c.   ⑪ 1 mi. = _____ ft.   ⑫ 1 pt. = _____ oz.

⑬ 1 gal. = _____ pt.   ⑭ 1 qt. = _____ oz.   ⑮ 1 gal. = _____ oz.

D Fill in the blanks with <, >, or =.

① 36 in. __=__ 3 ft.   ② 16 qt. _____ 5 gal.   ③ 39 oz. _____ 2 lb.

④ 24 pt. _____ 42 c.   ⑤ 3 mi. _____ 5,280 ft.   ⑥ 48 lb. _____ 800 oz.

⑦ 12 gal. _____ 96 c.   ⑧ 18 yd. _____ 54 ft.   ⑨ 10 qt. _____ 80 oz.

⑩ 6 yd. _____ 72 in.   ⑪ 20,000 lb. _____ 10 T.   ⑫ 112 c. _____ 224 oz.

⑬ 16 c. _____ 8 pt.   ⑭ 127 oz. _____ 1 gal.   ⑮ 100 in. _____ 10 ft.

E True or false.

__true__ ① Inches and fractions of inches are marked on a measuring tool called a ruler.

_____ ② An inch is 1/12 of a foot and 1/36 of a yard.

_____ ③ Ounces are included both in U.S. units of weight and in U.S. units of volume.

_____ ④ Half of a quart is a cup.

_____ ⑤ A cup is 1/16 of a gallon, and an ounce is 1/16 of a pint.

_____ ⑥ A yard is 12 times as long as a foot.

_____ ⑦ A quart is 1/4 of a gallon, and a cup is 1/4 of a quart.

_____ ⑧ To convert miles to inches, divide by 5,280.

_____ ⑨ A unit of volume tells how much is contained.

_____ ⑩ A foot is one unit of measure which tells how long.

Review of Metric Units of Measure

Unit 154

Learning Objective: *We will learn to recognize and utilize metric units of measure.*

A metric unit of measure is a unit of length, weight, or volume, which is used throughout the modern world.

EXAMPLE: Metric units of length include millimeters, centimeters, meters, and kilometers. Metric units of weight include grams, kilograms, and metric tons. Metric units of volume include milliliters, centiliters, and liters.

A Write the abbreviations for these units of measure.

_km_ ① kilometer _____ ② metric ton _____ ③ meter _____ ④ kilogram _____ ⑤ millimeter

_____ ⑥ milliliter _____ ⑦ centimeter _____ ⑧ gram _____ ⑨ liter _____ ⑩ centiliter

B Write the symbol ($\times$ or $\div$) for the mathematical operation used to convert one unit of measure to another.

$\times$ ① kilometers to centimeters _____ ② grams to kilograms

_____ ③ meters to millimeters _____ ④ centiliters to liters

_____ ⑤ metric tons to kilograms _____ ⑥ meters to kilometers

_____ ⑦ millimeters to kilometers _____ ⑧ millimeters to centimeters

_____ ⑨ centimeters to meters _____ ⑩ liters to milliliters

_____ ⑪ kilograms to grams _____ ⑫ milliliters to centiliters

_____ ⑬ milliliters to liters _____ ⑭ centimeters to kilometers

_____ ⑮ centimeters to millimeters _____ ⑯ kilometers to millimeters

_____ ⑰ centiliters to milliliters _____ ⑱ meters to centimeters

_____ ⑲ kilometers to meters _____ ⑳ kilograms to metric tons

_____ ㉑ liters to centiliters _____ ㉒ millimeters to meters

REMINDER: Write the definition of a metric unit of measure.

_____

_____

C Fill in the blanks.

① 1 km = __100,000__ cm 　　② 1 t = _____ g 　　③ 1 m = _____ mm

④ 1 kg = _____ g 　　⑤ 1 l = _____ ml 　　⑥ 1 cm = _____ mm

⑦ 1 t = _____ kg 　　⑧ 1 cl = _____ ml 　　⑨ 1 m = _____ cm

⑩ 1 l = _____ cl 　　⑪ 1 km = _____ m 　　⑫ 1 km = _____ mm

D Fill in the blanks with <, >, or =.

① 12 cm __=__ 120 mm 　　② 2,500 g _____ 25 kg 　　③ 200,000 mm _____ 2 km

④ 2,800 ml _____ 28 cl 　　⑤ 6 kg _____ 12,000 g 　　⑥ 800 cl _____ 8 l

⑦ 10,000 m _____ 100 km 　　⑧ 45 l _____ 500 cl 　　⑨ 25 km _____ 25,000 m

⑩ 16 t _____ 16,000 g 　　⑪ 400,000 cm _____ 4 km 　　⑫ 84 kg _____ 840 t

⑬ 92,000 ml _____ 920 l 　　⑭ 1,120 ml _____ 112 cl 　　⑮ 2,000,000 g _____ 2 t

⑯ 7,700 cm _____ 77 m 　　⑰ 39 g _____ 39,000 kg 　　⑱ 15 cm _____ 1,500 m

E True or false.

__true__ ① The prefix "kilo" means 1,000.

_____ ② A gram is 1/1,000 of a kilogram, and a kilogram is 1/1,000 of a metric ton.

_____ ③ It takes 1 million grams to equal a kilogram.

_____ ④ Divide by 1,000 to convert milliliters to liters, millimeters to meters, kilograms to tons, meters to kilometers, or grams to kilograms.

_____ ⑤ Multiply by 100 to convert kilometers to centimeters.

_____ ⑥ A centiliter is 1/10 of a liter, and a centimeter is 1/10 of a meter.

_____ ⑦ A ton is 1 million times the weight of a gram, and a kilometer is 1 million times the length of a millimeter.

_____ ⑧ A milliliter is a metric unit of measure which tells how heavy.

_____ ⑨ A meter is longer than a millimeter, but shorter than a centimeter.

_____ ⑩ A metric ton is the greatest metric unit of weight.

Units of Measure — A Review   Unit 155

Learning Objective: *We will learn to identify units of measure, to compare U.S. and metric units of measure, and to compare Fahrenheit and Celsius temperature measurement.*

A unit of measure is a specific quantity which has been adopted to describe length, weight, volume, and temperature.

EXAMPLE: A degree is a specific quantity which is used as a unit of temperature on both Fahrenheit and Celsius scales.

A Identify each of the following as a unit of length (l), weight (w), or volume (v).

__l__ ① kilometer	____ ② inch	____ ③ cup
____ ④ centiliter	____ ⑤ ton	____ ⑥ metric ton
____ ⑦ mile	____ ⑧ liter	____ ⑨ millimeter
____ ⑩ pound	____ ⑪ meter	____ ⑫ foot
____ ⑬ pint	____ ⑭ milliliter	____ ⑮ gallon
____ ⑯ kilogram	____ ⑰ yard	____ ⑱ quart
____ ⑲ centimeter	____ ⑳ gram	____ ㉑ ounce

B Fill in the blanks with < or >.

① 1 km __<__ 1 mi.	② 1 in. ____ 1 cm	③ 1 oz. ____ 1 cl
④ 1 g ____ 1 oz.	⑤ 1 lb. ____ 1 kg	⑥ 1 t ____ 1 T.
⑦ 1 m ____ 1 yd.	⑧ 5,280 ft. ____ 1 km	⑨ 36 in. ____ 1,000 mm
⑩ 1 mi. ____ 1,000 m	⑪ 2,000 lb. ____ 1,000 kg	⑫ 1 m ____ 3 ft.
⑬ 10 ml ____ 1 oz.	⑭ 100 cm ____ 1 yd.	⑮ 1,000,000 g ____ 1 T.
⑯ 1,000 kg ____ 32,000 oz.	⑰ 1 t ____ 32,000 oz.	⑱ 1 km ____ 1,760 yd.
⑲ 10 mm ____ 1 in.	⑳ 1 yd. ____ 1,000 mm	㉑ 1 mi. ____ 1,000,000 mm
㉒ 1 lb. ____ 1,000 g	㉓ 100 cm ____ 3 ft.	㉔ 2,000 lb. ____ 1 t
㉕ 1 T. ____ 1,000 kg	㉖ 36 in. ____ 1 m	㉗ 1 kg ____ 16 oz.

REMINDER: Write the definition of a unit of measure.

_____

_____

C Match equivalent Fahrenheit and Celsius temperatures.

① 194° F   167° F   ⑨ 85° C   55° C

② 30° C   100° C   ⑩ 77° F   185° F

③ 75° C   86° F   ⑪ 131° F   41° F

④ 212° F   90° C   ⑫ 5° C   25° C

⑤ 15° C   10° C   ⑬ 113° F   70° C

⑥ 50° F   65° C   ⑭ 35° C   68° F

⑦ 50° C   59° F   ⑮ 158° F   95° F

⑧ 149° F   122° F   ⑯ 20° C   45° C

°F	°C
212°	100°
203°	95°
194°	90°
185°	85°
176°	80°
167°	75°
158°	70°
149°	65°
140°	60°
131°	55°
122°	50°
113°	45°
104°	40°
95°	35°
86°	30°
77°	25°
68°	20°
59°	15°
50°	10°
41°	5°
32°	0°

D Complete the chart below and mark each statement true or false.

false ① The high temperature recorded for the year was 104° F.

_____ ② The high Celsius temperature was 113°.

_____ ③ Celsius temperatures went no higher than 30° in the months of April, May, and September.

_____ ④ The coldest high monthly temperature was recorded in January.

_____ ⑤ In every month but June, July, and August, Celsius temperatures did not rise above the freezing point.

_____ ⑥ Temperatures climbed steadily from January through August.

_____ ⑦ Between August and September, the high Fahrenheit temperature dropped 27 degrees.

_____ ⑧ The largest drop in monthly high Celsius temperatures occurred between September and October.

High Temperatures		
Month	° F	° C
January	32	0
February	50	
March		25
April	86	
May		30
June	104	
July		40
August	113	
September		30
October	50	
November		5
December	41	

Comprehension Check

A Study the partial Celsius thermometers below and fill in the blanks with the correct temperatures. Circle any temperature that is above the boiling point.

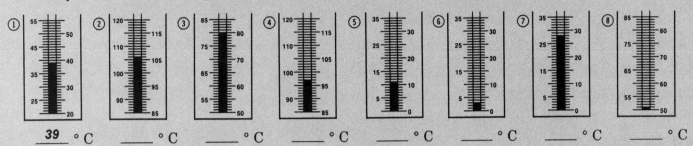

_39_ ° C   ____ ° C   ____ ° C   ____ ° C   ____ ° C   ____ ° C   ____ ° C   ____ ° C

B Fill in the blanks with <, >, or =.

① 105° F __>__ 39° C   ② 42° C _____ 42° F   ③ 59° F _____ 15° C

④ 72° C _____ 145° F   ⑤ 203° F _____ 89° C   ⑥ 67° C _____ 167° F

⑦ 3° C _____ 32° F   ⑧ 140° F _____ 60° C   ⑨ 80° C _____ 176° F

⑩ 196° F _____ 90° C   ⑪ 29° C _____ 94° F   ⑫ 40° F _____ 12° C

⑬ 21° C _____ 77° F   ⑭ 125° F _____ 59° C   ⑮ 48° C _____ 122° F

⑯ 86° F _____ 30° C   ⑰ 73° C _____ 175° F   ⑱ 150° F _____ 64° C

⑲ 60° C _____ 152° F   ⑳ 210° F _____ 95° C   ㉑ 88° C _____ 195° F

㉒ 177° F _____ 77° C   ㉓ 49° C _____ 113° F   ㉔ 68° F _____ 20° C

°F	°C
212°	100°
203°	95°
194°	90°
185°	85°
176°	80°
167°	75°
158°	70°
149°	65°
140°	60°
131°	55°
122°	50°
113°	45°
104°	40°
95°	35°
86°	30°
77°	25°
68°	20°
59°	15°
50°	10°
41°	5°
32°	0°

C Write the abbreviation or symbol for each of the following.

_pt._ ① pint   _____ ② centiliter   _____ ③ ton   _____ ④ millimeter

_____ ⑤ kilogram   _____ ⑥ cup   _____ ⑦ liter   _____ ⑧ foot

_____ ⑨ quart   _____ ⑩ yard   _____ ⑪ gram   _____ ⑫ meter

_____ ⑬ pound   _____ ⑭ Fahrenheit   _____ ⑮ inch   _____ ⑯ metric ton

_____ ⑰ ounce   _____ ⑱ degree   _____ ⑲ centimeter   _____ ⑳ mile

_____ ㉑ gallon   _____ ㉒ kilometer   _____ ㉓ Celsius   _____ ㉔ milliliter

   Test 31 cont'd ☛

D Identify each of the following as a unit of length (l), weight (w), volume (v), or temperature (t).

___l___ ① yard   _____ ② pint   _____ ③ millimeter   _____ ④ ton

_____ ⑤ kilometer   _____ ⑥ inch   _____ ⑦ metric ton   _____ ⑧ pound

_____ ⑨ gallon   _____ ⑩ quart   _____ ⑪ cup   _____ ⑫ milliliter

_____ ⑬ mile   _____ ⑭ centimeter   _____ ⑮ meter   _____ ⑯ degree

_____ ⑰ centiliter   _____ ⑱ liter   _____ ⑲ foot   _____ ⑳ kilogram

_____ ㉑ gram   _____ ㉒ ounce

E Write the symbol (× or ÷) for the mathematical operation used to convert one unit of measure to another.

___÷___ ① ounces to pounds   _____ ② meters to millimeters   _____ ③ kilometers to centimeters

_____ ④ grams to kilograms   _____ ⑤ inches to feet   _____ ⑥ centimeters to millimeters

_____ ⑦ gallons to cups   _____ ⑧ milliliters to liters   _____ ⑨ cups to quarts

_____ ⑩ millimeters to kilometers   _____ ⑪ miles to yards   _____ ⑫ metric tons to kilograms

_____ ⑬ quarts to pints   _____ ⑭ centimeters to meters   _____ ⑮ gallons to quarts

_____ ⑯ meters to kilometers   _____ ⑰ gallons to ounces   _____ ⑱ pounds to tons

_____ ⑲ yards to inches   _____ ⑳ ounces to cups   _____ ㉑ liters to centiliters

List 10 U.S. units of measure and 10 metric units of measure.

U.S.		Metric	
① _inch_	②	① _millimeter_	②
③	④	③	④
⑤	⑥	⑤	⑥
⑦	⑧	⑦	⑧
⑨	⑩	⑨	⑩

Geometric Shapes

Learning Objective: *We will learn to distinguish between similar and congruent forms.*

A geometric shape is a distinct form that is made up of curved or straight lines.

EXAMPLE: Figures A and B are similar. They have the same shape, but are not the same size. Figures C and D are congruent. They have the same shape and size.

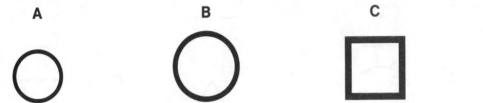

A   B   C   D

A In each row, circle the letter of the figure that is similar to the first figure in that row.

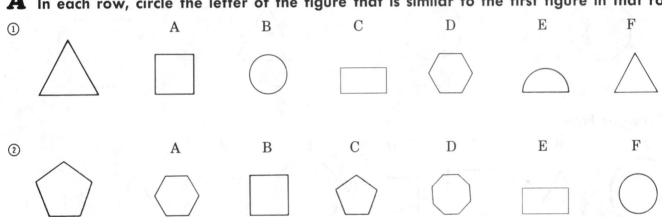

B In each row, circle the letter of the figure that is congruent to the first figure in that row.

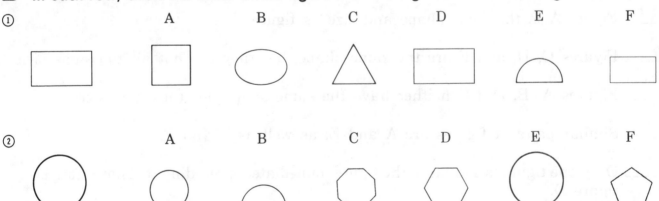

REMINDER: *Write the definition of a geometric shape.*

_____

_____

     Unit 156 cont'd ☞

C Label each pair of shapes (c) congruent or (s) similar.

① ___c___ ② _____ ③ _____ ④ _____

⑤ _____ ⑥ _____ ⑦ _____ ⑧ _____

D True or False

A B C D E F G H

① __F__ Figure A is the same shape and size as figure H.

② ____ Figures C, D, and F are the same shape, but they are not all the same size.

③ ____ Figures A, B, and C neither have the same shape nor the same size.

④ ____ Similar pairs of figures are A and E, as well as B and F.

⑤ ____ Only one figure is similar to the figure immediately preceding it. That figure is figure D.

⑥ ____ Congruent pairs of figures are A and E, B and G, and D and F.

⑦ ____ Figure E is congruent to figure A and similar to figure H.

⑧ ____ Figure F is congruent to figure C and similar to figure D.

378

Identifying Shapes

Learning Objective: *We will learn to identify nine geometric shapes, two types of lines, and three types of angles.*

A geometric shape is a distinct form that is made up of curved or straight lines.

EXAMPLE: A square is made up of four straight line segments that meet to form four square corners, or right angles.

A Identify the shapes.

circle

① A ___*triangle*___ is made up of three straight line segments.

triangle

② Only one shape, the _____, consists of both curved and straight lines.

rectangle

③ A _____ is formed by four straight line segments and has four right angles. The line segments may or may not be the same size.

④ A _____ is a special type of rectangle with four line segments of equal size.

ellipse

⑤ Five line segments and an equal number of angles make up the shape known as a _____ .

semi-circle

⑥ A _____ is made up of two congruent semi-circles and has only curved lines.

hexagon

⑦ The _____ has eight angles, though none are right angles.

⑧ Only a _____ has three angles.

pentagon

⑨ The _____, like the circle, has only curved lines and has no angles.

octagon

⑩ Six line segments and six angles form the _____ .

REMINDER: Write the definition of a geometric shape.

_____

_____

Unit 157 cont'd ☛

B Three types of triangles have one or more of the angles shown at left below. Study the angles and identify the types of triangles.

right angle   acute angle   obtuse angle   _____   _____   _____

C List the number of line segments and the number of angles that make up the shapes below.

① line segments: _____   ② line segments: _____   ③ line segments: _____   ④ line segments: _____
angles: _____   angles: _____   angles: _____   angles: _____

D Underline the correct answers.

① The (octagon, triangle, pentagon) has more angles than the hexagon.

② Both a square and a rectangle have four (right, acute, obtuse) angles.

③ The angles of a (circle, ellipse, pentagon) may be either acute or obtuse.

④ An acute (rectangle, triangle, semi-circle) has three angles, all of which are acute.

⑤ The (acute, obtuse) angle is greater than the right angle.

⑥ The (acute, obtuse, square) angle is less than the right angle.

⑦ Two (ellipses, octagons, semi-circles) of the same size form a circle.

⑧ The circle and the (ellipse, octagon, semi-circle) have no straight line segments

⑨ Three special types of triangles are the obtuse triangle, the right triangle, and the acute triangle. A (semi-circle, hexagon, square) is a special kind of rectangle.

⑩ The hexagon and the octagon lack the one kind of angle which forms both the (square and rectangle, triangle and semi-circle, circle and ellipse).

Drawing the Other Half

Learning Objective: *We will learn to recognize shapes, four types of lines, and three angles.*

A geometric shape is a distinct form that is made up of curved or straight lines.

EXAMPLE:

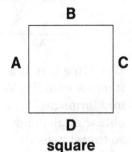

square

Two triangles may be arranged to form a square. In the figure at left, lines A and C are parallel; they will never meet no matter how far they are extended. Lines C and D are perpendicular; they meet to form a right angle.

A Identify the two shapes which, when joined, will form the complete shape.

A   B   C   D   E   F

  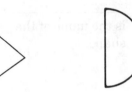 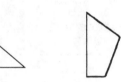

① __A__ , __D__ a circle   ② ____ , ____ a pentagon   ③ ____ , ____ a right triangle

G   H   I   J   K   L

   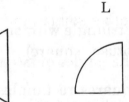

④ ____ , ____ a hexagon   ⑤ ____ , ____ a rectangle   ⑥ ____ , ____ a semi-circle

M   N   O   P   Q   R

  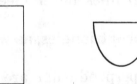 

⑦ ____ , ____ an ellipse   ⑧ ____ , ____ a square   ⑨ ____ , ____ a an octagon

REMINDER: Write the definition of a geometric shape.

      Unit 158 cont'd ☛

B Follow the instructions and identify the shapes.

①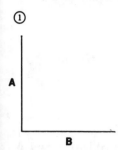

②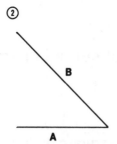

③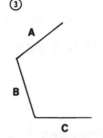

④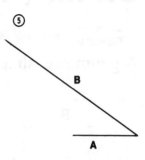

⑤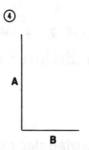

① Draw line C an equal size and parallel to line A. Draw line D an equal size and parallel to line B.

_____ is the name of the shape.

② Draw line C so that it is perpendicular to line A and so that it meets with line B to form an acute angle.

_____ is the name of the shape.

③ Draw line D an equal size as line B and forming an obtuse angle with line C. Draw line E so that it meets and forms obtuse angles with A and D.

_____ is the name of the shape.

④ Draw line C so that it is a size equal to line A and is perpendicular to line B. Draw line D an equal size and parallel to line B.

_____ is the name of the shape.

⑤ Draw line C so that it meets with line A and forms an obtuse angle, and so that it meets with line B and forms an acute angle.

_____ is the name of the shape.

C Underline the correct answers.

① A (triangle, circle, <u>square</u>) is made up of both parallel and perpendicular lines.

② A triangle with one angle that is greater than a right angle is called (acute, obtuse, square).

③ Squares, rectangles, triangles, pentagons, hexagons, and octagons are made up of three or more (curved lines, straight lines, obtuse angles).

④ Half a circle is (an ellipse, an octagon, a semi-circle).

⑤ (Curved, Perpendicular, Parallel) lines never meet.

⑥ Acute, obtuse, and right are types of triangles, as well as types of (circles, angles, lines).

⑦ Straight, curved, parallel, and perpendicular are types of (lines, angles, shapes).

⑧ A (pentagon, rectangle, square) has no parallel lines.

⑨ The (triangle, hexagon, ellipse) has no angles.

⑩ The (semi-circle, circle, ellipse) is made up of two types of lines.

382

Graphs

Learning Objective: *We will learn to plot number pairs on a graph.*

A graph is a visual aid for presenting numerical information.

EXAMPLE:

The table immediately to the right gives information in the form of number pairs. To the far right, the same information is presented on a graph.

Grade	Number of Sections
12	3
11	3
10	4
9	2

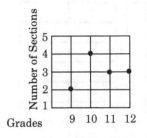

A The points on a graph indicate number pairs. Study the number pairs on the graphs below and record the information on the accompanying tables.

①
Sales Team	Subs. Sold
1	**6**
2	
3	
4	
5	
6	
7	
8	
9	
10	

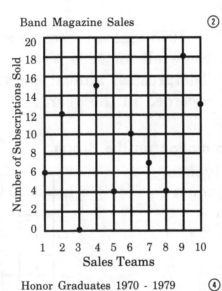

②
Club	New Members
1	
2	
3	
4	
5	
6	
7	
8	
9	
10	

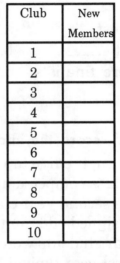

③
Year	Honor Grads
1	
2	
3	
4	
5	
6	
7	
8	
9	
10	

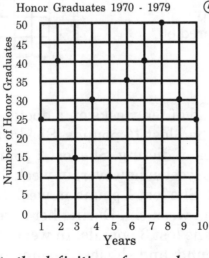

④
Day	Pizzas Sold
1	
2	
3	
4	
5	
6	
7	
8	
9	
10	

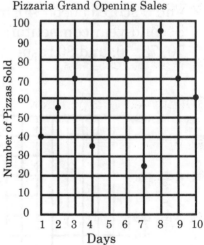

REMINDER: Write the definition of a graph.

Unit 159 cont'd ☞

B Study the tables and plot the number pairs on the graphs. Complete the statements that follow.

①
Finalist	Score
1	6
2	4
3	8
4	7
5	6
6	7
7	9
8	5
9	10
10	5

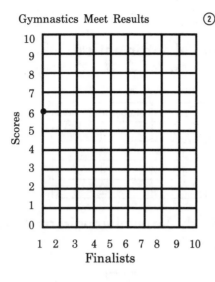

Gymnastics Meet Results

Scores / Finalists

②
Year	Inches of Snow
1	6
2	5
3	18
4	9
5	8
6	15
7	6
8	7
9	10
10	11

Annual Snowfall 1975 - 1984

Snowfall in Inches / Years

a. Finalist __9__ scored highest.
b. Low score went to finalist ____ .
c. Tying for fourth place were finalists ____ and ____ .

a. In 1975, ____ inches of snow fell.
b. Snowfall for 1984 was ____ inches.
c. The greatest annual snowfall was recorded in the year ____ .

C Study each paragraph and record the information on the graph.

① At the close of the school term, the five top typists from the first-year typing class competed against the five top typists from the second-year class. First-year students were assigned odd numbers for the competition. Second-year students were assigned even numbers. First-year typists 1, 3, 5, 7, and 9 scored 50, 65, 40, 50, and 60 respectively. Second-year competitors 2, 4, 6, 8, and 10 scored 60, 70, 75, 50, and 80 respectively.

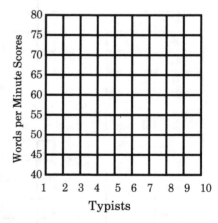

Words per Minute Scores / Typists

②

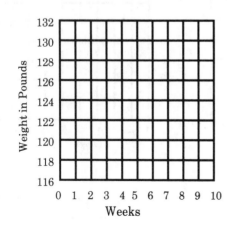

Weight in Pounds / Weeks

At the end of ten weeks on a doctor-approved diet, Miriam had lost 16 pounds. She lost 4 pounds her first week of dieting. She lost 2 pounds each of the next two weeks; however, in week four, she gained a pound. She lost 1 pound in week five and two pounds in week six. During her seventh week of dieting she lost 3 pounds. In week eight, Miriam lost 1 pound, and she lost 1 pound during each of of the last two weeks of the diet. At the beginning of the diet, Miriam weighed 132 pounds.

384

Line Graphs

Unit 160

Learning Objective: *We will learn to read and construct line graphs.*

A line graph is a graph on which points are connected with a line.

EXAMPLE:

Line graphs are ideal for illustrating change over a period of time. The graph at right shows one person's weight changes over a period of several years.

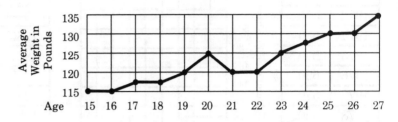

A Study the graphs and complete the tables.

①
Month	Low Temp.
9	**35°**
10	
11	
12	
1	
2	
3	
4	
5	
6	

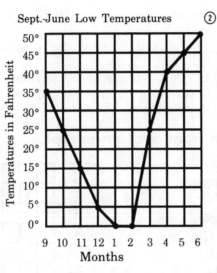

Sept.-June Low Temperatures

②
Year	Total Proceeds
1975	
1976	
1977	
1978	
1979	
1980	
1981	
1982	
1983	
1984	

1975-1984 Bike-a-thon Proceeds

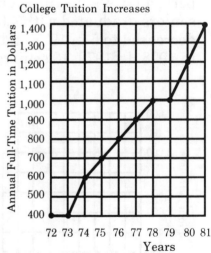

③
Class of	# Attendees
1970	
1971	
1972	
1973	
1974	
1975	
1976	
1977	
1978	
1979	

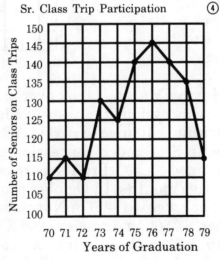

Sr. Class Trip Participation

④
Year	Annual Tuition
1972	
1973	
1974	
1975	
1976	
1977	
1978	
1979	
1980	
1981	

College Tuition Increases

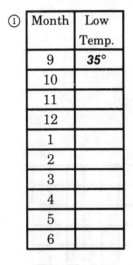

REMINDER: Write the definition of a line graph.

Unit 160 cont'd ☞

B Study the tables and construct line graphs with the same information.

①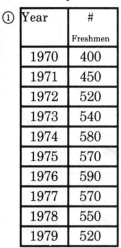

Year	# Freshmen
1970	400
1971	450
1972	520
1973	540
1974	580
1975	570
1976	590
1977	570
1978	550
1979	520

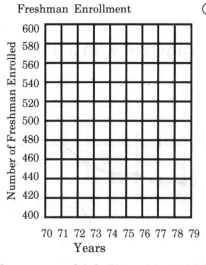

②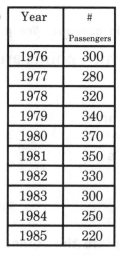

Year	# Passengers
1976	300
1977	280
1978	320
1979	340
1980	370
1981	350
1982	330
1983	300
1984	250
1985	220

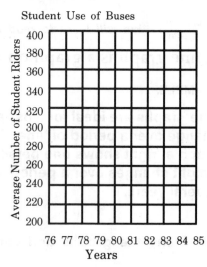

a. Freshman enrollment was highest in _____ .

b. Fewer freshmen enrolled in _____ than in 1971.

c. Freshman enrollment decreased steadily after it peaked at _____ students.

a. An average of _____ students rode buses in 1979.

b. The greatest use of buses by students was in _____ .

c. In _____ , fewer students rode buses than in any year shown on the graph.

C Construct a line graph with the information from each paragraph.

① In 1970, 4 of Smithton High School's seniors graduated with perfect 4.0 grade point averages. The number of graduates with perfect GPA's increased to 6 the following year, but decreased to 3 in 1972. For three years, beginning in 1973, the Smithton senior class included 7 students with perfect GPA's. In 1976, a record number of 15 seniors graduated with 4.0 GPA's. The number decreased to 5 in 1977 and dropped even more to 3 in 1978. In 1979, 10 seniors earned 4.0 GPA's.

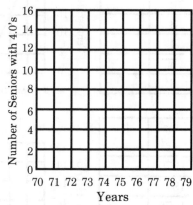

②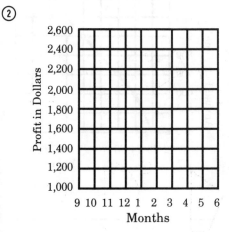

When Marsha Maroney took over management of a theater concession stand, she pledged to double profits within a 10-month period. When Marsha took over in September, concession profits for that month totaled $1,100. Profits increased steadily for the next five months. In October profits came to $1,300. They were $1,400 in November, $1,600 in December, $1,800 in January, and $2,000 in February. In March, a decline began with only $1,900 in profits for that month, $1,700 in profits for April, and $1,600 in May. The concession saw only $1,400 in profits in Marsha's tenth month of management.

Comprehension Check

A Circle two hexagons. Are they similar _____ or congruent _____ ? (Check one.)

① ② ③ ④ ⑤ ⑥ ⑦ ⑧

B Circle the two figures that have no straight lines. These are the _____ and _____.

① ② ③ ④ ⑤ ⑥ ⑦ ⑧

C Circle the lines that are parallel.

① ② ③ ④ ⑤ ⑥ ⑦ ⑧

D Circle the lines that are perpendicular.

① ② ③ ④ ⑤ ⑥ ⑦ ⑧

E Circle the obtuse triangle. Two other triangles are called _____ and _____.

① ② ③ ④ ⑤ ⑥ ⑦ ⑧

F Circle the square. It is a special type of _____.

① ② ③ ④ ⑤ ⑥ ⑦ ⑧

G Circle the two shapes that will join to form a pentagon.

① ② ③ ④ ⑤ ⑥ ⑦ ⑧

Test 32 cont'd ☞

H Study the number of pairs marked on the graphs below. Complete the tables.

①

Year	# Attendees
1975	**190**
1976	
1977	
1978	
1979	
1980	
1981	
1982	
1983	
1984	

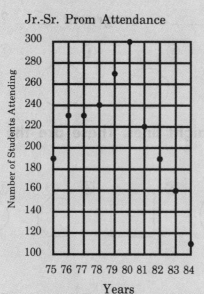

Jr.-Sr. Prom Attendance

②

Year	Students Driving
1966	
1967	
1968	
1969	
1970	
1971	
1972	
1973	
1974	
1975	

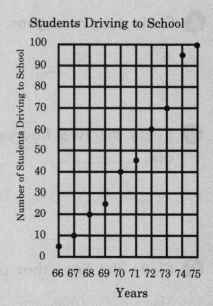

Students Driving to School

I Use the information from the tables to construct line graphs.

①

Year	Honor Graduates
1970	30
1971	20
1972	35
1973	10
1974	15
1975	40
1976	5
1977	20
1978	45
1979	25

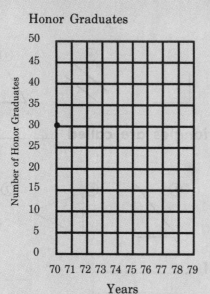

Honor Graduates

②

Day	$ Sales
1	$60
2	$80
3	$95
4	$90
5	$110
6	$100
7	$85
8	$75
9	$40
10	$25

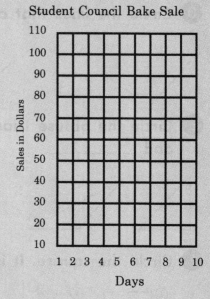

Student Council Bake Sale

Write a definition for each of the following.

① octagon _____

② right angle _____

③ semi-circle _____

④ graph _____

⑤ line graph _____

388

Bar Graphs

Learning Objective: *We will learn to read and construct bar graphs.*

A bar graph uses rectangles to show comparisons.

EXAMPLE:

Bar graphs are suited for comparisons of groups. The bar graph at the right illustrates average weights of various age groups of females.

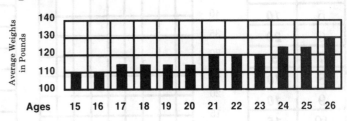

A Study the graphs and complete the tables.

①
Team #	$ Sales
1	**$40**
2	
3	
4	
5	
6	
7	
8	
9	

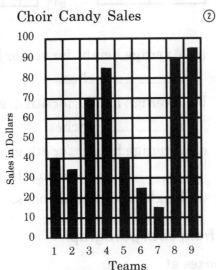

②
Precinct #	# Voters
1	
2	
3	
4	
5	
6	
7	
8	
9	

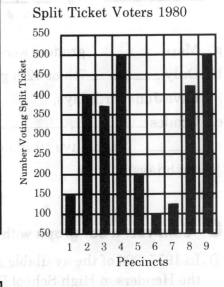

③
Grade	Books per year
4	
5	
6	
7	
8	
9	
10	
11	
12	

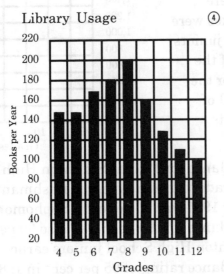

④
Team #	Fish Caught
1	
2	
3	
4	
5	
6	
7	
8	
9	

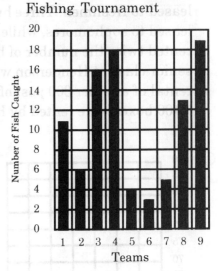

REMINDER: Write the definition of a bar graph.

B Use the tables to construct bar graphs.

①

Grade	# Students
4	15
5	10
6	20
7	5
8	10
9	10
10	15
11	35
12	5

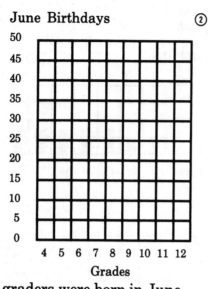

June Birthdays

Grades

a. More _____ graders were born in June.

b. Only _____ 7th or 12th graders have June birthdays.

c. Grades _____, _____, and _____ each have 10 students with birthdays in June.

②

Grade	Height in Inches
4	56
5	59
6	62
7	64
8	66
9	67
10	68
11	69
12	70

Average Heights of Boys

Grades

a. Average height for senior boys is _____ inches.

b. Average height for 4th grade boys is _____ inches.

c. Average height for 8th grade boys is _____ inches more than the average height of 6th grade boys.

C Construct a bar graph with the information from each paragraph.

① In 1977, 200 of the available 1,600 post office boxes at the Henderson High School Postal Station were leased to freshmen. Three hundred postal boxes were leased to sophomores, while Henderson High juniors rented twice the number of boxes. Members of the senior class at Henderson were responsible for the rental of another 300 post office boxes. A total of 1,400 boxes were rented by Henderson students.

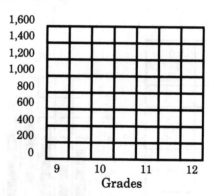

Grades

②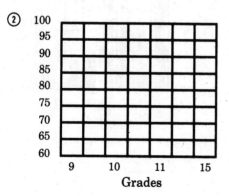

Grades

Student attendance for 1985 at Smithton High School varied from grade to grade. Average freshman attendance for 1985 was 90 per cent. Sophomore average attendance for the year was also 90 per cent per cent. Smithton High School juniors earned an average attendance rating of 95 per cent in 1985. Seniors had the lowest rate of attendance. Only 80 per cent average attendance was recorded for Smithton's senior class.

Maps

Learning Objective: **We will learn to distinguish between four types of maps.**

A map is a representation of an actual area.

EXAMPLE: A physical map shows features of the earth's surface, such as mountains, rivers, lakes, and plains. A political map shows such features as boundaries, cities, capitals, and roads and highways. A relief map shows the elevation of land. A simple reference map provides information about a certain area or region.

A Identify the following maps as (a) physical, (b) political, (c) relief, or (d) simple reference.

① _____

② _____

③ _____

④ _____

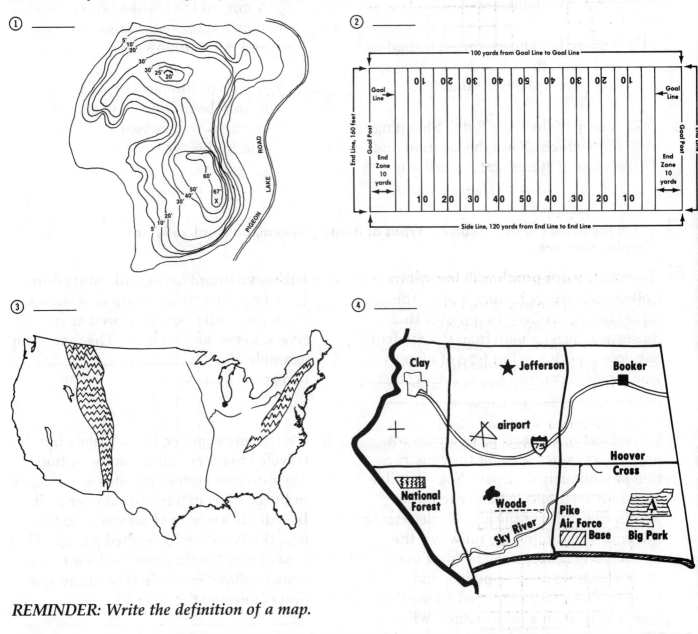

REMINDER: Write the definition of a map.

391

B Identify the following types of maps as (a) physical, (b) political, (c) relief, or (d) simple reference.

_d_ ① A map that shows the trails, picnic areas, campgrounds, restrooms, and parking lots at Green Springs Resort.

___ ② A map of the city of Casper and surrounding area. City boundaries are shown, as are roads and highways.

___ ③ A map that shows, through shading and color, the mountains, valleys, and plains of South America.

___ ④ A map of the Park Ridge Shopping Mall which shows the location and names of stores and restaurants.

___ ⑤ A map of the mountains and valleys, rivers and lakes of western Europe.

___ ⑥ A map that shows the location of bed and breakfast inns in the state of Washington.

___ ⑦ A map of the United States which shows state boundaries, capitals, and major highways.

___ ⑧ A map of Illinois which shows county boundaries and county seats, as well as roads and highways.

C Fill in the blanks with the correct types of maps: physical, political, relief, or simple reference.

① When Suzanne enrolled at Lewis State College, she easily became lost on the large campus. A friend suggested that Suzanne request a map from the Student Services Director. What type of map would help Suzanne? _____

② Hikers visiting Waynesville State Forest have been helped by a map that shows the forest's hilly areas, as well as its rivers, lakes, and streams. The map is an example of a _____ of a small region.

③ The Jonestown Board of Aldermen was asked to consider sites for the construction of a municipal airport. Four possible sites had been selected and each was within five miles of the city. To determine the land's suitability for runways, the board found it necessary to know the exact elevation of hills, plains, and valleys. The board requested a map that would provide this information. What type of map was needed? _____

④ During one summer, the Winslow family traveled to every capital in the nation. The different states and sites were visited in the comfort of a roomy camper-trailer. In order to know the best route for the trip, the Winslows consulted a map. What type of map would show the locations of state capitals, as well as the highways that connected the cities? _____

Maps to Scale

Learning
Objective: *We will learn to use a scale when reading maps.*

A scale tells us how the distances between objects on a map correspond to real distances.

EXAMPLE: If you measure the scale at right, you will find that it is 2 inches in length. It tells us that, on any map using this scale, 2 inches will equal 48 miles and 1 inch will equal 24 miles.

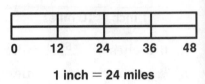

1 inch = 24 miles

A Use the scale above to determine distances.

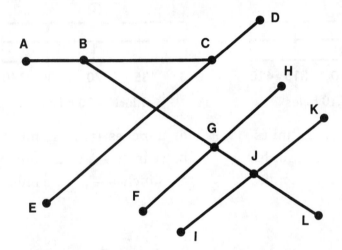

① The distance between points A and C is ___48___ miles.

② There are _____ miles between points B and L.

③ The distance between points F and H is the same as the distance between points I and K: _____ miles.

④ Points G and J are only _____ miles apart.

⑤ From point I to J to G is a total distance of _____ miles.

⑥ From Shelby School to the post office is _____ miles.

⑦ From the police department to the intersection of Shelby Drive and Airport Road is _____ miles.

⑧ The zoo entrance at the corner of Macon and Dover Streets is _____ miles from the post office.

⑨ If you drove from Shelby School past the fire department, turned right on Main Street and left on Airport Road, and continued to the zoo entrance at Park Drive, you would drive a total of _____ miles.

REMINDER: Write the definition of a scale.

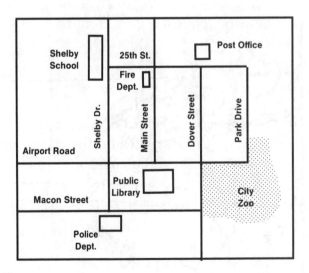

Unit 163 cont'd ☞

B Determine the distances.

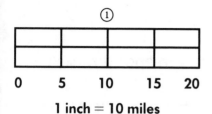

① 1 inch = 10 miles

a. 6 inches = __60__ miles
b. ½ inch = _____ miles
c. 4 inches = _____ miles

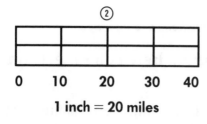

② 1 inch = 20 miles

a. 3 inches = _____ miles
b. 1½ inches = _____ miles
c. 8 inches = _____ miles

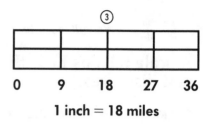

③ 1 inch = 18 miles

a. 5 inches = _____ miles
b. 3 inches = _____ miles
c. ½ inch = _____ miles

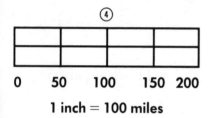

④ 1 inch = 100 miles

a. 12 inches = _____ miles
b. 1½ inches = _____ miles
c. 7 inches = _____ miles

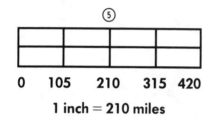

⑤ 1 inch = 210 miles

a. ½ inch = _____ miles
b. 1½ inches = _____ miles
c. 3 inches = _____ miles

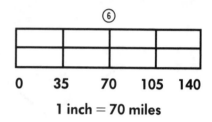

⑥ 1 inch = 70 miles

a. 2 inches = _____ miles
b. ½ inch = _____ miles
c. 8 inches = _____ miles

C Study the map and complete the statements.

Nautical Miles
0 200 400 600 800 1200   1 inch = 1,200 nautical miles

① If you were to sail from Guam to New Guinea, you would travel approximately _____ nautical miles.

② If you set sail at the mouth of Australia's Darling River and traveled to the point between the two islands of New Zealand, you would sail a total of _____ nautical miles.

③ From Wake Island to the Gilbert Islands is a nautical distance of _____ miles.

④ If a ship were to travel from the southern tip of New Zealand, to the west around the continent of Australia, and north to the southernmost islands of Indonesia, a distance of approximately _____ nautical miles would be logged.

394

Reading Maps

Learning Objective: *We will learn to use grids, indexes, and map legends.*

A map is a representation of an actual area.

EXAMPLES: A <u>grid</u> divides a map into sections. An <u>index</u> tells what section contains a specific point of interest. A <u>legend</u> explains any symbols that are used on a map.

A Complete the index by writing the grid letter and number next to each city.

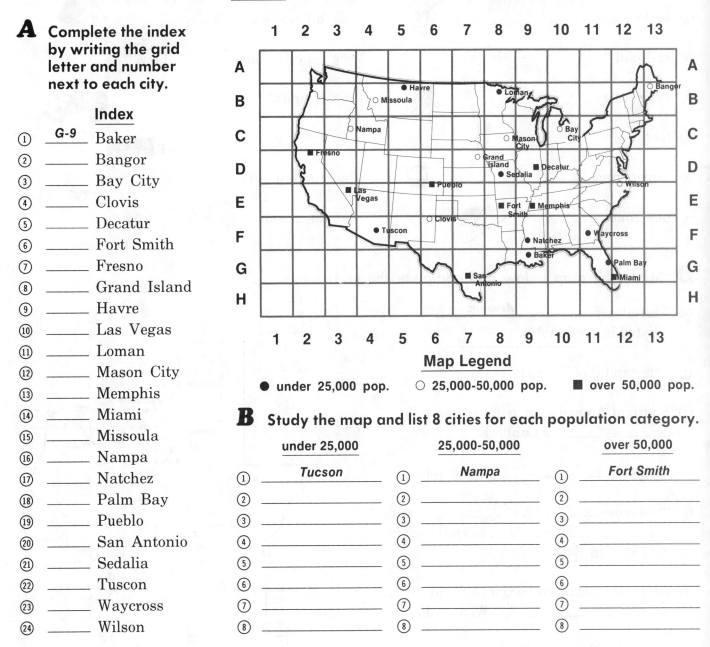

Index

1. _G-9_ Baker
2. _____ Bangor
3. _____ Bay City
4. _____ Clovis
5. _____ Decatur
6. _____ Fort Smith
7. _____ Fresno
8. _____ Grand Island
9. _____ Havre
10. _____ Las Vegas
11. _____ Loman
12. _____ Mason City
13. _____ Memphis
14. _____ Miami
15. _____ Missoula
16. _____ Nampa
17. _____ Natchez
18. _____ Palm Bay
19. _____ Pueblo
20. _____ San Antonio
21. _____ Sedalia
22. _____ Tuscon
23. _____ Waycross
24. _____ Wilson

Map Legend

● under 25,000 pop.   ○ 25,000-50,000 pop.   ■ over 50,000 pop.

B Study the map and list 8 cities for each population category.

under 25,000	25,000-50,000	over 50,000
1. *Tucson*	1. *Nampa*	1. *Fort Smith*
2. _____	2. _____	2. _____
3. _____	3. _____	3. _____
4. _____	4. _____	4. _____
5. _____	5. _____	5. _____
6. _____	6. _____	6. _____
7. _____	7. _____	7. _____
8. _____	8. _____	8. _____

REMINDER: Write the definition of a map.

_____

_____

Unit 164 cont'd

C Match the symbols with their meanings.

① mountain range

② airport

③ hunting area

④ state capital

⑤ railroad

⑥ ski resort

⑦ food

⑧ forest area

⑨ bus route

⑩ campground

⑪ highway

⑫ naval base

⑬ oil wells

⑭ bicycle route

⑮ hospital

⑯ truck route

⑰ fishing area

⑱ farmland

D Study the map below and complete the statements.

① The city of _____ **Amarillo** _____ is located in section A-4.

② The capital of Texas is _____.

③ South of Amarillo, in grid section _____, is Lubbock.

④ Dallas is _____ of Houston.

⑤ Two cities, _____ and _____, are situated in grid section E-8.

⑥ Along the northern border of Texas, in grid section _____, is Wichita Falls.

⑦ Forth Worth and Dallas are located in grid section _____.

⑧ Situated in grid section H-7 is the southernmost Texas city, _____.

396

Identifying Math Symbols

Unit 165

Learning Objective: *We will learn to identify and use 13 math symbols.*

A math symbol usually represents an operation or a relationship.

EXAMPLE: **The symbol $+$ represents the mathematical operation of addition.**
The symbol $=$ shows the relationship between two numbers or elements.

a.	b.	c.	d.	e.	f.	g.	h.	i.	j.	k.	l.	m.
$+$	$-$	$\times$	$\div$	$=$	$\neq$	$>$	$<$	$\subseteq$	$\in$	$\not\subseteq$	$\cap$	$\cup$

A Use the appropriate symbol for each problem.

① $289 \underline{\quad - \quad} 196 = 93$

② $730 \underline{\quad\quad} 5 = 146$

③ $113 \underline{\quad\quad} 12 = 1,356$

④ $2,016 \underline{\quad\quad} 312 = 2,328$

⑤ $291 \underline{\quad\quad} 614 = 905$

⑥ $648 \underline{\quad\quad} 350 = 298$

⑦ $702 \underline{\quad\quad} 9 = 78$

⑧ $294 \underline{\quad\quad} 98 = 3$

⑨ $64 \underline{\quad\quad} 21 = 1,344$

⑩ $134 \underline{\quad\quad} 128 = 6$

⑪ $11 \underline{\quad\quad} 573 = 6,303$

⑫ $93 \underline{\quad\quad} 91 = 184$

⑬ $62 + 75 \underline{\quad\quad} 137$

⑭ $133 \times 3 \underline{\quad\quad} 399$

⑮ $225 \div 9 \underline{\quad\quad} 32$

⑯ $3,114 - 105 \underline{\quad\quad} 3,009$

⑰ $2,968 \underline{\quad\quad} 33$

⑱ $912 \underline{\quad\quad} 913$

⑲ $1,877 \underline{\quad\quad} 1,900$

⑳ $2,778 \underline{\quad\quad} 2$

㉑ $412 \underline{\quad\quad} 312$

㉒ A = {10, 20, 30, 40, 50}
B = {10, 20}
C = {30, 40 50}
    $30 \underline{\quad\quad} B$

㉓ A = {2, 4, 6, 8, 10}
B = {6}
C = {2, 4}
    $2 \underline{\quad\quad} C$

㉔ A = {5, 10, 15, 20, 25}
B = {10, 20}
C = {5, 15, 25}
    $B \underline{\quad\quad} A$

㉕ A = {1, 3, 5}
B = {2, 4, 6}
A $\underline{\quad\quad}$ B = {1, 2, 3, 4, 5, 6}

㉖ A = {a, b, c, d}
B = {a, b, c}
A $\underline{\quad\quad}$ B = {a, b, c}

㉗ A = {20, 40, 60, 80}
B = {100}
A $\underline{\quad\quad}$ B = {   }

㉘ A = {9, 10, 11}
B = {6, 7, 8}
A $\underline{\quad\quad}$ B = {6, 7, 8, 9, 10, 11}

㉙ A = {3, 6, 9, 12}
B = {15}
A $\underline{\quad\quad}$ B = {3, 6, 9, 12, 15}

㉚ A = {1, 2, 3, 4, 5, 6}
B = {3, 4, 5, 6, 7}
A $\underline{\quad\quad}$ B = {3, 4, 5, 6}

REMINDER: Write the definition of a math symbol.

_____

_____

Unit 165 cont'd ☞

B Match the symbol with its meaning.

① ×　　　　is less than　　　⑤ ⊆　　　intersection of　　⑨ >　　　divided by

② =　　　　union of　　　　　⑥ ∩　　　minus　　　　　　⑩ ∈　　　is not a member of

③ <　　　　times　　　　　　⑦ −　　　is a subset of　　　⑪ ÷　　　is a member of

④ ∪　　　　is equal to　　　　⑧ ≠　　　is not equal to　　⑫ ⊄　　　is greater than

C Does the symbol show a relationship between two numbers or does it signify a mathematical operation?

① + ___*operation*___　　　② − _____　　　③ × _____

④ ÷ _____　　　⑤ = _____　　　⑥ ≠ _____

⑦ > _____　　　⑧ < _____　　　⑨ ⊆ _____

⑩ ∈ _____　　　⑪ ⊄ _____　　　⑫ ∩ _____

⑬ ∪ _____

D Study the symbols on page 397 and fill in the blanks with the appropriate letter.

① The symbol that instructs us to add one quantity to another is ___*a*___ .

② When one quantity or number has the same value as another, the symbol that stands between them is _____ .

③ All the members of one set plus all the members of another calls for the use of the symbol _____ to describe the result.

④ If one number has a lower value than another number, the symbol _____ is placed after the number of lesser value and before the other number.

⑤ When we want to show simply that two quantities do not have the same value, we use the symbol _____ .

⑥ The symbol that tells us to subtract one number from another is _____ .

⑦ The symbol that shows the relationship between two sets when a third set can be formed with common members is _____ .

⑧ If set B consists only of 2 members of set A, we use the symbol _____ to describe the relationship of B to A.

Comprehension Check

A Study the graphs and complete the tables.

①

Club	New Members
1	7
2	
3	
4	
5	
6	
7	
8	
9	

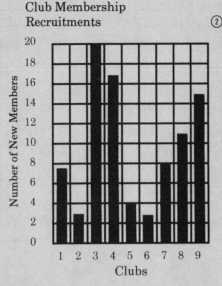

Club Membership Recruitments

②

Sales Team	$ Sales
1	12
2	
3	
4	
5	
6	
7	
8	
9	

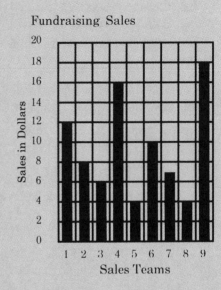

Fundraising Sales

B Construct bar graphs with information from the tables.

①

Finalist	Score
1	6
2	4
3	8
4	7
5	6
6	7
7	9
8	5
9	10

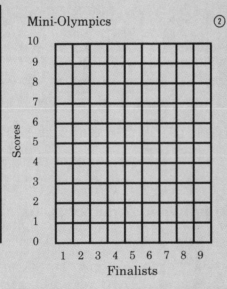

Mini-Olympics

②

Year	Inches of
65	6
66	5
67	18
68	9
69	8
70	15
71	6
72	7
73	10

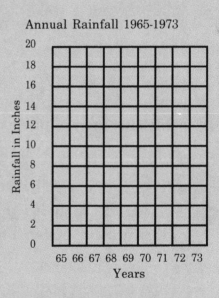

Annual Rainfall 1965-1973

C Identify the types of maps as (a) physical, (b) political, (c) relief, or (d) simple reference.

__d__ ① A map that shows only how to get from your house to a friend's house.

____ ③ A map that shows the location of books in a library.

____ ⑤ A map of the U.S., its state boundaries, state capitals, and major highways.

____ ② A map that shows elevation in a hilly region.

____ ④ A map of the counties that make up Arkansas, their county seats and roads.

____ ⑥ A map that shows a hiking trail surrounding a park. It shows rivers, lakes, streams, hills, and forests.

Test 33 cont'd ☛

D Determine the distances.

①


```
0    2    4    6    8
```
1 inch = 4 miles

a. 2 inches = __8__ miles
b. ½ inch = _____ miles
c. 1 ½ inches = _____ miles

②


```
0    25   50   75   100
```
1 inch = 50 miles

a. 3 inches = _____ miles
b. 2 inches = _____ miles
c. ½ inch = _____ miles

③


```
0    100  200  300  400
```
1 inch = 200 miles

a. 1 ½ inches = _____ miles
b. 6 inches = _____ miles
c. 4 inches = _____ miles

E Complete the index by writing the grid letter and number next to the city.

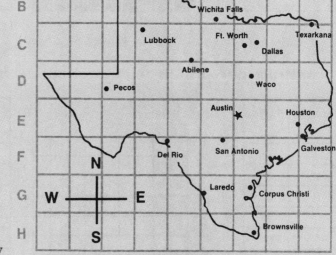

Index

C, D-5 ① Abilene   _____ ② Austin
_____ ③ Brownsville   _____ ④ Corpus Christi
_____ ⑤ Dallas   _____ ⑥ Ft. Worth
_____ ⑦ Galveston   _____ ⑧ Houston
_____ ⑨ Laredo   _____ ⑩ Lubbock
_____ ⑪ Pecos   _____ ⑫ San Antonio
_____ ⑬ Waco   _____ ⑭ Wichita Falls

F Match the map symbols and meanings.

① ●   city   ③ 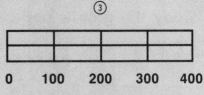   state highway
② ★   capital   ④ (45)   U.S. Highway

G Does the symbol show a relationship (R) between 2 numbers, or does it signify a mathematical operation (O)?

_R_ ① ∩   ___ ② ÷   ___ ③ >   ___ ④ ∪   ___ ⑤ −   ___ ⑥ =

___ ⑦ <   ___ ⑧ ×   ___ ⑨ ≰   ___ ⑩ ≠   ___ ⑪ ⊆   ___ ⑫ +

H Define these math symbols.

① ∉ _is not a member of_   ② ÷ _____   ③ ∈ _____

④ > _____   ⑤ ⊆ _____   ⑥ ∩ _____

⑦ − _____   ⑧ ≠ _____   ⑨ ∪ _____

⑩ < _____   ⑪ = _____   ⑫ × _____

400